International Government Information and Country Information
A Subject Guide

Andrea M. Morrison and Barbara J. Mann

How to Find It, How to Use It

GREENWOOD PRESS
Westport, Connecticut • London

Library of Congress Cataloging-in-Publication Data

Morrison, Andrea Marie, 1957–
    International government information and country information : a subject guide /
Andrea M. Morrison and Barbara J. Mann.
        p. cm. — (How to find it, how to use it)
    Includes index.
    ISBN 1-57356-479-6 (alk. paper)
    1. International agencies—Information resources. 2. Government information—
Handbooks, manuals, etc. 3. Electronic government information—Directories.
4. International agencies—Bibliography. 5. Non-governmental organizations—
Information resources. I. Mann, Barbara J. II. Title. III. Series.
    ZA5050.M67 2004
    025.04—dc20   2004000441

British Library Cataloguing in Publication Data is available.

Library of Congress Catalog Card Number: 2004000441
ISBN: 1–57356–479–6

First published in 2004

Greenwood Press, 88 Post Road West, Westport, CT 06881
An imprint of Greenwood Publishing Group, Inc.
www.greenwood.com

Printed in the United States of America

The paper used in this book complies with the
Permanent Paper Standard issued by the National
Information Standards Organization (Z39.48–1984).

10 9 8 7 6 5 4 3 2 1

Contents

Acknowledgments

First, I wish to acknowledge the support, love, and patience of my husband, Tom Morrison, during the course of this project. I thank him for the tremendous amount that he did and the support that he gave me, in order that I could write. Also, I am grateful to Peter and Emily Spadaro, my parents, for the educational opportunities they gave me and for their love and support. I especially thank my father for his professional research advice and example of persistence.

I wish to acknowledge my institution, Indiana University Libraries, Bloomington, Indiana, for their support of this project and the excellence of the collections in the GIMSS: Government Information, Microforms, and Statistical Services Department.

My colleague, Marian Shaaban, provided assistance and advice on IGOs throughout this project. I wish to acknowledge her mentorship and also to thank her as a friend.

This project was supported through a grant, the READEX/GODORT/ALA Catharine J. Reynolds Research Grant Award in 2000. I am grateful for the monetary assistance, but also for the belief in me that this award represented. The Government Documents Round Table (GODORT) has been a wonderful organization to work in, and I appreciate the professional opportunities it has provided for learning, contributing, sharing, and growing as a librarian.

I owe special thanks to my coauthor, Barbara Mann, who has grown to be a dear and close friend throughout this collaboration. Barb had a way of zeroing in on what is important and what is not. This book has become a reality because we worked as a team; however, most of all I treasured her friendship throughout this project.

Finally, I wish to thank my Creator for the learning and ability to complete this project. I sincerely hope that this book will be of service all over the world to those who wish to learn more about the rich and fascinating resources of international intergovernmental organizations and to also find more information about individual countries of the world.

Andrea Morrison

I want to first thank my coauthor and dear friend, Andrea Morrison, for her belief in my abilities to do this. Andrea asked me to collaborate with her on this project through blind faith in me. During the course of the project I have learned so much from her, and I will be ever grateful that she took a chance on me. Thank you, Andrea, for your belief in me, for your encouragement, for all you have taught me along the way, for all the laughter, and most of all for the gift of your friendship.

I want to thank Emory University for their support in this project. I was able to attend conferences where I continued to gain a better understanding of the resources that were available, and I was able to consult sources from the rich collections of the Robert W. Woodruff Library and Hugh F. MacMillan Law Library.

On a personal note, I want to thank my family for their support and encouragement. To my husband, Gary; my daughter and son-in-law, Jenny and Tim; my son, Andy, and my grandson, TJ; thank you for believing in me and being there for me. I also want to thank my parents, Robert and Carol Preikschat, for instilling in me the importance of education.

I, too, want to thank my Creator for the gifts He has bestowed on me that made all this possible.

Barb Mann

Introduction

Global issues are of paramount importance in a networked world of rapid, almost instant, dissemination of information via the Internet, and researchers, students, government officials, policy makers, and data users need access to a ready reference source to current government information on an international and national level. The purpose of this volume is to introduce the wide variety of international information resources that are available on a given subject, from such sources as international governmental organizations (IGOs), national governments, organizations, universities, and commercial publishers. IGOs in particular are rich resources of topical, statistical, and analytical information within the subject areas of economics, education, development, social and cultural affairs, health, trade, law, and much more. IGOs are also authoritative and prolific publishers of reliable information and data, especially on the Internet, where these resources are often available at the fingertips via full-text versions. Other resources are still in print format, but just as important in the research process.

Researchers at many different stages can benefit from *International Government Information and Country Information,* because it offers information to a wide range of users, from the beginning student to the advanced researcher. By offering quick access to titles and Internet addresses, summary descriptions, as well as detailed information and evaluation and research strategies, this book will help the following users find the international government information they need: college and university students; librarians for colleges, universities, junior and senior high schools, and public libraries; government documents and government information librarians as well as government information libraries; library schools; businesses and offices that work in international relations in many areas; teachers and professors; advanced data users; governmental officials; policy makers; high school, junior high, or prep school students; and Model United Nations and European Union programs.

The book is divided into two parts. Part I provides background on general information resources, and Part II contains 21 chapters, each on a different subject, with a wide array of resources included for each one.

Resources are usually described in two parts: a summary and a detailed description. The purpose, background, and mission of the organization are included in the summary. This guide is not intended to be a comprehensive listing of all the international resources available but is instead intended to be an introductory and intermediate guide leading to resources that provide even more resources. Each subject resource is described by type; for example, whether it is an Internet resource, a periodical, a database, or a yearbook. Unless otherwise specified, Internet resources are available for free on the World Wide Web. All included Internet sites were active as of February 2004. Most print resources, on the other hand, must be purchased, although this guide specifies if they are free on request. Each subject chapter also includes a Research Strategies section, which evaluates the resources in relation to specific research needs.

INFORMATION AND SUBJECTS INCLUDED IN THE BOOK

Part I: General Information

The first chapter of Part I describes general sources. This chapter is organized within these categories:

- Overview
- General Sources by Organization (includes descriptions of three of the most comprehensive IGOs: the United Nations, the European Union, and the Organization of American States, as well as the League of Nations)
- General Resources
- Biographical Sources
- Style Manuals

General Sources by Organization describes three major IGOs whose impact and scope of activities and research is global: the United Nations (UN), the European Union (EU), and the Organization of American States (OAS), as well as the League of Nations. This chapter is a broad introduction to these organizations and to some general resources, biographical sources, and style manuals that are useful as citation guides. Under each organization are separate sections for both resources published by the organization and reference sources about the organization. Each organization is described under the heading "About the Organization/Purpose of the Organization," followed by the descriptions of specific resources. Researchers should note that not all resources listed are annotated.

Resources for the United Nations are provided in three sections: United Nations Resources (published by the United Nations), United Nations Indexes (indexes to the UN material), and United Nations Reference Sources, both governmental and nongovernmental sources. After European Union and Organization of American State resources, annotations are included for the League of Nations and other general resources, biographical sources, and style manuals.

The chapter on general sources in particular includes significant research guides on the organizations for the serious, in-depth researcher; however, most information published by these organizations is described in the appropriate subject chapters. Cross-references from the subject chapters to other chapters guide the user to sections with other pertinent resources. Organizations with a specific area or subject focus are described under their most appropriate topic, for example, the International Bureau of Education in the Education chapter and the World Health Organization in the Health chapter.

Part II: Subject Chapters

Part II, the subject chapters, contains descriptions of resources based on the main subject covered:

- Agriculture and Food
- Communication
- Crime and Criminal Justice
- Development
- Economics and Business (includes finance)
- Education
- Energy
- Environment
- Government and Politics

- Health
- Human Rights
- International Relations (includes foreign affairs)
- Labor
- Laws and Treaties
- Science and Technology (includes natural sciences)
- Security, Peace, and Disarmament
- Social/Cultural Issues
- Statistics (includes broad statistical resources, population and census information; resources for statistics on an individual topic will be under that topic)
- Trade
- Transportation
- Women and Children

Each chapter follows a basic pattern by organizing information described under specific categories, beginning with a quick reference list of the resources discussed along with appropriate Internet addresses.

The following categories of information within most chapters provide users with different types of information and have different uses:

- Chapter Overview
- Governmental Sources Discussed
- Nongovernmental Sources Discussed
- Governmental Sources
- Nongovernmental Sources
- Research Strategies
- For Further Reading: Comprehensive Web Sites and Other Reference Sources

The Chapter Overview briefly discusses the authors' approach to the subject, defining it if necessary, and summarizes what is included in the chapter. Resources Discussed are lists of resources organized into two types, those published by IGOs or by the government of a country, which is the major focus of this book, under the category Governmental Sources Discussed, and those by nongovernmental organizations (NGOs), under Nongovernmental Sources Discussed. The list provides the resource name, publisher, and place of origin, along with the format(s), which is how the resource is accessed, whether paper, electronic, CD, or other. If they are accessed at no charge, just the URL is listed, and the researcher can assume that the resource is available at no charge unless otherwise noted.

These lists of resources may be very useful to sophisticated users who do not need a description and desire to quickly access a significant resource, either by Internet or print. Individual resources are then described immediately following the list of resources in the two subsequent sections entitled Governmental Sources and Nongovernmental Sources.

Following the initial list of resources discussed, each resource is fully described in three sections: Summary, Detailed Description, and Research Strategies. The Summary briefly explains what the resource covers and its major focus and how its information is organized. It includes the purpose of the organization, describing its background, mission, objectives, main area of activity, and except for large organizations, the member countries. Every effort has been made to give an idea of the usefulness and content of a resource in the Summary, however, for the most complete summary researchers should also read the first several paragraphs of the Detailed Description.

The Detailed Description continues to describe highlighted selected characteristics of the resources, covering publications, analysis of subjects and topics, online databases and other statistical data, bibliographies and indexes, portal Internet sites, libraries, directories, and links to other significant information. Major resources are highlighted, with content, type of information and organization, and dates covered. Information regarding preceding titles to journals is included when available.

The Research Strategies section provides users with introductory knowledge about the major resources described in the chapter, both governmental and nongovernmental, by explaining some of their strengths and weaknesses. Evaluation, comparisons, and recommendations are included. It warrants an individual section, because along with the Sources Discussed list at the beginning of each chapter, it provides information users a quick way of accessing the best resource for their purpose and guides the user to the appropriate resource for their level of information need. Resources are compared to each other on a basic level, and some guidelines are offered for which ones to consult first.

Although comparisons are made between resources, as well as their costs and their major features, only highlights are included. For further information, users may then consult the detailed information in the text of the description of the resources. The Research Strategies section also includes some guidelines for what resources are available on the Internet, and whether they are for sale or free.

This subject guide, intended to be a handbook for introductory and intermediate use of these sources, is therefore not comprehensive. There are many specific resources not mentioned or described. Users are encouraged to continue their research by further consultation of the resources themselves and of the research guides and general reference materials listed under For Further Reading.

The section of each chapter entitled For Further Reading: Comprehensive Web Sites and Other Reference Sources briefly describes Internet sites that are useful resources, but not described in the chapter. Other types of reference sources are also described, including traditional print titles, either serial or monographic, which are useful reference resources. Research guides specific for the chapter topic are included in For Further Reading, but the general research guides are found in the General Sources chapter. A few chapters, however, do not include this section because the resources themselves will lead researchers to many other reference sources. An example is the International Relations chapter.

When a resource clearly discusses two topics, both with significant information, for example, social and development issues, the resource is most fully described in one chapter, with a briefer description and a cross-reference from another chapter. Depending on the nature of the resources, some chapters do not warrant information in each area. General Sources, a chapter that is not intended to be comprehensive, but to introduce global information in other chapters, does not include the section on Research Strategies or For Further Reading.

Researchers should note that most of the resources described in this book have copyright statements. They clearly state the policies of the organizations in reproducing their information and for what purposes this is permitted. Often reproduction is permitted for research, where proper citation and credit is given.

Finally, the book concludes with an appendix listing selected acronyms of IGOs and a listing of selected IGOs and their Web site addresses. A general index provides access to titles, names, and subjects in the book.

CRITERIA FOR INCLUSION

Information was selected on the basis of type of author or publisher. The main focus was to include governmentally produced information from IGOs and national governments. Publications by national government agencies including the United States were included if the resources either contained important global perspectives or information about many individual nations of the world. A few selected nongovernmental publishers were included if the organizations contained research information in the subject field and contained information on individual countries. Also, the authors selected organizations that work in partnership with international intergovernmental organizations, provide information from IGO sources, or further link to IGO sources. The issues covered by the organization could either be global or regional in nature, but they had to cover a specific topical area for the organization of any type to be included in a subject chapter. Many of the organizations with a very specific regional focus were described in the For Further Reading section. Regional organizations with a few member countries were not included or described.

For the subject chapters, major IGOs focusing on the specific subject area are included. For each chapter, the authors also described the best resources for an overview, for data, for historical data users, for information by country, and for detailed policy and analysis of the subject. In some cases, significant IGO information is provided by an aggregator online resource, with numerous titles and databases. Sometimes these are subscription resources and often costly. If the aggregators contained significant IGO or individual country information and were typically used by researchers for this type of information, they were included, although the authors were very selective about including only the top percentage of the resources that fell into this category.

Finally, resources were included based on certain characteristics, such as whether they are ongoing or continually updated resources such as Web sites, periodicals, databases, and annual reports. Special attention was given to choose resources available electronically at no charge. Resources described may be published in the following formats:

- Electronic resources, including the Web sites of organizations, databases, interactive Internet sites, portal sites, and CD-ROMs.
- Serial publications, including ongoing periodicals, especially if the title was published online, annual or other regularly published reports, and titles published over many years.
- Monographic series—titles that were published with individual titles, but as part of a series of titles.
- Individual book titles. Special attention was given to include reference tools, bibliographies, directories, handbooks, manuals, guides, and indexes. Many of the individual book titles are included in

the For Further Reading category, with annotations describing them.

RESEARCH STRATEGIES FOR THE INTERNET

Information providers constantly change Web addresses and reorganize Web sites, and users of the book will find some addresses may be out of date or contain dead links. The authors recommend that users search on the Web address by deleting each last element of the Web address and running the search again. Many times, the domain of the provider is the same, but the folder structure of the address or the title of the file has changed. However, if this does not provide acceptable access, users should search using an Internet search engine, such as Google at <www.google.com> or Yahoo at <www.yahoo.com>, and usually the organization name will easily be found. We also recommend that the researcher go to the main page of the organization and run the search on the specific information they are interested in, if it has a fairly unique name, such as the name of a periodical or database. If the researcher is looking for nonspecific information, we suggest starting at a category of the home page linking further to Publications, Statistics, or Research Resources. A variety of links may lead to this type of information, but often there is a search engine specifically for publications on an organization's Internet site.

Some IGOs provide a depository library system, where cooperating libraries provide researchers with information from the organization. Contact information for these libraries may be found on the organization's Web site. Reference librarians at these libraries are experts who can help researchers through a phone call or an e-mail, regardless of whether the information seeker is connected to the library or research institution. Another option is for the researcher to contact the library or information service at the IGO itself. The online libraries are usually easy to find on an organization's Internet site, and they may also provide online research guides and contact information for reference service. Researchers may want to visit a research library in person to consult the print resources, as many of the publications are available in print and are a rich resource for historical data. Some valuable electronic resources may only be accessible from special locations, such as the library of an organization, and some libraries may even allow researchers to borrow resources in CD format for extended periods of time.

Finally, one characteristic that will greatly benefit a researcher in finding information in this area of governmental information is persistence, because obstacles can be expected. Much of the information is complex and detailed and takes more than one consultation to absorb. Internet sites change rapidly. They may be unavailable on certain days, and back again, or reconfigured under a different address. Researchers should first search the home page of the organization via a search engine or under the categories Research, Publications, Documents, Downloads, Statistics, Databases, and Resources, among a few, to try to find specific titles and information. However, some Internet information is lost because it is not preserved electronically on the Internet, and therefore, researchers must pursue other formats such as print or CD.

PART I
General Information

CHAPTER 1
General Sources

CHAPTER OVERVIEW

Unlike the other chapters of this book, which focus on the relevant sources of a particular topic, this chapter provides brief descriptions of sources that are general in nature and cover a variety of topics. The resources are organized into four main sections: General Sources by Organization, General Resources, Biographical Sources, and Style Manuals. Within each main section are both Web-based and print resources. Resources published by the organization and reference sources about the organization are listed separately, whether the title is governmental or nongovernmental.

The General Sources by Organization section describes these major international intergovernmental organizations: United Nations (UN), European Union (EU), Organization of American States (OAS), and League of Nations. The first three are included because they are the most broad based in their focus and mission. The League of Nations is included because of its status as the predecessor to the United Nations. The UN, EU, and OAS resources not only include their own comprehensive Web sites, but also dictionaries and bibliographies, tools useful to understand each one's unique vocabulary, to expand the research resources possibilities, and as most of these sources also include chronologies, as a way to understand each one's history. Many other important organizations are not covered in this general chapter because the main mission of the organization is focused on one or more specific subjects; they are described in the appropriate subject chapters.

The United Nations, by far the largest and most far reaching of these organizations, has the most complex, yet developed, indexing system, which is described here. A commercial online subscription database, *AccessUN,* and the catalog of the Dag Hammarskjöld Library in New York and Geneva UN Library, *UNBISnet,* have a more user-friendly interface to locate the extremely rich research resources found within the documents and publications of the United Nations. The *United Nations* Web site is a treasure

trove of research materials, especially as the United Nations is making much more of its resources available electronically. The various UN-generated and commercial publications described in this chapter provide great insight into the organizational structure and workings of the many bodies that comprise the United Nations system. For particular subject areas, researchers would be better served by consulting the resources of the relevant specialized agencies within the UN system. Information about these specialized agencies, their work, and the documents and publications they produce can be found in the United Nations-related handbooks and guides listed here, as well as on the *UN* Web site. *Basic Facts About the United Nations* and *The United Nations Handbook* are especially useful for understanding the organization and its structure. The *Annual Review of United Nations Affairs*, *A Global Agenda ...* and the *Yearbook of the United Nations*, also an annual publication, contain documents and information regarding the issues being addressed by the UN.

Both the European Union and Organization of American States are regionally focused compared to the United Nations, and neither has a comprehensive indexing component. The Web site of each contains the full text of many online documents and publications. Although there is no official *League of Nations* Web site, its documents and publications are available in a commercially produced microfilm collection with indexing from the accompanying guide. Two specialized digital collections are also described in this chapter.

The General Resources main section includes two Web sites, *International Documents Task Force Web Links* Web site, by the Government Documents Round Table of the American Library Association and *IONET: International Organization Network*[1] Web site, compiled by the International Organization Section of the International Studies Association. Both of these serve as online collections providing access to other international organization Web sites and also to materials in print format, such as dictionaries, encyclopedias, and directories. The dictionaries and encyclopedias not only serve to better understand the terminology, institutions, and legal documents, but also often contain chronologies and bibliographies. The directories have contact information and usually a description of the organization and its mission. Of special mention is the publication *International Information: Documents, Publications, and Electronic Information of International Government Organizations* by Peter I. Hajnal, 2nd ed. This two-volume set provides serious researchers with in-depth descriptions of the documents, publications, and electronic information produced by individual international intergovernmental organizations. Another excellent source to find explanation of the international intergovernmental organizations and their publications is *The Information Systems of International Inter-Governmental Organizations: A Reference Guide* by Robert V. Williams.

Biographical Sources, the third main section, describes some of the most useful resources in locating biographical information on world leaders and other individuals instrumental in the activities international organizations. The last main section, Style Manuals, lists two titles that are especially useful on how to cite governmental and international organization documents and publications. Although other style manuals, such as *The Chicago Manual of Style,* Turabian's *A Manual for Writers of Term Papers, Theses, and Dissertations,* and *Publication Manual of the American Psychological Association,* 5th ed., also cover citing these types of materials, they are not as comprehensive in documenting this format nor written specifically for this purpose and therefore are not included.

GENERAL SOURCES BY ORGANIZATION

United Nations Sources Discussed

United Nations Web site, New York.
  <http://www.un.org>

United Nations Indexes

AccessUN. NewsBank, Inc., 1946– (online subscription service and CD-ROM).
UNCAPS: United Nations System Shared Cataloguing and Public Access System Web site, New York. <http://uncaps.unsystem.org/>
UNDEX: United Nations Documents Index (1970–1978).

Subject (Series A), 1970–1978 (UN Document Symbol: ST/LIB/SER.1/A) (ISSN 0303-7118)
Country (Series B), 1970–1978 (UN Document Symbol: ST/LIB/SER.1/B) (ISSN 0303-7134)
List of Document Issued (Series C), 1974–1978 (UN Document Symbol: ST/LIB/SER.1/C) (ISSN 0303-7126)
UNDOC: United Nations Documents Index. New York: United Nations, Dag Hammarskjöld Library, 1979–1996 (ISSN 0250-5584).
United Nations Documents Index. New York: United Nations, Dag Hammarskjöld Library, 1998– (UN Document Symbol: ST/LIB/SER.N) (ISSN 1020-7090).
United Nations Documents Index. New York: United Nations (1950–1973) (UN Document Symbol: ST/LIB/SER. E) (ISSN 0041-7351).

United Nations Reference Sources

Annual Review of United Nations Affairs. Dobbs Ferry, N.Y.: Oceana Publications, 1949– (ISSN 0066-4340).
Basic Facts about the United Nations. New York: United Nations, 1947– (ISSN 0067-4419).
Encyclopedia of the United Nations and International Agreements, by Edmund Jan Osman´czyk, edited and revised by Anthony Mango. 3rd ed. New York: Routledge, 2003 (ISBN 0-41593-920-8) (4 vols.).
A Global Agenda: Issues Before the… General Assembly: An Annual Publication of the United Nations Association of the United States of America. Lanham, Md.: University Press of America, 1991–2000. Lanham: Rowman & Littlefield, 2001– (ISSN 1057-1213).
Historical Dictionary of the United Nations, by A. LeRoy Bennett. Lanham, Md.: Scarecrow Press, Inc., 1995 (Historical Dictionaries of International Organizations Series No. 8) (ISBN 0-81082-992-4).
Historical Dictionary of the United Nations Educational, Scientific and Cultural Organization (UNESCO), by Seth Spaulding and Lin Lin. Lanham, Md.: Scarecrow Press, Inc., 1997 (Historical Dictionaries of International Organizations Series No. 13) (ISBN 0-81083-288-7).
United Nations Handbook. Wellington, N.Z.: Ministry of Foreign Affairs and Trade, 1961– (ISSN 0110-1951).

United Nations System, by Joseph Preston Baratta. New Brunswick, N.J.: Transaction Publishers, 1995 (International Organizations Series: No. 10) (ISBN 1-56000-216-6).

Yearbook of the United Nations. Lake Success, N.Y.: Dept. of Public Information, United Nations, 1946/1947– (ISSN 0082-8521).

About the Organization/Purpose of the Organization: Established in 1945 with the ratification of the 111-article *Charter,* drawn up by 50 countries, the United Nations was created to foster peace through the stabilization of international relations. The United Nations works for world peace through its peacekeeping efforts and promotes human rights, health, development, independence, the environment, and many other issues through its various programs and agencies. The structure of the United Nations system is complex because, in addition to having major organs (institutional bodies) that do the main work of the organization, there are also many specialized bodies that are within the United Nations system that work in specific areas, such as the Food and Agriculture Organization, the World Health Organization, and many others.

The United Nations consists of six principal organs: General Assembly, Security Council, Economic and Social Council, Trusteeship Council, International Court of Justice, and the Secretariat. The General Assembly, comprised of one representative from each of the 191 member countries, is the "main deliberative body," although the "decisions of the Assembly have no legally binding force for Governments, they carry the weight of world opinion on major international issues, as well as the moral authority of the world community."[2]

The Security Council is the body responsible for maintaining peace and security. There are 15 members, the permanent members, China, France, Russian Federation, United Kingdom, and the United States, and the other 10 members, elected for two-year terms by the General Assembly. The Economic and Social Council (ECOSOC) coordinates the economic and social work of the UN and its specialized agencies and institutions, under the authority of the General Assembly, with a membership of 54. The Trusteeship Council was established to oversee the independence/self-government of trust territories and was disbanded in 1994 upon successful completion of its mission. The International Court of Justice, the world court, is described in the Law and Treaties chapter. The Secretariat, headed by the Secretary-General, handles the daily work of the UN. The Official Records of the Principal Organs, in the form of meeting records, both verbatim and summary, resolutions and decisions, reports from other UN bodies, and indexes are published in print format and are accessible at major research libraries as well as designated UN Depository Libraries <http://www.un.org/Depts/dhl/deplib/countries/index.html>.

In addition to the Principal Organs, the United Nations is comprised of programs and funds, functional commissions, regional commissions, specialized agencies, related organizations, research and training institutes, and other entities. A comprehensive list of these subsidiary organizations is available on the *UN* Web site at <http://www.un.org/aboutun/chart.html>.

United Nations Sources

United Nations Web site, New York.
 <http://www.un.org>

Summary: The home page of the United Nations (UN), available in the six official United Nations languages (English, Arabic, Chinese, French, Russian, and Spanish), is comprised of a wide variety of access points, many of which are described in other chapters. The focus of this discussion will be on the home page headings: UN News Centre; About the United Nations; Main Bodies; Documentation, Maps; Publications, Stamps, Databases; Issues on the UN Agenda and *Cyber School Bus.* *Cyber School Bus* is the United Nation's comprehensive Web site and searchable database for youth schools, with country and subject information, games, and curricula. The UN site is searchable, and a site index is available.

Detailed Description: UN News Centre, a home page heading, features full text of up-to-date news, press releases, statements, transcripts, radio broadcasts, and other materials. Researchers can subscribe to an e-mail news alert service. There is also an archive with an accompanying search engine, which can search the various news categories up to 45 days previous.

About the United Nations, another home page heading, is a comprehensive source of information about the United Nations, subdivided into a variety of information access points. One such access point is entitled Background Information and features links to descriptions taken from the print edition of *Basic Facts about the United Nations* including ordering information. Links to the UN's history, departments, emblem, and flag are also found here, along with a link to *About the UN,* information in 21 nonofficial languages. Another access point is a link to the home page heading, Main Bodies, which is discussed in the next paragraph. The

Main Documents access point has a link to the *UN Charter, Statutes of the International Court of Justice, Universal Declaration of Human Rights,* and other documents as well as a link to nongovernmental organizations and their UN affiliation. Guided Tours is also an access point and has information about the UN headquarters in New York and offices in Vienna and Geneva, and United Nations Online Tours provides online tours of the New York and Geneva offices. Who's Who, another access point under About the United Nations, contains links to pages on the President of the General Assembly, Secretary-General, Deputy Secretary-General, and previous Secretary-Generals. In addition, other access points include a link to Member States, various staff services, the UN mailing address, and a live webcam from New York.

Main Bodies, the third home page heading to be discussed, links to the home pages of the six Principal Organs. From these pages the full texts of documents, reports, and minutes can be accessed. Of special note is the accessibility of the full text of resolutions for the United Nations General Assembly (1946–) and the United Nations Security Council (1946–) from each of these organs' home page.

Documentation, Maps, another UN home page heading, is an especially useful place to begin the research process. It contains access to *UNBISnet,* the online catalog; *UN Documentation: Research Guide;* Documents Alert*; UN-I-QUE: UN Information Quest;* Maps and Geographic Information; *UN Journal,* a periodical; UN Webcasts; Library; Documents in German; and links to the Principal Organs. *UNBISnet* indexes United Nations documents as well as UN and non-UN publications (1979–) contained in the Dag Hammarskjöld Library in New York and the Geneva UN library. The catalog is being expanded as older documents are also being systematically added. In addition, voting records of the General Assembly (1983–) and Security Council (1946–) are included as well as General Assembly, Security Council, and Economic and Social Council speeches (1983–). Searching is by keyword or browsing, and a thesaurus is available. The *UN Documentation: Research Guide* is an especially useful online research tool as it provides in-depth understanding of what are and how to use UN document symbols, basic research tools, and indexes, as well as how to research the General Assembly, Security Council and Economic and Social Council, and press releases. Each topic includes embedded links to relevant materials. The *Research Guide* also contains special topic research guides on disarmament, human rights, international law, and peacekeeping. Documents Alert is a handy source of citations to electronic documents made recently available online and are kept on this site for two months. *UN-I-QUE (UN Info Quest)* (1946–), created by the Dag Hammarskjöld Library, serves as ready-reference file for frequently asked questions regarding recurring publications. Although full-citation information is not available, materials included do contain the document number/sales publication number. Searching *UN-I-QUE* is by keyword or phrase. Also included under the Documentation, Maps home page heading is the subheading Maps and Geographic Information, a rich source of PDF maps from the UN Cartographic Section. These maps are grouped into three main categories of country profiles, thematic, and peacekeeping as well as including information from the various working groups. *UN Journal,* another subheading, links to the current issue, in PDF format, of this daily publication, which highlights the activities of the UN. UN Webcasts features the archived video of meetings, conferences, and events. The subheading Library links to *UNBISnet,* various resources produced by the Dag Hammarskjöld Library, and information about the Library.

The Publications, Stamps, and Databases home page heading links to the UN publications catalog of books, periodicals, microfiche, and electronic products. Ordering information is included. There is also a link to available online publications along with one to the UN Online Bookshop from which books, posters, postcards, and emblem items can be ordered. The stamps segment is a link to the page of the United Nations Postal Administration where ordering and information about stamps is located. The Databases section links to a topical list of relevant databases, many of which are described in other chapters.

The final UN home page heading to be discussed is Issues on the UN Agenda, which contains a topical list of subjects linking to the home pages of relevant United Nations agencies. This heading is especially useful in the research process because it allows the researcher to hone in, through the agency home page, to all kinds of pertinent information.

United Nations Indexes

AccessUN. NewsBank, Inc., 1946– (online subscription service and CD-ROM).

Summary: An online subscription-based indexing source to both current and historical United Nations documents (1946–), *Access UN* indexes documents and publications from the Principal Organs in the form of official records, sales publications, restricted and limited distribution documents, as well as documents from the various related committees, commissions, conferences, and regional organizations. The search boxes have pull-down menus, which allow the searching choices: in all fields, subject, session/agenda, author, title, text, document number, UN Sales Publication number, document type, and country. Searches can be further limited by type of document, date, and full text. Results are comprised of document number, date, body, session/agenda, meeting date, corporate author, title, document type, physical description (number of pages), language, country of document (where relevant), and subjects. The full text of some documents is included along with links to the full-text version if it is available on the Internet.

UNCAPS: United Nations System Shared Cataloguing and Public Access System Web site, New York. <http://uncaps.unsystem.org/>

Summary: The *UNCAPS* Web site allows for searching the library catalogs, databases, and holdings, including full text and archives, of the Food and Agriculture Organization (FAO); International Civil Aviation Organization (ICAO); International Fund for Agriculture Development (IFAD); International Labour Organization (ILO); International Maritime Organization (IMO); *JOLIS* (World Bank and International Monetary Fund catalog); *UNBIS* (catalog of the Dag Hammarskjöld Library); United Nations Educational, Scientific, and Cultural Organization (UNESCO); United Nations Population Fund (UNFPA); and World Intellectual Property Organization (WIPO). Single organizations, selected organizations, or all organizations can be searched. Searching can be done by title, author, keyword, advanced, and browsing.

UNDEX: United Nations Documents Index (1970–1978).
Subject (Series A), 1970–1978 (UN Document No.: ST/LIB/SER.1/A) (ISSN 0303-7118).
Country (Series B), 1970–1978 (UN Document No.: ST/LIB/SER.1/B) (ISSN 0303-7134).
List of Documents Issued (Series C), 1974–1978 (UN Document No.: ST/LIB/SER.1/C). (ISSN 0303-7126)

Summary: *UNDEX,* also produced by the Dag Hammarskjöld Library, is the next iteration of United Nations indexes for Principal Organ and Specialized Agencies documents and publications. Entries are indexed into three series: *Subject (Series A), Country (Series B),* and *List of Documents Issued (Series C)* published in separate volumes. Cumulative volumes are available for Series A (1978), Series B (1978), and Series C. Series C has the most comprehensive cumulative index, entitled *UNDEX "Series C" Cumulative Edition* (1974–1978) and contained in four volumes: Volume 1: General Assembly; Volume 2: Economic and Social Council Series, regional economic commissions; Volume 3: Security Council, Trusteeship Council, International Court of Justice, documents issued in all other series, consolidated list of periodicals; and Volume 4: consists of the subjects covered in the other three volumes for the year 1978 only.

UNDOC: United Nations Documents Index. New York: United Nations, Dag Hammarskjöld Library, 1979–1996 (ISSN 0250-5584).

Summary: *UNDOC,* a product of the Dag Hammarskjöld Library, indexes documents and publications of the Principal Organs and Specialized Agencies of the United Nations. It was published monthly (1979–1986) and then quarterly (1987–1996), with an annual cumulative issue (in microfiche only). Each edition of the index is published in two volumes: Documents and Publications, Personal/Corporate Name Index, Title Index (Part I) and Subject Index. (Part II). Documents and Publications in Part I also encompasses the Official Records, Sales Publications, republished documents, and maps. Each entry contains the full bibliographic citation, and some entries are also annotated. Personal/Corporate Name, Title, and Subject entries include the title, author, and entry number for Documents and Publications. The subsequent *United Nations Documents Checklist* (1996–1997) served as an interim publication.

United Nations Documents Index. New York: United Nations, Dag Hammarskjöld Library, 1998– (UN Document No.: ST/LIB/SER.N) (ISSN 1020-7090).

Summary: The latest indexing iteration is the *United Nations Documents Index (1998–),* which serves as a continuation of *UNDOC,* in the same format. It is published quarterly with an annual subject index cumulation.

United Nations Documents Index. New York: United Nations (1950–1973) (UN Document No.: ST/LIB/SER. E) (ISSN 0041-7351).

Summary: Compiled by the United Nations Library (1950–1962), later know as the Dag Hammarskjöld Library (1963–), this monthly index is comprised of 24 volumes. Volumes 1–13 (1950–1962) contain bibliographic citations of documents and publications of Principal Organs and Specialized Agencies arranged by issuing agency. Some entries also contain annotations, and there is a subject index. Volumes 14–24 (1962–1973) are arranged by document series symbol and listed in three separate sections: Checklist, which contains the bibliographic description; Cumulative Subject Index; and Listings of Documents Received, Documents Republished, Sales Publications, New Document Symbols, and Libraries and Information Centers that Received United Nations Materials. Some entries in all volumes contain annotations. An alphabetically arranged subject list of documents is available in *United Nations Documents Index Cumulated Index* Volume 1–13 1950–1962.

United Nations Reference Sources

Annual Review of United Nations Affairs. Dobbs Ferry, N.Y.: Oceana Publications, 1949– (ISSN 0066-4340).

Summary: Published annually in multiple volumes, this publication reprints the major reports, meeting records, and resolutions of the five main bodies of the United Nations, arranged by body. Selected annual reports from subsidiary organizations are also included.

Basic Facts about the United Nations. New York, 1947– (ISSN 0067-4419).

Summary: An annual publication about the United Nations by the United Nations, which provides a description of the organization and its main bodies, including purpose, membership, official languages, structure, and related organizations. In addition, it discusses major initiatives and describes the relevant participating bodies. The UN budget as well a listing of information centers and offices is also included along with a short bibliography, arranged by subject.

Encyclopedia of the United Nations and International Agreements, by Edmund Jan Osman´czyk, edited and revised by Anthony Mango. 3rd ed. New York: Routledge, 2003 (ISBN 0-41593-920-8) (4 vols.).

Summary: This third edition, expanded into four volumes from the original one volume (1985, 1990 editions), is comprised of alphabetically arranged entries on the UN system and specialized agencies, international governmental organizations, and nongovernmental organizations that cooperate with the UN, full and partial texts of international agreements and treaties, and term explanations. Most entries also include a list of sources. The third edition is an extensive revision of the first two, with some entries deleted and others added. At the beginning of volume 1 is a listing of included articles, and volume 4 contains the index.

Global Agenda: Issues Before the... General Assembly: An Annual Publication of the United Nations Association of the United States of America. Lanham, Md.: University Press of America, 1991–2000. Lanham: Rowman & Littlefield, 2001– (ISSN 1057-1213).

Summary: Using a theme approach, this annual reference source describes the work of the current General Assembly in detail. Included is a description of the General Assembly's activity, as well as citations to relevant United Nations and other organization/news source documents and publications that are included in the text.

Historical Dictionary of the United Nations, by A. LeRoy Bennett. Lanham, Md.: Scarecrow Press, Inc., 1995 (Historical Dictionaries of International Organizations Series No. 8) (ISBN 0-81082-992-4).

Summary: A publication of the *Historical Dictionary Series,* this volume follows the usual format of a chronology; introductory essay focusing on background, structure, and initiatives; a dictionary of terms, individuals, organizations, events, and issues; and a nonannotated bibliography. This bibliography is subdivided into Official Publications, Other Basic General Sources, Reference Works, Background, Structure of the UN, Membership Issues, Peace and Security Activities, Arms Control and Disarmament, Legal Activities, Economic and Social Development, Human Rights Activities, Independence and Self-Government, UN Leadership and the Secretary-General, Evaluation and Prospects, and Specialized Agencies and Other Bodies. Reprints of the *Charter* and *Universal Declaration of Human Rights* as well as lists of member countries, presidents of the General Assembly, and Secretary-Generals are found in the appendices. A few black and white photographs of leaders and main bodies in session are also included.

Historical Dictionary of the United Nations Educational, Scientific and Cultural Organization (UNESCO), by Seth Spaulding and Lin Lin. Lanham, Md.: Scarecrow Press, Inc., 1997 (Historical Dictionaries of International Organizations Series No. 13) (ISBN 0-81083-288-7).

Summary: Included here are a comprehensive, annotated timeline; introductory essay outlining the organizations' structure; a dictionary of terms, individuals, organizations, events, and issues; and a nonannotated bibliography subdivided into General and Miscellaneous; Education; Science; Social and Human Sciences; Culture; Communication; Documentation, Libraries, Archives; and Serial Documents of UNESCO. An extensive section of appendices is also provided that reprints the text of relevant documents along with lists of officers, prizes, and conferences.

United Nations Handbook. Wellington, N.Z.: Ministry of Foreign Affairs and Trade, 1961– (ISSN 0110-1951).

Summary: An excellent source of quick and comprehensive information about the workings of the UN, this annual publication is divided into the main bodies of the United Nations. Each main section includes membership, officers, committees, and subsidiary and related bodies. Following the main bodies are relevant information subdivided into Other Bodies, Subsidiary and Regional Development Banks, and Budget and Scales of Assessment.

United Nations System, by Joseph Preston Baratta. New Brunswick, N.J.: Transaction Publishers, 1995 (International Organizations Series: No. 10) (ISBN 1-56000-216-6).

Summary: This especially useful annotated bibliography is subdivided into UN, Organs of UN Organizations, Closely Associated Entities, Functions of the UN Organization, and Functions of the UN System. Each entry contains full citations as well as the annotation. Also included is a shorter general bibliography and author and subject indexes.

Yearbook of the United Nations. Lake Success, N.Y.: Dept. of Public Information, United Nations, 1946/47– (ISSN 0082-8521).

Summary: This subject-oriented, unofficial record based on official sources is an invaluable tool for tracking major initiatives of the United Nations. Each subject contains reprints and/or brief citations embedded in the text of relevant documents, publications, and news sources. An index of resolutions and decisions is included along with a subject index.

European Union Sources Discussed

Chronological History of the European Union, 1946–2001, by Willem Frans Victor Vanthoor. Northampton, Mass.: Edward Elgar, 2002 (ISBN 1-84376-101-7).

Dictionary of the European Union, by David Phinnemore and Lee McGowan. London: Europa, 2002 (ISBN 1-85743-145-6).

Documentation of the European Communities: A Guide, by Ian Thomson. London; New York: Mansell, 1989 (ISBN 0-72012-022-5).

Encyclopedia of the European Union, edited by Desmond Dinan. Boulder, Colo.: Lynne Rienner Publications, 1998 (ISBN 1-55587-634-X).

Eurojargon: A Dictionary of European Union Acronyms, Abbreviations and Sobriquets, edited by Anne Ramsay. Chicago, Ill.: F. Dearborn, 2000 (ISBN 1-89886-967-7 or 1-57958-274-5).

Europa: European Union Online Web site, European Union Publications Office, Brussels, Belgium. <http://www.europa.eu.int>

European Communities, compiled by John Paxton. New Brunswick, N.J.: Transaction Publishers, 1992 (International Organizations Series No. 1) (ISBN 1-56000-052-X).

The European Union Encyclopedia and Directory. 3rd ed. London: Europa Publications, 1999 (ISBN 1-85743-056-5).

European Union in the United States Web site, Delegation of the European Commission. Washington, D.C. <http://www.eurunion.org/>

European Union Web Sites. Public Documents and Maps Department, Perkins Library. Duke University. Durham, N.C. <http://docs.lib.duke.edu/igo/guides/euindex.html>

Guide to the Official Publications of the European Communities, by John Jeffries. 2nd ed. London: Mansell, 1981; New York H. W. Wilson [distributor], 1981 (ISBN 0-72011-590-6).

Historical Dictionary of the European Communities, by Desmond Dinan. Metuchen, N.J.: Scarecrow Press, 1993 (International Organizations Series No. 1) (ISBN 0-81082-666-6).

The Penguin Companion to European Union, by Timothy Bainbridge. 3rd ed. London: Penguin, 2002 (ISBN 0-14100-769-9).

About the Organization/Purpose of the Organization: Established originally as a way to place the production of European steel and coal under one authority, the European Coal and Steel Community Treaty (Treaty of Paris) was signed by France, Belgium, Federal Republic of Germany, Italy, Luxembourg, and the Netherlands (signed April 18, 1951; into force July 23, 1952). The European Economic Community (EEC) and European Atomic Energy Community were created by the same six countries via the Treaties of Rome (signed March 25, 1957; into force January 1, 1958). In 1958 the Parliamentary Assembly and Court of Justice were put into place to oversee all three Communities, and the *Official Journal of the European Communities* began publication. The Treaty of the European Union (Treaty of Maastricht, February 7, 1992; into force November 1,1993) changed the European Economic Community to the European Community and established the three pillars known as the European Union (EU). The European Community and Economic and Monetary Union initiatives are the first pillar, followed by creation of the intergovernmental cooperatives Common Foreign and Security Policy (pillar two) and Justice and Home Affairs Policy (pillar three). The Treaty of Amsterdam (signed October 2, 1997; into force May 1, 1999) and the Treaty of Nice (signed February 26, 2001; into force February 1, 2003) continued the reforming process as the EU membership prepares to again expand.

Qualifications to join the EU are "stable democratic government, a good human rights record, a properly functioning market economy, and sound macroeconomic policies. Candidates must also have the capacity to fulfill and to implement existing EU laws and policies (known as the *acquis communautaire*)."[3] The original membership of six countries has grown since its inception with the additions of: Denmark, Ireland, and the United Kingdom (1973); Greece (1981); Spain and Portugal (1986); and Austria, Finland, and Sweden (1995). Future membership is in negotiation at the time of this writing and includes Bulgaria, Czech Republic, Estonia, Cyprus, Latvia, Lithuania, Hungary, Malta, Poland, Romania, Slovenia, Slovakia, and Turkey. The official languages of the European Union are: Danish, German, English, Spanish, Finnish, French, Greek, Dutch, Italian, Portuguese, and Swedish.

Governing of the European Union is overseen by five main bodies: European Parliament (elected by the population of each member country), Council of the Union (governmental representation from each member country), European Commission (executive body),

Court of Justice (judicial body), and Court of Auditors (oversee budget). Other component bodies constitute the European Union. The European Parliament and Council are discussed in the Government and Politics chapter; Commission and Court of Justice are discussed in the Law and Treaties chapter; and Court of Auditors is discussed in the Economics chapter.

Unlike the United Nations, the European Union does not have a centralized indexing system. Finding materials can be challenging. The European Union chapter in the publication *International Information: Documents, Publications, and Electronic Information of International Government Organizations* by Peter I. Hajnal is an excellent source for understanding how to access this information.

European Union Sources

Chronological History of the European Union, 1946–2001, by Willem Frans Victor Vanthoor. Northampton, Mass.: Edward Elgar, 2002 (ISBN 1-84376-101-7).

Summary: This title contains an annotated chronology of the European Union. A predecessor volume was published in 1999 covering 1946–1999, and the current volume covers the period ending December 31, 2001. A brief narrative history that focuses on the political and economic background of the EU precedes the chronology. A reprint of the articles of the Treaty establishing the European Economic Community (March 25, 1957) constitutes the appendix. A brief bibliography and index are also included.

Dictionary of the European Union, by David Phinnemore and Lee McGowan. London: Europa, 2002 (ISBN 1-85743-145-6).

Summary: Featured in this publication is an alphabetical listing of terms, events, organizations, reports, countries, meetings, and individuals relevant to the EU. Each entry is about a paragraph in length.

Documentation of the European Communities: A Guide, by Ian Thomson. London; New York: Mansell, 1989 (ISBN 0-72012-022-5).

Summary: Written to update *A Guide to the Official Publications of the European Communities,* this volume provides an overview of the available documentation and then moves into more specific information arranged by topics. These topics include European Community Legislation, European Community, Commission-Bibliographical Documentation, Commission-General Documentation, Commission-Directorate-General Documentation, Commission-Eurostat Documentation, Commission-Spokesman's Service/Information Offices, Council of Ministers, European Parliament, Economic and Social Committee, Court of Justice of the European Communities, Court of Auditors, and Other EC Organizations. Each topic contains a description of relevant publications. Appendices are also included such as the especially useful listing of major periodicals, reports, and statistical publications that are published on a regular basis, arranged by subject. Other appendices contain listings of information offices and depository libraries/information centers. There is also an index.

Encyclopedia of the European Union, edited by
    Desmond Dinan. Boulder, Colo.: Lynne Rienner
    Publications, 1998 (ISBN 1-55587-634-X).

Summary: This encyclopedia is organized by topic, A-Z, of relevant terms, individuals, organizations, countries, events, and treaties, accompanied by an annotated chronology and a section of abbreviations and acronyms. The appendices are especially useful as they list representation in EU institutions; membership in international organizations; Directorate-Generals; Presidents; dates of Summits of Heads of State and Government (1961–1998); and renumbered articles, titles, and sections of the Treaty on the European Union.

Eurojargon: A Dictionary of European Union
    Acronyms, Abbreviations and Sobriquets, edited
    by Anne Ramsay. Chicago, Ill.: F. Dearborn, 2000
    (ISBN 1-89886-967-7 or 1-57958-274-5).

Summary: Alphabetically arranged by acronym or term, each entry includes a brief definition of terminology used in the activity of the European Union, including acronyms, abbreviations, and phrases. A short bibliography is also included.

Europa: European Union Online Web site, by the
    European Union Publications Office, Brussels,
    Belgium. <http://www.europa.eu.int/>

Summary: Launched originally in 1995, *Europa* serves as a portal to online information pertaining to the European Union's various components. Information can be accessed in all 11 of the official languages. The site is arranged into four main headings: Activities, Institutions, Documents, and Services. Links to information about the European Union (EU), living in the EU, and contacting the EU are also found on the home page as well as links to current affairs and news. Advanced searching, an index, and a text version are also available.

Detailed Description: Activities, the first main home page heading, is divided into major topics addressed by the EU. Topics range from agriculture, business, culture, economics, health, information society, justice, security, transport, and much more. Each topic is linked to Latest Developments (key sites and documentation) and *A Comprehensive Guide to EU Law* (summaries and legal texts). The documentation section under Latest Developments provides full-text access to relevant press releases and significant current sections of the *Bulletin of the European Union* and *General Report on the Activities of the European Union.* Another main heading on the *Europa* home page Institutions contains a link to *How the European Union Works: A Citizen's Guide to the EU Institutions,* as well as links to the Web sites of various bodies that constitute the EU.

The next main home page heading is Documents. Arranged under the categories of European Law, Documents Common to All Institutions, and Documents of Individual Institutions are links to related Web sites. Of special note is the European Law section, which includes links to the major law databases *EUR-LEX, CELEX, ŒIL: The Legislative Observatory,* and *Pre-Lex,* all discussed in the Laws and Treaties chapter. The Publications Portal, under Documents Common to All Institutions, provides access to a thematic index covering European Union policies and activities and also to an alphabetical list of all the Web sites referenced in the portal. From the Documents heading researchers may also find more information about the Historical Archives of the European Union.

Also, Documents leads to the full text of the monthly *Bulletin of the European Union,* which reports the activities of the Commission and other institutions of the EU. The online version is in HTML format (1996–) and provides a search engine, annual cumulative indexes, glossary and FAQ, and also links to other documents such as COM documents. The print version of the *Bulletin* covers 1994– (ISSN 0378-3693); researchers may note that the earlier title of the *Bulletin* was the monthly *Bulletin of the European Communities* (1968–1993) (ISSN 0378-3693).

Yet another title available online under Documents is the annual title *General Report on the Activities of the European Union,* which supplements the *Bulletin* and provides an overview of the activities of the previous year. It is searchable from 2003–. The print version is available from 1994 (ISSN 1608-7321), with the preceding title, *General Report on the Activities of the Communities,* covering 1967–2003 (ISSN 0069-6749).

The last main home page heading is Services, which has links to the EU Bookshop, statistics, opinion polls, the EU Directory, contacts, and access to internal documents. The online EU Directory is entitled *IDEA: The Electronic Directory of the European Institutions* and allows searching by persons, organizations, and organizational hierarchy, and also includes an interinstitutional directory (PDF format).

The news link, All the News, also found on the home page, is worth mentioning here. This link includes access to upcoming events, the latest EU press releases, and the online archive of electronic full-text press releases back to 1985 in its *RAPID Database.* The full text of the *Europa Newsletter,* a biweekly information source of the EU's activities and issues, is available online back to Issue 1, November 2002 and also has an e-mail subscription. All the News also links to EbS (Europe by Satellite, the TV news agency of the EU) and press information including theme-based press packs and links to the online press of other EU institutions.

European Communities, compiled by John Paxton. New Brunswick, N.J.: Transaction Publishers, 1992 (International Organizations Series No. 1) (ISBN 1-56000-052-X).

Summary: An annotated bibliography of materials written about the European Union, this volume is divided into sections entitled Introduction; Chronology; History; Biographies; Member States; Institutions of the Communities; Regional Policy; International Market and Customs Union; Political Union; Community and Third World; Community Agriculture and Fish Policy; Law; Industry; Social, Labour, Environmental and Education Policy; Transportation Policy; Energy Policy; Economic, Financial and Fiscal Affairs; European Communities Publications; Periodicals; Directories; and Bibliographies and Databases. The entries in each subject area are arranged alphabetically by title. Indexes for authors, titles, subjects, and maps are also included.

The European Union Encyclopedia and Directory, 3rd ed. London: Europa Publications, 1999 (ISBN 1-85743-056-5).

Summary: Originally published in 1992 under the title *The European Communities Encyclopedia and Di-**rectory* and renamed *The European Union Encyclopedia and Directory* with the second edition of 1996, this volume provides a chronology of the European Union; a brief A to Z dictionary of EU terms, organizations, and individuals; essays regarding political and social issues, including brief bibliographies; and a directory of officers and contact information for the various components of the EU. It also contains a statistical survey arranged by topics such as demographics, agriculture/forestry/fishery, industry, financial, trade, tourism, health, environment, and education. A fourth edition, 2004, is now available and some libraries would consider this title a regularly published serial.

European Union in the United States Web site, by the Delegation of the European Commission, Washington, D.C. <http://www.eurunion.org/>

Summary: Originally established 1954 as an information office, the Washington Delegation of the EU gained diplomatic status in 1971 and ambassadorial status in 1990. This embassy serves as the EU representative to the United States. An office was also opened in New York in 1964 and now functions as a delegation to the United Nations.

This site, developed by the Library of the Delegation of the European Commission to the United States, serves as another excellent source of online information pertaining to the EU, especially for users in the United States. Information is accessible through the home page headings of A to Z Index of the *EU* Web site, EU Basics, EU Law & Policy Overviews, EU Member Countries, EU Offices & Services in the U.S., EU Research Tools, EU-U.S. Partnership, EU for Young People, Help/Queries/ Comments, Publications, Sitemap, Search. The home page itself also links to current news highlights and hot topics. For the most part, the focus of the information on this page is that of European Union–U.S. relations and issues.

Detailed Description: For the purpose of this discussion, only the most relevant of the home page headings will be discussed. The rest are fairly self-explanatory. The A to Z Index home page heading serves as a rich research resource as it provides links to not only Delegation of the European Commission to the United States sites, but also to those of the European Union. EU Basics, another home page heading, contains a link to History of the European Union, a year-by-year chronology, updated monthly, and European Union at a Glance, which was described in the *European Union* Web site entry.

Another home page heading, EU Offices & Services in the U.S., links to the full text of news releases (1995–); speeches (1996–); and radio programs (online audio) and free educational videos. Also provided are links to the *RAPID* press release database as well as to press releases of the Council of Ministers and European Parliament.

EU Research Tools, another home page heading, contains an especially useful tool *The European Union: A Guide for Americans* in full text including PDF format, that discusses the history, policies, and initiatives of the EU as well as providing Web sites and publications information. Under the EU Research Tools heading also are links to general information, EU policies and legislation, Green Papers (1984–, some full text, 1994–), White Papers (1985–, some in full text), and sources (Web sites, video, publications, etc.) arranged into Internet and Electronic Resources, Business and Employment Resources, and Research and Academic Resources.

Publications is the last home page heading discussed. There are links to the various EU Depository Libraries in the United States, particularly useful in locating comprehensive holdings of EU research materials, as well as links to business sources, free videos and publications, official publications, online publications, periodicals, and reading lists. Publications provides links to two ceased yet important titles, *EUROCOM* newsletter of the New York Delegation, full text (1995–2003) and to *EUROPE* magazine, online (1996–2003).

European Union Web Sites, by the Public Documents and Maps Department, Perkins Library, Duke University, Durham, North Carolina. <http://docs .lib.duke.edu/igo/guides/euindex.html>

Summary: Compiled by the Public Documents and Maps Department of Duke University's Perkins Library, this Web site serves as an aggregator of other Web sites pertaining to the European Union. The alphabetically arranged list of links contains brief annotations.

Guide to the Official Publications of the European Communities, by John Jeffries. 2nd ed. London: Mansell, 1981; New York: H. W. Wilson [distributor], 1981. (ISBN 0-72011-590-6).

Summary: The predecessor to the *Documentation of the European Communities: A Guide,* this publication has an overview of the major bodies of the European Communities and their official publications. The documentation is divided into subject-based chapters: Publications of the European Communities; Commission-General Publications; Commission-Non-statistical Publications; Eurostat-Publications of the Statistical Office of the European Communities; Council of Ministers; European Parliament; Court of Justice of the European Communities; Other Bodies; and Bibliographic Aids. Each subject area lists and describes relevant publications. Appendices provide address information for Commission Information Offices and Depository Libraries/Documentation Centers.

Historical Dictionary of the European Communities, by Desmond Dinan. Metuchen, N.J.: Scarecrow Press, 1993 (International Organizations Series No. 1) (ISBN 0-81082-666-6).

Summary: An alphabetically arranged dictionary of terms, individuals, bodies, organizations, and treaties, each entry is approximately a paragraph in length. A narrative essay introduces the book and provides historical and economic context. Also, there is a bibliography divided into official documents; reference; overview; external relations; history; institutions and decision making; member states, politics, and political movements; and policies and programs. The appendices have a chronology and tables and graphs.

The Penguin Companion to European Union, by Timothy Bainbridge. 3rd ed. London: Penguin, 2002 (ISBN 0-14100-769-9).

Summary: First published in 1995, with a second edition in 1998, this third edition has 60 new entries defining terms and discussing individuals, institutions, organizations, and events pertaining to the European Union. The entries are alphabetically arranged and consist of narrative descriptions, ranging from a paragraph to approximately a page and a half. A bibliography, with brief annotations, is also included, subdivided into sections on General Reference, History, the United Kingdom and Europe, Institutions of the European Union, Law, Economics and Single Market, Politics and Political Parties, Memories and Biographies, General Studies, and Periodicals.

Organization of American States (OAS) Sources Discussed

Classification Manual for the OAS Official Records Series: A Manual for the Maintenance of the Series. 2nd ed. Washington, D.C.: General Secretariat, Organization of American States, 1996 (ISBN 0-82703-637-X).

Organization of American States (OAS) Web site, Washington, D.C. <http://www.oas.org>

The Organization of American States: A Bibliography by Thomas L. Welch and René Gutiérrez. Washington, D.C.: Columbus Memorial Library, Organization of American States, 1990 (Hipólito Unanue Bibliographic Series No. 7).

The Organization of American States by David Sheinin. New Brunswick, N.J.: Transaction Publishers, 1996 (International Organizations Series No. 11) (ISBN 1-56000-243-3).

About the Organization/Purpose of the Organization: The history of the Organization of American States (OAS) began with the Congress of Panama (1826), the first step in officially organizing countries of the Western hemisphere. Then followed the International Union of American Republics and its Secretariat, the Commercial Bureau of American Republics (1890). The next step was the Pan American Union (1910), which then transformed into the Organization of American States via the adoption of the *OAS Charter* (April 30, 1948). Twenty-one countries adopted this *Charter:* Argentina, Bolivia, Brazil, Chile, Colombia, Costa Rica, Cuba, Dominican Republic, Ecuador, El Salvador, Guatemala, Haiti, Honduras, Mexico, Nicaragua, Panama, Paraguay, Peru, United States, Uruguay, and Venezuela. The membership has now expanded to 35 member countries with the addition of Barbados, Trinidad and Tobago (1967); Jamaica (1969); Grenada (1975); Suriname (1977); Dominica, Saint Lucia (1979); Antigua and Barbuda, Saint Vincent, and the Grenadines (1981); The Bahamas (1982); St. Kitts and Nevis (1984); Canada (1990); Belize and Guyana (1991). The official languages of the Organization of American States are English, Spanish, French, and Portuguese.

Headquartered in Washington, D.C., each member nation has a single vote. The OAS has a General Assembly, consisting of foreign ministers, that meets annually to discuss policies and planning. Its decisions are carried out by the General Secretariat. A Permanent Council, made up of an ambassador from each member country, meets regularly for the political and administrative functions. Other specialized agencies are also part of the OAS. Areas of work include trade, sustainable development, education, and democracy.

Organization of American States Sources

Classification Manual for the OAS Official Records Series: A Manual for the Maintenance of the Se- *ries.* 2nd ed. Washington, D.C.: General Secretariat, Organization of American States, 1996 (ISBN 0-82703-637-X).

Summary: First published in 1960 with the title *Guide, Outline and Expanded Tables for OAS Record Series,* the first edition of the current title became available in 1977. The second edition is a useful source for identifying the document numbers for the various Official Record Series.

Organization of American States (OAS) Web site, Washington, D.C. <http://www.oas.org>

Summary: The *Organization of American States (OAS)* Web site provides access to documents, publications, video and audio material, and news. Information is divided in to the main headings of News, About the OAS, General Assembly, Publications, Opportunities, Documents, Webcast, Library, Museum, IACD, Democratic Charter, and OAS Structure. The site is available in all four official languages: English, Spanish, French, and Portuguese. At the top of the page, a pull-down menu of OAS issues links to the relevant OAS resources.

Detailed Description: News is the first home page heading and consists of news highlights, press releases, video and audio broadcasts, the full text of the current newsletter, *OAS News,* and the eZine *American Forum.* About the OAS, another home page heading, contains information regarding the work of the organization and contact information.

General Assembly, the third home page heading, makes available materials from the most recent General Assembly session such as press releases, speeches, videos, and documents. An archive of full-text resolutions and declarations is available from 1995 forward. Documents may be searched by language, title, document number, date, agenda, type, and area.

Also from the home page, the heading Publications links to much online information published by OAS. Here are found the full text of the Secretary-General's *Annual Report* (2001–2002 in PDF and Microsoft WORD; 1997–2001 in full text; 1996–1997 in Spanish only); the full text of a special publication of the Secretary-General outlining the work of the OAS in *Toward the New Millennium: The Road Traveled 1994–1999;* the full text of *America's Magazine* (1997–); and *OAS News.* Of special interest is the AICD Digital Library, a collection of full-text publications. Many of these titles are now out of print, and they are organized under the subheadings OAS Collection and Links to Publications of Interest. The OAS Collection has four groups: the Spanish language education journal, *La Educación* (1995–); *Inter-American Review of Bibliography,* which contains specialized information in the Humanities and Social Sciences (in Spanish); *Interamer,* which features issues on cultural, education, and special issues; and the publication *Trends for a Common Future.* Links to Publications of Interest contains publications in the eight areas of interest of the Inter-American Council for Integral Development (CIDI). Available vacancies and internships are found in the Opportunities home page heading.

Documents, another home page heading, features the full text of the *OAS Charter* and *Democratic Charter* and also links to the OAS *Annual Reports.* In addition, the heading Documents links to Official Documents (laws, treaties, statutes and regulations of organs, resolutions, etc.), Reference Documents (links to specialized agencies), another access point to Resolutions and Declarations, Treaties and Conventions (described in the Law and Treaties chapter), OAS Archives, and Speeches (2000–). The Webcast main heading is another access point to audio and video broadcasts as well as live transmission of meetings in session.

The Library main heading links to the Columbus Memorial Library of the OAS. This is a comprehensive and rich research resource. Under the Library heading are descriptions of the various Library collections, publications, and services, as well as links to other related Web sites. There is also a link to the catalog, which is available for searching the Library's holdings. Museum is the main heading link to the Arts Museum of the Americas. Artwork can be viewed online, and a virtual gallery is included. Information about the collections, exhibits, and services is also available.

The Inter-American Agency for Cooperation and Development is described in the Development Chapter.

The Organization of American States: A Bibliography, by Thomas L. Welch and René Gutiérrez. Washington, D.C.: Columbus Memorial Library, Organization of American States, 1990 (Hipólito Unanue Bibliographic Series No. 7).

Summary: This brief bibliography contains a listing of books and periodical articles arranged by author last name. Although there are no annotations, a subject and title index is included.

The Organization of American States, by David Sheinin. New Brunswick, N.J.: Transaction Pub-

lishers, 1996 (International Organizations Series No. 11) (ISBN 1-56000-243-3).

Summary: This title is an annotated bibliography divided into the following sections: Introduction, Acronyms, Chronology, Reference Works, General Works, History, Events, Pan-Americanism, OAS in Inter-American Politics, and Issues. Entries under each subject are alphabetically arranged by title. Also included are indexes to authors, titles, and subjects.

League of Nations Sources Discussed

League of Nations Documents 1919–1946: A Descriptive Guide and Key to the Microfilm Collection, by Edward A. Reno, Jr. New Haven, Conn.: Research Publications, 1973–1975.

League of Nations Photo Archive Web site, Indiana University Center for Global Change, Bloomington, Ind. <http://www.indiana.edu/~league/>

League of Nations Statistical and Disarmament Documents Web site, Government Publications and Maps Department, Northwestern University Library, Evanston, Ill. <http://www.library.northwestern.edu/govpub/collections/league/>

About the Organization/Purpose of the Organization: Created as a way of promoting international peace and cooperation, the League of Nations was established on January 10, 1920, with headquarters in Geneva, Switzerland, and is the predecessor organization to the United Nations. In 1920, 63 countries were members, including major European countries, but not the United States. The main organs of the body were a Council, Assembly, and Secretariat. The League of Nations dissolved on April 18, 1946, and was assumed by the United Nations, which was established in 1945.

League of Nations Sources

League of Nations Documents 1919–1946: A Descriptive Guide and Key to the Microfilm Collection, by Edward A. Reno, Jr. New Haven, Conn.: Research Publications, 1973–1975.

Summary: The microfilm collection published by Research Publications is an excellent source for accessing League of Nations documents and serial publications. This guide indexes the microfilm collection and is arranged by the following subject categories: Administrative Commissions (IA), Minorities (IB), Financial Section and Economic Intelligence Service (IIA), Section of Economic Relations (IIB),

Health (III), Social Questions (IV), Legal Questions (V), Mandates (VIA), Slavery (VIB), Political Section (VII), Communications and Transit (VIII), Disarmament (IX), Financial Administration of the League of Nation (X), Traffic in Opium and Other Dangerous Drugs (XI), Intellectual Cooperation (XIIA), International Bureau (XIIB), Refugees (XIII), and General Questions—Documents from the Secretariat (G). The number of the section helps the researcher access the microfiche. Within each year are Circular documents, Assembly documents, and Council documents.

League of Nations Photo Archive Web site, by the Indiana University Center for Global Change, Bloomington, Ind. <http://www.indiana.edu/~league/>

Summary: Digital photographs from the League of Nations Archives are provided by this archive. An Introduction explains the project and has links to *The Illustrated Album of the League of Nations* and *League of Nations: A Pictorial Survey,* both also digitized. The collection is divided into the headings: Personalities, Assemblies, Councils, Commissions and Committees, Conferences, Secretariat, Delegations, Permanent Court of International Justice, International Labour Organization/Bureau International du Travail, and last of all, one entitled Various. Each heading contains a description and link to the relevant photographs. A Sources section links to other sites, a research guide, timeline, and bibliography.

League of Nations Statistical and Disarmament Documents Web site, by the Government Publications and Maps Department, Northwestern University Library, Evanston, Ill. <http://www.library.northwestern.edu/govpub/collections/league/>

Summary: This digital collection has the full text of 260 documents pertaining to disarmament from the League of Nations. A search engine is available to browse the collection online. The full text of the *Statistical Yearbook of the League of Nations* (1926–1944) is also included and can be downloaded or viewed in PDF.

General Resources Discussed

Database of International Organizations, compiled by the Union of International Associations (online subscription version). <http://www.uia.org/organizations/ybonline.php>

Encyclopedia of Associations: International Organizations. Detroit: Gale Research Co., 1960– (ISSN 0071-0202).

The Europa Directory of International Organizations. London: Europa Publications, 1999– (ISSN 1465-4628).

Guide to Country Information in International Governmental Organization Publications, by Marian Shaaban. Chicago: American Library Association Government Documents Round Table, 1996.

Historical Dictionary of European Organizations, by Derek W. Urwin. Metuchen, N.J.: Scarecrow Press, 1994 (Historical Dictionary of International Organizations Series No. 4) (ISBN 0-81082-838-3).

Historical Dictionary of Inter-American Organizations, by Larman C. Wilson and David W. Dent. Metuchen, N.J.: Scarecrow Press, 1998 (Historical Dictionaries of International Organizations Series No. 14) (ISBN 0-81083-381-6).

Historical Dictionary of International Organizations, by Michael G. Schechter. Metuchen, N.J.: Scarecrow Press, 1998 (Historical Dictionaries of International Organizations Series No. 16) (ISBN 0-81083-479-0).

The Information Systems of International Inter-Governmental Organizations: A Reference Guide, by Robert V. Williams. Stamford, Conn.: Ablex Publishing Corporation, 1998 (ISBN 1-56750-339-X).

International Documents Task Force Web Links Web site, by the Government Documents Round Table of the American Library Association (GODORT). <http://www.library.uiuc.edu/doc/idtf/links.htm#igos>

International Information: Documents, Publications, and Electronic Information of International Government Organizations, by Peter I. Hajnal. Englewood, Colo.: Libraries Unlimited, 1997–2001, 2 vols. (ISBN 1-56308-147-4 [v.1]; 1-56308-808-8 [v. 2]).

International Organizations: A Dictionary, by Giuseppe Schiavone. 4th ed. New York: Stockton Press, 1997 (ISBN 0-33367-591-6).

International Organization and World Order Dictionary, by Sheikh R. Ali. Santa Barbara, Calif.: ABC-CLIO, Inc., 1992 (ISBN 0-87436-572-4).

IONET: International Organization Network Web site, compiled by the International Organization Section of the International Studies Association. <http://csf.colorado.edu/isa/sections/io/internet.html>

Yearbook of International Organizations: Guide to Global Civil Society Networks, compiled by

Union of International Associations, 1967– (print title) (ISSN 0084-3814).

Yearbook Plus of International Organizations and Biographies, compiled by Union of International Associations. München; New Providence: K. G. Saur, 1990s–(annual CD-ROM and title).

GENERAL RESOURCES

Database of International Organizations, compiled by the Union of International Associations (online subscription version).

<http://www.uia.org/organizations/ybonline.php>

Summary: A federation since 1910, the Union is a nonprofit clearinghouse for information on over 40,000 international organizations and constituencies and maintains consultative status with the United Nations Economic and Social Council since 1953. Its goals include promoting recognition and understanding of international organizations by making the information available as well as encouraging meetings of these organizations and undertaking research studies and surveys. This annual, multivolume directory, published since 1967 in print, provides up-to-date and comprehensive profiles of nonprofit international organizations, both governmental and nongovernmental. Detailed information, easily accessed, concerning international organizations and their names, purposes, activities, and publications is provided. Many types of organizations are included, from professional to recreational, excluding for-profit enterprises. There are also CD-ROM and online (by subscription only) versions. In addition to this title, the Union publishes other databases in many formats, listed and described following and also at <http://www.uia.org/services/databases.php>, which is searchable alphabetically or by subject.

Detailed Description: Volume 1 (in two parts) includes organization descriptions in alphabetical order for quick reference and cross-references between organizations. The description provided for each organization includes names, addresses, officers, aims, history, structure, finances, activities, publications, member countries, and links among organizations. Volume 2 provides a country directory of participation in international organizations. It helps users to find out which organizations are active in a specific country or region. Volume 3 is the global action networks index, a classified subject guide and index that users can use to locate organizations by region or subject.

Volume 4 is a bibliography and resource guide that cites the research publications of the international organizations as well as research citations by subject heading. Volume 5 includes statistical tables organized by geographic regions and subject interests in which organizations are involved. Illustrations of the statistical data accompany the tables as well as historical statistical summaries and analyses. Within the tables, organizations are clearly specified as to type and whether they are intergovernmental (IGO) or nongovernmental (NGO).

The CD-ROM version, in English, French, and multilingual languages edition, is accessible using a self-installing database access program called FolioBoundVIEWS. Text is hyperlinked to related organizations, officers, and other relevant information. Biographical information is based on *Who's Who in International Organizations.*

The online subscription version of the database entitled *Database of International Organizations,* provides direct links to the Internet sites of international organizations and is kept up-to-date. Some additional information may be included in this format that is not available in the CD-ROM or paper versions because of space constraints.

Encyclopedia of Associations: International Organizations. Detroit: Gale Research Co., 1960– (ISSN 0071-0202).

Summary: Published annually since the 1960s, the volumes related to International Organizations are arranged in a subject format. Each numbered entry, arranged alphabetically within the subject designation, contains contact information, description of the organization, major publications, and meeting information. Geographic, executives, and name and keyword indexing provide information necessary to locate the entries.

Europa Directory of International Organizations. London: Europa Publications, 1999– (ISSN 1465-4628).

Summary: Published annually since 1999, this directory provides comprehensive coverage of international organizations in five major parts. This discussion is based on the fourth edition, 2002. Part 1, Background Information, features an essay about international organizations and gives a chronology and listing of international observances. Part 2, United Nations, contains comprehensive information of the United Nations itself, the Principal Organs, UN Regional Commissions,

Other UN Bodies, and Specialized Agencies within the UN System. Part 3, Major Non-UN Organizations, is arranged alphabetically and includes a lengthy description of the organization and its activities. Part 4, Other International Organizations, lists the organizations by subject and includes a brief descriptive entry. Part 5, Who's Who in International Organizations, is also arranged alphabetically and contains brief entries.

Guide to Country Information in International Governmental Organization Publications, by Marian Shaaban. Chicago: American Library Association Government Documents Round Table, 1996.

Summary: This volume provides an annotated bibliography of major intergovernmental organization publications pertaining to regions of the world and, in some cases, individual countries. Publications are either those issued by the organization itself or those of commercial publishers on behalf of the organization. Print and electronic resources are found here, dating from 1988 through 1994, unless earlier issues were of such significant importance to also be included. Some new publications and CD-ROM products, dating through December 1995, are also listed.

The volume is divided into eight sections: Worldwide/Multiregional; Africa; Asia/Pacific; Europe; Latin America/Caribbean; Middle East; North America; and Guides, Catalogs, and Indexes. Within each section, the entries are arranged topically and contain annotated citations of relevant sources. Because there is some overlapping, the researcher should consult both the Worldwide/Multiregional section and the specific region of interest. Topics include: General; Agriculture/Fisheries/Forestry; Children/Youth; Crime/Narcotics Control; Culture, History/Social Sciences; Development/Assistance; Economic Affairs; Education/Training; Energy; Environment/Natural Resources; Finance/National Accounts; Food/Nutrition; Health; Housing/Construction; Human Rights/Racial Discrimination; Industry; International Trade; Labor/Social Security; Laws/Treaties; Mass Media/Communications; Peace/Disarmament/Military Affairs; Population/Migration/Refugees; Research and Development/Science/Technology; Transportation; and Women. However, not all regions include all topics. Indexing is available by issuing sources and titles. A listing is also provided of selected IGOs and the countries of membership of each.

Historical Dictionary of European Organizations, by Derek W. Urwin. Metuchen, N.J.: Scarecrow Press,

1994 (Historical Dictionary of International Organizations Series No. 4) (ISBN 0-81082-838-3).

Summary: Featured in this volume are acronyms and abbreviations; a post-1941 chronology; a brief introductory essay of the political history; and in the main body, a dictionary of terms, individuals, organizations, and issues, usually a paragraph in length, pertaining to European organizations. Although there is no index, the accompanying appendices include the institutional structure of the European Community and presidents of the EC, ECSC High Authority, EURATOM Commission, and Secretary Generals of NATO. A nonannotated bibliography concludes the volume and is divided into: Europe; International and European Organizations; Cold War; German Question; North Atlantic Treaty Organization; Defense and Deterrence; East European Security; Arms Control; Disarmament; European Integration Before 1957; European Economic Community; European Atomic Energy Community; European Community: General; European Community: Structures; European Community: Policy Areas; European Free Trade Association; Nordic Cooperation; Space; Franco-German Relations; and Eurocommunism.

Historical Dictionary of Inter-American Organizations, by Larman C. Wilson and David W. Dent. Metuchen, N.J.: Scarecrow Press, 1998 (Historical Dictionaries of International Organizations Series No. 14) (ISBN 0-81083-381-6).

Summary: Following the standard *Historical Dictionaries of International Organizations Series* format, this volume is comprised of a list of abbreviations and acronyms; chronology of organizations and events; maps; introductory essay of issues, history, and organization participation; dictionary of terms, individuals, organizations, and issues, with each entry a paragraph in length. The included appendices focus more on the Organization of American States and provide listings of officers and structure, as well as the *Charter of the OAS* text. The volume concludes with a bibliographic essay subdivided into General Topics, Inter-American and International Relations; Regional Organizations; Global and Universal Organizations; Latin American/Caribbean Relations with the World; Nongovernmental Organizations; Guides to Professional Journals; Inter-American Organizations, and the Internet, immediately followed by a nonannotated bibliography subdivided by these same topical headings.

Historical Dictionary of International Organizations, by Michael G. Schechter. Metuchen, N.J.: Scarecrow Press, 1998 (Historical Dictionaries of International Organizations Series No. 16) (ISBN 0-81083-479-0).

Summary: The bulk of the volume consists of the dictionary of terms, individuals, and organizations of international organizations. An acronyms and abbreviations listing begins this volume, followed by a selected chronology of international organizations and key events. The historical context, trends, and future are discussed in the narrative introduction. There is also a nonannotated bibliography subdivided into General Works on International Organizations; United Nations (Major Organs); Specialized and Related Agencies of the United Nations; Regional Organizations; Non-United Nations, Nonregional Intergovernmental Organizations (includes the League of Nations); and International Nongovernmental Organizations.

Information Systems of International Inter-Governmental Organizations: A Reference Guide, by Robert V. Williams. Stamford, Conn.: Ablex Publishing Corporation, 1998 (ISBN 1-56750-339-X).

Summary: An excellent reference source for finding publications of intergovernmental organizations, this volume is divided into three parts with descriptive entries in each: United Nations and United Nations Subsidiary Bodies; United Nations Specialized Agencies, the IAEA, and Related Organizations; All Other Inter-Governmental Organizations. Each entry includes all or some of the following elements: address, description, overview of the information systems, Internet access, major libraries and documentation centers, how to acquire publications and documents, list of publications, and publications and documents indexes. A compilation of Web sites gathered during the research of this book is available at <http://www.libsci.sc.edu/bob/IGOs.htm>, however, it has not been updated since 2001.

International Documents Task Force Web Links
Web site, by the Government Documents Round Table of the American Library Association.

<http://www.library.uiuc.edu/doc/idtf/links.htm#igos>

Summary: Compiled by the Government Documents Round Table of the American Library Associ-ation, this site brings together other aggregations of international organizations including Northwestern University Library, Union of International Associations, and University of Michigan Library Documents Center. Nongovernmental organization aggregation sites are also included. Also included are links of interest to information professionals in the area of international and foreign (non-U.S.) government information.

International Information: Documents, Publications, and Electronic Information of International Government Organizations, by Peter I. Hajnal. Englewood, Colo.: Libraries Unlimited, 1997–2001, 2 vols. (ISBN 1-56308-147-4 [v.1]; 1-56308-808-8 [v. 2]).

Summary: An outstanding, detailed research resource for understanding the publishing and accessibility of international documentation, this volume provides in-depth coverage of the documents, publications, and electronic information produced by international organizations (IGOs). Volume 1 is divided into three parts; the first part, Institutions, examines and describes the United Nations, European Union, Organization for Economic Co-operation and Development, League of Nations, International Development Research Centre, and the G7 (now the G8). Resources, the second part, examines the electronic information sources of the United Nations family of organizations, the document resources of the Dag Hammarskjöld library, and other United Nations research tools. The third part, Processes, examines the library processes of collection development and reference and information work. An extensive nonannotated bibliography is also included.

Volume 2 updates and augments the information in volume 1 for institutions, resources, and library processes, also including a bibliography. The institutions it covers in detail are the International Monetary Fund; the General Agreement on Tariffs and Trade (GATT) and its successor organization the World Trade Organization (WTO); La Francophonie—officially called the Organisation internationale de la Francophonie (OIF); and international selected nongovernmental organizations and civil society. Also covered in this volume is an examination of the role of IGO as publishers; microform documents; maps and other cartographic materials; IGO archives; UN information gathering in the area of peace and security; trends in reference services for UN system materials; and forms of citation of IGO documents, publications, and electronic information.

International Organizations: A Dictionary, by Giuseppe Schiavone. 4th ed. New York: Stockton Press, 1997 (ISBN 0-33367-591-6).

Summary: This is an alphabetically arranged dictionary of international organizations, which also includes an introductory narrative essay providing a historical context. Each dictionary entry contains descriptions of the origin of the organization and its development, objectives, structure, activities, and contact information. In addition, there is a table of international organizations memberships, classification of countries and membership of major groups, and two indexes (classified and names).

International Organization and World Order Dictionary, by Sheikh R. Ali. Santa Barbara, Calif.: ABC-CLIO, Inc., 1992 (ISBN 0-87436-572-4).

Summary: This dictionary is a straightforward A to Z listing of organizations, arranged alphabetically, with each entry describing the organization and its significance. An index is also included.

IONET: International Organization Network Web site, compiled by the International Organization Section of the International Studies Association. <http://csf.colorado.edu/isa/sections/io/internet.html>

Summary: Established in 1959 and based at the University of Arizona, this organization brings together international relations scholars. The Web site serves as an aggregator of subject-based resources organized into the categories: International Governmental Organizations; Nongovernmental Organizations, UN Conferences, Academic Associations, Africa, Asia, Electronic Discussion Groups, Environment and Development; Europe, General Global Politics Resources, Governments, Human Rights and Humanitarian Issues, International Law, Journals and Other Electronic Repositories, Latin America, Middle East, News Sources, Security, Universities, Other Resources, and Search Engines. Each subject contains links to other relevant sites. The frequency of updates is not available and some links were broken at the time of this writing.

Yearbook of International Organizations: Guide to Global Civil Society Networks, compiled by Union of International Associations, 1967– (print title) (ISSN 0084-3814).

Yearbook Plus of International Organizations and Biographies, compiled by Union of International Associations München; New Providence: K. G. Saur, 1990– (annual CD-ROM title).

BIOGRAPHICAL SOURCES

Biography and Genealogy Master Index. Detroit, Mich.: Gale Research Co., 1980– (ISSN 0730-1316) (print); (ISSN 1066-7695) (online subscription).

Encyclopedia of World Biography, edited by Paula K. Byers. 2nd ed. Detroit, Mich.: Gale Research Co., 1998 (ISBN 0-78762-221-4).

Who's Who in International Affairs. 3rd ed. London: Europa Publications Ltd., 2003 (ISBN 1-85743-156-1).

Who's Who in International Organizations: A Biographical Encyclopedia of More Than 13,000 Leading Personalities, prepared by Nancy Carfrae. 2nd ed. München; New Providence: K. G. Saur, 1996 (ISBN 3-59811-239-4) (set).

Who's Who in the World. Chicago: Marquis Who's Who, Inc. (ISSN 0083-9825).

Biography and Genealogy Master Index. Detroit, Mich.: Gale Research Co., 1980– (ISSN 0730-1316) (print); (ISSN 1066-7695) (online subscription).

Summary: Available in print and electronic (subscription) formats, this index to biographical publications is alphabetically arranged by last name. Each entry lists biographical sources to consult.

Encyclopedia of World Biography, edited by Paula K. Byers. 2nd ed. Detroit, Mich.: Gale Research Co., 1998, 18 vols. (ISBN 0-78762-221-4).

Summary: This 18-volume set contains narrative biographical entries, alphabetically arranged, as well as a brief further readings list. The eighteenth volume is a supplement published in 1999 with updates and name / subject index.

Who's Who in International Affairs. 3rd ed. London: Europa Publications Ltd., 2003 (ISBN 1-85743-156-1).

Summary: The alphabetically arranged entries contain birth date, education and career highlights, publications, and contact information. The first edition was published in 1990.

Who's Who in International Organizations: A Biographical Encyclopedia of More than 13,000 Leading Personalities, prepared by Nancy Carfrae.

2nd ed. München; New Providence: K. G. Saur, 1996 (ISBN 3-59811-239-4) (set).

Summary: Comprised of three volumes, volumes 1 and 2 contain biographical sketches with education, career, field of work, highlights of honors, and contact information. The third volume contains indexes: name by organization, area of concern, and country of citizenship.

Who's Who in the World. Chicago: Marquis Who's Who, Inc., 1995– (ISSN 0083-9825).

Summary: An annual publication since 1995 and a biennial publication from 1971–1994, this source provides brief biographical sketches including name, occupation, family, education, position, organization memberships, awards, and contact information. A professional index is also included.

STYLE MANUALS

Complete Guide to Citing Government Information Resources: A Manual for Social Science & Business Research, by Debora Cheney, Diane L Garner, and Diane H. Smith. 3rd ed. Bethesda, Md.: LexisNexis, Congressional Information Service, 2002 (ISBN 0-88692-586-X).

Complete Guide to Citing Government Information Resource: A Manual for Writers & Librarians, by Diane L. Garner, Diane H. Smith, with additional chapters by Debora Cheney and Helen Sheehy for the Government Documents Round Table, American Library Association. Rev. ed. Bethesda, Md.: Congressional Information Service, 1993 (ISBN 0-88692-254-2).

The Complete Guide to Citing Government Information Resources: A Manual for Social Science & Business Research, by Debora Cheney, Diane L Garner, and Diane H. Smith. 3rd ed. Bethesda, Md.: LexisNexis, Congressional Information Service, 2002 (ISBN 0-88692-586-X).

Complete Guide to Citing Government Information Resources: A Manual for Writers & Librarians, by Diane L. Garner and Diane H. Smith, with additional chapters by Debora Cheney and Helen Sheehy for the Government Documents Round Table, American Library Association. Rev. ed. Bethesda, Md.: Congressional Information Service, 1993 (ISBN 0-88692-254-2).

Summary: Both of these publications contain information on how to cite all types of government information resources, including paper books and periodicals, electronic online and CD formats, and part of an aggregator sources, databases, Web sites, and much more. Many examples are included.

NOTES

1. Sometimes referred to as *IONet.*
2. "About the General Assembly," *United Nations* Web site, New York, <http://www.un.org/ga/57/about.htm> (accessed February 27, 2004).
3. "What is the European Union?" *European Union in the United States* Web site, by the Delegation of the European Commission, Washington, D.C., <http://www.eurunion.org/infores/euguide/Chapter1.htm#Chapter%201:> (accessed February 27, 2004).

PART II
Subject Chapters

CHAPTER 2
Agriculture and Food

CHAPTER OVERVIEW

Agriculture is defined as the science or art of cultivating crops, raising livestock, and other farming. It is a major worldwide industry that affects nations both rich and poor. This chapter focuses on these topics and also includes some information on nutrition and food. Major statistical sources on agriculture are included in this chapter. Both governmental and nongovernmental organizations promote their mission through their information, are politically active, and seek to influence governments' policies in the field of agriculture.

Other agricultural information can also be found in the trade chapter resources covering trade of agricultural commodities. Also, because agriculture is an industrial sector, economic resources will often cover agriculture as well as many other economic factors.

Governmental Sources Discussed

Food and Agriculture Organization of the United Nations Resources (FAO)

FAOSTAT Web site, by the Food and Agriculture Organization (FAO) of the United Nations. <http://apps.fao.org/>

Food and Agriculture Organization (FAO) of the United Nations Web site, Rome. <http://www.fao.org>

State of the.... FAO World Review Series Web site, by the Food and Agriculture Organization (FAO) of the United Nations, including the following titles <http://www.fao.org/sof/index_en.htm> (all print and online titles):

   State of Food and Agriculture (SOFA) (ISSN 0081-4539) (print annual title and online since 1994).

   State of Food Insecurity in the World (SOFI) (print annual editions and online since 1999).

   State of World Fisheries and Aquaculture (SOFIA) (ISSN 1020-5489) (print irregular editions and online since 1998).

   State of the World's Forests (SOFO) (ISSN 1020-5705) (print biennial titles and online since 1995).

OECD Agricultural Outlook, by the Directorate for Food, Agriculture, and Fisheries, Organisation for Economic Co-operation and Development (OECD). Paris. (print annual title and online subscription).

FAS Online: United States Department of Agriculture Foreign Agricultural Service Web site, by the U.S. Dept. of Agriculture. <http://www.fas.usda.gov/>

Nongovernmental Sources Discussed

CGIAR (Consultative Group on Agricultural Research) Web site, Washington, D.C. <http://www.cgiar.org/>

Food First Web site, by the Food First/Institute for Food and Development Policy, Oakland, Calif. <http://www.foodfirst.org/>

Future Harvest Web site, Washington, D.C. <http://www.futureharvest.org/>

GOVERNMENTAL SOURCES

Food and Agriculture Organization of the United Nations Resources (FAO)

FAOSTAT Web site, by the Food and Agriculture Organization (FAO) of the United Nations.

<http://apps.fao.org/> (online and online subscription service).

Summary: *FAOSTAT* is a resource of online multilingual databases that contain over 1 million time series records covering international statistics in the following areas: production, trade, food balance sheets, fertilizers and pesticides, land use and irrigation, forest products, fishery products, population, agricultural machinery, and food aid shipments. The left sidebar leads the user to the databases and a section on What's New. A list of all databases is available. (Note that the databases are unavailable late Sunday to early Monday central European time.) Databases are produced in French, Spanish, Arabic, and Chinese.

The FAO, as part of its mission, compiles and analyzes data and information from countries on various aspects of food and agriculture. The country-level data in *FAOSTAT* is collected through surveys and visits to countries. Statistical data is disseminated to the public in a broad variety of ways, including paper publications, CD-ROMS, diskettes, and the Internet.

Detailed Description: Querying the databases allows users many options. A user may select elements from country/region/organization, item, data type, and year to formulate a query and can select output as a table or CSV file. Some of the databases go back to the 1960s. The annual subscription service provides extended query and download capabilities. Also of note is the *FAOSTAT 200 CD-ROM: FAO Statistical Databases,* Rome, 2001, multilingual (ISBN 9-25004-535-2) which contains more than a million time-series records in the areas of agriculture, fisheries, forestry, and nutrition.

Food and Agriculture Organization (FAO) of the United Nations Web site, Rome. <http://www.fao.org>

Summary: This is a comprehensive searchable Web site of an international governmental organization devoted to agriculture, forestry, fisheries, rural development, and nutrition. Researchers may consult the FAO catalog online or even search the *FAO* Web site for periodical or monographic titles on the topics of their choice. There are many statistics available under *FAOSTAT,* described as a separate resource in this chapter. Other major resources are also separately described. Users will find many titles full text online appropriate for high school users and older. The Web site is available in English, French, Spanish, Arabic, and Chinese. The FAO was founded in 1945 with a mandate to raise levels of nutrition and standards of living, to improve agricultural productivity, and to better the condition of rural populations. Today FAO is one of the largest specialized agencies in the United Nations system with 187 member countries plus one member organization, the European Union.

Detailed Description: The FAO home page leads to many resources on agriculture. Some of the content-rich links from the left sidebar buttons of this Web page are links to: Statistical Databases; Agriculture; Economics & Nutrition; Fisheries; Forestry; Sustainable Development; Technical Cooperation; Programme, Budget and Evaluation; Legal Office; Decentralized Offices; Employment; Interdisciplinary Activities; Trade; Biotechnology; Gender; Country Information; Virtual Library; Publications; and more. Look for articles on hot topics in the midsection of the home page, such as bird flu virus, AIDS, and toxic pesticide waste dumps. These news stories are archived by year under Newsroom back to 2002. On the right side of the page are links to special programs of the FAO.

Country-rich resources include the *State of the....FAO World Review Series,* under the Publications section, and other home page links to Selected Key Programmes and other Conferences, such as the FAO World Food Summits 1996 and 2002. Statistical Databases links to *FAOSTAT,* which is covered in this chapter as an individual resource. Of particular note to researchers is the home page link to the World Agricultural Information Center, an online resource which helps users access agricultural information. It links to an online *Glossary of FAO Databases and Information Systems,* a list of annotated hot linked resources, including these few sample resources: *FAOLEX,* which stores full-text copies of international treaties, laws, and regulations related to food, agriculture, and renewable natural resources; *FAOTERM,* a multilingual dictionary of agricultural terms; and *FAO Country Profiles and Mapping Information System,* which groups FAO information by country.

The search engine allows simple searching for word or phrase free text and advanced searching capabilities by many elements for documents and publications, Web pages, photos, press releases, and free text. It also provides a browse-by-topic feature, help tips, and search examples. The advanced search for documents is taken from the Corporate Document Repository, but the entire FAO bibliography is available from the *FAO Catalogue On-Line,* <http://www4.fao.org/faobib/>, which is searchable by many types of functions, including advanced, simple, and command searching. The *Catalogue* includes documents and publications produced by FAO since 1945, as well as other publication titles. It also provides a thesaurus and a database of new books and new serials. Full-text links are provided for documents in electronic formats, or a researcher may order the title in print or microfiche.

By accessing the Economics and Nutrition link on the left sidebar of the home page, then following the Nutrition link, users may find online nutrition country profiles under Human Nutrition and *INFOODS,* the *International Network of Food Data Systems,* under Nutrition Assesment *INFOODS* provides data on the nutrient composition of foods on a partnership site with information from all over the world. This information is critical to many areas of agriculture and food production, including the labeling nutrition contents of food for the consumer.

Other resources from the FAO Newsroom include the FAO online photograph archive *Mediabase,* which contains more than 3,000 photos and was launched in 1996. Thumbnail photos and basic information can be clicked for more textual information about the photo. It is searchable by type of format, phrase, and region and provides an Index. (For example, try format—photos, with subject—AIDS and Region—Africa to retrieve a list of thumbnail photos.)

The link to the section FAO Regional Conferences from the home page allows the researcher to search and discover major topics and issues worldwide, by region, or by country. The date, place, and a list of documents on the conference are available for the current year's conferences, which are held by region. The conferences offer introductions, country statements, discussion items, and conclusions and recommendations. Appendices are available and also a list of the FAO member countries of that particular region.

The home page links to FAO Key Selected Programmes, which include: SPFS: Special Programme for Food Security; EMPRES: Emergency Prevention System for Transboundary Animal and Plant Diseases; GIEWS: Global Information and Early Warning System on Food and Agriculture; and Special Relief Operations. SPFS provides general information, procedures, objectives, and support for the program and also online case studies. These case studies are available for programs in specific countries, for example, fish farming in Zambia under "SPFS," "Case Studies," and "Zambia."

FAO reports regularly worldwide meetings of government leaders on food issues under the section World Food Summit. Watch for audio and video files especially in this area. The Global Watch link from the home page provides specific articles about problem areas in the world and crises archived back to 1996.

State of the.... FAO World Review Series Web site, by the Food and Agriculture Organization (FAO) of the United Nations, including the following titles: <http://www.fao.org/sof/index_en.htm> (all print and online titles):

State of Food and Agriculture (SOFA) (ISSN 0081-4539) (print annual title 1947– and online 1994–).
State of World Fisheries and Aquaculture (SOFIA) (ISSN 1020-5489) (print irregular title and online 1998–).
State of the World's Forests (SOFO) (ISSN 1020-5705) (print biennial titles and online 1995–).
State of Food Insecurity in the World (SOFI) (print annual title and online 1999–).

Summary: In its *World Review Series,* FAO disseminates recent information and analyses on subjects covered by its mission, such as food and agriculture, fisheries and aquaculture, forests, and food insecurity. These titles discuss the subjects on a worldwide level. The text is clear and understandable from a high school level on up. Overall, these are good introductory, explanatory sources for current conditions in the world.
Detailed Description: Statistics, tables, graphs, and illustrations supplement the text. All of these titles are available in English, French, Spanish, Arabic, and Chinese. Some of the titles are available for ordering as a time series on a diskette. Researchers must consult their libraries for the information prior to the few current years posted on the Internet. FAO documents are usually owned by research institutions that have an international, agricultural, business, or economics focus.

- *State of Food and Agriculture (SOFA)* (ISSN 0081-4539) (print annual title 1947– and online 1994–).

  This is an annual report on developments and policies affecting world agriculture, with each year focusing on a special topic of current interest at the world and regional level. It covers environmental issues and provides statistics and country information.
- *State of Food Insecurity in the World (SOFI)* (print annual title and online 1999–).
- *State of World Fisheries and Aquaculture (SOFIA)* (ISSN 1020-5489) (print irregular title 1996– and online 1998–).

  This title is published every two years in order to provide policy makers and civilians within this industry with a comprehensive, global view of capture fisheries and farm fisheries (aquaculture).
- *State of the World's Forests (SOFO)* (ISSN 1020-5705) (print biennial title and online 1995–).

  Published every two years, this report gives a comprehensive, global, statistical view of the developments in forestry and the state of the world's forests.

This annual report covers global and national efforts to reach the goal set by the 1996 World Food Summit to reduce the number of malnourished people in the world by half by the year 2015 and to relieve food insecurity (when people live in hunger and fear starvation).

FAS Online: United States Department of Agriculture Foreign Agricultural Service Web site, by the U.S. Dept. of Agriculture. <http://www.fas.usda.gov/>

Summary: This resource is a comprehensive English Web site authored by the U.S. federal government that collects data about agriculture in other countries to assist in providing financial support, among other reasons. Two of its major resources are *World Production, Market, and Trade Reports* and *World Agricultural Production,* but many more sources of information from the Foreign Agricultural Service (FAS) are listed in the Detailed Description. There are online databases, periodicals, and reports available online. The FAS search engine searches text by word or phrase with Boolean logic and tips are available.

Part of its mission is to provide links to international organizations and world resources and assist in building a spirit of cooperation. It helps U.S. companies get access to foreign markets for their products. It analyzes production and trade and reports on trends in policies and developments worldwide that affect U.S. trade policy.

Detailed Description: The Foreign Agricultural Service provides information market intelligence and access; provides trade policy formulation and monitoring; collects data; distributes food aid around the world; and provides financial support to U.S. companies. The FAS home page provides links to information about countries and commodities; import and export programs; news and information; and a magazine index. Users may select the Countries or Commodities sections from the top of the home page to select specific countries and products to research for import/export potential. The section on Countries includes links under individual countries and contains new reports released within two weeks. The Trade Policies and Negotiations section provides information about agricultural trade policies around the world. Food Aid covers information on FAS food aid programs around the world.

Here are some specific titles that are available from *FAS Online.* A researcher with a specific title in mind may first consult *FAS Publications and Reports Index* online at <http://www.fas.usda.gov/info/pubindex/pub-a.html>, which lists reports, fact sheets, and periodicals alphabetically by title. However, it is not very efficient for browsing. The series of specialized reports on trade called *World Market and Trade Reports* contains titles that include commodity, trade, and market information by country worldwide. They cover specific agricultural products such as tobacco, sugar, dairy, or livestock. Each title is issued periodically, and researchers may see the list at <http://www.fas.usda.gov/info/circular.html>. Researchers note that with the transition from paper to online titles, the titles changed. Similar information is available historically published by the FAS with titles such as *World Market Report: Tobacco* or *World Market Report: Sugar* and are available from federal depository libraries in paper or microfiche. Try the *World Market and Trade Short Reports* for summaries about specific agricultural products in specific countries (arranged chronologically from the latest). Other search options are available at the *Attache Reports* Web page, <http://www.fas.usda.gov/scriptsw/attacherep/default.asp>, which allows the user to select on the commodity, country and date, or subject, or AGR number to search 22,705 reports online from 1995 as of February 10, 2004. These are available in a PDF format to display visuals such as charts and graphs or in a downloadable text version.

AgExporter, a monthly magazine published by FAS from 1989, is available full text online from 1996 at <http://www.fas.usda.gov/info/agexporter/agexport.html> or <http://purl.access.gpo.gov/GPO/LPS1647>. The image of the latest issue is available from the home page; a Magazine Index link below the image provides access to older issues. Although geared to U.S. agricultural producers and exporters, it provides information for businesses selling farm products overseas, including tips on exporting and descriptions of markets.

OECD Agricultural Outlook, by the Directorate for Food, Agriculture, and Fisheries, Organisation for Economic Co-operation and Development (OECD), Paris (print annual title and online subscription).

Summary: First published in 1995 in English and French, this annual title analyzes how global and domestic forces shape agricultural markets over the five previous years of each edition. It provides statistics and analysis of agricultural trends and future prospects for regions and countries, especially for the member states of the OECD.

Detailed Description: This title covers specific subjects in chapters with a statistical annex. The chapters are well illustrated with figures and tables and analyze specific commodities and sometimes the current agricultural conditions and prospects of a specific country. A glossary and references are included. The statistical tables cover about a decade of projections of production for specific agricultural commodities for OECD countries. Tables are included with projections for other selected countries and commodities.

In addition to publishing this title, OECD publishes much more information on agriculture, especially on agricultural markets, policies, and special issues that affect the industrialized member states of the OECD. These include its many databases, such as the *Agricultural Commodities Outlook Database,* statistics, publications and documents, and information by country. This information is available from the OECD Web site at <http://www.oecd.org/agriculture> and also through its online subscription resource SourceOECD.

NONGOVERNMENTAL SOURCES

CGIAR (Consultative Group on Agricultural Research) Web site, Washington, D.C. <http://www.cgiar.org/>

Summary: The combined efforts of CGIAR and its partners have increased food productivity in developing countries. Other goals that CGIAR works on and provides information about are increased farm income, reduced prices of food, better food distribution systems, better nutrition, more rational agricultural policies for nations, and stronger agricultural institutions. CGIAR provides information online about specific programs in these areas and has a range of publications, databases, and periodicals provided from its main page or from the Web pages of the many specialized institutes under the main organization. Historical documents in full text are available back to 1971.

Established in 1973, CGIAR is an informal association of 63 members supporting agricultural research and related activities carried out by 16 autonomous research centers. Individual members are from both the public and private sector. The World Bank, the Food and Agricultural Organization (FAO) of the United Nations, and the United Nations Development Programme (UNDP) are cosponsors of the CGIAR. The mission of this organization is to contribute to food security and assist in eradicating poverty in developing countries through research, partnership, capacity building, and policy support. The CGIAR promotes the environmentally sound management of natural resources in working for sustainable agricultural development. Built into its organizational structure, the CGIAR supports international centers as part of a global agricultural research system. One of its main functions is assisting in seeing that international scientific effort is spent on the world's disadvantaged.

Detailed Description: Programs carried out by CGIAR-supported centers fall into six broad categories. Information on these topics is available from the home page.

- **Productivity Research:** Creating or adopting new technologies (such as the "dwarf" varieties of wheat and rice that brought about Asia's and Latin America's green revolution) to increase productivity on farmers' fields
- **Management of Natural Resources:** Protecting and preserving the productivity of natural resources on which agriculture depends
- **Improving the Policy Environment:** Assisting developing countries to formulate and carry out effective food, agriculture, and research policy
- **Institution Building:** Strengthening national agricultural research systems in developing countries
- **Germplasm Conservation:** Conserving germplasm and making it available to all regions and countries
- **Building Linkages:** Helping to create or strengthen linkages between developing country institutions and other components of the global agricultural research system. <http://www.worldbank.org/html/cgiar/report1.html>

The CGIAR Secretariat is the publisher of the organization. The Publications section includes the CGIAR Annual Reports, the *CGIAR News* (a newsletter), news releases, meeting documents, *Crawford Lectures, Issues in Agriculture, Gender Program papers, Study Papers,* and more. One major database is the *CGIAR Core Collection Database,* which is a compendium of historical documents of the CGIAR, 1971–2000, which allows the user to search under author, title, descriptor, year, and document type. In addition to this database, the Publications section lists the Institutes under CGIAR and organizes the documents under the Institutes that issue them.

The Institutes under CGIAR cover a whole range of topics including forestry, tropical and desert agriculture, wheat, potato, rice, livestock, plant genetics, and water management. Under their topics, the institutes provide further bibliographic information, full text of documents online, many within series, and other specific databases, all with a scientific research focus for developing countries.

Users looking under specific institutes can find many rich resources and full texts of research publications. For example, the International Food Policy Research Institute <http://www.ifpri.cgiar.org/> features the title *2020 Global Food Outlook: Trends, Alternatives, and Choices,* which is available in full-text, online summary or to order from CGIAR. The title assesses the future food situation of the world and includes appendices and references.

Food First Web site, by the Food First/Institute for
   Food and Development Policy, Oakland, Calif.
   <http://www.foodfirst.org/>

Summary: This nongovernmental organization is a people-supported, nonprofit think tank and education center. These Web pages provide information on the availability of food and the issues of hunger and poverty and produce books, resources, and articles on these topics, some of which are available online. Food First is a reliable source, known for its independent, well-documented research in its publications. This resource is useful for all levels of users for getting updates on current hunger issues.

Food First, a politically active organization, was formed by Frances Moore Lappé and Joseph Collins following the international success of the book, *Diet For a Small Planet.* First formed in 1975, it is also called the Institute for Food and Development Policy. The focus of its mission is to help establish food as a fundamental human right and assist in finding solutions to hunger and poverty worldwide. The FoodFirst Information and Action Network (FIAN) is the action and campaigning partner of the Institute.

Detailed Description: Some articles are reprinted full text online, with news updates about hot topics available from the home page. Useful links from the top bar of the home page are Bookstore, Resource Library, and Programs. Bookstore provides an online catalog of books, videos, backgrounders, development reports, policy briefs, and fact sheets. Unfortunately, most publications are not available online, but must be purchased. Individuals may join Food First to support its mission. Recent publications can be ordered at a minimal cost. The Resource Library section has a subject index and list of links, which are not in depth and offer only general interest information. Users can sign up online for *Food Rights Watch,* its bimonthly free electronic newsletter.

Future Harvest Web site, Washington, D.C.
   <http://www.futureharvest.org/>

Summary: The homepage of this nongovernmental charitable and educational organization leads the user to information about the future of agriculture, new agricultural research, agricultural development, and information on its own charitable research projects. Future Harvest was formed in 1998 by 16 Future Harvest Centers, known as the Consultative Group on International Agricultural Research (CGIAR). This organization's mission is to educate and promote awareness, advance debate, and build financial support for charitable projects and scientific agricultural research. It is based on the belief that future agriculture is linked to peace, growth, less poverty, and a healthier people and environment worldwide.

Detailed Description: The *Future Harvest* Web site provides the following links and content: what's new on the Web site, video messages, a search engine, a site map, and spotlighted topics, which lead to discussions of current issues and hot topics. Some full-text online publications are available from Future Harvest pages. For example, in a 2001 study commissioned by FH and the IUCN, the World Conservation Union issued the title *Common Ground, Common Future: How Ecoagriculture Can Help Feed the World and Save Wild Biodiversity.* This significant title is available in English and other languages online. It is a comprehensive summary of the interactions between wild biodiversity and agriculture worldwide. It includes an introduction, definitions, strategies of ecoagriculture, information about ecotourism, and maps. A full report of the two-year study this summary is based on was published in 2001.

RESEARCH STRATEGIES

For up-to-date explanations of current conditions of agriculture, fisheries, forestry, and the food supply worldwide and as a starting point for comparable country statistics from the high school level on, users should consult the **State of the….FAO World Review Series** by the Food and Agriculture Organization (FAO) of the United Nations <http://www.fao.org/sof/index_en.htm>. This series includes these titles: **State of Food and Agriculture (SOFA); State of Food Insecurity in the World (SOFI); State of World Fisheries and Aquaculture (SOFIA);** and **State of the World's Forests (SOFO).** Other beginning resources include the title *World Agricultural Production,* the best starting place for worldwide agricultural production information.

The other online FAO resources discussed in this chapter, the *Food and Agriculture Organization (FAO) of the United Nations* Web site at <http://www.fao.org> and its Statistics Database, *FAOSTAT,* are both appropriate for beginning users who expect a high level of complexity and comprehensiveness. Users can select an agricultural topic from the left sidebar, do a general search on their topic, or consult the *FAO Catalogue Online,* which leads to many online full-text documents. Also go to the FAO home page, especially for a photo resource, *Mediabase,* and hot topics and current issues. The *FAOSTAT* Web site is the resource for researchers needing historical sets of statistics on crop and livestock production, trade, commodities, food supply, food aid, fisheries, forestry, pesticides, and drugs. This is not a resource for the beginning user who only needs a few basic or comparative statistics. For that, users should consult the *State of the.... FAO World Review Series* from the main FAO home page.

These two nongovernmental resources have partisan, current, and thorough discussions of food and agriculture issues. Go to the *Food First* Web site for up-to-date explanations of current hunger issues worldwide. The *Future Harvest* Web site is specifically best for discussion of trends in agricultural research that will affect world food supply. Both of these resources are appropriate for high school level and above and as beginning resources because they offer such a range of type of document from general to specific. For statistical facts, and more research and trends coverage of the issues, consult the governmental resources in combination with these. Food First and Future Harvest do have a narrow focus and provide limited online texts compared to the other resources. Users should also be aware of the activist perspectives of these two organizations.

For scientific research information about specific agricultural topics, college-level researchers who require country and project detail may supplement the FAO titles with titles from the *CGIAR (Consultative Group on Agricultural Research)* Web site by checking the full-text monographs, bibliographic databases, and other documents under the Institutes on its publications page. Users cannot be sure of getting full text online, but may continue their research in other library catalogs by performing searches using the term CGIAR as author or keyword along with the keyword for the agricultural topic desired.

For trade by specific commodity and basic information worldwide about markets for specific agricultural products, consult the *World Market and Trade Reports,* published by the Foreign Agricultural Service of the United States. It also contains information on food aid for countries worldwide from the United States, world agricultural production, and global crop conditions.

FOR FURTHER READING: COMPREHENSIVE WEB SITES AND OTHER REFERENCE SOURCES

AgriSurf.com Web site. <http://www.agrisurf.com>

This online directory allows the user to select their agricultural subject and link further to organizations and publications on that subject. Subjects of note are Research & Education, Publications, and Catalogs, as well as topics such as environment, marketing, aquaculture, and much more. Foreign government Web sites and international organizations' information is included. Of note to researchers is a link to countries information on the *AgriSurf* Web site (under an icon of a globe) that links further to all the databases on the Web site from that individual country.

AGROVOC: Multilingual Agricultural Thesaurus,
   by the Food and Agriculture Organization (FAO) of the United Nations. <http://www.fao.org/agrovoc/>

This online searchable thesaurus of agricultural vocabulary is published in English, Chinese, Arabic, French, Spanish, and Portuguese. The terms found in *AGROVOC* are used for the description of information sources in the field of agriculture, fisheries, forestry, nutrition, food safety, and related subjects, such as the environment. The thesaurus standardizes terms used in indexing, which results in simpler and more efficient searching. Each descriptor has an equivalent in the other languages. Researchers must apply for a user name and password by e-mail, which then allows them to download the database locally and use it.

European Programme for Food Aid and Food Security Web site, Brussels, Belgium. <http://europa.eu.int/comm/europeaid/projects/foodsec/index_en.htm>

This worldwide food program acts to bring assistance to developing countries facing food deficit problems. Under the umbrella of the EuropeAid Co-operation Office, which handles all the European Union's external aid, this program publishes information on its organization, information on how it uses country indicators in its work, a few online documents and reports, and links to *RESAL,* the European Network of Food Security at <http://europa.eu.int/comm/europeaid/projects/resal/>. *RESAL* is an independent network of information financed by the European Commission, which provides general information on countries and national policies in the area of food security.

World Agriculture Towards 2015/2030: An FAO Perspective [sic], edited by Jelle Bruinsma. London: Earthscan, 2003 (ISBN 9-25104-835-5).

This report on trends in world agriculture updates an earlier FAO report issued in 1995 entitled *World Agriculture: Towards 2010.* Each chapter reports on global prospects of an area of agriculture, including food and nutrition, agriculture as commodity, crop production, forestry, livestock, fisheries, globalization, poverty and agriculture, and much more. Projects, analysis, and statistical tables with some information concerning individual countries are included. FAO periodically issues studies on global agriculture, and researchers may want to search the FAO Web site for the latest publication. The 1995 edition is available on the Internet at <http://www.fao.org/docrep/v4200e/v4200e00.htm>.

CHAPTER 3
Communication

CHAPTER OVERVIEW

This chapter provides information on resources related to the study and research of communication and information. Included are statistical sources on basic communications and media worldwide published by international governmental organizations, along with information about governments' electronic information initiatives, strategies, and e-government policies. So many significant titles of international intergovernmental organizations exist that no nongovernmental sources have been described. The resources included are major reference sources, mostly periodicals, such as journals or annual titles, or continually updated Web sites.

Governmental Sources Discussed

Information Society Web site, by the European Commission, Brussels, Belgium.
<http://europa.eu.int/information_society/>

International Telecommunications Union Resources

International Telecommunications Union Web site, Geneva, Switzerland. <http://www.itu.org>
ITU News, by the International Telecommunication Union, Geneva, Switzerland, 1996– (ISSN 1020-4148) (print and online 1996–).
<http://www.itu.int/itunews/>
World Telecommunication Development Report, by the International Telecommunication Union, Geneva, Switzerland, 1994– (print and online annual title 1999–). <http://www.itu.int/>
World Telecommunication Indicators by the International Telecommunication Union (ITU), Geneva, Switzerland, 2000– (print title). Some sections available at <http://www.itu.int/ITU-D/ict/publications/wtdr_02/index.html>
World Telecommunication Indicators Database. Free download of 2002 edition at <http://www.itu.int/publications/online/index.html> and electronic subscription through ITU.

Yearbook of Statistics, by the International Telecommunication Union (ITU), Geneva, Siwtzerland, 1986/1995– (print annual title, CD, and online sales title).

Organisation for Economic Co-operation and Development (OECD) Resources

Communications Outlook/Perspectives des communications, by the Organisation for Economic Co-operation and Development, Paris, 1990– (print biennial title and online subscription resource through *SourceOECD*).
OECD Information and Communications Technologies Web site, by the Organisation for Economic Co-operation and Development, Paris. <http://www.oecd.org> (select Browse by Topic: Information and Communications Technologies).
OECD Information Technology Outlook, by the Organisation for Economic Co-operation and Development, Paris, 2000– (print biennial title and online subscription resource through *SourceOECD*).

United Nations Information and Communication Technologies Task Force Web site, New York. <http://www.unicttaskforce.org>
Universal Postal Union Web site, Bern, Switzerland. <http://www.upu.int/>
World Intellectual Property Organization (WIPO) Web site, Geneva, Switzerland. <http://www.wipo.int/>

GOVERNMENTAL SOURCES

Information Society Web site, by the European Commission, Brussels, Belgium.
<http://europa.eu.int/information_society/>
Summary: The *Information Society* Web site, developed by the European Commission, a division of the European Union, was conceived to support, promote, and orient public and private actions relating to the in-

formation age within the European Union, and this searchable Web site provides a guide to users through the many aspects of the information society by providing information on information practices and policies concerning regulations, standardization, statistics, topics, European Commission programs, and electronic communications networks and services. The site is arranged into four main categories: Our Institution, Topics, News Room, and Services. Every Web page on this site is in three formats: standard, low-tech equivalent, and printer friendly.

Detailed Description: Our Institution, the first home page category for discussion, provides an overview and the history of the organization. The home page category Topics guides users to policies, references, and links in the areas of e-business, education, culture, health care, international efforts, development, research, and telecommunications through major European Commission programs listed and in some cases even hosted here. These include eContent, Safer Internet Action Plan, IST Research, eTen, Go Digital, safety, and other programs. Each of these programs then links to relevant documents, publications, and links.

Services, another home page category, provides users with an archive of information, FAQs, a glossary, links, statistics, and technology tools and software. Archives connect users with the former *DG Information Society* Web site. The last home page category, Newsroom, is grouped into library, research information, multimedia resources, and reference documents on the Web site, which are searchable by information theme and year.

International Telecommunication Union Resources

International Telecommunications Union (ITU)
  Web site, Geneva, Switzerland.
  <http://www.itu.org>
Summary: This is the major international intergovernmental organization that focuses and publishes statistics and analysis on communication issues worldwide. Major publications include telecommunications standards and regulations, telecommunications indicators and statistics, policy and analysis documents, and a global directory. Regional statistical telecommunications reports are issued regularly in print and online for a fee, including such titles as *African Telecommunication Indicators, Asia-Pacific Telecommunication Indicators, Americas Telecommunication Indicators,* and *African Telecommunication*

Indicators. Some online access is provided for summaries and table of contents of reports. The ITU provides a search engine for its site and a site map, as well as publications, information about the organization, and information about current events concerning telecommunications in the world.

Detailed Description: ITU provides some free online publications as well as summaries of its publications, but most of its information is for sale through its online catalog. Publications are offered in a variety of formats, including hard copy (print), CD-ROM, and Internet subscription. For example, a recent title covering countries worldwide *Trends in Telecommunications Reform: Country Profiles,* 2000, is available only electronically in CD-ROM and in an electronic interactive form through subscription.

One interesting free online resource is the ITU's *Country Case Studies* database at <http://www.itu.int/osg/spu/casestudies/index.html>. The research was done in collaboration with national governments. The studies define the issues and analyze the current conditions and possible strategies to address the specific issue for that country. They identify the individual country's obstacles and experiences. Users can access the case studies by region of the world, by country, or by telecommunications topic including: 3G mobile, broadband, effective regulation, fixed-mobile interconnection, Internet diffusion, IP telephony, trade in telecommunications, and critical network infrastructure.

The ITU's regional statistical telecommunications reports are among its major publications. The *African Telecommunication Indicators,* 5th ed., 2001, is a comprehensive reference book of telecommunication facts and figures for the African region available in English and French. The fourth edition of the ITU's *Asia-Pacific Telecommunication Indicators,* 2000, provides an analytical overview, regional statistics, and a directory of telecommunication organizations in the Asian region. The statistics cover fixed, mobile, Internet, and broadcasting data for year-end 1999, where available. This title is available only in English.

The regional telecommunications report for the Americas is *Americas Telecommunication Indicators.* This first report is available in English and Spanish. It reviews developments of the telecommunications sector in developing countries of the Western Hemisphere (primarily Latin America but also the Caribbean) and also provides a comprehensive and comparable set of current key telecommunication indicators for the region. In addition, the report includes analysis of trends in privatization, mobile, Internet, and regulatory and policy issues and a directory with names and Web sites of telecommunication ministries, regulators, and operators in the region.

The publications of the ITU are organized by year and theme on its publications page. Users should check under their topic of interest because some reports are available for free download, for example, recent ITU reports on the Internet such as the title *Internet for a Mobile Generation, 2002.*

ITU News, by the International Telecommunication Union, Geneva, Switzerland, 1996– (ISSN 1020-4148) (print and online 1996–). <http://www.itu.int/itunews/>

Summary: Previously published as the *Newsletter of the International Telecommunications Journal* (1994–1995) and as a monthly journal entitled *Telecommunications Journal* (1962–1993), this newsletter is available at no charge on the Internet or through a print subscription. Published 10 times a year, it covers the activities of the International Telecommunications Union and also issues of interest worldwide in the broad telecommunications industry. Articles are about policy, regulatory, legal, economic, and social aspects of telecommunications, especially with an emphasis on international telecommunications with each specific issue focusing on a theme in telecommunications. Official announcements and ITU highlights are included, and it is available in English, French, and Spanish editions.

World Telecommunication Development Report, by the International Telecommunication Union, Geneva, Switzerland, 1994– (print and online annual title 1999–). <http://www.itu.int/>

Summary: Published since 1994 in print format, each annual report focuses on a specific theme in the area of telecommunications. Text, analysis, statistics, and case studies are provided on the theme of the issue, and each issue also contains a second part, the latest comparable data on the development of communications services in some 200 economies worldwide. Beginning in 1999 a free download of the table of contents and executive summary is available in English, French, and Spanish. An online version may be purchased. Each chapter usually includes an introduction, discussion, conclusions, and bibliography on a specific issue of the major theme, for example, the trends, the industry, regulations, prices, and outlook

for the industry. Issues also contain a glossary, abbreviations, and acronyms.

World Telecommunication Indicators, by the International Telecommunication Union (ITU), Geneva, Switzerland, 2000– (print title).
Some sections available at <http://www.itu.int/ITU-D/ict/publications/wtdr_02/index.html>

World Telecommunication Indicators Database. Free download of 2002 edition at <http://www.itu.int/publications/online/index.html> and electronic subscription through ITU.

Summary: The *World Telecommunication Indicators* is available in both print and online versions, and both provide similar basic information, although the content and delivery detail may vary. The executive summary and others sections are available free of charge.

The print publication contains the ITU's authoritative telecommunication indicators, including data by nation of the world. It provides the most current statistics that monitor the main indicators of telephone network growth, mobile services and communications, traffic, pricing, revenues and investment for 200 plus economies worldwide. The ITU online database contains historical or time series data for the years 1960, 1965, 1970, and annually (1975–) for the same information as the paper. A broader range of selected demographic, macroeconomic, broadcasting, and information technology statistics are also included in the online version compared to the paper edition.

Detailed Description: Detailed statistical tables for both print and online versions include data on the following: basic indicators, main telephone lines, waiting list, local telephone network, tele-accessibility, largest city main lines, telephone tariffs, cellular subscribers, cellular tariffs, ISDN, international telephone traffic, telecommunication staff, telecommunications revenue, telecommunications investment, equipment trade, information technology, television, network growth, projections, top 20 PTOs by revenue, cellular subscribers, and international traffic. Some statistics are free on the International Telecommunication Union's Internet site at its free statistics Internet page.

The online database *World Telecommunication Indicators Database* uses a powerful software, the World Bank's Socio-economic Time Series Access and Retrieval System (WIN*STARS v4.2), to provides users with sophisticated mapping and charting, a choice of data selection techniques, versatile display options, and several data export formats. A users' guide is available online. It also includes statistical tables from the ITU *Yearbook of Statistics* from 1991 on and from the *World Telecommunication Development Report* starting in 2002, and is available for an annual subscription fee. The 2002 edition (6th) is available at no charge in English for downloading in PDF, text, or WORD formats. Previous versions of the indicators were published by the ITU on CD-ROM and diskette. The ITU does offer a free summary version of this title online, *World Telecommunication Indicators Handbook,* available in HTML format, in English, French, and Spanish online, which includes an introduction, basic telecommunications statistics, a bibliography, and definitions.

Yearbook of Statistics, by the International Telecommunication Union (ITU), Geneva, Switzerland, 1986/1995– (print, CD, and online sales title).
Summary: The *Yearbook of Statistics* was previously entitled the *Yearbook of Common Carrier Telecommunication Statistics* or *ITU Statistical Yearbook* (covering the years from 1965–). The online title is *ITU Yearbook of Statistics: Telecommunications Services.* The 2002 electronic edition is a free download and the 2003 edition is a sales title. The statistical data have been collected and processed by the Telecommunication Development Bureau (BDT) from replies received to ITU questionnaires sent to telecommunication ministries, regulators, and operating companies. As such, the ITU statistical yearbook provides the most authoritative source of data about the evolution of the public telecommunications sector available anywhere. Online subscription versions of the *Yearbook* are available in English, French, and Spanish.
Detailed Description: Statistics are presented by country to allow users to review the evolution of telecommunication services in a country. Statistics are provided for the latest 10-year period. The *Yearbook* includes some general country statistics on population and economy, and then for most countries of the world where data is available, it includes statistics on telephone networks, mobile and other services, traffic, quality of services, tariffs, revenue, capital expenditures, broadcasting, information technology, and telephone lines and cellular telephone subscriptions. Inclusion of selected television broadcasting and information technology time series provides a wider picture of a country's communication sector.

The *Yearbook* is available online in PDF format for a one-time purchase or a subscription fee at <http://www.itu.int> (search under Publications).

The data included in the *Yearbook* are also contained in the *ITU World Telecommunication Indicators Database,* also described in this chapter.

Organisation for Economic Co-operation and Development (OECD) Resources

Communications Outlook/Perspectives des communications, by the Organisation for Economic Co-operation and Development, Paris, 1990– (print biennial title and online subscription resource through *SourceOECD*).
Summary: Each biennial report provides statistical data focused on a specific current theme in the communications field and provides comparable data on the performance of the communication sector in OECD countries and on the national policies of the OECD countries. The data is used to evaluate the national policy performance and covers the years from 1980 to the present. This is a standard reference source.
Detailed Description: The data in the *Communications Outlook* is based on the OECD's *Telecommunications Database,* a source containing time series of statistics for OECD countries from 1980 to the present. It contains telecommunications and economic indicators, such as network dimension, telecommunications infrastructure, revenues, expenses, investment, trade in telecoms equipment, and employment. The *Telecommunications Database* is available online through subscription or on CD-ROM (earlier on diskette), and it is produced in association with the title *Communications Outlook.*

The title is published in several volumes, the first providing a comprehensive overview of the communications industry, with chapters on significant subjects and the text accompanied with many supplementary figures and statistical tables. Most of the data is on a country-by-country basis. The second volume, which is alphabetically organized by country, provides information on regulatory policy in the telecommunications and broadcasting sectors of OECD countries. For the first time in 1997 this title included data and analysis of broadcasting, cable television, and the Internet.

OECD Information and Communications Technologies Web site, by the Organisation for Economic Co-operation and Development, Paris, France. <http://www.oecd.org> (select Browse by Topic: Information and Communications Technologies).
Summary: The *OECD Information and Communications Technologies* Web site guides users to links on themes under the topic of communications. These in-

clude e-government; information and communication technology and learning; security; privacy and consumer protection online; information and communications policy; innovation and education research and development; measuring the information economy; and teaching, learning, and schools for the future. Under each link is an explanation of the topic as well as the OECD's work in the area. Also provided are links to OECD publications specifically on the theme. Articles on what's new for each theme covers conferences, OECD projects, new publications, studies, and news items. Some reports and studies are available free online, but current and major publications are usually available on a fee base.

OECD Information Technology Outlook, by the Organisation for Economic Co-operation and Development, Paris, 2000– (print biennial title and online subscription resource through *SourceOECD*) (free download of 2000 ed.).

Summary: In this title, the OECD provides analysis of significant current issues in public communications services in OECD member countries. Published every other year, this title covers trends in information technology, globalization, and the impact on the way people live and work. It describes the rapid growth in the demand for information technology goods and services, especially in the industrialized countries of the OECD and also describes their role in the Internet economy. The *Outlook* examines the emerging uses of information technology and makes use of the new official national sources of data and is available in English and French. Statistical tables accompany the text highlighting the development of the information economy in 12 OECD countries and summarizing the countries' national information policies.

This title was preceded by an earlier title, *Information Technology Outlook,* 1992–1997. On occasion both titles are in English and French and sometimes the language editions are issued separately. The 2000 edition is available in PDF from the *OECD Information and Communications Technology* Web site also described in this chapter.

United Nations Information and Communication Technologies Task Force Web site, New York. <http://www.unicttaskforce.org>

Summary: The overall mission of this task force, begun in 2001, involves efforts to bridge the global digital divide, foster digital opportunity, and promote the service information and communication technolo-gies in the development for all. The Web site offers the user a solid base of information about news, conferences and meetings, regional networks, the background of the task force, recent initiatives by region, a discussion forum, and a section with members-only information. The Web links to such important meetings as the World Summit on the Information Society, 2003–2005, which includes issue papers and reports full text online. The full text of reports, speeches, and documents can be found here, some in PDF format.

Universal Postal Union Web site, Bern, Switzerland. <http://www.upu.int/>

Summary: The Universal Postal Union (UPU), established in 1874 and named a specialized United Nations agency in 1948, serves as a cooperative mechanism between the postal services of the countries of the world. Its Web site provides information about conferences and meetings; publications; statistics; activities, projects, and information of the organization; postal addresses; and stamp collecting, all available in English and French language versions. The site is arranged into four main headings: About Us, What We Do, Resources, and Contacts and Links. There is also a site map.

Detailed Description: The About Us home page heading contains an overview, frequently asked questions, full text of speeches (2001–) and press releases (2002–) as well as the most current annual report. The What We Do category provides basic information about the organization and how it works.

Resources, another home page category, features publications and documents. Publications can be accessed online in full text, usually PDF, or ordered. Documents are password protected and not accessible. Also included here are Postal Statistics, which have been published by UPU since its beginning in 1874. UPU's objective in gathering postal statistics is to provide an analytical working tool at both the international level to analyze trends and means for handling postal traffic and at the national level to be used by postal administrations as an efficient management and planning tool for their services. The UPU's statistical database contains data from over 200 countries or territories and includes 100 statistical indicators from 1980 on topics such as postal establishments, delivery, traffic, parcels, special treatment, and financial services.

Contacts and Links, the last home page category, links to postal administrations of member countries and their Web sites, philatelic sites, and other postal-related sites.

World Intellectual Property Organization (WIPO)
Web site, Geneva, Switzerland.
<http://www.wipo.int/>

Summary: The *World Intellectual Property Organization (WIPO)* Web site provides users with information about the concept and regulations governing intellectual property and copyright. Available in English, Arabic, French, Spanish, and Russian, the site is organized into four main categories: About WIPO, About Intellectual Property, News and Information Resources, and Activities and Services.

Detailed Description: The About WIPO home page category contains an overview of the organization and its work, budget and program information, full text of relevant treaties, and the full text of annual reports (1998–). Of special mention regarding the About Intellectual Property home page category is no-charge access to the full-text publication (PDF) *WIPO Intellectual Property Handbook: Policy, Law, and Use* and links to resources pertaining to industrial property and copyright/related rights.

The News and Information Resources home page category is of special note. Here are found full-text press releases and updates (1998–) as well as an e-mail notification system, an electronic bookshop that allows browsing by type along with an e-mail notification system for new titles, full text of the *WIPO Magazine* (2000–) and the periodical *Intellectual Property Laws and Treaties* (2002–, plus cumulative index) under the link IPLT Periodical, and links to related Web sites. The Intellectual Property Digital Library, Documents, Library, and *Collection of Laws for Electronic Access* database are also accessible here. The Intellectual Property Digital Library is WIPO hosted "intellectual property data collections," which are available at no charge and can be browsed and searched. Documents database provides access to the full text of meeting documents and links to the PCT Patent Database and Treaties and Laws collection. The Library links to *UNCAPS: United Nations System Shared Cataloguing and Public Access System* described in the General Sources chapter and the Web sites of related libraries and research institutes. *The Collection of Laws for Electronic Access (CLEA)* database contains bibliographic information and the full text of treaties with a search engine available.

Activities and Services is the last home page category. Patent information including the text and related information pertaining to the Patent Cooperation Treaty is provided here. Information technology projects are discussed in this category as well as global intellectual property issues.

RESEARCH STRATEGIES

The **International Telecommunication Union (ITU)** is the major international intergovernmental organization that provides global communication information and country-level statistics. Users have access to some free information on the *ITU* Web site, including full texts of some reports online and some data; however, the majority of the statistics are available through print or online subscriptions, with some online titles being available for a one-time purchase. Data for countries are provided depending on their availability. The ITU is a major provider of regulations and standards, as well as statistical databases.

Two of the International Telecommunications Unions periodicals are particularly good for quick reference and for both titles some sections are available at no charge online. *World Telecommunication Development Report,* a theme-related report, provides a global overview and analysis of telecommunications and quick current statistics by country. The *World Telecommunication Indicators* is the title to check for up-to-date statistics by country and is very useful for comparative research and for evaluating telecommunication trends. For researchers who require sophisticated levels of communication statistics and the ability to manipulate the statistics, the source of choice is the International Telecommunications Union's *World Telecommunications Indicators Database,* which is available online through subscription only. For information on current trends in information and communication technology, the best resource to consult would be the *Communications Outlook* biennial reports, by the **Organisation for Economic Co-operation and Development (OECD),** with each focusing on a special theme of current interest in the field. Comprehensive analysis and data are available, but mostly only for the OECD countries.

The *Organisation for Economic Co-operation and Development Information and Communications Technologies* Web site links users to OECD publications on communication and information technology. This organization focuses particularly on the progress of its member nations on the development of communication. Member nations of the OECD are industrialized countries such as the United States and European countries. OECD also provides statistics and documents on information technology analysis for developing national policies. Although many publications are available only through online subscription, particularly through *SourceOECD,* users still can find full text of significant documents in the area of communications from this Web site.

The *Information Society* Web site by the European Commission is a good source for researchers interested in the European experience with information and information policy. It provides much information about policies, action plans, and programs, but only publishes a small selection of online titles. Users and researchers at all levels interested in copyright and intellectual property should consult the Internet site and publications of the **World Intellectual Property Organization (WIPO).** Those interested in postal statistics and trends should consult the publications and Web site of the **Universal Postal Union.** All three of these organization's Web sites have the advantage of being free online resources.

In addition, researchers should consult general international governmental organization resources and statistical titles. For example, to use online publications on this subject by the **World Bank,** researchers can go to its home page at <http://www.worldbank.org/> and search under the Publications category by the subject Telecommunications and Technology. The World Bank categorizes its publications online by subject, and many significant titles in this area are published online at no charge. Also, the World Bank's Documents and Reports category will link researchers to more information. This strategy can be used with any of the other international governmental organizations or in searching for information-, communications-, or technology-focused government agencies of nation states.

FOR FURTHER READING: COMPREHENSIVE WEB SITES AND OTHER REFERENCE SOURCES

Atlas of the World's Languages in Danger of Disappearing, by Stephen A. Wurm. 2nd ed. Paris: UNESCO, 2000 (ISBN 9-23103-798-6).
This study describes the phenomenon of the death of languages and reports on the efforts of the scientific community in cooperation with UNESCO with the intention to describe, record, and introduce threatened languages into the data bank. It also provides an atlas of selected threatened languages currently identified. Endangered languages under region and country are described in the text.

UNESCO currently has a special project entitled The Red Book of Languages in Danger of Disappearing, which focuses on gathering information, studying the languages, and activities of preservation and protection. This atlas is one outcome of that project and is now in its second edition.

Digital Opportunity Initiative (DOI) Web site.
<http://www.opt-init.org/>
The Digital Opportunity Initiative was a public private partnership of Accenture, the Markle Foundation, and the United Nations Development Programme (UNDP) that began at the G-8 Okinawa Summit in 2000. Its objectives were to identify the roles that information and communication technologies (ICT) can play in fostering sustainable economic development and enhancing social equity. *Creating a Development Dynamic: Final Report of the Digital Opportunity Initiative,* the main report generated by this group and available in full text, examines the use of information and communication technologies in a broad range of developing nations and provides case studies and analyses of specific national e-strategies in information and communication technologies. The Global Digital Opportunity Initiative is a continuation, formed in 2002, by the Markle Foundation and the United Nations Development Programme (UNDP). For more information users may consult the *UNDP* Web site <http://www.undp.org>.

Telecommunications Directory. Detroit: Gale Research, 1991– (ISSN 1055-8454).
This print reference title, issued biennially since 1991, provides information on companies in international telecommunications that provide a range of products and services from cellular communications and local exchange carriers to satellite services and Internet service providers. Organized alphabetically by organization name, each directory entry includes a list of products and services, contact information (including URL), and a summary of the organization's activities. Issued in two volumes, Volume 1 covers the United States and Canada and Volume 2 covers the world except the United States and Canada. It includes a glossary that defines more than 500 terms, acronyms, concepts, standards, and government rulings.

World Communication Report: The Media and the Challenge of the New Technologies. 2nd ed. Paris: UNESCO, 1997 (ISBN 9-23103-428-6).
A reference work for decision makers, planners, researchers, students, media professionals, and the general public on worldwide communication issues, this

report provides discussion and analysis of new information and communication technologies, changes in media environments, and media and democracy. It discusses written press, news agencies, radio, and television and highlights major new problems such as the regulation of networks, media attitudes to violence, standards in news reporting, and access of women to the media. The report includes a summary, introduction, conclusion, bibliography, footnotes, and glossary. Graphs, charts, and data illustrate the text.

World Media Handbook, by the United Nations Dept. of Public Information, New York, 1990– (ISSN 1014-871X) (print).

A biennial publication, this directory provides a summary of selected media and related data covering countries around the world. Information for each country includes demographic data, communications indicators, and a list of media organizations, press associations, and communication education institutions. The title was prepared primarily as a reference tool for public information professionals within the United Nations system and other media specialists. The countries profiled are mostly the United Nations member states. Although it is no longer in print, this is still a useful reference tool available in research libraries and United Nations depository libraries.

The information is arranged alphabetically by country. A section entitled Membership Brief includes a summary of the country's involvement in the main organs of the United Nations, such as the General Assembly and the Security Council, and particularly those that contribute to the development of communication. It includes information on each country's participation in intergovernmental organizations that focus on media development and the improvement of international communication.

CHAPTER 4
Crime and Criminal Justice

CHAPTER OVERVIEW

The sources described in this chapter represent a sampling of governmental sources available on the topic of international crime and criminal justice. They were chosen because of their comprehensiveness, both in supplying information and documents and in related links to other sites. The United Nations is well represented, as it is a major player in countering global crime. Main topics covered include drugs, corruption, and terrorism, although other aspects of crime such as art theft, information technology crime, and human trafficking are also discussed. Because there is such a wealth of government sources in this area, related to the cooperative efforts between governments and international governmental organization, no nongovernmental sources were included.

Governmental Sources Discussed

AnCorRWEB—Anti-Corruption Ring Online Web site, by the Organisation for Economic Cooperation and Development (OECD), Paris, France. <http://www1.oecd.org/daf/nocorruptionweb/>

Bureau for International Narcotics and Law Enforcement Affairs Web site, by the U.S. State Department, Washington, D.C. <http://www.state.gov/g/inl/>

Estimated World Requirements of Narcotic Drugs. International Narcotics Control Board. New York: United Nations, 1946– (ISSN 1013-3453).

Europol (European Police Office) Web site, The Hague, The Netherlands. <http://www.europol.eu.int/>

ICPO-Interpol (International Criminal Police Organization) Web site, Lyons, France. <http://www.interpol.int/>

International Review of Criminal Policy. Department of Economic and Social Affairs. New York: United Nations, 1952– (ISSN 0074-7688).

United Nations Center for International Crime Prevention Web site, Vienna, Austria. <http://www.uncjin.org/CICP/cicp.html>

United Nations Interregional Crime & Justice Research Institute Web site, Turin, Italy. <http://www.unicri.it/index.htm>

United Nations Office on Drugs and Crime Web site, Vienna, Austria. <http://www.unodc.org/anodc/index.html>

GOVERNMENTAL SOURCES

AnCorRWEB—Anti-Corruption Ring Online Web site, by the Organisation for Economic Cooperation and Development (OECD), Paris, France. <http://www1.oecd.org/daf/nocorruptionweb/>

Summary: An excellent source of bibliographic information in the subject area of corruption compiled by OECD's Anticorruption Division, this Web site is divided into eight major sections: About, Corruption, Bribery, Business Integrity, Good Governance, Money Laundering, World Regions, and Law. Each of the sections is subdivided, with some having yet another layer of subdivisions. Entries are arranged alphabetically by author and include title, publisher, publication date, and number of pages as well as an assigned subject heading. Some citations also include annotations and a few even link to the full text of the publication.

Detailed Description: About, the first home page sections discussed, provides background information about *AnCorRWEB*. The next section, Corruption, is subdivided into Definition, Causes, Impacts, Survey, and Prevention. The third section, Bribery, is divided into Actors, Practices, and Remedies. Business Integrity, section four, includes Self-Regulation, Corporate Governance, Disclosure, and links to OECD Instruments on Combating Bribery. Good Governance, the fifth section, contains Public Ethics and Public Management and links to the home page of the OECD Public Management Committee.

The sixth section, Money Laundering, also includes Money Laundering as a subtopic along with Offshore Banking and E-Crime. World Regions, section seven, is comprised of the subtopics Transition Economies,

OECD, Latin America, South Eastern Europe, Africa and the Middle East, Asia and Pacific, Network for Transition Economies Stability Pact for South Eastern Europe, and Asia-Pacific Web.

Law, the last section, is more complex. The subtopics here are Comparative Legal Analysis, International treaties and Conventions, OECD Convention Signatory States, Asia and the Pacific, Africa, Central and Eastern Europe, South Eastern Europe, and Central and Latin America.

Bureau for International Narcotics and Law Enforcement Affairs Web site, by the U.S. State Department, Washington, D.C.
<http://www.state.gov/g/inl/>

Summary: The Bureau serves as a policy development advisory body for the President, Secretary of State, Department of State, and other governmental agencies. The information found here is useful in researching how the United States is working with the governments of foreign countries in combating drug trafficking and corruption. The site is divided into the major headings Congressional Budget Justification, *International Narcotics Control Strategy Report (INCSR)*, INL Regional Programs, International Law Enforcement Academies (ILEA), International Civilian Police Program (CivPol), Anticorruption Programs, Narcotics Rewards Programs, Advance Fee Business Scams, Travel Warnings on Drugs Abroad, Photo Gallery, Related Site, Releases, and Archive: 1997–2000.

Detailed Description: Congressional Budget Justification Budget, the first home page heading discussed, provides information relating to the Congressional Budget Justification and is for fiscal year 2002–. Included here is the full text (also in PDF format) of the report, arranged by regional initiative and then individual country. Each section outlines the funding amount request, along with an explanation of the objectives, justification, programs, and effectiveness measurements for each country or subregion, in dealing with drug trafficking and other crimes. Various other related full-text reports are also found here.

International Narcotics Control Strategy Report (1999–) is the next home page heading. The bulk of this report documents activities within the regions of the world. Each region is broken down into specific countries and includes a summary and also further information on the status, actions against drugs, and United States policy initiatives and programs for each country. A section on money laundering is also included. This report is in full text, both HTML and PDF formats.

INL Regional Programs, another home page heading, is responsible for the narcotics control component of foreign assistance. This section has fact sheets, press releases (full text, 2001–), op-eds and articles, and reports, including the full text of *End-Use Monitoring* (2001–2002). Information describing its work is also included.

The International Law Enforcement Academies (ILEA) home page heading provides an overview and statement of purpose for this program and has links to the various academies worldwide. The International Civilian Police Program, established as a participatory police organization with local agencies in eastern European regions, also a home page heading, links to full text of relevant press releases, remarks, reports, and fact sheets (2000–).

Anticorruption Programs, another home page heading, contains full-text reports, fact sheets, and press releases, as well as an archive by type of material (1996–2000). Special note should be taken of the International Anticorruption Initiatives Timeline and the anticorruption links sections. The Narcotics Rewards Program home page heading features a listing of criminals wanted for their participation in drug trafficking and a brief description of the individual along with his/her photograph.

From the home page heading, Advance Fee Business Scams is information on how to identify such a scam, types, and real-life examples. Contact information to verify the authenticity of a business proposal is also included. The home page heading Travel Warning on Drugs Abroad is a fact sheet. The Photo Gallery home page has links to color photographs of major related events (2001–).

Related Sites, another heading, provides links to U.S. government agencies and international organizations, especially related to drug enforcement. The Releases home page heading has the full-text of *Narcotics Control Reports* (1999–2002) and remarks, fact sheets, press releases, op-eds and articles, and other reports (all dating 2001–). Previous editions of all of these publications are included in the Archives, the last home page heading, dating from 1996–2000. The home page also features links to recent highlights.

Estimated World Requirements of Narcotic Drugs.
International Narcotics Control Board. New York: United Nations, 1946– (ISSN 1013-3453).

Summary: An annual publication, published since 1946 with varying titles, the *Estimated World Requirements of Narcotic Drugs* provides statistical information, by country, on the production of narcotic drugs for medical and scientific purposes. In addition, an estimate of opium production is also included. This publication is mandated by various United Nations conventions and protocols, beginning with Article 5 of the Convention of July 13, 1931.

Europol (European Police Office) Web site, The Hague, The Netherlands. <http://www.europol. eu.int/>

Summary: The law enforcement agency of the European Union was established as part of the Maastricht Treaty on European Union in 1992. The Web site is divided into Europol at a Glance, Publications, Management and Control, Legal, Press Releases, and Job Opportunities. The home page also contains a Frequently Asked Questions section; a search engine; contact information; links to the Web sites of other European Union law enforcement agencies, arranged alphabetically by country name; and a site map, all of which have a link that appears on every page.

Detailed Description: Europol at a Glance, the first major home page section, provides the "nuts-and-bolts" information about Europol in the form of mission, history, mandate, computer system, budget, personnel, and guidance and management. Publications is the second major home page section and features the full text of annual reports (1998–); organized crime reports (2000, 2002–); budget reports (2002–, PDF format); and serious crime overviews, which includes *Trafficking in Human Beings: Child Abuse, Forgery of Money, Illegal Immigration, Terrorism, Trafficking of Stolen Vehicles,* and *Money Laundering.*

Management and Control, the next major home page heading, provides a brief description of the administrative bodies. Legal, the fourth major section, includes the full text of the Europol Convention along with regulations as published in the *Official Journal of the European Communities* (PDF format). The home page section Press Releases includes the full text of press releases, dating from 1998 to the present.

ICPO-Interpol (International Criminal Police Organization) Web site, Lyons, France. <http://www. interpol.int/>

Summary: Interpol, the premier global international law enforcement system, promotes international police cooperation among its 181 member countries. The *Interpol* Web site provides information under fifteen major headings: Interpol Information, Terrorism, Wanted, Children and Human Trafficking, Works of Art, Drugs, Financial Crime, Corruption, International Crime Statistics, Forensic, Vehicle Crime, Regional Activities, Information Technology Crime, Weapons/Explosives, and Criminal Intelligence Analysis. Each section is then further subdivided. The entire Interpol site can also be searched, and the search button is found on every page.

Detailed Description: Interpol Information is the first major home page heading. This heading has been subdivided into Governance, Legal Materials, Member States, Publications, Recruitment, Media Releases, Fact Sheets, Tenders, Speeches, Links, and Distinctive Signs. The General Assembly, Executive Committee, and Secretary-General govern Interpol. Under the Governance subcategory are a listing of agendas, reports, and full-text resolutions for the General Assembly (1996–); the full text of documents such as articles and the constitution relevant to the Executive Committee, the deliberative body; and the full text of regulations under the Secretary-General section. Legal Materials has the full text of the constitution and regulations, cooperation agreements, and related international conventions. Member States is a listing of Interpol member countries. The Publications category provides an annotated listing of print and CD-ROM titles, along with ordering information. Media Releases contains the full text of releases (2000–) in English, French, and Spanish. Full-text Fact Sheets in English, French, Spanish, and Arabic provide information on topics relevant to the times. The Speeches category has the full text of speeches (2001–). Links are to international cooperation organizations and to police-justice organizations, arranged alphabetically by country. Distinctive Signs explains each sign. The full text (PDF) of annual reports (1998–) is also available from the Interpol Information section Web page.

Terrorism, the second major home page heading, is subdivided into Fusion Task Force, Financing, Terrorist Attacks, and Resolutions. Given the relationship between organized crime and terrorism, the Fusion Task Force was created to investigate such linkages in order to break them up. This section features an overview and objectives. Financing states Interpol's position, but of particular interest to researchers are links to the United States Treasury Department's Office of Foreign Assets Control alphabetical master list of Specially Designated National and Blocked Persons and to the Council of the European Union adopted decisions. Terrorist Attacks includes the full text of press releases, speeches, fact sheets, and articles (1998, 2001–). The Resolutions section provides the full text of all Interpol resolutions dealing with terrorism.

Wanted, the third major home page heading, has an explanation of red notices, which are issued for individuals wanted by national jurisdictions. In addition a wanted search criteria form and photographs/brief descriptions of current individuals wanted by Interpol are found here, as well as links to national wanted Web sites, arranged alphabetically by country.

Children and Human Trafficking, the fourth major home page heading, is subdivided into Crimes Against Children, Trafficking in Women, People Smuggling, and *Project Bridge*. Of special note are the Crimes Against Children and People Smuggling subsections. The Crimes Against Children subsection has a lengthy explanation of Interpol's work in this area, along with a search form for Interpol's database of missing and abducted children. Photographs/brief descriptions of children currently missing are found here. Also included are links to full-text legislation of each member country, arranged alphabetically by country name, for national legislation and on the topic of sexual abuse, and the full texts of *International Conventions for the United Nations, Hague Conference on Private International Law*, and the International Labour Organization. People Smuggling, the other subsection of special note, has information on the broad topic, smuggling routes, and trends.

Works of Art, another major home page category, has photographs of recent thefts, discovered artwork, and unclaimed items. Posters with photographs of stolen art can be downloaded (PDF format) from this site. Object ID, a project that was undertaken to establish standardization for documentation of stolen art, is described here, along with the full texts of *International Conventions for United Nations Education, Scientific and Cultural Organization* and the International Institute for the Unification of Private Law. A listing of African heritage objects that could be targets of looters is also included. Because of the war in Iraq, information has been added regarding Iraqi stolen art works and at-risk antiquities. Lastly, a frequently asked questions section is provided.

The Drugs major home page heading contains information about Interpol's work in controlling drug trafficking. The category is subdivided into Cannabis, Cocaine, Heroin, and Synthetic Drugs, with a description of each type and information about drug trade activity.

Financial Crime, another major home page heading, is subdivided into Payment Cards, Money Launder-

ing, and Intellectual Property Crime. Each category details Interpol's endeavors in these areas. The Money Laundering subdivision also provides links to the various organizations and initiatives discussed in this section. Of special mention is IMoLIN, the Information Money Laundering Information Network.

Corruption, the eighth major home page heading, is the Web page for the Interpol Group of Experts. Here is found the mission statement, codes, standards, calendar of events, and links to the home pages for International Anti-Corruption Conference, Transparency International, Independent Commission Against Corruption, Metropolitan Police (United Kingdom), World Bank, Federal Bureau of Investigation, ACA Malaysia, and United Nations Office on Drugs and Crime (UNODC).

International Crime Statistics is the ninth major home page heading. These statistics have been published since 1950 (every two years until 1993, when it became annual). Statistics of types of crimes are available, alphabetically by country, as a downloadable file (PDF format). The date coverage is 1995–2002, although date coverage within this span varies from country to country.

Forensic, the next home page heading discussed, is subdivided into Fingerprint, DNA, Disaster Victim Identification, and International Forensic Science Symposium. This section is more technical in nature. The Fingerprinting subsection deals with system "development and implementation" and has a reference documents subsection to obtain full text (PDF) of *Data Format for* the *Interchange of Fingerprint, Facial and SMT Information*. The DNA subdivision has documentation from the Expert Group, along with minutes and presentations from conferences and the full-text PDF format of the *Interpol Handbook on DNA Data Exchange and Practice*. Disaster Victim Identification provides the full text of the *Disaster Victim Identification Guide* and forms. The International Forensic Science Symposium section has materials, many in full text, from the 13th (2001) and 14th (2004) symposiums.

Vehicle Crime, another major home page heading, provides information on how to prevent vehicle theft and procedures for recovering stolen vehicles from abroad from individual countries, via an alphabetical listing. Regional Activities, the twelfth major category, is subdivided into Africa, Americas, Asia, Europe, Middle East and North Africa, and Frequently Asked Questions. Each regional section contains information on the structure, objectives, and meetings of that region.

Information Technology Crime, the thirteenth home page category, provides a description of the four Regional Working Parties (European, American, African, and Asia–South Pacific) and Steering Committee. Of special note are in-depth information on security and crime prevention in the way of explanations and checklists, both for companies and individuals, along with a frequently asked questions section.

Weapons/Explosives, the fourteenth major home page heading, and Criminal Intelligence Analysis, the final major home page heading, each have a short description of the efforts of Interpol in these areas. The *Interpol* home page also has a listing of recent updates and additions. Shortcuts to various subjects included on the *Interpol* Web site are provided at the bottom of the home page.

International Review of Criminal Policy. New York: United Nations Department of Economic and Social Affairs, 1952– (ISSN 0074-7688).

Summary: Mainly an annual publication, each issue of the *International Review of Criminal Policy* is devoted to a single topic. One issue worth special mention is no. 47–48 for 1996–1997, entitled *The United Nations and Criminals, 1946–1996: Resolutions, Reports, Documents and Publications.* Included are a narrative overview and a bibliography of UN-related publications listed by title/description. The bibliography is subdivided into the topics of Legislative Mandates, Reports, Ministerial Meetings and Conferences, UN Congresses on the Prevention of Crime and Treatment of Offenders, Committees on Crime Prevention and Control, Regular Publications, Other Publications, and Publications of UN Interregional Crime and Justice Research Institute and Affiliated Regional Institutes.

United Nations Center for International Crime Prevention Web site, Vienna, Austria.
    <http://www.uncjin.org/CICP/cicp.html>

Summary: Crime prevention, criminal justice, and criminal law reform are the focus of this United Nations office, a unit of the United Nations Office for Drug Control and Crime Prevention, described separately in this chapter. The home page contains the sections Overview, The Center, Action Orientation, Commissions, 10th Congress, and Contact.
Detailed Description: Overview and The Center, the first two home page sections, briefly describe the purpose and work of the Center. Action Orientation, the

next home page section, links to Crime Prevention and Criminal Justice Standards and Norms, Technical Cooperation, and the full text, in PDF format, of reports on three main global programs: Global Program against Corruption, Global Programme against the Trafficking in Human Beings, and Assessing Transnational Organized Crime Groups: Dangerousness and Trends.

The Standards link also provided leads to Crime Prevention and Criminal Justice Standards and Norms, United Nations rulings, and the home page of the *UN Criminal Justice Standards for Peace-Keeping Police* (English and French), as well as the full text, in PDF form, of this publication (English, French, Spanish, English-Croatian, and Arabic); documents from the fifth through seventh sessions of the Commission on Crime Prevention and Criminal Justice; a link to the International Victimology Web site; and the full text, in PDF, of *Handbook on Justice for Victims* and *Guide for Policy Makers.*

The Commissions home page section links to documents and other materials pertaining to the Commissions on Crime Prevention and Criminal Justice (5th–10th, 1996–2000), Congresses on the Prevention of Crime and Treatment of Offenders (8th–10th, 1990, 1995, 2000), and *Draft Conventions Against Transnational Organized Crime* (1999–2001). Links to Publications including *Crime Prevention and Criminal Justice Newsletter* (PDF, 1993–1996), *Trends: United Nations Crime and Justice Information Network: Crime and Justice Letter* (full text, 1993, 1995), *United Nations Action Against Corruption and Bribery* (PDF), and *United Nations Crime and Justice Information Network: Providing Information to and from Developing Countries* (full text) are also available here. The 10th Congress home page section contains documents, press releases, photographs, and the audio recording from this meeting held in Vienna, April 10–17, 2000.

United Nations Interregional Crime & Justice Research Institute Web site, Turin, Italy. <http://www.unicri.it/index.htm>

Summary: Originally located in Rome and moved to Turin in 2000, the Institute was established as the United Nations Social Defense Research Institute (1968) for crime behavior and prevention. The addition of developing countries to the membership of the United Nations expanded the work of the Institute, acknowledged in its name change in 1989 to the United Nations Interregional Crime & Justice Research Institute (UNICRI). The *UNICRI* Web site is divided into the major headings of About Us, Projects, Publications, Documentation Center, Crime Programme, Links, News, and Contacts. A search engine is available from the homepage.

Detailed Description: About Us, the first home page heading discussed, provides a brief history of the organization along with its objectives and context. Projects, the next section, has the full text of ongoing projects; a listing of pipeline projects, those that have been designed but not yet funded; and completed projects for 1998–, arranged by year.

Publications, another home page heading, is subdivided into UNICRI Publication Series, Issues and Reports, Special Editions, *UNICRI Journal*, and ordering information. The UNICRI Publication Series (1969–2000) includes a list of publications with ordering information and the table of contents. Many of these are out of print, especially from 1997 and preceding years. However, the New York Office may be a source of acquiring those that are out of print. Issues and Reports, nos. 1–12 (1994–1998), are available in English Digital text format. These publications are on a variety of topics ranging from crime in various world areas to child abuse and family violence. Special Editions (1993–2000) are publications published by commercial vendors; this section only includes a list of the titles with ordering information. The *UNICRI Journal* (2002–), published twice a year, is available in full-text format and documents UNICRI activities.

The Databases home page heading is subdivided into Bibliographic Database (LMS), *UNICRI Thesaurus,* and *World Directory of Criminological Resources.* Searching the LMS database can be done by keyword, author, series, publisher, and title. Information on how to search and the thesaurus is also found under Databases. The *World Directory of Criminological Resources*, with information on 470 institutions in 70 countries, is also a searchable database. Searching can be done by keyword, country, name, or free text. In addition, a keywords list is provided. An update service that sends weekly e-mail updates of new library additions is also included.

The Crime Programme home page heading is divided into the United Nations Crime Prevention and Criminal Justice Programme Network, *World Directory of Criminological Resources,* and links from the UNODC official Web site, all discussed elsewhere in this chapter.

News, another home page heading, provides links to selected information regarding conferences, initia-

tives, and the full text (PDF, 2001) of the *Report of the Board of Trustees.* The last home page heading, Contacts, lists the UNICRI address and phone numbers, as well as e-mail addresses for the various programs. Also available from the home page (right side) are further links to information on Trafficking in Human Beings, the Probate and Parole Web site, *International Crime Victims Survey,* and Terrorism Prevention Unit.

United Nations Office on Drugs and Crime (UNODC) Web site, Vienna, Austria. <http://www.unodc.org/unodc/index.html>

Summary: Established in 1997 as the primary office of the United Nations devoted to the prevention and eradication of drug use and international crime, this Web site is a comprehensive source of information on such topics as drug abuse and demand reduction, terrorism, organized crime, related treaties and legal affairs, as well as providing links to related commissions. The site itself is divided into the main headings of News and Publications; Drug Abuse and Demand Reduction; Drug Supply Reduction; Terrorism, Corruption and Human Trafficking; Treaty and Legal Affairs; Analysis and Statistics; About Us; Crime Commission (CCPCJ); Commission on Narcotic Drugs (CND); Global Youth Network; Information Services for Member States; UN News Service Global News Coverage; UN-Wide Calendar.

A site map, links to other related United Nations agencies arranged by topic, contact information, and a search box are also included on the home page. A pull-down menu, also on the home page, provides links to the various UNODC Country Offices and the information provided from there. Each section also has an Email Document Utility and a printer-friendly version.

Detailed Description: The first section, News and Publications is chock-full of information. Here are found Press Releases (full text, 1997–), Speeches and Statements made by current and previous executive directors (full text, 1999–), Events (1998–), Newsletters, the UNODC Update (full text, 2000–), Multimedia, Publications, and Promotional Materials. Multimedia includes the *UNODC Film and Video Catalogue* (in PDF format) and video clips of public service announcements. The Publications and Promotional Materials subsections require more in-depth descriptions.

The Publications subsection is especially extensive, with publication dates varying. An abstract and ordering information is provided for each listed publication. Individual titles are grouped into topical headings. These headings include Alternative Development; Analysis and Statistics, which also includes the full text of the *Bulletin on Narcotics* (1949–); Commission on Narcotic Drugs; Corruption; Crime and Criminal Justice; Drug Abuse and Demand Reduction; Drug Supply Reduction; Human Trafficking; Illicit Crop Monitoring Programme, arranged by country; Scientific Support; Treaty and Legal Affairs; *World Drug Report,* which includes the full text (PDF), as well as executive summary and highlights (both in Arabic, Chinese, German, English, Spanish, French, and Russian); and Other. Links are provided to International Narcotics Control Board and United Nations Interregional Crime & Justice Research Institute (UNICRI) publications.

Promotional Materials, the last subsection under News and Publications, provides the full text, in PDF format, of brochures; color images of posters; and the full text, again in PDF format, of informational postcards. Some of these postcards are available in languages other than English. The color images of the posters could be especially useful for school or public library educational displays.

Drug Abuse and Demand Reduction is the second major section discussed linked from the home page. This section provides in-depth coverage and has links to the full text of major publications embedded in the narrative. It is divided into six subsections. The first subsection is Drugs of Abuse—the Facts. Here is found information relating to the types and effects of the three main drug categories: depressants, stimulants, and hallucinogenics. Links to relevant UN conventions are imbedded in the text. Of special interest is the link to the publication *Terminology and Information on Drugs* compiled by the Scientific Section (Laboratory) Policy Development and Analysis Division for Operations and Analysis (October 1998). This publication is divided into two parts. Part I details the major drug groups of Cannabis, Coca, Opium, Opioids, CNS Depressants, Amphetamine-Type Stimulants, and Hallucinogens. Information for each group includes chemical constituents, pharmacological effects, medical use, and chemical structure. Part II is composed of a glossary of terms derived from WHO's *Lexicon of Alcohol and Drug Terms,* Geneva, 1994.

Global Youth Network is another subsection of Drug Abuse, and its focus is on drug use by children and young adults, with drug trends, information on drugs, a newsletter, events, tools, programs, and links. Here are found full-text publications, mainly in PDF

format, including *Youth and Drugs: A Global Overview* (1999), *World Situation with Regard to Drug Abuse, in Particular Among Children and Youth* (2000), and *Prevention of the Recreational and Leisure Use of Drugs Among Young People* (2001). Also found here are the full-texts, in PDF format, of the newsletter *Connekt,* (June 2000–). Lastly, a listing of links to other relevant Web sites is also included.

Global Assessment Programme is the third subsection. The topic Who Is Using Drugs contains embedded links to the full text, in PDF format, of major UN drug publications. Publications included here are *World Situation with Regard to Drug Abuse* from the Commission on Narcotic Drugs and the annual *Global Illicit Drug Trends.* Another full-text, PDF, major report is *World Drug Report for 2000,* available in English with an Executive Summary and Highlights in Arabic, Chinese, German, English, Spanish, French, and Russian.

Also located here is the topic of Harmonizing Global Drug Abuse Data, which includes the Annual Report Questionnaire and the methods on how drug abuse data are collected. The standardization of data collection information systems is discussed in *Drug Information Systems: Principles, Structure and Indicators,* as well as the significance of collecting comparable data.

Partners in Prevention, the fourth subsection, discusses programs that counteract drug demand and use. There are also links to examples of programs.

Access to Treatment and Rehabilitation, the fifth subsection, describes the various steps in this process. The full texts (PDF) of *Evaluation Guidelines, Facilitator's Workshop Guide,* and nine workbooks are also included: *Framework, Planning, Implementation, Needs Assessment, Process Evaluations, Cost Evaluations, Client Satisfaction Evaluations, Outcome Evaluations,* and *Economic Evaluations.* There are also links to the full text of publications within the Drug Abuse Treatment Tool Kit. The last subsection of Drug Abuse and Demand Reduction is HIV/AIDS and Other Diseases. Here is found narrative linking drug abuse and AIDS. Links are provided for global status by region, UNAIDS (Joint United Nations Programme on HIV/AIDS) cosponsoring agency Web sites, extent of HIV/AIDS and intravenous drug use by region, and UNODC's ongoing activities.

The third section from the home page is Drug Supply Reduction. This section is divided into two subsections: Alternative Development and Law Enforcement. Alternative Development pertains to developing legitimate crops instead of drugs. Included here is a link to the *Action Plan on International Cooperation on the Eradication of Illicit Drug Crops and on Alternative Development* (June 1998) and the *Alternative Development Database,* which provides the project summary for various countries. Also found here is a pull-down menu to the full text of the Alternative Development Projects and Strategic Studies Series. Law Enforcement provides a brief narrative and then links to Law Enforcement Project Summaries for Africa, Central Asia, East Asia, Latin America and the Caribbean, and Europe. Also included is a link to the Annual Reports Questionnaires, divided into three parts. This information is available via Word format or PDF in English, French, and Spanish.

Terrorism, Corruption and Human Trafficking, the fourth major section discussed from the UNODC home page, is subdivided into Crime Programme, *United Nations Crime and Justice Information Network* (UNCJIN), Terrorism, Corruption, Organized Crime, and Trafficking in Human Beings. Crime Programme refers to the Center for International Crime Prevention, which has been described separately in this chapter. *United Nations Crime and Justice Information Network* (UNCJIN) links to a comprehensive PDF listing of related international organizations and their URLs. The Terrorism subsection has the full text of 12 terrorism-related conventions (1963–1999), as well as links to various General Assembly and Security Council resolutions and documents and the full-text PDF of the *Global Programme against Terrorism.* There are also links to various terrorism conventions and seminars. Corruption, another subsection, includes the full text, in PDF format, of the *Global Programme against Corruption: An Outline for Action,* causes of corruption, and a link to the Utstein Anti-Corruption Resource Center. The Corruption page provides access to Country Projects, Interagency Coordination, Judicial Integrity, Global Trends, an *Anti-Corruption ToolKit,* and further links. The Organized Crime subsection also features information on the UN Convention against Transnational Organized Crime, as well as other publications, reports, and information sources on organized crime. The link under UN Convention against Organized Crime provides access to the text of the treaty, the *International Convention against Transnational Organized Crime,* background information, and speeches. Trafficking in Human Beings, the last major subdivision of the Terrorism, Corruption and Human Trafficking home page heading, features Background on the Protocol; *Protocol to Pre-*

vent, Suppress and Punish Trafficking in Persons; Technical Cooperation Projects, Awareness-Raising Campaigns; FAQ; Trafficking Links; TV Campaign; and United Nations Crime and Justice Information Network (UNCJIN). The *Protocol* supplements the *United Nations Convention against Transnational Organized Crime* by clarifying the United Nations stance on trafficking. Of special note is the TV Campaign section, which features real video public service announcements (2001–). By selecting the Internet-based United Nations Crime and Justice Information Network (ICJIN) under the Crime Programme subsection of the Terrorism, Corruption and Human Trafficking heading, researchers may find an online directory of links for this topic and others.

Treaty and Legal Affairs, another major section from the UNODC home page, is divided into four subsections: UN Treaties, Legal Advisory Programme, Legislation/Legal Library, and Money Laundering. UN Treaties and Resolutions, the first subsection, has the full text of *Single Convention on Narcotic Drugs 1961, Convention on Psychotropic Substances 1971,* and *Convention Against the Illicit Traffic in Narcotic Drugs and Psychotropic Substances 1988.* Also found here are the full text of related resolutions and decisions (1946–) from the General Assembly, Economic and Social Commission, and Commission on Narcotic Drugs. Legal Advisory Programme is the second subsection and has information pertaining to legal assistance including links to other intergovernmental legal bodies. This section is further subdivided into Achievements, Country and Regional Projects, Tools, and UNODC and Drug Treatment Courts. The Legislation subsection provides access to the UNODC legal library to research legislation. Along with standard searching there are also keyword, country, and year indexes. Money Laundering, the last subsection, lists the Ten Fundamentals of Money Laundering, publications (some in full text), and further links through a pull-down menu to the Money Laundering Home Page, GPML Technical Assistance, GPML Research, GPML Reports, and About IMoLIN.

Analysis and Statistics, yet another major section from the home page, is divided into Research, Scientific Support, and Illicit Crop Monitoring. Research provides access to resources already described, including full texts of *Annual Reports Questionnaires; Global Illicit Drug Trends* (PDF, 1999–); *Crime Statistics, Research and Analysis; Bulletin on Narcotics;* and *World Drug Report* (PDF, 1997–). Also found here are a series of full text, in PDF format, of books in UNODC's "Studies on Drugs and Crimes." Scientific Support provides brief information on UN laboratory services and quality assurance. Publications that are included here link back to publications previously discussed in the News and Publications section. *Crime Statistics, Research and Analysis* includes the *United Nations Survey on Crime Trends and the Operations of Criminal Justice Systems* (1970–). Illicit Crop Monitoring provides a description of this program, as well as links to the full text of annual survey reports, arranged by country.

The last major home page heading discussed, About Us, links to the pages regarding Leadership, Drug Programme, Crime Programme, Commission on Narcotic Drugs, International Narcotics Control Board, UN Commission on Crime Prevention and Criminal Justice, Goodwill Ambassadors, NGO and Civil Society, FAQs, and Job Opportunities. Each of these subsections contains a description and relevant links embedded in the text.

The other home page categories, Crime Commission (CCPCJ), Commission on Narcotic Drugs (CND), Global Youth Network, Information Services for Member States, UN News Service Global News Coverage, and UN-Wide Calendar, provide links to information already mentioned elsewhere in this chapter.

RESEARCH STRATEGIES

With drugs being the major crime emphasis of this chapter, the best place to begin the research process is with the *United Nations Office on Drugs and Crime* Web site, especially given the international stature of the United Nations and its far-reaching bounds. This site provides in-depth coverage of the various categories of drugs including definitions, chemical structure, and pharmacological effects via the full-text version of the *Terminology and Information on Drugs.* Here also are found the publications *World Situation with Regard to Drug Abuse, Global Illicit Drug Trends,* and *World Drug Report* along with the full text of many other related publications. The effects of drugs on youth is also discussed along with furnishing the full text of such publications *Youth and Drugs: A Global Overview* (1999), *World Situation with Regard to Drug Abuse, in Particular Among Children and Youth* (2000), and *Prevention of the Recreational and Leisure Use of Drugs Among Young People* (2001). The full texts of related resolutions and decisions

(1946–) from the General Assembly, Economic and Social Commission, and Commission on Narcotic Drugs are all included here. The description of the UNODC site provides an in-depth description of the wealth of research material available from the UN.

The *Bureau for International Narcotics and Law Enforcement Affairs* Web site of the United States State Department is also useful for researching the criminality of drugs. Under the Congressional Budget Justification section is the full text of reports outlining the objectives, justification, programs, and effectiveness measures for individual countries in their dealings with drug trafficking. The annual *Narcotics Control Report* outlines both the efforts by individual countries to combat drugs and U.S. policy initiatives and programs in that area. This site also includes a listing of links to the Web sites of other related U.S. government agencies and international organizations. **ICPO-Interpol** also presents its work in controlling drug trafficking.

Corruption is another major theme. OECD's *AnCorRWEB—Anti-Corruption Ring Online* Web site serves as a comprehensive bibliography of research sources arranged by topic. Although only some of the titles are annotated, this source will still prove to be a rich resource of references. The *Bureau for International Narcotics and Law Enforcement Affairs, ICPO-Interpol,* and *United Nations Center for International Crime Prevention* Web sites all contain sections addressing the subject of corruption and include the full text of publications.

Europol and ICPO-Interpol are police organizations, and therefore their coverage of crime is much broader. Europol includes the *EU Organized Crime Situation Report* along with its annual reports and related EU regulations.

ICPO-Interpol is very extensive in its coverage, including such topics as children and human trafficking, art theft, information technology crime, and weapons/explosives. This site also includes statistics on crime via *International Crime Statistics,* which have been published since 1950.

The subject of terrorism is also addressed by ICPO-Interpol, United Nations Center for International Crime Prevention, and United Nations Office on Drugs and Crime. The United Nations Office on Drugs and Crime is especially useful because it provides the full text of 12 terrorism conventions (1993–1999), along with a description of terrorist weapons.

The *United Nations Interregional Crime & Justice Research Institute* Web site is a good source for locating publications useful for research. Most, however, are only in citation form. Of special note for this site is the database *World Directory of Criminological Resources,* providing information on more than 450 institutions in 70 countries. The *United Nations and* *Criminals, 1946–1996: Resolutions, Reports, Documents and Publications,* issue 47–48, 1996–1997 of **International Review of Criminal Policy,** is another excellent bibliographic source of United Nations publications related to crime.

CHAPTER 5
Development

CHAPTER OVERVIEW

"Development cannot be defined in any simple way. It is a political and cultural term, and therefore heavily disputed.... Since the establishment of the Bretton Woods System, development has referred to the process whereby poor countries or communities are able (from within their own resources) or enabled (by others) to improve their situation economically, socially, and culturally."[1] This chapter covers resources addressing the economic and social growth of nations, particularly those nations that have developed the least in these two areas. Economic development is often viewed in terms of the measure of goods and services available per person in each country, as measured by per capita income. Also included in this chapter is information on the topic of sustainable development, defined as involving "notions of patterns of economic and industrial development that do not entail substantial ecological damage and/or consume only those natural resources that can be renewed or replaced without great difficulty."[2] Other terms researchers will discover in using the resources in this chapter are social development and human development, which both describe the economic growth of a country as measured by indicators that illustrate the social well-being of a country.

Statistical indicators play an important role in reporting on development; therefore researchers will find the resources in this chapter rich in data. Related information is found especially in these other chapters: Economics and Business, General Resources, Health, Human Rights, Social/Cultural Issues, and Statistics. Lending institutions that provide economic assistance are a good resource for online development information, among them the Web sites of the *Inter-American Development Bank (IADB)*, the *International Monetary Fund*, the *World Bank*, and the nongovernmental organization the *European Bank for Reconstruction and Development*. Selected *International Monetary Fund* Web site resources and *United Nations Industrial Development Organization* Web site resources are described here; the rest are covered in the Economics and Business chapter.

Governmental Sources Discussed

Asian Development Bank (ADB) Web site, Manila, Philippines. <http://www.adb.org/>

ELDIS Web site, by the Eldis Programme at Institute of Development Studies, University of Sussex, Brighton, United Kingdom. <http://www.eldis.org/>

Geographical Distribution of Financial Flows to Aid Recipients, by the Organisation for Economic Co-operation and Development, Paris, 1974– (ISSN 1015-3934). (print annual title, CD, and online subscription title).

Inter-American Agency for Cooperation and Development (IACD) Web site, by the Organization of American States, Washington, D.C. <http://www.iacd.oas.org/>

Inter-American Development Bank (IDB) Web site, Washington, D.C. <http://www.iadb.org/>

International Monetary Fund Web site, Washington, D.C. <http://www.imf.org/>

SD Dimensions, a Web site by the Sustainable Development Department, Food and Agriculture Organization (FAO) of the United Nations, Rome, Italy. <http://www.fao.org/sd/>

United Nations Development Programme (UNDP) Resources

Human Development Report, by the United Nations Development Programme. New York: Oxford University Press, 1990– (ISSN 0969-4501) (print annual title 1990–, CD, and online 1995–). <http://www.undp.org/hdr/>

United Nations Development Programme (UNDP) Web site, New York. <http://www.undp.org/>

United Nations Industrial Development Organization (UNIDO) Web site, Vienna, Austria. <http://www.unido.org/>

US AID Web site, by the United States Agency for International Development, Washington, D.C. <http://www.usaid.gov/>

World Bank Group Resources

African Development Indicators. New York: United Nations Development Programme; Washington, D.C.: World Bank, 1992– (ISSN: 1020-2927) (print and CD-ROM).
  Global Development Finance and *GDF Online* (print, CD-ROM, and online subscription).
  Global Development Finance. Washington, D.C.: World Bank (ISSN 1020-5454) (print version).
  Global Development Finance. Washington, D.C.: World Bank, 2002– (ISBN 0-82135-083-8) (CD-ROM).
  GDF Online. World Bank Group, 2000– (online subscription).
PovertyNet Web site, Washington, D.C. <http://www.worldbank.org/poverty/>
World Bank Atlas. Washington, D.C.: World Bank, 1967– (ISSN 0085-8293) (print annual title and CD-ROM).
  World Bank Group Web site, Washington, D.C. <http://www.worldbank.org/>
  World Development Indicators (print, CD-ROM, and online subscription).
  World Development Indicators. Washington, D.C.: World Bank, 1978– (print edition).
  World Development Indicators CD-ROM. Washington, D.C.: World Bank, International Economics Dept., Development Data Group, 1990–
WDI Online. Washington, D.C.: World Bank, International Economics Dept., Development Data Group, 2002– (online subscription).
World Development Report, published for the World Bank by Oxford University Press, 1978– (ISSN 0163-5085) (print, CD-ROM, and online). <http://econ.worldbank.org/wdr/> (online full text from 2002; editions 1992–2001, online content varies according to year).

Nongovernmental Sources Discussed

Development Gateway Web site, Washington, D.C. <http://www.developmentgateway.org/>
European Bank for Reconstruction and Development (EBRD) Web site, London, United Kingdom. <http://www.ebrd.com/>

GOVERNMENTAL SOURCES

Asian Development Bank (ADB) Web site, Manila, Philippines. <http://www.adb.org/>

Summary: The Asian Development Bank (ADB) emphasizes specific areas in fulfilling its mission to reduce poverty in Asia and the Pacific, and, therefore, its Web site contains information on these subjects for the region: economic growth, human development, gender and development, good governance, environmental protection, private-sector development, and regional cooperation. Users may search by subject under the home page category Topics. Also, under the home page category Regions and Countries, researchers will find countries listed alphabetically, with many resources and reports on poverty, finance, and development for individual countries, as well as links, poverty statistics, and online photographs available for each country. Other main categories on the home page are Economic & Statistics and Publications, as ADB is its own publisher and distributor. The Web site of the Asian Development Bank is searchable and has a site map and index.

ADB is a multilateral development finance institution owned by 61 members dedicated to reducing poverty in Asia and the Pacific. Members' countries are mostly from Asia and are listed on its Web site. ADB's priority mission is to reduce poverty in Asia and the Pacific and to improve the quality of people's lives by providing loans and technical assistance for a broad range of development activities. Users may select either a specific country/region or topic from a drop-down box on the home page to find key indicators/statistics, projects, programs, and news information.

Detailed Description: Under the home page category Publications, researchers may find information on publications for sale in its catalog and also a separate list of publications available online at no charge. Under the link to ADBI Publications, articles from the Bank's professional journal, the *Asian Development Bank Review,* are also available online at no charge in PDF format from 2001 on. The ADB's Depository Library Program offers the public a worldwide network of more than 162 libraries, which assists the public in obtaining free access to ADB documents and publications. Up-to-date economic forecasts for ADB countries and regions are available in the *Asian Development Outlook*, a print annual title (ISSN 1655-4809) (1989–), CD, and online (1996–) with summaries and updates (varying HTML and PDF formats).

The home page category Regions & Countries provides access to detailed online information through the sections Country Reports and Country Economics Review (CER). Country Reports provides information on economic performance and assessing economic needs, and Country Economics Review reports on current economic conditions and trends.

ELDIS Web site, by the Eldis Programme at Institute of Development Studies, University of Sussex, Brighton, United Kingdom. <http://www.eldis.org/>

Summary: *ELDIS* is a comprehensive development portal describing and linking to Internet resources on development and the environment and is continually updated. Information includes: country information, resource guides, electronic research documents, development data links, Internet sites for development organizations, development related databases, library catalogs, bibliographies, electronic communications forums, research projects, information about maps, and news. In cases in which no Internet link is available, information on a resource's availability in tangible electronic formats is included (CD-ROMS, etc.). *ELDIS* also hosts development databases produced by other organizations and is available at no charge to researchers, officials, and students. Advanced searching is available, and the Web site is published in English and Spanish.

ELDIS is hosted by the Institute of Development Studies, Sussex, and is core funded by three national government agencies for development: Danida (Denmark), Norad (The Norwegian Agency for Development Cooperation), and Sida (Sweden).

Geographical Distribution of Financial Flows to Aid Recipients, by the Organisation for Economic Co-operation and Development (OECD), Paris, 1974– (ISSN 1015-3934) (print annual title, CD, and online subscription).

Summary: Published annually, this statistical reference book, in English and French, contains data on financial aid disbursements of many types to individual developing countries and territories. Historical time series data back to 1960 is provided. It is also available for purchase as part of the information on OECD's *International Development Statistics CD-ROM* and through OECD's electronic subscription service *SourceOECD,* or through subscription to the OECD's online database, *International Development Statistics Online.*

The OECD's Development Assistance Committee works to improve access to financial support by developing countries. This statistical report supports the Committee's work in reviewing the amount and nature of their contributions to bilateral and multilateral aid programs. The members of the Development Assistance Committee are Australia, Austria, Belgium, Canada, Denmark, Finland, France, Germany, Greece, Ireland, Italy, Japan, Luxembourg, the Netherlands, New Zealand, Norway, Portugal, Spain, Sweden, Switzerland, the United Kingdom, the United States, and the Commission of the European Communities.

Detailed Description: Information is provided in three sections. The main section of each issue has data summary tables by individual countries receiving aid on official development assistance and official aid net disbursements to developing countries, with data provided for five-year periods. Disbursements are the actual international transfer of financial resources. These countries are on the Committee's List of Aid Recipients.

In addition in separate parts, aggregate data is provided for countries classified as the least-developed countries and in another section for countries and territories in transition. The definition of least-developed countries (LLDCs) follows the United Nations definition as of 1999 and includes 48 countries. An annex gives the full List of Aid Recipients and also definitions of concepts used in the report.

This title succeeds the earlier titles, *Geographical Distribution of Financial Flows to Less Developed Countries: Disbursements-Commitments* that covered 1960–1967 (Statistical series B—Development Assistance Committee) and *Geographical Distribution of Financial Flows to Developing Countries.* The 2003 CD-ROM edition, *International Development Statistics CD-ROM* includes statistics from this title 1960–2001 and includes a free annual subscription to the online database, *International Development Statistics Online.*

Inter-American Agency for Cooperation and Development (IACD) Web site, by the Organization of American States, Washington, D.C. <http://www.iacd.oas.org/>

Summary: With development activities in the Americas as its mission, this Web site highlights its activities through reports, press releases, video, and links to other sources. For the purpose of this discussion, the focus will be on the IACD Projects, Government Best Practices, New Initiatives, News, and Links home page categories. This entire site, also available in Spanish, is searchable, with the search engine found on every page. A site map is available from the home page.

Created in 2000, the IACD's mission is to forge new private-/public-sector partnerships through the capabilities of the member and observer states of the OAS to help the people of the Americas overcome poverty, benefit from the digital revolution, and advance their economic and social development.

Detailed Description: The IACD Projects home page category provides information about how projects are developed and presented to the IACD and then funded. A chart, in PDF format, lists in Spanish the project name, area, funding, participants, institutions, and objectives. The full-text publication, in PDF, of how to present proposals is also included in this category.

Government Best Practices, another home page category, has a description of the program as well as a full-text, PDF copy of the report *Profiles of Electronic Government Procurement Systems.* New Initiatives features the full-text, PDF copy of the report *Rural Connectivity and Energy Initiative Program* (no date).

The News home page category contains press releases (2000–), video, full text PDF of annual reports (2000–), the full text of sponsored studies reports, and the full text of *IACD Bulletin* (2002–). Links is the last home page category, and here are found links to the home pages of National Agencies of International Cooperation in Latin America, arranged by country name.

Inter-American Development Bank (IDB) Web site, Washington, D.C. <http://www.iadb.org/>

Summary: The mission of the Inter-American Bank (IDB) is to reduce poverty and promote economic and social growth, as well as to strengthen democratic institutions in Latin America and the Caribbean. The IDB provides online publications and reports, updates on conferences and events, feature articles, major online journals such as *IDBAmérica*, news, country information, and project reports. The organization's Web site is available in English, French, Spanish, Portuguese, and Japanese, and a text format is available. Comprehensive search aids include search tips, a simple and advanced search engine, a site map, a drop-down box of searching by preselected topics, as well as by subtopic. IDB is its own publisher and distributor and provides an online bookstore under the Publications category.

The Inter-American Development Bank, the oldest and largest regional multilateral development institution, was established in 1959 to help accelerate economic and social development in Latin America and the Caribbean. It is the principal source of multilateral financing for economic, social, and institutional development projects in Latin America and the Caribbean. The Bank provides loans and technical assistance using capital provided by its member countries; it also promotes and participates in a significant number of projects as a cofinancer with other multilateral, bilateral, and private organizations. Of the Bank's affiliates, the Inter-American Investment Corporation (IIC) finances small- and medium-scale private enterprises, and the Multilateral Investment Fund (MIF) promotes investment reforms and private-sector development.

Detailed Description: Main categories of information on this Web site are Inside the IDB, Projects, Resources, IDB Periodicals, Documents, and Country Focus (Country Web Pages). In addition, the Web site offers links to feature articles, featured Web pages, news, and special events. Inside the IDB includes information about its organization and activities under the subcategories About Us, Calendar of Events, Press, Countries, Sectors and Topics, Employment and Scholarships, Policies, Staff and Structure, and Annual Report.

The Projects Category includes this type of information on IDB projects under the subcategories Projects Background, Projects Documents, Private Sector Projects, MIF Projects, IIC Projects, Business Opportunities, and *IDB Projects Online. IDB Projects Online* is a subscription database on current projects funded, contracts, and awards.

The category Resources includes the subcategories Library, *IDBAmérica Magazine,* Publications, Investor Information, Photo Library, Public Information Center, Cultural Center, INDES, INTAL, and E-Courses. The Publications subcategory is an online bookstore for English and Spanish titles available for purchase in print or electronic format. Searching by keyword and by topic is available. The Photo Library is a searchable database of electronic and print pictures. Under certain conditions, images may be freely used and can be searched by country, subject, or topic. Under Resources, INDES links to The Inter-American Institute for Social Development, (INDES), an integral part of the Inter-American Development Bank, which functions as a training center for policy design and management, assists establishing national programs, and functions as a discussion forum.

Also under the category Resources, INTAL links to the Institute for the Integration of Latin America and the Caribbean, an international organization with over a hundred research centers participating in projects and publishing research. INTAL provides researchers with papers, studies, and databases online, with most information in Spanish, some in Portuguese and English. Integration, globalization, and trade are its focus. Although INTAL provides some titles online at no charge, most are available through purchase or subscription. INTAL is a comprehensive Web site offering in-depth information on integration and providing links to other integration Web sites for the Latin America and Caribbean areas.

The Country Focus category from the home page of the Inter-American Development Bank provides an online database and resource entitled Country Web Pages providing summary information about IDB's activities concerning Latin American and Caribbean countries, in English and Spanish. Information for each country includes an overview with statistics, online articles about IDB's activities in that country, and links to projects for the individual country in different stages, including projects online. Also available are online resources for each country, such as a Web directory of government, finance, research, and news organizations for that nation, as well as a listing of the IDB country office and the IDB's lending portfolio to the country.

The category Documents lists featured online titles available at no charge in PDF or HTML format, including such titles as *Facing the Challenges of Sustainable Development*. The Country Focus category includes Country Web Pages, Press Releases, Proposed & Approved Projects, and the IDB Country Strategy & Country Economic Assessment.

The IDB Periodicals category links to four major journals of the bank. Its flagship periodical, the monthly *IDBAmérica,* (1997–, Internet edition only since January 2001) is richly illustrated with articles on comprehensive sectors of life in Latin America and the Caribbean relating to development, including health, education, civil society, democracy, microenterprise, information technology, finance, arts, crime, and justice, as well as news about the organization. Available electronically in English, French, Spanish, and Portuguese, the journal is searchable and features a searchable online archive of monthly issues dating back to 1997. An e-mail notification service providing monthly headlines from *IDBAmérica* is available. Also available is a searchable digital PDF archive 1963–1997 to articles from *IDBAmérica* and the earlier title, the *IDB Newsletter.* The newsletter *Latin American Economic Policies* reports recent research on major economic and social problems affecting both Latin America and the Caribbean. Articles are by authors independent of the

IDB. *Microenterprise,* a biennial periodical (1998–), provides an in-depth discussion of innovation and issues in microenterprise development in Latin American and the Caribbean. Also available is the monthly newsletter of the *Institute for the Integration of Latin America and the Caribbean* (PDF format, 2000–).

International Monetary Fund (IMF) Web site, Washington, D.C. <http://www.imf.org>

Summary: The home page of the International Monetary Fund, available in English, French, Spanish, and Arabic, provides access to information about its work, finances, news and events, publications, as well as current highlights. A site map and index along with a first-time visitor's section are also included. A pull-down menu of individual country names allows for finding information about the IMF's work in that country. A search engine is available for searching the entire site and is found on every page.

For the purpose of this chapter the entire *IMF* Web site will not be described. The main focus will be on the home page categories IMF at work, Country Information, and Publications. IMF at work provides information under the subheading Lending, and further links to the topics Poverty Reduction and Growth Facility, Debt Relief Initiative, and Emergency Assistance. Lending also links to Crisis Resolution topics, including Sovereign Debt Restructuring Mechanism, which is discussed here. For more information about the IMF, researchers should consult the Economics and Business chapter.

Established in 1945, the IMF began functioning in 1947 and currently has 184 member countries. As a financial-based international organization, the IMF seeks to assist with economic growth and stability, including balance of payment loans as well as fostering "international monetary cooperation."

Detailed Description: The IMF at Work category on the home page links to rich information on finances of developing countries. Under Crisis Resolution, Sovereign Debt Restructuring provides information about the problem that countries face, both as creditors and debtors, when restructuring a country's debt. The IMF strives to help prevent financial crisis. It provides fact sheets on this topic, the full text of relevant papers, speeches, and a questions-and-answer section. The IMF at work also provides detailed information on the financial organization and operations of the IMF.

Poverty Reduction and Growth Facility, a topic under Lending, contains fact sheets, papers, and reports. Of particular importance is the *Poverty Reduction Strategy Papers (PRSP)* series, available in full text. These papers are prepared by the member countries in association with external development partners, such as the World Bank and International Monetary Fund. Updated every three years with annual progress reports, *PRSP*s describe the country's macroeconomic, structural, and social policies and programs over approximately three years and how these promote broad-based growth and reduce poverty. They also identify external financing needs and major sources of financing for countries. The reports are accessible by country name, arranged alphabetically, or by policy. Other related documents are also included in this section.

Debt Relief Initiative is another topic under Lending. Like the other two, this section has fact sheets, papers, and reports. In this section also are documents related to the Heavily Indebted Poor Countries (HIPCs) Initiative in the form of documents and country reports arranged alphabetically by country name.

Country Information is a main top-page heading on the IMF home page that provides an alphabetical listing of world countries, with each country's name linking to relevant full-text materials regarding the IMF's relationship with that particular country. These materials include reports, working papers, transcripts, press briefings, and statements, although not all countries will contain all material types.

Publications is the last main heading from the home page that will be discussed in this chapter. A search engine is found on this page that allows for browsing by title, author, and subject as well as searching by title, author/editor, and subject. Pull-down menus are included for series selection and date criteria selection, and sorting is also available by date, author, and title. The latest publications catalogue is found here in PDF format. Publications can also be located via the subheadings of recent titles, periodicals, research, and work in progress.

The periodical subheading under Publications lists the various periodical titles published by IMF, which link to the various full-text issues, mainly in PDF format. Date coverage varies. The quarterly periodical *Finance and Development* covers major development topics concerning the IMF's mission, such as debt and poverty, and other monetary and financial issues. It is available in print (1968–) and online (1996–) in varying formats. The current online issues provide the articles in PDF format. The content is scholarly, providing supporting statistics and bibliographical cita-

tions. The print issues are indexed in the December issues, and the Web site provides searching and advanced searching by date, year, and title.

The section Research at the IMF includes working papers (full text 1997–, citation and abstract 1991–1997), occasional papers (full text late 1996–, citation and abstract 1991–1996), policy discussion papers (full text 1999–), ongoing research projects, and a full-text description of research activities. Ongoing research projects features a search engine, which allows searching by author, title, projects relate to…, countries, and IMF department. Work in progress links to the same search engine described under ongoing research projects. Country intention documents are arranged alphabetically by country name. Topical searching is also possible, and a search box is included. A link to many of the various publications already mentioned can also be found on the main publications page.

SD Dimensions Web site, by the Sustainable Development Department, Food and Agriculture Organization (FAO) of the United Nations, Rome, Italy. <http://www.fao.org/sd/>

Summary: The relationship between agriculture and food security and development is important in order to ensure that the natural resource base remains productive for the future and that rural development and agricultural are sustained. This Web site, available in English, French, Spanish, and Arabic, provides a global reference center for knowledge on sustainable development in the areas of biophysical, biological, socioeconomic, and social dimensions of sustainable development. Information is arranged into four main categories: Environment, Knowledge, Institutions, and People. The Web site is searchable by keyword and allows browsing by keyword and by theme. Each category links to publications relevant for the specific theme, resources (periodicals, etc.), forums for the exchange of information, and related Web sites.

Created by the FAO in 1995 to provide development support and poverty alleviation, *SD Dimensions* focuses on key areas of activity; promoting sustainability strategies and methods for sustainable livelihoods; gender and population issues; agrarian transformation and institutional reform; research, extension, education, and communication; and natural resource monitoring and management. The Sustainable Development Department coordinates FAO's follow-up to the United Nations Conference on Environment and

Development (UNCED); conventions related to these conferences; and the international summits on population, social development, and women.

Detailed Description: Environment, the first main category on the Web page of *SD Dimensions,* contains information on Conventions and Agreements, Energy and Technology, Geoinformation Monitoring and Assessment, and Policy and Integrated Management. The next main category, Institutions, covers information under Land Tenure, Public Institutions, and Rural Organizations. Land Tenure, under the subheading Land Reform, links to the *Land Reform Bulletin,* a periodical in English, French, and Spanish, with an index by author (1990–2001), which links to individual articles or a chronological index by issue back to 1996. The articles are full text online at no charge and in either HTML or PDF format.

The third main category on the Web page of *SD Dimensions,* Knowledge, includes information under Communication for Development, Education, Extension, and Research and Technology. Of special note is the CD-ROM entitled *Communication for Development,* available for purchase or online at no charge, which contains English, French, and Spanish publications from the FAO Communication for Development Group. It contains a wide range of searchable topics related to communication for development in many countries. The titles included were selected for types of experiences that assist policy makers, planners, educators, extension workers, and others on how to effectively use communication to inform and educate people about new ideas and technical innovations in agriculture.

The last main category from the home page, People, includes subsections on Gender and Development, Participation, Population, and Sustainable Livelihood. Under Gender and Development are resources such as the *Database on the Rural Disabled* and policy information on the following plans of action: *Plan of Action for People's Participation in Rural Development*; *FAO Plan of Action for Gender and Development* (2002–2007); *FAO Plan of Action for Women in Development* (1996–2001); and *FAO People's Participation Programme.* Also under the category People are links to projects such as the *Dimitra project,* which is a tool for women and their organizations to make their voices heard at the national and international level. The project provides rural populations with easier access to information and assists women's organizations in highlighting the extent and value of women's contributions. *Dimitra* provides an online database with publications and contact information for organizations that work with rural women and development.

Another program of note under the category People/Gender and Development is a program called SEAGA, Socio-Economic and Gender Analysis Program, which was established in 1993 as a cooperative effort to promote gender awareness when meeting development challenges. Articles published under SEAGA are available back to 1998.

In addition to the main categories of information previously described (Environment; Institutions, Knowledge; and People,) the Web site also provides highlights for each area, as well as a long list of hot links to related sites. Researchers interested in environment and development information and reports for individual countries could consult the FAO information on two of the major Internet resources listed concerning environmental conferences: the World Summit on Sustainable Development (Earth Summit +10), and the earlier conference, Earth Summit +5. More information on these summits is located in the Environment chapter.

United Nations Development Programme (UNDP) Resources

Human Development Report, by the United Nations
    Development Programme. New York: Oxford University Press, 1990– (ISSN 0969-4501) (print annual title 1990–, CD, and online 1995–).
    <http://www.undp.org/hdro/>

Summary: The purpose of this annual report is to provide an independent, critical analysis of human development across the globe aimed at assisting the growth of human development, as well as providing detailed country data focusing on human well-being, along with economic trends. It is not a formal policy statement for the UNDP. Each report has a specific theme concerning the topic of development. Chapters focus on topics within the theme and are well illustrated with boxes, figures, and data. Each report contains an overview, bibliography, illustrations, and a significant section of statistical tables on human development indicators.

Detailed Description: The text of the *Human Development Report* is accompanied by tables, figures, boxes, and special articles, which are also listed separately for easy access. The statistical data provides references, definitions of statistical terms, and an HDI

(Human Development Index). Tables cover indicators for monitoring development, demographic trends, knowledge trends, access to resources, security, equality for the genders, and human and labor rights instruments for individual developing countries, as well as basic indicators for other UN member countries. Tables are organized by ranking in human development index by grouping indictors for countries in high, medium, and low human development rank. Because of lack of reliable data, 18 UN member countries are excluded from the HDI. Statistical tables are indexed. Data in the *Human Development Report* should not be expected to conform to those in other publications because of the methodology used. The report also includes a list of countries and regions that have produced human development reports.

Reports are available full text on the Web site from 1994 on. The CD-ROM version permits researchers to produce customized statistical tables and color charts. It contains the full text of reports in HTML and PDF formats. It allows searching of all reports.

United Nations Development Programme (UNDP)

Web site, New York. <http://www.undp.org/>

Summary: The United Nations Development Programme (UNDP) is the major development arm of the United Nations and a publisher of significant research development reports. Its Web site provides developing countries with a global development network or forum for discussion and activities. The UNDP publishes significant referent titles, such as the *Human Development Report,* also described in this chapter, regional development reports, journals, such as *Choices,* fact sheets, and much online information, some available at no charge. Its searchable Web site, in English, French, and Spanish, highlights major publications, news, press releases, and categorizes information under UNDP topics. Only selected development topics are described here.

The UNDP is the United Nations global development network, advocating for change and connecting countries to knowledge, information, and resources to help people lead a better life. The UNDP works in approximately 166 countries, through 131 country offices, and devotes its activities to these areas: Democratic Governance, Poverty Reduction, Crisis Prevention and Recovery, Energy and Environment, Information and Communications Technology, and HIV/AIDS. In addition, it also promotes human rights, the empowerment of women, technical cooperation about developing countries, and the ability of countries to attract and use aid effectively.

Detailed Description: Major highlighted activities and publications include full text of its annual report, the *Human Development Report* (1994–), also described in this chapter. Millennium Development Goals, Choices Magazines, Newsfront, the UNDP's latest annual report, Jobs, and the UNWorks. Most of this information is also accessible under the topical categories. Highlighted articles and current news in brief are on the home page.

UNDP categories of information on its Web site include: UNDP by Region, Development Policy, Strategic Partnership, Human Development Reports, UNDP Thematic Trust Funds, Netaid, UN Volunteers (UNV), UN Capital Development Fund, UNIFEM, UN System Organizations, Executive Board, Newsfront, Speeches & Statements, Press Releases, For Journalists, Publications, Events, Jobs, Discover UNDP, Frequently Asked Questions, Enquiries & Comments, and Copyrights & Terms of Use.

The Publications category allows researchers to search for publications by theme and by region and also lists general publications. General publications include its *Annual Report* online since 2001 and its *Results Oriented Annual Report (ROAR),* online since 1999, which analyze results of UNDP supported development throughout the world in relationship to the Millennium Development Goals. *Choices* is the flagship quarterly magazine of UNDP. Each issue focuses on a specific country program that illustrates UNDP's key practice areas. Other major titles are *World Energy Assessment,* an analysis of current energy trends in relationship to redevelopment; *World Resources,* a study of the state of the environment in response to increasing world resource demands; and other major reports on specific themes such as poverty and corruption. The Publications category also links to UNDP online fact sheets on specific subjects, such as the role of UNDP in the fight against AIDS.

In addition to *Choices,* the major journals published by UNDP include its *Cooperation South Journal* and *Development Policy Journal,* both new in 2002. The themes that publications are organized by include democratic governance, poverty reduction, crisis prevention & recovery, energy & environment, information & communications technology, HIV/AIDS, Gender in Development, Strategic Partnerships, South-South Cooperation, and Capacity Development.

Publications also links to regional development reports, such as the ***Arab Human Development Report*** online 2002– (downloadable for a fee). English, French, and Arabic language versions are available. Users may also link to the National (individual country) human development reports; however, only some are online, in full text or summary versions.

United Nations Industrial Development Organization (UNIDO) Web site, Vienna, Austria. <http://www.unido.org/>

Summary: UNIDO acts as both a global forum and a technical cooperation agency with its 169 member states, disseminating knowledge, creating partnerships, and designing and implementing programs. UNIDO's information services and databases cover industrial development abstracts, industrial statistics, business environment, finance, industrial technology, energy, agro-industries, and biosafety. A major publisher, one of UNIDO's significant publications is its annual *Industrial Development Report.* On UNIDO's searchable Web site, information is organized under these categories: Services Overview, Media, What We Do, About UNIDO, UNIDO Weekly News, Hot Topics, Publications, Integrated Programmes, and Topics and Initiatives. Advanced searching is also available. Created in 1966, UNIDO's mission focuses on helping developing countries and countries with economies in transition toward goals of improved productive employment, a more competitive economy, and a cleaner environment. More information about UNIDO is covered in the Economics and Business chapter.

Detailed Description: The category Publications links to information concerning the products of UNIDO. UNIDO is a publisher and distributor of its own works and provides an online catalog of sales publications, as well as a link to downloadable no-fee documents. One current title full text online at no charge from the home page and under the Publications category is its *Industrial Development Report* (2002/2003–) an annual report that continues earlier titles available back to 1985, including UNIDO's *Industrial Development Global Report.* This reference title provides industrial indicators by country and other analysis and is available in many languages. Other information under Publications includes links to UNIDO databases, UNIDO reports and documents online, and video publications. A separate section (entitled Full Texts Available Online) allows access to a small number of free online publications in PDF format, but UNIDO is planning on adding more titles in the future. Also from the Publications category, re-

searchers may find some online Documents, the internal official working documents of UNIDO from 2001 on, and a section for just new documents.

Publications also links to databases, such as the *Industrial Development Abstracts (IDA) Database,* a unique database that contains more than 11,000 fully indexed abstracts of UNIDO documentation from 1981 on. It includes descriptions of major studies and reports and proceedings of working groups and seminars. There is no charge for searching the database; copies of the full reports may be ordered in microfiche or electronic format.

UNIDO's other major industrial databases are available on a subscription CD-ROM entitled *Databases of Industrial Statistics.* These permit users to search for industrial statistics by date (1984–), by country, and by different levels of ISIC (Industrial Classification of All Economic Activities).

The category Services Overview provides business and research information and is organized under Agro-Industries, Industrial Energy and Kyoto Protocol, Industrial Governance and Statistics, Investment and Technology Promotion, Montreal Protocol, and Small Business Development. These topics provide development, industrial, and environmental research information by linking to full-text documents, statistics, project information, and news.

Some miscellaneous features of the UNIDO Web site are news by e-mail, information about jobs, contact, and a registered users site. About UNIDO explains the organization's objectives, its core structure, and facts and figures about it. The UNIDO Weekly News category links to an electronic weekly newsletter entitled *UNIDOscope,* archived since 2002.

From the home page, Media provides electronic press releases, highlighted publications currently released, the Director-General's speeches, and a press room. Also from the home page, the category What We Do is mainly about UNIDO's services. The category About UNIDO provides detailed information about its mission, objectives, structure, and more.

USAID Web site, by the United States Agency for International Development, Washington, D.C. <http://www.usaid.gov/>

Summary: From 1961, USAID has been the principal U.S. agency to extend assistance to countries recovering from disaster, working to develop economically, and engaging in democratic reforms. USAID works specifically in four regions of the world through its field offices: sub-Saharan Africa, Asia and the Near

East, Latin America and the Caribbean, and Europe and Eurasia. It reports on assistance to countries through its searchable Internet site, organizing information under About USAID, Our Work (specific development topics), Locations (information on the regions and countries getting assistance), and Policy (business, policies, and procedures). The home page features articles on specific development activities within countries, as well as links to press information and *USAID News.* The site is searchable, has a site map, and provides a drop-down Country Locator box and USAID keyword browsing.

USAID is an independent federal government agency that works to support long-term economic growth and advancing U.S. foreign policy objectives through supporting: economic growth, agricultural and trade, global health, promotion of democracy, conflict prevention, and humanitarian assistance. About USAID links to key online USAID documents.

Detailed Description: Under Our Work on the home page users may link to information on Agriculture, Democracy & Governance, Economic Growth & Trade, Education & Universities, Environment, Global Partnerships, Health, Humanitarian Assistance, and Cross-Cutting Partnerships. Each section has news, current highlights, and links to publications. The home page category Locations links to a Web site for each region of the world. Each site is searchable and features information organized in various ways, usually with links to country and topical information, specific activities, progress reports, publications, photo galleries, and news. Many publications are free (PDF format), and others may be ordered through USAID's *Development Experience Clearinghouse (DEC),* which supplies USAID-funded, international development documentation.[3] USAID reports available at no charge in PDF format may be searched online in the *Development Experience System (DEXS)* database, actually a family of bibliographic databases for about 100,000 USAID technical and program documents. *DEXS* also provides searching by country or by topics and provides other USAID links. Other format USAID publications (paper, electronic, and CD) may be ordered through *DEC* online.

Under the category Our Work/Global Partnerships, USAID reports on a new initiative, Global Development Alliance (GDA). This alliance helps to coordinate and mobilize the ideas, efforts and resources of the public sector with those of the private sector and non-governmental organizations. The aim of this partnership is to maximize aid given to developing coun-

tries. Alliance partners make a formal agreement with USAID on development efforts.

World Bank Resources (Washington, D.C.)

African Development Indicators. New York: United Nations Development Programme; Washington, D.C.: World Bank, 1992– (ISSN: 1020-2927) (print and CD-ROM).

Summary: First published in 1992, this annual title provides detailed development data on Africa in one volume from the *World Bank Africa Database.* Macroeconomic, sectoral, and social data are provided on 53 African countries in annual time series dating from 1970 and are organized in separate statistical tables on topics of development.

Detailed Description: Topics of development covered in this title are grouped into chapters including: selected background data; national accounts; prices and exchange rates; money and banking; external sector; external debt and related flows; government finance; agriculture; power, communications, and transportation; public enterprises; labor force and employment; aid flows; social indicators; environmental indicators; and Heavily Indebted Poor Countries (HIPC) debt initiatives. Each chapter contains an introduction, defines the data, and provides statistical tables, charts, and technical notes. Introduction, bibliography, and acronyms are included.

A separate CD-ROM subscription product of *African Development Indicators* offers annual time series of most development topics and chapters back to 1970, providing a database of historical statistics. Data is also provided in 20 country groups. A sample of statistics are available on the *World Bank* Web site at <http://www.worldbank.org/> (search for the title).

Global Development Finance and *GDF Online* (print, CD-ROM, and online subscription).
Global Development Finance. Washington, D.C.: World Bank (ISSN 1020-5454) (print version).
Global Development Finance. Washington, D.C.: World Bank, 2002– (ISBN 0-82135-083-8) (CD-ROM).
GDF Online. World Bank Group, 2000– (online subscription).

Summary: *Global Development Finance (GDF)* provides statistical tables on external debt for 138 countries, organized alphabetically by country. Each country table provides summary statistical data with standard economic indicators and debt indicators, as well as repeated standard statistical tables. Summary tables for regional groups of developing countries and for groups of country by income level are also included. Background on methodology, sources, and definitions are included for the data. The print edition is published in March of every year since 1997. The CD-ROM edition of this resource provides more coverage of data over a period of years and more data, with linking to sources. The online edition provides more data like the CD-ROM, plus the ability for researchers to create their own tables from country and topical tables information.

Detailed Description: *GDF Online* provides access to time series statistical data for the 138 countries that report public and publicly guaranteed debt to the World Bank Debtor Reporting System. Information is organized into country tables and summary tables. An online index can be viewed in a tree view, hierarchical view, or alphabetical view. Summary tables are preformatted with popular information organized under individual countries and for topics for all developing countries. By selecting country tables, researchers can create their own statistical tables by selecting countries, series (which are topics of statistics desired for the country), and years covered. Series topics covered in the database include external debt stocks and flows, major economic aggregates, key debt ratios, average terms of new commitments, currency composition of long-term debt, debt restructuring, and scheduled debt service projections. An online help section is provided.

The CD-ROM title is a database of indicators available from 1970 on for at least 218 statistical indicators, including more information in year coverage and topic coverage than is possible to publish in the annual print title. The country tables link directly to country notes, source notes, and definitions.

PovertyNet Web site, by the World Bank, Washington, D.C. <http://www.worldbank.org/poverty/>

Summary: *PovertyNet*, the World Bank's main Web page on poverty, is its own searchable site, organized by poverty-related topics and containing resources and support for people working to understand and alleviate poverty. Here are links to online articles, various newsletters, and publications, such as a major series of papers entitled the *Poverty Reduction Strategy Papers (PRSP).*

Detailed Description: In addition to the access by many poverty topics, *PovertyNet* includes sections of

information under major categories such as Data; Library; Web Guide; Learning; and World Bank Activities. Also highlighted are sections such as the *PovertyNet Newsletter;* Understanding Poverty; the Literature of Poverty; the World Bank Mission; Features, or highlighted publications on poverty; and What is *PovertyNet,* a section that contains a list of described resources organized by either student/general public or researcher. *PovertyNet Newsletter,* online at no charge in full-text format since 1998, provides a monthly report on poverty news and resources available through *PovertyNet.*

The *Poverty Reduction Strategy Papers (PRSP),* in English, French, Spanish, and Russian, are available from the list of poverty topics on the home page of *PovertyNet.* They are online at no charge in varying formats (PDF and HTML), searchable by country of interest, and describe a country's macroeconomic, structural and social policies and programs to promote growth and reduce poverty, as well as associated external financing needs. *PRSPs* are prepared by governments through a participatory process involving civil society and development partners, including the World Bank and the International Monetary Fund (IMF). These are organized under a *PRSP Documents Library,* which permits researchers to browse by document type and includes other documents in addition to the *PRSPs* and also to browse by country. Also online at the *PRSP* strategies Web site, is the *Poverty Reduction Strategy Sourcebook,* a guide to assist countries in the development and strengthening of poverty reduction strategies, links to other publications, including major reference titles such as the *World Development Report on Poverty,* and the *PRSP Newsletter,* an e-newsletter available at no charge and online since 2000.

World Bank Atlas. Washington, D.C.: International Bank for Reconstruction and Development, 1967– (ISSN 0085-8293) (print annual title and CD-ROM).

Summary: This annual publication is a quick reference title that presents information in graphical form with accompanying statistics. It includes easy-to-read, colorful world maps, tables, charts, and graphs highlighting key social, economic, and environmental data for over 200 countries. The *Atlas* contains summary information relating to the six thematic sections of the larger reference title published by the World Bank, the *World Development Indicators:* World View, People, Environment, Economy, States and Markets, and

Global Links. Although the *Atlas* is not online, it is provided for purchase in a CD set with a related statistical reference title from the World Bank, entitled the *Little Data Book* 2002, which is a pocket-sized ready reference on key development data by country, with 54 indicators for 206 countries and regional and income country groups. Both these titles could be considered quick or "pocket" reference tools, suitable for the readers of the *World Development Indicators,* as well as for instructors, researchers, and students. The *Atlas* is also included in the *World Development Indicators* CD-ROM from the World Bank.

World Bank Group Web site, Washington, D.C.
 <http://www.worldbank.org/>

Summary: In its role as a key player in providing development assistance throughout the world, the *World Bank Group* Web site provides comprehensive documentation of its work and is a major publisher in the field of development. Available in English, Spanish, French, and Russian, the home page of the World Bank is divided into 11 main sections: About Us, Countries and Regions, Data and Statistics, Documents and Reports, Evaluation, Learning, News and Media, Opportunities, Projects and Policies, Publications, Topics in Development, and Resources for.... It also links to e-newsletters, events, and discussions, as well as a Frequently Asked Questions section and site index. A search engine is found on every page that allows for searching the entire site, as well as by publications, documents and reports, and projects.

Established in 1944 at a conference of world leaders in Bretton Woods, New Hampshire, the World Bank became affiliated with the United Nations in 1947 and now has a membership of 184 countries. The World Bank supports national and international efforts to improve statistics, establishing standings, sharing knowledge, and coordinating the collection and dissemination of international statistics in order to understand economic and social development and improve growth and performance. The World Bank Group is made up of five organizations: the International Bank for Reconstruction and Development (IBRD), the International Development Association (IDA), the International Finance Corporation (IFC), the Multilateral Investment Guarantee Agency (MIGA), and the International Centre for Settlement of Investment Disputes (ICSID), of which the IBRD and IDA will be included in this description, whereas IFC, MIGA, and ICSID will be described in the Economics and Business chapter. Links to all of these are available on the World Bank home page.

Detailed Description: About Us, the first main section of the World Bank home page, includes basic facts; links to more information regarding its subsidiary bodies, strategies, policies, projects, products, and services; organizational information; the full text of annual reports (1996–); description of major funding areas; and a link to its comprehensive archive under the Archives and History subsection. This subsection provides a history and chronology of the World Bank's activities. Also of special mention are the catalog, oral history program, and exhibits. The catalog allows for keyword searching and extensive limiting options. The oral history subsection includes the full text, PDF format, of *The World Bank Since Bretton Woods,* authored by Edward S. Mason and Robert E. Asher (1973, Brookings). Exhibits are online and provide texts, photographs, and publications centered around particular themes.

Countries and Regions is the second major section and provides in-depth coverage of the World Bank's activities within individual countries. Access is either by region (Africa—Sub-Saharan, East Asia and the Pacific, Europe and Central Asia, Latin America and the Caribbean, Middle East and North Africa, and South Asia) or by individual country, arranged alphabetically by country name. There is no standardization of what information is provided for each country. Types of information may include data, project descriptions and/or reports, publications, related links, news and events, and quick information about the country.

Data and Statistics, the third main section, is a rich resource of statistical data, which supplements the subscription-based *World Development Indicators (WDI). WDI* will be described separately in this chapter. The most useful collections of information on this page are the subcategories: Country Data, Data by Topic, Online Databases, Country Classification, Quick References Tables, Maps, and Publications. Country Data provides access to several other databases: Data Profile Tables, ICT (Information and Communication Technologies) at a Glance, Country at a Glance, EdStats, GenderStats, HNP (Health, Nutrition, and Population) Stats, African Development Indicators (also described separately), and Other Resources in the form of links. Each database contains relevant social and economic indicators and has an explanation of what is included. Data by Topic is subdivided topically with links to appropriate data and other resources. Online Databases contains subscription information for *World Development Indicators* and *Global Development Finance* as well as no-charge access to *Data Query,* which allows searching on five years of 54 statistical indicators from *WDI.* Country Classification provides an explanation of the terminology. Quick Reference Tables has the latest regional comparison data from the *World Development Indicators* in the areas of people, environment, economy, states and markets, and global links. Country comparisons can also be made within regions. The section Maps has indicators from the current *World Bank Atlas* and is interactive. The indicator subheadings are the same as found in Quick Reference Tables. Data Publications contains another access point for the major databases already mentioned. In addition, an archive of *World Development Indicators, World Bank Atlas,* and *African Development Indicators* (1998–) is also included.

Evaluation is the fourth main home page section and is part of the Operations Evaluation Department of the World Bank. Publication is one of the elements of this section and includes the full text of reports, working papers, and proceedings. A search engine is available that searches, via pull-down menus, for series, subject, region/country, language, and date or searches by keyword. Also contained in the Evaluation section are descriptions and links to tools, approaches, and partnerships, along with related links to bilateral agencies subsection. A search engine is included that searches the entire Evaluation section.

Main section number five is Learning, which links to information from the World Bank Institute on courses and seminars (some available via distance education); publications in the form of citations and annotations as well as ordering information; full text and graphics of the most recent *Development Outreach;* clips from the offerings of *Global Link Television;* and a description and highlights of the 17 themes associated with Learning Programs.

News, main section number six, is chock-full of various full-text media. Included are press releases, feature stories, press preview, loans and credits, speeches, and transcripts. Most date from 1995 forward and can be found by date, region/country, and topic. Also contained here, but without specific dates, are issue briefs, project profiles (searchable by country/region or topic), experts (name, topic, or language), multimedia products that are available, and a speaker's bureau.

The seventh main section from the World Bank home page is Opportunities, the area to search for employment and internship offerings. Projects, Policies and Strategies, the eighth main section, provides de-

scriptions and relevant materials, many in full-text format, of these activities and initiatives.

Publications, the ninth main section, includes citations/annotations of featured, top selling, and recent title publications. Browsing is available by subject, region, country, and e-books and data. Also found here is a listing of electronic newsletters and the opportunity to subscribe at no cost as well as a link to the InfoShop, the online and retail bookstore for development information. Bank documents are also available for download and can be searched/browsed via a search engine. The World Bank also has depository libraries in many countries, and this information is accessible at <http://www.worldbank.org/html/extpb/libraries/libdir.htm>.

Research is the tenth main section and is subdivided into What's New, Key Outputs, Research Program Web Sites, and Topics. The full text of relevant documents and publications are found under each subdivision. Topics also include data sets as well as working papers and abstracts of current studies. Pull-down menus allow for searching by topics, key outputs, and programs. Featured research resources are highlighted.

Topics in Development is the last main section of the World Bank's home page. A pull-down menu allows for choosing a particular topic to then access that information. In addition, major topical headings are hot linked to the relevant materials. Materials under each topic, however, are not standardized in format.

Also of special interested is the Hot Topics category, located on the home page, which links to rich content on the following topics: Comprehensive Development Framework, Debt Relief/HIPC, Millennium Development Goals, Reconstructing Afghanistan, Trade, and West Bank & Gaza. Under Comprehensive Development Framework, researchers will find feature articles, speeches, presentations, and reports on the topic of addressing countries' development priorities through an overall conceptual framework, or vision, that provides the direction, consistency, and focus essential to sustain any long-term process. Debt Relief features information regarding Heavily Indebted Poor Countries, including progress of debt relief strategies by country, country cases, and articles in a periodical title, *HIPC Review,* online since 1999. Millennium Development Goals are summarized by topic, such as poverty, education, and child mortality, and by region of the world, providing reference information, partners, achievements, data, and research materials. Reconstructing Afghanistan has an overview, data, publications, news, and links. Trade contains in-depth categories of trade topics, research, features, and data. West Bank and Gaza is comprised of a country overview, projects, reports, publications, links, press releases, and of special note, the Palestinian Development Gateway, a source of information on topics, projects, and links to the gateways of other countries.

The International Bank for Reconstruction and Development (IBRD) and International Development Association (IDA) are two of the organizations comprising the World Bank Group. Both share the same leadership, staff, and location. A country must be a member of IBRD in order to join IDA. The IBRD is responsible for lending as a way of reducing poverty in its middle-income member countries. On its Web site is information about the organization and its policies, articles of agreement, membership, and links to the World Bank annual reports. The IDA lends to poor developing countries. Its Web site features links to project profiles arranged by region and then by individual countries, full text (PDF) of reports, reports and documents pertaining to the IDA13 initiative, and links to miscellaneous other full-text reports.

World Development Indicators (print, CD-ROM, and online subscriptions).
World Development Indicators. Washington, D.C.: World Bank, 1978– (print edition).
World Development Indicators CD-ROM. Washington, D.C.: World Bank, International Economics Dept., Development Data Group, 1990–.
WDI Online. Washington, D.C.: World Bank, International Economics Dept., Development Data Group, 2002– (online subscription).

Summary: This is a major reference title on the global economy that provides accompanying background and analysis of issues concerning economic and social development and statistical tables for individual countries. The print edition has been available in varying forms since 1978. Broader coverage in years is possible in the CD-ROM and online editions. Time series data are available in the *World Development Indicators* CD-ROM and *WDI Online,* which has preformatted tables for ease of use with information back to 1970. The *online* edition provides links, full methodology and source information, and the ability to reformat personalized tables or view the standard tables. The CD-ROM edition can be purchased for single-use or multiple-use purposes.

Detailed Description: The paper edition of *World Development Indicators* reports data on global development, social, poverty, and environmental issues and places these in relation to set, measurable targets for development, such as the Millennium Development Goals. Specific key indicators of development included are gross national product, population growth, mortality, life expectancy and income distribution, economic activity, trade, aid, and finance. Most of the statistics included are produced by national statistical agencies. Issues are discussed in the following sections: World View, People, Environment, Economy, States and Markets, and Global Links, each with its own introduction and divided into subsections by topic. Each subsection defines and describes the data and includes data sources, then provides the statistical tables. Most tables provide data alphabetically by country with two years of statistics, the latest and an earlier benchmark year. Data is shown for 152 economies with populations of more than 1 million, with other selected indicators for small economies (territories that report separate social or economic statistics, not a country with political independence).

The paper edition was issued as a statistical annex in *World Development Report,* 1978–1996; as of 1997, the *World Development Report* included only selected indicators. The earlier versions did not include as much social and environmental indicators. In 2002, information was added on the digital divide and gender issues. The section with selected world development indicators provides statistics for the latest year, sometimes two years, in tables arranged alphabetically by country name. Statistical methodology is described.

The paper edition is also published in pocket-sized ready reference versions, *Little Data Book,* 2000– ; and: *Little Green Data Book,* 2002– (with environmental indicators). The purpose is to provide reliable quantitative evidence for understanding economic and social development, in order to set policies, monitor progress, and evaluate results.

WDI Online, the online edition of this title, contains 575 data series for 225 countries and 18 regions, 1960–. Data includes social, economic, financial, natural resources, and environmental indicators, with all the published information from the print edition, but with the additional ability to manipulate and personalize tables. Data selection screens are formatted for ease of use and allow for selecting of countries, series, and years. The data can then be manipulated via scaling, percentage change, or indexing against a particular year. The results can be viewed or exported in to Excel or ASCII.

The CD-ROM version varies somewhat from the online version. There are four main tabs to choose from: Query, to conduct the search; Results, which provides a spreadsheet for compilation; Map, a map of the world; and Tables. The section Tables features seven theme-based categories containing preselected data on that theme. These themes are: Country-at-a-Glance, key social and economic development indicators; Economic Time series Tables, dating from 1970 and covering 200 economies; Social Indicators Datasheets, covering fertility, mortality, literacy, and gross domestic product for social expenditures for 190 economies; *World Bank Atlas*; *World Development Indicators*, the text and indicators from the print version; Population Projections; and Education Tables, which include 29 indicators for 180 countries. The date coverage in the CD-ROM version is not as current as the online by a few years and provides a few less data series choices.

World Development Report, published for the World Bank by Oxford University Press, 1978– (ISSN: 0163-5085) (print, CD-ROM, and online). <http://econ.worldbank.org/wdr/> (online full text from 2002; for editions 1992–2001, online content varies according to year).

Summary: A major reference title published annually since 1978 by the World Bank, the *World Development Report* provides a comprehensive look at development, with each edition devoted to a particular theme. Coverage of the theme is comprehensive in analytical text with accompanying selected world indicator data tables covering over 140 economies and 14 country groups. Extensive bibliography and technical notes are included. Some print editions can now be accessed via netLibrary, a subscription-based electronic books collection from OCLC.

For earlier information and historical runs of data or time series, users must consult a library with the title or CD-ROM. The CD-ROM, *World Development Report with Selected World Development Indicators, Indexed Omnibus CD-ROM* edition, includes over 550 time series indicators from 1960– with the full text of the paper title and in addition, it includes some quick reference tables with country and per capita information. A preview, a list of countries, and a list of indicators is online under World Bank publications to assist users to determine whether the scope of the CD-ROM title would be most useful to them.

Detailed Description: Most of the text from the publications section is available with sample data and the bibliography, index, errata, acronyms and abbreviations, and terminology. The full text of the publication is only available through ordering the hard copy or the CD-ROM product. Order information is available online at the World Bank publications address. Only the latest year's issue was online. An online users' guide will assist any new user in determining this title's relevance as it gives details about the methodology, collection, and presentation of the data.

NONGOVERNMENTAL SOURCES

Development Gateway Web site, Washington, D.C. <http://www.developmentgateway.org/>

Summary: The *Development Gateway* is an interactive portal Web site on sustainable development and reduction of poverty issues that includes country overviews, data, and statistics in a collaborative effort. It provides information, resources, and tools that allow users and those in the development field to share their own knowledge and experience and to problem solve. The *Gateway* gathers information on ideas; good practices in development; information about development activities; trends, funding, and commercial opportunities on individual developing countries for countries, the official donor community, civil society, the private sector, and others. Topics covered include poverty, gender, environmental issues, food security, law, and much more. Major categories provided on the *Development Gateway* site are its Exchange Ideas & Information, Find Development Projects, Explore Business Opportunities, and Country Gateway. Also available are sections on About Us, My Gateway, Feedback, and Online Bookstore, as well as news and announcements. This searchable site provides an index and FAQs and is available in English, French, and Spanish.

The *Development Gateway* was initially funded by the World Bank in collaboration with members of the public and private sectors and civil society groups and is to be administered by the Development Gateway Foundation, an independent nonprofit organization dedicated to reducing poverty and bridging the digital divide by promoting development-related technology and communication initiatives.

Detailed Description: The first category, Exchange Ideas & Information, contains a drop-down box of links to development topics with online information, highlights, links to new topics pages such as Gender and Development, and Data and Statistics. The topics links are a rich source of information, with articles. The Data and Statistics page offers a selection of online data tables by region and country and a comprehensive list of links to online data in the area of development provided by the World Bank, the United Nations, the International Monetary Fund, other international intergovernmental organizations, regional development agencies, and nongovernmental organizations.

The second category, the Find Development Projects, contains an online directory of records on these projects entitled AIDA, an extensive searchable directory with historical and current information on development activities from participating sites, which includes highlights of projects, reports, and donor information. AIDA ready-made Country or Topic views allow users to search the site to get information on a wide range of sectors, topics, and countries

The third category, Business Information, contains an online marketplace entitled DGMarket, with searchable market opportunities, and also highlights for this area. It is searchable by keyword and country/region and offers many more services.

The Country Gateways category on the home page provides browsable access to country information. The country search brings together information on individual countries under the categories ideas and knowledge, business, development projects, and publications. These Gateways are planned to be based on local content—from governments at all levels, from communities, from civil society, and from businesses—with the objectives to strengthen networks of development communities, to help people interact with each other most effectively, and to build on the efforts of those working in development.

The section About Us provides a history of the *Gateway,* key documents such as its business plan and online fact sheets, and what's new in the *Gateway.* Under the section My Gateway, researchers who sign up for a free log-in will receive an e-newsletter. The online Bookstore is searchable by country, by region, and by topic. This site will also report on the newly formed conference hosted by the Development Gateway Foundation, entitled *ICT Development Forum of the Development Gateway Foundation,* first held in 2003.

European Bank for Reconstruction and Development (EBRD) Web site, London, United Kingdom. <http://www.ebrd.com/>

Summary: This organization provides project financing for banks, industries, and businesses in developing countries and promotes governmental policies that bolster the business environment. Reports on these activities are available through its Web site in English, French, German, and Russian. Featured on the home page are news articles about the work of the EBRD and highlighted press releases and publications. Major categories of information linked from the home page are: About the EBRD, Press Centre & Events, Publishing & Analysis, Countries & Sectors, Projects, Environment & Safety, Apply for Financing, and Opportunities.

The European Bank for Reconstruction and Development was established in 1991 when communism was crumbling in central and Eastern Europe and ex-Soviet countries needed support for economic transition. As the largest single investor in this region, the EBRD builds market economies through financing and assists with additional financing. It only works in countries committed to democratic principles.

Detailed Description: The category About the EBRD provides basic facts and information on the management of the bank, strategies, policies, and applying for financing. The category Press Centre & Events provides press releases, both current and archived; news announcements; the Bank's annual reports online; and a photo library.

Of particular interest to researchers is the category Publishing & Analysis, which contains online documents and reports searchable by topic, by strategies, or in a list of new titles. The Bank published many documents in its series of *Working Papers.* Its biennial periodical, *Environments in Transition: The Environmental Bulletin of the EBRD,* is available in PDF online from 1994 on, both in English and Russian, and provides articles on economic development in the former Soviet Union countries. Some documents are online in HTML or PDF full-text format and are available at no charge. Some titles are available in languages other than English. The Bank also has an online bookstore for ordering publications.

The category Countries & Sectors allows a researcher to search for specific project information, either by country or by sector, and provides information geared toward investors on the EBRD's projects in that area, including a summary showcase of past projects and signed projects. Other project information is available through the category Projects, providing summaries, case studies, documents, and evaluations on projects. The environmental impact assessments of projects are also online under the category Environment & Safety. In addition, this category also provides publications by topics (some only are online), nuclear energy information, and environmental partnerships. One partnership, the Northern Dimension Environmental Partnership, was launched by the EBRD in a joint effort to strengthen and coordinate important environmental projects with an impact on northern Europe and northwest Russia.

RESEARCH STRATEGIES

To begin to understand the concept of development, perhaps the most useful starting resources are the *World Development Reports* and *Human Development Reports.* These reports, being theme based and comprehensive, provide an in-depth look at the various aspects of development. The statistics included are available by individual country and assist users in understanding significant issues.

The Web sites of the *United Nations Development Programme (UNDP)* and the *World Bank Group* are the next places to conduct generalized research, as both of these organizations, agencies of the United Nations with a worldwide focus, are key players in development. Coverage is both comprehensive and extensive. Both contain major publications and reports, many of which are available in full-text format, detailing their efforts in individual countries.

Gateways serve as a way to bring information from a wide variety of locations into one central Web site. *ELDIS,* government sponsored, and the *Development Gateway,* a nongovernmental organization product, both bring together resources that are Internet-available such as databases, library catalogs, research projects, and publications. Both are also excellent places for accessing more generalized information.

Various aspects of development can be researched in other sources included in this chapter. For regional coverage, the governmental agencies **Inter-American Development Bank (IDB),** which works with countries in Latin America and the Caribbean, **OAS's Inter-American Agency for Cooperation and Development,** with an emphasis on the Americas, and **European Bank for Reconstruction and Development (EBRD),** a nongovernmental agency that focuses its activities on central Asia and central Europe, are sources to consult. The **IADB's** work is discussed through its various publications, reports, and searchable databases. **EBRD,** with an emphasis on financial assistance, also features online, full-text publications and project reports. The United States government, through **USAID (United States Agency for International Development)** works with sub-Saharan Africa, Asia and the Near East, Latin America and the Caribbean, and Europe and Eurasia. However, its focus is more specialized as it works with countries in these regions recovering from disaster. Searchable Web sites for each region allow for more specialized research.

The full-text publications available here document its work.

SD Dimensions Web site, published by the Sustainable Development of the Food and Agriculture Organization of the United Nations, provides valuable online information in forums, projects and links, and especially publications on agriculture and development, women and development, and rural populations and development. Its focus makes its relatively few publications a valuable resource to researchers.

The *United Nations Industrial Development Organization (UNIDO)* Web site deals with the industrial and business side of development. It provides information in the form of project reports and a searchable database of publications, some of them available for a fee.

The *International Monetary Fund (IMF)* Web site provides more specialized information regarding the financial aspects of development, especially poverty and debt relief. Country-specific information is available here as well as the full text of publications and reports.

To specifically address the issue of poverty, the World Bank's *PovertyNet,* is an excellent source to consult. Of special note on this Web site are the *Poverty Reduction Strategy Papers* available in full-text format and prepared by various governments.

Statistics are especially valuable in understanding the various aspects of development. The World Bank's *World Development Indicators* (print, CD-ROM, and online subscription), as well as its more specialized *African Development Indicators* (print and CD-ROM) and *Global Development Finance* (print, CD-ROM, and online subscription), contain extensive and comprehensive coverage of development activities in the world. Summary data can be found in the *World Bank Atlas.*

FOR FURTHER READING: COMPREHENSIVE WEB SITES AND OTHER REFERENCE SOURCES

Canadian International Development Agency (CIDA) Web site, Quebec, Canada. <http://w3. acdi-cida.gc.ca/home>

The mission of this Canadian development agency is to develop sustainable development and poverty reduction in countries of the world in order to contribute to a more secure, equitable, and prosperous world. On its home page, under the category Resources, are global Web links and publications. Under the category Regions and Countries, CIDA reports on its activities within regions of the world, providing an overview of activities, project reports online, stories, and photographs. Under CIDA's Development Information Program from its home page are learning resources for journalists, students, and mass media. Also a Youth Zone link from the home page helps youth explore international development issues and provides information geared to students.

One of its notable Web resources is a subject guide to international development available in English and French: *Canada's Virtual Thematic Library for International Development* Web site at <http://w3.acdi-cida.gc.ca/virtual.nsf>, which is produced by the International Development Information Centre (IDIC) of the Canadian International Development Agency (CIDA). This site provides a collection of hot links to international development resources on the Internet. Access is organized under topics, countries, regions, organizations, and development reference desk.

Department for International Development (DFID) Web site, London, United Kingdom. <http://www.dfid.gov.uk/>

This government department works to promote sustainable development to alleviate poverty globally. All publications are free of charge and can be searched in an online catalog by country, subject, or document type. DFID publishes a periodical entitled *Developments: The International Development Magazine,* archived online since 2001, and other reports online, such as *Statistics on International Development 1997/ 1998–2001/2002* <http://www.dfid.gov.uk/sid2002/>, a report published regularly on the British financial aid throughout the world continuously for 37 editions.

Directory of Development Organizations, by Burt Wesselink. <http://www.devdir.org/>

This online directory is a comprehensive list of organizations and government agencies involved in private-sector development, poverty alleviation, microfinance, and small enterprise development in low-income countries. Useful for researchers, policy makers, and students, it is arranged geographically by world regions and is available in English, French, and Spanish, with information in HTML or PDF format. Users may download, copy, and reprint information from the site for noncommercial purposes as long as the source is cited. The Directory lists 29,500 contacts of organizations that offer (non-) financial support, market access, information, and advice to the enterprise and poverty-reducing sectors in low-income countries. The information was collected mainly through the Internet. Each entry contains the organization's mail and street address, telephone and fax numbers, e-mail address, and Web page details, if available.

Group of 77 at the United Nations Web site, New York. <http://www.g77.org/>

Established in 1984 by 77 developing countries, this organization now represents 133 developing countries, in a third-world coalition of the United Nations (UN). It aims to promote the collective economic interests of its members, advocate within the UN, and assist all developing countries with economic and technical growth. The Ministerial Meeting is convened annually and is the major decision-making body of the Group of 77. On its Web site are a few publications including news, statements and speeches, and reports on conferences, meetings, and programs of interest to the Group of 77.

Institute for Development Studies, University of Sussex Web site, Brighton, United Kingdom. <http://www.ids.ac.uk/ids/>

The Institute for Development Studies is the United Kingdom's leading center for research and teaching in the field of international development studies and organizes access to research topics by theme and by resource. Under the category Information Services on the home page, researchers will find links to significant development resources, including:

- BLDS, an online catalog of Europe's largest library on international development
- *ELDIS*, an Internet development portal site, also described in this chapter
- BRIDGE an information and analysis service on development and gender
- ID21, a forum for communicating United Kingdom research on development <http://www.id21.org/>
- *Livelihoods Connects*, an online resource for sharing information on promoting sustainable livelihoods to break the cycle of poverty <http://www.livelihoods.org/>

International Conference on Financing for Development Web site, by the United Nations Department of Economic and Social Affairs, New York. <http://www.un.org/esa/ffd/>

The International Conference on Financing for Development, held in Monterey, Mexico, in 2002, was the first United Nations–sponsored conference on this theme. Attended by many heads of government and organizations (over 800 participants) involved with development, it provides summaries of development finance topics and other conference documents online at no charge, including a conference report in PDF and WORD formats. The Web site is available in English, French, Spanish, and Russian and follows up on postconference work.

Sustainable Development Strategies: A Resource Book, compiled by Barry Dalal-Clayton and Stephen Bass. Paris: OECD, Earthscan, and UNDP, 2002 (ISBN 1-85383-946-9).

This resource book with accompanying CD provides guidance on developing, implementing, and assessing national sustainable development strategies (NSDs) based on an analysis of past and current practice, in both developed and developing countries. It sets out principles in separate stand-alone chapters and also provides background and introductory material for the concepts in the book. Topics covered are sustainable development and the need for strategic responses, current practice in sustainable development, key steps, analysis, decision making, communications, financing, and monitoring and evaluation systems. Selected case studies and examples of individual countries are included, as well as many resources in the area of sustainable development. Figures, statistical data, and bibliographical references accompany the text.

The CD includes the full text of the report and extensive related documents. This resource book builds on and complements a project report from the OECD Committee on Development Assistance's Working Party on Development Cooperation and Environment entitled *DAC Guidelines on Strategies for Sustainable Development,* OECD, 2001.

Water for People, Water for Life: A Joint Report by the Twenty-Three UN Agencies Concerned With Freshwater, by the United Nations World Water Assessment Programme. New York: UNESCO Publications and Berghahn Books, 2003 (ISBN 9-23103-881-8).

This first edition of the United Nations *World Water Development Report* series analyzes and reports on global water problems, especially in relation to sustainable development, and provides recommendations. It was generated from the World Water Assessment Programme, a long-term project started in response to decisions of the United Nations General Assembly and the Commission on Sustainable Development. The report emphasizes how human development is stifled without adequate supply of suitable quality water. The report will be issued periodically, giving a global picture of the state of the world's freshwater resources and global stewardship of them. It is a richly illustrated reference resource with accompanying statistical tables, charts, graphs, and bibliographic references.

NOTES

1. R. J. Barry Jones, *Routledge Encyclopedia of International Political Economy,* Volume 1 (New York: Routledge, 2001), 337.

2. Ibid., Volume 3: 1529.

3. USAID, *Development Experience Clearinghouse (DEC)* <http://www.dec.org>.

CHAPTER 6
Economics and Business

CHAPTER OVERVIEW

International intergovernmental organizations and national level governments are heavy producers of business and economics information. The focus of this chapter is on the following business and economics topics: balance of payments, banking, business, commerce, national economic policy, economic statistics, finance, government finance, industrial classification, industrial production, industrial statistics and development, money and investments, national accounts, and tourism. Because of the wide variety of resources available on these topics, this chapter includes sources that are excellent for both beginning and more advanced research needs. Types of resources include Web sites, periodicals, a variety of references sources, and statistical yearbooks. They will provide basic information and data and also guide users to many more sources of information.

Researchers should note that business and economics information is also discussed in many of the other related chapters, such as Communication, Development, General, Law and Treaties, Social/Cultural Issues, Statistics, Trade, and Transportation. Even some of these same resources (i.e., Web sites) are discussed in other chapters, but always with the focus on the subject of the chapter. Therefore, researchers may want to consult several chapters at the same time. Researchers should also note that these resources often do include general demographics, population, social, and trade information and statistics, among other topics covered, but they were selected for this chapter because of a primary focus on business and economics. Regional information is included in the section later in the chapter entitled For Further Reading: Comprehensive Web sites and Other Reference Sources, which contains significant titles especially on economic conditions for regions of the world, such as Europe, Latin America, Africa, Asia, and North America.

Governmental Sources Discussed

Asia-Pacific Economic Cooperation (APEC) Web site, Singapore. <http://www.apecsec.org.sg/>

Asian Productivity Organization (APO) Web site, Tokyo, Japan. <http://www.apo-tokyo.org/>

Association of Southeast Asian Nations (ASEAN) Web site, Jakarta, Indonesia. <http://www.aseansec.org/>

Bank for International Settlements (BIS) Web site, Basel, Switzerland. <http://www.bis.org/>

BISNIS Web site, by the United States Department of Commerce, International Trade Administration, Washington, D.C. <http://www.bisnis.doc.gov>

Country Commercial Guides, by the U.S. Embassy Staff and the U.S. Trade Administration published by STAT-USA and U.S. Trade Administration, Washington, D.C. <http://www.export.gov> (select Market Research: Country & Industry Market Reports) and <http://www.stat-usa.gov/tradtest.nsf> (online database) (both subscription sites conditionally available at no charge).

European Union Resources

Europa: Activities of the European Union: Economics and Monetary Affairs Web site, Brussels, Belgium. <http://www.europa.eu.int/pol/emu/index_en.htm>

European Central Bank Web site, Frankfurt am Main, Germany. <http://www.ecb.int/>

European Court of Auditors Web site, Brussels, Belgium. <http://www.eca.eu.int/>

European Investment Bank Web site, Luxembourg. <http://www.eib.org/>

G8 Information Centre Web site, by the University of Toronto Library and the G8 Research Group at the University of Toronto. <http://www.g8.utoronto.ca/>

International Monetary Fund Resources

International Monetary Fund Web site, Washington, D.C. <http://www.imf.org>

Balance of Payments Statistics and *Balance of Payments Statistics Yearbook* (print annual title,

1946/1974–) (ISSN 0250-7374) (monthly print title, 1981–).

Direction of Trade Statistics and *Direction of Trade Statistics Yearbook.* Washington, D.C.: International Monetary Fund, 1994– (ISSN 0252-306X).

Government Finance Statistics and *Government Finance Statistics Yearbook* (1977–) (ISSN 0250-7374).

International Financial Statistics, International Monetary Fund, Washington, D.C. (monthly print subscription periodical, 1948–) (ISSN 0250-7463) (CD-ROM, 1991–).

International Financial Statistics Yearbook (annual print subscription cumulative title) (1961–) (ISSN 0250-7463).

International Financial Statistics Online (IFS Online) (subscription online database through IMF Online services) (2000–). <http://www.imf.org> (select Publications: IFS Online services).

World Economic Outlook (Occasional Paper Series) (ISSN 0256-6877) (paper semiannual title).

World Economic Outlook Databases (online subscription resources). <http://www.imf.org/external/pubs/res/index.htm>

Organisation for Economic Co-operation and Development (OECD) Resources

Organisation for Economic Co-operation and Development (OECD) Web site, Paris. <http://www.oecd.org>

International Direct Investment Statistics Yearbook (1993–) (print and online subscription title and database).

Main Economic Indicators (1962–) (ISSN 0474-5523) (monthly print and subscription online title).

National Accounts Statistics (1955–) (ISSN 0256-758X) (print, online, and CD-ROM subscription title).

OECD Economic Outlook (1967–) (ISSN 0474-5574) (print and online subscription title).

OECD Economic Studies (ISSN 0255-0822) (semiannual print and subscription online title).

OECD Economic Surveys (1968–) (print and online subscription title by individual country). <http://ww.oecd.org> (search the home page or select Publications: Country Surveys).

OECD Observer (1962–) (ISSN 0029-7054) (bi-monthly print and subscription online title).

OECD Papers (2000–) (ISSN 1609-1914) (print and subscription online title).

OECD Small and Medium Enterprise Outlook (2000–) (biennial print and online subscription title).

Pacific Islands Forum Secretariat Web site, Suva, Fiji. <http://www.forumsec.org.fj/>

United Nations Regional Economic Commissions Resources

United Nations Economic Commission for Africa (UNECA) Web site, Addis Ababa, Ethiopia. <http://www.uneca.org/>

United Nations Economic and Social Commission for Asia and the Pacific (UNESCAP) Web site, Bangkok, Thailand. <http://www.unescap.org/>

United Nations Economic Commission for Europe (UNECE) Web site, Geneva, Switzerland. <http://www.unece.org>

United Nations Economic Commission for Latin America and the Caribbean (UNECLAC) (English) Web site, Santiago, Chile. <http://www.eclac.cl/> (select English language).

United Nations Economic Commission for Western Asia (UNESCWA) Web site, Beirut, Lebanon. <http://www.escwa.org.lb/>

United Nations Resources

Industrial Commodity Statistics Dataset (online and CD sales product).

Industrial Commodity Statistics Yearbook, by the United Nations Statistics Division Energy and Industry Statistics Section, New York, 1976– (ISSN 0257-7208).

National Accounts Database (online subscription).

National Accounts Statistics: Main Aggregates and Detailed Tables, by the United Nations Statistics Division National Accounts Section, New York, 1957– . <http://unstats.un.org/unsd/nationalaccount/default.htm>

United Nations Economic and Social Council (ESOSOC) Web site, New York. <http://www.un.org/esa/coordination/esosoc/>

World Commodity Survey, by the United Nations Conference on Trade and Development (UNCTAD), New York, 1999/2000– (print annual title).

World Economic and Social Survey, by the United Nations Department of Economic and Social Affairs, New York, 1994– (print annual title). <http://www.un.org/esa/analysis/wess/> (selected sections online, including Chapter 1, "The State of the World Economy").

World Investment Report, by the United Nations Conference on Trade and Development (UNCTAD), New York (United Nations document no: UNCTAD/WIR/YEAR) (1991–) (print annual title and online, 2001–). <http://www.unctad.org/wir>

United Nations Industrial Development Organisation (UNIDO) Web site, Vienna, Austria. <http://www.unido.org/>

World Bank Resources

Countries & Regions Web site, by the World Bank, Washington, D.C. <http://www.worldbank.org/> (select Countries & Regions).
World Bank Web site, Washington, D.C. <http://www.worldbank.org/>

World Tourism Organization Resources

World Tourism Organization (WTO) Web site, Madrid, Spain. <http://www.world-tourism.org/>

Compendium of Tourism Statistics, 1986– (print subscription title).
WTO Statistics—Basic Set, 2003 (CD-ROM sales) (ISBN 9-28440-609-9).
Yearbook of Tourism Statistics, Madrid (ISSN 1011-8977) (print and annual subscription title) (1986–).

Nongovernmental Sources Discussed

EIU.com Web site, by the Economist Intelligence Unit, New York. <http://www.eiu.com>
World Economic Forum Web site, Geneva, Switzerland. <http://www.weforum.org/>

GOVERNMENTAL SOURCES

Asia-Pacific Economic Cooperation (APEC) Web site, Singapore. <http://www.apecsec.org.sg/>
Summary: APEC is a major international forum for facilitating economic growth, cooperation, trade, and investment in the Asia-Pacific region. Information is organized on the *APEC* Web site into the following categories: About APEC, Member Economies, APEC activities, Business and Investment, Community Interest, Publications and Library, Databases and E-IAPs, and News and Events. The latest news concerning the organization is highlighted from the home page. It also provides searching, a glossary, links, a site map, and restricted members' information. Twenty-two economic jurisdictions have membership in APEC, and

these include: Australia, Brunei Darussalam, Canada, Chile, People's Republic of China, Hong Kong, China, Indonesia, Japan, Korea, Malaysia, Mexico, New Zealand, Papua New Guinea, Peru, Philippines, Russia, Singapore, Chinese Taipei, Thailand, United States, and Viet Nam.
Detailed Description: Under the home page section Publications and Library, researchers may link directly to free downloads (organized by year of publication), search lists of publications and new publications, order publications for sale, or consult a Meeting Documents Centre with downloadable documents of meetings in WORD format. *Key APEC Documents* is an annual reference collection of policy, meetings, and initiative documents of APEC. The annual statistical reference titles *APEC Outcomes and Outlooks* and *APEC Economic Outlook* are available free online.

Asian Productivity Organization (APO) Web site, Tokyo, Japan. <http://www.apo-tokyo.org/>
Summary: The APO focuses in the areas of industry, service, and agriculture and provides Web site information through basic research studies, surveys, symposia, study meetings, seminars, technical expert services, study missions, publications, and audiovisual training materials. This searchable site is published in English and Japanese. Sections include: About APO; Secretary-Genera's Statements (current and archived); National Productivity Organizations (NPOs); Upcoming Projects; Participants' Corner; Publications, E-books, and Videos; Productivity Resources; and Contact Us. Other highlights include the full-text newsletter *APO News,* Special Events (which includes links to current conferences and workshops), and Special Features.

Established by convention in 1961, the Asian Productivity Organization (APO) is an intergovernmental regional organization with a mission to increase productivity in the countries of Asia and the Pacific region through mutual cooperation. The APO serves as regional advisor, think tank, and clearing house for productivity information to member countries, assisting them through human resource development, technical expert assistance and dissemination of knowledge on productivity. APO membership is open to all Asian and Pacific governments that are members of the United Nations' Economic and Social Commission for Asia and the Pacific (ESCAP); however, governments outside Asia and the Pacific may become Associate Members. APO member countries are

Bangladesh, Republic of China, Fiji, Hong Kong, India, Indonesia, Islamic Republic of Iran, Japan, Republic of Korea, Lao People's Democratic Republic, Malaysia, Mongolia, Nepal, Pakistan, the Philippines, Singapore, Sri Lanka, Thailand and the Socialist Republic of Vietnam.

Detailed Description: The Publications section leads to sales publications, except for e-books, which lists free online titles (in PDF format). APO is a modest publisher and publishes all titles in English. In addition to the sales publications are reports and other online documents and titles. For every APO project, each participant is required to present a country paper that reports on the current situation or practice in the country on the subject under study. The Productivity Resources section from the home page includes Articles and Commentaries (online); Project Reports (online); and Productivity Links.

Association of Southeast Asian Nations (ASEAN)
Web site, Jakarta, Indonesia.
<http://www.aseansec.org/>

Summary: On its searchable Web site, the Association of Southeast Asian Nations (ASEAN) provides information under the categories ASEAN Summits, ASEAN Projects, ASEAN Statistics, Publications, and Speeches and Papers. It is a rich source of statistics, news, and publications for this region of the world. The home page highlights current trends, issues, and news. Established in 1967, ASEAN is focused on improving collective political and economic cooperation and foreign relations in the Asian region, with cooperative peace and shared stability its fundamental goals. Joining the five original Member Countries of Indonesia, Malaysia, Philippines, Singapore, and Thailand are Brunei Darussalam (1984), Vietnam (1995), Laos and Myanmar (1997), and Cambodia (1999).

Detailed Description: Under the home page heading of Publications are ASEAN annual reports, archived online in full text since 1980, and a series of individual titles are available under Public Information Series, a subheading of Publications. *Business ASEAN: A Quarterly Newsletter of the ASEAN Secretariat* is also available online since its beginning in May 2000.

ASEAN has several specialized bodies and arrangements promoting intergovernmental cooperation in various fields: ASEAN University Network, ASEAN-EC Management Centre, ASEAN Centre for Energy, ASEAN Agricultural Development Planning Centre, ASEAN Earthquake Information Centre, ASEAN

Poultry Research and Training Centre, ASEAN Regional Centre for Biodiversity Conservation, ASEAN Rural Youth Development Centre, ASEAN Specialized Meteorological Center, ASEAN Tourism Information Centre, and ASEAN Timber Technology Centre. These may be consulted for publications, documents, and other online information in their field.

Bank for International Settlements (BIS) Web site,
Basel, Switzerland. <http://www.bis.org/>

Summary: The Bank for International Settlements (BIS) is an international organization established in 1931 that fosters cooperation toward monetary and financial stability among central banks and other agencies and serves as a bank for central banks. BIS also works on issues of monetary policy, the structure and functioning of financial systems, and the developments of international financial market and provides research and analysis for these issues. The Bank organizes information concerning monetary and financial cooperation among central banks on its searchable Web site in the categories: About BIS, Press and Speeches, Links to Central Banks, Banking Services, Forum for Central Banks, Basel Committee, Financial Stability Institute, and Publications and Statistics. Also featured here are What's New, Key Topics, and advanced search capabilities. The focus of this discussion will be the publications and statistics made available to researchers from the organization.

To fulfill its mission, the Bank acts as a forum to promote discussion, a center for monetary and economic research, and an agent or trustee in international financial operations. Much of this activity is coordinated through the Bank's Monetary and Economic Department. In addition, the Bank's Secretariat Services assists the various committees and working groups of central bank officials that meet on a regular basis to work on policy issues. Regular meetings for central bank governors and senior central bank officials take place on the occasion of the meetings of the BIS Board, where they work on the monitoring of foreign exchange market activities (Committee of Experts on Gold and Foreign Exchange), the surveillance and analysis of financial market developments (Committee on the Global Financial System), and the oversight of payment and settlement systems (Committee on Payment and Settlement systems).

Detailed Description: The home page category Publications and Statistics provides researchers with access to Regular Publications, BIS Papers, Committee

Publications, Working Papers, International Financial Statistics, and Other Publications. Researchers should note that for many titles online data is published over a number of years, providing longer time series and allowing users to manipulate the figures. The subsection Regular Publications provides access to the full text (HTML format) of BIS annual reports in English, French, German, Italian, and Spanish back to 1997. No-charge access to the full text of the *Quarterly Review: International Banking and Financial Market Developments* (1996–) is also under the regular publications link. Available in English, French, German, and Italian, it covers international banking and financial market developments and has special issue articles on banking all over the world. The statistical annex is a separate feature of each issue. Also available from the *Quarterly Review* page are full-text Central Bank articles and speeches back to 1996. Another regular full-text (PDF) publication is *BIS Consolidated International Financial Statistics* (1996–) on consolidated statistics on the maturity, sectoral, and national distribution of international bank lending. This report includes supplementary information about countries' external indebtedness, comprehensive explanatory notes for the statistics, and separate statistical tables. One other regular database is its *Joint BIS-IMF-OECD-World Bank Statistics on External Debt,* with online information from 1996, which provides the current international data, mainly from creditor sources, on the external debt of developing and transition countries and territories. It is available in PDF, EXCEL, and some data in HTML format, with a background summary and metadata describing each of the 14 data series presented. The print title related to this database is the joint *BIS–OECD Statistics on External Debt.*

Researchers may subscribe to a free BIS e-mail alert to be notified when relevant new information is published on the *BIS* Web site.

Also from the category Publications and Statistics, under the BIS Papers section, researchers may access online at no charge, the full text of the BIS working papers and the earlier series of conference and policy papers. All titles in these series are unique and cover banking issues, monetary policy, and financial statistics. The link to Committee Publications under the category Publications and Statistics contains selected online committee publications for three committees, whereas the section Working Papers contains the papers online back to about 1996 and lists the earlier ones, which are only available in hard copy. Working

Papers are on very specific, very detailed monetary and financial research. The section entitled International Financial Statistics links to statistical press releases, international banking statistics (an online database from the statistical annex of the *BIS Quarterly Review*), consolidated banking statistics, securities statistics, derivatives statistics, and methodology. Statistics are downloaded in zip, CSV, and PDF formats. BIS publishes methodology for its statistics. Other Publications link to general information titles such as on methodology and to titles from its working with the G-10 on financial issues.

Linked from the home page, the page for the Financial Stability Institute (FSI) was created in 1999 to assist supervisors around the world in improving and strengthening their financial systems. Its activities include offering workshops, seminars, and information training to supervisors. Publications made available on this Web site include its Occasional Papers (2000–), its Award Papers, and a searchable database entitled *Training Supervisors Information Directory.* Also worthy of note is the information from the home page on the Basel Committee Banking Supervision. Its series of publications are published online since no. 1, 1982. The Basel Committee was established by the Central Bank Governors of the Group of Ten countries at the end of 1974, meets regularly, and has about 30 technical working groups and task forces that also meet regularly on topics concerning banking supervisory standards and guidelines and best practices. They report and recommend practices to nations based on their findings.

BISNIS Web site by the United States Department of Commerce, International Trade Administration, Washington, D.C. <http://www.bisnis.doc.gov>

Summary: This Web site is a gateway to information about doing business with the former Soviet Union countries, particularly for international trade and current market assessments. The purpose of the U.S. Department of Commerce, International Trade Administration in providing the *BISNIS* Web site is to support U.S. businesses and trade with research information and counseling for doing business in this area of the world. The online resource contains detailed country reports, news stories, industry reports, trade leads, an events calendar, information on export financing, and more available on this Web site. Under the category Country Reports, information is provided about Russia and the countries called the Newly Independent States, including Armenia, Azerbaijan, Belarus, Georgia, Kazakhstan, Kyrgyz Republic, Tajikistan and Turkmenistan, Moldova, Ukraine, and Uzbekistan.

Detailed Description: From the *BISNIS* home page, Country reports link to a variety of business and commercial information on specific countries, particularly a commercial overview of the country that provides economic, business, trade, and environmental information relating to international business and also business funding and leads. Each country report also includes information in a section called Market Updates, which are published several times a year and contains a report on specific economic and commercial market highlights within the country. Other sections include industry reports, general reports, region specific reports, events, and links to directory information. Interested researchers may subscribe to market updates by e-mail.

Another category from the home page are the Industry reports, which are organized by industry name, such as automotive, chemicals, computers, consumer goods, natural resources, and telecommunications. The monthly periodical the *BISNIS Bulletin* addresses the interests of U.S. companies operating in the Newly Independent States by providing current reports on market developments, business practices, the regulatory environment, financing, U.S. government programs, upcoming trade events and conferences, and other business resources. It is available at no charge, and issues are archived on the site back to 1997.

Country Commercial Guides, by the U.S. Embassy Staff and the U.S. Trade Administration. Washington, D.C.: STAT-USA and U.S. Trade Administration. <http://www.export.gov> (select Market Research: Country and Industry Market Reports) and <http://www.stat-usa.gov/tradtest.nsf> (online database) (both subscription sites conditionally available at no charge).

Summary: This regularly updated U.S. government guide to the commercial environment of countries provides access to current and retrospective country reports containing economic, political, and market analysis. It provides an excellent quick resource to updated economic conditions in countries of the world. Each country report in this series includes an executive summary and chapters that provide a comprehensive look at the country's commercial environment. Because the reports are clearly organized, it is easy for users to go right to the section they are interested in from the table of contents, particularly the economic, commercial, or trade statistics or political analysis.

These annual reports provide users with the information they need to understand a country's commercial environment. This includes analysis of the market trends and strategies that would affect businesses engaged in trade and other political, economic, and legal conditions and factors affecting business and trade in a specific country. Each report contains the same chapters as well as appendices including marketing, trade regulations, investment climate, and business travel.

The U.S. Trade Administration provides this service to assist U.S. businesses with overseas trade and also to assist students and researchers. To access *Country Commercial Guides* free on the *Export.gov* Web site, businesses, students, and researchers must register online. *STAT-USA/Internet* is a subscription service that is also provided free of charge to U.S. depository libraries. The location and other directory information for federal depository libraries is online at <http://www.gpoaccess.gov/libraries.html>.

Detailed Description: *Country Commercial Guides* provides an alphabetical listing by country of business and economics reference information. In addition to countries, information is provided for the Bahamas, EBRD (European Bank for Reconstruction and Development), European Union, West Bank, and Gaza. Each country report in this series includes an executive summary and chapters that present a comprehensive look at the country's commercial environment. Because the reports are clearly organized, it is easy for users to go right to the section they are interested in, particularly the economic, commercial, or political analysis. Each chapter includes analysis and statistics in a dense form, but not too difficult to read and understand. Each report includes chapters on economic trends and outlook, political environment, marketing U.S. products and services, leading U.S. imports and exports, trade regulations, investment climate, financing, business travel, statistics, contacts (directory information), and even trade events and schedule.

The executive summary contains an easier to understand summary and explanation of the country's commercial environment and current markets and issues, political, trade, or business. For more specific information, researchers may jump from the Table of Contents to the chapters, which offer detailed information and analysis of the topic with text and statistics.

Frequently updated, current global business, economic, and trade online databases in addition to the *Country Commercial Guides* are available through this service. *STAT-USA/Internet* provides commercial databases in its Market and Country Research section and Global Business Leads section, *Globus & NTDB.* This description will focus on the business and economic aspects of the resources. More information is also available in the Trade chapter. It provides the *Market Research Reports,* a significant resource for online economic trends for specific markets in individual countries. Also available are the *International Market Insight (IMI) Reports* (Archive), which is alphabetical by country and reports on the economic conditions of trade for a certain commodity in that country, and the *Industry Sector Analyses (ISA) Reports* (Archive), which provide market analysis of an industry in a country, such as the environmental industry in Dubai, and are available by country and by date. *Industry Sector Analyses* (ISAs) are in-depth profiles of a selected industry subsector. They include an analysis of the market opportunities, end users, competitors, market access, distribution channels, market barriers, and financing options and economic trends. All of these databases were available and issued as a CD-ROM entitled *National Trade Data Bank,* 1990–2001.

European Union Resources

Europa: Activities of the European Union: Economics and Monetary Affairs Web site, Brussels, Belgium. <http://www.europa.eu.int/pol/emu/index_en.htm>

Summary: The *Europa* Web site, of which this is a section, has been described in the General Sources chapter. Only business and economics information is described in this section. This is an aggregator Web site for the European Union on this topic. The full text of relevant news headlines and brief notes is located here as well as the subheadings of Latest Developments and A Comprehensive Guide to European Union Law. Latest Developments is subdivided into Key Sites and Documentation. Key Sites links to the relevant pages of the Commission on Economic and Financial Affairs, European Parliament, Council of the European Union, and European Central Bank. Documentation links to relevant press releases, sections of the *Bulletin of the European Union* and *General Report on the Activities of the European Union* as well as publications and statistics. A Comprehensive Guide to European Union Law is subdivided into Summaries and Legal Texts. The Summaries section includes relevant sections of the online publication *Panorama* and information related to the European Monetary Union. Legal

Texts has selected instruments of the Treaty Establishing the European Community, legislation in force, and links to the Web sites of other EU legislative bodies. As the law affects business, economics, and trade so much, researchers may want to consult the Laws and Treaties chapter for more information.

European Central Bank Web site, Frankfurt am Main, Germany. <http://www.ecb.int/>

Summary: Because of its central role within the financial system of Europe's central banks and Europe's monetary policy as an institution of the European Union, the European Central Bank is a provider of publications and statistics on monetary policy and financial statistics. It also covers the European Monetary Institute, TARGET (the European Union wide system for monetary payments with the euro). Its searchable Web site is organized into featured information and categories on the sidebar, which cover About the ECB, Press Release, Key Speeches, Calendars and Events, Publications, Statistics, EURO Banknotes and Coins, MFIs and Eligible Assets, TARGET, Job Opportunities, Contact Us, Links to EU Central Banks, EMI Publications, and Copyright and Disclaimer.

Featured information includes the categories: the EURO (links to the official EURO Web site available in the European member countries' languages at <http://www.euro.ecb.int/>); Figures at a Glance; and What's New from the European Central Bank—in Periodical Publications, Statistical Press Releases, Public Consultations, Legal Documents, Research Conferences and Seminars and Call for Papers, and ECB Working Paper Series; TARGET; Other Publications of Interest; and Other Items. This discussion will focus on the publications and statistics of the European Central Bank. Most of the documents and publications are available in the languages of the national central banks: English, Danish, Dutch, Finnish, French, German, Greek, Italian, Portuguese, Spanish, and Swedish.

The European System of Central Banks (ESCB) is composed of the European Central Bank (ECB) and the national central banks (NCBs) of all 15 EU member states. The "Eurosystem" is the term used to refer to the central banks and the national central banks of the member states that have adopted the euro. The Governing Council and the Executive Board and the European Central Bank are the central decision-making bodies of the Eurosystem. The national central banks of the member states that do not participate in the euro area, however, are members of the ESCB with the right to participate concerning national monetary policies, but not in the decision making and activities concerning the single monetary policy for the euro area. The primary objective of the Eurosystem is first to maintain price stability, then to support the general economic policies in the Community and to act in accordance with the principles of an open market economy.

The ESCB advises the European Community and national authorities on matters that fall within its field of competence, particularly where Community or national legislation is concerned. Finally, the European Central Bank, assisted by the NCBs, collect the necessary statistical information, either from the competent national authorities or directly from economic agents.

Detailed Description: The home page category Figures at a Glance provides the lending rates of the Bank, the publication of the irrevocable euro conversion rates fixed by regulation between the euro, and the currencies of the Member States adopting the euro monetary unit on 31 December 1998 and the current euro foreign exchange reference rates. About the ECB, another category on the home page, provides online access to background legal documents and regulations and organizational and mission documents.

From the Publications home page category researchers can access the subcategories Periodical Publications, Working Paper Series, Occasional Paper Series, Legal Documents, Documents for Public Consultation, Other Publications organized by year from 1999, and finally, Documents of the EMI (European Monetary Institute). Listed under the section Periodical Publications are the titles the *Monthly Bulletin;* the European Central Bank's *Annual Report,* and its *Convergence Report.* The *Monthly Bulletin* is available in PDF format back to January 1999 and includes articles and statistics on money and financial policies, the economic developments in the euro areas, the euro, financial statistics, exchange rates, financial markets, as well as a list of documents published by the ECB. The *Annual Reports* are available online in PDF back to 1999, and the *Convergence Report* is required by treaty every several years to report on the progress made by member states to fulfill their obligations regarding the achievement of monetary and economic union. It covers the key aspects of economic convergence, status of national legislation, related legal information, and a summary of progress made by individual nations. To this date,

only the 2000 and 2002 reports are available online in full-text format.

The Working Paper Series of titles disseminates the results of research conducted within the ECB on those concerns relevant to the issues of the Eurosystem. Each number in the series is a unique title, and from 1999 on these are mostly available in full text (PDF) online at no charge. Individual titles within the Series are listed chronologically by year, by number. The Occasional Paper series presents policy-relevant topics to a wide audience, including other policy makers, academics, the media, and the general public. The ECB Occasional Papers series make public material used by the ECB and the Eurosystem, and they contain work carried out by ECB. Unlike the Working Papers, the Occasional Papers are not intended to present original contributions to economic theory, and therefore, include old and new economic theories and empirical methodologies used by authors to present their results or to support their conclusions. Also, all the more than 200 titles in this series are available online in PDF format at no charge from number 1, 1999, forward. All documents in both series are also available as hard copies, free of charge, from the European Central Bank.

Also under the category Publications, Legal Documents includes online documents for this information: Statute of the ESCB and the ECB, Statutes/Laws of the National Central Banks, Legal Instruments of the ECB (guidelines, decisions, and regulations), and Other Relevant Legal Instruments of the EU (European Union) Council. These titles are also available free of charge in print from the European Central Bank on request. Documents for Public Consultation is a subcategory under Publications where the European Central Bank posts topics on which they request interested parties to comment. They may relate to the Bank's work in a policy area, in financial development, pertaining to a conference such as on e-payments, and much more. Responses are made public by consent from this Web site. Also under the subcategory Other Publications are titles listed in reverse chronological order by date. Many concern specific aspects of the ECB's work—its monetary policy, the euro, and its TARGET program and are available in PDF format online, with accompanying press releases.

Under the home page category Statistics, the organization provides overview statistics, statistical press releases, Statistics On-Line, Euro Area Statistics, Euro Foreign Exchange Reference Rates, access to historical financial data series, time management, and international reserves. Statistics On-Line gives researchers access to the *ECB Statistical DataBank,* used for searching, displaying, and saving statistical series online using a dedicated Java browser and also for subscribing to data sets and downloading predefined sets of data. Some databases may be downloaded in CSV format. Statistical data sets are free of charge, although users must register.

From the home page, the category Euro Banknotes and Coins links to further information, images, and answers to frequently asked questions about the euro and its chronological development. The category MFI and Eligible Assets provides general information, data sets that can be searched and downloaded, and online publications from the Monetary Financial Institutions, which are central banks, credit institutions, money market funds, and other institutions resident in the European Union (EU) and report monthly or quarterly balance sheet statistics. Another category from the home page TARGET, which stands for Trans-European Automated Real-time Gross settlement Express Transfer system, is an EU-wide system for euro payments. This category links to general information, basic texts, payment statistics, cross-border collateral statistics, and a hotline. Also from the home page, the Links to European National Central Banks links to each specific Web site. Finally, the category EMI (European Monetary Institute) Publications contains general information and basic legal texts concerning the Institute. The European Monetary Institute was set up under the Maastricht Treaty to deal with preparing for Economic and Monetary Union in 1994, primarily to set up the European System of Central Banks and the European Central Bank (ECB). Once the ECB was operational, the Institute was made redundant.

European Court of Auditors Web site, Brussels, Belgium. <http://www.eca.eu.int/>

Summary: The European Court of Auditors is an institution of the European Union (EU) that carries out its auditing work within the EU independently and autonomously and publishes its auditing reports and special subjects report on its Web site. On the English Web site information is available under the following categories: Court of Auditors, Reports & Opinions, Audit Report, Press Room, Calendar, Want to Know More, Recruitment and In-service Training, Tenders, What's New, and Annual Report. Also additional information and service is provided under the links to Important Legal Notice, Contact, Other Sites, Search, and Home. The Web site is published in the 11 European Union languages,

The mission of the European Court of Auditors is to audit independently the collection and spending of European Union funds, to assess the way that the European institutions are functioning, and to analyze financial operations in terms of economy, efficiency, and effectiveness. In fulfilling its two main tasks of auditing the accounts and implementing the budget of the European Union, the court may audit any persons or organization receiving funds from the European Union. It is required by treaty to produce annual reports, special subject reports, and opinions. The Court has 15 members from 15 different member countries, each appointed for six-year terms, and they serve independently from the other European Union institutions to maintain the independence and objectivity of the Court. The Court is mandated to inform the citizens of Europe of its work in reports. Within the institutional framework of the European Union, the European Court of Auditor is one of the five major institutions, among them the European Commission, the European Council, the European Parliament, and the European Court of Justice, which are independent and represent the interests of the Union as whole, its member countries, and its citizens.

Detailed Description: Information about the European Court of Auditors and its relationships as an organization with the European Union is found under the category Court of Auditors on the home page, which contains under the section Presentation two online brochures with background on the Court and its purpose and its functions. The category also contains an organization chart, the treaty mandate and rules of procedure of the organization, its code of administrative conduct, its communication policies and standards, and finally, the external auditor's report.

The major publications of the Court are available online under the category Reports & Opinions from the home page, including a PDF file with a bibliography of the Court's Reports and Opinions from 1997–2002. The page also features publications under the sections Annual Reports, Special Reports, Specific Annual Reports, and Opinions. Annual Reports on the European Union budget are archived by year back to 1996 and link to the online full-text version (HTML) available through the *Official Journal of the European Communities* online. Special reports, specific annual reports, and opinions are both in PDF format full text online back to 1997. These reports are also published in the *Official Journal of the European Communities* in all the Community languages.

In addition to these publications, the category Press Room on the home page contains a photographic library, press releases (1997–), summaries of reports (1997–), and speeches (1999–). The photographs are organized into subjects such as events, officers, the court, and archives. Under the home page category Want to Know More?, the Court provides information on the right of access to documents; services in answering questions; a bibliography of literature on the Court in an alphabetical list; and information on enlargement and the cooperation between the supreme audit institutions of candidate countries for membership in the European Union with the European Court of Auditors. It also links to feedback Internet sites *Dialogue* and *Europa Chats. Dialogue* on Europe contains public comment and debate, and *Europa Chats* is a cyberchat site on the European Union. Finally, from the home page, the section What's New contains news announcements archived back to 2001.

European Investment Bank Web site, Luxembourg.
 <http://www.eib.org>

Summary: The European Investment Bank is the European Union's long-term financing institution, whose task is to contribute toward the integration, balanced development, and economic and social cohesion of the European Union member countries through sound investment. It finances capital projects according with the objectives of the Union. The Web site is available in English, French, and German and features searching, a site map, a drop-down box of quick topics, contact information, press releases, news, and events. Information is organized into the following categories: About EIB, Info & News, Projects & Loans, Capital Markets, Publications, Jobs, and FAQ. Member nations include Austria, Denmark, Germany, Finland, France, Greece, Italy, Portugal, Spain, and Sweden, with some access to EIB information under the languages of these nations.

Detailed Description: The home page category About EIB is comprised of the mission statement, objectives, information about partners, and structure and key data about current Bank activity. The category Info & News provides some background information, information on specific projects funded by the Bank, and current news. Under the Projects & Loans category are a list of current Bank projects, information about project appraisals, loan activities, and evaluation. Related press information, news, and FAQs are also available.

On its Capital Markets site, another home page category, the European Investment Bank offers information about the EIB as an issuer of products to investors focusing on its financial products, ongoing financing operations, and details of outstanding securities as well as information about its bond markets and bond issue.

As a publisher, the EIB publishes for both professionals and the public in electronic format, and its titles are also available at no charge on request in hard copy. The Publications home page category is subdivided into General, Strategies, Thematic & Procedures, Country Fact Sheets, Technical Studies, Economic Reports, and Ex-Post Evaluations. The EIB *Annual Report* is available from 1999 online under the General Publications subdivision. Also under General Publications are the *EIB Bulletin,* a bulletin featuring topical articles on EIB activity; a video library; and the EIB's statutes and rules of procedures. Country Fact Sheets are provided for each member country and for EIB lending in Central European countries, Balkan countries, and other parts of the world. Technical Studies contains a few published policy papers available online on industries that affect the mission of the European Investment Bank. The category Economic Reports links to research publications produced by the Economic and Financial Studies (EFS). The twice-annual *EIB Papers* presents the results of research carried out by EIB staff together with contributions from external scholars and specialists. These are available online at no charge back to 1996 in PDF format or free on request from EFS. *The Economic and Financial Reports,* an EFS working paper series, contains economic research on topics related to the operations of the EIB and are available online at no charge back to 1999, no.1, or free on request from EFS.

G8 Information Centre Web site, by the University of Toronto Library and the G8 Research Group at the University of Toronto. <http://www.g8.utoronto.ca/>

Summary: Since 1975, in annual summit meetings and ministerial meetings, the G7 and G8 Summit has dealt regularly with macroeconomic management, international trade, and relations with developing countries, as well as addressing specific issues such as security, crime, terrorism, environment, energy, and development. Since 1998, the G7 has officially become G8. When referring to both organizations, G7/G8 is used in this description. Although each G8 summit of industrialized nations has its own Web site, this research and information center on the G7/G8 is an excellent source of information, documents, and analysis of activities from this intergovernmental international organization's annual summits and ministerial meetings. It is an authoritative, permanent, and archival online resource, with the mission to serve as a comprehensive, independent source of information, analysis, and research on the G8 Summit. It is intended to serve scholarly, research, and public education needs.

The G7/G8 provides an important occasion for world leaders to discuss complex international issues and to develop the personal relations that help them respond in effective collective fashion to sudden crises. At the summits, governments set priorities, define new issues, provide guidance to established international organizations, and arrive at decisions to pressing problems, meeting on an ad hoc basis as needed. The original member countries were France, the United States, Britain (now United Kingdom), Germany, Japan, and Italy, joined later by Canada (1976), by the European Community (1977), and finally by Russia (1998, with full membership by the year 2006).

The Web site is available in English, Dutch, Russian, French, Spanish, Italian, and Japanese languages and provides online help and searching by keyword, subject, and country. In addition to providing links to current news and research on the G8, the Web site organizes information into the following categories: [Current summit by name], Summit, Meetings & Documents of G7/G8, Scholarly Writings & Policy Analyses, G8 Research, Scholarships, Links to Other G7/G8 Related Sites, G20, and Sponsors. This discussion will focus on the documents, scholarly writings, and research.

Detailed Description: Two categories of information in sidebars of the Web site, What's New in the G7/G8 and What's New in the G7/G8 Research, feature current news and research in dated entries and link to further information. Research also highlights current books and articles of interest published by the Information Centre. Also in addition to the central categories of information on the home page, there is a link to Help, and under Have a Question, there is an e-mail answering service. The Help page provides G7/G8 background information and links to documentation of the summit and ministerial meetings provided by the Information Centre and others. It also gives tips on searching and using the Web site.

The category on the current summit meeting is featured at the top of the home page and has links to the current Web site. These summits are held in locations based on a rotation schedule for the countries, changing every year, and their Web sites give background information on previous summits and the G8. Researchers may also find current speeches and summaries relating to the summit and also to archived documents. For example, the French summit site for 2003 links to archived G8 documents back to 1996.

Summits, Meetings & Categories, a category on the home page of the *G8 Information Centre,* contains information and links to Delegations & Documents, Ministerial Meetings, Officials-Level Meetings, and What is the G8? The section Delegations & Documents provides this information for each summit back to 1975: Delegations, communiqués, political declarations, other official releases, documents released by national delegations at summits, and available transcripts of summit news conferences. Ministerial Meetings links to both regular and ad hoc meetings and provides further information here as well as under Officials-Level Meetings, such as press releases, statements, summaries, and reports.

The category Scholarly Writings & Policy Analyses contains the sections Analytical Studies, Fact Sheets, Bibliography, Latest Citations, Conferences, Publications & Papers, G8 Governance Working Papers, G8 & Global Governance Book Series, and Oral History. Analytical Studies includes the analytical assessments back to the 1996 summit on issues, compliance, performance, and more. Fact Sheets are on summit achievement grades (1975–), ministerial institutions and meetings (1975–), and performance assessment by country (1996–). The *Bibliography,* compiled by Peter J. Hajnal, University of Toronto, provides a selective list of monographs, articles in periodicals, governmental and international organization publications, and Internet Resources that deal entirely or partly with the G7 or with G7-related issues. Latest Citations collects references to current information sources. Under the section Conferences are a collection of online programs, speakers' biographies, and papers from the conferences (1997–). Publications & Papers is a collection of online papers by individual authors, most provided in full-text PDF or HTML formats, in English, although some are in other languages (1988–). G8 Governance Working Papers are original articles by individual authors also full text online concerning the G8 and/or governance issues. Oral History provides online verbatim, unedited interviews with individuals who have played a key role in the development of the G7/G8 and the G20 (2001–).

The home page category G8 Research contains G8 Online, News Releases (2001–), the G8 Research Group (background information on the group), Professional Advisory Council, Special Advisors, Teaching Program, the G7/G8 Research Library Collection, Speakers' Series (speakers' presentations online), Sponsorship, Photos, and Partnership Institutions. G8 Online is an online, Internet-based, university-level course taught by different professors for the University of Toronto.

Other miscellaneous information available from the G8 Information Centre home page includes the Links to Other G7/G8 Sites, organized under the types governmental, international organization, nongovernmental, and media. The category G20 links to information from meetings, documents and background information, and a bibliography about the Group of 20 (G20). The G20 is a forum of finance ministers and central bank governors created at the September 25, 1999 meeting of the G7 Finance Ministers with the intent to broaden discussion on key economic and finance policy issues. It includes the G8 and other countries. Finally the category G8 in the News contains information from the *G8 Bulletin,* the *G20 Bulletin,* the *G8 Online,* and the *Financial Post.* The *G8 Bulletin* is published weekly with special issues and is available full text online back to vol.1, 1997. Its purpose is to summarize news highlights concerning the G8 and its activities and analyze, report, and summarize the pressing themes in G8-related news in world media. *Financial Post* links to a section providing full-text articles on G7/G8 in a chronological list back to 1975 courtesy of the *Financial Post.*

International Monetary Fund Resources

International Monetary Fund Web site, Washington, D.C. <http://www.imf.org>

Summary: The International Monetary Fund (IMF) is an international organization that has a strong publishing commitment and history since its beginning in 1945. Of special note are its publications on global economics, economic and business statistics, and information about the economic growth and economic policies of its member countries. Information is available at no charge on its Web site and also through subscription for print and electronic publications. The IMF Web site, available in English, French, German, and Spanish, is searchable and provides a site map and a site index. Information is organized under the categories About the IMF, IMF at Work, IMF Finances, Country Information, News and Events, Publications, and What's New. IMF information on individual countries is available through a drop-down box of countries listed alphabetically. A Current Highlights section features publications, events, and topics of current interest. For more information about the IMF's role in debt restructuring, debt relief, and poverty reduction, researchers should consult the Development chapter.

The International Monetary Fund (IMF) is an international organization of 184 member countries from around the world that was established in 1945 to promote international monetary cooperation, exchange stability, and orderly exchange arrangements; to foster economic growth and high levels of employment; and to provide temporary financial assistance to countries to help ease balance of payments adjustment. A specialized agency within the United Nations system, the IMF is governed by a Board of Governors, an Executive Board, and an International Monetary and Financial Committee. Also called the central institution of the international monetary system, the IMF is the system of international payments and exchange rates among national currencies that enables business to take place between countries, and aims to prevent crises in the system by encouraging countries to adopt sound economic policies. It also is a fund that can be tapped by members needing temporary financing to address balance of payments problems. It specifically helps its member countries by surveillance, financial assistance, and technical assistance, including the following:

- Reviewing and monitoring national and global economic and financial developments. Advising members on their economic policies and exchange rate policies.
- Lending countries hard currencies to support adjustment and reform policies designed to correct balance of payments problems and promote sustainable growth.
- Offering a wide range of technical expert assistance, including training for government and central bank officials.

The IMF's main business is macroeconomic performance (performance of an economy as a whole) and the financial sector policies of its member countries. In this function, it reviews total spending; employment; the balance of payments (the balance of a country's transactions with the rest of the world); macroeconomic policies, mainly policies relating to the government's budget; the management of money and credit; and the exchange rate. It also works in the area of financial sector policies, including the regulation and supervision of banks and other financial institutions, and in the area of structural policies that affect macroeconomic performance, such as labor market policies that affect employment. The IMF advises members on how to improve policies in these areas to achieve goals such as better and more sustainable economic growth.

Detailed Description: The What's New feature on the home page lists news by date in either descending or ascending order from May 1999. It also provides access by category of information such as speeches, press releases, or recent titles. Current Highlights, another feature of the IMF's home page, focuses on publications, topics, and events and offers a free subscription e-mail notification of what's new on the Web site. The category About the IMF presents a comprehensive collection on its organization, structure, and history; selected legal documents, bylaws, decisions, and statutes; resources (financial); access to its online annual reports and topic issue briefs; contact and visitor information; information about IMF photos and videos; evaluations of the IMF; IMF community activities; and working at the IMF. Of particular interest to researchers is its online *Glossary of Selected Financial Terms,* an alphabetical online dictionary of words and phrases, and users may suggest additional terms. Also available is the title *IMF Terminology: A Multilingual Directory.* Also very useful is the Web page for First Time Visitors to the IMF Web site. Note that the small video collection can be downloaded and viewed with the free media player or real player software. The IMF photos online are in the public domain and free to use for publication purposes. The IMF annual reports are online in various languages back to 1996. Information for students is contained in the section IMF in Action.

Country information from the International Monetary Fund is available through the home page drop-down box or also from the category entitled Country Information, which links to a *Country Information* Web site http://www.imf.org/external/country/index. htm>. Researchers may select their country from an alphabetical list, but in addition to nations, other entities and organizations are included. This resource provides access by individual country to lists of documents and publications published by the International Monetary Fund concerning that specific country. Documents are listed in reverse chronological order and most of the titles are available full text online at no charge back to the early 1990s. Specific information provided includes each country's exchange rate and position in the fund. Also the IMF publishes several series of titles that update economic and statistical reports on countries, policy discussions, and papers on specific issues. Researchers may look for these titles in these lists, especially when they are interested in specific countries. Ordering information for sales publications is available. Libraries of research institutions and business libraries are likely to own International Monetary Fund titles.

The Publications category from the home page also allows a researcher access to many of the documents and publications also accessible from the category Country Information, described earlier. Highlighted titles and a publications sales catalog are available. Also, users may browse publications by title or by author/editor and by subject in a searchable interface that covers from 1981 on in a variety of languages, which allows results to be sorted. Searching is also provided within the IMF's major series of titles, including the following: *Policy Discussion Papers, Working Papers, Economic and World Financial Surveys,* and *Occasional Papers,* as well as others. These series are an excellent source of information on individual countries, as every title published in these series has its own unique title and subject and often reports on a region or specific country. Users may access some of these titles, *Country Reports* and *Working Papers,* for example, both rich sources of information about individual countries, under the series name on the Publications page. Within each year back to 1997, the titles are listed alphabetically and provided full text at no charge.

Also linked from the Publications category are some of the IMF's online periodicals. These are, among others, the *IMF Survey,* the *IMF Staff Papers,* the *IMF Research Bulletin,* and *Finance & Development.*

The IMF is a rich source of financial data. Researchers can find comparable data in historical time series on economic subjects published by the IMF, including economic indicators such as Gross Domestic Product (GDP), taxes, finance, pensions, exchange rates, and labor. Some of the IMF's major statistical serial titles include the following.

- ***Balance of Payments Statistics Yearbook.*** Washington, D.C.: International Monetary Fund, 1981– (ISSN 0252-3035) (previously issued as *Balance of Payments Yearbook,* 1946/1974– [annual] which split into this annual yearbook and monthly issues, *Balance of Payments Statistics*). *The Balance of Payments Statistics Yearbook* contains balance of payments statistics for over 165 countries and international investment position data for over 80 countries and is published annually. English, French, and Spanish editions are available. Issued in three parts, the first part contains country tables, the second part contains world and regional tables, and the third part contains methodologies, compilation practices, and data sources. This title is also issued annually in CD-ROM format with historical statistics and methodology.

- *Direction of Trade Statistics.* Washington, D.C.: International Monetary Fund, 1994– (ISSN 0252-306X). This quarterly periodical contains statistical dates with current data (or estimates) on the value of imports and exports to their most important trading partners. Also, it provides summary tables for the world, industrial countries, and development countries. A yearbook (covering at least 7 years) and a CD-ROM version are available. This title is further described in the trade chapter of this book.

- *Government Finance Statistics Yearbook.* Washington, D.C.: International Monetary Fund, 1977– (ISSN 0250-7374). This annual title contains world tables and statistical tables for individual countries with central government revenue, expenditure, lending minus repayments, financing and debt for over 115 countries and for a period of 10 years, if available. Information for the yearbook is obtained primarily through means of questionnaire responses from ministers of finance or statistics divisions of individual countries.

International Financial Statistics, International Monetary Fund, Washington, D.C. (monthly print subscription periodical, 1948– (ISSN 0250-7463) (CD-ROM, 1991–).

International Financial Statistics Yearbook (annual print subscription cumulative title) (1961–) (ISSN 0250-7463).

International Financial Statistics Online (IFS Online) Database, (2000–) (subscription online database through IMF Online services).
<http://www.imf.org> (select Publications: IFS Online Services).

Summary: This serial title, known as *IFS*, is one of the premier sources for international financial statistics, current and historical. It is published in a variety of formats (print, CD-ROM, online subscription), languages (English, French, Spanish), and frequency (monthly, annual). "International Financial Statistics is a standard source of international statistics on all aspects of international and domestic finance. It reports, for most countries of the world, current data needed in the analysis of problems of international payments and of inflation and deflation, i.e., data on exchange rates, international liquidity, international banking, money and banking, interest rates, prices, production, international transactions, government accounts, and national accounts."[1]

Included in this title, in any of the formats, are statistics for the world and regions of the world, with statistical tables accessible by individual country. In paper, *IFS* is published as a monthly periodical, with an accompanying annual print *Yearbook*. Historical statistics and data manipulation are available in the CD-ROM and online versions.

Detailed Description: The *International Financial Statistics* print monthly periodical provides country data tables for the International Monetary Fund member countries, as well as for Aruba, the euro area, and the Netherlands Antilles, for approximately six current months of data, as well as the earlier year and a half. Coverage of data in the alphabetical country tables includes an overview; exchange rates; International Monetary Fund accounts; international liquidity; money and banking; interest rates; prices, production, and labor (consumer price index and more); international transactions (external trade); government finances; and national accounts and populations. World and area tables are also provided. The *Yearbook,* which began in 1961, provides approximately 30 years of statistical data for individual countries in the country tables and general world and region financial tables. Country notes and methodology are included.

The monthly issues report monthly, quarterly and annual data, whereas the *Yearbook* reports selected annual data. Most annual data on the CD-ROM and Internet begins in 1948, with quarterly and monthly data beginning mostly in 1957 and most balance of payments data in 1970.

The *International Financial Statistics Online* database contains time series data from 1948 in a Windows interface software available for network or individual subscription. Users may select specific countries to view country, world, and commodity prices tables and other economic information. Specific data can be viewed within a table presentation, and data and metadata may be saved in a variety of formats. Queries and queries for selected time series may be saved. Browsing, searching, saving settings, and online help are all available as options.

Users may select time series of interest, displaying the selected series in a spreadsheet format, and export the data. The system is similar to the *IFS* CD-ROM software, supporting downloading in CSV format.

The *IFS Online* provides similar data to the CD-ROM. It contains approximately 32,000 time series covering more than 200 countries and areas, including all series appearing on the IFS Country Pages; exchange rate series for all Fund member countries; major Fund accounts series; and most other world, area, and country series from the IFS World Tables.

International Financial Statistics on CD-ROM includes historical data not found in the monthly print issues. Software supports data extraction and downloading in CSV format provides English, French, and Spanish instructions and help screens. It is available through subscription for either network or individual PC licensing, including documentation.

World Economic Outlook, by the International Monetary Fund, Washington, D.C. (Occasional Paper Series) (ISSN 0256-6877) (paper semiannual title).

World Economic Outlook Databases (online subscription resources). <http://www.imf.org/external/pubs/res/index.htm>

Summary: The *World Economic Outlook* provides analysis and projections of economic developments at the global level and for major country groups. It analyzes major economic policy issues and economic developments and prospects, and therefore serves as a basic, economic reference title. Usually published semiannually, this title is available online in PDF format from 1997 on, along with the year 1993. In addition, this title was published semiannually September 1984–October 1996 and annually from 1980–1984. Historical information and statistical data sets are available through an online subscription resource, the *World Economic Outlook Databases.* For more information, researchers should check on the *IMF* Web site at <http://www.imf.org/> under the category Publications: Research at the IMF.

Organisation for Economic Co-operation and Development (OECD) Resources

Organisation for Economic Co-operation and Development (OECD) Web site, Paris. <http://www.oecd.org/>

Summary: The OECD is an international organization of industrialized governments worldwide that is well known for its work in reporting and monitoring policies and statistics, reviewing economies, and publishing country surveys. This discussion will focus particularly on the OECD's publications and work in the field of economics. It publishes many top-quality periodicals and books in this area—many important titles are described following, whereas other titles of a more global or general nature are described separately in this chapter.

The OECD's key objective is to help governments ensure the responsiveness of key economic areas by monitoring key economic policy areas, reporting on emerging issues, and identifying government policies that work in the most current environments. The OECD produces internationally agreed instruments, decisions, and recommendations to promote cooperation in areas in which multilateral agreement is necessary for individual countries to make economic progress. The OECD promotes sharing the benefits of economic growth in its activities in assisting emerging economies, promoting sustainable development, and providing aid:

> The OECD groups 30 member countries sharing a commitment to democratic government and the market economy.... With active relationships with some 70 other countries, NGOs and civil society, it has a global reach. Best known for its publications and its statistics, its work covers economic and social issues from macroeconomics, to trade, education, development and science and innovation.[2]

OECD member's countries are Australia, Austria, Belgium, Canada, Czech Republic, Denmark, Finland, France, Germany, Greece, Hungary, Iceland, Ireland, Italy, Japan, Korea, Luxembourg, Mexico, Netherlands, New Zealand, Norway, Poland, Portugal, Slovak Republic, Spain, Sweden, Switzerland, Turkey, United Kingdom, and United States.

Detailed Description: The home page category entitled Member Countries links to each country, arranged alphabetically, and to all the OECD documents pertaining to that country, including a list of Web links. Publishing is one of the OECD's strengths, and many of its titles are significant reference resources in the areas of economics, business, and statistics. These are listed alphabetically following with summary descriptions, except for the *OECD Economic Outlook,* which is described separately in this chapter. Most of the titles or resources are available electronically, may be in CD, as a single-title subscription, or are available through *SourceOECD,* the subscription publications and data Internet service of the OECD; for updated information, researchers should check the OECD Web site.

- ***International Direct Investment Statistics Yearbook*** (1993–) (print and online subscription title and online subscription database). An annual title published with English and French text, the *Year-*

book provides statistical tables on foreign direct investment (particularly to and from OECD member countries and developing countries). Part I includes summary tables and Part II tables by individual OECD country. The statistics are internationally comparable, and the online database permits users to build and download their own tables and graphs.

- *Main Economic Indicators* (1962–) (ISSN 0474-5523) (monthly print and subscription online title). This monthly bulletin of key short-term economic indicators provides international comparable statistics for the 30 Organisation for Economic Cooperation and Development (OECD) member countries and also the non-OECD member countries, Brazil, Bulgaria, China, Estonia, India, Indonesia, Latvia, Lithuania, Romania, Russian Federation, Slovenia, and the Ukraine. It is published in English and French. The content in *Main Economic Indicators* covers quarterly national accounts, business surveys, retail sales, industrial production, construction, consumer prices, employment and unemployment, interest rates, money, domestic and foreign finance, foreign trade, and the balance of payments. The nonmember countries' monthly bulletin provides current official monthly, quarterly, and annual economics indicators by country for Brazil, China, India, Indonesia, the Russian Federation, and South Africa. Volumes with historical statistics are available.

- *National Accounts Statistics* (1955–) (print, online, and CD subscription title) (ISSN 0256-758X). Published in English and French text in two volumes, Part I covers main aggregates and national accounts by individual country for each year of the last 10 years, and Part II has detailed tables with national comparative statistics for OECD member countries. National accounts indicators include gross domestic product, employment, and prices. Related titles are the *Quarterly National Accounts—OECD* (1976–), and *Quarterly National Account: Historical Statistics* for data 1960–1976, and overall, they provide a rich source for historical data on national accounts of the industrialized countries of the OECD.

- *OECD Economic Outlook* (1967–) (ISSN 0474-5574) (print and online subscription title). The *OECD Economic Outlook* is issued twice a year in English, French, and German and is available in print, CD, or electronic online formats in a variety of subscription packages from *SourceOECD*. It analyzes prospective global and country-specific economic trends, particularly for the upcoming two years within the context of the world economy for the OECD member economies and for certain non-OECD member economies. Each issue provides an assessment of the world economic situation, development in individual OECD countries, current top-

ics, and a statistical annex with detailed tables. Statistical modeling and analysis is also included along with the short- and medium-term economic projections and prospects. Certain issues are discussed as reoccurring themes in semiannual issues.

- *OECD Economic Studies,* by the Economics Department, OECD Secretariat (1983–) (ISSN 0255-0822) (semiannual print and online). This research journal is published twice a year with articles on applied macroeconomic and statistical analysis, particularly with an international or cross-country perspective. Articles are generated from the work of the OECD's intergovernmental committees.

- *OECD Economic Surveys* (1968–) (print and online subscription titles for individual country) (search the home page or select Publications: Country Surveys). The OECD's Dept. on Economics and Statistics publishes this important series with individual annual surveys on member countries. Many surveys began in 1968, although for countries joining the OECD post 1968, their surveys begin when they joined. These surveys are an excellent source of economic information on countries. They present information on economic assessment and recommendation for the country in text with supporting figures and statistical tables. Content covers macroeconomic performance and prospects, macroeconomic policy, productivity and growth, and managing public expenditure. Supporting the textual analysis are bibliographical references and notes, a glossary, and other appendices.

- *OECD Observer* (1962–) (ISSN 0029-7054) (bimonthly print and subscription online title) (1962–). This bimonthly journal provides analysis of world economic and social issues in sections on economy, society, development, trade & investment, government, resources, and science & technology. Each issue contains a separate annex of statistical indicators as well as tables and graphs within the articles. More information from its content is available at <http://www.oecdobserver.org>, where searching by keyword, by section, country, and hot topic is available, as well as current subscription information. Electronic full text of articles between 1996–2000 are archived at <http://www1.oecd.org/publications/observer>. Earlier archive editions in English and French are available on request.

- *OECD Papers* (2000–) (ISSN 1609-1914) (print and subscription online title). This monographic series is a compilation of individual titles on current research in economics, including research, analyses, forecasts, policy, and statistics. Economics and industrial policies, as well as energy, employment, education, environment, trade, science and technology, aid, development, agriculture, urban studies, economies in transition, and more are covered.

- *OECD Small and Medium Enterprise Outlook* (2000–) (biennial print and online subscription title). Another useful title on business within the member countries of the OECD is this biennial report on the economic performance of small and medium-size enterprises within OECD countries (which represents over 95% of business enterprises in most OECD countries). It reports on small and medium-size business policy trends by individual OECD countries and also reports on findings in the areas of taxation, entrepreneurship, environmental management, and restructuring. International comparisons of key small and medium-size enterprise indicators and their trends are also included.

Pacific Islands Forum Secretariat Web site, Suva, Fiji. <http://www.forumsec.org.fj/>

Summary: Topics on the Pacific Islands Forum Secretariat Web site cover socioeconomic activities and publishes in the areas of these resources: fisheries, forestry, minerals, water and land, and conservation in regard to all of them. Information on the Web site is categorized under About the Forum, Divisional Information, General Information, Funding Assistance, Employment Opportunities, Calendar of Meetings, Forum Documents, Forum News, and Photo Gallery. The Forum provides a Fiji site and a U.S. mirror site, but only the Fiji site is described here.

The Pacific Island Forum represents the heads of government of all the independent and self-governing Pacific Island countries, as well as Australia and New Zealand, and was formerly known as the South Pacific Forum Secretariat. Since 1971 it has provided member nations with a forum to express their joint political views and to cooperate politically and economically. Within the Pacific Islands Forum Secretariat, governments actively cooperate with nongovernmental organizations and international organizations as well. Member countries include Australia, Cook Islands, Federated States of Micronesia, Fiji, Kiribati, Nauru, New Zealand, Niue, Palau, Papua New Guinea, Republic of the Marshall Islands, Samoa, Solomon Islands, Tonga, Tuvalu, and Vanuatu.

Detailed Description: Under the home page category Forum Documents are online publications including general documents, annual reports, a news bulletin Trends and Development, South Pacific Trade Director, forum papers, full legal texts, FAQs, and the monthly *Forum E-Bulletin,* online since April 2002. The *Forum Review, Trends and Developments*, a news bulletin published three times a year by the Development and Eco-nomic Policy Division, covers international events and socioeconomic trends that may be of interest within the region, major meetings organized or attended by the Secretariat, and recent economic or development news from within the Forum region. Under the Divisional Information home page category is a section on Surveys and Databases, providing access to the Regional Trade and Investment Database, South Pacific Trade Directory, Business Cost Survey, and also on Regional Trade Agreements—PACER and PICTA (Full Legal Texts and Frequently Asked Questions).

United Nations Regional Economic Commission Resources

The work of the United Nations Economic Commissions that report to the United Nations Economic and Social Council (ESOSOC) is extensive, and they provide much information on specific regions on Web sites and through print and electronic publications. Although a very rich source of information, these commissions and their activities are only briefly described here.

United Nations Economic Commission for Africa (UNECA) Web site, Addis Ababa, Ethiopia. <http://www.uneca.org/>

Summary: Established in 1958 and based in Addis Ababa, Ethiopia, the United Nations Economic Commission for Africa (UNECA) is the regional arm of the United Nations for the African region, including 53 member states. The entire list of members is available on its Web site. It is mandated to support the economic and social development of these countries, foster regional integration, and promote international cooperation for Africa's development. Major activities and objectives include advocacy and policy analysis, convening stakeholders and building consensus, technical cooperation and capacity building, and enhancing the UN's role in Africa.

Available in English and French, this organization provides resources, newsletters, links, quick links drop-down box, searching, programs, information from subregional centers, and initiatives reports from its Web site. Under Related Initiatives are links to organizations under the ECE including: AISI (African Information Society Initiative), SIA (Special Initiative for Africa), ADF (African Development Forum), ITCA (Information Technology Center for Africa), AKNF (African Knowledge Networks Forum), and POPIA (Population Information Africa). The African Development Forum's major objectives are to coordinate and provide the results of current research and opinion on key developments to the key stakeholders in African development in order to formulate shared goals, priorities, and action plans.

Under the home page category Resources are selected UNECA documents (accessible by theme and by year), a news archive (back to 2000), speeches and statements, selected publications, press releases, meetings and events, ECA Databases, and ECA Library. Most publications are sales publications. Key periodicals include the annual *Economic Report on Africa* (available online back to 1998) and the *Africa Economic and Population Bulletin*. UNECA also organizes and reports on a regularly held conference, the African Development Forum.

United Nations Economic Commission for Asia and the Pacific (UNESCAP) Web site, Bangkok, Thailand. <http://www.unescap.org/>

Summary: The regional arm of the United Nations Secretariat for the Asian and Pacific region, with a membership of 52 countries and 9 associate member countries, is the United Nations Economic and Social Commission for Asia and the Pacific (UNESCAP), and its main purpose is to promote economic cooperation and development in the region. It provides advisory services, development assistance, research, special programs, and coordinating services with other organizations and countries.

Major categories available on the UNESCAP Web site include About Us, Media Centre, Members, Programmes, Secretariat, and Publications. UNESCAP News is featured on the Web site and also links to topical information covered in the activity of the organization. These topics are Poverty Development; Poverty and Development; Statistics; Managing Globalization; Environment and Sustainable Development; Information, Communication, and Space Technology; Trade and Investment; Transport and Tourism; Addressing Emerging Social Issues; and information about developing countries. Users may sign up for an e-mail newsletter. The home page category Publications includes online documents of the Commission and links to its major divisions, such as the Statistics Division, as well as to its Library.

UNESCAP published a significant title providing a report of the economic conditions of the region, with economic analysis and data, in its *Economic and Social Survey of Asia and the Pacific* (1974–). Data is available back to 1947 in the earlier title, *Economic Survey of Asia and the Far East*.

United Nations Economic Commission for Europe (UNECE) Web site, Geneva, Switzerland. <http://www.unece.org>

Summary: As one of five regional commissions of the United Nations, the UNECE's primary goal is to encourage greater economic cooperation among its member states, within the areas of economic analysis, environment and human settlements, statistics, sustainable energy, trade, industry and enterprise development, timber, and transport. Its activities include policy analysis, development of conventions, regulations and standards, and technical assistance. It has 55 member states, some whose membership in UNECE dates back to its beginning in 1947; however, all interested United Nations member states may participate in its work.

The UNECE's searchable site features news and highlighted articles. The Information Resources category contains ECE Weekly (an online newsletter), Publications, Press Releases, and a Photo Gallery. Other categories include Programmes, Meetings, and Statistical Data Online. Subjects are generally economic, environmental, and social topics, also including statistics, energy, agriculture, and gender activities. In addition, a site map is available to help the researcher navigate through the many resources.

The UNECE is a major publisher and also collects, analyzes, and reports many statistics on the region. Under the Publications subsection are lists of publications, many of which are sales publications, but some significant titles are also online at no charge, including its *Economic Survey of Europe* (1948–). This title provides comprehensive analyses of economic developments and prospects in the entire ECE region, with a particular focus since 1989 on the process of transition to market economies in Central and Eastern Europe. It contains a statistical appendix accompanying the text and is online in full text for current years and in part for earlier years back to 1998. More statistics are found in the *Economic Bulletin for Europe* (1949–) an annual title published in English and French, which analyzes the current economic situation in the European Commission region and provides data by individual country in a statistical annex. Another significant series is the UNECE's *Environmental Performance Reviews (EPRs)* by individual country. Each assesses a country's efforts to reduce its overall pollution burden and manage its natural resources, to integrate environmental and socioeconomic policies, to cooperate with the international community, to harmonize environmental conditions and policies throughout Europe and North America, and to contribute to sustainable development in the ECE region. One more series of note is the UNECE's *Country Assessment Reports,* which are assessments of the communication, e-knowledge, and networking capabilities of individual countries in transition, and all titles are downloadable at no charge in PDF format.

A major statistical publication is its annual title, *Trends in Europe and North America: The Statistical Yearbook of the Economic Commission for Europe* (1995–) (print with the current issue free online to users who register). This statistical reference resource contains country profiles by subject for the 55 ECE member countries. There are many other electronic resources and titles produced by this agency; they are too numerous to describe here.

United Nations Economic Commission for Latin America and the Caribbean (UNECLAC) (English) Web site, Santiago, Chile.
<http://www.eclac.cl/> (Spanish language; select English language).

Summary: Previously known as the Economic Commission for Latin America (ECLA) when it was established in 1948, it changed its name to the Economic Commission for Latin America and the Caribbean (ECLAC) in 1984. The Spanish acronym, CEPAL, has remained constant all these years. ECLAC is one of the five regional commissions of the United Nations. Headquartered in Santiago, Chile, it was founded for the purposes of contributing to the economic development of Latin America and the Caribbean, coordinating actions directed toward this end, and reinforcing economic relationships among the countries and with the other nations of the world. The promotion of the region's social development was later included among its primary objectives. The mandate of its guiding organ, the Secretariat, is to provide research, information dissemination, and advisory services, promote development, and much more.

The Economic Commission for Latin America and the Caribbean (ECLAC) has 41 member states; 33 countries of Latin America and the Caribbean are member countries of ECLAC. In addition, there are member countries of ECLAC from North America and Europe because of the many historical, economic, and cultural ties of their countries with the region, and these include Canada, France, Italy, Netherlands, Portugal, Spain, the United States, and the United Kingdom. Finally, seven nonindependent territories in the Caribbean are associate members of the Commission.

The comprehensive Web site of ECLAC, available in English and Spanish, provides information under the categories About ECLAC, Office of the Executive Secretary, Press Centre, Analysis & Research, Divisions, Publications, and Statistical information and features news, headlines, and highlighted documents. As a major publisher, ECLAC makes its catalog available on the Web under Publications, and although many are sales publications, many of the major periodicals and documents of the organization are available electronically at no charge. Occasionally, just a summary of the title will be available online. Much more information is published than is covered in this description.

ECLAC's journal, the *CEPAL Review* (1976–), studies the economic and social development problems of the region in articles by individual authors, is archived online since no. 56, August 1985, and is published in English and Spanish three times a year. One significant annual title, the *Statistical Yearbook for Latin America and the Caribbean,* is downloadable at no charge from 1998 in PDF format, and the latest edition contains historical data series back to 1980, which can be downloaded in Excel format. The *Yearbook* contains a selection of the main statistical series available on economic and social trends in the countries of the region. Another significant annual title is the *Social Panorama of Latin America,* which covers the condition of the populations of the region, including poverty levels.

Finally, another significant annual title, the *Economic Survey of Latin America and the Caribbean* (1982–), is available in print format with accompanying CD and online in PDF format at no charge beginning with 1998/1999 linked under the Publications category of UNECLAC's home page. Part 1 of this annual title covers regional issues, including current economic conditions and outlook for the year; economic policy; significant economic variables; and external sectors such as trade, capital flows, and balance of payments. Part 2 contains country information in an alphabetical list with this same content. The CD contains a statistical appendix with over 400 tables of recent data, which permits the creation of spreadsheets. The previous title, *Economic Survey of Latin America,* was published between 1948–1981.

Also available from the *ECLAC* Web site are the speeches, presentations, and reports from the Office of the Executive Secretary; many more statistics and publications; a searchable online library catalog of

ECLAC publications; information by subject under the category Analysis & Research; and FAQs. The site is searchable and has a site map.

United Nations Economic Commission for Western Asia (UNESCWA) Web site, Beirut, Lebanon. <http://www.escwa.org.lb/>

Summary: Created in 1973 particularly for many of the Arab countries of the Middle East, the Web site for this regional economic and social development Commission contains documents and publications (not many in full text online) listed under the various themes and divisions. However, many of the publications may be ordered at no charge. The searchable Web site also provides news and highlighted features of the activities of the organization and its separate divisions.

Of special note is the link under the category Information Resources, which leads to sections on Publications, Press Releases, Declarations & Agreements, ESCWA Library, and Meetings and Events. The Publications section guides researchers to many of the significant publications of UNESCWA, including the annual title *Population Bulletin of ESCWA* (from 1971–, under different titles), a journal concerned with population, demographic studies, and related issues relevant to the Arab countries. Another significant publication with economic statistical data by individual country of the region is the annual title *Statistical Abstract of the Region of the Economic and Social Commission for Western Asia,* which has text in Arabic and English (1983–). An online library catalog is also available for searching.

United Nations Resources

Industrial Commodity Statistics Dataset (online and CD sales product).

Industrial Commodity Statistics Yearbook, by the United Nations Statistics Division, Energy and Industry Statistics Section, New York, 1976– (ISSN 0257-7208).

Summary: Since 1976, the *Industrial Commodity Statistics Yearbook,* published in English and French, provides statistical data on world industrial production by region and country of the world for individual commodities. About 530 industrial commodities are reported, including 10 years of data for each issue. Regional and world totals are included. Information about the print publication is available on the Internet at <http://unstats.un.org/unsd/industry/yearbook/yearbookreadme.htm>, including a complete list of all commodities, sorted alphabetically and by industry, and a sample page of the printed publication.

The United Nations Statistics Division (UNSD) is engaged in the collection and dissemination of data, an important support of the UN mission, and this Division concentrates on the production of major industrial commodities in physical quantities. By linking to the Statistics Division home page, researchers will discover many other economic and production compilations of statistics, and also they can consult the Statistics chapter in this book.

Detailed Description: A compilation of the entire data set of the print *Yearbook,* the *Industrial Commodity Statistics Dataset* is an online CD subscription product in Access format that provides the entire database of industrial commodity statistics covering the period 1950–2000. Although not an interactive database, it comprises five tables and two queries, and researchers may develop other queries for extracting data. Customized subsets of the database are available on request.

The data on Industrial Commodity Statistics is collected through a yearly questionnaire sent to national statistical offices and also from specialized and intergovernmental agencies both within and without the United Nations system of organizations. Questionnaires are published on the Web site along with other information about the publication.

The coding system used for the commodities throughout the *Dataset* and *Yearbook* is based on the International Standard Industrial Classification of All Economic Activities (ISIC), Revision 2. A correspondence table between these ISIC Rev.2-based codes and the corresponding codes in the Standard International Trade Classification (SITC, SITC Rev.2, SITC Rev.3) and the Harmonized System (HS 1996) is also available from the agency's page on the product at <http://unstats.un.org/unsd/industry/yearbook/default.htm>.

An additional source of United Nations statistics on industries and related economic topics is the *Monthly Bulletin of Statistics,* by the United Nations Statistical Division, which is also available in an online edition and provides over 30 years of historical data on industries, prices, products, basic population, employment, mineral industries, trade, and more by individual country. For more information, researchers may consult the Statistics chapter.

National Accounts Database (online subscription).

National Accounts Statistics: Main Aggregates and Detailed Tables, by the United Nations Statistics Division National Accounts Section, New York, 1957– (print annual title). <http://unstats.un.org/unsd/nationalaccount/default.htm>

Summary: The Statistics Division's National Accounts Section collects and estimates national accounts statistics from individual countries and publishes them in the annual *National Accounts Statistics,* a bilingual reference publication in English and French. This source has been published since 1957 under variant titles, such as the *Yearbook of National Accounts Statistics.* The National Accounts Section also maintains the updating of the Web resource *System of National Accounts (SNA) 1993,* as well as handbooks and training materials on it. The 1993 *SNA* on the Web incorporates updates as soon as they are approved, and in addition, it is searchable and contains a glossary of term. The Division also provides links to reference sources for International Economic and Social Classifications, along with a glossary of classification terms.

United Nations Economic and Social Council (ESOSOC) Web site, New York. <http://www.un.org/esa/coordination/esosoc/>

Summary: A main organ of the United Nations, the United Nations Economic and Social Council organizes information on its Web site under the following selected categories: About ECOSOC, UN Conferences, Documents and Resolutions, DESA Issues, UN ICT Taskforce, NGO Participation, ECOSOC Archives, UN System, ECOSOC Secretariat, Publications, and Press Releases.

The main Web site to a subcategory, the links *United Nations Economic and Social Development (ESOSOC)* Web site at <http://www.un.org/esa/>, which links further to programs, publications, and activities of the United Nations in the area of economic and social development that are related to, but not specifically under the United Nations Economic and Social Council's oversight. This discussion will focus on its documents, publications, and archives. The *Council* Web site is a rich source for documents on the activity of the organization, but most publications are issued by the organizations under it and not by the Council itself.

The Economic and Social Council was established by the Charter as one of the principal organs of the United Nations, under the authority of the General As-

sembly, in order to promote higher standards of living, full employment, and economic and social progress; solutions to international economic and social problems; and universal respect for, and observance of, human rights and fundamental freedoms for all. The Council's 54 members each serve three-year terms, and various commissions carry out the work of the Council. The Economic and Social Council coordinates the work of 14 UN specialized agencies, 10 functional commissions, and 5 regional commissions; receives reports from 11 UN funds and programs; and also issues policy recommendations to the UN system and to Member States.

Detailed Description: From its searchable Web site, ESOSOC features news on conferences, programs, and reports from its meetings. The ESOSOC Archives category links to resolutions of the Council from 1982 online, documents from 1994, and decisions from 1995, with earlier in text format and later information in PDF format. The category Documents also links to current documents and decisions of the Council, as well as sessional documents, background information, and its rules of procedure. From the Publications category on the home page, a few online full-text electronic publications are available. These tend to be general in nature, as most of the publications issued under ESOSOC are issued by individual organizations that report to it.

World Commodity Survey, by the United Nations Conference on Trade and Development (UNCTAD), New York, 1999/2000–.

Summary: This annual title provides global statistics on key commodities, or commercial products, within the context of the trends and growth in world commodity markets and crises. The information covers aspects of commodity production, processing, financing, marketing, prices, and trade. Specific subjects include market crises, fundaments, electronic trading, agriculture and fishing industries, metals industries, energy, major industrial products and services, megamergers, and acquisitions. This title has a supplement entitled *Commodities World Trends.* Each issue provides information in approximately 13 parts with an index and accompanying statistical tables, charts, figures, graphs, and index, and each includes specific themes. One part contains an overview of the world economic environment by region of the world.

World Economic and Social Survey, by the United Nations Department of Economic and Social Affairs, New York, 1994– (print annual title).

<http://www.un.org/esa/analysis/wess/> (selected sections online, including Chapter 1, "The State of the World Economy").

Summary: A reference title published in two parts; this report is the United Nations' annual analysis of current developments in the world economy, emerging policy issues, review of major developments in international trade, and financial resources of developing countries. It contains a forecast of short-term global and regional economic trends. Statistical tables, boxes, and figures in the text give standardized data on macroeconomics, international trade, and finance. A separate annex of statistical tables presents data on global output and macroeconomic indicators over a period of approximately 10 years, with world, regional, and individual country data.

This title is published in two parts, part 1 focusing on the state of the world economy and part 2 on social goals. This annual title has been published in print since 1932 under various titles and under the title *World Economic and Social Survey* since 1994. From 1932–1944 it was published as *World Economic Survey* by the League of Nations, from 1948–1954 as the *World Economic Report,* and from 1955–1993 under the title *World Economic Survey.* Further detailed description of this title is available in the Social/Cultural Issues chapter.

World Investment Report, by the United Nations Conference on Trade and Development (UNC-TAD), New York (Document No: UNCTAD/WIR/ YEAR) (1991–) (print annual title and online 2001–). <http://www.unctad.org/wir/>

Summary: This annual report analyzes global and regional investment trends and statistics, the role of transnational corporations, and the role of policy measures in the context of world and regional economics trends. A statistical annex accompanies the text. Each issue reports on a special theme within the area of foreign direct investment (FDI), such as trends in international production. It is produced in English, Arabic, Chinese, French, English, Russian, and Spanish.

UNCTAD serves as a focal point for the United Nations on all matters of foreign direct investment and transnational corporations, publishing many individual titles in this area. A list of publications is available as an appendix to each of these reports or on the UNCTAD home page under Publications.

Detailed Description: In addition to linking to the full-text reports that are downloadable in sections in PDF (2001–), the Web site provides press releases, overview, and table of contents for every issue back to 1991. Each issue contains figures and bibliographical references that support the text.

United Nations Industrial Development Organisation (UNIDO) Web site, Vienna, Austria. <http://www.unido.org/>

Summary: UNIDO produces information services, databases, publications, and newsletters and provides a forum to fulfill its mission in promoting industrial development. Topics covered in its information products, some which are online at no charge, include industrial development abstracts, industrial statistics, business environment, finance, industrial technology, energy, agro-industries, globalization, National Cleaner Production Centres, and biosafety. Publications of UNIDO include its annual title, *World Industrial Development Report,* the *International Yearbook of Industrial Statistics,* and its electronic weekly newsletter, *UNIDOSCOPE.* Also notable for researchers is its *Industrial Statistics Database.* Searching and advanced searching of the Web site is available, as well as a quick find drop-down box. For more information, researchers should consult the Development chapter. The UNIDO Web site is available in English, Chinese, French, German, Italian, Russian, and Spanish.

UNIDO is an international organization with 170 member countries, which was created in 1966 with the mission to help developing countries and countries with economies in transition in their fight against marginalization in today's globalized world. It mobilizes knowledge, skills, information, and technology to promote productive employment, a competitive economy, and a sound environment. UNIDO assists in relieving poverty by fostering productivity growth.

Through its programs, UNIDO promotes international industrial cooperation among developing countries, between developed and developing countries, and also between developing countries and countries with economies in transition. Its activities focus on the strengthening of industrial activities and cleaner and sustainable industrial development. UNIDO became a specialized agency of the United Nations in 1985. UNDIO supports 35 regional offices throughout the world, as well as other promotion and technology offices.

Detailed Description: Information is organized on the *United Nations Industrial Development Organisation's* (UNIDO) Web site under the following categories: *UNIDO Weekly News* (electronic newsletter); Events; Publications; Services; Media Corner; About

UNIDO; Offices Worldwide; Hot Topics; and Topics and Initiatives. There is a calendar of live links to current and upcoming events. Publications links to sales publications, databases, and reports and documents, which are either online or free except for shipping and handling charges, as well as a downloadable catalog and online ordering form. A special section exists for Free Publications for Download (PDF format reports available at no charge). Reports and Documents contains UNIDO's annual report online back to 1998 and also titles listed under topics such as industry and development, small and medium industries, industrial policies, industrial development reviews (by individual country), the role of women in industrial development, and industry and the environment. This is a rich online resource for these topics and more concerning industrialization and development issues. Under the section on sales publications, researchers may find more about the annual subscription periodical *Industrial Development Report* (2002/2003–). This title was previously published for UNIDO by the Oxford University Press under the title *Industrial Development Global Report,* which continued the earlier title *Industry and Development: Global Report* (1985–). These are available from 1985 on in English, French, and Spanish, although language editions may vary from year to year. Also, UNIDO's *Industrial Development Abstracts* database may be accessed and searched from under the Publications category. It contains over 11,000 abstracts and full-text reports of UNIDO's development projects from around the world (for more, see the Development chapter). New publications are also listed separately, and reports from this database may be ordered.

On the home page under the category Services, UNIDO links to information on doing business in the following areas: Agro-Industries, Industrial Energy & Kyoto Protocol, Environmental Management, Industrial Governance and Statistics, Investment and Technology Promotion, Montreal Protocol, Quality and Productivity, and Small Business Development. Each area links further to selected events, projects, databases, business tools, online publications, and program information from UNIDO on that topic. Databases are usually searchable by topic or country.

In the section Industrial Statistics, under the Industrial Governance and Statistics Service category, researchers will find databases, publications, and selected country industrial statistics. Three major UNIDO databases are:

- *UNIDO Industrial Statistics Database* at the three-Digit Level of ISIC (Revision 2)
- *UNIDO Industrial Statistics Databases* at the four-Digit Level of ISIC (Revision 2 and 3)
- *UNIDO Industrial Demand-Supply Balance Database.*

In the three-digit level database, data is consistent and comparable between countries and over time. With statistics for 175 countries from the current year back to 1963, the data is available in Excel, ASCII, or CSV (comma separated values) files. For the four-digit level database, seven indicators are provided for individual countries from 1990 on. The third database covers industrial output, trade, and apparent consumption. All three databases are available for purchase on CD-ROM. Since 1994, the United Nations Industrial Development Organization (UNIDO) has become responsible for the collection and dissemination of general industrial statistics of the United Nations, which were previously collected and disseminated by the United Nations Statistics Division. See this agency described, which is also in this chapter.

Also under the Industrial Governance and Statistics section on the home page researchers can access information on the annual sales title *International Yearbook of Industrial Statistics* (1995–), which was formed by the union of three titles: *Industrial Statistics Yearbook,* v. 1: *General Industrial Statistics,* and *Handbook of Industrial Statistics,* which combined provide researchers with information back to the early decades of the 1990s and are available in hard copy in research libraries. The *Yearbook* provides worldwide statistics on current performance and trends in the manufacturing sector. It covers countries and areas worldwide and gives up-to-date statistical indicators on the manufacturing sector. The statistical data is harmonized and adjusted to the requirements of international comparability and to standards set by the United Nations. Also for quick statistics by country, researchers can search Selected Industrial Country Statistics.

From the home page, under the category Weekly News, is the electronic weekly newsletter about the current activities of the organization *UNIDOSCOPE* archived online back to June 2002. It also includes press releases, a feature story on a current topic, illustrations, and links to other industry newsletters. The home page category About UNIDO contains the history, strategic guidelines, business plan, constitution, and organization chart of UNIDO.

World Bank Resources

Countries & Regions Web site, by the World Bank, Washington, D.C. <http://www.worldbank.org> (select Countries & Regions).

Summary: The *Countries & Regions* Web page organizes information by a clickable map, an alphabetical list for choosing a country or region, or by a list of links to specific regional initiatives. The main search engine for the World Bank and its site index are available in button form at the bottom of the page. A user new to the World Bank will see from the map that the developing economies that are its focus are in color and linked. Industrialized economies are not colored on the map.

This online resource leads to many online country and regional profiles and full-text publications. Regional initiatives include the Brazilian rain forest, Country assistance strategies, Early Childhood Development in Africa, European Union Enlargement, Indigenous Knowledge, and other initiatives involving immunization, transportation, and reconstruction. Depending on the size of the regional initiatives the online links lead to a variety of text and photos describing it, including some of online texts of proposals, newsletters, or periodicals for several years; free publications; news; and video clips. For example, the *Country Assistance Strategies* offers definitions and free online strategy reports from 1998–2001, listed by year and by country. Once a country has been selected, there is a choice of format display (for textual information or data). The *Country Assistance Strategies* are an excellent resource for seeing a summary of progress by government and civilians in the area of sustainable economic development within a country. A beginning user of this information can expect to find explanations of successes and challenges for the country developing its labor force, improving its finances, and eliminating poverty.

World Bank Web site, Washington, D.C. <http://www.worldbank.org/>

Summary: The World Bank works in over 100 developing economies with a goal to improve living standards and eliminate poverty through finance and ideas. It works with government agencies, nongovernmental agencies, and the private sector to plan assistance strategies. This description will focus on the economic information of the World Bank, a major publisher, and will describe the *World Bank* Web site's information resources, features, publications, and data in the field of economics and business. This Web site is provided in English, French, Spanish, and Russian, with other language information available through regional offices. It provides searching, site index, help, and Frequently Asked Questions.

Established in 1944 at a conference of world leaders in Bretton Woods, New Hampshire, the World Bank became affiliated with the United Nations in 1947 and now has a membership of 184 countries. The World Bank supports national and international efforts to improve statistics, establishing standings, sharing knowledge, and coordinating the collection and dissemination of international statistics in order to understand economic and social development and improve growth and performance. The World Bank Group is made up of five organizations: the International Bank for Reconstruction and Development (IBRD); the International Development Association (IDA); the International Finance Corporation (IFC); the Multilateral Investment Guarantee Agency (MIGA); and the International Centre for Settlement of Investment Disputes (ICSID). IFC, MIGA, and ICSID are described in this chapter, whereas the other organizations are described in the Development chapter. Links to all of these are available from the *World Bank* home page.

Detailed Description: The International Finance Corporation (IFC) an organization within the World Bank group, with its own Web site at <http://www.ifc.org/> was established in 1956 as the largest multilateral source of loan and equity financing for private-sector projects in the developing world. It promotes sustainable private-sector development primarily by financing projects and providing advice. On its searchable Web site, it also provides specialized searching under categories including projects by keyword and searching by sector, by resource, and by program. More information is available in the sections on the home page under IFC projects, Doing Business With IFC (Investor information), Sustainability Resources, Media, and Research. Of special note under research are the IFC library, an online searchable library catalog with hot-linked titles, environmental resources, and publications, along with the IFC catalog. The IFC publishes a *Review of Small Business Activities*, its annual reports online since 1995, *Impact—Private Sector Partners* (a review of private-sector investment in infrastructure archived online since 1998), and many other online publications at no charge, organized by topic. IFC Discussion Papers and IFC Technical Papers are two major series of publications, issued with individual titles.

The Multilateral Investment Guarantee Agency (MIGA) member of the World Bank Group has promoted foreign direct investment into emerging economies since 1988 in order to improve people's lives and reduce poverty. Its Web site <http://www.miga.org/> leads to online publications, full-text reports and brochures, online short videos, and an online newsletter *MIGA News* archived from 1997.

ICSID, another member of the World Bank Group <http://www.worldbank.org/icsid>, was established to assist in mediation or conciliation of investment disputes between governments and private foreign investors. Hearings from specific cases, current and archived news, and regulations are available online.

World Tourism Organization Resources

World Tourism Organization (WTO) Web site, Madrid, Spain. <http://www.world-tourism.org/>

Summary: This organization serves as a global forum for tourism and is a prolific publisher on tourism research, policy, and statistics. It highlights news, recent publications, projects, activities, latest facts, and conferences. Information is provided on its Web site under the categories Infoshop (Publications & Electronic Projects), Facts & Figures, Statistics & Economic Measurement of Tourism, Quality in Tourism Development, Sustainable Development of Tourism, About WTO, Newsroom, Employment, Programme Activities, and Regional Activities. A separate section links to information on current conferences and meetings. Although most of the publications are subscription title, researchers may find some online information and statistics. Some significant publications of the WTO are the annual *Yearbook of Tourism Statistics, Compendium of Tourism Statistics,* and the triannual *Travel and Tourism Barometer.*

Programme activities links to Documentation, a section with *Lextour,* an online database of tourism legislation, as well as to WTO depository libraries and a thesaurus of tourism terms. The Statistics & Economic Measurement of Tourism section leads to current and historical data, methodology, and statistical publications.

The World Tourism Organization is an international intergovernmental body within the United Nations family with the responsibility of promoting and developing tourism as a global forum for tourism policy issues and know-how. Begun in 1925 as the International Union of Official Tourist Publicity Orga-

nizations, it was renamed World Tourism Organization in 1975, and it currently includes 132 countries and more than 350 affiliate members.

Detailed Description: The section Facts & Figures leads to latest data, trends in worldwide tourism, and trends by country. Major publications of the World Tourism Organization, found under the Infoshop Category on the WTO home page, include the following:

- ***Compendium of Tourism Statistics*** (print subscription title) (1986–). Previously the *Tourism Compendium* (1975–1986) published in English and French, this title contains statistical indicators on inbound tourism by type of transportation of arriving tourist, domestic tourism, outbound tourism, tourism activities, and basic economic indicators.
- ***WTO Statistics—Basic Set*** (CD-ROM sales title). 2003– (ISBN 9-28440-609-9). An essential and invaluable tool for everyone dealing with tourism issues, this CD set includes the best-selling *Yearbook of Tourism Statistics* and the famous *Compendium of Tourism Statistics,* which are together the most comprehensive collection of current tourism statistics by the WTO providing access by country and region.
- ***Yearbook of Tourism Statistics*** (1986–) (ISSN 1011-8977) (print and annual subscription title). Published annually in two volumes with text in English, French, and Spanish, it provides detailed statistical tables on tourism for over 190 countries. For individual countries and territories, it contains international inbound tourism for five years by country of origin of the tourists. It also provides data on tourists and visits from abroad; length of stay and historical data is available. This title continues the earlier titles, *World Travel and Tourism Statistics* and *World Tourism Statistics,* and other titles back to 1937 when it was first issued by the International Union of Official Travel Organizations and World Tourism Organization.

NONGOVERNMENTAL SOURCES

EIU.com Web site, by the Economist Intelligence Unit, New York. <http://www.eiu.com>

Summary: EIU delivers business, economic, and political information to companies managing operations across national border in many formats: printed reports, newsletters, CD-ROMs, electronic feeds, online services, and customized briefings on what they name their "virtual library" site. They provide research and analysis on business operations and environment of countries, on strategic industries, and on developments in management thinking, striving for global coverage and impartial analysis. In addition to written analysis, EIU sponsors or takes part in international forums, government roundtables, and conferences on key areas of business, politics, and economics, and its many publications are for sale on its Web site. Although many of the services are subscription, its *EIU ebusiness Forum* is a free Web site on global business issues that is searchable by country. This description will focus on the e-business Forum and other EIU databases and services available on a subscription or pay-on-demand basis.

Founded in 1946, the Economist Intelligence Unit (EIU) is an information provider for companies establishing and managing operations across national borders anywhere in the world. It produces objective and timely analysis and forecasts of the political, economic, and business environment and also reports on certain strategic industries.

Detailed Description: EIU provides a collection of subscription databases of worldwide economic and market indicators by individual country, including historical time series of economic and demographic data (annual, monthly, and quarterly). Results may be sorted and exported into a spreadsheet format. Its *EIU ViewsWire* <http://www.viewswire.com> is a subscription daily intelligence service on almost 200 countries on aspects of economy, finance, regulations, and industries, including background information, forecast, and news analysis. A small amount of information is available at no charge online. The *Executive Briefing* is a recent online service offering industry and strategic intelligence for senior executives on 60 leading world markets, organized around eight key industries.

EIU ebusinessforum <http://www.ebusinessforum.com/> is a portal to global analysis on e-business available at no charge online. It offers significant coverage of global business issues, searchable by country name, along with e-business strategies, which can be searched by type of industry. The type of information covered includes market trends on e-business conditions in regions or countries, doing e-business in (explores how specific industries and companies are pursuing e-business opportunities), executive surveys and benchmarks, and resources (links to Web sites devoted to e-business). Under e-business this information is provided under five areas: Thought Leadership, Research, Best Practice, Doing e-business in…, and

Latest Development. Thought leadership features the interviews and analytical essays of leaders in the field of e-business on the implications of the Internet for business strategy. Research provides a wealth of analytical material specifically assessing the impact of e-business on specific industries, countries, and corporate functions. Best practice contains dozens of case studies of leading. Doing e-business in…assesses the prospects for e-business growth in 60 countries, with updates on information needed to implement e-business, such as government policy, tax questions, regulatory problems, and infrastructure constraints you need to follow to do e-business around the globe. Latest Development are the latest daily updates on e-business.

As the business information arm of the Economic Intelligence Group, EIU takes part in the group that publishes the *Economist* newspaper.

World Economic Forum Web site, Geneva, Switzerland. <http://www.weforum.org/>

Summary: For information on international business, the *World Economic Forum* is a rich Internet source of business and economics information. It provides online reports at no charge under one of its initiatives, the Global Competitiveness Programme, which provides analysis for global and regional economic transition and competitiveness in today's global economic market. It organizes information on its searchable Web site under the categories About Us, Initiatives, Events, Media Centre, Knowledge Navigator, and Members. Its publications are available for sales, but many are also online at no charge.

This independent international organization is committed to improving world economy by providing world leaders with a forum to address global issues and to work with business partners and corporate members to improve the state of the world. The WEF is an organization of international companies that calls itself a platform for discussion, debate, and action on the key issues of the global agenda, and it provides special member services online.

Detailed Description: The Media Centre provides press releases and press kits. The Events category reports on economic and business summits and meetings from all over the world, organized by date and by region of the world. The *Knowledge Navigator* Web site is an information resource available at no charge containing reports on aspects of international business, such as competitiveness profiles of individual countries from the Forum's Global Competitiveness Programme reports. Researchers may also access information by theme, region, and industries. *Worldlink* at <www.worldlink.co.uk> is the World Economic Forum's searchable online magazine, providing analytical articles on global business, archived online back to 1998, and available at no charge.

RESEARCH STRATEGIES

This discussion will provide a summary overview of how researchers may use selected resources described in this chapter, especially economic surveys, statistical data, country information, regional information, and information by topic, such as industry, tourism, money, and investment. To begin with, researchers may want to consult very broad summaries of economic conditions in the world. The ***World Economic and Social Survey,*** a subscription print title by the United Nations, provides an excellent annual overview of economic and social conditions for individual countries, and the first chapter on the state of the global economy is a summary available online at no charge. The International Monetary Fund's subscription print title ***World Economic Outlook*** and its online subscription ***World Economic Outlook Databases*** can be beginning resources but are also very rich in historical data for serious researchers. ***Country Commercial Guides,*** by the U.S. Embassy Staff and the U.S. Trade Administration, offers practical information to U.S. businesses on doing business in other countries of the world and provides excellent updated information on economic, political, and social conditions that affect business, and it is a resource available at no charge. **The United Nations Economic and Social Council (ESOSOC)** Web site is included as a beginning place for researchers to investigate the economic resources of the United Nations. The Council provides many online economic internal documents concerning the Council's activities. Although it does not publish economic information and titles, it leads to many wonderful and rich resources published by the agencies that report to it.

For statistics, one of the best initial sources to consult in the research process is the subscription resource from the International Monetary Fund, the ***International Financial Statistics,*** available in print, CD-ROM, or online database formats and depending on the format, it is published on a monthly, quarterly, and annual basis. It is easy to use, covers a broad range of countries with comparable statistics between countries, and has a wide range of time series data. Also many individual yearbooks and titles are described within this chapter and can be found by a quick review of the governmental sources discussed. This chapter provides many statistical sources for countries provided through international intergovernmental organizations, including some statistical yearbooks through the United Nations system of organization on specific business topics, such as national accounts, but researchers should also consult the Statistics chapter for even more information published by the United Nations Statistics Division.

The **Organisation for Economic Development and Cooperation (OECD)** is a major provider of economic information for the serious researcher; however, much of its information is available by subscription only, in print or through various online subscriptions, including its product SourceOECD, which allows access to electronic documents and statistical data. The ***OECD's Economic Outlook*** is excellent for its analysis of OECD member and nonmember countries in a global context and provides a useful introductory overview of global conditions in its introductory material. The organization also publishes regular analytical titles for individual OECD countries in its series entitled *OECD Economic Surveys* and statistical data in its periodical *Main Economic Indicators.*

Researchers needing either a specific country or more detailed information should consult the ***International Monetary Fund*** Web site ***Country Information*** category. Each member country of the IMF has similar financial and economic information, including exchange rates. For detailed information about a country in general, economic and financial information, and practices, one of the major resources would be reports in the series called ***IMF Country Staff Reports,*** and the current reports are accessible from ***Country Information.*** For financial data about a country, try the Special Data Dissemination Standard (SDDS) links. For some of the major countries, it will link directly to the National Summary Data made available by that country. The **World Bank** Web site category Countries and Regions is an excellent beginning place for country information on developing or poorer countries. The organization **World Economic Forum** provides business competitiveness analyses for individual countries, and the Web site of the Economic Intelligence Unit provides information about e-business in countries of the world, both also at no charge for selected information.

More specialized information concerning regions of the world can be found in a variety of sources. The Web sites of these international intergovernmental organizations, the **European Union, G8,** the **Organisation for Economic Co-operation and Development,** as well as the various United Nations regional economic organizations (**United Nations Economic Commission for Africa [ECA], United Nations Economic Commission for Asia and the Pacific [ESCAP], United Nations Economic Commission for Europe [ECE], United Nations Economic Commission for Latin America and the Caribbean [ECLAC],** and **United Nations Economic Commission for Western Asia [ESCWA]**), all contain a wealth of publications, many of which are full text, and links to other sources. Most of them also publish economic surveys or economic statistical bulletins with historical economic, financial, social, and demographic indicators over a number of years. These are often subscription publications, either in print or electronic format, but well worth consulting. In addition, the **IGO Asia-Pacific Economic Cooperation (APEC)** provides an excellent comprehensive Web site and publishing on economic information for countries of Asia and Pacific that are members of the organization, including many years of historical data and economic outlooks. For information concerning the former Soviet Republic, the U.S. online resource *BISNIS* is an excellent place to begin. The Web site resource of the European Union, entitled *Europa: Activities of the European Union: Economics and Monetary Affairs,* is excellent for legal documentation online concerning the economic policies of the European Union.

For information on global tourism, researchers should start with the *World Tourism Organization's (WTO)* Web site. Several serial titles published by the WTO are excellent compilations of statistics for countries of the world, including its *Yearbook of Tourism Statistics*.

Industry and production is another subtopic under economics and business. For researchers interested in these specific areas, the United Nations *Monthly Bulletin of Statistics* and *Yearbook of Industrial Production* provide excellent production statistics by country. The *World Commodity Survey,* by the **United Nations Conference on Trade and Development (UNCTAD),** covers prospects of production of individual commodities, whereas the *Industrial Commodity Statistics Yearbook,* by the United Nations Statistics Division, provides production by country. The Asian Productivity Organization offers much information about industry, production, and related sectors on its Web site and in its publications.

The bank resources described in this chapter are excellent sources for monetary, financial, and investment information. The Web sites of the **Bank for International Settlements,** the **European Central Bank,** and the **European Investment Bank** are resources for researching banking issues, monetary policies, and financial statistics. These sources contain reports, publications, and statistics, many of which are available online in full-text format. The Bank for International Settlements (BIS) specifically covers issues that concern central banks of countries and the development of policy, the European Central Bank covers monetary policy and financial issues for the European Union, and the European Investment Bank is particularly focused on financial aid of European Union countries for developing nations. Also investment information may be found in the annual title *World Investment Report.* The European Court of Auditors is the financial arm of the European Union and monitors and reports on the spending of the organization as a whole.

This brief summary of sources is not intended to be comprehensive. Researchers are encouraged to consult the research guides from the resources described and from the Web sites and titles described in the For Further Reading section.

FOR FURTHER READING: COMPREHENSIVE WEB SITES AND OTHER REFERENCE SOURCES

Business Information: How to Find It, How to Use It, by Michael R. Lavin. 3rd ed. Phoenix, Ariz.: Oryx Press, 2002 (ISBN 1-57356-213-0).

This handbook on business resources is a beginning guide for researchers that combines in-depth descriptions of major business publications and databases with explanations of concepts that are essential for using them effectively. It includes many international intergovernmental organization resources.

Economic and Social Committee of Europe Web site, Brussels, Belgium. <http://www.ces.eu.int/pages/en/home.asp>

Founded in 1957 by treaty, the European Economic and Social Committee is an advisory body representing the views and interests of organized civil society in relationship to the Commission, the Council, and the European Parliament. It ensures that the various economic and social interest groups (employers, trade unions, farmers, consumers, etc.) are represented in the institutional framework of the European Union. It advises the larger European Union institutions and must be consulted on matters relating to economic and social policy. It also issues opinions on its own initiative. News, information about its activities, documents, and a few publications are available on its searchable Web site, and publications are free on request.

Economic Survey of Europe, prepared by the Research and Planning Division, Economic Commission for Europe. Geneva: United Nations, 1945– (ISSN 0070-8712).

Issued three times a year since 1997 and annually prior to 1997, this title reports on the European economy in three parts: recent economic development and short-run outlook in the region of the Economic Commission for Europe; special issues related to economic conditions and prospects; and a statistical appendix, providing over 10 years of data by country. In addition to its review of economic developments in Europe, this title regularly covers the CIS and North America. Other information related to the United Nations Economic Commission for Europe may be found on its Web site at <http://www.unece.org/>.

Field Guide to the Global Economy, by Sarah Anderson and John Cavanagh with Theo Lee and the Institute for Policy Studies. New York: New Press, 2000 (ISBN 1-56584-421-1).

This basic handbook and guide to the study of international trade defines economic globalization and discusses what's new about the global economy and worldwide responses to it. Ten claims about globalization are discussed, including issues of free trade, trade and its relationship to democracy, living standards, better jobs, workers, and the effect of trade to the good of a country. An introduction, conclusion, appendices, references, and directory of organizations are included.

Wilton Park Papers (Series) Web site, United Kingdom. <http://www.wiltonpark.org.uk/web/welcome.html>

This Web site is a good source for online reports and significant economic information in its series on broad international affairs. Wilton Park is an academically independent and nonprofit making Executive Agency of the British Foreign and Commonwealth Office, being established in January 1946 as part of an initiative by Winston Churchill to promote the establishment of a successful democracy in Germany after the Second World War. Key issues of international concern discussed include the Middle East, peace, China, Africa, global trade, and the environment.

World Economy: A Millennial Perspective, by Angus Maddison. Paris: OECD, 2001 (Development Centre Studies) (ISBN 9-26418-608-5).

This reference on global economic development provides a comprehensive view of the growth and levels of the economic performance of nations over the very long term, including world population since the year 1000. It discusses the gaps between rich countries and those lagging behind in development and identifies the forces explaining the reasons for success and obstacles to development. Lastly, it scrutinizes the interaction between the rich nations and other nations and assesses the degree to which their relationship was exploitative.

World Public Sector Report: Globalization and the State. New York: United Nations, Division for Public Administration and Development Management, Dept. of Economic and Social Affairs, 2001– (UN Sales No.: E.01.II.H.2) (UN Document No: ST/ESA/PAD/SER.26) (biennal paper and online title). <http://bibpurl.ock.org/web/4815>

This inaugural issue of the report contains information, data, and research on public-sector issues, with a specific focus on the theme of globalization. The first part provides background information and current issues on globalization, as well as the impact of globalization on nation states, social perspectives, and future prospects. Part 2 contains information on defining and measuring the state, presenting data on the public sector and measurement tools with analysis and technical and statistical tables. The introductory material and table of contents are available on the Web at <http://www.unpan.org/>.

NOTES

1. "About the IFS Online Service," by the International Monetary Fund. *International Monetary Fund Web site*, <http://ifs.apdi.net/imf/about.asp>.

2. "About OECD," by the Organisation for Economic Co-operation and Development. *Organisation for Economic Co-operation and Development (OECD) Web site, Paris,* <http://www.oecd.org/> (Browse: About OECD).

CHAPTER 7
Education

CHAPTER OVERVIEW

Education is an area of great interest to the world at large. An educated population reduces poverty levels, increases productivity, and promotes human rights and democracy. Resources in this chapter describe the work of such intergovernmental organizations as the United Nations Educational, Cultural and Scientific Organization (UNESCO), Organisation for Economic Co-operation and Development, European Union, Council of Europe, and the World Bank. Full-text reports, publications, documents, and statistics can be found on the Web sites of each, with the focus on various educational aspects such as initiatives, innovations, eLearning, and national systems. The nongovernmental Web site *Social Science Information Gateway: Education* provides links to a plethora of Internet resources.

Governmental Sources Discussed

Council of Europe. ECC [European Cultural Convention]: The Europe of Cultural Cooperation: Education Web site, Strasbourg, France. <http://culture.coe.int/T/E/Cultural_Co-operation/education/>

Education and the World Bank Web site, Washington, D.C. <http://www1.worldbank.org/education/>

European Commission. Directorate-General for Education and Culture Web site, Brussels, Belgium. <http://europa.eu.int/comm/dgs/education_culture/index_en.htm>

International Bureau of Education Web site, United Nations Educational, Scientific and Cultural Organization, Geneva, Switzerland. <http://www.ibe.unesco.org>

OECD Directorate for Education, Web site, by the Organisation for Economic Co-Operation and Development, Paris, France. <http://www.oecd.org> (select Browse: by Department, then EDU: Directorate for Education).

United Nations Educational, Scientific and Cultural Organization (UNESCO): Education Web site, Paris. <http://www.unesco.org/education/>

Nongovernmental Source Discussed

Social Science Information Gateway: Education Web site, by the Institute for Education, University of London. <http://www.sosig.ac.uk/education/>

GOVERNMENTAL SOURCES

Council of Europe. ECC [European Cultural Convention]: The Europe of Cultural Co-operation: Education Web site, Strasbourg, France. <http://culture.coe.int/T/E/Cultural_Co-operation/education/>

Summary: The **Council for Cultural Co-Operation** oversees educational and cultural programs with an emphasis on learning as a way of promoting democracy and human rights. This Web site, available in English and French, encompasses the education program of the Council of Europe's Europe of Cultural Co-operation. Included here are reports, publications, and links to other resources. The site is arranged into seven main headings: Cooperation Programme, Standard Setting and Policy Development, Better Understanding Our Work, News, Conferences, Committees, and Partners.

Detailed Description: Cooperation Programme is the first main home page heading and is further subdivided into Education of Roma/Gypsy children in Europe, Teaching Remembrance, Education for Democratic Citizenship and Human Rights, History Teaching, Intercultural Education, Languages, Higher Education, Partnerships for Educational Renewal, and In-Service Training Programme for Teachers. The subdivision of Education for Democratic Citizenship and Human Rights is of especial importance. Included here are links to activities and publications. These publications, accessible by type, subject, or language, are in full-text format, and include annual reports (1997–), other reports, studies, recommendations, and resolutions. Each of the other subdivisions is linked to further information.

Standard Setting and Policy Development, the second home page heading, contains Conventions and Recommendations of the Committee of Ministers. These "standard setting instruments" are in full-text format.

Better Understanding Our Work is the third home page heading and features the full text of the most current Activity Report written by the Directorate of Strategic Planning for the Council of Europe's Secretary-General. It is included here because of the section that discusses education initiatives.

News, another home page heading, contains the full text (PDF) of the most recent issues of the *Newsletter Education*. Also located here is the publications catalog. Each catalog entry includes annotations and the table of contents.

The home page heading Conferences has both the Standing Conferences of European Ministers of Education (1959–) and Informal Conferences of Ministers of Education of South-East Europe. Both of these subdivisions contain the full text of resolutions or declarations.

The Committee home page heading is subdivided into Steering Committee for Education, Steering Committee for Higher Education and Research, and Lisbon Recognition Convention Committee. The Steering Committee for Education section contains a description of its work and the membership, but does not have any documents or publications. A restricted site accompanies this committee that may very well be the location for the documentation. The links for the other two committees were broken at the time of this writing.

Partners is the final home page heading and includes contact information and links to other Ministries of Education and other relevant international organizations.

Education and the World Bank Web site, Washington, D.C. <http://www1.worldbank.org/education/>

Summary: As the world's "external funding agency" of education, this Web site contains reports and other publications detailing its work in this area. Much of the material is in full-text, usually PDF, format. Some materials are available in other languages. The home page is divided into the main headings of Overview, Strategy, Themes, Regions & Countries, Data & Statistics, Documents and Reports, Projects, News and Events, and Related Links. The Web site is searchable and provides a site map, Frequently Asked Questions, and a Help/Web guide. Under Contact Us is an Educational Advisory Service to help users access information.

Detailed Description: The home page heading Overview provides a brief synopsis of the World Bank's work in the field of education. Strategy, the next home page heading, provides the full text (PDF) of strategy papers, from both a global and regional perspective. Themes, the third home page heading, has a pull-down menu listing various educational topics, each linking to further online information. Education for All encompasses the subheadings of Girls' Education, Early Childhood Development, Effective Schools and Teachers, Adult Education, and School Health. Education for the Knowledge Economy is comprised of Secondary Education, Tertiary Education, Science & Technology, Education and Technology, Global Distance Education, Global Education Reform, Economics of Education, and Public Examination System. Each of these subheadings is linked to a Web page that describes the initiative and contains relevant documentation and publications.

Regions and Countries is divided into the regions of Africa—Sub-Saharan, East Asia and Pacific, Europe and Central Asia, Latin America and the Caribbean, Middle East and North Africa, and South Asia. Each of these regions is hot linked to descriptions of initiatives in that region. Also located here are links to regional projects, regional data, and regional publications.

Data and Statistics, another home page heading, links to the World Bank's education database, EdStats. The database includes the categories country data, thematic data, regional indicators, World Bank lending, country at a glance, and links to other sources. Data is either in full text or can be downloaded into Microsoft Excel, depending on the category. Links to other sources is a listing of Web sites of relevant organizations.

The Documents and Reports home page heading links to relevant material subdivided into Informal Disclosure, Regional Publications, World Bank Documents, and Reports and Infoshop (the World Bank Bookstore). Each subdivision has its own search engine to access full-text documents by type and topic.

Projects, yet another home page heading, links to a database of project documents that allows searching by browsing education projects by region, educational sector, or country. Advanced keyword searching is provided for multiple categories including country, region or sector, product line, goals or themes, lending instruments, and years.

Related Links, the final home page heading, is divided into World Bank Resources and Related Topics.

European Commission. Directorate-General for Education and Culture Web site, Brussels, Belgium. <http://europa.eu.int/comm/dgs/education_culture/index_en.htm>

Summary: The European Commission is the executive body of the European Union comprised of 20 commissioners. The commissioners' administrative staff includes 36 Directorate-Generals, who oversee various European Union (EU) initiatives, including a Directorate-General for Education and Culture. This Web site of the Directorate-General for Education and Culture highlights the education objectives and initiatives of the European Union. For this discussion, the focus will be on the Programmes, Actions and Initiatives, and Publications home page headings, which contain the bulk of the material on the topic of education. A search engine is available from the main page. This site is available in all 11 of the official EU languages: Danish, German, English, Spanish, Finnish, French, Greek, Dutch, Italian, Portuguese, and Swedish.

Detailed Description: Programmes, one of the home page headings, is subdivided into Socrates (Comenius; Erasmu; Grundtvig; Lingua; Minerva; Observation and Innovation: Eurydice, Arion, and Naric; Joint Actions, and Accompanying Measures); Leonardo da Vinci, Youth, and Tempus; EU/Canada Cooperation; and EU/USA Cooperation.

Socrates is the European Community action programme in the field of education for 2000–2006 with the goal to build cooperation across Europe through funding and support for all aspects of education, including innovation, equal opportunities, and language learning. These objectives are to be accomplished through eight actions. The first action, COMENIUS, deals with school education from preschool through secondary and encompasses language learning, "learning in a multi-cultural framework," and participation by all members of the education community. The COMENIUS section of the *Socrates* Web site includes information about the program, links, keywords, lists of projects and course, and tools for current COMENIUS projects and mobility, which includes publications mostly in PDF format.

ERASMUS, the second action, covers both university and nonuniversity higher education through ideas such as quality improvement, curriculum development, faculty and department exchanges for language coursework, and "thematic network projects." Information about the programs, activities, projects, statistics, studies/publications (either the full text in PDF format or a listing of titles), related sites, and latest news related to this action are found here.

GRUNTDTVIG, the third action, deals with enhancement of adult education (generally, culturally, and socially) though European cooperation. A description of the action including legal and policy documents in PDF format, project themes, proposal writing assistance, selected projects, and links are available here.

LINGUA, the fourth action, has to do with language education and supports the first three actions. Information in this area covers language learning/teaching promotion and development. Of special note is the *Lingua Compendia,* with full-text PDF format materials pertaining to the objectives.

MINERVA, the fifth action, focuses on the educational aspects of Open and Distance Learning (ODL) and Information and Communication Technology (ICT). MINERVA action resources consist of the Socrated/ODL/Minerva projects database publications, in PDF format (1998–) and links to relevant Web sites.

Observation and Innovation, the sixth action, has the goals of educational systems quality improvement and European educational innovation. Three major initiatives have been developed to help fulfill these goals. One such initiative is EURYDICE, the Information Network on Education in Europe, available in English, French, and German. Here are found publications, including the current version of *Key Data on Education in Europe* and the Eurybase system, arranged by country, comprised of bibliographies, institutions, legislation, glossary, and searching by both free-text and keyword for each country. ARION, another initiative, is a "European Community action of study visits for education specialist and decision makers."[1] Included here are themes of study, facts and figures, annual reports, and a catalogue of ARION study visits (PDF). NARIC, National Academic Recognition Information Centres, was "created in 1984 to help in regulating title recognition and facilitating the integration of national educational systems."[2] There is also a link to *Guide to Higher Education Systems and Qualifications in the EU and*

EEA Countries (PDF) for each country and *Recognition of Diploma* (PDF) for each country.

Joint Action, action seven, has to do with community programmes [sic]. Accompanying Measures, action eight, covers additional activities that fall outside the scope of the other actions.

Another area under the Programmes home page heading is Leonardo da Vinci, which focuses on vocational training. Resources included in the First Phase (1995–1999) are guides and handbooks for compiling reports (in Microsoft WORD and PDF formats); Council Decisions (Microsoft WORD format); annual Compendium of Projects, arranged by country and in PDF format (1995–1997); a searchable database of Project Compendium; and statistics on vocational training. The Second Phase (2000–2006) includes the guides and handbooks, along with application forms, information, photos, studies, and reports in full-text PDF format.

Youth, another Programmes area, deals with young people (ages 15–25) and includes news, white papers, conferences and documentation on this topic, and links to full-text documents through its catalog. It also contains a site map and an index with a glossary and links to national youth agencies. The Tempus Programme pertains to overall European cooperation in the area of education and provides information on Council Decisions and participating countries. The EC/Canada Cooperation and EC/USA Cooperation Programme areas both include press releases, application forms, guidelines, and lists of project selections (1996–).

Actions and Initiatives is another home page heading. Only those subdivisions dealing with education will be discussed here and include eLearning, Les Netd@ys Europe, *Jean Monnet Project,* and Libraries.

ELearning, was initiated "to adapt the EU's education and training systems to the knowledge economy and digital culture. This initiative has four components: to equip schools with multimedia computers to train European teachers in digital technologies, to develop European educational services and software, and to speed up the networking of schools and teachers."[3] The eLearning actions include an overview of the initiative, Compendium of Projects (PDF format), Projects (alphabetical Web links with descriptions), Documents (PDF format), and a link to the eLearning portal.

Les Netd@ys Europe deals with the use of technologies in the learning process. Included here is a description of the initiative and links to the full text (PDF) of reports documenting the progress.

Jean Monnet Project provides funding for studies of European integration at the university level. "The term European integration studies is taken to mean the construction of the European Community and its related institutional, legal, political, economic and social developments."[4] This site includes an application form, listing of publications, links to relevant conferences, directory, and the *EURISTOTE* database. The *EURISTOTE* archive version (1960–1994) allows for searching by research topic or university. The New *EURISTOTE* (1994–) has a more complex search form, and searching can be done by subject, free-text, country, author, supervisor, language, and university. There is also a *Jean Monnet Project* search form allowing for searching by country, city, university, professor/name, specialization, subject, and type.

The Libraries subdivision provides a link to the Central Library catalog, ECLAS, which "covers the Union's official publications and documents of most intergovernmental organizations, commercial, academic and government presses, and selected periodical articles of lasting interest. In ECLAS you will find material on European integration, the political objectives and activities of the Union institutions and material on Member States of the EU, in particular their institutional, legal and socioeconomic structures or technical material necessary to the work of the various Commission departments, ranging from legal documentation to scientific and technical research papers."[5]

Publications is the last main home page heading included in this discussion of education sources. Here is found a listing, with annotations, of brochures, leaflets, newsletters, reports, and CD-ROMs of relevant publications. Many are available in full text (PDF).

International Bureau of Education Web site, United Nations Educational, Scientific and Cultural Organization, Geneva, Switzerland. <http://www.ibe.unesco.org>

Summary: Although originally founded as a private institution (1925–Geneva), the International Bureau of Education (IBE) became the first intergovernmental organization devoted to education when it added governments to its membership roster (1929), subsequently becoming a part of UNESCO (1969). The *IBE* Web page provides access to databases that focus on comparisons of national education systems and their best educational practices. These are major information sources available at no cost. The full-text publications related to education from individual countries can be found here. In addition, other materials related to international activities, country-specific activities, and regional programmes [sic] are also included. Information on this page is available in English, French, and Spanish languages. The home page of this Web site is divided into three main headings: International Activities, Regional Programmes, and Country-Level Activities. In addition, at the bottom of the page are links to What's New, About IBE, Publications, Databanks, Documentation Services, ICE (International Council on Education), IBE Council, Search, Site Map, Index, and Links.

Detailed Description: International Activities, the first home page heading, contains the major information sources of the Web page and for this discussion will focus on databases and publications. There are six databases or databanks located here: *Country Dossiers, INNODATA, World Data on Education, IBEDOCS, RelatED,* and *Global Content Bank: International Clearinghouse on Curriculum for HIV/AIDS.*

Country Dossiers, also available in French, contains information on more than 100 countries. A listing of the countries to be added next is also included. Each dossier is comprised of Profile, Reports, Educational Innovations, Official Documents, Selected Bibliography, Statistics, and Links.

INNODATA, begun in 1993, is a source of information on educational innovations concerning the content and methods of education at the primary and secondary levels. Information here is archival, as this database is no longer being updated and has been integrated into the *RelatED* database, which records good practices in learning and school-based initiatives worldwide. Searching in *RelatED* can be done by Country, Region, Area of Innovation, Keywords, Target Population, Title, and Free Text. The data is subdivided into Areas of Innovation, Keywords, Target Population, Description, Evaluation, and Administrative Information. Although most of these reports are in English, there are a few from Spanish- and French-speaking countries in their native language.

World Data on Education is a continually updated databank of annual reports and profiles of national educational systems (organization and function). This database has three parts: Educational Profiles, National Reports, and Web Resources. Educational Profiles contains 168 national education systems profiles that appear in English, French, or Spanish, according to the country, arranged by geographical region. These profiles describe the educational system's organiza-

tion and function. National Reports are on the subject Development of Education, arranged alphabetically by country in full text (PDF), from the September 2001 meeting of the International Conference on Education. Web Resources contains links to other sites arranged into general information (statistics and databases on educational systems) and official information sources, arranged by world region.

IBEDOCS is the IBE bibliographic catalog, and searching can be done to find documents, publications, books, articles, journal titles, and reports dating from 1971. The full text of IBE publications is included, as well as the full text of ICE conference documents.

RelatED is a database of school-based initiatives bringing together *INNODATA* and *BRIDGE* (good practices in education). Searching can be done by country/region, title of project/program, area of good practice, target group, keywords, and starting date.

Global Content Bank: International Clearinghouse on Curriculum for HIV/AIDS contains links to education-related databases, publications, and photographs. The publications section provides citations and annotations.

Regional Programmes, the next main home page heading, features information on the most current projects. Country-Level Activities, the last home page heading, details the current projects under way in specific countries divided into operational, seminars/workshops/technical assistance, and agreements.

The What's New home page category, located at the bottom of the page, offers a month-by-month listing of new publications, conferences, and updates. Publications, also one of the categories found at the bottom of the home page, provides no-cost access to online publications as well as listing those for sale. The online versions, usually in PDF, include Educational Innovation publications, the *Educational Practices Series, INNODATA* Monograph Series, workshop reports, and *Thinkers in Education.* Sales publications, available for purchase, are the quarterly comparative education journal, *Prospects,* and the *Studies in Comparative Education* series.

The Databanks category is another access point to the previously described databases. The Documentation Service home page category includes links to the previously described IBE databases and to the Documentation Centre page. The Documentation Centre collects policy documents and journals related to comparative education and educational system development. A historical archive (1925–1968) link is also included.

ICE (International Conference on Education) category provides a history and information on this regular event and includes electronic access to the proceedings of the 44th Session (1994), 45th Session (1996), and 46th Session (2001). The Search category consists of a search criteria box with opportunities to limit the search by global, international, regional, or country levels. The Links category provides access to other related Web sites, arranged by subject.

OECD Directorate for Education Web site, by the Organisation for Economic Co-operation and Development, Paris, France. http://www.oecd.org/> (select Browse: by Department, then EDU: Directorate for Education).

Summary: Produced by the Directorate for Education, this Education section of the *OECD* Web site, in English and French languages, contains information regarding publications and documents pertaining to education. Much information is online, full text at no charge, although most titles are sales publications. The home page of this Directorate includes links to these major headings: Themes, About, Publications and Documents, and Statistics and Information by Country. A search engine is also available.

Detailed Description: The home page heading About provides an overview of the work of this Directorate. The Statistics home page heading contains links to various statistical tables from the *Education at a Glance* database, available for downloading in Microsoft Excel format. Publications and Documents, also a home page heading, provides links to the full text, mainly PDF format, of annual reports, case studies, country survey/reviews/guides, directories, events/conferences/meetings, guidelines, manuals /sources/methods, news releases, newsletters/ brochures, other OECD documents, policy briefs, publications, questionnaires, reports, speeches, staff papers/presentations, and statistics/data/indicators. Working papers that are focused on either countries or territories are also included. The Publications and Documents heading contains the greatest amount of materials for researchers.

The home page also features links to information and full-text publications on the specific topics of Brain and Learning, Economics and Management of Knowledge, Education and Skills, Education in Non-Member Economies, Human and Social Capital, and trade in Education Services. Don't Miss, another heading on the home page, links to the *OECD Online Education Database* as well as information about spe-

cific educational programs of the OECD. The online subscription service *SourceOECD* provides the full text of many education-related books, periodicals, and statistical sources that are not available from the OECD Education site. Many research institutions have access to this service.

United Nations Educational, Scientific and Cultural Organization (UNESCO): Education Web site, Paris. <http://www.unesco.org/education/ index.shtml>

Summary: Established by the signing (1945) and ratifying of its Constitution (1946), UNESCO was formed to promote peace through educational, scientific, and cultural collaboration. The Education section of the UNESCO Web page highlights the various educational activities and programs of this organization. The information is arranged by broad subjects: In Focus, News, UNESCO & Education, Global Monitoring, Meetings, and New Publications. Links to UNESCO Institutes relevant to education are included along with an archive. The site is available in both English and French. A search engine is included.

Detailed Description: The *UNESCO Education* Web site links to many topics on education including: Right to Education, Education Plans & Policies, Early Children & Family, Primary Education, Secondary Education, Higher Education, Technical & Vocational Education, Science & Technology Education, Non-Formal Education, Inclusive Education, Cultural & Linguistic Diversity in Education, Education and ICTs, Education in Situations of Emergency, Crisis & Reconstruction, Physical Education and Sport, Peace & Human Rights Education, and Nonviolence Education. Each of these topics contains relevant online information and publications.

Education Networks is another heading on the *UNESCO Education* Web site. Three networks are highlighted: Associated Schools Project Network (ASPnet), International Centre on Technical and Vocational Education and Training (UNEVOC), and UNESCO Chairs-UNITWIN Networks, an inter-university cooperative initiative.

Information regarding the mission and focus of this organization is also included on the home page under the heading UNESCO & Education. Also available are links to programs, budgets, and Web sites of related institutions. Of special note on the home page are links to information and materials related to the major initiatives of Education for All, the United Nations Literacy Decade (2003–2012), and the United Nations

Decade of Education and Sustainable Development (2005–2014). Education for All links to full-text documents and reports of major global world conferences on education.

NONGOVERNMENTAL SOURCE

Social Science Information Gateway: Education
Web site, by the Institute for Education, University of London. <http://www.sosig.ac.uk/education/>

Summary: Compiled by the Institute for Education at the University of London, this site links to Internet resources arranged into the categories: editor's choice (key resources), bibliographic databases, bibliographies, books/book equivalents, data, documents/digests, educational materials, government publications, governmental bodies, journals (contents, abstracts, and full text), mailing lists/discussion groups, news, organizations/societies, papers/reports/articles (collections), reference materials, research projects/centers, resource guides, and software. The topic of education is subdivided into Adult Education, Educational Policy, Educational Theory, Elementary Education, Further Education, Higher Education, Primary Education, Secondary Education, Special Education, Teaching Methods, Training of Teachers and Educators, and Vocational Education. Each of these topics links to the same types of Internet resources, although not all categories may contain all types.

RESEARCH STRATEGIES

The *International Bureau of Education* Web site, with its more global focus, is an excellent place to begin the research process. The various databases, especially *Country Dossiers, World Data on Education,* and *RelatED,* included on this site provide access to information about educational systems for individual countries. Comparisons of systems can also be made here. In addition, the bibliographic catalog *IBEDOCS* can be searched for the full text of publications.

The *UNESCO* Web site is another source with a global focus. Information can be accessed on a variety of topics. The *World Bank's Education* Web site also uses a themed approach to describe its initiatives.

The nongovernmental *Social Science Information Gateway: Education* Web site is a comprehensive source of relevant Internet sites for a variety of material types. In addition to the broad heading of Edu-

cation, resources can be identified for more specialized education subject areas.

For more regional coverage, especially for Europe, the *Council of Europe* and *European Commission* Web sites both are the best starting places. The European Commission site, in particular, provides in-depth coverage of the many educational initiatives being conducted across Europe.

All of the sites include statistical coverage, but for the most in-depth statistics, the *Organisation for Economic Co-operation and Development's OECD Directorate for Education* Web site is the place to go. Many of the statistics can be downloaded into Microsoft Excel and cover a broad range of subjects. The *World Bank's Education* Web site also is a statistical resource, especially its *EdStats* database.

FOR FURTHER READING: COMPREHENSIVE WEB SITES AND OTHER REFERENCE SOURCES

Education at a Glance: OECD Indicators, compiled by the Centre for Educational Research and Innovation. Paris: Organisation for Economic Co-operation and Development, 1992–.

This annual publication, published since 1992, provides statistical indicators and background information on international education. Topics covered include demographic, social, and economic context; financial resources; access to education; learning environments; achievement; graduates; and labor market outcomes. The date of coverage varies according to the topic, and there are also graphs and tables to supplement the statistics.

Southeast Asian Ministers of Education Organization (SEAMEO) Web site, Bangkok, Thailand. <http://www.seameo.org/>

Established in 1965 as a chartered international organization, the *Southeast Asian Ministers of Education Organization's (SEAMEO)* purpose is to promote cooperation in education, science, and culture in the Southeast Asian region. There are 10 member countries as well as associate and affiliate member countries. Members include Brunei Darussalam, Cambodia, Indonesia, Lao PDR, Malaysia, Myanmar, Philippines, Singapore, Thailand, and Viet Nam. Associate member countries include Australia, Canada, France, Germany, Netherlands, and New Zealand and one affiliate member, the International Council for Open and Distance Education (ICDE). Of special importance are the Publications and Virtual Library home page categories. From both of these points the full text of many reports, monographs, and documents are available online at no charge. The Library category includes a search engine that allows searching by title, author, subject or keyword, and year.

Statistical Yearbook/Annuaire Statistique, by the UNESCO Institute for Statistics. Paris: UNESCO Publishing, 1963–1999 (ISSN 0082-7541).

Statistical Yearbook has been published annually since 1963, and the 1999 edition was the last in this format. This volume presents statistical tables on different educational and related subjects, with education comprising the bulk of the publication. Statistics for education include literacy, enrollments, distribution, and public expenditure. The time period coverage varies according to the statistical table.

World Education Encyclopedia: A Survey of Educational Systems Worldwide, edited by Rebecca Marlow-Ferguson. Farmington Hills, Mich.: Gale Group, 2002 (ISBN 0-78765-577-5).

Arranged alphabetically by country name, this three-volume set, provides a narrative essay on each country's educational system. Each entry also includes a brief bibliography. Educational statistical tables are proved in the appendices, and there is an index.

NOTES

1. European Commission, Directorate-General for Education and Culture, *Education and Training Programmes and Actions Home Page: Socrates: Arion* Web site, <http://europa.eu.int/comm/education/socrates/arion/index_en.html>.

2. European Commission, Directorate-General for Education and Culture, *Education and Training Programmes and Actions Home Page: Socrates: NARIC (National Academic Recognition Information Centre)* Web site, <http://europa.eu.int/comm/education/socrates/agenar.html>.

3. European Commission, Directorate-General for Education and Culture, *Education and Training Actions and Initiatives Home Page: eLearning: Overview* Web site, <http://europa.eu.int/comm/education/elearning/intro_en.html>.

4. European Commission, Directorate-General for Education and Culture, *Education and Training Actions and Initiatives Home Page: Jean Monnet Project: Introduction to the Jean Monnet Project* Web site <http://europa.eu.int/comm/education/ajm/ajm/index_en.html>.

5. European Commission, Directorate-General for Education and Culture, *Education and Training Actions and Initiatives Home Page: Libraries: European Commission Central Library: European Commission Union Catalogue (ECLAS)* Web site, <http://europa.eu.int/comm/libraries/catalogues/index_en.htm>.

CHAPTER 8
Energy

CHAPTER OVERVIEW

Energy and its future is an increasing concern in global affairs. Conventional sources, such as oil and coal, are in danger of being depleted, and even water, a source of hydroelectricity, is becoming scarce in some areas. The instability of governments whose countries are chief producers of oil increases concern about ready supplies of one of the chief sources of energy for the world. Science is constantly working to develop new sources, but the use and disposition of by-products of sources such as nuclear energy are another set of problems addressed by international government agencies.

This chapter discusses major international intergovernmental and nongovernmental agencies, such as the *International Energy Agency,* that either monitor or are involved with producing the various types of world energy sources. These agencies document their work through data, reports, publications, legal instruments, and major conferences.

Governmental Sources Discussed

Activities of the European Union: Energy Web site, by the European Union, Brussels, Belgium. <http://europa.eu.int/pol/ener/index_en.htm>

European Energy Foundation Web site, Brussels, Belgium. <http://www.f-e-e.org/>

International Atomic Energy Agency (IAEA) Web site, Vienna, Austria. <http://www.iaea.org/>

International Energy Agency Resources

International Energy Agency (IEA) Web site, Paris, France. <http://www.iea.org/>

World Energy Outlook, by the Economic Analysis Division, International Energy Agency. Paris: Organisation for Economic Co-operation and Development, 1977– (print annual title and online subscription; earlier issues free of charge online). <http://www.worldenergyoutlook.org/weo/pubs/index.asp>

OECD Nuclear Energy Agency Web site, by the Organisation for Economic Co-operation and Development (OECD), Paris, France. <http://www.nea.fr/>

Organization of the Petroleum Exporting Countries (OPEC) Web site, Vienna, Austria. <http://www.opec.org/>

Organization of Arab Petroleum Exporting Countries (OAPEC) Web site, Kuwait City, Kuwait. <http://www.oapecorg.org/>

United Nations Resources

Energy Statistics Yearbook, by the Department of Economic and Social Information and Policy Analysis, Statistical Division, United Nations. New York: United Nations, 1982– (print periodical title and CD) (ISSN 0256-6400).

United Nations Statistics Division Energy Statistics Web site, New York. <http://unstats.un.org/unsd/energy/>

United States Energy Information Agency International Web site, Washington, D.C. <http://www.eia.doe.gov/emeu/international/>

Nongovernmental Sources Discussed

World Energy Council Web site, London. <http://www.worldenergy.org/>

World Nuclear Association Web site, London. <http://www.world-nuclear.org/index.htm>

GOVERNMENTAL SOURCES

Activities of the European Union: Energy Web site, by the European Union, Brussels, Belgium. <http://europa.eu.int/pol/ener/index_en.htm>

Summary: A comprehensive portal reporting on the energy policy of the European Union (EU), available in all 11 official languages of the EU, this site links to energy information within the EU and through its many organizational units, including the European Commission and Council of Europe. Categories include In Brief, Latest Developments (with sections entitled Key Sites and Documentation), and *A Comprehensive Guide to European Law* (with sections entitled Summaries and Legal Texts). Also provided are a category on What's New, searching of the entire *EU* Web site, a glossary, and the basic links available from all the major *EU* Web sites, including News, Activities, Institutions, The EU at a Glance, Official Documentation, Information Sources, and links to 30 theme Web sites on varying subjects of importance within the EU, including this one on energy.

Detailed Description: The home page category In Brief links researchers to an overview of the energy policies and concerns of the EU and related documents, including links to texts of other strategy papers and the treaties behind the energy policies of this organization.

Another home page category is Key Sites, which links to the European Commission's Energy theme page, a rich source of information on energy policy, markets, nuclear security, oil and gas, infrastructure, and the effect of war on energy. The European Commission is the executive body and driving force for the EU, and much of this information is produced by the European Commission's Directorate-General for Energy and Transport (TREN). This energy theme page also provides detailed information on energy sources and demand management in the following areas: coal, oil, gas, electricity, nuclear energy, as well as new and renewable energy sources and energy demand management. For each link to an energy source such as oil, detailed information is available, including background documents, legislation, treaties, and price and market information. The European Commission's Energy theme page also provides information under the category Support Programmes, which are links to Web sites on European Commission energy programs such as its Trans-European energy networks "TEN-E"; RTD Framework Programmes; "Energy" Framework Programme" (1998–2002); European Local & Regional Energy Management Activities; and Intelligent Energy for Europe 2003–2006. Under Newsletter, the European Commission's energy site links to an online monthly newsletter entitled *Energy and Transport in Europe Digest* (beginning with no. 1, April 2002), a look at background information and weekly energy developments in Europe, and there are also links to press releases and to EU publications specifically relating to energy, some of which are available at no charge, either in print or online.

In addition to linking to the energy theme page of the European Commission, the category Key Sites also links to energy information for the European Parliament, the Council of the European Union, the European Ombudsman, EURATOM, the European Investment Bank, and AGORES. The European Parliament links to the Committee on Industry, External Trade, Research and Energy and permits researchers access to online documents, committee hearings, and news from the European Parliament on energy and other concerns of this committee. The link for the Council of the European Union leads researchers to online documents concerning energy, as well as transports and telecommunications, and the documents are available full text in PDF format at no charge. EURATOM leads to the European Atomic Energy Community (Euratom) Supply Agency, whose mission is to ensure a regular and equitable supply of nuclear fuels for community users. The European Investment Bank's mission is to further the objectives of the European Union by making long-term finance available for sound investment, and it publishes documents and information on projects and loans in the area of energy. Finally, there is a link to AGORES, a global overview of renewable energy sources, which is described separately in this chapter and is an effort under the Directorate-General for Energy and Transport.

The home page category of Documentation provides further access to information on energy published by the European Union, including press releases; a link to its journal, the *Bulletin of the European Union;* a link to the section on energy from the current issue of its *General Report on the Activities of the European Union;* publications (specifically energy); statistics (including some free data and statistical publications online); and information and publications on the European Coal and Steel Community (ECSC), established by treaty for 50 years, 1952–2002.

Another major category from the home page is the pertinent subsections of *A Comprehensive Guide to European Law* that apply to energy such as summaries of legislation and legal texts. The summaries of legislation contain an overview of energy policies, programs, and actions within the European Union and summaries for the topics: security of energy supply, internal market in energy, energy and sustainable development, energy efficiency, renewable energy sources, taxation of energy products, Trans-European networks, relations with third countries, and applicant countries. Legal texts provide researchers ready access to legal research within the European Communities on energy, including treaties, and legislation in force. The treaties are the Treaty establishing the European Atomic Energy Community (EURATOM), the Treaty establishing the European Coal and Steel Community, and the Treaty establishing the European Community (Title III, Title XV, Title XIX). Legislation is under legislation in force and legislation in preparation and monitoring of the decision-making process between institutions, including Commission proposals; Search in the Legislative Observatory of the European Parliament; Search in the Public Register of the Council of the European Union; Search in PreLex; Opinions of the European Economic and Social Committee; Opinions of the Committee of the Regions; Recent Case Law of the Court of Justice and the Court of First Instance; and Recent Case Law of the Court of Justice and the Court of First Instance. Of particular note is the online title *The ABC of Community Law,* which serves as background reading for understanding legal research.

European Energy Foundation Web site, Brussels, Belgium. <http://www.f-e-e.org/>

Summary: This organization provides a neutral information forum on energy being discussed within the political arena of the European Union. Its Web site facilitates the exchange of information between parliamentary representatives, members of the European Commission, European civil servants and other authorities, and principally, the industrial and scientific sectors and all other interested parties. The site is organized into categories that include About EEF, Agenda, Newsletter, Files, Forum, Members, Links, and Site Map. For the purpose of this discussion, the categories of Agenda, Newsletter, and Files will be described.

Detailed Description: The Agenda home page category features summary reports of EEF's presentations at meetings and summary reports on projects. Under the Newsletter home page link is the EEF's *Monthly Newsletter,* which is archived online, described in highlights, and contains summaries of administrative and legal texts; case law of the Court of Justice of the European Union; press releases; links to information from conferences, meetings, and other events; news; and official documents, such as COM documents. Much of the information is linked from the HTML newsletter online.

The category Files provides researchers with a searchable database of online publications. This section compiles the publications from the EEF (articles from the administrative and legal texts newsletter and from the general newsletter and the summaries of debates and visits). The news sources found here include: European Institutions' Web sites (mainly the *Official Journal of the European Communities,* the Commission's *Bulletin,* press releases, and databases); Correspondents' Web sites (chiefly the Energy Charter Treaty, the International Atomic Energy Agency, the International Energy Agency, the Organisation for Economic Cooperation and Development / Nuclear Energy Agency, the Organisation of Petroleum Exporting Countries, and the World Energy Council); EEF members' Web sites; and finally, general or specialized media Web sites.

International Atomic Energy Agency (IAEA) Web site, Vienna, Austria. <http://www.iaea.org/>

Summary: The International Atomic Energy Agency (IAEA) acts as the world's central intergovernmental forum for scientific and technical cooperation in the atomic energy field. Although it is in the United Nations family, it is an independent intergovernmental agency focused on nuclear cooperation. The home page provides information under the categories: About the IAEA, Our Work, News Center, Publications, and Data Center. Searching of the site is provided on the home page, as well as an A–Z index and an e-mail news service. The organization sells books, periodicals, and multimedia online. All electronic documents on the Web site may be downloaded free of charge and are in PDF format. Its main periodical, the *IAEA Bulletin,* is available online at no charge.

Detailed Description: The home page category About the IAEA provides a profile of its resources and organizational structure and links to information on its policy-making organs, the IAEA General Conference, the IAEA Board of Governors, and its member states. It also contains information on the organizations mission, mandates, history, and strategy documents. The Our Work home page category organizes information under Promoting Safeguards and Verification, Promoting Safety and Security, and Promoting Science and Technology, with each section leading to information on the programs and activities of the IAEA, including online documents and publications, articles, guidelines, and even texts of treaties.

The News Center home page category provides full-text access to the latest top stories (2000–), feature stories, press releases (1995–), media advisories (2001–), events calendar (current year), multimedia such as photos, film and video clips (1928–), and transcripts of briefings and interviews. In addition there is a section titled In Focus, with links to documents and publications pertaining to the IAEA and Iran, the Democratic People's Republic of Korea, Iraq, and the Nuclear Non-Proliferation Treaty.

The Publications home page category contains scientific and technological publications; international standards, guides, and codes; IAEA reports and reviews; IAEA documents and conventions; magazines, journals, and newsletters; booklets and topical articles; fact sheets and FAQ; and education, training, and related resources. Some sales publications provide a link to full text. Special interest publications are also featured, as well as new publications. The documents and conventions subcategory includes the IAEA's *Annual Report* in full text from 1999 on; Information Circulars, searchable by year, by category, by number, and by country; and Legal Agreements, as well as the text of the IAEA state and the Nuclear Non-Proliferation Agreement. The Information Circulars are available from 1996 forward in full-text PDF format, with a few published in 1995, and cover topics of general interest that the IAEA wishes to bring to the attention of its member states. Also under the documents and conventions subcategory is the section Legal Agreements which includes full text of Conventions & Agreements under IAEA auspices; IAEA Related Treaties and Conventions; and also UN Security Council Resolutions in PDF format and in selected languages.

From the home page under Publications, the magazines, journals, and newsletters subcategory provides access to the *IAEA Bulletin: Quarterly Journal of the IAEA,* the flagship journal of the International Atomic Energy Agency, available in print and online formats. Articles from the *IAEA Bulletin* are online at no charge in PDF format. Published four times a year since 1959 in English, French, Spanish, Russian, and Chinese editions, the *IAEA Bulletin* features articles covering various applications of nuclear energy, as well as IAEA programs and projects. Of special mention is the link to the IAEA library and its online catalog, which allows searching by title, author, subject, and free-text keyword.

Data Center is the final home page category discussed. This category is divided into statistics and forecasts, IAEA databases, scientific networks and services, and program sites. IAEA databases contain information about atomic energy for countries of the world. Some of the major databases include: Atomic Molecular Information System (AMDIS), Interna-

tional Nuclear Information System (INIS), Global Network of Isotopes in Precipitation (GNIP), Nuclear Data Information System (NDIS), Power Reactor Information System (PRIS), and others. A listing of online databases in a *Directory of IAEA Databases* provides a name and acronym list and allows full text searching.

International Energy Agency Resources

International Energy Agency (IEA) Web site, Paris, France. <http://www.iea.org/>

Summary: The International Energy Agency (IEA), with a membership of 26 countries, serves as an "energy forum." This comprehensive, searchable Web site provides access to global energy information and to many of the publications and statistics of the International Energy Agency. It includes news articles, highlights of publications and statistics, and information on energy in many forms, including oil, gas, coal, and electricity. Categories on the *International Energy Agency* home page include Statistics, *Oil Market Report, World Energy Outlook,* About IEA, Energy Information Centre, News & Events, Publications & Online Bookshop, and For Delegates. Also highlighted on the home page are news and topics of the month. Publications are available online at no charge as well as fee-based publications that are downloadable and available in varying formats.

Detailed Description: This discussion will focus on the information organized under the following major home page categories: Energy Information Centre, News & Events, Publications & Online Bookshop, Statistics, *Oil Market Report,* and *World Energy Outlook.* The Energy Information Centre home page category features a topics list with links to relevant documents, publications, and Web sites. Keyword and country searching is also included.

The News & Events home page category links to the full text of various newsletters and reports. Search engines are available for press releases, speeches, and presentations.

Publications & Online Bookshop, another home page category, provides information pertaining to sales publications and subscription titles. Access to publications is organized under Statistics, Country Reviews, Studies, Free Publications, Papers and Documents, *Monthly Oil Market Report,* and Forthcoming Publications. Keyword searching is included via a pull-down menu of terms. The Free Publications subcategory links to some online issues of the country review series of reports (PDF format), which focus on the energy policies of IEA member countries. It also provides full text of the current annual report entitled *Key World Energy Statistics* (PDF format) and other reports and studies on specific countries at no charge.

Some of the IEA's most significant titles from a library reference point of view are its publications on energy statistics. These include titles with similar coverage: *Energy Statistics of OECD Countries* and *Energy Statistics of Non-OECD Countries* (also available in CD-ROM). They contain data for individual countries on energy supply and demand for coal, oil, gas, electricity, heat, waste, and combustible renewables, along with historical data tables. Definitions of products and flows and explanatory notes on individual country data are also included. The CD-ROM includes a greater range of historical data back to 1960. Along with several other CD-ROM titles, these make up the CD subscription service *World Energy Statistics,* intended to be used in conjunction with the related paper titles for an impressive resource on world energy. It contains annual energy statistics and energy balances for 30 OECD countries for the years 1960– and energy statistics and balances for more than 100 non-OECD countries for the years 1971–.

Linking under the Statistics home page category are some free statistical publications. One is the online reference title *Key World Energy Statistics,* published annually, which provides summary information of supply, transformation, and consumption of major energy sources, free online in PDF format. It includes an energy outlook, statistics, and a glossary. Another free annual title, first published in 2002, is the *Renewables Information,* which contains comprehensive information on the use of renewables and waste in the OECD region, covering principles issues, analysis, and detailed country statistical tables. The first issue is provided free of charge and can currently be ordered in print, although this may not continue. In addition, free online monthly titles with statistics are *Monthly Electricity Survey, Monthly Price Statistics, Monthly Natural Gas Survey,* and *Monthly Oil Survey,* all available in PDF or Microsoft Excel formats.

Subscription services available from the Statistics category are IEA's *Online Data Services.* Serious statistical researchers may purchase access to query IEA's many online statistical databases on energy. These data may be downloaded in several different formats for file manipulation. Another database made available free of charge is on government budget for research and development in the energy field. In English and French, this database includes government energy and technology research and development budgets and economics indicators (used for deflating and currency conversion) by country, by product, and more. Finally the Statistics category has a Unit Converter for energy, mass, and volume.

A separate category from the IEA home page, the *Oil Market Report* is a monthly report on oil highlights, world overview, prices, demand, supply, trade, and statistics that is available online from 2001 at no charge. Related information on oil supply security is under the category of the same name from the home page and gives further information on this topic, including a free download of the comprehensive title *Oil Supply Security: The Emergency Response Potential of IEA Countries in 2000,* which IEA publishes every five years.

The reference title *World Energy Outlook,* by the International Energy Agency, also a category from the home page, is described separately in this chapter. *Country Studies,* also a category on the home page, links to sales titles for individual countries that analyze and review the country's energy policy. Each is titled *Energy Policies of IEA Countries* (country's name). A small bit of information provided online includes a table of contents, executive summary and sample statistical tables. Environment is a separate subject category that organizes sustainable development information and climate change information from the agency, including links to publications, news, and conference and activity reports. This is also how the subject categories from the home page on Energy Markets, Energy Technology, Renewable Energy, and Energy Efficiency organize access to information.

Finally the category About IEA contains its objective and background, member countries, a three-volume online history, goals, speeches, organization, and press releases. Also included is information on IEA workshops and conferences and its committees.

World Energy Outlook, by the Economic Analysis Division, International Energy Agency. Paris: Organisation for Economic Co-operation and Development, 1977– (print annual title and online subscription; earlier issues free of charge online). <http://www.worldenergyoutlook.org/weo/pubs/index.asp>

Summary: A reference title on global energy issues covering the world and 18 major regions, the *World Energy Outlook* presents projections for approximately 25 years on the supply and demand of oil, gas, coal, renewable energy sources, nuclear power, and electricity. It also analyzes energy security, trade and investment, and global efforts to reduce energy-related carbon dioxide emissions. Statistical data and charts support the text. From 1997–1993 publication was irregular, but beginning in 1993 it became an annual publication.

Detailed Description: Some earlier issues are available in full-text PDF format free of charge. For subscription issues, this Web site provides information such as press releases, table of contents, executive summary, and sample charts from the title, but for full text online, the title must be purchased. Also available from this site are presentation papers from workshops and conferences relating to the data in this title.

A related series of sales publications is the IEA's *World Energy Outlook: Insights* series, which reports on a single aspect of energy such as subsidies (1999 issue) and global supply (2001 issue).

OECD Nuclear Energy Agency (NEA) Web site, Paris, France. <http://www.nea.fr/>

Summary: The Nuclear Energy Agency, a specialized agency of the Organisation for Economic Co-operation and Development (OECD), provides information for the nuclear energy related activities of the member nations of OECD. It is a major publisher in this area, but most publications are sales and available online at no charge. The Web site is available in English and French, is searchable, and provides a site map. Information is organized under the categories About (the agency), Themes, Databank, Publications, Search, and Delegates' Area, along with highlights of press releases and new publications. Researchers may link directly to its major periodical online, *NEA News,* and to nuclear facts and figures. Also the home page highlights the work areas of the OECD, organizing access to information under Nuclear Safety, Radioactive Waste, Radiation Protection, Nuclear Development, Nuclear Science, Nuclear Law, Data Bank, Joint Projects, Sustainable Development, and Civil Society.

Detailed Description: About, a category on the main home page, links to the organizational information, including its mission, a list of member countries, staff and budget, areas of work within the organization (linking references for additional information), and the strengths of the agency, with general information on nuclear energy. The home page category Search provides searching capabilities by keyword of the *Nuclear Energy Agency* Web site and a searchable direc-

tory of addresses, as well as a site map with links to the various subjects contained on the Web site. These same topics are included in the Themes and Publications home page categories. The category Themes links to further information about these subjects: nuclear safety, radioactive waste, radioactive protection, nuclear development, nuclear science, nuclear law, joint projects, and Eastern Europe, and under these subjects, further links to goals, objectives, projects, conference activities, news, reports, documents, and publications.

The Publications category organizes information in the sections By Subject, Recently Published, and NEA News and Policy Papers. By Subject provides an alphabetical list of available titles as well as a detailed publications list by year, with each entry comprised of full citation, annotation, and whether it can be obtained for a fee or for free. Recently Published is arranged the same way as By Subject.

NEA News, linked on the home page and under the Publications category, is the journal of the NEA. It features articles on current nuclear energy issues, radiation protection, radioactive waste management, nuclear safety, and nuclear legislation. Each issue provides facts and opinions about nuclear energy, along with an update of NEA activities, news, and recent publications. Only the table of contents (PDF format) and several sample articles from the latest issues are provided at no charge, as this is a subscription title available in print and online formats. Earlier issues (1993–1999) have the table of contents listed online. The subcategory NEA Policy Papers, which is linked from the home page and under the Publications category, provides online summary information on various topics, including general interest, nuclear safety and regulation, radioactive waste management, and radiation protection. These provide an overview of research and policy on current topics and are available in PDF format, mostly in English and French. A subsection of earlier similar papers provided under a link at the bottom of the page is under *NEA Issue Briefs* (1987–1994).

Data Bank is another home page category. Use of the online services in the Data Bank are subject to authorization procedures, which involve contacting the NEA Data Bank or the liaison officer of the user's establishment to obtain permission. In order to protect the Data Bank's collection of data and programs, users are assigned a confidential password only through agreed nomination procedures. Special authorization is required for access to restricted services. Various subscription distribution lists are available for news and updates.

Nuclear Facts and Figures is a category of information featured on the home page of the NEA that contains a table of current statistics on and links to several complete reports, including the title *Nuclear Energy Data,* which provides detailed data covering total and nuclear electricity generation and capacity, the status of nuclear power plants, and supply and demand for nuclear fuel cycle services. Another category on the NEA's home page NEA Press Room provides press kits with introductory information on nuclear issues, which can be searched by keyword and register. Latest news is also featured, along with a news archive and access to news organized by theme.

The OECD Energy Directorate icon at the top of the NEA page links to other energy-related information from the OECD, including information organized under climate change, energy, and transportation, and links back to the Nuclear Energy Agency and to the International Energy Agency. It features OECD sales publications on energy and also may be accessed through <http://www.oecd.org/> under the energy link.

Organization of Arab Petroleum Exporting Countries (OAPEC) Web site, Kuwait City, Kuwait.
<http://www.oapecorg.org>

Summary: This Arab cooperative organization was established in 1968 with a membership of 11 countries. The Web site, available in English and Arabic, organizes its content under the major categories About OAPEC, OAPEC Activities, 7th AEC (the current conference), Publications, OAPEC Awards, Seminars, and Links. The Web site is searchable and provides a link to searching capabilities and a link to Contents, an online contents index.

Detailed Description: The About OAPEC home page category links to brief information about member countries, OAPEC organizational structure, joint Arab action, and Arab and international relations. The latter explains the role OAPEC plays in joint sponsorship of the regular meeting called the Arab Energy Conference, sponsored in partnership with the Arab Fund for Economic and Social Development, which first met in 1979. The second category, OAPEC Activities, leads to a brief online report of current concerns and issues OAPEC and its ministers are involved with and recent meetings attended.

The category, 7th AEC, or Arab Energy Conference, reports on the background and history of this regular meeting, specifically on the 7th meeting held in Cairo,

April 2002, and on earlier meetings. It contains information including the conference program (English), conference conclusions (PDF report in Arabic only), and statements of conference participants in Arabic.

Under the home page category Publications, OAPEC provides online access to many periodical titles and also publishes monographs in English, Arabic, and French. Titles included are *Secretary General's Annual Report* (online free of charge, 1998– in English and Arabic), *Annual Statistical Report* (online 1999– in PDF format with both English and Arabic in one volume), *OAPEC Monthly Bulletin* online 2002– in English), *Oil and Arab Cooperation* (abstracts of articles online 1998– in Arabic), *Energy Resources Monitor* (print format only), and *Arab Energy Data* (online at no charge in English and Arabic and in PDF format).

Other miscellaneous information from the OAPEC home page includes information on awards, seminars, and conferences to be held by OAPEC and links to the Ministry of Oil, Kuwait.

Organization of the Petroleum Exporting Countries (OPEC) Web site, Vienna, Austria.
<http://www.opec.org/>

Summary: With a membership of 11 countries (Algeria, Indonesia, Iran, Iraq, Kuwait, Libya, Nigeria, Qatar, Saudi Arabia, the United Arab Emirates, and Venezuela), OPEC's primary mission is to promote stable and fair oil prices that benefit both oil producers and consumers by balancing the oil market. Information on the Web site is organized under these categories: About OPEC, News & Info, Member Countries, Meetings, OPEC/NA, Publications, FAQs, and Contact OPEC. In addition to these categories, the Web site provides general information and information on current oil prices, climate change, and OPEC statistics. Statistical periodicals on oil markets and production are online at no charge, as well as being available on paper for a subscription fee.

Detailed Description: The home page category About OPEC describes the organization and also links to members and general information available elsewhere on the site. The category News & Info provides access to three types of information under press releases, speeches, and general information. Press Releases links to details of the organization's agreements to limit crude oil output and other important decisions, whereas the speeches online are from OPEC's senior officials. General information is a link to an online booklet with general information about the founding, background, aims, and objectives of OPEC. From the home page, the category Member Country also links to the clickable map for information concerning each member country (text links available), including basic facts and figures, links to the country's Web site and directory information on the country's OPEC governor, national representative, and national oil company.

Under the home page category Meetings is a calendar of world oil and energy events and detailed information on OPEC conferences, including information on ministers and press releases for conferences. OPEC/NA links to OPEC's News Agency, which provides e-mail and paper subscription news.

The Publications home page category lists the following titles, available both online at no charge in PDF format or in print for a subscription fee: *Monthly Oil Market Report, Annual Statistical Bulletin,* the *OPEC Annual Report,* the *OPEC Statute,* and the monthly *OPEC Bulletin.* An interactive CD is also available for purchase, which features tables, charts, and graphs detailing the world's oil and gas reserves, crude oil and product output, exports, refining, tankers, plus economic and other data. OPEC's main periodical, the monthly *OPEC Bulletin,* features news from member countries, articles, analysis of current and topical issues, and a review of the oil market (available online in PDF format or on Zip file for downloading). The *OPEC Review* is a quarterly academic journal featuring research articles on energy economics and related issues from around the world and is available only through subscription through a private publisher, Blackwell Publishers, and a link is provided for more information. The *Annual Statistical Bulletin* contains nearly 150 pages of tables, charts, and graphs detailing the world's oil and gas reserves, crude oil and product output, exports, refining, and tankers, plus economic and other data, and also is available in PDF or Zip formats from 1999 forward. The *Monthly Oil Market Report,* available in PDF, also is archived online from January 2000 on and covers developments in the world economy, data on oil prices, supply and demand, crude and product stocks, and much more. *OPEC's Annual Report* is online in PDF and Zip for 2001 and contains reviews of OPEC member countries' economic performances and the world oil market, activities of the OPEC Secretariat, and listings of OPEC officials. The *OPEC Statute* is a PDF document outlining the organization's principle aims. The General Information booklet is also available from this Publications category.

The category FAQs provides information about OPEC and also about the petroleum industry as well as crude oil and its uses. The petroleum industry links to brief discussions on 14 issues concerning global oil reserves, the global oil market, oil prices, and related issues. Questions can be submitted by e-mail.

United Nations Resources

Energy Statistics Yearbook, by the Department of Economic and Social Information and Policy Analysis, Statistical Division, United Nations. New York: United Nations, 1982– (print periodical title and CD) (ISSN 0256-6400).

Summary: This basic reference of statistical tables on power resources and energy industries contains text in both English and French. The *Yearbook* is a historical, comprehensive, and reliable reference source for global comparable data on energy, reporting on long-term statistical trends in the production, supply, and consumption of mainly commercial, primary, and secondary forms of energy. Valuable and precise data for each type of fuel and aggregate data for the total mix of commercial fuels for individual countries and areas are summarized into regional and world totals. Statistics for five years are reported for more than 215 countries and areas in the world, including data on production, trade, and consumption of solid, liquid, and gaseous fuels and electricity.

Detailed Description: This annual title has been published since 1950 under various titles: the *Energy Statistics Yearbook* (1982–), the *Yearbook of World Energy Statistics* (1979–1981), and the *World Energy Supplies* (1950–1978). The United Nations document number is a constant, being ST/ESA/STAT/SER.J/ with the number of edition after the last slash. More information about the Yearbook and the CD (a noninteractive electronic data), including ordering information, can be found on the agency's Web page.

United Nations Statistics Division Energy Statistics Web site, New York. <http://unstats.un.org/unsd/energy/>

Summary: As the main statistics collection agency of the United Nations, one such statistical area for which it collects and disseminates data is in the area of energy, including information on energy balances and electricity profiles. Energy statistics are collected from more than 190 countries. It also maintains the Energy Statistics Database, a comprehensive statistical database with energy statistics from

1950 for individual countries, which is available through purchase.

Information on this agency's Web site is organized under the following categories: Description of Activities, Energy Yearbook, Energy Balances and Electricity Profiles, Energy Statistics Database on CD and in Electronic Format, Joint Oil Data Initiative (JODI) Database, UNSD Annual Energy Questionnaires, Publications, and Contact Us. The Energy Yearbook links to further information on the reference title *Energy Statistics Yearbook,* described separately in this chapter.

Detailed Description: The home page category on Energy Balances links to downloadable online information from the agency's regularly published biennial publication, *Energy Balances and Electricity Profile* (New York: United Nations, 1980–). This title contains energy data for selected countries, including energy production, conversion, and consumption for fuels utilized in the country. The following sections of only the most recent title are online: concepts and definition, table notes, abbreviations, conversion factors, and tables. Tables may be downloaded in Microsoft Excel format.

Another link from the home page, the *Energy Statistics Database,* contains comprehensive energy statistics on more than 215 countries, regions, and areas for new and renewable sources of energy and energy production, trade, and consumption. Information entered into the database is gathered through a questionnaire sent to statistical offices and ministries of energy or otherwise responsible for energy statistics in a country. The data set from 1950 on is available for purchase in CD or other electronic formats.

The home page category Joint Oil Data Initiative (JODI) links to another activity of the United Nations Statistics Division within the scope of energy statistics: its project on monthly oil statistics. The United Nations Statistics Division collaborates with five other international organizations involved in oil statistics (Asia Pacific Energy Research Center [APERC], EUROSTAT, International Energy Agency [IEA/OECD], Latin American Energy Organization [OLADE], and Organization of Petroleum Exporting Countries [OPEC]), which aims to investigate the differences in definitions, unit of measurement used, and methodologies.

Publications, another category on the home page, lists selected energy publications published by the United Nations Statistics Division. Sales prices are listed, but many publications are also available free of charge online in PDF format and in various languages, especially English, French, and Spanish. Other major publications produced by this agency include a good source of energy data in the monthly title *Monthly Bulletin of Statistics* (1946–), which presents statistics on coal, crude petroleum, and electricity data, along with many other economic statistics. Covering 60 subjects from over 200 countries and territories, together with special tables illustrating important economic developments, it regularly provides quarterly data for significant world and regional aggregates and is available online as a subscription title.

From the home page, the category Questionnaire on Energy Statistics links to the questionnaire with which the agency collects data. It is available in PDF format in English, French, and Spanish.

United States Energy Information Agency International Web site, Washington, D.C.
<http://www.eia.doe.gov/emeu/international/>

Summary: Providing significant reference information via its online country database and publications, this statistical agency of the U.S. Department of Energy is an excellent source for international energy information, particularly in its online country database and publications. The site is searchable through its parent body, the Energy Information Agency. Featured topics from this page are the latest OPEC Fact Sheet, Country Analysis Briefs, Energy Chronologies, Energy Fact Sheets, Energy Supply Security, Energy Finance, Energy Data Exchanges, and the titles *International Energy Annual* and *International Energy Outlook.*

Detailed Description: Researchers may select individual countries from a drop-down box on the home page to view related statistical data on energy. Also specific energy topics, such as total energy, petroleum, natural gas, electricity, coal, prices, environment, and forecasts/analyses, can be selected in order to view statistical reports. The reports, located under the countries and topics, may be in HTML, PDF, or Microsoft Excel formats. Country reports lead to data and country analyses briefs, including energy balance sheets.

International Energy Annual, another link from the home page, has been published in print from 1979– and online since 1993– in PDF format. The current report is linked from the home page and earlier reports under Publications, then Archived Publications. This annual title provides information, trends, highlights, and data for petroleum, electricity, natural gas, coal, consumption, production, energy reserves, CO_2 emissions, population and GDP, and global energy prices. E-mail updates, a glossary, and related material supporting this title are also available online. One related publication is the *International Petroleum Monthly,* also available online.

A related title and another home page link, the annual publication *International Energy Outlook* is a significant reference title published in print 1985–, and the entire report is available free of charge online in PDF format 1995–, with the current issues in HTML and PDF. It contains highlights, outlook for world energy demand, growth in world energy use, energy prices, world consumption by energy resource, outlook for transportation energy use, and international energy forecasts as well as reporting on natural gas, coal, electricity, nuclear power, oil, hydroelectricity, and other renewable resources. Coverage of environmental issues and energy use is also included.

NONGOVERNMENTAL SOURCES

World Energy Council Web site, London.
  <http://www.worldenergy.org/>

Summary: As the "foremost global multienergy organization," this Web site contains information on all types of energy. Information is categorized into WEC Information, Energy Information, News and Events, Publications, Member Services, and GHG Reduction Projects. All information found on this site can be printed using the printer-friendly version.
Detailed Description: Energy Information, a home page category, is a source for statistical information. Links to the full text of principal publications, including *Survey of Energy Resources 2001* (the most current at the time of this writing), in full text has commentary and statistics, arranged by energy type; *Energy Efficiency Policies and Indicators* (2001), a study report published as the result of major energy conferences; *Energy Technologies for the 21st Century,* a research and development study; and *WEC/IIASA Scenarios,* which contains global energy scenarios/projections up to 2050. The Energy Information category also provides statistical searching via pull-down menus to view data by country, region, or fuel type. Combining search elements is not allowed. The results are comprehensive containing statistics and explanatory notes. A search box is also available. There are links to regional energy information and to

purchase information for the *2001 Survey of Energy Resources* CD-ROM.

News and Events is also a home page category. The WEC News section is only available to WEC members and requires registration. Energy News, another section, features reprints of relevant news articles from other news sources arranged by subject. Information pertaining to the most recent conference is also included.

The Publications home page category allows for browsing of titles and provides ordering information, although many are available in full text online at no charge. A link to online full-text free publications is also included. Publications are also categorized into Speeches, Congress Papers, Other Papers (those presented at meetings sponsored solely by WEC or in partnership), and Archives (press releases, speeches, technical papers) in full text. The full-text WEC Annual Reports from 1998 are also available here.

The final category, GHG Reduction, "is an industry initiative led by the WEC to record, on an interactive electronic database, the projects in which the global energy industry is involved and the reductions in Greenhouse Gas (GHG) emissions they are expected to achieve."[1] A brief explanation is included, as well as a search box/link to relevant WEC Congress papers.

World Nuclear Association Web site, London.
  <http://www.world-nuclear.org/index.htm>

Summary: The World Nuclear Association is an independent, nonprofit organization, funded primarily by membership subscriptions, whose Web site provides a Nuclear Portal containing an Introduction to Nuclear Energy for educational and school purposes, policy documents, information, reports and projects, and linking to other Web sites on nuclear energy. It lists and provides full text for major national and multinational policy documents and international treaties under the Policy Documents and Treaties link from the home page. The Nuclear Portal is regularly updated and strives to be comprehensive.

Other information on the home page is a list of the world's nuclear power reactor. Also, access to the nuclear energy theme information is available under an A–Z alphabetical list.

RESEARCH STRATEGIES

For basic energy information on nations of the world, a good place to begin is the *United States Energy Information Agency International* Web site under its link to online country information in the category Country Analysis Briefs. Users may select the country of choice from a drop-down box to see basic energy information on that country, information pulled from the International Energy Agency and other reliable sources.

Another global reference resource on energy with a focus on projected energy needs is the International Energy Agency's annual title *World Energy Outlook.* It projects energy needs for countries and regions for 25 years and for different types of energy (oil, gas, etc.) and provides statistical data along with analysis. This title is available in paper and electronically via subscription, although older editions can be accessed online at no charge. The International Energy Agency also publishes research publications on a wide variety of energy topics and provides a well-organized, searchable Publications category on its Web site that allows researchers to search by subject, by type of publication, and by publications that are online at no charge and those that are electronic subscriptions.

The nongovernmental organization the **World Energy Council** provides access to energy information across a wide range on its Web site, including reports, programs, case studies, and research. It provides information from a different point of view from the governmental agencies, and one of its objectives is outreach to the public.

For statistical data, the *International* Web site of the **United States Energy Information Agency** is a good place to start. Researchers will find historical data in its online annual and monthly publications, and if need be, they can retrieve older historical data by consulting these titles in print format prior to the electronic editions. Data is available for nations of the world and for monthly and annual statistics. Of particular note are these titles: the *International Energy Outlook* for forecasting energy use and production and the *International Energy Annual* for a global overview of types of energy and prices. The United States Energy Information Agency also publishes information monthly, such as its title *International Petroleum Monthly,* a source for global petroleum statistics. Researchers should check for its publications on other energy forms. Also, the preceding titles will footnote the sources of specific energy data and will lead researchers to titles with more information.

An international intergovernmental source for comparative energy data is the United Nations. The *United Nations Statistics Division Energy Statistics* Web site provides some free online data; however, most of its print and electronic publications are by subscription only. The major reference title *Energy Statistics Yearbook* is an excellent starting point for comparative global energy information by country and regions of the world, and because it has been published for many years, the CD version or the print versions will provide researchers with authoritative historical data. This agency is well known for its attention to methodology and harmonizing data.

The previously mentioned **International Energy Agency** is also an excellent source for comprehensive energy data. Some of its statistical reports are available online at no charge, including the title *Key World Energy Statistics,* with data by country. Its statistical journals by type of energy (i.e., oil, gas) are also online at no charge. However, its databases and major statistical publications and CD-ROMs are sales and subscription publications. A collection of statistical subscription publications in print and CD entitled *World Energy Statistics* and the IEA's databases online offer researchers historical energy information by individual country in different file formats. The agency also offers the option of purchasing data access privileges online for querying the IEA databases. The nongovernmental **World Energy Council** also provides in-depth statistical information and explanatory notes. Searching can be done by country, region, or fuel type.

For energy policy the best resource is again the **International Energy Agency (IEA),** which acts as a forum for coordinating the energy policies of 26 industrialized countries. It publishes regular editions of energy policies for individual member nations, and although the full titles are sales publications, summaries for each country are available online. The IEA addresses all types of energy sources; however, for specific types of energy, it is best to consult agencies focused on that type. Following are the major international intergovernmental agencies for nuclear energy and for oil.

The **Organisation for Economic Co-operation and Development (OECD)'s Nuclear Energy Agency (NEA)** specializes in coordinating activities on nuclear-related issues for the 28 OECD member countries.

The **International Atomic Energy Agency** is the premier international agency concerned with nuclear energy. Its Web site is a highly recommended beginning place for researchers at any level in the field of nuclear energy. Those interested in treaties and IAEA's reports on international conventions concerning nuclear arms and energy should consult the Documents category. Advanced researchers may want to immediately select the IAEA's Reference Center to consult its databases and to check out its directory of databases. It is notable that the agency provides all electronic documents on the Web site free of charge in PDF format. Its major journal, *IAEA Bulletin,* is also available online at no charge and is searchable, covering nuclear energy in a research context and reporting on projects and programs of the IAEA.

A nongovernmental resource for nuclear energy information is the **World Nuclear Association** Web site and its online Nuclear Portal. It links to a very wide variety of information, such as energy policies and treaties, and includes educational information.

For the subject of oil and petroleum production and revenue, researchers should consult the Web sites of the specific organizations, the **Organization of the Petroleum Exporting Countries (OPEC),** which provides basic introductory information and statistical data on its Web, and the organization for Arab oil-producing nations, the **Organization of Arab Petroleum Exporting Countries (OAPEC).** The *OAPEC* Web site also provides a wealth of electronic journal articles and statistical data on its Web site concerning oil and petroleum. Historical data is not provided electronically from these organizations, especially before 1998, but it is available in earlier print editions of the titles.

For regional specific energy statistics, users will want to consult the Web sites of the organizations concerned with energy in those regions, in particular for Europe, the *Activities of the European Union: Energy* Web site. Also described briefly under For Further Reading in this chapter are Web sites for the *Latin American Energy Organization* and the *Asia Pacific Economic Research Center (APERC).*

FOR FURTHER READING: COMPREHENSIVE WEB SITES AND OTHER REFERENCE SOURCES

Asia-Pacific Energy Research Center (APERC) Web site, Tokyo, Japan. <http://www.ieej.or.jp/aperc/>

The Asia Pacific Energy Research Centre (APERC) was established in 1996 in Tokyo as an affiliated body to the Institute of Energy Economics, Japan, following the Action Agenda adopted by the APEC Economic Leaders at the Osaka Meeting in November 1995. Its prime objective is to foster member economies' understanding of future energy supply, demand, trends, and associated energy policy implications. Activities include conducting joint energy research activities

and preparing reports on energy supply, demand, and outlook. APERC authors the title *APEC Energy Demand and Supply Outlook,* coordinating work with the Asia Pacific Economic Co-operation (APEC) organization and also providing access to the title electronically on its own Web site. The Web site provides a list of Web links of authoritative sources of energy information.

BP Amoco Statistical Review of World Energy Web site. <http://www.bp.com/worldenergy/>

This Web site provides a global statistical review of energy on the Web, which includes information on resources and energy use. Online access to information in the print publication is provided through different formats: Microsoft Excel and PowerPoint as well as PDF.

Comprehensive Nuclear Test Ban Treaty (CNTBT) Web site. <http://www.un.org/Depts/dda/WMD/ctbt/article_iv/index.html>

This treaty, which was opened for signatures in 1996, was not yet in force by the end of 2001. This Web site provides background information on the treaty, the issues, information about meetings, its status, and the draft final statement.

Energy.gov Web site, by the United States Department of Energy, Washington, D.C. <http://www.energy.gov>

Included in this resource are links to energy under World for national energy information and an A–Z index that covers national and worldwide energy topics. Under Resources on the top left are links to a National Library for energy resources on the Internet and free subscriptions. At the A–Z index, a user should check International energy for links to general information; *International Energy Supply Outlook,* an annual title; and individual nation fact sheets. Also under International Energy Initiatives, users will find topics of broad interest to many countries, including international agreements, power plant safety, international clean cities, and international sustainable energy development, as well as many others.

Center for Renewable Energy and Sustainable Technology (CREST) Web site, Washington, D.C. <http://www.crest.org/>

Information pertaining to renewable energy, energy efficiency, and sustainability available on the Internet is indexed here. Includes *Global Energy Marketplace (GEM),* a database that helps researchers find data, documents, and contacts on a worldwide level concerning renewable energy and energy efficiency.

Latin American Energy Organization Web site, San Carlos, Ecuador. <http://www.olade.org.ec/>

Energy statistics for Latin America and the Caribbean are published on this Web site, providing data for individual countries as well as textual summaries of the characteristics of the energy sector and the use of different power resources in each country. More information is available in the categories from the English home page: Publications, Documents and Reports, Energy Statistics, and Documentation Center. It also maintains a subscription resource entitled the *EEIS,* the *Energy Economic Information System,* as a comprehensive source of energy data for Latin America and the Caribbean. The Web site is published in English, French, Spanish, and Portuguese. Most of the publications are sales publications and are not available in English.

Technical Information (OSTI) by the United States Department of Energy, Office of Scientific and Technical Information (OSTI) Web site, Washington, D.C. <http://www.osti.gov/energycitations/>

This online searchable database is free online at no charge and contains bibliographic records for energy and energy-related scientific and technical information from the Department of Energy (DOE) as well as its predecessor agencies, the Energy Research & Development Administration (ERDA) and the Atomic Energy Commission (AEC). Many of these titles relate to international energy concerns and fall within these disciplines: chemistry, physics, materials, environmental science, geology, engineering, mathematics, climatology, oceanography, computer science, and related disciplines. It includes citations to report literature, conference papers, journal articles, books, dissertations, and patents. It contains citations from 1948 to the present and is currently kept updated. Researchers may search on bibliographic record, title, creator/author, subject, identifier numbers, publication date, system entry date, resource/document type, research organization, sponsoring organization, language, country, and/or combinations. It gives information on full-text availability.

NOTE

1. *World Energy Council* Web site, London. <http://www.worldenergy.org/wec-geis/ghg2001/ghgmain.asp>

CHAPTER 9
Environment

CHAPTER OVERVIEW

Included in this chapter are environmental resources that report and/or analyze environmental conditions and trends with a global emphasis. Environmental treaties (conventions) are covered either by description or through the links of the major resources described. Most resources in this chapter also provide information for many countries individually through the organization's Web site or in their major reports and databases. Environmental information related to specific topics is included and available through other chapters in this book, including agriculture, energy, development, general, health, science and technology, statistics, and transportation. Users are recommended to consult these chapters for a full overview of environmental information available from international governmental sources. Forestry is covered in the agriculture chapter. A note about sustainable development and the resource described in this chapter pertaining to it, *World Summit on Sustainable Development (RIO + 10)*—this resource is described here because the national reports that issue from this environmental conference and earlier related conferences are excellent for environmental research.

Governmental Sources Discussed

Arctic Council Web site, Reykjavik, Iceland. <http://www.arctic-council.org/>

European Environment Agency (EEA) Web site, Copenhagen, Denmark. <http://www.eea.eu.int/>

Global Environment Facility (GEF) Web site, Washington, D.C. <http://www.gefweb.org>

Helsinki Commission (HELCOM) Web site, Helsinki, Finland. <http://www.helcom.fi/>

Organisation for Economic Co-operation and Development (OECD) Resources

OECD Environment Web site, by the Environment Directorate of the Organisation for Economic Co-operation and Development (OECD), Paris. <http://www.oecd.org/env/>

OECD Environmental Outlook. Paris: Organization for Economic Cooperation and Development (OECD), 2001 (print title with summary online). <http://www.oecd.org/env/outlook/> (Executive summary, highlights, and order information only).

UNESCO Water Portal Web site, by the United Nations Educational, Scientific, and Cultural Organization. <http://www.unesco.org/water/>

United Nations Economic and Social Commission for Asia and the Pacific,(UNESCAP), Environment and Sustainable Development Division Web site, Bangkok, Thailand. <http://www.unescap.org/esd/main.asp/>

United Nations Framework Convention on Climate Change (UNFCC) Web site, Bonn, Germany. <http://www.unfccc.int/>

United Nations Environment Programme (UNEP) Resources

Global Environment Outlook (GEO), by the United Nations Environment Programme (UNEP). New York: Oxford University Press, 1997– (ISSN 1366-8080) (print biennial title and online database). <http://www.unep.org/GEO/>

Our Planet: The Magazine of the United Nations Environment Programme, by UNEP Information and Public Affairs, Nairobi, Kenya, 1989– (print and online magazine) (ISSN 1013-7394). <http://www.ourplanet.com/>

United Nations Environment Programme (UNEP) Web site, Nairobi, Kenya. <http://www.unep.org/>

World Bank Environment Web site, Washington, D.C. <http://www.worldbank.org/environment/>

World Summit on Sustainable Development (RIO + 10) Web site. <http://www.johannesburgsummit.org/>

Nongovernmental Sources Discussed

IUCN, the World Conservation Union Web site, Geneva, Switzerland. <http://www.iucn.org/>

Nature Conservancy Web site, Arlington, Virginia. <http://nature.org/>

World Resources Institute Resources

World Resources: A Report by the World Resources Institute and the International Institute for Environment and Development. New York: Basic Books, 1986– (print biennial title) (ISSN 0887-0403).

World Resources Institute Web site, Washington, D.C. <http://earthtrends.wri.org/>

World Wildlife Fund (WWF) Web site, Washington, D.C. <http://worldwildlife.org/>

Worldwatch Institute Web site, Washington, D.C. <http://www.worldwatch.org/>

GOVERNMENTAL SOURCES

Arctic Council Web site, Reykjavik, Iceland. <http://www.arctic-council.org/>

Summary: The Web site of the Arctic Council provides information about the Arctic region under these categories: What's New, About, Member States, Permanent Participants, Meetings, Activities, Archives, Links and Acronyms, Site Map, Contact, Search, A–Z, ITC Conference, Photo Gallery, and Password Area. For the purpose of this discussion, the focus will be on the Activities, Archives, and Links and Acronyms home page categories. The Arctic Council is a high-level intergovernmental forum that provides a mechanism to address the common concerns and challenges faced by the Arctic governments and the people of the Arctic. Arctic Council Member Countries are: Canada, Denmark, Finland, Iceland, Norway, the Russian Federation, Sweden, and the United States of America.

Detailed Description: The Activities category describes specific projects including the Arctic Monitoring and Assessment Program (AMAP) (described in the next paragraphs); the Conservation of Arctic Flora and Fauna (CAFF), a working group of the Arctic Council, with responsibilities to facilitate the exchange of information and coordination of research on species and habitats of Arctic flora and fauna; Emergency Prevention, Preparedness and Response (EPPR), a working group with responsibilities to provide a framework for future cooperation in responding to the threat of Arctic environmental emergencies; the working group Protection of the Arctic Marine Environment (PAME), with responsibilities to take preventative and other measures, directly or through competent international organizations, regarding marine pollution in the Arctic, irrespective of origin; and the Sustainable Development Working Group (SDWG), responsible for the economies, culture, and health of Arctic residents. Project descriptions are included for each of these groups.

The Archives category contains the full text of Founding Documents, Arctic Environmental Protection Strategy Documents, Declarations, Meeting materials such as minutes and reports, and Statement by the Chairman of the Senior Arctic Officials. The Links and Acronyms category provides access to Web sites of the representative countries and to related topical Web sites.

The Arctic Monitoring and Assessment Program (AMAP) has its own searchable Web site at <http://www.amap.no/>. AMAP, established in 1991, is charged with implementing components of the Arctic Environmental Protection Strategy (AEPS). The members of AMAP are the Arctic rim countries: Canada, Denmark/Greenland, Finland, Iceland, Norway, Russia, Sweden, and the United States. Now under the umbrella of the Arctic Council, AMAP's current objective is to produce information pertaining to the Arctic environment and threats from pollution. This body is also charged with recommending actions to reduce the risks to Arctic ecosystems. According to their Web site, the objectives of the Arctic Environmental Protection Strategy (AEPS) are to protect the Arctic ecosystems, including humans, protect and restore environmental quality, work with indigenous peoples, review the state of the Arctic environment, and eliminate pollution in the Arctic.

AMAP publishes documents and reports online, including a significant reference *Arctic Pollution Issues: A State of the Arctic Environment Report* (1997–, PDF format, title varies: *Arctic Pollution*), as well as AMAP Assessment Reports, maps, fact sheets, graphics, and symposia abstracts. A project directory search form is available that allows searching by country, project status, region, and key words. Of special note is the Map and Graphics Database of 381 maps and other graphics. A query builder of thematic keywords, geographic area, time period, and product type is provided to obtain the information.

European Environment Agency (EEA) Web site, Copenhagen, Denmark. <http://www.eea.eu.int/>

Summary: The European Environment Agency (EEA) provides decision makers in 31 European member countries with the information needed for making sound and effective policies to protect the environment and support sustainable development through its searchable Web site and publications. The major sections that constitute this Web site are Products, Browsing, Networks, and Press Room. Other Web site options include searching a glossary of terms used on the page, a section of Frequently Asked Questions, and a site map. The About Us section provides online documents on the EEA, including regulations, strategies, programs, brochures, and annual reports (back to 1997).

Detailed Description: The home page highlights environmental themes, including air, water, waste, transport, and climate change, but more theme pages are also available. The Products section is a significant section that features an Overview, Indicators, Reports, Maps and Graphs, Data, the *EEA Multilingual Environmental Glossary,* and the *State of the Environment Reporting Information System (SERIS)* online database. *SERIS* is an inventory of the national state of the environment reports. In an alphabetical list by country it provides summaries and links to the national environmental reports online from 1997 and to the main organization involved in the report. Multinational reports are included. The *EEA Multilingual Environmental Glossary* is a searchable glossary online that allows users to find definitions to environmental terms in many of the European Union languages.

From the home page, the Browsing section provides browsing by themes/topics or by countries. The selected item then links to a summary of environmental conditions, related themes, data, full-text reports, fact sheets, links, and data. The Networks section on the home page leads users to online databases, including the *European Environment Information and Observation Network (EIONET). EIONET* is an online gateway to information by topic, country, Geographic Information Systems, data, and reports. It provides an online newsletter, information on environmental acronyms, and a users' guide. The Networks section also leads users to other online databases on the topics of biodiversity, desertification, and business.

Also in the EEA Networks section is access to *EnviroWindows,* <http://www.ewindows.eu.org/>, the information "marketplace" for European businesses and local authorities, which organizes access to companies' information on products, best practices, use of natural resources, and corporate environmental performance, thereby helping local authorities to communicate with concerned public, governments, and businesses. Only a few online publications are available, but the depth of the links and information is comprehensive for its purpose.

The Press Room section of the home page of the *European Environment Agency* Web site includes online news, reports, press releases, and speeches.

Global Environment Facility (GEF) Web site, Washington, D.C. <http://www.gefweb.org>

Summary: The *Global Environment Facility* Web site provides information about financing environmental projects and publishes documents and reports online. It finances environmental projects, especially on biodiversity, climate change, and persistent organic pollutants, international waters, and the ozone layer. Many of its reports are available full text online at no charge, and the Web site links to many other environmental resources. Available in English, French, and Spanish, this resource provides news, a site index, highlights, a section on frequently visited pages, and links to information under the GEF Assembly. Information is organized into nine main categories: Participants, Operational Policies, Projects, Project Database, Partners, Documents, Outreach and Publications, Results and Impacts, and Replenishment. A text version of the Web site and help guide "How Do I?" are also available from the home page.

Established in 1991, the Global Environment Facility brings together over 100 member countries, nongovernmental organizations, and international governmental organizations (IGOs) to address complex environmental issues and national sustainable development through financing projects that protect the environment. Three IGOs assist in implementing and managing GEF projects: the United Nations Development Programme (UNDP), the United Nations Environment Programme (UNEP), and the World Bank.

Detailed Description: The site index is one of the best ways of understanding and finding the information presented on this Web site, as the sections interconnect with each other. From the home page, the Participants section describes and lists the member countries, agencies, nongovernmental organizations, and other members involved in GEF and hot links to them. Under the Projects link, GEF provides general information about projects and their focal areas and intends to publish a GEF Country Profiles database online. From the home page Project Database section is an online database, searchable by country, focal area, agency, project type, and keywords, providing online project concepts and financing documents (PDF).

The Documents section is a rich source of full-text documents from the GEF council, final projects documents, project proposal, and legal instruments; however, this is very specific information on the workings of the GEF as an organization. For more public information there is the Outreach and Publications section, which includes fact sheets, a GEF glossary, media, videos, information on meetings, and country dialogue workshops. Media contains press releases, tip sheets, and project stores. The Results and Impacts section includes evaluation documents such as projects' performance reviews and reports; the series *GEF Lessons Notes,* which analyzes project lessons; and also provides summary conclusions from projects. Finally, the Replenishment section from the home page concerns the refinancing and support of GEF.

Helsinki Commission (HELCOM) Web site, Helsinki, Finland. <http://www.helcom.fi/>

Summary: The Helsinki Commission, or HELCOM, works to protect the marine environment of the Baltic Sea from all sources of pollution and to restore and safeguard its ecological balance. HELCOM is the governing body of the Convention on the Protection of the Marine Environment of the Baltic Sea Area, entered into force on May 3, 1980 and commonly called the Helsinki Convention, through intergovernmental cooperation among Denmark, Estonia, the European Community, Finland, Germany, Latvia, Lithuania, Poland, Russia, and Sweden. One of its guiding principles is to act responsibly as individual countries or jointly in order to restore the ecosystem of the Baltic Sea area and prevent and eliminate pollution by all appropriate legislative, administrative, or other measures.

This searchable site organizes information under the topics: Helsinki Commission, Recommendations, Publications, Meeting Documents, HELCOM News, Baltic News, Hot Stories, and *HELCOM Atlas.* A pulldown menu at the top of the Web page allows users to select sections on eMeetings, Press Room, Pollution, Environment, Man and the Baltic, and Ship Waste Handling. The section eMeetings allows for separate public and password-protected access to ongoing work, notices, and background papers of the HELCOM working groups.

Detailed Description: The Publications section provides searching by topic and includes brochures, reports, and proceedings. *Baltic Sea Environment Proceedings* in full text (PDF format) are also available here (1987–), as well as the *Clean Seas Guide: The Baltic Sea Area,* which provides information for

mariners on the Baltic Sea. An online interactive and searchable bibliography entitled *Baltic Marine Environment Bibliography* enables researchers to find all available literature about Baltic marine topics. The *Bibliography* also includes HELCOM publications as well as other publications, mainly in English. Of special note is an interactive map service the *HELCOM Atlas,* linked from the home page as well, that requires a Flash plug-in and allows users access to maps and graphical representations of the Baltic's environmental issues, including Baltic Sea Protected Areas (BSPAs) and oil spills.

Organisation for Economic Co-operation and Development (OECD) Resources

OECD Environment Web site, by the Environment Directorate of the Organisation for Economic Co-operation and Development (OECD), Paris. <http://www.oecd.org/env/>

Summary: The Environment Directorate provides governments with the analytical basis to develop environmental policies that are effective and economically efficient through individual country performance reviews, data collection, policy analysis, projections, and the development of common approaches. These activities provide a means for international cooperative efforts in addressing the complex problems facing the world's environment today, especially through government policy changes. Its Web site provides conference reports, news, publishing information, and especially much information under its thematic Web pages on specific environmental themes. The OECD publishes some major titles and a database on the environment. Of special note are its *OECD Environmental Indicators,* a resource with statistics by country, and its report on environmental trends, the *OECD Environmental Outlook.* OECD is a major publisher in this field, but most books and periodicals are available only for purchase, whereas conference reports and summaries of the thematic environmental issues are usually found online. The Web site is available in English and French.

Detailed Description: The Environment Directorate provides information under environmental themes in these categories: Biosafety—BioTrack Online; Chemical Safety; Climate Change, Energy, and Transport; Environment in Emerging and Transition Economies; Environmental Impacts of Production and Consumption; Environmental Performance, Indicators, and Outlooks; Environmental Policies and Instruments;

Environmental–Social Interface; Natural Resource Management; Trade, Investment, and Environment; and Waste. For each theme, the Web site summarizes the issue, provides information about OECD reports on the topic, and gives links to online information. There are links to what's new within the theme and to related themes. The theme BioTrack Online provides online documents related to the regulatory oversight of products of biotechnology, including a product database. The Climate Change theme page provides analytical studies online on international and national policies concerning climate change from 1998–, linking to projects, conference information, and guidelines on environmentally sustainable transport.

A rich number of resources are under the theme Environmental Performance, Indicators, and Outlooks. The Environmental Performance Reviews program regularly reviews environmental conditions and progress for each member country. OECD undertakes outlooks of environmental trends and works with its member countries to develop principles, regulations, policies, and strategies for the effective management of the main environmental problems they face. This program analyzes the efforts of individual countries to meet domestic environmental objectives and international commitments and recommends changes that could lead to better progress. Researchers may find online environmental performance reviews by country, linking to full-text surveys, reports, publications, and abstracts for each country.

Also found under the theme Environmental Performance, Indicators, and Outlooks are four sections on data, indicators, outlooks, and performance reviews. Under Data is found selected environmental, social, and economic data online, along with methodology of the data collection. Researchers will find a major report on the environment, published by the OECD Environment Directorate every two years, entitled *OECD Environmental Data Report,* available in print and PDF format through purchase online. However, free data and reports are made available in this section. Also found here is a database with environmental tax information jointly published by the OECD and the European Commission, *Environmentally Related Taxes Database.*

Under the section on Indicators, researchers will find free online indicators and reports, including the annual report *OECD Environmental Indicators,* which provides environmental data for OECD member countries. Every issue focuses on specific environmental themes, for example, the theme for 2001 was sustainable development. Core environmental indicators are presented in categories by issues such as climate change, air pollution, biodiversity, water resources, and waste. The report is available only in print and through subscription full text (PDF format) through the Web site.

Also Under the theme Environmental Performance, Indicators, and Outlooks, the section on Environmental Outlooks highlights the report *OECD Environmental Outlook,* first published in 2002 and described next.

OECD Environmental Outlook. Paris: Organization for Economic Cooperation and Development (OECD), 2001 (print title with summary online) (ISBN 9-26418-615-8). <http://www.oecd.org/env/outlook/> (Executive summary, highlights, and order information only).

Summary: This report contains projections of environmental issues, reports on environmental changes, analysis, and environmental conditions to 2020 for the OECD member countries. The projections are based on key economic sectors from industry sectors, including agriculture, forestry, fishery, transport, and energy. Changes in the state of the environment are investigated for selected environmental issues, including freshwater, biodiversity, climate change, air quality, and waste. It assesses the institutional reasons behind environmental problems and proposes strategies and policy packages to address improvements. The executive summary, highlights, and order information only are available online.

Under the theme from the main page Environmental–Social Interface is found information about employment and the environment. The Natural Resource Management theme pages links to information on water management and biodiversity. The theme Waste focuses on the prevention and management of waste and the transboundary movement of waste.

UNESCO Water Portal Web site, by the United Nations Educational, Scientific, and Cultural Organization. <http://www.unesco.org/water/>

Summary: This searchable Web portal is intended to enhance access to information related to freshwater available on the Internet. The site provides links to current UNESCO and UNESCO-led programs on freshwater and serves as an interactive point for sharing, browsing, and searching Web sites of water-related organizations, government bodies, and nongovernmental organizations. Sections included cover water links, water events, water celebrations, learning modules, a glossary, and other resources. The Web site is available in English, French, and Spanish. In Focus, Resources, and News are sections highlighted on the home page, with additional categories of information in a side panel including About the Water Portal, IHP (International Hydrological Programme), WWAP (World Water Assessment Programme), Water Events, Water Links, and Water Celebrations.

Detailed Description: The Resources category includes an *International Glossary of Hydrology* available in 11 languages and contributed by the French National Hydrology Committee. Also included is a link to UNESCO water photos within the UNESCO Photobank and to UNESCO publications specifically on water.

The category IHP (International Hydrological Programme) leads to reports of national committees and an online database searchable and browsable by region, by country, and by keyword search. The category WWAP (World Water Assessment Programme) leads to a collection of online pilot case studies. Some case studies are also reported in the title *World Water Development Report (WWDR),* which is scheduled to be published at regular intervals and to be available online <http://www.unesco.org/water/wwap/wwdr/index.shtml>. The first issue of the report was published in March 2003. This report reviews the global water system, providing indicators, methodology, and analysis that will identify, diagnose, and assess human water stewardship, the state of the global water system, and critical water problems.

The category Water Events organizes information by theme, by geographic region, by date, by organizers, and by type of events. The category Water Links organizes information by theme, by geographic scope, and by type of organization. Themes include climatic zones, ecosystems land forms and land use, extreme water events, hydrological cycle, irrigation and drainage, water and society, water quality and contamination, water-related processes, water resources system, water supply and sanitation, and water use. The category Water Celebration includes information on the *International Year of Rice* and World Day for Water.

United Nations Economic and Social Commission for Asia and the Pacific (UNESCAP), Environment and Sustainable Development Division Web site, Bangkok, Thailand. <http://www.unescap.org/esd/main.asp>

Summary: This searchable Web site provides the latest news, publications, and information about activities in the area of environment for the region of Asia and the Pacific. The Web site contains three major focus areas: Energy Resources, Environment, and Water Resources. Users will also find a directory, a calendar, highlights of publications, and special online activities. For the purposes of this chapter, the Environment focus area will be described, although much related information is also accessible. This Division of UNESCAP has an overall goal to strengthen national capacity in achieving environmentally sound and sustainable development in accordance with Agenda 21 adopted by the United Nations General Assembly in 1997. A site map and a site index are provided.

Detailed Description: The home page provides access to the online newsletter (2001–) the *Environment and Natural Resources Development News* which reports on conferences and major publications and activities in the environment for the Asia and Pacific region. The Water Resources focus area reports on water and minerals in Asia and the Pacific, new publications, and activities and conferences in this area, as well as on natural disaster planning and regional networking. The Environment focus area of this Web site links to information pertaining to environmental initiatives. It reports on workshops such as the Asia-Pacific Workshops on the Clean Development Mechanism and the regional World Summit on Sustainable Development <http://www.rrcap.unep.org/wssd/>. It also reports on the activities and documents of important environmental meetings, such as the annual Ministerial Conference on Environment and Development in Asia and the Pacific (online full text).

The Publications category on the home page provides ordering information for reports, environmental handbooks, and information brochures, however, many of these are not available online. One major print report entitled *State of the Environment in Asia and the Pacific,* by the United Nations Economic and Social Commission for Asia and the Pacific in cooperation with the Asian Development Bank, is published every five years (1995, 2000). This report includes articles on environmental conditions and consequences, best trends, policies, and outlook for the nations in this region. It identifies the environmental challenges related to sustainable development in the region. The report is also well illustrated with figures, boxes, and photographs and includes many statistical tables and bibliographical references.

United Nations Framework Convention on Climate Change (UNFCC) Web site, Bonn, Germany. <http://www.unfccc.int/>

Summary: This searchable Web site publishes much information directly related to treaty negotiations for the Convention on Climate Change for involved governments, for researchers, and for environmentalists through the secretariat of the Convention, which provides support and information for the Parties to the Convention. It directly links to the information on the latest round of environmental negotiations, under the section named Convention Kyoto Protocol. Other emphasized sections are statements, press releases, and topical highlights on Greenhouse Gas Emissions, National Communications, and the Development and Transfer of Technologies. The home page also contains the following sections: Documents, Convention Parties/Observers, Calendar, the Secretariat, Library, Issues, Sessions/Workshops, Press, Webcast, Site Info, and Text Version. Some materials are available in French and Spanish. For the purpose of this discussion only selected sections will be described.

Detailed Description: The National Communications section contains the online statements and presentations of governments, in English and PDF format, that either are parties or nonparties to the convention. The Issues section provides online documents with background and status information for each item currently under discussion concerning the Convention. Among many issues, this links to online status reports by individual countries of greenhouse gases. Under the Convention Kyoto Protocol section are the full text of the original 1992 United Nations Framework Convention on Climate Change and the Kyoto Convention and their signatories. Another link supplies information on Convention parties and observers worldwide.

The Documents section leads to online documents, mostly in PDF format, concerning the implementation of the Convention. It contains documents organized by date, official documents, and in-depth reviews that are available online in a number of languages. The Library section also leads to publications and information available through the UNFCC Library and Documentation Centre. The library catalog is online, and reference service is available to virtual users who can send their questions online. The Press section includes news, press releases, background information, and accreditations. Background information defines and summarizes topics under the convention, including emissions, CO_2 trading, energy, and COP7. Also available are a glossary of treaty terms and explanations on the background of the Convention and the Kyoto Protocol.

The Greenhouse Gas Emissions highlighted topic on the home page contains two sections, GHG Information and a GHG Database, which leads to the Greenhouse Gas Inventory Database (GHG) <http://ghg.unfcc.org/>.

United Nations Environment Programme (UNEP) Resources

Global Environment Outlook (GEO), by the United Nations Environment Programme (UNEP). New York: Oxford University Press, 1997– (ISSN 1366-8080) (print biennial title and online database). <http://www.unep.org/GEO/>

Summary: This reference title is a comprehensive global state of the environment report that assesses the environmental crisis faced by humanity. It is an interactive online resource (frequently updated) and also issued as a print report. Each print report summarizes global environmental issues by region and country of the world. This report is based on contributions from UN agencies, many individuals, and 30 environmental institutes. Each report defines the forces affecting our global environment—political and economic problems made worse by rapid population growth. These are comprehensive resources and provide statistics and rich illustrations, including graphs and photographs.

Detailed Description: Each section contains conclusions and references. The complete report is available online only in English, French, and Spanish (PDF and HTML format); however, a report summary is available in other languages. This searchable Web site also provides other information in addition to the reports, including a *GEO Data Portal* and GEO-3 Data Compendium, education, news, and highlights. It also provides a kids' page with a simplified version of the report, named *Pachamama: Our Earth, Our Future.* Technical and Regional reports section links to PDF files of regional reports, technical reports, and alternative policy studies. From this Web site, researchers also will find order information, press releases, and links to mirror sites.

The latest *Global Environment Outlook* report in print (2002) begins with a synthesis of the main issues covered, including regional trends. Also under the introduction, this text covers data access, quality, and availability issues. In chapters on the state of the environment and national policy response, it provides an overview of the state of the environment in regions of the world and individual countries. It covers these regions: Africa, Asia and the Pacific, Europe, Latin America and the Caribbean, North America, and West Asia. The state of the environment provides a summary social and economic background, driving forces, land and food, forests, biodiversity, freshwater, marine and coastal areas, atmosphere, urban areas, and references. For each region, it also offers a section on key facts. The chapter on national policy response covers laws, social issues, treaties, and environmental action and education.

Two final chapters cover future perspectives and policies and outlook and recommendations. The report concludes by giving recommendations for immediate, integrated action. An appendix of acronyms is included, as well as a list of figures.

UNEP provides special copyright information stating on this Web site that this publication may be reproduced in whole, in part, or in any form, for educational or nonprofit purposes without special permission from the copyright holder.

The *GEO Data Portal* is an authoritative source for data sets used by UNEP in the *Global Environment Outlook (GEO)* report and in other assessment. Searchable by keyword, it contains more than 400 different variables presented in national, subregional, and global statistics, and geospatial data sets (maps) covering themes such as freshwater, population, forests, emissions, climate, disasters, health, and GDP. Data can be manipulated; displayed as maps, graphs, or raw values; or downloaded in different formats.

Our Planet: The Magazine of the United Nations Environment Programme, by UNEP Information and Public Affairs, Nairobi, Kenya, 1989– (print and online magazine) (ISSN 1013-7394). <http://www.ourplanet.com/>

Summary: The focus of this bimonthly magazine, first published in 1989, is to inform nations and peoples on environmental issues and trends and on environmentally sustainable development in order to assist them to improve their environment and their quality of life. Each issue of this bimonthly magazine deals with a specific theme on a current topic, perhaps an environmental conference currently being held, or an event or issue. It reports on international developments, reviews current thinking, suggests solutions, and debates key issues. Full-text issues are free online since May 1996.
Detailed Description: From this Web site users may clearly see in a grid the theme of each issue of every year online since 1996. Some of these themes are disasters, hazardous wastes, climate change, tourism, oceans, and ozone, among many others. Each issue contains a table of contents, an editorial, and articles by prominent leaders, scientists, business leaders, and environmentalists from around the world. The articles are illustrated with photographs. The magazine *Our Planet* is also highlighted on UNEP's home page with a link from the bottom of the page.

United Nations Environment Programme (UNEP) Web site, Nairobi, Kenya. <http://www.unep.org/>

Summary: The Web site of this organization provides comprehensive information on the state of the global environment, covering both countries and regions. UNEP's mission is to be a world leader in environmental quality protection and improvement. Available in English and French, this searchable Web site provides significant online publications and also provides highlights, news, in-depth articles, and media information. The home page headings are: About UNEP, UNEP Offices, News Centre, Milestones, Publications, Conferences and Meetings, Events and Awards, as well as Resources For: Government, Scientists, Journalists, Children and Youth, Business Persons, and Civil Society. Clickable images on the home page under Issues leads to information pertaining to the focus areas of Environmental Assessment, Biodiversity, Chemicals, Freshwater, Marine and Coastal Areas, Land, Atmosphere, Energy, Urban Issues, Civil Society, Business and Industry, Governance and Law, and Sustainable consumption. UNEP is a significant publisher on global environmental issues, providing both research sales publications and significant full-text online information at no charge.
Detailed Description: About UNEP, the first home page heading discussed, pertains to the functioning of this organization and includes the mission, links to the various organizational and governing bodies, partnerships, the functional structure, and the library. The full text of annual reports (PDF format) are also available here (2000–). UNEP Offices, the next home page heading, links to divisions, regional offices, liaison and other specialized offices, other collaborating centers and agencies, and Convention Secretariats.

The home page heading News Centre features a photo gallery, videos, broadcasts, full-text press releases (1999–), and speeches (2000–). Milestones, another home page heading, provides the full text to key

UNEP documents such as the *World Summit on Sustainable Development* (2002), *Malmo Declaration* (2000), *Nairobi Declaration* (1997), *Rio Declaration* (1992), *Agenda 21* (1992), United Nations General Assembly XXVII, and *Stockholm Declaration* (1972). Links to related topics are also included.

The Publications heading on the home page links to sales and online no-fee publications, such as the reference resource described also in this chapter, the *Global Environmental Outlook*. A printable catalog is available online. Many of UNEP's publications are available for purchase through EarthPrint, a central and official online bookshop for UNEP and environmental publications from other international organizations, at <http://www.earthprint.com/>. publications is subdivided into categories for what's new, best sellers, latest reports, UNEP Annual Reports, Periodicals, a kids section by kids and individual titles. Many of these publications are available online in full text.

The Resources for different groups features materials relevant to each particular audience. The section Resources for Scientists provides many significant online resources on the environment. These are especially in-depth and include maps, graphics, a variety of publications, documents, and other sources. The section Resources for Journalists includes press releases back to 1999 and the newsletter *Information Notes* archived online back to 1997. This section also contains speeches and audiovisual resources. The section Resources for Youth links to a recent online environmental magazine for youth entitled *Tunza: The UNEP Magazine for Youth* (ISSN 1727-8937), available also in French and Spanish.

Resources of special note to researchers are included in the Biodiversity Issues area, under the Select an Issue drop-down box on the home page. The first is the *UNEP World Conservation Monitoring Centre* Web site at <http://www.unep-wcmc.org/>, which has its own searchable site with online publications and information. The Centre was established in 2000 as UNEP's world biodiversity information and assessment center and to provide informational support for policy and action to conserve the living world. It provides information through inquiries, publications, its library, and electronic communications services. The Centre also assesses the status, value, and management of biological diversity and endangered species and works with organizations on conventions. Under the World Conservation Monitoring Centre's Resources section, researchers will find publications such as the *Biodiversity Series* and the magazine *Bio-diversity Bulletin*. Also under the Resources section, researchers will find an online library catalog, links, and a section entitled Country Information Sources that lists national environmental reports and other information by country name. Another significant section is *IMAPS*, which provides interactive map-based conservation data on the Internet. Researchers select specific topics to display maps. Global topics are included, for example, under the title *World Atlas of Biodiversity*, also available in print, and there are many conservation maps. The print source is a rich reference title.

Earthwatch, <http://earthwatch.unep.net/>, a United Nations initiative to coordinate and share UN-wide information on the global environment, which includes data and indicators, assessments, searching by issue and by region, and online official documents, is a resource of special note. It is a searchable Web site with a site index.

World Bank Environment Web site, Washington, D.C. <http://www.worldbank.org/environment/>

Summary: This searchable environment Web site of the World Bank provides access to an overview of the Bank's work on environmental and related issues and activities. It contains information in documents, publications, analytical studies, partnerships, projects, training, and also information on the World Bank's environmental strategies and policies. Also highlighted is information under Environmental Themes and Environment in the Regions. The World Bank is a major publisher, and some of the information is online in full-text format.

Protecting the environment is one of six main principles in the World Bank's mission to alleviate poverty and to sustain the quality of development. The World Bank promotes and finances environmental upgrading in the developing world because it recognizes that sustainable development will help alleviate poverty and balance economic development, social conditions, and environmental protection. It focuses on three objectives: improving the quality of life, the quality of economic growth, and protecting the quality of shared resources, such as forests, water, climate, and biodiversity.

Detailed Description: A Help/FAQ index feature contains a frequently asked questions list, a site index, site map, a list of World Bank country offices, language resources for non-English speakers, and links. The following discussion will describe only specific sections of the home page.

The section on Environmental Themes provides summary information of the World Bank's activities by theme, the significance of the theme, and highlights, linking to Web sites or other information. It does not include publications, but directs users to some World Bank thematic titles. Environmental Themes organizes information in the subsections: Natural Resources Management, Pollution Management, Environmental Economics and Indicators, and Global Environmental Management. Through these sites the World Banks supports and/or contributes to 12 thematic Web sites on: biodiversity, forests and forestry, land, resources management, pollution managements, environmental economics and indicators, climate change, the Montreal Protocol and ozone depleting substances, persistent organic pollutants, environmental assessment, the World Bank—Global Environment Facility, and the Trust Fund for Environmentally and Socially Sustainable Development. The World Bank is one of the three implementing agencies of the Global Environmental Facility (GEF), which is described separately in this chapter <http://www.gefweb.org/>.

The section Environmental Strategy contains documents on the World Bank's strategies, also on regional strategies, implementation, and development. Its Strategy Papers and Notes subsection features online full-text (PDF) documents in its *Environment Strategy Paper* series, the *Environment Strategy Note* series, and background papers that discuss a wide range of environmental issues and provide background on the issues.

The section Environment in the Region reports on specific projects, activities, and lessons of the World Bank on environmental issues in over 100 developing countries. It is organized by region of the world. The section Projects provides access to specific projects by theme, by a reference list, and through an *Environmental Projects in the World Bank Projects Database* that provides keyword search capability. One collaborative project of note, *Mapping the Global Environment* <http://www.worldbank.org/nipr/Atrium/mapping.html>, aims to illustrate environment-related threats through an interactive map with data and maps by region.

The section on Publications allows users to access World Bank environment-related publications, research, and other documents and reports. By selecting a link, an automatic search returns environment information within that category. Categories under the Publications section include: World Bank Environment Related Publications, World Bank Environment Related Economic and Sector Work, World Bank Environment Related Research, World Bank Environment Related Documents and Reports, and World Bank Documents and Reports Database. Documents and Reports are usually online in PDF or text format and can be ordered. Searching in Documents and Reports can be customized. Publications are usually sales publications only and not online. By searching in World Bank Environment Related Publications, users can customize their search by keyword searching or by browsing by country, region, or e-book/data. E-book data links to data publications, online databases, and free online PDF documents. A search under the World Bank Environment Related Research allows researchers to browse World Bank environment working papers (online in PDF), abstracts of current studies, evaluations of research, and data sets on environmental issues and highlights important new environmental studies. Four environmental data sets are online free to users. One significant title is the World Bank's *Environment Matters,* published online (PDF and text) since 1996. This is an annual report on the Bank's work in environment and the challenges that lie ahead in the environmental area. Past reports examined the World Bank's environment strategy and its commitments to sustainable development, the challenges of equitable development, and resource use efficiency.

One resource of note within the World Bank under Environment Related Research is the *Environmental Agencies of the World,* by David Shaman <http://www.worldbank.org/nipr/epas.htm>. It is an online directory of agencies and contact information, organized by region and country name, and it has a feature entitled Environmental Agencies on the Net, which provides highlights of what environmental agencies around the globe are placing online.

World Summit on Sustainable Development (RIO + 10) Web site. <http://www.johannesburg summit.org/>

Summary: This official United Nations Web site for the World Summit on Sustainable Development (WSSD) meeting in Johannesburg in 2002 provides users with background information and documents, such as the national and regional documents prepared for the summit, publications and reports from the summit, media information, and links. The site gathers information to provide a comprehensive and honest review of the important past earth summit conferences. This particular conference was a summit gathering from September 2–11, 2002, in Johannesburg, South Africa, of world governments, concerned citizens, United Nations agencies, multilateral financial institutions, and other major actors to assess global change since the historic United Nations Conference on Environment and Development (UNCED) of 1992. Postconference information is provided on the *United Nations Division of Sustainable Development* Web site at <http://www.un.org/esa/sustdev/index.html>. Users are offered a choice of format of Web site, either a Java-enabled interactive Web site or a traditional Web site with the same, searchable content.

Detailed Description: To use these related resources successfully, it is very important to understand the background and impact of the earth summit conferences before the Johannesburg conference. The United Nations Conference on Environment and Development (UNCED), also known as the "Earth Summit," was held in Rio de Janeiro, Brazil, June 3–14, 1992. This global conference brought together policymakers, diplomats, scientists, media personnel, and nongovernmental organization representatives from 179 countries in a tremendous effort to coordinate governments to halt environmental pollution and the degradation of natural resources. The challenge was to rethink approaches to socioeconomic development in relation to environmental concerns. The size and scope of this significant event was unprecedented. The Earth Summit influenced all subsequent United Nations conferences.

Links to information on these conferences is available from the United Nations Economic and Social Council. They are a very rich reference resource for national government reports on environmental issues. United Nations Conference on Environment and Development (UNCED), Rio de Janeiro 1992, is available at <http://www.un.org/esa/sustdev/agenda21.htm>. This site provides information on Agenda 21, an agreement that was a major result from this conference. Agenda 21 is a comprehensive plan of action to be taken globally, nationally, and locally by organizations of the United Nations System, governments, and major groups in every area in which humans impact on the environment. It was agreed at the 1992 conference that a five-year review of Earth Summit progress would be made in 1997 by the United Nations General Assembly meeting in special session, and this is the meeting Earth Summit + 5, New York, 1997 <http://www.un.org/esa/earthsummit/>, and users may compare the national reports after five years to the earlier reports. The World Summit on Sustainable Development

strongly affirmed the principles of Agenda 21 and the commitments to the Rio principles. Full reports (PDF format) are available under the section Documents and Publications. See national assessment reports for the list of full-text country reports already submitted to the summit. Some include annexes as well as the text of the report. Some of the documents prepared for the summit are also available in French and Spanish.

The *Report of the World Summit on Sustainable Development: 26 August – 4 September, Johannesburg, South Africa* reports on the specific work of this major conference on the environment. For further information, researchers may consult the agency, the United Nations Commission on Sustainable Development, which was created to follow up the commitment to Agenda 21, review progress, promote policies and activities, and implement partnerships for these principles. The agency's home page is at <http://www.un.org/esa/sustdev/csd.htm>.

NONGOVERNMENTAL SOURCES

IUCN, the World Conservation Union Web site, Geneva, Switzerland. <http://www.iucn.org/>

Summary: This Union of organizations, established to promote global conservation by working with governmental and nongovernmental organizations, is a publisher of note in the field of conservation. It publishes the *World Conservation Journal* three times a year, a subscription journal also online back to 1999 in PDF, with articles on conservation themes. Included on this Web site is an online bookstore, library, and information about its Depository Library system worldwide. Of special note is the section Our Work which provides information on conservation themes, with some internal documents online and a directory of its regional offices throughout the world, which also provide environmental information within their region.

Nature Conservancy Web site, Arlington, Virginia. <http://nature.org/>

Summary: This organization works in the regions of Asia Pacific, the Caribbean, Central America, North America, and South America to conserve land and water through conservation ownership. It reports on current environmental issues online and in its magazines and newsletters. The scope of this Web site is conservation of a general nature. The Nature Conservancy, a nonprofit group of more than a million members, has worked with businesses, people, and communities to protect land and water since 1951, raising funds to purchase property to conserve and protect land and preserve plants, animals, and natural communities that represent the diversity of life on earth. The top of the page features the main categories of How We Work, Where We Work, News Room, and About Us. Also featured are the *Online Field Guide* to global Nature Conservancy projects, online greeting cards, and information about events.

Detailed Description: How We Work, the first home page category discussed, describes conservation by design, the "science-based planning process," as well as conservation methods and partnerships. Also included is information pertaining to the five priority initiatives of climate change, fire, freshwater, invasive species, and marine. Where We Work, the next home page category, lists the regions with links to a clickable map of the region to gain information about the Conservancy's program in that geographic area.

The News Room includes full-text press releases (2001–), contact information, public service announcements, annual reports (PDF, 2001–), information about the leadership, fact sheets, and links to news stories. About Us, the last home page category, provides an overview and facts.

The left hand side of the home page also contains useful links. Activities links to abstracts of book reviews by the Nature Conservancy. Magazine provides full-text access to current and back issues (2002–) of the magazine *Nature Conservancy*. Science Publications has abstracts of relevant publications. Registration to receive the free e-newsletter is available under Newsletter.

World Resources Institute Resources

World Resources: A Report by the World Resources Institute and the International Institute for Environment and Development. New York: Basic Books, 1986– (print biennial title) (ISSN 0887-0403).

Summary: This biennial publication is a comprehensive report on the global environment, with data tables, reports, and analysis of environmental global conditions and conditions by country. It discusses environmental issues; suggests strategies for improving world environment, climate, and ecosystems; and assesses environmental governance. Older issues are available in full text online (2000–2001), whereas for newer issues, some data tables are available at no charge online.

Detailed Description: This title is issued by the World Resources Institute biennially in collaboration with the United Nations Environment Programme and the United Nations Development Programme from 1990 on and in collaboration with the World Bank from 1996 on. Each individual title provides a wealth of articles, statistics, an environmental theme, and illustrations. The volume for 2002–2004, *A Guide to World Resources 2002–2004: Decisions for the Earth: Balance, Voice, and Power,* focuses on good environmental governance.

World Resources 2000–2001: People and Ecosystems: The Fraying Web of Life is a comprehensive guide to the global environment. It assesses five of the world's major ecosystems: agricultural, coastal and marine, forest, freshwater, and grassland ecosystems.

World Resources 1998–99: Environmental Change and Human Health is an issue that focuses on global environmental trends, especially critical issues of environment affecting human health.

World Resources 1996–97: The Urban Environment, available in full text (PDF) online, assesses urban environmental conditions in developing and developed countries and suggests policies for improving them.

World Resources Institute (WRI) Web site, Washington, D.C. <http://www.wri.org/>

Summary: This searchable Web site provides information under the categories of About WRI, Global Topics, EarthTrends: The Environmental Information Portal, Newsroom, Publications and Media, and Taking Action. It is a good source of summary information and links, especially by environmental topic under the categories Global Topics and EarthTrends, because one of WRI's major goals is to guarantee all people's access to environmental information. However, information available for free is limited, and the major recent titles are for sale. A site index is provided.

World Resources Institute is a global think tank dedicated to improving the world's environment and ecosystems by reducing waste, safeguarding the environment, and providing information on the world's environmental condition to all peoples. It is a major publisher of environmental information and often collaborates with international intergovernmental organizations.

Detailed Description: From the home page, researchers may sign up for an e-mail newsletter or view the WRI Annual Report, spotlight issues, a calendar, and what's new. Under the Publications and Media category is an online bookstore and titles organized under environmental topic. The Newsroom contains press releases, media kits and previews, and a newsroom archive. Under the category Global Topics, it lists environmental topics Web pages from which users may find news, projects, a summary of the topic, links, and some online full-text documents in HTML and PDF. The environmental topics include Agriculture and food; Biodiversity and protected areas; Business and economics; Climate change and energy; Coastal and marine ecosystems; Forests, grasslands, and drylands; Governance and institutions; Population, health, and human well-being; Resource and materials use; and finally, Water resources and freshwater ecosystems.

One major information resource available on the Web site is *EarthTrends: The Environmental Information Portal* <http://earthtrends.wri.org>, a free online environmental information resource that organizes information under environmental topics. For each topic it provides a searchable database, data tables, country profiles, and features (text analysis and graphic of key segments of the topic). It also links to articles and news and provides quick links to WRI sites and is regularly kept up to date.

A major title available on the Web site is *Guide to Global Environmental Statistics,* by the World Resources Institute at <http://www.wri.org/statistics/environment.html>. This online directory provides summary information on statistical programs covering the environment in over 30 different international organizations. It includes an index of key subject terms and a description of the purpose and major activities of each organization's statistical program. Detailed information on the data collection, processing, and analysis is also provided.

World Wildlife Fund (WWF) Web site, Washington, D.C. <http://worldwildlife.org/>

Summary: The WWF releases information, news, publications, resources, links, and reports on the following themes: endangered species and spaces, forests, climate change, oceans, toxic chemicals, education, and community outreach. Also under each theme, it provides analysis and update on government and international governmental organization activity in that area, including updates on treaties, current policies, and environmental disasters. Publications and reports are usually in full text online in English and in other languages, with summaries in additional languages. The Web site is searchable and provides an index.

The mission of the World Wildlife Fund, established in 1961, is to protect the world's wildlife and wild lands, including endangered species and the places where they live, and also to educate and be active against all global threats that put all living things in harm's way.

Detailed Description: Under the Ocean category on the home page, WWF publishes its online *WWF Global Network's Endangered Seas* Web site, which features additional WWF marine publications and news on European and global issues. The Education category links to a kids' site with fun and interactive online educational activities, fact sheets summarizing environmental issues, and *Windows on the Wild,* WWF's core environmental education program.

Worldwatch Institute Web site, Washington, D.C. <http://www.worldwatch.org/>

Summary: Founded in 1974, this independent environmental research organization provides environmental writing and research in the form of an online journal, summaries of environmental issues, updates, press information, research center, bookstore, and Worldwatch Live (section of interview transcripts) on its Web site. The site also contains breaking news, featured publications, searching, a site index, and highlights of upcoming events, such as environmental conferences. The Worldwatch Institute strives to have a nonpartisan perspective and reports on many government-supported environment initiatives. It has a global focus, especially on the idea of attaining an environmentally sustainable and socially just society.

Detailed Description: The Research Areas section provides minitopic sites on people, nature, economy, and energy. Under each topic are subtopics that contain Worldwatch publications, which are for purchase only; online free resources, such as discussions and press releases; and links to other informational Web sites on the topic. Subtopics include under energy (climate change, energy, materials, and energy); under economy (globalization and governance, sustainable economics, information technology, security, and consumption); under people (population, urbanization, food, and water); and finally under nature (freshwater ecosystems, natural disasters, bioinvasion, pollution, forests, oceans, diseases, and species).

Major titles published by Worldwatch Institute can be found in the Bookstore online for a fee and include the *State of the World, Vital Signs,* the *World Watch* magazine, the *Worldwatch Paper* series, and the CD-ROM *Signposts.* Also linking directly from the home page, the bimonthly *World Watch* contains feature issues on global environmental problems, essays, and editorials and is archived online back to 1995. Most articles are available electronically for a fee, although a few are free online. *Vital Signs* is authored in cooperation with the United Nations Environment Programme and analyzes environmental, social, and economic trends and challenges for the future. Highlights, an overview, and table of contents only are online. The *State of the World* current edition is available online for a fee, while the year-old edition may be downloaded at no charge. The *State of the World* provides information on climate change, farming, toxic chemicals, sustainable tourism, population, resource conflicts and global governance, and reports on special meetings such as the 2002 United Nations World Summit on Sustainable Development. The illustrated, searchable CD-ROM, *Signposts,* includes time series of data back 50 years, environmental trends for 40 years, and full text of several editions of *State of the World* and *Vital Signs.*

RESEARCH STRATEGIES

Excellent beginning reference sources for the topic of the environment are the following titles, both available in print and electronic form: **Global Environment Outlook** (free online), by UNEP, the **United Nations Environment Programme** Web site; the **OECD Environmental Outlook,** and the **World Resources: A Report by the World Resources Institute and the International Institute for Environment and Development. OECD Environmental Outlook,** which is particularly good for the industrialized OECD countries, is available through online purchase or the subscription of *SourceOECD.* **World Resources** is also a subscription electronic title. These titles all include summary analyses of global environmental trends and issues, data, and country information.

For a comprehensive beginning Web site resource, consult the **United Nations Environment Programme (UNEP)** Web site, which contains free documents, reports, data, and links. It is a good place to begin for environmental law, treaties, and regulations. It is particularly strong on information by environmental topic and by country of the world. UNEP's magazine, **Our Planet,** is a good beginning place for articles on worldwide environmental issues and concerns. The **World Resources Institute** is a nongovernmental organization that has comprehensive environment information on its Web site, but it does not have as much information available at no cost online, although it

does have **EarthTrends,** an environmental information portal.

For more in-depth research, other international governmental organizations' environmental Web sites, such as OECD's and the World Bank's, are very strong. For researchers looking for environmental statistics, the OECD resources are among the strongest. Consult these two titles first: **OECD Environmental Data Report** and its annual report, **OECD Environmental Indicators,** which have data for countries, before exploring the many databases available through this organization. OECD is also noted for its **Environmental Policy Reviews** by OECD country, each a comprehensive report on a country's environment incorporating analysis with statistics. The World Bank publishes many reports and documents in the environment field, in order to support its main objectives in sustainable development. World Bank documents and publications catalogs are easily searched online and link to many online documents, but may be best to consult as secondary bibliographic sources. The World Bank's strength lies in the area of the relationship of the environment to sustainable development and financing environmental projects, and its magazine **Environmental Matters** is a good online source for this type of information.

For researchers interested in regional environment concerns, consult a regional environmental organization; several are described in this chapter. For European environmental information, consult the **European Environment Agency (EEA)** Web site for a portal to information and databases and access by country and environmental themes. However, this agency is best for organizing access to information, and it is not the best resource to begin with to find environmental issues and problems in Europe summarized. Instead, start with the general environment references resources and Web sites. For Asia and the Pacific environmental information, consult the **United Nations Economic and Social Commission for Asia and the Pacific, Environment and Sustainable Development Division** Web site.

Other options for researchers include starting with a thematic environmental resource, such as the **UNESCO Water Portal** Web site, or consult a general reference resource or Web site and look under specific themes such as acid rain, water pollution, or biodiversity. For environmental treaty information, consult Web links from UNEP or other organizations on legal information, which will lead users to specific Web sites, such as on the Conventions on Climate Change or Biodiversity.

Often treaties require national reports from governments on their implementation; these are a good source of information, and the reports are often full text online. For very up-to-date environmental information and concerns, a good resource is the latest Web site for the *World Summit on Sustainable Development.* The summit held in Johannesburg in 2002, *(RIO + 10),* was a major global environmental conference with reports from many national governments provided online. Another specific environmental resource is the *Global Environment Facility (GEF)* Web site, which is an excellent source for descriptions, summaries, and conclusions from environmental projects worldwide.

The nongovernmental resources described in this chapter are mostly Web sites of organizations that focus on specific environmental concerns. Consult the *Nature Conservancy* Web site for issues broader than governmental environmental conservation of land, water, and so on. For wildlife and wild lands conservation, consult the Web site of the *World Wildlife Fund (WWF).* The *Worldwatch Institute* Web site publishes several excellent reference titles of broad focus, available only through subscription and covering the environment along with social and economic global concerns.

FOR FURTHER READING: COMPREHENSIVE WEB SITES AND OTHER REFERENCE SOURCES

Commission for Environmental Cooperation of North America (CEC) Web site, Montréal, Québec, Canada. <http://www.cec.org/>

This Commission is an international organization created by Canada, Mexico, and the United States under the North American Agreement on Environmental Cooperation (NAAEC) in order to address regional environmental concerns, help prevent potential trade and environmental conflicts, and promote the effective enforcement of environmental law. The Web site reports on programs and projects especially in the areas of environment, economy, and trade; conservation of biodiversity; pollutants and health; and law and policies. Its Publications and Information Resources section provides online publications and research studies, laws, treaties, and agreements, especially under NAFTA, the North American Agreement on Environmental Cooperation, Eco Region, and a current newsletter entitled, *TRIO,* all available in English, French, and Spanish.

Convention on Biological Diversity Web site. <http://www.biodiv.org/>

This searchable site provides information about the implementation of this treaty, including conferences, meetings, full text of the legal instruments, documents, strategic plan, and participation of countries as signatories to the treaty. Information concerning national reports on the implementation of the convention agreements are available from this site. It provides a site index.

International Council for Local Environmental Initiatives Web site, Montréal, Québec, Canada. <http://www.iclei.org/>

ICLEI is the international environmental agency for local governments, whose mission is to build and serve a worldwide movement of local governments to improve global environment and sustainable development conditions through cumulative local actions. Its Web site provides documents, links to conference events, and other Web links.

Intergovernmental Panel on Climate Change Web site, Geneva, Switzerland. <http://www.ipcc.ch/>

The Intergovernmental Panel on Climate Change (IPCC) was established by the World Meteorological Organization (WMO) and the United Nations Environment Programme (UNEP) and collects and evaluates scientific, technical, and socioeconomic information pertaining to climate change. Its searchable Web site contains online news, publications, press releases, speeches, presentations, and documents. One title of note is a series of publications on the *IPCC Third Assessment Report: Climate Change 2001.* It is available full text online in many languages.

National Council on Science and the Environment (NCSE) Web site, Washington, D.C. <http://ncse online.org/>

Formerly known as Committee for the National Institute for the Environment, this organization has been working since 1990 to improve environmental decision making. NCSE maintains the *National Library for the Environment* as a universal, timely, easy-to-use, single-point entry to quality environmental data and information for public use. The online Library includes directories of academic environmental programs, journals, conferences, news sources, laws and treaties, reports, references materials, and more. NCSE works to ensure that users understand the context and quality control relevant to all information provided. Under the journals section, it maintains a list of environmental journals on the Internet, including information about which journals are available in full text and those available in part such as abstracts, tables of contents, or selected articles. Of special note in the online library is its electronic list of national State of the Environment Reports organized alphabetically by country at <http://www.ncseonline.org/SciencePolicy/StateofEnvironment.cfm>. Most national reports are in English, some in the country's major language, and some in both. Many were facilitated by the United Nations Environment Program through its Global Resources Information Database (GRID) center in Arendal, Norway. Reports from international organizations, countries, states, and regional governments are all included.

North America's Environment: A Thirty-year State of the Environment and Policy Retrospective, by the United Nations Environment Programme. Nairobi: UNEP, 2002 (ISBN 9-28072-234-4).

This report analyzes 30 years of progress in North America in addressing environmental problems that challenge the atmosphere, biodiversity, coastal and marine areas, freshwater, land, forests, disasters, human health, and urban areas. It provides policy options and is well illustrated with figures and statistical tables.

Review of World Water Resources by Country. Rome: Food and Agriculture Organization of the United Nations, 2003 (*Water Reports* 23) (ISBN 92-5-104899-1).

Prepared within the framework of the FAO Land and Water Development Division's Aquastat Programme, this reference report proves a summary of world water resources and overviews of water resource management for regions and countries. It reports on water management and major characteristics and trends of water use within countries and regions. Concepts, definitions, glossary, illustrations, maps, and statistical tables accompany the text. Other information produced by the FAO's Aquastat programme are also available on CD-ROM or on the Internet at <http://www.fao.org/ag/agl/aglw/aquastat/main/index.stm>.

Stockholm Environment Institute Web site. <http://www.sei.se>

This is a comprehensive searchable online resource for research and publications in environmental areas. The Institute's objective is to bridge science and policy in the field of environment and development in local, national, regional, and global arenas. Users may download free full-text publications, many with a global theme, from lists organized by year of publication, by program, or by title. Online fact sheets (PDF) and a library catalog are also available.

CHAPTER 10
Government and Politics

CHAPTER OVERVIEW

To include all official Web resources from the various governments of the world would fill a book all by itself. Therefore, as in the chapter on International Relations, Web site aggregators are described in this chapter. These nongovernmental aggregators, *Foreign Government Resources on the Web, Governments on the WWW, Latin American and Caribbean Government Documents Project,* and *Web Sites of National Parliaments,* bring together links to official governmental Web sites of the countries of the world. Two online resources from the U.S. Central Intelligence Agency have also been included because of their global reach.

The major governmental sources described are the Inter-Parliamentary Union, a parliamentary organization with 144 member nations as well as five regional associate members, and the European Union, because of its central governing bodies that oversee its current membership of 15 member states (with the possibility of 13 more), namely the Council of the European Union, European Council, and European Parliament, all of which work together. In addition, the collaborative work of the Western hemisphere, with a membership of 35 countries, is found on the Web site of the Organization of American States Permanent Council. The rest of the chapter is devoted to print resources. Most of the print sources discussed are annual publications. Not only do they contain fairly current information, but also older editions can be used to trace the governmental history and political situations of particular countries. The primary citation indexes for this subject area have also been included.

All of these sources combined provide a comprehensive look at the governments and politics of the countries of the world. The chapters on General Resources, International Relations, and Laws and Treaties also contain information related to government and politics. The sources used in those chapters were not duplicated here.

Governmental Sources Discussed

Chiefs of State and Cabinet Members of Foreign Governments Web site, by the U.S. Central Intelligence Agency, Washington, D.C. (online directory). <http://www.odci.gov/cia/publications/chiefs/index.html>

Council of the European Union Web site, Brussels, Belgium. <http://ue.eu.int/en/summ.htm>.

European Council (hosted by current president's country) Web site. <http://ue.eu.int/en/Info/eurocouncil/index.htm>

European Parliament: EUROPARL Web site, Brussels, Belgium. <http://www.europarl.eu.int/>

Inter-Parliamentary Union Web site, Geneva, Switzerland. <http://www.ipu.org/>

Organization of American States: Permanent Council Web site, Washington, D.C. <http://www.oas.org/consejo/default.htm>

World Factbook. Washington, D.C: Central Intelligence Agency (print annual title 1981– and online). <http://www.cia.gov/cia/publications/factbook/index.html>

Nongovernmental Sources Discussed

ABC Pol Sci: Advanced Bibliography of Contents: Political Science and Government. Santa Barbara, Calif.: ABC-Clio, Inc., 1969–2000.

CSA Political Science and Government: A Guide to Periodical Literature. Bethesda, Md.: Cambridge Scientific Abstracts, 2001– (ISSN 0001-0456).

Directory of European Union Political Parties, by Alan J. Day. London: John Harper, 2000 (ISBN 0-95362-786-1 or 0-95362-785-3 [pbk.]).

Europa World Year Book. New York: Europa Publications, 1926– (ISSN 0956-2273).

Foreign Government Resources on the Web Web site, by the University of Michigan Documents Center, Ann Arbor, Mich. <http://www.lib.umich.edu/govdocs/foreign.html>

Government Gazettes Online Web site, by the University of Michigan, Ann Arbor, Mich. <http://www.lib.umich.edu/govdocs/gazettes/index.htm>

Governments on the WWW, compiled by Gunnar Anzinger. <http://www.gksoft.com/govt/>

Guide to Official Publications of Foreign Countries, edited by Gloria Westfall. 2nd. rev. ed. Chicago: American Library Association, Government Documents Roundtable, 1997.

Information Sources in Official Publications, edited by Valerie J. Nurcombe. West Sussex, United Kingdom: Bowker-Sauer, 1997 (ISBN 1-85739-151-9).

International Bibliography of Political Science, by the International Political Science Association. Chicago: Aldine Publishing Company, 1951–.

International Political Science Abstracts. Paris: International Political Science Association, 1951– (ISSN 0020-8345) (paper and online subscription title produced by Silver Platter International).

International Year Book and Statesmen's Who's Who. West Sussex, United Kingdom: Reed Business Information, 1953– (print annual title).

Latin American and Caribbean Government Documents Project Web site, Cornell University, Ithaca, N.Y. <http://www.library.cornell.edu/colldev/ladocshome1.html>

Political Handbook of the World, edited by Arthur S. Banks and Thomas C. Muller. Binghamton: New York: CSA Publications, 1975– (ISSN 1093-175X).

The Statesman's Yearbook, edited by Barry Turner. New York: Palgrave Macmillan Ltd., 1864– (ISSN 0881-4601).

Web sites of National Parliaments, by the Weidenbaum Center on the Economy, Government, and Public Policy, Washington University, St. Louis, Mo. <http://wc.wustl.edu/parliaments.html>

World Encyclopedia of Parliaments and Legislatures, by George Thomas Kurian. Washington, D.C.: Congressional Quarterly, Inc., 1998 (ISBN 0-87187-987-5).

World Encyclopedia of Political Systems and Parties, edited by George E. Delury. 3rd. ed. New York: Facts on File, 1999 (ISBN 0-8160-2874-5).

Worldmark Encyclopedia of the Nations, edited by Moshe Y. Sachs. Farmington Hills, Mich.: Gale Group, 1960– (ISSN 1531-1635).

Worldwide Government Directory with International Organizations. Washington, D.C.: Keesings Worldwide, L.L.C. (ISSN 0894-1521).

GOVERNMENTAL SOURCES

Chiefs of State and Cabinet Members of Foreign Governments Web site, by the U.S. Central Intelligence Agency, Washington, D.C. (online directory). <http://www.odci.gov/cia/publications/chiefs/index.html>

Summary: Previously a monthly publication published in paper since the mid 1950s, this directory is now kept up to date on the Internet on a weekly basis. "The directory is intended to be used primarily as a reference aid and includes as many governments of the world as is considered practical, some of them not officially recognized by the United States. Regimes with which the United States has no diplomatic exchanges are indicated by the initials NDE."[1] It is available online in text and PDF versions. Abbreviations are provided, and the directory is searchable online.

Detailed Description: Access to information for governments is alphabetical by commonly used form of the country's name. Also, an A–Z quick links to countries is provided. Information provided includes the government position and the full name of the person in that position for heads of government, including the top executive officials and heads of major government agencies. The U.S. ambassador is listed, as well as the country's representative to the United Nations. No addresses or contact information are included.

Council of the European Union Web site, Brussels, Belgium. <http://ue.eu.int/en/summ.htm>.

Summary: As the legislative and decision-making body of the European Union, the *Council of the European Union* Web site is a comprehensive documentation of its activities and is updated daily. Materials are available in the 11 official languages (Danish, German, English, Spanish, Finnish, French, Greek, Dutch, Italian, Portuguese, and Swedish). The site is divided into the main categories of Council, The Secretary-General, Activities, Transparency, Public Relations, and References. At the top of the page are links to the full text of latest news, press, and agendas. In addition, icons that link to what's new, contacts/e-mail, and help are found on every Council-created page.

Detailed Description: Council, the first main category, has links to the European Council, discussed as a separate entry, and the Council of the European Union (EU). The Council of the EU subsection has an overview of the organization, complete with functions, composition, and working methods. Also as part of the

Council main category is a link to the home pages of all who have served as president along with a link to the membership directory. The Secretary-General, the second main category, links to the home page of the current Secretary-General. Here are found the full texts, usually in PDF format, of speeches, articles, press releases, and reports. Activities is the third main category and links to the thematic Web sites of Community Policies, Common Foreign and Security Policy (CFSP), EU Police Mission in Bosnia-Herzegovina (EUPM), Justice and Home Affairs (JHA), Economic and Monetary Affairs (EMU), and Scientific and Technical Research (COST). Each of these Web sites describes the activities of the Council through online documents, publications, and descriptions.

Transparency, main category number four, has the full text of minutes, summary of Council Acts, press releases, timetable, and agendas and an overview of legislative procedures. This material dates from 1999 to the present, but is not considered official. Only the material published in the *Official Journal,* which is accessible via the *EUR-Lex* online resource <http://europa.eu.int/eur-lex/en/index.html> (this source will be fully described in the Laws and Treaties chapter) is regarded as official.

Public Relations is the fifth main category and links to a Frequently Asked Question sections along with the schedule of open Council debates, information on how to visit the Council, and job postings. Of special note is the link to BookShop Online. Here are found titles and ordering information for free and for-fee publications along with links to the EUR-OP Office for Publications, Commission Publications, and Parliament Publications.

The last main category is References. This category is multifaceted. It contains the full text, in PDF format, of selected Treaties, a searchable database of Agreements, and links to the Web sites of the European Convention, Fundamental Rights, Europa On-line (European Union home page), European Union @ United Nations, Governments On-line (the home pages of the member countries), and a searchable terminology database, used by terminologists and translators.

European Council (hosted by current president's country) Web site. <http://ue.eu.int/en/Info/euro-council/index.htm>

Summary: Although not legally an institution of the European Union, the European Council serves as an advisory body. The Web site, available in all 11 of the European Union official languages (Danish, German,

English, Spanish, Finnish, French, Greek, Dutch, Italian, Portuguese, and Swedish), outlines its work such as intergovernmental cooperation on a multitude of issues. The site is divided into five main categories: Summary, Presentation, Next European Council, Presidency Conclusions, and Photographic Library.
Detailed Description: Summary, the first main category, provides an overview of the Council's work. Embedded within this text are links to presentation, presidency, photographs, and *Presidency Conclusions.* Also in this section are links to the Future of the Union, a discussion of reforming the EU; Presidency Work Programme, a schedule of events; and Presidency Home Page.

Presentation, the second main category, contains more in-depth discussion regarding the Council. Here are found the full text of three major presentations: *European Council's Unique Role in European Union Decision-Making, The European Council Fireside Chats Within a Media Event,* and *Is the European Council an Indispensable Political Gathering?* The third main category is Next European Council. This category links to the home page of the current president and includes information regarding the Council's meeting.

Presidency Conclusions, the fourth main category, is the "meat" of this Web site. Here are found the reports that document the annual work of the Council. Available in full text, for the most part in all official languages, they date from 1994 to the present. Photographic Library, the last main category, provides images of the various Council meetings, dating from 1999 to the present.

European Parliament: EUROPARL Web site, Brussels, Belgium. <http://www.europarl.eu.int/>

Summary: Membership, numbering 626, consists of seven political groups, representing more than 100 national political parties. The Parliament is the main source of law passage and ranks equally with the Council of Ministers. The Web site of the European Parliament (EP), *EUROPARL,* brings together, into one location, the vast information of this legislative body. The site itself is divided into the main categories of President, Political Groups, Press, ABC, Activities, and References. In addition, there are also links to Your *EUROPARL,* Who's Who, Election of the Ombudsman, Citizens' Portal, The Future of Europe, 15+ Enlargement, and Freedom, Security, and Justice. This site is available in the 11 official languages of the European Union: Danish, German, English, Spanish,

Finnish, French, Greek, Dutch, Italian, Portuguese, and Swedish. The *EUROPARL* home page is also available in Bulgarian, Czech, Estonian, Latvian, Lithuanian, Hungarian, Maltese, Polish, Romanian, Slovak, Slovenian, and Turkish. A pull-down find menu at the top allows the researcher to choose the topics of What's New, Your *EUROPARL*, Site Map, Index, Search Guide, FAQ, ABC, Press, Activities, or References and then be connected directly to that topic's section on the Web site. This menu is available on every page of this Web site.

Detailed Description: President is the first main category discussed, and a link to this is found on the top of the home page. Information is given on the current elected President. This section contains current agendas, press releases, and speeches, with an archive for each going back to the time of the president's election. There is also a multimedia subsection with images and audio/video clips. A subsection entitled the President provides a welcome letter, biography, description of functions, cabinet membership, and images of previous presidents, with their dates and party affiliation. In addition, the main President category includes links to the Conference on Presidents and the current president's contact information and personal Web site.

Political Groups, the second main category linked from the top of the home page, is comprised of links to the home pages of the seven major political groups: Group of the European People's Party (Christian Democrats) and European Democrats (PPE-DE); Group of the Party of European Socialists (PSE); Group of the European Liberal Democrat and Reform Party (ELDR); Group of the Greens/European Free Alliance (Verts/ALE); Confederal Group of the European United Left/Nordic Green left (GUE/NGL); Union for a Europe of Nations Group (UEN); and Group for the Europe of Democracies and Diversities (EDD). Each of these home pages contains a wealth of information relating to its activities.

Press, the third main category discussed, is linked from the body of the home page and is subdivided into Major Topics, Our Publications, Who to Contact, Search, Audiovisual Service, and Other Sources. Major Topics provides the full text, in PDF format, of *The Charter of Fundamental Rights of the European Union,* adopted on December 7, 2000, along with accompanying explanations and links. Our Publications has the description of, including languages, and the full text of the current year's individual issues of *News Report, The Briefing, News Alert, The Daily Notebook, Background Notes,* and *The Week.* An archive of each

title is available from 1996 forward. Who to Contact has names, e-mail addresses, and phone numbers for individual sections and language editors. Search is a keyword search engine used to find Press Service documents. Audiovisual Services has television coverage of the video magazine *Parlamento* (requires Quick-Time 4); Europe by Satellite, which provides coverage of European Parliament activities via television and Internet in all 11 official languages; radio clips; and photograph archive of portraits and locations. Other Sources links to the Web sites of other European Union press services.

ABC, the fourth main category, again found in the body of the EP home page, provides in-depth coverage of the European Parliament. Here are found an Overview, including powers, responsibilities, organization, and operation; the official membership list, complete with contact information, photographs, and vitas, along with the ability to search by name, country, political group and parliamentary committee; and contact information for the European Parliament, as well as links to the Web sites of Information Offices and other European institutions. In addition, this category contains information useful to the citizens, including a portal, submission of petition information, and searching for and requesting official documents. Of special note in this category is the Search Guide that explains the different types of documents and how to search for them. There is also a link to the News Archive (1996–2000) and a Frequently Asked Question section.

Activities is the fifth main category, and here is found the "meat" of the European Parliament's Web site as this section details the work of the organization. This category is subdivided into Plenary Sessions; Parliament's Governing Bodies; Meetings and Agendas; Legislative Observatory (OEIL); Committees; Delegations; Conciliation Committee; Delegation to the Convention; Parliamentary Questions; Written Declarations; International Cooperation; and Hearings, Conferences, and Summits. Plenary Session is subdivided into Agendas, Calendars (1999–), Reports, Minutes, Debates, Rules of Procedure, Texts Adopted, and Consolidated by COD Number. Each subdivision not only has the full-text documents, but also allows searching by various components, depending on the type. Of special mention are the minutes and reports. The minutes of the plenary sessions date back to 1994 and are grouped according to whether the session was held in Strasbourg or Brussels. They are in full-text format, usually PDF and HTML. Committee reports are also in full text, in this case most are available as either PDF, WORD, or HTML format. Materials found under all the other subheadings are either full-text documents generated by that body or explanations of the work of that body.

References is the last main category and also is subdivided into Key Topics and EU Policies, Treaties and Basic Documents, Rules of Procedure, Official Journals, Interinstitutional Agreements, Bulletins of European Institutions, Studies and Background Documents, Code of Conduct, and Scientific and Technological Options Assessment (STOA). Current key topics include the Euro, Intergovernmental Conference and Treaty of Amsterdam, and enlargement of the Union. The full text of relevant documents and other informational materials are included, as is the case of the archives, which dates back to 1995. The full-text of the *Interinstitutional Agreement of 20/11/2002 Between the European Parliament and the Council Concerning Access by the European Parliament to Sensitive Information of the Council in the Field of Security and Defence Policy* is available in all 11 official languages. Bulletins provides the full text of European Parliament special editions and activities publications (1999–) and links to the *Bulletin of the European Union.* Studies and Background Documents provides the catalogue and full text of working papers from the Directorate-General for Research (DG4) along with fact sheets. In addition there is information on the Benes-Decree pertaining to issues of ethnic cleansing in Czechoslovakia during the middle part of the twentieth century. STOA has to do with research in science and technology and of special note is the full text of many research papers. Code of Conduct is the full-text document for officials and other workers of the EP, available in all the official languages.

Also available from *EUROPARL's* home page are other links. One such link is Your *EUROPARL*, which allows researchers to set up their own portal. Who's Who, another link, is a quick way to access member and contact information. The Citizens' Portal brings together information needed by citizens of the European Union in understandings and working with their government, such as correspondence, how to access documents, and file petitions. The Future of Europe makes available information on the convention established to reform the European Union, and included here are news, archives, delegate lists, and proposals. Enlargement has to do with expansion of the European Union, and this section contains candidate coun-

try information, statistics, calendar of meetings, press reviews, and archives. Finally, the Freedom, Security, and Justice link has to do with an initiative being pursued in this area. Here are found information, newsletter, the fundamental rights, and public hearing information. Of special note for this section is reference texts and sites, which provides documents and other information produced by the bodies involved in this initiative.

Inter-Parliamentary Union Web site, Geneva, Switzerland. <http://www.ipu.org/>

Summary: With a membership of 144 national parliaments and 5 regional associate memberships, the Inter-Parliamentary Union (IPU) is indeed a worldwide governing body. This "site on parliamentary democracy" provides access to documents, publications, databases, and other resource detailing its work.

The home page, also available in French, is divided into 16 main headings: *Quarterly Review,* What's New, Quick Search, Information on Parliaments, What is the IPU, Functioning and Documents, Main Areas of Activity, Future Meetings, Statutory Assemblies, Specialized Meetings, Governing Council, Committees and Working Groups, Publications, Press Releases, ASGP, and Useful Links. Many of these headings also appear on every page of this Web site, although often varying from page to page. A link to the current hot topic is also found on the home page.

Detailed Description: *Quarterly Review,* the first main heading of the home page, features the full-text monthly Web publication, *Journal of the Inter-Parliamentary Union,* dating from May 1999 until February 2001. Beginning with the April 2001 issue, the Web version of this publication became quarterly with a new title of *The World of Parliaments—The IPU Quarterly.* The Web versions are abridged, but the print version is available from the Secretary-General at no charge. This journal includes such materials as topical articles and interviews, opinion pieces, gender issues, and parliamentary developments.

What's New, the second main heading, provides access to new materials that have been posted in the areas of recent events, publications, future activities, and press releases. The Quick Search, the third main heading, is the search engine for the entire site and includes a "tips on searching" section.

Information on Parliaments is the fourth main heading discussed, and here are found the *PARLINE, PARLIT, Women in Politics,* and *Women in Parliaments* databases along with parliamentary Web sites and statistics on women in politics. The *PARLINE* database contains: "general information on each of the Parliament's chambers, description of the electoral system, results of the most recent elections, information on the presidency of each Chamber, and information on the mandate and status of members of Parliament"[2] on all countries with national legislatures. It is updated regularly according to information received from the various national parliaments. The search engine allows searching by country, region, and subregion, all via pull-down menus, along with free-text searching and advanced searching. "*PARLIT* (a derivative of Parliaments and Literature) is a unique database of bibliographic references on the role, structure and working methods of national parliaments, and on electoral systems, constitutional law, history and political science."[3] Articles and books, dating from 1992 to the present, are included. Searching can be done by country, parliamentary organization, subject, author, specialized periodical, year of publication, and language. Pull-down menus are available for all categories except author. Free-text searching is also allowed. The *Women in Politics* database is also a bibliographic reference database, this time for books and articles on women and politics. For this database, searching can be done by type of document, geographic keyword, organization keyword, subject, author, title of periodical, year of publication, and language, all with pull-down menus except author. Free-text searching is also available. This bibliography had been available in print form only until 2000. The Parliamentary Web sites section provides a link to countries with national legislatures via an alphabetical list. The *Women on Parliaments* database consists of current data by number of seats, number of women, and percentages by world classification, world and regional averages, and regional parliamentary assemblies. An archive of data (1997–) is also included.

The last set of main headings contains overlapping information. What is the IPU, the fifth main heading, explains the history of the organization and lists the individual member countries and associated members. Functioning and Documents, the sixth main heading, contains the full text of descriptions and relevant documents, along with membership lists, where relevant, for Statutes, Inter-Parliamentary Council and its rules (1996–), Executive Committee and its rules, Inter-parliamentary Conference and its rules (1991–), Resolutions of Statutory Conferences (1991–), and Specialized Meetings (1992–). Also included under this heading are List of Future Meetings, Committees

and Working Groups, Financial Regulations, IPU Headquarters, IPU Secretary-General (biographical information and list), Rules of the IPU Secretariat, Job Vacancies, and link to the previously mentioned Current Membership lists.

Main Areas of Activity is the seventh main heading. Activity areas are Representative Democracy; International Peace and Security; Sustainable Development; Human Rights and Humanitarian Law; Women in Politics; and Education, Science, and Culture. Each of these areas provides an explanation and links to relevant reports, publications, and other Web sites.

The next five main headings (numbers 8 through 12) are Future Meetings, Statutory Assemblies, Specialized Meetings, Governing Council, and Committees and Working Groups. Each of these is the same as discussed under main heading number six, Functioning and Documents.

Publications, main heading number 13, is subdivided into Reports and Surveys, Periodicals, Books, and Handbooks. Each subdivision provides a list of titles, with brief annotations. Ordering information is included, along with price, although many are available at no charge.

Press Releases, the 14th main heading discussed, has the full text of press releases from 1996 to the present. They are arranged topically; however, a chronological list is also accessible. ASGP (Association of Secretaries General of Parliaments) is the 15th main heading. This body serves as a consultative body. In this section are found the membership list, rules, working methods, chronology of reports (titles, a few in full text, and rapportuers), studies and discussions (topics and rapportuers), and minutes of last session (full text in PDF format). The final heading is Useful Links, which provides links to the Web sites of other international regional parliamentary assemblies as well as other organizations that cooperate with IPU.

Organization of American States: Permanent Council Web site, Washington, D.C.
<http://www.oas.org/consejo/default.htm>

Summary: A governing body of the Organization of American States with membership consisting of an ambassador from each member country, the Permanent Council's site provides information about its work through agendas, minutes, resolutions, and declarations. The site contains information about the Council divided into the headings of About, Agendas and Notices, Authorities, Calendar of Meetings, Resolutions and Declarations, and Minutes. Each committee also has a link form this home page. The committees are: General Committee; Committee on Juridical and Political Affairs; Committee on Administrative and Budgetary Affairs; Committee on Hemispheric Security; Committee on Inter-American Summits, Management and Civil Society Participation in OAS Activities; and Permanent Council Working Groups. Each committee links to its page where minutes, order of business, and documents can be found.

Detailed Description: About, the first Council home page heading, gives an overview of its work, including a list of member states and permanent observers. In addition, the full text of the *OAS Charter,* Statutes, and Rules of Procedure are found here. Agendas and Notices, the next heading, contains the full text of these documents. Although a log-in and password are requested, the documents are accessible without one. Authorities, the third main home page heading, lists the current chairs and vice chairs as well as the permanent representatives by date of accreditation. The Calendar of Meetings home page has access to a monthly calendar as well as searching by meetings (day, month). Exact coverage dates are not given.

Resolutions and Declarations, another main heading, provides the full text of these documents from 1999 to the present. Minutes, the last main home page heading, also contains the full text, PDF, dating from 1999 to the present.

World Factbook. Washington, D.C: Central Intelligence Agency (print annual title 1981– and online). <http://www.cia.gov/cia/publications/factbook/index.html>

Summary: Produced by the U.S. Central Intelligence Agency, *The World Factbook* is an annual publication, both in print and Web formats, which serves as a source of "finished intelligence" on foreign countries. It was first published in 1962, but not unclassified until June 1971. In 1975, it became available for sale through the U.S. Government Printing Office and has been a major reference tool for libraries and researchers since then. Selected data from the Web version is periodically updated during the year.

The home page includes a pull-down menu to select a country. It also contains reference maps, roles and definition, history of the *Factbook,* flags of the world, the ability to download the page, and a link to submit factual updates. The material is updated periodically during the year. Print versions of this publication are available at all U.S. federal depository and other libraries.

Detailed Description: Each country entry is comprised of information on that country's background, geography, people, government, economy, communications, transportation, military, and transnational issues. For the sake of this discussion, the focus will be on the government section. Here is found information on the type, administrative divisions, independence, national holiday, constitution, legal system, suffrage, executive branch, legislative branch, political parties and leaders, political pressure groups and leaders, international organization participation, diplomatic representation in the United States, and flag description.

NONGOVERNMENTAL SOURCES

ABC Pol Sci: Advanced Bibliography of Contents: Political Science and Government. Santa Barbara, Calif.: ABC-Clio, Inc., 1969–2000.

Summary: Published since March 1969, with eight issues per year, this publication indexes U.S. and foreign periodical literature in the areas of political science and government. Citations, without annotations, are arranged by journal name. A CD-ROM version, updated three times a year, is also available. This publication ceased in 2000 when it was assumed by Cambridge Scientific Abstracts and became *CSA Political Science and Government: A Guide to Periodical Literature.*

CSA Political Science and Government: A Guide to Periodical Literature. Bethesda, Md.: Cambridge Scientific Abstracts, 2001– (ISSN 0001-0456).

Summary: This publication continues *ABC Pol Sci: Advanced Bibliography of Contents: Political Science and Government* and is published five times per year. Entries are now arranged by subject, but still not annotated. An annual cumulative index is also produced. An online version is available as *Worldwide Political Science Abstracts.* The online version, dating from 1975–current, does provide abstracts along with the citations.

Directory of European Union Political Parties, by Alan J. Day. London: John Harper, 2000 (ISBN 0-95362-786-1 or 0-95362-785-3 [pbk.]).

Summary: This directory contains an alphabetical listing of each member country, with a description of the various political parties as well as contact information for that country.

Europa World Year Book. New York: Europa Publications, 1926– (ISSN 0956-2273).

Summary: An annual publication, published since 1926, the *Europa World Year Book* provides in-depth coverage of the government and politics of individual countries. Published in two volumes since 1960, it is divided into two main parts: International Organizations and Countries. A late information section is also included. There is an index of international organization names and an index of territories.

Detailed Description: Part One: International Organizations is subdivided into the United Nations, United Nations Regional Commissions, Other United Nations Bodies, and Specialized Agencies within the United Nations System. Included for each entry are contact information, membership, organization description, activities, finance, and publications.

The bulk of this publication is Part Two: Countries. Countries are arranged alphabetically. Each entry is comprised of a narrative introductory overview of recent history, followed by short paragraphs on government, defense, economic affairs, education, public holidays, weights, and measures. The next section is a statistical survey encompassing area and population, health and welfare, agriculture, forestry, fishing, mining, industry, finances, external trade, transport, tourism, communications, media, and education. Lastly, information is provided regarding the constitution, government (authority, ministries, and legislature), political organizations, diplomatic representation, judicial system, religion, press, publishers, broadcasting and communication, finance, trade and industry, transport, and tourism.

Foreign Government Resources on the Web Web site, by the University of Michigan Documents Center, Ann Arbor, Mich. <http://www.lib.umich.edu/govdocs/foreign.html>

Summary: A product of the Documents Center of the University of Michigan's Hatcher Library, this site provides links to relevant government and related Web sites. The site is launched in a frames version; however, a no frames version can be selected. There are three major categories of resources: Foreign Government Web Sites, Related Foreign Information, and Additional Web Pages.

Detailed Description: The first major category, Foreign Government Web Sites, is arranged by world region: Africa (Sub-Saharan), Asia and the Pacific, Central/South America, Europe, Middle East/North Africa, and North America. The countries within each region are arranged alphabetically with links to relevant resources. The comprehensiveness of coverage varies by country.

Related Foreign Information, the second main category, is subdivided into Background; Comprehensive Listing of Foreign Governments; Constitutions, Laws, and Treaties; Embassies; News; and Statistics (Demographic, Economic, Health, Military). Background consists of links to various Web resources devoted to country information, biographies, human rights, and politics/elections. The Comprehensive Listing of Foreign Governments provides links to aggregations of foreign government Web sites arranged by national or local governments. Constitutions, Laws, and Treaties provide links to aggregations of sites devoted to this area. In the Embassies subsection are found links to various listings of embassies along with links to local government sites. News links to media sources, both comprehensive and individual, some of which are restricted to the University of Michigan community only. Lastly, Statistics brings together many statistical sources, again some restricted to the University of Michigan community only, pertaining to various aspects of governments.

The frames version of this site also provides additional access points to the information available on this site. A scroll-down menu is found on the left-hand side arranged by World Regions/Countries (with A–Z choices), Subjects, World Regions, Countries, and Related Sites.

Government Gazettes Online Web site, by the University of Michigan, Ann Arbor, Mich. <http://www.lib.umich.edu/govdocs/gazettes/index.htm>

This research aid online lists official government gazettes, the means by which countries communicate with officials and the general public and their Internet address. Gazettes are listed by country, and annotations include the title, URL, price, language, frequency, time coverage, and contents.

Governments on the WWW Web site, compiled by Gunnar Anzinger. <http://www.gksoft.com/govt/>

Summary: Compiled by Gunnar Anzinger of Germany, this Web site is a "comprehensive database of governmental institutions on the World Wide Web: parliaments, ministries, offices, law courts, embassies, city councils, public broadcasting corporations, central banks, and multigovernmental institutions. Includes also political parties. Online since June 1995. Contains more than 17,000 entries from more than

220 countries and territories as of February 2002."[4] Criteria for inclusion are

- "institutions of the legislative branch (parliaments)
- institutions of the executive branch (ministries, agencies, administrations, offices, institutes, councils, committees and others)
- institutions of the judicative branch (law courts)
- governmental representations in foreign countries (embassies, consulates and others)
- some other government-related institutions
- political parties and party alliances (on national, regional and municipal level)
- parliamentary groups, youth organizations etc. of political parties (only on national level)."[5]

One word of caution in using this site. Although it is updated, this is not done on a frequent basis.

Detailed Description: Governments on the WWW is subdivided into four main categories: Overview with Links to Individual Countries, Some Categories of Institutions, History of the Web site, and Additional Information. Overview with Links to Individual Countries is further subdivided into the subcategories of Worldwide, European, Africa, Asian, and Oceania governments. Each subcategory is arranged alphabetically by country and also includes the number of entries, file size, and date of last change. Each country entry is then arranged by national, regional, and municipal institutions; representation in foreign countries; and additional information such as general, political, from other sources, tourism, and human rights. Comprehensiveness of coverage varies from country to country, with entry numbers ranging anywhere from 4 to over 1,800.

Some Categories of Institutions, the second main category, is also subdivided. These subcategories are: Parliaments, Law Courts, Representation in Foreign Countries, Political Parties, and Institutions in the Area of: Auditing, Broadcasting, Currency, Elections, Statistics, and Tourism. Each subcategory is arranged alphabetically by country, although not all countries are represented. A link or links to the relevant Web source is then included for each entry.

History of the Web site, the third main category, is a monthly list of updates to the Web site itself. Additional Information, the last main category, provides information on what is included and how to suggest sites to be included.

Guide to Official Publications of Foreign Countries, edited by Gloria Westfall. 2nd rev. ed. Chicago:

American Library Association, Government Documents Roundtable, 1997.

Summary: First published in 1990, this publication highlights the "most important titles produced by each country in a number of categories and provides translations of titles and agency names, as well as descriptions of contents and means of access to them, in English."[6] This edition encompasses publications published between 1990 and January 1997, with 178 countries being included. Dependent territories and sovereign nations with populations smaller than 100,000 have been excluded.

Detailed Description: Arranged alphabetically by country name, each country entry lists and describes publications, when available, in the categories of Bibliographies and Catalogs, Sources of General Information on the Country; Government Directories and Organization Manuals; Statistical Yearbooks; Laws, Regulations, and Constitutions; Legislative Proceedings; Statements of the Head of Government; Economic Affairs; Central Bank Publications; Development Plans; Budget; Census; Health; Labor; Education; Court Reports; Environment; and Human Rights and Status of Women. Each entry includes the bibliographic citation and annotation.

Publications of intergovernmental organizations have not been included unless they have been a joint publication between a particular country and organization. An index of titles by country is also available, which gives researchers a listing of titles.

Information Sources in Official Publications, edited by Valerie J. Nurcombe. West Sussex, United Kingdom: Bowker-Sauer, 1997 (ISBN 1-85739-151-9).

Summary: Written in narrative form, this volume describes official publications (i.e., government documents or publications), arranged by world region: North America, Central America and Hispanic Caribbean, the Commonwealth Caribbean, South America, Australasia, Asia, Africa, the Former Soviet Union, Eastern Europe, Western Europe, and the Middle East. A chapter on the United Nations and Other International Organizations is also included. Each region is then arranged by countries within that region. Government-related publications included pertain to the "legislative process, executive or departmental and agency publications, and judicial publications where appropriate."[7] Some statistical information may be separately described. The titles and publishing history are included.

International Bibliography of Political Science, by the International Political Science Association. Chicago: Aldine Publishing Company, 1951–.

Summary: Part of the *International Bibliography of Social Science* series, this annual publication indexes journal articles and monographs and provides citations only, no abstracts. Some of the entries are in the original language of the article. Access to these resources is available online through the database *International Bibliography of the Social Sciences,* with coverage dating 1981 to the present. This database provides abstracts along with the citations.

International Political Science Abstracts. Paris: International Political Science Association, 1951– (ISSN 0020-8345) (paper and online subscription title produced by Silver Platter International).

Summary: Citations and abstracts to major political science journals and yearbooks are included in this index, first published in 1951. Citations are grouped by major categories. A subject index is included. Online access is available through the database *International Political Science Abstracts,* containing both citations and abstracts. Coverage is from 1989 to the present.

International Year Book and Statesmen's Who's Who. West Sussex, United Kingdom: Reed Business Information, 1953– (print annual title) (each year has separate ISBN).

Summary: An annual publication, with the 47th edition published in 2000, the *International Year Book and Statesmen's Who's Who* is divided into four main sections: International Organizations, Other International and National Organizations, States of the World, and Biographical Section. Organizations that are included are either of a political, commercial, scientific, or charitable nature. There is no index.
Detailed Description: The International Organizations section focuses mainly on the United Nations with some other intergovernmental organizations included. The information for each organization centers on its purpose, structure, and function. The address of the chief officer(s) is found here. The Other International and National Organizations section is structured the same way.

States of the World is arranged alphabetically by country. For each country there is a brief statistical and textual overview, followed by brief descriptions of the constitution and government, legal system, local government, economy, health, religion, communications, and education. The Biographical Section contains brief entries of politicians, diplomats, and businesspeople, arranged alphabetically.

Latin American and Caribbean Government Documents Project Web site, by Cornell University, Ithaca, N.Y. <http://www.library.cornell.edu/colldev/ladocshome1.html>

Summary: Developed by Cornell University and last updated in 1999, the *Latin American and Caribbean Government Documents Project* brings together official state documents from these two regions that are available on the Internet. The documents are arranged into categories of National and International Statistics, National Legislative Documents, Inactive Legislative Documents, Subnational Documents, Inactive Subnational Documents, National Executive and Ministerial Documents, Inactive National Executive and Ministerial Documents, National Judicial Documents, and Inactive Judicial Documents. Each category is arranged alphabetically by country with a link to the agency and a brief summary of the contents of the documents.

Political Handbook of the World, edited by Arthur S. Banks and Thomas C. Muller. Binghamton, N.Y.: CSA Publications, 1975 (ISSN 1093-175X).

Summary: Originally published as *A Political Handbook of Europe* 1927, this publication became *Political Handbook of the World* in 1928, although occasionally over the years the name has varied as have publishers and editors. According to the 1998–1999 issue, this is an annual publication, with the exception of the biennial issues of 1982–1983 and 1984–1985. *Political Handbook of the World* is a comprehensive source of government and political information for each country. The book is divided into two main parts: Governments and Intergovernmental Organizations. An index is also provided.
Detailed Description: Governments, the first main section, comprises the bulk of the book. Countries are arranged alphabetically by country name. Here is found a brief overview of the political status, area, population, major urban centers, languages, and monetary unit, and a brief narrative about the country. A more in-depth narrative is then provided that discusses the background setting, political parties and groups, legislature, cabinet, news media, and intergovernmental representation.

Intergovernmental Organizations, the second main section, alphabetically lists major organizations and includes date established, purpose, budget, membership, language, origin, and development. Appendices are also included and cover such topics as chronology of major international events, chronology of major international conferences sponsored by the United Nations, membership of the United Nations, and its specialized and related agencies.

The Statesman's Yearbook, edited by Barry Turner. New York: Palgrave Macmillan Ltd., 1864– (ISSN 0881-4601).

Summary: Published annually since 1864, this book is divided into two main parts: International Organizations and Countries of the World. International Organizations is subdivided into United Nations-related, European, Americas, Asia/Pacific, Middle East, Africa, and other. Within each subdivision are the organizations relevant to that area. A short description is included for each organization.
Detailed Description: Countries of the World is comprised of an alphabetical listing of countries. For each country short information is provided on the topics of key historical events, territory and population, social statistics, climate, constitution and government, current administration, defense, international relations, economy, energy and natural resources, industry, international trade, communications, social institutions, culture, diplomatic representation, and further reading. There is an index of place and international organization names.

Web Sites of National Parliaments Web site, by the Weidenbaum Center on the Economy, Government, and Public Policy, Washington University, St. Louis, Mo. <http://wc.wustl.edu/parliaments. html>

Summary: Included here is an alphabetical listing of individual country parliament Web sites. In addition there are links to International and Regional Parliamentary Institutions and Additional Information about Parliaments and Domestic Political Systems.

World Encyclopedia of Parliaments and Legislatures, by George Thomas Kurian. Washington, D.C.: Congressional Quarterly, Inc., 1998 (ISBN 0-87187-987-5).

Summary: This volume provides in-depth coverage of world country government and political situations through signed narrative essays. A general background essay begins the book, followed by essays for each individual country, listed alphabetically. These essays include historical background, a relevant discussion, and a bibliography.

Topical essays included are on the European Parliament, Executive–Legislative Relations, Legislative Committees, Legislative Voting Behavior, Legislators and Constituents, Lobbying, Parliamentary Libraries: Information on the Legislative Process, The Parliamentary Ombudsman, The Parliaments of New Democracies, The Experience of Central Europe, Second Chambers, Systems of Representation for Legislature in Democracies, Televising Parliaments, The United Nations General Assembly, and Women and Minorities in Parliaments and Legislatures. There are also a glossary of terms and index.

World Encyclopedia of Political Systems and Parties, edited by George E. Delury. 3rd ed. New York: Facts on File, 1999 (ISBN 0-8160-2874-5).

Summary: Published first in 1983 and then again in 1989, this third edition is comprised of three volumes. The entries are arranged alphabetically by country and include a description of that country's system of government and political parties and suggested further reading sources. An index is also available.

Worldmark Encyclopedia of the Nations, edited by Moshe Y. Sachs. Farmington Hills, Mich.: Gale Group (ISSN 1531-1635).

Summary: First published in 1960, the 10th edition is dated 2001. This six-volume set provides in-depth coverage on countries and the United Nations. Volume 1 is on the United Nations and consists of narrative describing the principal organs and subsidiary bodies. Volume 2 is on Africa, volume 3 on Asia, volume 4 on Asia and Oceania, and volume 5 on Europe. Each region volume contains information on the countries within that region. Volume 6 is devoted to world leaders. It is arranged alphabetically by country and includes political and personal background, policy, and references.

Worldwide Government Directory with International Organizations. Washington, D.C.: Keesings Worldwide, L.L.C. (ISSN 0894-1521).

Summary: First published in 1981, this publication provides a description of 199 countries and territories as of October 2001. It is divided into two parts: Countries and International Organizations. The country section, arranged alphabetically by country name, contains brief information on the head of state, cabinet, defense forces, state agencies and corporations, legislature, judiciary, Central Bank, United Nations missions, general data, international and regional memberships, forms of address, and foreign diplomatic missions.

The International Organizations section, arranged alphabetically by organization, has contact information, member states, and name of highest-ranking official.

RESEARCH STRATEGIES

Because the political situation and government of a country can change suddenly, up-to-date information is particularly important. This can be found via the official Web site of an individual country. To find this information, the best place to go is the aggregator Web sites: *Foreign Government Resources on the Web, Governments on the WWW,* and *Web sites of National Parliaments.* The *World Factbook* is another good source of current information and, as it is published by the U.S. government, is considered authoritative.

With its worldwide membership of national parliaments, the *Inter-Parliamentary Union* Web site is an excellent resource on the workings of multicountry governmental cooperative efforts. In addition, this site provides access to publications and documents as well as links to the Web sites of the member national parliaments. The *Latin American and Caribbean Government Documents Project* Web site provides information on a more specific area with coverage of particular types of official documents. However, this site has not been updated in several years. To understand the political and governmental situation in Europe, the *Council of European Union, European Council,* and *European Parliament (EUROPARL)* Web sites are the best place to begin researching this region of the world. The *Organization of American States Permanent Council* Web site covers the Western hemisphere's collaborative political and governmental situation.

Journal articles are another way to keep abreast of current governmental and political affairs. *CSA Political Science and Government, International Bibliography of Political Science,* and *International Political Science Abstracts* provide citations to current writings in both print and electronic formats. The online versions will most likely be found in college and university libraries and may be restricted to that community only due to licensing requirements. These three indexes along with *ABC Pol Sci* also serve as sources of historical information, especially useful in tracking the changes in a government or political situ-

ation. *World News Connection* and its predecessor, *FBIS (Foreign Broadcast Information Service) Daily Reports,* both described in the International Relations chapter, should also be considered for historic information. **World News Connection** is also a source for current information. In addition, such annual sources as *Europa World Year Book, International Year Book and Statesmen's Who's Who, Political Handbook of the World, Statesman's Yearbook,* and *The World Factbook* also can serve the same purpose, as they provide a level of detail necessary to understanding. Although they are published annually, they are not as up to date due to the delay in publishing. Most of these publications also detail international organizations, especially the United Nations, a key player in the area of international government affairs.

Although not published annually, *World Encyclopedia of Parliaments and Legislatures, World Encyclopedia of Political Systems and Parties, Worldmark Encyclopedia of the Nations,* and *Worldwide Government Directory with International Organizations* also supply another level of detail to the understanding of international governments and politics, along with coverage of international organizations

To find particular titles the *Information Sources in Official Publications* and *Guide to Official Publications of Foreign Countries, 2nd rev. ed.,* should be consulted. Although both sources are a few years old, they nevertheless contain the titles of important governmental publications of particular countries.

All the sources mentioned complement each other in the level of comprehensiveness they bring. All should be consulted to obtain an accurate picture of current political issues. In addition, some of the sources described, especially *International Year Book, Statesmen's Who's Who,* and *Worldmark Encyclopedia of the Nations,* contain information on the world leaders themselves. The *Chiefs of States and Cabinet Members of Foreign Governments* Web site provides an up-to-date listing of world leaders.

NOTES

1. *Chiefs of State and Cabinet Members of Foreign Governments* Web site, Washington, D.C., U.S. Central Intelligence Agency (online directory), <http://www.odci.gov/cia/publications/chiefs/index.html>.

2. *Inter-Parliamentary Union* Web site, Geneva, Switzerland, <http://www.ipu.org/parline-e/parline-search.asp>.

3. *Inter-Parliamentary Union* Web site, Geneva, Switzerland, <http://www.ipu.org/parlit-e/parlitsearch.asp>.

4. *Governments on the WWW* Web site, compiled by Gunnar Anzinger, <http://www.gksoft.com/govt/>.

5. *Governments on the WWW* Web site, compiled by Gunnar Anzinger, <http://www.gksoft.com/govt/en/contents.html>.

6. *Guide to Official Publications of Foreign Countries*, edited by Gloria Westfall. 2nd rev. ed. (Chicago: American Library Association, Government Documents Roundtable, 1997), xiii.

7. *Information Sources in Official Publications,* edited by Valerie J. Nurcombe (West Sussex, United Kingdom: Bowker-Sauer, 1997), xxiv.

CHAPTER 11
Health

CHAPTER OVERVIEW

Health, as defined in the WHO Constitution, is "a state of complete physical, mental, and social well-being and not merely the absence of disease or infirmity."[1] This chapter encompasses health subjects and statistics that fall under this definition. It also covers information about diseases, national health policy, and some human biology and science issues that affect the future development of health. Medicine as a topic is not covered in this chapter, although some of the resources and databases can be searched for medical information. Major international governmental organizations working in this field are the World Health Organization and the Pan American Health Organization. Also covered are the health-related activities of the United Nations and the Organisation for Economic Cooperation and Development (OECD).

Governmental Sources Discussed

Globalhealth.gov Web site, by the Office of Global Health Affairs, U.S. Department of Health and Human Resources, Washington, D.C. <http://www.globalhealth.gov>

Health in the Americas, by the Pan American Health Organization (PAHO), Washington, D.C., 1998– (print title with next-to-latest edition full text online; latest edition available online by subscription). <http://www.paho.org/English/SHA/HIA_1998ed.htm>

ICD-9-CM, International Classification of Diseases, 9th rev., Clinical Modification, by the U.S. National Center for Health Statistics and the Health Care Financing Administration, Hyattsville, Md. (print 1994–, CD and online title). <http://www.cdc.gov/nchs/icd9.htm#CD-ROM> (some issues) or <http://purl.access.gpo.gov/GPO/LPS8749>

OECD Health Data, by the Organisation for Economic Cooperation and Development, Paris, 1997–. (CD-ROM/interactive online subscription resource).

Pan American Health Organization (PAHO) Web site, Washington, D.C. <http://www.paho.org>

U.S. Centers for Disease Control and Prevention. Division of International Health (DIH) Web site, Atlanta Ga. <http://www.cdc.gov/epo/dih/index.htm>

UNAIDS Web site, by the Joint United Nations Programme on HIV/AIDS, Geneva. <http://www.unaids.org/>

World Health Organization Resources

Bulletin of the World Health Organization: The International Journal of Public Health, by the World Health Organization, Geneva, 1948– (ISSN 0042-9686) (print and online periodical). <http://www.who.int/bulletin>

Country Information Web site, by the World Health Organization, Regional Office for Europe. <http://www.euro.who.int/countryinformation>

International Digest of Health Legislation (IDHL), by the World Health Organization (WHO), Geneva, 1948– (ISSN 0020-6563) (print and online). <http://www.who.int/idhl/>

Library & Information Networks for Knowledge (LNK) Web site, by the World Health Organization library, Geneva, Switzerland. <http://www.who.int/hlt/>

Weekly Epidemiological Record, by the World Health Organization (WHO), Geneva, Switzerland, 1948– (ISSN 0049-8114) (print and online periodical). <http://www.who.int/wer/>

WHO Statistical Information System (WHOSIS) Web site, by the World Health Organization, Geneva, Switzerland. <http://www3.who.int/whosis/>

World Health Organization Web site, Geneva, Switzerland. <http://www.who.org>

World Health Report, by the World Health Organization, Geneva, Switzerland, 1995– (ISSN 1020-3311) (print and online annual title). <http://www.who.int/whr/>

World Health Statistics Annual, by the World
Health Organization, Geneva, Switzerland, 1962–
(ISSN 0250-3794) (paper and online in a different format). <http://www3.who.int/whosis/
menu.cfm?path = statistics,whsa&language =
english> (Online as the *WHO Database* on the
WHOSIS database page, 1997–. <http://www.
who.int/whosis/>).

Nongovernmental Source Discussed

Project HOPE Web site. <http://www.projhope.
org/>

GOVERNMENTAL SOURCES

Globalhealth.gov Web site, by the Office of Global
Health Affairs, U.S. Department of Health and
Human Resources, Washington, D.C.
<http://www.globalhealth.gov>

Summary: This is a portal health Internet site that
addresses global health and provides the link between
U.S. and international health issues, especially of
global health concern. This searchable site provides
key messages and speeches, news, a calendar, reports
and publications, travel information, data resources
under countries and statistics, Internet links, and
medical literature. The U.S. Department of Health
and Human Resources involvement in global health
initiatives and policies supporting health worldwide
serves the health interests of the United States; this
site links to all the Department's agencies, to their
global activities, and to selected worldwide health resources.

Detailed Description: This site organizes information
under these major sections: About Global Health,
What's New, Archives Data Resources, International
Travel, Links & Dialogue, and Search. About Global
Health provides information about the office and its priorities. Similar home page links provide even more information about the office, its agency partners,
frequently asked questions, and global health partnerships between the United States and other organizations. Under What's New is information about the
Department's activities around the globe and a calendar
of events. Users also find news, statements, speeches,
reports, and publications in this section. Under Data
Resources users may also link to information about
refugee health worldwide, as this office acts as liaison
to organizations on this topic. The Reports and Publications section is a compilation of links to major health

reports. U.S. reports are listed first, followed by those
published by other agencies and organizations such as
the United Nations, the World Bank, and the World
Health Organization. This page links to the full text of
most reports unless otherwise noted. It also links to
publication catalogs.

The Data Resources section also links to Country
Information, World Health Statistics, Global Health
Topics, and Fact Sheets. Under country information
users may click on a map or a region of the world, then
select a country, or select a country from a drop-down
box. The information provided for each country is a
link to the country's embassy, background information (*Background Notes,* by the U.S. Department of
State), international travel (*CDC's Travelers Health,*
by the U.S. Centers for Disease Control), and the Department of Health and Human Services projects in
that country. The Data Resources section also links to
World Health Statistics, a list of important resources
online, and links to many full-text statistical reports
on health, some of which are described in this chapter.
Global Health Topics includes information on Biotechnology, Bioterrorism, Food Safety, HIV/AIDS,
Tobacco, Tuberculosis, SARS, and Bird Flu.

International Travel links to the U.S. Department of
State for general travel warnings and the U.S. Centers
for Disease Control for disease and country specific
information for travelers. The Links & Dialogue section provides selected Internet links to other key
global health organizations and health-related list-
servs.

The Search section *Globalhealth.gov* is searchable
by keyword or advanced search options of words,
phrases, and dates. Medical/Health Literature links to
two important U.S. resources: the U.S. National Library of Medicine, with full-text and bibliographic information, and *MEDLINE/PubMed*, with references
and abstracts from over 4,000 biomedical journals.

Health in the Americas, by the Pan American Health
Organization (PAHO), Washington, D.C., 1998–
(print title with next-to-latest edition full text online; latest edition available online by subscription). <http://www.paho.org/English/HIA1998/
HealthVol1.pdf>, <http://www.paho.org/En-
glish/HIA1998/HealthVol2.pdf>

Summary: This is an authoritative reference of health
indicators and trends for countries of the entire Region of the Americas. Information is provided under
country name. Also published in Spanish, this title is
published every four years, in two volumes, and is

available in print. The 1998 edition is available electronically in full-text format. The latest edition is available online for a fee or through a database subscription; the introduction is available at no charge.

Detailed Description: Formerly published as *Health Conditions in the Americas* (1964–1994), this reference provides a comprehensive analysis of the health situation of the countries of the Americas. Volume 1 covers analysis of health situation trends, health by population group, diseases or health impairments, and the response of health systems. Finally, it covers technical and financial external cooperation on health. Volume 2 provides information under individual country name organized alphabetically. Online users may choose to download each volume fully or select just a country profile. The first edition under its newer title, published in 1998, contains information for 1993–1996.

The country profiles are organized by topic and contain both analysis and statistics in the same text. Each profile covers general health situation and trends in the country and health problems of specific population groups, such as women, children, and the elderly. It provides an analysis by specific disease or health impairment, broken down into communicable and noncommunicable disease sections. Coverage focuses on the health sector, the organization of the national health system, health regulation and policy, and health services and resources, including water supply, waste disposal, food safety, food aid, and pollution.

To fulfill its mission of health for all in the Americas, the Pan American Health Organization publishes many other books on health in the Americas. Others may be found in their searchable online bookstore. Also, users may link to full-text online publications by searching PAHO's Institutional Memory Database of bibliographic records and digital collections from 1902. In addition, users may search a Virtual Health Library.

ICD-9-CM, International Classification of Diseases, 9th rev., Clinical Modification, by the U.S. National Center for Health Statistics and the Health Care Financing Administration, Hyattsville, Md. (print 1994–, CD and online title). <http://www. cdc.gov/nchs/icd9.htm#CD-ROM> (some issues) or <http://purl.access.gpo.gov/GPO/LPS8749>

Summary: This title, abbreviated as *ICD-9-CM,* is based on the World Health Organizations' ninth revision, *International Classification of Diseases (ICD-9).* *ICD-9-CM* is the official system of assigning codes to diagnoses and procedures associated with hospital utilization in the United States. It is used to code and classify mortality data from death certificates. On CD-ROM, this title contains the complete official version of the ninth revision. Some years are also available online at the National Center for Health Statistics Web site and through a PURL assigned by the U.S. Government Printing Office. The U.S. agencies, the National Center for Health Statistics and the U.S. Health Care Financing Administration, are responsible for overseeing all the changes and modifications of the *ICD-9-CM.*

Detailed Description: This title provides access through a tabular list containing a numerical list of the disease code numbers; a tabular list of surgical, diagnostic, and therapeutic procedures with an alphabetic index; and an alphabetical index to the disease entries. Appendices include a glossary, classification of drugs, classification of industrial accidents, and the morphology of neoplasms.

The database is searchable by words, phrases, and numbers. In the CD-ROM version, the search history can be saved, and records can be tagged to print or save. This is not available online. However, some of the online files can be downloaded by ftp in rich text files, as well as be viewed in HTML.

OECD Health Data, by the Organisation for Economic Cooperation and Development, Paris, 1997– (CD-ROM/interactive online subscription resource).

Summary: This CD-ROM/interactive title provides access to comparative health data for 30 OECD countries for the 1990s on with some indicators in time-series back to 1960. It is intended to be published annually and is run under Windows software. Free updating is available to purchasers through the Internet. It provides printing and exporting capabilities, and it is available in English, French, Spanish, and German.

In 2001, the OECD embarked on a three-year project on health and health analysis because the organization recognizes that health systems are crucial to the OECD economies. The project's goal is to provide policy guidance for health systems, because of the money spent on health in the service sector and also because the health of the population as citizens, workers, and consumers is very important to the economy. OECD also sponsors conferences on health, and more information is available on the OECD's searchable Web site at <http://www.oecd.org>.

Detailed Description: *OECD Health Data* provides data coverage in these areas: health status, such as mortality and injury; health care resources, such as medical technology and health employment; health care utilization; expenditure on health; financing and remuneration; social protection; pharmaceutical market; nonmedical determinants of health; demographic reference; and economic references. It includes three-dimensional tables that display several indicators simultaneously for multiple countries and years.

The data covers over 1,200 indicators and allows complex queries. Key topics span the period 1970 to present, although some historical series are available from 1960. Users have options to query the database through modules, save tables, and access information by country group. This software package also provides links to valuable Internet sites in this area. Sample tables, definitions, methodology, and ordering are available through the OECD Web site.

Some of this information is available free online through OECD's Internet site on health, <http://www.oecd.org/> (OECD home, select By Topic: Health). Full text of selected titles on health issues under OECD's series *Health Working Papers* is made available in PDF or Word format.

Pan American Health Organization (PAHO) Web site, Washington, D.C. <http://www.paho.org>

Summary: PAHO is an international public health agency whose essential mission is to strengthen national and local health systems and improve the health of the peoples of the Americas, and it provides a comprehensive Web site on health in the Americas in English and Spanish. It contains information on health topics such as diseases and nutrition, health data, and information resources online including periodicals, books, and databases. News and articles are available from the home page. A quick search option from the home page allows users to search for a specific topic. Also a section on countries and regions of the Americas lets users find health information and data online about specific countries in the Americas. The major information sections discussed following are Health Data, Health Topics, and Information Resources.

With more than 90 years of experience, PAHO works with national Ministries of Health, international agencies, and many other groups to improve health and living standards of the countries of the Americas. It serves as the Regional Office for the Americas of the World Health Organization and is part of the United Nations system.

Detailed Description: The *PAHO* Web site provides sections on Health Data, Health Topics, Information

Resources, Online Bookstore, and About PAHO linked from a topbar, which lists detailed subsections. Also available from the left sidebar is information about training programs, grants, news and public information, and links back to WHO. The center text of the home page features many articles on organization activities in current concerns, which could range from research collaboration to disaster and crisis treatment systems. Only the beginning paragraph of the articles is shown with a link to the rest in either HTML or PDF versions. On the right of the home page, users may find and implement a quick search. Below quick search is a link to advanced search options, press releases, announcements, and what's new. The advanced search lets users select language, date, type of publication of interest, and specific country to limit their search. Finally, there is a section of buttons on the right side that leads users to special programs like measles eradication, World Health Day, proceedings, and new books of interest.

About PAHO provides a list of the country offices that work in the member countries of the organization, which serves as a further resource for health information. The Health Data section leads to full text and statistics available online under the subsections: Atlas of Inequities, Basic Health Indicators, Core Health Data, Country Health Profiles, and Trends and Situation Analysis. Parts of the section also list major titles of interest and describe them, but do not make them fully available online. Basic Health Indicators and Core Health Data are both brief subsections. Country Health Profiles gives a detailed online summary online for individual countries, linking to the countries in an alphabetical list. General demographics, socioeconomic and health risks, and mortality for the country data is listed first, followed by a summary of health trends and situation in the country, an analysis of specific health problems of groups, like children, and specific diseases, such as AIDS. Finally, it summarizes the national health policy of the country and its health systems, its organization, and resources.

Health Topics is a major source of information available from the *PAHO* home page. These major topics follow a link to specific topics, and from there to information mostly in HTML or PDF formats from PAHO's technical documentation, resolutions, summaries of meetings, periodical articles, links to database, multimedia (including videos), and announcements. Major health topics links from the home page include: Disasters, Diseases, Prevention/Control, Environmental Health, Epidemiology/Biostatistics, Equity and Human Development, Health

Groups, Health Promotion, Health Systems and Services, Health Technology, Mental Health, Nutrition and Food Protection, Other Topics, Research, Vaccines & Immunizations, and Zoonoses/Animal Health.

The Information Resources Section from PAHO's home page links to different types of information: Technical Documentation, Books, Periodical Publications, Multimedia, Databases, Announcements, Other Resources, and Community Interaction. Under periodicals, users can find full text in PDF format of PAHO's *Pan American Journal of Public Health,* a peer-reviewed journal on public health research, combating disease, emerging health trends, and news in the Americas. Published in English and Spanish, abstracts of the research articles are available online.

U.S. Centers for Disease Control and Prevention, Division for International Health (DIH) Web site, Atlanta, Ga. <http://www.cdc.gov/epo/dih/>

Summary: In working with partner countries to improve public health systems, this U.S. agency publishes specific project information on their activities on their home page. These relate to specific countries and regions all over the world, and many of the publications are free, online full text. The Web page of DIH is searchable, provides a site map, and users may link to the Centers for Disease Control and Prevention's A–Z subjects on health on the top bar.

The main goal of the U.S. Centers for Disease Control and Prevention, Division for International Health is to assist countries in the development and implementation of dynamic, cost-effective public health systems and health information systems for reporting and measuring public health. DIH also helps partner countries improve their health organizations in their function, activities, training, and communication.

Detailed Description: The *U.S. Centers for Disease Control, Division of International Health* Web site is divided on the left sidebar into the categories: What We Do, How We Work, Where We Work, Partners, Publications, Site Map, and Contact information. What We Do links to information about major programs in countries all over the world and links to training information and online training materials for certain health problems, such as the disease yellow fever. Also under What We Do are reports on DIH's work as Public Health Systems consultants, for example in assisting with a new national health surveillance program in Brazil.

How We Work reports on the mission, goals, strategies, evaluations, and achievements of the organization. This includes summaries of the major projects around the world. Where We Work links to a clickable world map and more information geographically organized. From the home page side bar, Partners links to the partner agencies of this organization in the private, public, and nongovernmental sectors.

UNAIDS Web site, by the Joint United Nations Programme on HIV/AIDS, Geneva, Switzerland.<http://www.unaids.org/>

Summary: This cooperative agency of many agencies dealing with HIV in the world publishes statistics and information on HIV/AIDS and promotes awareness and education. The Web site provides latest news, what's news, conference information, and information for journalists. Of special interests are the publications and worldwide statistics available in full electronically and the HIV/AIDS information that is available by subject and by country. The site is searchable and provides a site map and help.

UNAID considers itself a leading world advocate of action against the HIV/AIDS epidemic. It leads global response, prevention, support, and alleviation efforts in a joint program of seven organizations. In the beginning of the epidemic around 1986, the World Health Organization led the United Nations efforts against AIDS, but it became necessary to draw on more resources in the mid-1990s. The original joint organizations in UNAID are UNICEF, UNDP, UNFPA, UNESCO, WHO, and the World Bank, which were joined in April 1999 by UNDCP.

Detailed Description: News and current events are the focus of the main part of the UNAIDS home site. This organization sponsors a World AIDS Day and provides information about it, including an update of the epidemic and a press kit for journalists. Also available is information about the organization's yearly campaign against AIDS. Joint UNAIDS/WHO press releases are provided in English, French, Spanish, and Russian.

Home page categories include About UNAIDS, Geographic Area, In Focus, Resources, Media, Events, and Special Sections. These provide more detailed information. An advanced search allows users to search by topic, region, or organization. Media links to information for journalists including press releases, speeches, video/sound clips, and fact sheets. The information about the organization itself is under About UNAIDS.

The category In Focus provides news and links to complete AIDS topics. Full-text documents on AIDS are available here under topics such as access to drugs, human rights, care and prevention of the disease, children, surveillance and reporting (statistics), and many more. Documents are provided mostly in English and PDF format, with some other languages and formats such as HTML.

Under Resources, the section on Terminology provides an online glossary and another section Questions and Answers, an instructional guide. An important subsection on Epidemiology provides detailed statistics on AIDS through online documents and statistical reports. It links to recent online full-text publications such as *AIDS Epidemic Update* and epidemiological fact sheets that provide AIDS statistics by country. Also available are HIV/AIDS trends and outlooks and downloadable epidemiological software, graphics, and slides. It links to more information from the WHO HIV/AIDS Department.

Miscellaneous information is provided in the link from the home page under Events. It provides information on conferences, World AIDS Day, and other special initiatives and programs.

World Health Organization Resources

Bulletin of the World Health Organization: The International Journal of Public Health, by the World Health Organization, Geneva, Switzerland, 1948– (ISSN 0042-9686) (print and online periodical). <http://www.who.int/bulletin>

Summary: This monthly periodical is a leading research journal in the area of world health. WHO was formed in 1948 and from that year has published the *Bulletin* specifically to help the organization promote and coordinate biomedical and health services research; stimulate and advance work on the prevention and control of epidemics and other diseases; and act as the directing and coordinating authority on international health work. The *Bulletin* includes biomedical and scientific research, as well as social and behavioral science articles. By including scientific research findings and policy-relevant discussions in the same publication, the *Bulletin's* goal is to provide the best scientific evidence for guiding public health policy and practice, and also to encourage closer links between scientific investigation and the art of helping populations to lead healthier lives. Special theme issues explore public health issues in-depth; for example, volume 78, no. 9, 2000, focuses on Environment and Health. Full-text articles are available online from volume 77, no.1, 1999, and can be searched with the World Health Organization (WHO) search engine available from the *Bulletin's* home page. It is published in English, with French and Spanish summaries for each article.

Detailed Description: Established for more than 50 years as a leading research journal, the *Bulletin* was expanded in 1999 to publish more quickly, moving from bimonthly to a monthly publication and enlarging its editorial scope. It broadened its traditional coverage of biomedical and scientific research to include social and behavioral science articles, linking science and policy. Coverage prioritizes original research findings that improve understanding of health problems and ways to solve them, especially for concerns of health and disease shared by many countries. In the year 2001, readers will notice these added features: special theme issues, up-to-date reviews on clinical problems and policy issues, expanded world coverage, updates on the initiatives and views of WHO, and interviews with leading figures in public health.

The *Bulletin's* issues include editorials, subject papers by individual authors, reprinted public health classics, research, policy and practices articles, news, perspectives, letters, and special themes, often accompanied by graphs, charts, and tables, and bibliographies and footnotes. A list of forthcoming special themes for individual issues is listed on the home page. Articles are available online in PDF format.

The home page links to the current issue, including the table of contents and text for the current issue. Users may link to previous issues online back to 1947, under the link titled Volumes (for previous volumes). This month's Features is a section that provides highlights (PDF) for the current issue. A link to the *SCI-ELO* site allows readers to search the *Bulletin* by keyword, issue, and author, 2000–.

The *Bulletin's* home page also links to some other major health research resources under the category Publications including: WHO Publications Catalog, Just Published, *World Health Report* (also described in this chapter), and Search Medline. The Just Published section leads the user to new materials published in paper and electronically in the PDF format.

Country Information Web site, by the World Health Organization, Regional Office for Europe. <http://www.euro.who.int/countryinformation>

Summary: This online resource provides Country Highlights, with health and health-related information by European country, with some comparative information. It also provides annual reports for the region and statistical databases. The World Health Organization, Regional Office for Europe, promotes health in European nations and compiles information.

Detailed Description: *Country Information* has three main sections: Country Information, Health Topics, and Information Sources. Country Information provides highlights of health information for individual countries and compares them to other European countries. The files are mostly in English, French, Dutch, and Russian languages and are available in full text via PDF format, with some in HTML. They cover the country and people, health status, environment, lifestyle, health systems, and include references and a map. These are informational informal publications produced in collaboration between the WHO Regional Office for Europe and the member countries, and not formal statistical publications.

Information Sources links to the latest edition online of full-text reports in PDF format on trends in health in the European region. The current title, *Health in Europe,* is available in English, French, German, and Russian and covers status, trends, principles, and practice of health in Europe and includes color graphs, charts, and statistics. Appendices are also provided containing basic socioeconomic indicators and progress reports on health for all in the region. Earlier reports must be purchased from the WHO sales office. Also available are links to data and the *Statistical Atlas of Health in Europe,* 2002 (PDF). The Health Topics section provides information by subject, including programs and reports.

International Digest of Health Legislation (IDHL), by the World Health Organization (WHO), Geneva, Switzerland, 1948– (ISSN 0020-6563) (print and online). <http://www.who.int/idhl/>

Summary: This quarterly periodical provides up-to-date information on health-relevant legislation, including new national and international legislation, as part of WHO's mission is to compile and disseminate health information to its member states. Concerning new national and international legislation, WHO informs members of the frequency of adoption, amendment, and repeal of legislative provisions. It also includes studies on current problems in health legislation, news and views, and book reviews and abstracts. A subject index is available, and this title is currently available online only starting April 2000. This title is available in

English and French editions. For those who do not have access to the Internet, WHO will furnish printed copies of sections of the electronic version.

Detailed Description: The texts of the health legislation are reproduced or translated in full or exact form and also summarized. Each issue begins with a chronological index. The subject index is published in the last issue of each volume of the printed title, however, the online title allows a site search for the entire periodical. Also for the online version in English, searching is available across successive issues by country, by subject, by volume, by issue, by keyword, and by subject notes. Each issue is organized into chapters by subject of the legislation, such as cloning, nutrition, consumer protection, human reproduction, radiation, health information, or statistics. Each issue also provides a literature section that abstracts significant titles in the health field, whereas the actual book review provides more detailed information than the abstracts.

This title mainly includes the official publications and documents forwarded by the WHO member states according to the constitution of WHO. Volume 50, no. 4, 1999, was the last issue of the *Digest* in printed form.

Library & Information Networks for Knowledge (LNK) Web site by the World Health Organization library, Geneva, Switzerland. <http://www.who.int/hlt>

Summary: *LNK* is a World Health Organization Internet resource that links the user to world health information, databases, library catalogs and *WHOLIS,* WHO documentation, WHO's Virtual Reference Desk, resources specifically for country support, and historical information. Access to information about Library collections is available through the *WHOLIS* electronic library database. The page is available in English and French and offers a text version.

LNK provides the information resources and knowledge needed by all WHO members, but also has a policy of providing free access for all to current public health information. The resource also supports the work of WHO in providing technical cooperation to help improve the transfer of health information in developing countries.

Detailed Description: *WHOLIS,* the library catalog, is linked right from the home page of *LNK.* It allows the user to search by quick and complex searches and to set preferences for searching. *WHOLIS* also provides an Information Desk and user services buttons for further information about how to use it. The Information Desk has a Booklist that lists new titles.

Weekly Epidemiological Record, by the World Health Organization (WHO), Geneva, Switzerland, 1948– (ISSN 0049-8114) (print and online periodical). <http://www.who.int/wer/>

Summary: This weekly report on cases and outbreaks of infectious diseases is available in both paper and online formats, allowing health workers in the government and private sectors and citizens to stay informed about health threats. It reports on those infectious diseases monitored under International Health Regulations or on newly emerging diseases that pose a threat to human health. Published in bilingual English/ French, an electronic edition is free of charge in PDF format dating back to 1996.

Detailed Description: A News section on disease outbreaks, information on international health regulations, and chapters on specific diseases are the main components of this periodical. Users will find reports on disease trends in specific regions or countries of the world, reports on immunization, vaccinations, and surveillance efforts, and maps of disease incidence by country. Some statistics are provided within the text of the bulletin. Each yearly volume has an index by subject, including diseases and country. A free e-mail subscription service is available that provides table of contents information and brief epidemiological bulletins.

This title continues the *Weekly Epidemiological Record,* published by the League of Nations 1928–1946.

WHO Statistical Information System (WHOSIS)
Web site, by the World Health Organization, Geneva, Switzerland. <http://www3.who.int/whosis/>

Summary: This is a searchable Internet database of selected health, epidemiological, and health-related statistical information from the WHO Global Programme on Evidence for Health Policy. One of WHO's major objectives in order to fulfill its mission in world health is to provide important statistical information as a resource for decision and policy makers in the area of health. Users may search under many categories, particularly statistical information on topic and disease and journals on specific subjects (such as *HIV/AIDS Statistics*). Keyword searching through the entire *WHO* Web site is available with the capability of linking to other Internet health re-

sources. Some individual resources are described in this chapter.

Detailed Description: *WHO Statistical Information System (WHOSIS)* is basically a list of links to full information resources, with a focus on statistics, especially epidemiological. Links to Other Sources of Health Information are grouped and listed by category. A *WHOSIS* query service will give additional tips to users who need assistance in finding information in the databases provided. Searches may be limited to pages with only the specific words and phrases. Users may also search throughout WHO. A Frequently Asked Questions section is available.

The information that *WHOSIS* links to and provides searching for includes online titles and information in the following categories:

- Contact *WHOSIS*
- External sources for health-related statistical information
- *Global Alcohol Database*
- Global Programme on Evidence for Health Policy—*Discussion Papers*
- Health personnel
- HIV/AIDS Statistics
- Immunization Statistics
- International Classifications and Terminology
- Links to National Health-related Web sites
- New health life-expectancy rankings, with press releases and country rankings
- Population Statistics
- Severe Acute Respiratory Syndrome (SARS)
- Statistical Annexes from the *World Health Report*
- Statistics by Disease or Condition
- *Weekly Epidemiological Record;* International Travel and Health; *Global Burden of Disease and Injury Series*
- WHO Library and Information services (library catalog is included)
- *WHO Mortality Database*
- WHO Publications (a publications catalog)

World Health Organization Web site, Geneva, Switzerland. <http://www.who.org>

Summary: The World Health Organization (WHO) is considered the premier international health organization in the world. Its Web site is available in English, French, and Spanish. Prominently across the top of the page, the user will find a site index, a search engine, and information about WHO as an organization. Notable is the ability of the user to search specific sections of the WHO Web pages; search links to the advanced search option. From the home page the user may choose selections such as Health Topics A–Z, Emergencies, and Disease Outbreaks right from the front page that quickly lead to worldwide information about specific diseases, health problems, and events that affect health. The Research Tools link connects the user to important periodicals that are full text on the Web. Research Tools also leads to several important resources described separately in this chapter, *WHOLIS,* the library database, and *WHO Statistical Information System (WHOSIS).*

WHO's mission is to function as the directing and coordinating authority on international health work. It supports its main objective of health for all peoples by a variety of work such as supporting research, assistance to governments, promoting cooperation, publishing, and proposing agreements and standards in the field of health.

Publications is a major category on the home page. WHO publishes and distributes its materials via an online bookshop and other vendors.

Detailed Description: Basic links from the home page of *WHO* include the following categories: WHO Sites, Disease Outbreaks, Emergencies, the Press Media Center, Research Tools, Governance (information about the working of the organization), Regional Committees, and Travellers' Health. Three vertical text columns cover current news and events and highlight the activities and information found through this organization. Significant news coverage begins in text on the home page.

Health Topics A–Z provides an alphabetical list of diseases and a separate category list for users to choose from. It allows users to search just the Health Topics. Under each topic is a reference page with links to *WHO Fact Sheets,* publications, statistics, surveys, surveillance, and more information. Each topic has a varying degree of coverage, usually with a simple definition or summary of the issue, and then links to publications about the disease or issue. Publications often include very specific examples and facts from countries around the world. For example, the health topic "food safety" links to a program and much more information on this topic. Cancer links to a well-developed page listing specific databases and publications concerned with cancer. The topic Women, Health & Environment provides an anthology of related information.

Research Tools links to full text of major periodicals and reports of WHO, including these major titles, which are all described separately in this chapter:

- *Bulletin of the World Health Organization*
- *ICD-10 International Statistical Classification of Diseases & Related Health Problems* (lists health conditions)
- *Weekly Epidemiological Record* (provides information on the outbreak of diseases worldwide in a bilingual English/French edition)
- *World Health Report*

Research Tools also links to *WHOLIS,* the library database, and from there to the *Library and Information Networks for Knowledge (LNK)* (covered as a separate resource in this chapter), as well as the Media Center, and Related Links. The Media Center includes audio and video clips, and photographs from the organization and its regional offices. The latest fact sheets and press releases are available from the Centre. The fact sheets are available by number or by alphabetical order and in English and French. They cover basic facts about health topics, such as blindness, drinking water, and electromagnetic fields, and even about health topics in specific countries.

From the Publications category, researchers should take note of the WHO online bookshop which is much more than a simple online catalog. The catalog links to databases, which contain bibliographic details for all publications issued by WHO since its beginning in 1948. The catalog also leads to a full-text searchable *Multilingual List of Publications* issued since 1950 and an alphabetical list of subjects for titles still in print. A Free Documents section is available consisting of mostly current titles in PDF format.

World Health Report, by the World Health Organization, Geneva, Switzerland, 1995– (ISSN 1020-3311) (print and online annual title). <http://www.who.int/whr/>

Summary: This *Report* covers health issues and services worldwide. Published since 1948, it is available on the Internet from 1995 forward. The title's objective is to help policy makers in the field of health to make wise choices and therefore to assist in fulfilling WHO's objective, the attainment by all peoples of the highest possible level of health. From 2000 on, individual issues have distinctive titles and specific subjects, with individual chapters analyzing specific health issues. The statistical appendix in each issue provides country statistics on diseases and other health subjects.

Detailed Description: Issues have distinctive titles and focus on special subjects; for example, 2003 is on shaping the future of global health systems, 2001 covers mental health. The 2000 report is on health systems: improving performance. It provides expert analysis of the influence of health systems in the daily lives of people worldwide and aims to stimulate debate in order to improve health systems. The 1999 issue focuses on how health can make a difference in humanity's continuing progress. This report shows how the pursuit of lasting improvements in health along with improved national health policies can affect social and economic improvements. The 1998 report is on the assessment of the global health situation with projections of health trends to the year 2025 and includes some time series of data back to 1955.

Each issue of the *Report* contains an overview, index, graphics, references, and a statistical annex. The statistical annex of tables provides statistics for WHO regions and WHO member countries for specific health topics and diseases.

The statistical tables from the report may be searched and retrieved from a section of the *WHO Statistical Information System (WHOSIS)* called *Statistical Data: New Measures for Health and Health Systems* at <http://www.who.int/whosis/>. This is available for the 2000 *Report* and planned for future reports. The user may search the tables by keyword or phrase, go directly to the table through a table of contents, or choose specific countries and indicators to retrieve. Additional choices include World Maps, which show the distribution of selected indicators, and terminology, with definitions in English and equivalents in official languages.

World Health Statistics Annual, by the World Health Organization (WHO), Geneva, Switzerland, 1962– (ISSN 0250-3794) (paper and online in a different format). <http://www3.who.int/whosis/menu. cfm?path = statistics,whsa&language = english>. Online as the *WHO Database* on the *WHOSIS* database page, 1997–. <http://www.who.int/ whosis/>

Summary: This statistical database in English and French contains the latest data from WHO's mortality database, including causes of death, infant causes of death, life expectancy, and age-standardized death rates. This online version of the *World Health Statistics Annual* contains all data that has been received since the publication of the last print edition, issued in early 1998, which covered the year 1996. It follows the same format in tables and organization of data, therefore users may use comparative data across the

years in both print and online versions. The data is reported to WHO from the official national statistical offices of about 70 countries. Most member countries supply the data to WHO on national mortality statistics and cause of death, but WHO compiles and utilizes validated data of good quality in the *WHO Mortality Database.*

Detailed Description: The 1997–1999 *World Health Statistics Annual* online as *WHO Mortality Database 1997–1999* is available in four tables, with data provided for individual countries. Table 1 has numbers of deaths and deaths rates by cause, sex, and age. Table 2 covers infant deaths. Table 3 covers life expectancy, and table 4 age-standardized death rates. Several years are available for each country, from the current year, back to at least the last print edition in 1996. International Classification of Diseases (ICD) codes for diseases are used in the tables. On the *WHOSIS* page, users will find *WHO Mortality Data,* the online version of the *World Health Statistics Annual,* listed last.

Even more detailed information on death data for specific countries is available through the *WHOSIS* statistical database through downloadable files of mortality data in the *WHO Mortality Database.* This database is the underlying source containing all WHO's mortality statistics by country, age group, sex, and year and cause of death. Also, *WHOSIS* provides users with search by keyword for the entire WHO Web site, including these tables, and is separately described in this chapter.

The annual print publication, *WHO Health Statistics Annual,* is available in research and health libraries back to 1962, with a previous title also in English and French back to 1949: *Statistiques épidémiologiques et démographiques annuelles/Annual Epidemiological and Vital Statistics.* Users should note that when the publication or online database does not include a country's information, that specific country did not report the data to WHO for the time period. *WHO Health Statistics Annual* contains a Section A with several very general health and demographic data tables listing data by country and a Section B organized by individual country by region of the world with the following data:

- Numbers of deaths and mortality rates by country, age group, sex, year and cause of death
- Causes of infant deaths by age (under one year) and sex
- Life expectancy, by sex
- The probability of dying at different ages due to major cause-of-death groups, by sex
- Age-standardized death rates for major cause-of-death groups, by sex

NONGOVERNMENTAL SOURCES

Project HOPE Web site. <http://www.projhope. org/>

Summary: Project HOPE's searchable Web site provides information on its activities and functions by the categories: health education, humanitarian relief, and health systems development. The home page heading How We Help provides access to the current issue and abstracts of articles of older issues of Project HOPE's subscription print and online journal, *Health Affairs: The Policy Journal of the Health Sphere. Health Affairs* also publishes Web-only articles free in HTML or PDF format on its Web site.

Project HOPE is a privately funded organization that meets the health needs of 28 developing countries by health education, primary care, humanitarian care, health systems development, health policy analysis, and health research. Its mission is to achieve sustainable advances in health care around the world by these means to contribute to human dignity, promote international understanding, and enhance social and economic development. HOPE stands for Health Opportunities for People Everywhere.

Detailed Description: Information on projects in individual countries may be accessed through the link Hope Around the World from the Home Page. Also available from the home page are the photo gallery, a sign-up for their electronic newsletter, site map, text version, search engine, and its annual reports. Following the links from the broad categories on *Project HOPE's* Web site, such as training and humanitarian care, are details and descriptions of projects at the country level, organized by topic.

RESEARCH STRATEGIES

The premier world international intergovernmental organization on health is the **World Health Organization.** Its Web site can be an excellent starting place for beginning to advanced researchers. Certainly for current health news and emergencies, users should begin here, and also for health topics such as diseases, all users should consult the Health A–Z Topics on WHO's home page. If a user wants to learn the site better and begin to use it, the ***Library & Information Networks for Knowledge (LNK)*** will be of assistance to help navigate to the correct resource. Using the *WHO* Internet site does require some knowledge of moving about a complicated Web site, and the time spent

searching it for information is not always needed, so students to researchers are recommended to start with the specific titles that meet their needs. Here are some hints.

For general statistics by country, a recommended starting place is the statistical tables available in every annual edition of **World Health Report,** available online from 1995. It is also the best resource to check for statistics on many countries because the tables are easy to consult. Researchers may also consult this title back to 1948 for health trends in countries. For help in finding detailed statistical health information, and if users are unsure where to start, consult **WHO Statistical Information System (WHOSIS)** Web site, which lists many links to statistical searchable databases and other information.

If a user needs detailed statistics, it is best to go to the specific resource that provides it first, bypassing the general information resources just listed. For mortality statistics and cause of death, all users should use the **World Health Statistics Annual.** If electronic data is needed by researchers, the online version will provide downloadable data through the **WHO Mortality Database.** If historical data is needed, users must consult the print title available in many university libraries that goes back annually to 1962 and before then in a different title. For worldwide AIDS data by country, the **UNAIDS** Web site is best, and for cases and outbreaks of infectious diseases worldwide, WHO's **Weekly Epidemiological Record.** Users may view this title electronically back to 1996, but only if they have the capability of viewing PDF format files online.

Discussion of general health issues that affect national policy, such as access to clean water or women and health is best covered in a general way in the **World Health Report,** and this title is a good indicator of what issues were important in worldwide concerns about health. For information in this area of a current nature, and in the form of more detailed articles and research, policy, and for editorials on health issues, users should consult the monthly **Bulletin of the World Health Organization.**

After first consulting the general statistical information for information about specific areas of the world or a specific health topic, the general health information is not as useful. Instead users should try these resources for these topics. For information about Latin American and Caribbean countries, for beginners to researchers, the best beginning resource is *Health in the Americas,* the annual publication available in print and electronically that is current and provides health issue coverage for the area and also statistics. Another starting place for Internet users is the Web site for the *Pan American Health Organization,* because it is a well-organized site that provides easy access to both health data and public health topics. The *Pan American Journal of Public Health* provides up-to-date monthly research needed if the user's focus is on this part of the world. The *International Classification of Diseases* is a title for researchers to use with health resources containing this classification of diseases when they are working on a detailed research level.

For current information about Europe, the *Country Information* from the Regional Office for Europe gives an excellent access point for beginning to intermediate students, as it provides both health information in its country highlights and reports on trends and issues in European health in online titles such as *European Health Report.* Most of this information would only be available in print in major university and research libraries that purchase European Union and World Health Organization information and is not suited for detailed research. For this, consult the *OECD Health Data 2001* online resource, usually only available in research libraries. This provides electronic data from 1970 on, with some time series back to 1960, on many health topics for all OECD countries. This is a complex resource, therefore researchers may need to consult information specialists and librarians for assistance in its use. Users should remember that OECD is an organization whose members are industrialized countries in Europe and around the world, including the United States.

For the topic of international health issues, a good beginning resource for any level of user is *Global-health.gov* health portal of the U.S. government to international health issues. Some students researching international health issues may find the Globalhealth.gov Web site a less complex site to navigate than the World Health Organization, and therefore a better place to begin.

For legislation on an international and national level, consult the *International Digest of Health Legislation (DHL).* A resource to use after the first choices have been consulted is the Internet site for the *U.S. Centers for Disease Control and Prevention, Division of International Health (DIH)* for two types of information, diseases A–Z, and U.S.

health projects and health programs in other countries.

FOR FURTHER READING: COMPREHENSIVE WEB SITES AND OTHER REFERENCE SOURCES

Annual Consumers Guide to Health & Medicine on the Internet 2000, by James B. Davis, Ed. Los Angeles: Health Information Press, 2000 (ISBN 1-88598-718-8).

This title reports chapter by chapter on specific disease or health topic with brief entries for the Internet resources. It includes an introduction and index. It covers Internet resources from international intergovernmental organizations.

Directory of NGOs in Official Relations With WHO Web site, by the World Health Organization. <http://www.who.int/civilsociety/en/dto-ngo1st.doc>

This online directory is both a summary of the health-related objectives and activities of 193 nongovernmental organizations (NGOs) in official relations with World Health Organization (WHO) and of their recent contributions in the work for health for all. The directory describes the nature and interests of NGOs in official relations with WHO, from fields such as medicine, science, education, law, labor, industry, professional and occupational societies, families, women, children and youth, as well as humanitarian and development organizations. The descriptions are limited to the scope and form in which collaboration takes and does not discuss the significant roles NGOs take in planning and delivering health services and health systems development and in developing and revising international health and health-related guidelines.

Emergency Nutrition Network Online Web site, Dublin, Ireland. <http://www.ennonline.net/>

The Emergency Nutrition Network (ENN), which began in 1996, aims to improve the effectiveness of emergency food and nutrition interventions by providing a forum for exchange of information, ideas, applications, and current research. The issues of their online newsletter, *Field Exchange* (1997–), issued every 3–4 months, are available from the home page with an archived index (in HTML and PDF). On its searchable site, it provides short articles on fieldwork in the nutrition sector of emergency response, research, news and information, a profile of an agency in the field, evaluation of current activities in different areas of the world, and other full-text reports on emergency nutrition. Also available is their *Resource Database* a searchable catalog of all the documents used in their research.

International Bulletins Web site, by the U.S. Centers for Disease Control, Atlanta, Ga. <http://www.cdc.gov/mmwr/international/world.html>

This Internet site provides a list and links to the major epidemiological health bulletins of countries, organized by region of the world. If there is no direct link to a title, it links to the agency within the country responsible for this information.

Links to National Health-Related Websites, by the World Health Organization (WHO). <http://www3.who.int/whosis/> (select National Health-Related Web sites).

This site provides links to health ministries and central statistics office where available. It is kept updated, as a service to WHO online users, but WHO has no control over the validity of the data for users who follow the links and use the national health information available from the countries themselves.

MEDLINE/PubMed Web site, by the U.S. National Library of Medicine. <http://www.pubmed.gov>

This online database provides access to over 11 million *MEDLINE* citations back to the mid 1960s and additional life science journals. *MEDLINE* is the National Library of Medicine's database of references to journal articles. *PubMed* is available in English and French, and it also links to many sites providing full-text articles. *Pubmed Central* is its free, unrestricted online archive of journal articles at <http://www.pubmedcentral.nih.gov/>. Users may search all journals or select a title.

World Cancer Report, edited by Bernard W. Stewart and Paul Kleihues, Lyon, France: IARC Press, 2003 (ISBN 9-28320-411-5).

This report provides a comprehensive overview of global cancer for health care professionals, students, and the general reader. Sponsored by the International Agency for Research on Cancer (IARC), World Health Organization, it covers the causes of cancer, prevention and screening, human cancers by organ site, cancer management and control with many color illustrations, and statistical tables. The report also documents the frequency of cancer, cancer trends, cancer prevention activities, and cancer mortality in individual countries of the world.

NOTE

1. *World Health Organization* Web site, *About WHO,* Geneva, Switzerland, <http://www.who.int/aboutwho/en/definition.html>.

CHAPTER 12
Human Rights

CHAPTER OVERVIEW

The protection and promotion of human rights has been a global issue for over 60 years, beginning with the signing of the *Charter of the United Nations* (June 1945). The adoption of the landmark United Nations document *Universal Declaration of Human Rights* (December 1948) codified the rights of all humans and has now been translated into 300 languages.

This chapter details global and regional human rights efforts. Official documents, international instruments, and publications provide comprehensive coverage of the work of both international and nongovernmental organizations as well as individual countries. The United Nations is still the leader in worldwide efforts especially through its United Nations High Commissioner for Human Rights and Human Rights Committee. Regionally, the Council of Europe and the Organization of American States are leading the pack in ensuring human rights. In addition, the nongovernmental agencies Amnesty International, Human Rights Internet, and Human Rights Watch, all of which are described in this chapter, provide a different perspective and serve as watchdogs.

Governmental Sources Discussed

Council of Europe Commissioner of Human Rights Web site, Council of Europe, Strasbourg, France. <http//www.coe.int/T/E/Commissioner_H.R/Communication_Unit>

Council of Europe Directorate General of Human Rights (DGII) Web site, Strasbourg, France. <http://www.coe.int/T/E/Human_rights/>

Country Reports on Human Rights Practices, by the U.S. Dept. of State. Washington, D.C.: U.S. Government Printing Office, 1979–. <http://purl.access.gpo.gov/GPO/LPS1236> or <http://www.state.gov.g/drl/hr/c1470.htm>

European Court of Human Rights Web site, Strasbourg, France. <http://www.echr.coe.int/>

Human Rights: A Compilation of International Instruments, by the United Nations Centre for Human Rights, 2002 (ISBN9-21154-1441; UN Sales Number: E.02.XIV.4).

Inter-American Commission on Human Rights Web site, by the Organization of American States, Washington, D.C. <http://www.cidh.oas.org/>

International Instruments of the United Nations: A Compilation of Agreements, Charters, Conventions, Declarations, Principles, Proclamations, Protocols, Treaties Adopted by the General Assembly of the United Nations, 1945–1995, by Irving Sarnoff. New York: United Nations, 1997 (ISBN 9-21100-612-0; UN Sales Number E.96.I.15).

United Nations High Commissioner for Human Rights Web site, by the United Nations High Commissioner for Human Rights, Geneva, Switzerland. <http://www.unhchr.ch/>

Yearbook of the Human Rights Committee, by the United Nations Human Rights Committee, 1977/1978–1987 (ISSN 0256-9639).

Official Records of the Human Rights Committee, by the United Nations Human Rights Committee, 1987/1988– (ISSN 0256-9639).

Nongovernmental Sources Discussed

Amnesty International (AI) Web site, by the International Secretariat, London. <http://www.amnesty.org>

Human Rights Internet Web site, by the Human Rights Internet, Ottawa, Ontario. <http://www.hri.ca/>

Human Rights Watch (HRW) Web site, by Human Rights Watch, New York. <http://www.hrw.org>

GOVERNMENTAL SOURCES

Country Reports on Human Rights Practices, by the U.S. Dept. of State. Washington, D.C.: U.S. Government Printing Office, 1979–. <http://purl.access.gpo.gov/GPO/LPS1236> or <http://www.state.gov/ >

Summary: This annual report, prepared by the Department of State, provides short, but detailed information by country on the status of human rights for all nations that are members of the United Nations and a few others, including those nations that receive United States assistance. The purpose of this report is to provide information that may be used to assist members of the U.S. Congress in shaping policy, in conducting diplomacy, and in consideration of legislation, especially foreign aid. More specifically, it is intended for the use of the Committee on Foreign Relations of the U.S. Senate and the Committee on International Relations of the U.S. House of Representatives and is issued from these Committees as a joint committee print.

The printed text of the *Country Reports* was published in two volumes for 1998 and is now fully accessible on the Internet in HTML, gopher and ftp. This report is available electronically back to 1993. For full historical use, researchers will want to consult the paper editions, which are available yearly back to 1979 and are available in many academic libraries. Libraries with specific human rights collections may want to order the paper edition to ensure permanent access to their users. The latest print editions can be easily ordered through the *Sales Product Catalog* of the Government Printing Office <http://bookstore.gpo.gov>.

Detailed Description: The overall introduction reviews human rights worldwide for the previous year, highlighting specific developments and providing an analysis and conclusions. The entries for the countries are arranged alphabetically under regions of the world, which allows for easy access. For each country, the government's human rights record is evaluated.

Each country's report begins with an introduction containing an overview of human rights developments for that country within the previous year. It covers how the political process, the economy, and security issues affect human rights specifically in that country and also highlights significant events such as elections and foreign relations, in order for human rights practices in that nation to be understood within the overall context of human rights. Also included are the governments' attempts to improve human rights practices and problem areas of human rights with specific examples. Each government's human rights record is then evaluated.

Under each country, an analysis of six specific human rights topics follows the introduction. These topics include religious freedom and the rights of women and minorities; developments in democracy, including elections and laws passed; and developments in labor, such as worker rights and child labor. Information is also provided on internationally recognized individual, civil, political, and worker rights, as set forth in the *Universal Declaration of Human Rights*. For each topic, very detailed examples, dates, and incidents are provided for human rights violations.

Specific human rights topics are covered for each country. (1) *Respect for the integrity of the person (including freedom from)* covers political and other extra-judicial killing; disappearance; torture and other cruel, inhuman, or degrading treatment or punishment; arbitrary arrest, detention, or exile; denial of fair public trial; and arbitrary interference with privacy, family, home, or correspondence. (2) *Respect for civil liberties* includes freedom of speech and press; freedom of peaceful assembly and association; freedom of religion; and freedom of movement within the country, foreign travel, emigration, and repatriation. (3) *Respect for political rights: the rights of citizens to change their government* provides detailed information about elections, political parties, and government opposition. (4) *Governmental attitude regarding international and nongovernmental investigation of alleged violations of human rights.* (5) *Discrimination based on race, sex, religion, disability, language, or social status.* Women and ethnic minorities are covered in this section, which tries to provide the cultural background on the specific country and how it affects human rights in all of these areas. (6) *Worker rights* includes the right of association; the right to organize and bargain collectively; prohibition of forced or compulsory labor; status of child labor practices and minimum age for employment; and acceptable conditions of work.

Several appendices include how the report was prepared; a chart listing International Human Rights Conventions; a chart that shows which country is party to specific conventions, and a list of those conventions; and the text of the *Universal Declaration of Human Rights.*

Council of Europe Commissioner of Human Rights
Web site, by the Council of Europe, Strasbourg, France. <http://www.coe.int/T/E/Commissioner_H.RCommunication_Unit>

Summary: The Commissioner of Human Rights was established in 1999 by the Council of Europe Comissioner to promote his activity on human rights within its member countries. The commissioner focuses on hurman rights awareness, law, and the promotion of human rights to all members of the Council of Europe. Information on the Web site, also available in French, is arranged into four main categories: Commissioner, Documents, Press Room, and Links.

Detailed Description: The home page category Commissioner consists of an overview (history, election, objectives and principles, and activities), biography, mandate, and staff listing, complete with photographs and contact information. The next home page category is Documents, and materials found here are arranged by country, year (1999–), and series (annual reports, visit reports, National Institutes for Human Rights, ombudsmen, opinions, recommendations, seminars, visit reports). Each document is in full text. At the time of this writing, many of the countries represented did not include any documents.

The Press Room home page category is further subdivided into agendas, news, press releases, speeches/articles/interviews, photos/videos. Each of these subdivisions contains full-text materials that are from the current year. Links, the last home page category, provides links to other Council of Europe bodies as well as other international organization and nongovernmental organizations that focus on human rights.

Council of Europe Directorate General of Human Rights (DGII) Web site, Strasbourg, France. <http://www.coe.int/T/E/Human_rights/>

Summary: As the body that oversees the Council of Europe's human rights policies and standards, the Web site of the DGII explains the mandate and details its activities. The site, also available in French, contains four main headings: Activities, Topics, Publications, and Recent Developments. A link to an in-depth description of its mandate is found at the bottom of the page.

Detailed Description: The Activities home page heading is further subdivided into Human Rights Convention; Economic and Social Rights; preventing torture; national minorities; combating racism; equality between women and men; protecting media freedom; law, policy, intergovernmental cooperation, and awareness. Each subdivision links to a Web site devoted to this topic that includes documents and publications. The Topics home page heading is also subdivided into police programme, ECHR (European Court of Human Rights) reform, and fight against trafficking. Like those in Activities, each of these subdivisions links to a Web site of relevant materials.

The Publications home page category includes the full text, PDF, of *Guidelines on Human Rights and the Fight Against Terrorism* (in English, French, Spanish, German, Dutch, Czech, Russian, and Serbian) as well as the full text of *Human Rights Handbooks, Human Rights Files,* and *Human Rights Information Bulletin* (1997–). A listing of other publications available for purchase is also included such as the annual *Yearbook of the European Convention on Human Rights and Fundamental Freedoms* (1955/1957–).

The final home page heading, Recent Developments, includes a brief summary, located on the home page and arranged chronologically, of the item and then a link to its text.

European Court of Human Rights Web site, Strasbourg, France. <http://www.echr.coe.int/>

Summary: Established in 1959 as the body to deal with issues of violation of the *European Convention on Human Rights of 1950,* the Web site, also available in French, contains documentation of its work. The site is grouped into the main categories of General Information, Pending Cases, Judgments and Decisions, Basic Texts, Press Releases, and Library.

Detailed Description: General Information, the first home page category, provides in-depth information regarding the Court's composition and history. In addition, information regarding case law, practice direction, consultation of files, applying to the Court, dates of ratification of the Convention, traineeships, and employment are included. The home page category Pending Cases lists those cases to appear before the Grand Chamber as well as the current listing of scheduled public hearings.

Judgments and Decisions, another home page category, contains much useful information regarding the working of the Court. The Press Releases subcategory (1998–) lists each case with such details for each as facts, proceedings, summary, and decision. Free-text searching of these is also available. *Effects of Judgments or Cases 1969–1998,* another subcategory, summarizes these points. The subcategory, Publisher Information, includes a listing of judgments and decisions to be published. The final subcategory, Subject Matter of Judgments Delivered by the Court, is an annual listing in table form (1999–) of the case name and its subject.

The Basic Texts home page category contains the full text of the Convention in 29 European languages, as well as the Rules of the Court (English). The Press Releases home page category is another access point to the Press Releases, found under the Judgments and Decisions home page category.

Library, the last home page category discussed, links to information about the library. Users can search the catalog and an online thesaurus is available.

Human Rights: A Compilation of International Instruments, by the United Nations Centre for Human Rights, 2002 (ISBN 9-21154-144-1; UN Sales Number: E.02.XIV.4).

Summary: This two-volume set is a comprehensive catalogue containing the full text of universal and regional instruments pertaining to human rights. Instruments are defined as "(1) written legal document that defines rights, duties, entitlements or liabilities, such as a contract, will, promissory note, or share certificate and (2) A means by which something is achieved, performed, or furthered."[1] *Human Rights: A Compilation of International Instruments* includes protocols, covenants, and conventions that are legally binding among the states that ratify them; and principles, standard rules, recommendations, and declarations, which are not legally binding. The United Nations regularly revises this title and issues it in a new edition.

Detailed Description: Volume I, Parts 1 and 2, contain the full text of international instruments with adoption dates up to December 18, 2002. Other editions were published in 1968, 1973, 1978, 1983, 1988, 1994. This edition was expanded to also include United Nations instruments and documents that have been adopted by UNESCO (United Nations Educational, Scientific, and Cultural Organization), Office of the High Commissioner for Refugees, and the International Labour Organization.

Volume II includes adopted documents from regional intergovernmental organizations that date from May 2, 1948, to April 4, 1997. This is the first issuance of such a collection, and this volume was published in 1997.

The instruments in Volume I are categorized under a major topical heading. Under each heading are the instruments that pertain to that category. The headings are: to that International Bill of Human Rights; World Conference and Millennium Assembly; The Right of Self-Determination; Rights of Indigenous Peoples and Minorities; Prevention of Discrimination; Rights of Women; Rights of the Child; Rights of Older Persons; Rights of Persons with Disabilities; Human Rights in the Administration of Justice: Protection of Persons

Subjected to Detention or Imprisonment; Social Welfare; Progress and Development; Promotion and Protection of Human Rights; Marriage; Right to Health; Right to Work and to Fair Conditions of Employment; Slavery, Slavery-like Practices, and Forced Labour; Rights of Migrants; Nationality, Statelessness, Asylum, and Refugees; (P16) War Crimes and Crimes Against Humanity, including Genocide; and Humanitarian Law.

Each instrument includes the date of adoption, the date of entry into force, and the full text of the instrument itself. No background information or discussion of the content is included. A "List of Instruments in Chronological Order of Adoption" is found at the end of each Part. This is particularly useful in viewing the chronology of human rights efforts. There is no index.

The organizations included in Volume II are the Organization of American States, Council of Europe, Organization of African Unity, Conference on Security and Co-operation in Europe, and Organization of the Islamic Conference, arranged according to the establishment date of the organization itself. The instruments within each organization are listed chronologically by their date of adoption. As in the first volume, no background information, discussion of the contents, or index is included.

Inter-American Commission on Human Rights Web site, by the Organization of American States: Inter-American Commission on Human Rights, Washington, D.C. <http://www.cidh.oas.org>

Summary: The Inter-American Commission on Human Rights, founded in 1959, is charged with advancing and protecting human rights and carries out this charge through visiting and reporting on the work in individual countries, examining pertinent subjects and reporting on the findings, conducting meetings and conferences, and making recommendations. Information found on this Web site documents human rights activities within the Organization of American States and the 35 countries it represents. The home page is divided into the main categories of What's the IACHR, Basic Documents, Annual Reports, Special Reports, How to Present a Petition, Press Releases, Cases Published by the IACHR, Responses of States to Recommendations of the IACHR, Composition, Speeches, Onsite Visits, and Rapporteurships. In addition, a link to Publications, Links, and a search engine are also available from the home page. Information on this site is available in the official OAS languages of English, Spanish, Portuguese, and French.

Detailed Description: The home page category What's the IACHR provides both a narrative overview of the IACHR, including contact information, and a history of the Inter-American Human Rights System. The Basic Documents home page category contains links to core human rights documents, including *American Declaration of the Rights and Duties of Man, American Convention on Human Rights, Regulations of the Inter-American Commission on Human Rights,* and several others.

The Annual Reports category has the full text of annual reports dating back to 1970. However, some of the earlier versions are in Spanish only. The Annual Reports are very important sources of information about the work of the IACHR and include highlights of the IACHR sessions, highlights of the OAS General Assembly session and the texts of resolutions pertaining to human rights; reports on Petitions and Cases Declared Admissible, Petitions and Cases Declared Inadmissible, Friendly Settlements, and Reports on the Merits; Human Rights Developments in the Region; Follow-up on IACHR Recommendations on its Reports on Member States; Special Studies; and Report of the Office of the Special Rapporteur for Freedom of Expression. The Annual Reports for the IACHR are also available in paper format.

The Special Reports home page category includes the full text of reports on individual countries (1962–) as well as other specialized reports. Some of the earlier issues are also only available in Spanish. The How to Present a Petition category pertains to documenting human rights violations and provides instructions and a copy of the form. Press Releases, another home page category, contains the full text of Press Releases arranged by date (1993–). The Cases Published by the IACHR category (1975–) lists each case for that year with a link to the summary and IACHR resolution. Response of States to Recommendations of the IACHR is subdivided into Special Reports and Individual Cases. The Composition category lists the membership by name, country, and term. Speeches, another category, provides the full text of various speeches by officers and members of the Commission (1999–current). The On-site category is just a listing of date, places, and a short phrase observation.

The Rapporteurships home page category is much more in-depth. Subdivided into Freedom of Expression and Rapporteur on the Rights of Women, each contains reports, documents, press releases and publications, related to its work.

The Publications home page link is found on every page. It provides another access point to annual reports, country reports, and other publications, all already described. The Links home page link is to the Web sites of other international organizations pertaining to human rights. Of special note is the link to the Inter-American Court of Human Rights and the Publications category that contains the full text of Judgments and Opinions (1981–current).

International Instruments of the United Nations: A Compilation of Agreements, Charters, Conventions, Declarations, Principles, Proclamations, Protocols, Treaties Adopted by the General Assembly of the United Nations, 1945–1995, by Irving Sarnoff. New York: United Nations, 1997 (ISBN 9-21100-612-0; UN Sales Number E.96.I.15).

Summary: Authored by the founder of Friends of the United Nations, a nongovernmental organization, this publication contains a compilation of "norms and standards adopted by the General Assembly during its first 50 years of work."[2] These "norms and standards" are in the form of full-text documents, referred to as instruments. Roughly half of the international instruments included in this publication deal with human rights issues. Instruments are defined as "A written legal document that defines rights, duties, entitlements, or liabilities, such as contract, will, promissory note, or share certificate...[and] a means by which something is achieved, performed, or furthered."[3]

Detailed Description: The book is divided into four major sections: The General Assembly of the United Nations; Treaties, Conventions, Protocols, Agreements, Declarations, Proclamations, Charters, and Resolutions of the General Assembly; Charter of the United Nations; and Statute of the International Court of Justice. A brief Overview of Terms is located at the beginning of the book. This six-page section is useful because it explains the different types of documents included in the book and defines key terms. Knowing the types of documents and their definitions will help users understand the importance of each document and its binding legality. A list of legal sources cited and additional reference sources is located at the end of the Overview.

As the General Assembly is a major player in the area of human rights, an understanding of its structure and subsidiary and ad hoc bodies is extremely helpful. Brief descriptions of the various bodies and phone numbers are contained in the first section, which includes Charter Provisions, Membership, Sessions and Officers, Structure, and Subsidiary and Ad Hoc Bodies. This information was taken, with permission, from the New Zealand Ministry of Foreign Affairs and Trade's *United Nations Handbook* (1996).

The second section, Treaties, Conventions, Protocols, Agreements, Declarations, Proclamations, Charters, and Resolutions of the General Assembly, comprises the bulk of this publication. It contains the full text of the instruments grouped by topical headings. These headings are: Disarmament, Security, and Political; Human Rights; Economic and Development Issues; Social Issues; Space; Information; Mercenaries; Environment; and Legal Questions and International Law. The pertinent instruments under each topic are then arranged chronologically. No background information or discussion of the contents is included for any of the documents.

The Human Rights subsection contains 21 instruments dating from December 1948 to December 1992. Other human rights instruments are also found predominately in the Social Issues and Legal Questions and International Law subsections and also scattered among the other subsections.

The other two major sections of this publication are Charter of the United Nations and Statute of the International Court of Justice, with only the full text of the instruments themselves included, and no additional background information or content discussion.

Appendices are located after the four major sections. In the area of human rights, two of the appendices are of particular interest. The first Appendix is Selected List of Instruments Adopted by United Nations Agencies and Programs. Human rights is one of the categories and has five items listed. However, other human rights documents are included under other subheadings, such as Traffic in Persons and Obscene Publications. Some of these documents are dated in the early 1900s. All of these documents are not in full text, and no selection criteria are included.

Appendix 6 is a chart of the United Nations Human Rights System. This chart helps the reader to visually understand how the various components of the United Nations System work together to support and further the cause of human rights.

No index is included. Although having an index would make it easier to find particular instruments, the Contents page does list each instrument under its main topical heading. In searching for human rights instruments, the user needs to read all the titles be-

cause relevant human rights instruments are not always listed under the Human Rights topical heading.

United Nations High Commissioner for Human Rights Web site, by the United Nations High Commissioner for Human Rights, Geneva, Switzerland. <http://www.unhchr.ch/>

Summary: The United Nations High Commissioner for Human Rights is the UN body responsible for supporting and promoting universal human rights efforts through education, preventative measures, and development. This Web site, available in English, French, or Spanish, provides up-to-date coverage of human rights information and activities in full-text format. The home page of this site is divided into the following categories: Welcome Center, Sections, General Information, Highlights, Issues in Focus, Children's Rights, Human Rights Bodies, and Human Rights Education and Training. Search boxes for the Treaty Bodies and Charter-based Bodies Databases, latest news highlights, site map, and index are also available on the home page.

Detailed Description: The Welcome Center home page category lists the latest updates to the site. The full-text text of the *Universal Declaration of Human Rights* is also available here in over 300 languages.

The Sections home page category is further subdivided into About Us, Field Presences, Issues, Documents, Treaties, Meetings/Events, and Press Room. About Us includes the organizational structure, field presences (also accessible via the Field Presences subdivision), human rights issues, technical cooperation, and other related topics. The Field Presences subdivision is arranged by region (Africa; Arab Region; Asia/Pacific Region; Europe, Central Asia, and the Caucasus; Latin America and the Caribbean). Contact information is given for specific countries within each region. In addition, the full text of the most recent quarterly reports are included for each region. The Issues subdivision is an alphabetical listing of various human rights issues with a link to relevant sites within the *UNHCHR* Web site. The Documents subdivision has a section about United Nations Documents Symbols to aid the user in understanding the UN document numbering system as well as a description and links to the Treaty Bodies and Charter-based databases. The Treaty-based database (1992–) links to relevant documents produced by the six committees established to monitor the implementation of the principal international human rights treaties. Full-text searching is available as well as finding information by committee member, documents, reporting status, ratifications, and reservations. It is also possible to sign up for an e-mail notification of additions to this database. The Charter-based database (1994–) has the relevant documents produced by the General Assembly, Commission on Human Rights, and Subcommission on the Promotion and Protection of Human Rights. Searching can be done by country, mandate, subject, symbol, year, and body. The Treaties subdivision contains links to the full text of International Human Rights Instruments. Meetings/Events has the past year and current calendar of events as well as links to other events. Press Room, the last subdivision, has the full text of current press releases and includes searching by type, country, symbol, date, subject, and mandate. Current statements, also in full-text format, allows searching by official, subject, country, date, or mandate possible.

The General Information home page category features information regarding fund-raising, civil society support initiatives, vacancies, and internships and fellowships. In addition, publications can be found here grouped into fact sheets, training and educational materials, special issue papers, promotional materials, and reference materials. Most are full text and are available in English and one or two other languages.

The Issues in Focus, Children's Rights, and Human Rights Bodies home page categories contain links to Web sites of relevant materials. The Human Rights Education and Training category pertains to the UN Decade for Human Rights Education (1995–2004), and of special mention is the Database on Human Rights Education that allows searching by institution, materials, programs, and scholarships.

Yearbook of the Human Rights Committee, by the United Nations Human Rights Committee, 1977/1978–1987 (ISSN 0256-9639).

Official Records of the Human Rights Committee, by the United Nations Human Rights Committee, 1987/1988– (ISSN 0256-9639).

Summary: The *Yearbook/Official Records of the Human Rights Committee* is the Committee's annual publication, published in two volumes. Volume I contains the summary record for each public meeting for the United Nations session covered. Included in this volume is an introductory note, membership of the Committee, officers, agendas, and the summary records. Volume II includes the Report of State parties; public documents considered for the sessions

covered for each issuance period; Report of the Committee to the General Assembly; and reservations, declarations, notifications, and communications relating to the *International Covenant on Civil and Political Rights and the Optional Protocol.*

Detailed Description: The first two-volume set, covering the period 1977/1978, was published in 1986. Subsequent volumes followed for 1979/1980 (1988), 1981/1982 (1989), 1983/1984 (1991), 1985/1986 (1992), and 1987 (1993). In 1988, The Human Rights Committee changed the title to *Official Records of the Human Rights Committee.* The new title commenced with the issuance of the 1987/1988 (1993) edition, and subsequent editions were published for 1988/1989, 1989/1990, 1990/1991, and 1991/1992, all published in 1995, and 1992/1993 (1996).

Both annual volumes also include the same two annexes. Annex I is entitled Consideration of Reports Submitted by State Parties and contains the State party, the document symbol for Committee comments, session number, meeting number, dates, report number with the UN document symbol, and the paragraph number(s) in which it is found. Annex II is the Check-list of Documents. This Check-list includes the document number, title, and the page number. Beginning with the 1981/1982 *Yearbook* and continuing with the subsequent years, a third annex is also found in both volumes. Annex III, Records and Documents of the Human Rights Committee Published in the *Yearbooks/Official Records* of the Committee, contains a listing by report, session, and meeting numbers; dates; publication title; symbol; and sales number of all records and documents from the first session to the current session included in each volume.

NONGOVERNMENTAL SOURCES

Amnesty International (AI) Web site, by the International Secretariat, London, United Kingdom. <http://www.amnesty.org>

Summary: A worldwide grassroots activist organization with an emphasis on the international protection of human rights, the Web site *Amnesty International* provides information on human rights all over the globe. The Web site itself is in English, but also provides information in Spanish, French, and Arabic. In addition, the various annual reports are also available in other languages. Of particular interest for this discussion are the home page categories About AI, Library, Campaigns, Resources and Links, and News.

The home page also contains a site map and contact information. The latest news highlights are also featured on the home page.

Detailed Description: About AI, the first home page category to be described, details its work, includes the full text of the Universal Declaration of Human Rights, Statute of Amnesty International, Recommendations for the Protection and Promotion of Human Rights as well as Facts and Figures and Frequently Asked Questions.

The Library category is an archive of reports, news releases, and activities (1996–) with browsing by region, subregion, country, or theme possible. An individual can also sign up on the update listserv in order to be notified of new document additions. The full text of annual reports (1996–) is also available here.

The Campaigns category includes links to current and previous campaigns (2000–) and are for reference purposes, as most are out of date. Resources and Links, another home page category, contains links to other Amnesty International Web pages, human rights-related Web pages, and Amnesty International contact points as well as a place to order publications. The News category contains a video archive with a search engine to locate materials.

Although not available electronically, Amnesty International also publishes *Amnesty International News* (London: Amnesty International, 1995–). This is a bimonthly periodical covering political prisoners and torture and other human rights violations around the world.

Human Rights Internet Web site, by Human Rights Internet, Ottawa, Ontario. <http://www.hri.ca/>

Summary: Originally called *Internet: The International Human Rights Documentation Network,* HRI was begun in 1976 in the United States, but is currently located in Ottawa, Canada. The mission of this nongovernmental organization is to empower organizations and governments in the promotion and education of human rights. The site provides much information regarding human rights. For the sake of the discussion the focus will be on the home page categories About HRI, Thematic Programs, Publications and Bookstore, For the Record, and HR Databank. Web highlights and a search engine are also available on the home page.

Detailed Description: The About HRI home page category provides background, staffing, and a site map. The category Thematic Programs is subdivided into Children's Rights, Freedom of Religion or Beliefs, Racism, Women's Rights, Forum for Citizen's Diplomacy, and Information Technology and Human Rights. Each subdivision links to a relevant Web site of publications and program materials.

Publications and Bookstore, another home page category, contains many subdivisions. Under the All Publications subdivision is a general outline of the types of publications available: New Human Rights Releases, HRI Human Rights Directories, Regular HRI Publications, Special HRI Publications, and Order HRI Publications. New Human Rights Releases is a misnomer. There are titles included here dating back to 1997. HRI Human Rights Directories has brief annotations and sales information for human rights directories published by HRI.

The Regular HRI publications subdivision of the Publications and Bookstore home page category contains the full text of many publications. *Human Rights Tribune* (1992–) is published three times a year and reports on the happenings of international organizations such as the United Nations and other individuals involved in human rights. Online, full-text access is available (1995–). The archives are searchable by keyword. In 2001 HRI reinstituted its *Occasional Papers Series,* and the full text of these papers are found here as well as a title listing of previous issues (1992–1996). A new electronic newsletter, *H.R. Eye,* which documents HRI activities, was begun in December 2002, and the full-text issues are accessible here. Full-text annual reports are also included (1999–). *Human Rights Internet Reporter* was a print publication. Beginning with volume 11, an annual paper supplemental publication, *Masterlist,* provided names and addresses of organizations reviewed in the *Reporter.* The serial subscription for the paper version of the *Reporter* ended with volume 16. However, information regarding the special issue, *Special Issues in Human Rights Education* (January 1999, Volume 16, no. 2), is included. HRI also publishes *Human Rights Documentation on Microfiche,* a comprehensive microfiche collection of the full text of publications, both published and unpublished, from nongovernmental organizations that emphasize human rights. This collection dates from 1980 and is regularly updated. The *Cumulative Guide* serves as the indexing tool. A *Directory of Microfiche Organizations,* available on this Web site, features a searchable database of institutions pertaining to human rights. Search fields include name, acronym, organization type, issues these organizations deal with, country organization is interested in, and the country organization resides in.

The home page category *For the Record: The UN Human Rights System* is another annual HRI publication, which began in 1997. This publication is available in paper, CD-ROM, and Web formats, in both English and French, and reports on the progress, based on UN documentation, of human rights by country and theme for that year. A special edition in 2000 and 2001 featured European Human Rights Systems within the Council of Europe.

The last category for discussion is HR Databank. Free-text searching can be done by global search, organization, job board, *Tribune,* urgent alerts, Web sites, world calendar, human rights education, bookstore, and E-Doc Center. The E-Doc Center is arranged thematically, with links to relevant full-text publications.

Human Rights Watch (HRW) Web site, by Human Rights Watch, New York. <http://www.hrw.org>

Summary: Human Rights Watch serves as both a supporter and watchdog of international human rights. The organization has now grown to include Africa, Americas, Asia, Europe and Central Asia, and Middle East divisions along with three thematic divisions, Arms, Children's Rights, and Women's Rights. Further background information is available in the About home page category. This Web site is available in English, Arabic, Russian, Chinese, Spanish, French, and Portuguese. For the purpose of this discussion the focus will be on the home page categories of Publications, Information by Country, and Global Issues. A site map, search engine, and contact information are also available from the home page. The search engine can search in English, Spanish, French, or Portuguese, as well as by keyword or concept.

Detailed Description: Publications, a home page category, includes the current and back issues of the *Human Rights Watch World Report* (1997–), an annual publication that surveys the human rights events of the previous year. This publication is also available in paper format (1990–; ISSN 1054-948X). The report is divided into geographic areas with a narrative overview of events and the work of regional organizations for that particular region followed by reports of human rights developments and the work of international and nongovernmental organizations in individual countries within that region. Also available under the Publications category are full-text e-books, thematic reports (children, women, arms), and country reports (alphabetically by country). All of the information included in the subcategories is annotated.

The most recent Publications Catalogue, available in PDF, is also included.

The Information by Country category is subdivided into the regions of Africa, Americas, Asia, Europe/Central Asia, Middle East/North Africa, and the United States. Each region includes the full text of relevant press releases, briefing papers, reports, and letters. Also found here are annual overviews of human rights developments (late 1980s to current—depending on the region) and depending on the region, individual country information.

Global Issues, the last category for discussion, is subdivided into arms, children's rights, HIV/AIDS, international justice, prisons, refugees, and women's rights, United Nations, and a link to additional topics. Each topic may contain publications, press releases, letters, reports, regional coverage, thematic coverage, related links, excerpts from applicable sections of the *Human Rights Watch,* and overview of human rights developments. Not every topic includes each of these materials.

RESEARCH STRATEGIES

Country Reports on Human Rights Practices provides a quick way to obtain country information on human rights. The alphabetical arrangement by country under regions of the world is easy to use. The report is well suited for information seekers on all different levels because it includes basic information such as general analysis and background information, along with specific examples and facts for those who need more detail. A wide range of users, from high school and college students to librarians and advanced scholars will also find this title useful to check among the first because of its up-to-date nature, availability online, and detail. Users should be aware that this is the United States' viewpoint on human rights in other countries, and the United States as a country is not covered.

The United Nations is the best place for the global approach to human rights. An excellent beginning point is the ***United Nations High Commissioner for Human Rights*** Web site. The two databases, Treaty-Based and Charter-Based, provide full-text access at the fingertips to a host of official documents, and each has searching capabilities for easier access.

The ***Yearbook of the Human Rights Committee/ Official Records of the Human Rights Committee*** documenting the work of the United Nations Human Rights Committee is a major research tool for all seekers of human rights research information, especially for those interested in United Nations activities in the field of human rights and the implementation of human rights instruments. This print source provides a single source for the full texts of both the summary record for each public meeting and reports and public documents. In addition, the annexes provide important bibliographic information, directing the user to specific United Nations documents that pertain to human rights. Although much of this information has previously only been available at large research institutions, the United Nations has recently committed to publishing the documents of the General Assembly on the Internet. The records are indexed online at the *UN* Web site by *UNBISnet,* for those who need to do broader bibliographic research.

Those who need to consult a major instrument on human rights from the United Nations should consult *Human Rights: A Compilation of International Instruments* first, before trying the more comprehensive *International Instruments of the United Nations. Human Rights* is easier to find and use, and it focuses strictly on human rights and also includes human rights instruments for the Organization of American States, Council of Europe, Organization of African Unity, Organization for Security and Co-operation in Europe, and Organization of the Islamic Conference.

Researchers with a broader focus will want to go to *International Instruments of the United Nations,* as it contains instruments on many topics and includes more detailed information for each instrument. However, only about half of the instruments included in this title deal with human rights issues. Also, neither of these two titles on instruments have an index.

For regional coverage, the *Council of Europe's Commissioner of Human Rights, Directorate General of Human Rights,* and *European Council of Human Rights* Web sites and the *Organization of American States' Inter-American Commission on Human Rights* Web site are the sources to use. All contain documents and publications detailing the problems and accomplishments in the area of human rights for this geographic area of the world.

Nongovernmental sources are also excellent sources of information regarding human rights practices and violations. The *Amnesty International* Web site, *Human Rights Watch* Web Site, and *Human Rights Internet* Web site all contain comprehensive publications and reports regarding countries and human rights issues, many in full text. Each also provides full-text access to annual reports, important sources of documenting their activities in promoting and protecting human rights

FOR FURTHER READING: COMPREHENSIVE WEB SITES AND OTHER REFERENCE SOURCES

Black's Law Dictionary, by Henry Campbell Black. St. Paul, Minn.: West Group, 1999.

Blackstone's International Human Rights Documents, edited by P. R. Ghandi. 3rd ed. Oxford: Oxford University Press, 2002 (ISBN 0-19925-530-X).

Contains reprints of international instruments arranged in chronological order and divided into five parts: International Instruments, United Nations Procedure for Handling Human Rights Complaints, Regional Instruments, United Nations World Conference on Human Rights Instruments, and Domestic Legislation. A title/keyword index is included.

Historical Dictionary of Human Rights and Humanitarian Organizations, by Robert F. Gorman. Lanham, Md.: Scarecrow Press, 1997 (Historical Dictionaries of International Organizations no. 12) (ISBN 0-81083-263-1).

This dictionary, arranged alphabetically, compiles information on historical background of human rights organizations, concepts, people, and documents. It also includes a listing of abbreviations and acronyms; a timeline of twentieth-century human rights events (1903–September 1995); and an introduction, which provides a historical overview.

Human Rights Encyclopedia, edited by James R. Lewis and Carl Skutsch. Armonk, N.Y.: M. E. Sharpe, Inc., 2001 (ISBN 0-76568-023-8).

Comprised of three volumes, this encyclopedia covers the human rights situations in individual countries, alphabetically arranged, and discusses particular issues and individuals. Each entry also includes a brief bibliography.

Human Rights: The Essential Reference, by Carole Devine, Carol Rae Hansen, and Ralph Wilde. Phoenix: Oryx Press, 1999 (ISBN 1-57356-205-X).

This publication provides an in-depth look at human rights, beginning with a history of human rights from the Greek and Roman traditions up to the end of

World War II, and ending with discussion of the current issues. It includes a detailed analysis of the *Universal Declaration of Human Rights,* an overview and discussion of the various movements, directory and description information on pertinent government and nongovernmental organizations, and brief biographies of human rights activists.

NOTES

1. Henry Campbell Black, *Black's Law Dictionary* (St. Paul, Minn.: West Group, 1999), 801.

2. Irving Sarnoff, *International Instruments of the United Nations: A Compilation of Agreements, Charters, Conventions, Declarations, Principles, Proclamations, Protocols, Treaties Adopted by the General Assembly of the United Nations, 1945–1995* (New York: United Nations, 1997) iii.

3. Black, *Black's Law Dictionary,* 801.

CHAPTER 13
International Relations

CHAPTER OVERVIEW

This chapter is different in format than most of the others. Most of the resources described in this chapter are aggregators. They bring together a comprehensive collection of the most important Web-based research sources and arrange them in categories for ease of use. They are mainly nongovernmental resources that include much government information either as a free resource on the Internet or as a fee-based product. These aggregator resources provide or link to Web sites for the U.S. federal government, international, and nongovernmental organizations and also to search engines, news sources, discussions lists, and the abstracts and/or full texts of articles. As the area of international relations is constantly changing, research sources need to be particularly up to date. One of the major attributes of the Internet is the ability to make available current research resources. These resources have been selected because of the information they provide and their standards in keeping information current.

This chapter does not cover the wealth of material on international relations within international intergovernmental agencies. Users would do best to approach the information resources of these agencies (i.e., the United Nations and European Union) through specific content, or a chapter topic of this book, or also through the general introduction to international agencies. The resources in the Government and Politics chapter also relate closely to the study of international relations and serve as a way to find such information as hearings, testimony, and laws concerning foreign affairs and foreign policy within the legislative documents of a country. Please see this chapter for a list of possible resources.

Governmental Sources Discussed

World News Connection, by the United States Department of Commerce. Springfield, Va.: National Technical Information Service (online subscription service; free online through U.S. depository libraries). <http://wnc.fedworld.gov/>

World News Connection. *Dialog.* Cary, N.C. (online subscription service). <http://wnc.dialog.com/>

Nongovernmental Sources Discussed

Canadian Institute of International Affairs: Links to Other Sites on International Relations Web site, Glendon College, Toronto, Canada. <http://www.ciia.org/links.htm>

Columbia International Affairs Online (CIAO), by Columbia University, New York. <http://www.ciaonet.org/> (online subscription service).

OCLC Public Affairs Information Service, New York. <http://www.pais.org> (print index and online subscription service also known as *PAIS*).

Royal Institute of International Affairs (RIIA) Web site, London. <http://www.riia.org/>.

Social Science Information Gateway: Politics: International Relations Web site, by the U.K. Resource Discovery Network, University of Bristol, Bristol, U.K.<http://www.sosig.ac.uk/roads/subject=listing/World=cat/intrelations.html/> or <http://www.sosig.ac.uk/> (select politics, then international relations).

WWW Virtual Library: International Affairs Resources Web site, by the Department of Political Science, Elizabethtown College, Elizabethtown, Penn. <http://www.etown.edu/vl/>

GOVERNMENTAL SOURCES

World News Connection, by the United States Department of Commerce. Springfield, Va.: National Technical Information Service (online subscription service; free online through U.S. depository libraries). <http://wnc.fedworld.gov/>

World News Connection. *Dialog.* Cary, N.C. (online subscription service). <http://wnc.dialog.com/>

Summary: *World News Connection (WNC)* provides translations of foreign press and broadcast media for the purposes of the U.S. federal government via the

Foreign Broadcast Information Service (FBIS), an agency of the U.S. federal government. Compiled from thousands of non-U.S. media sources, *WNC* covers issues and events in the areas of socioeconomics, politics, science, technology, military, and the environment. Information is generally available within 24–72 hours from the time of original broadcast or publication. WNC coverage is from July 1994 to the present. Earlier indexes and the full text of *FBIS Daily Reports* are available in larger U.S. Federal Depository Libraries (see <http://www.gpoaccess.gov/libraries.html> for contact information). Some libraries may also subscribe to the microfiche and on-line index (1975–1996) produced by Newsbank, Inc.

Detailed Description: *WNC* is also available via Dialog. It offers three methods of searching: simple, advanced, and region/topic. FBIS has divided the world into eight regions: Central Eurasia, China, East Asia, East Europe, West Europe, the Americas, Near East and South Asia, and sub-Saharan Africa. Simple search allows for searching by entire article, headline and lead paragraph, or publication date. Advanced searching contains the same components as simple search as well as words in headlines, publication, city/source, geographical name, *WNC* insert date, topic, and region. The region/topic searching allows for combining particular regions with particular topics. The search results from all three methods are in mainly full-text format, although some records are only in summary form, of newspaper articles, conference proceedings, television and radio broadcasts, periodicals, and nonclassified technical reports. Users may also set up alerts. An added feature is WNC Latest Headlines, which allows the user to pull up the latest headlines from the eight regions.

NONGOVERNMENTAL SOURCES

Canadian Institute of International Affairs: Links to Other Sites on International Relations Web site, Glendon College, Toronto, Canada.
<http://www.ciia.org/links.htm>

Summary: Founded in January 1928, the Canadian Institute of International Affairs (CIIA), was established to assist Canadians in the understanding and promotion of international relations, is in affiliation with the Royal Institute of International Affairs and Institute for Pacific Relations. The home page of the CIIA contains a section entitled Links, added in July 1998 and updated frequently, which will be the focus of this discussion. Links provides a comprehensive listing of outstanding Internet research sources for international relations. In addition, there is an index listing the resources in subject categories: Conferences and Meetings; Government: Canadian, American and Foreign Sites; International Law; International, Multinational and Non-governmental Organizations; Journals, Magazines, and E-Zines on Foreign Policy and the Internet; Newspapers and News Services; Other Institutes, Research Centers, Think Tanks and Foundations in Canada, the USA and Around the World; Popular Search Engines for the WWW; Scholarly E-Mail Discussion Lists; Selected Libraries, On-line Databases, Archives, and Primary Source Documentation; Subject Related Collections, Sites & Internet Resource Guides; University Programmes; and Jobs/Employment in International Affairs. Each section contains an excellent selection of related Web sites. Sites new to this page are so marked. None of the links, however, are annotated.

Columbia International Affairs Online (CIAO) Web site, by Columbia University, New York.
<http://www.ciaonet.org/> (online subscription service).

Summary: CIAO was established through a grant from the Andrew W. Mellon Foundation as a collaboration between Columbia University Press and the Columbia University Libraries. This online subscription service provides access to a collection of full text of working papers, and some monographs and journals published by several leading International Relations university departments, think tanks, and research institutes, both domestic and foreign. Publications date from 1991 to the present. The contents include topics such as security, wars and conflicts, diplomacy, and international relations theory and each section is updated monthly.

Detailed Description: Working Papers, the first major CIAO component, provides access to the full text, some in PDF format, of working papers from 100 institutes devoted to the study of international relations. In addition to the actual working papers, the purpose of each institute is briefly described along with a link to its home page and the resources available there:

Journals, another major section, includes abstracts of articles from a variety of international relations journals. The date coverage varies, and in some cases the full text is available. Books, another section, has full-text access to titles published by various institutions, although the offerings are quite limited.

Policy Briefs is also a major section. Like Working Papers, the full text is included, along with a link to the institution, but the number of institutions represented is much more limited.

The whole CIAO site can be searched and limited to types of materials (e.g., papers/conferences, books). There is also a link to the online version of the most current *CIA World Factbook*.

Unique to this site is its adaptability for use in the classroom. Online case studies and course packs can be used on a variety of topics.

OCLC Public Affairs Information Service, New York. <http://www.pais.org> (print index and online subscription service also known as *PAIS*).

Summary: The *PAIS* index is the most important indexing source for international relations materials and is published by OCLC Public Affairs Information Service, founded in 1914. The print index was first published in 1915 and continues in this format on a monthly basis. Citations do not include an abstract. Most research libraries have this index as a part of their holdings.

The online version is available from a variety of vendors and includes abstracts: OCLC First Search, DIALOG, Silver Platter's ERL (Electronic Reference Library), Gale Group's InfoTrac Searchbank, Cambridge Scientific Abstract's Internet Database Service, and OVID Technologies. All vendor versions have contents dating from 1972 to the present.

The *PAIS* Web site contains information of interest about its products. Of special interest to researchers on this site is the Hot Topics link, which links to relevant sites of both recent and archived events. The *PAIS* Web site provides a listing of the 24 broad subject headings used in indexing. This topics listing is also available in French, German, Italian, Portuguese, and Spanish. Each broad topic can be further subdivided into 306 subtopics. The listing of all the journal titles included in the *PAIS* index is also found on the Web site.

Royal Institute of International Affairs (RIIA) Web site, London. <http://www.riia.org/>

Summary: The *Royal Institute of International Affairs (RIIA)*, or Chatham House, as it is often called due to its physical location, was established in 1920 with a focus of promoting the understanding of international issues. Funding for the RIIA is from sources outside the political and governmental arenas. For this chapter only the most relevant sections of the *RIIA* Web site will be discussed. They are Research, Publications, Library & Information Services, and Press & Media. Abbreviated information about the RIIA and contact information can also be found on the home page.

Detailed Description: Research, the first home page section discussed, contains descriptions of the various research programs. These are arranged alphabetically and include a mix of world geographic areas and topics. The programs are: Africa, Americas, Asia, Europe, International Economics, International Law, Middle East, Russia & Eurasia, Sustainable Development, and Directory of Experts. This grouping not only provides brief descriptions, but also an annotated listing of pertinent books and a link to the full text of Briefing Papers that will be described further in the next paragraph. The Directory provides contact information for various projects and programs undertaken by the RIAA.

Publications is the next major section of the home page. Issues of the monthly magazine *The World Today* and the quarterly journal *International Affairs* are available electronically to members of the RIIA for free and can be accessed here. Most major research institutions probably subscribe to both publications in print and/or electronic format. *International Affairs* has had several name changes since its beginning in 1922. Originally entitled *Journal of the British Institute of International Affairs* (1922–1926), it became *Journal of the Royal Institute of International Affairs* (1926–1930), followed by *International Affairs: Journal of the Royal Institute of International Affairs* (1931–1939), *International Affairs Review Supplement* (1940–1943), and finally *International Affairs* (1944–). Briefing Papers are published annually in response to significant events. The full text (PDF format) of these Briefing Papers, arranged in groupings according to the year, dating from 1999 is also available here. A listing of the books, also found on the Research section, along with forthcoming titles, is another part of the Publications section. Annual report links are also included. Lastly, contact information is provided.

Library & Information Services, the next major section, provides online access to the RIIA catalog. Older journal information can be found in the print volumes *Index to Periodical Articles 1950–1964 in the Library of the Royal Institute of International Affairs*. Updates to this index were also published for the time periods 1965–1972 (1973) and 1973–1978 (1979). Entries include article title, journal title, date, and page numbers arranged by entry number. Entries are classified according to the Chatham House method, which is described in the volumes. Many major research institutions include these volumes as part of their holdings. The *RIIA* Web site also houses a members only archive consisting of meeting transcripts (1920–)

under the Meetings category, as well as files of the study groups, conference reports of the Institute of Pacific Relations, and British Commonwealth Relations conferences. Records are released from restriction after 30 years. The Library & Information services section does include special bibliographies on timely subjects, listing sources held by the RIIA. Unfortunately, these sources are not annotated.

Press & Media is the final major section for discussion. Located here are Current Focus, Media Diary, Press Releases, Press Archive, Photo Library, Contacts, and *Chatham House Newsletter.* The current issue of the *Newsletter* is available in PDF format and details events, speakers, new publications, and research news.

Mention should be made of the Meetings and Conferences sections of the *RIIA* home page. Here are found brief descriptions of these events, including speakers. This information may be useful in locating the names of experts in the field or as a way of taking the pulse of hot topics in international affairs. Membership in the RIIA is possible, and information and fee structure is available from this Web site.

Social Science Information Gateway: Politics: International Relations Web site, by the U.K. Resource Discovery Network, University of Bristol, Bristol, U.K. <http://www.sosig.ac.uk/roads/subject=listing/World=cat/intrelations.html/> or <http://www.sosig.ac.uk/> (select politics, then international relations).

Summary: Edited by the British Library of Political and Economic Science of the London School of Economics, this Web site presents an excellent place for international relations research because of its comprehensiveness, the added value of the record detail information provided by the *SOSIG Internet Catalogue,* and the ability to both search and browse through the Social Science Search Engine. The Internet resources comprising this site are arranged by topic and by type. Each title includes a short record detail comprised of author, brief description, appropriate keywords and subject sections, the resource type, administrator's name and administrator's e-mail (when available), language, and the URL. Clicking on the title will pull up its record. This information is part of the *SOSIG Internet Catalogue* that features both browsing and searching by subject area. To the left of each title is an upward arrow symbol; by clicking on this icon the user will bypass the record information and go directly to either the full text of the item or information about the item produced by its author/publisher.

The topic section is subdivided into Foreign Policy of African Nations; Foreign Policy of Asian Nations; Foreign Policy of Australia, Australasian, and the Pacific Islands [sic]; Foreign Policy of Individual European Nations; Foreign Policy of North American Nations (including Mexico); Foreign Policy of South American Nations; Foreign Policy of the European Union; Conflict and Security; International Peace-keeping; and Philosophy and Theory of International Relations. The Internet titles are then arranged by resource type within each topic. These types include: Editor's Choice (sites deemed especially good), Bibliographic Databases, Books/Book Equivalents, Companies, Data, Educational Materials, Government Publications, Governmental Bodies, Journals (Contents and Abstracts), Journals (full text), Mailing Lists/Discussion Groups, News, Organisations [*sic*]/Societies, Papers/Reports/Articles (collections), Papers/Reports/Articles (individual), Reference Materials, Research Projects/Centres, and Resource Guides. Not all sections contain all resource types.

Under Internet Resources by Type, the user can select those for the World, for Europe, and specifically for the United Kingdom.

WWW Virtual Library: International Affairs Resources Web site, by the Department of Political Science, Elizabethtown College, Elizabethtown, Penn. <http://www.etown.edu/vl/>

Summary: Created and edited by Wayne A. Selcher, Professor of International Studies at Elizabethtown College in Elizabethtown, Pennsylvania, the *WWW Virtual Library: International Affairs Resources* Web site is a valuable source of international relations information relating to international and nongovernmental organizations along with regions and countries. This award-winning site contains more than 2,600 annotated links divided into five major categories: Getting Started, Media Sources, Organizations, Regions and Countries, and Topics. Each category is then further subdivided.

Detailed Description: Getting Started, the first major category, provides starting tips for research on the Internet, along with directories, gateways, and major libraries for virtual library access. A link to search engine directories, portals, and other sources for maps is also found here.

Media Sources is the second major category. Included here are the subdivisions News Sources, International Radio and Television Broadcasts, and

International Relations Journals and Magazines. News Sources has search engines and links to sources. International Radio and Television Broadcasts contains both Web and audio links where applicable. International Relations Journals and Magazines has both search engines and links to foreign policy journals that have free access to their "significant content."

The third major section, Organizations, has several subcategories: United States Government, Research Institutes; Nongovernmental Organizations; United Nations; European Union; and Other Intergovernmental Organizations. Each of these subcategories contains search engines and links to various relevant Web-based resources.

Regions and Countries, the fourth section, is comprised of the subcategories Global and Cross-Cultural Issues, Western Europe, Eastern Europe, Latin America, Africa, Asia, Middle East, General Resources for All Countries, and Resources for Selected Countries. Each subcategory again has relevant search engines and Web links.

The last category is Topics and contains the most subcategories. Included here are International Business and Economics; International Communications; Global Environment; Human Rights and Humanitarian Affairs; French Language; International Development; World Religions; Peace, Conflict Resolution, and International Security; International and Comparative Education; Spanish Language; General Foreign Languages; Study, Work, Internships and Service Abroad; Public Health; International and National Law; American Foreign Policy; and German Language. As with the other categories, each topic contains search engines, directories, and Web links.

The comprehensiveness of this site, the fact that all included links were selected because of their apparent long-term value, and the annotations for each source make this yet another rich source for international relations research on the Internet.

RESEARCH STRATEGIES

For many users, the first place to start in researching international relations is with several current reference resources about countries and government. The chapter on Government and Politics provides a listing of valuable sources to use as a place to begin research. International governmental agencies that have legislative bodies are also a good source of information for international relations. Users may check the chapter on Laws and Treaties in this book for sources in this area with information for researchers on international relations. However, *World News Connection* and *Columbia International Affairs Online* are also good places to begin, as they provide full text and/or abstracts to current news sources, working papers, and conference proceedings.

In this area of study, international relations, close attention must be paid to the bias of information provided by the organization. The *Canadian Institute of International Affairs: Links to Other Sites on International Relations* Web site is an outstanding Internet resource because of its comprehensive content, its promotion of the understanding of international affairs, and its nonpartisan approach to delivery of the information.

For more in-depth bibliographic research, the *PAIS* index is one of the most significant indexing resources available in the field of international relations. Users may search for government and nongovernment titles and titles of different formats, books, journals, and documents. However, as the online version is a fee product, users who do not have access through a research institution may prefer to use some of the Internet resources listed in this chapter, such as *Social Science Information Gateway: Politics: International Relations* Web site and the *WWW Virtual Library: International Affairs Resources.* Also, researchers may note that the *Social Science Information Gateway: Politics: International Relations* Web site has a section specifically on Internet resources for the philosophy and science of international relations.

Finally, within many of the aggregators and complex Internet sites covered in this chapter, are the rich resources of journals and other periodicals that users may want to consult. *Columbia International Affairs Online* Web site contains abstracts to many of the most important journals in this area. In addition to the ones listed here are many others published by Ministries of Foreign Affairs, several of which can be found on the Internet. As an example, this chapter described the **Royal Institute of International Affairs'** titles, the monthly *World Today,* and the quarterly *International Affairs.* Typically, a government agency for foreign affairs will report on a nation's policies within the arena of international relations and also publish a public affairs-type magazine to update the public on these issues. Most scholarly journals on international relations are privately published. Researchers may find these in research or university libraries.

CHAPTER 14
Labor

CHAPTER OVERVIEW

The focus of this chapter on labor is on the Web sites of international intergovernmental organizations (IGOs) that collect and disseminate labor and employment information. It covers major labor resources such as annual periodicals, journals, and magazines; statistics and databases; publications, books, and documents; and Web sites. These resources cover specific labor issues of global concern, including child labor; globalization, labor laws and standards, wages, employment and unemployment characteristics, labor policy issues, living and working conditions, occupational safety and health, labor unions, emerging technology's impact on labor and employment, and specific labor-related events and conferences. Resources are grouped under several major international governmental organizations (IGOs) actively working on labor concerns. The main source for labor information is the International Labour Organization (ILO). Many other IGOs support objectives in activities and publishing related to labor. The Organisation for Economic Co-operation and Development (OECD) focuses on labor in industrialized countries, whereas the European Foundation for the Improvement of Living and Working Conditions focuses on Europe. By consulting the resources described in this chapter, users will find information for individual countries of the world, global concerns, and also specific titles covering geographic regions.

Governmental Sources Discussed

European Foundation for the Improvement of Living and Working Conditions Web site, Dublin, Ireland. <http://www.eurofound.eu.int/>

International Labour Organization Resources

Encyclopaedia of Occupational Health and Safety, by the International Labour Organization (ILO). 4th ed. 1998. (ISBN 9-22109-203-8) (print). <http://www.ilo.org/public/english/support/publ/ encyc/index.htm> (subscription online resource; also available as CD-ROM).

International Labour Organization (ILO) Web site, Geneva, Switzerland. <http://www. ilo.org/>

International Labour Review. Geneva, Switzerland: International Labour Organization (ILO), 1921– (ISSN 0020-7780) (print and online subscription 1999–).

Key Indicators of the Labour Market (KILM). Geneva: International Labour Organization (ILO), 1999– (select Resources, ILO Databases, KILM) (print, CD-ROM, and subscription online resource).<http://www.ilo.org/public/english/ employment/strat/kilm/index.htm> or <http://www.ilo.org/>

LABORSTA Web site. <http://laborsta.ilo.org/>

World Employment Report. Geneva, Switzerland: International Labour Organization (ILO), 1998– (print biennial title, limited sections only are online). <http://www.ilo.org/public/english/ employment/strat/stwer/>

World of Work: The Magazine of the ILO, by the International Labour Office, Geneva,Switzerland, 1992– (ISSN 1020-0010) (print and online periodical). <http://www.ilo.org/public/english/ bureau/inf/magazine/>

Yearbook of Labour Statistics. Geneva: International Labour Organization (ILO), 1936– (ISSN 0084-3857) (print and CD-ROM).

OECD Labor and Statistical Labor Resources

OECD Directorate for Employment, Labour, and Social Affairs Web site, Paris, France. <http://www.oecd.org/> (search Browse: By Department).

OECD Employment Outlook. Paris: Organisation for Economic Co-operation and Development (OECD), 1983– (print and online subscription title).

OECD's Labour Market Statistics (CD-ROM), by the Organisation for Economic Co-operation and Development.

Labour Force Statistics. Paris: Organisation for Economic Co-operation and Development, 1966– (ISSN 0474-5515) (print annual).

Labour Force Statistics Online Databases Web site. <http://www.oecd.org/> (search Find: statistics).

Quarterly Labour Force Statistics. Paris: Organisation for Economic Co-operation and Development, 1983– (ISSN 0255-3627) (print).

Nongovernmental Sources Discussed

International Labor Rights Fund (ILRF) Web site, Washington, D.C. <http://www.laborrights.org/>

LabourNet: The International Labor Solidarity Web site, United Kingdom. <http://www.labournet.org/>

GOVERNMENTAL SOURCES

European Foundation for the Improvement of Living and Working Conditions Web site, Dublin, Ireland. <http://www.eurofound.eu.int/>

Summary: The European Foundation for the Improvement of Living and Working Conditions, a tripartite European Union body, is actively engaged in programs, research, analysis, and publications for European countries on areas including living conditions, working conditions, and industrial relations. The site is searchable, includes a site map, and is available in English and French. Some of the major programs include the European Monitoring Centre on Change (EMCC), a European information resource and Web portal, and an Observatory on Industrial Change. At this organization's publications Web site, a searchable catalog links to many publications. Some publications are full text online, free of charge, and some are available only through purchase.

Detailed Description: The link on the home page to Newsroom provides press releases, news, and press reporting for this organization. From the section Industrial Relations, the Web site links to a knowledge base of information and reports on information through these databases: *EIROnline: The European Industrial Relations Observatory, EMIRE: The European Employment and Industrial Relations Glossaries, EWC: The European Works Councils Agreements* full text online, and *PECS: Pacts for Employment and Competitiveness* online collection of case studies. It also reports on work in progress. The *EIROnline: European Industrial Relations Observatory On-Line,* available at <http://www.eiro.eurofound.ie/>, is an online resource worth noting. It is a database of articles on national, EU level, and comparative industrial relations, providing up-to-date information and analysis continuously since 1987. One of the titles available here is *EIRObserver,* the bimonthly bulletin of the European Industrial Relations Observatory, which contains feature articles and news, based on some of the reports from the *EIROnline* database over each two-month period. Registered users may sign up for automatic e-mail delivery of *EIRObserver. EIRObserver* is available for downloading as an Adobe Acrobat (PDF) file back to 1997. The online casebook of *PECS* links to national reports and a database of pacts for employment and competitiveness that is searchable by country and by sector.

The home page section Living Conditions also reports on work in progress and provides a knowledge base, as well as the section on Working Conditions. Within these knowledge bases, research results and survey results are posted online. The section on the Foundation's European Monitoring Centre on Change (EMCC) has a Web portal at <www.emcc.eurofound.eu.int> that aims to provide European institutions, public authorities, social partners, and companies with the data and information they need to anticipate and manage change. EMCC was established in 2001 with many partners at the European level as a place for exchanging practice, information, and ideas on the management and anticipation of change.

Copyright restrictions of the European Foundation for the Improvement of Living and Working Conditions are stated on its Web site: "The Foundation holds the copyright of all its publications and of this Web site. Reproduction is authorized for personal or internal use, provided the source is acknowledged, clearly stating the Foundation's full name. In all other cases, the Foundation is happy to receive a request for permission...."[1]

International Labour Organization Resources

Encyclopaedia of Occupational Health and Safety, by the International Labour Organization (ILO). 4th ed. 1998. (ISBN 9-22109-203-8) (print). <http://www.ilo.org/public/english/support/publ/encyc/index.htm> (subscription online resource,; also available as CD-ROM).

Summary: The 4th edition of this reference book for occupational health and safety was published in 1998 in four volumes. It contains chapters with articles that analyze the following topics: work, workers, and the working environment; the chemicals workers are exposed to at work and their hazards; occupational disease and injury; methods of treatment and prevention; and existing protective legislation.

The *Encyclopaedia* contains chapters with detailed articles covering specific industries, occupations, and hazards; medicine and hygiene; and social policy issues. It includes a guide to chemicals providing information on more than 2,000 chemicals. Authors of the sections are experts from the areas of government, employers' organizations, professional organizations, and labor unions from around the world. The very first edition was published in 1930, and much information has been added in the latest edition.

The four volumes of the revised and expanded 4th edition cover different topics. Volume I defines and describes health and management issues, including medical issues, policy issues, management of occupational disease and hygiene, and occupational health services. Volume II provides a detailed analysis of hazards, including general hazards, environmental, accidents and safety management, and psychosocial and organizational factors. Volume III covers activities and substances related to work in major industries broken down by type of industry. These include the biological industries such as farming and food and beverage; natural resources industries such as mining, oil exploration, and power generation; chemical industries; manufacturing industries; textiles and apparel industries; transport industries; construction industries; and services industries and occupations. Volume IV contains guides and indexes to help users access the information in the *Encyclopaedia*. These include the Guide to Occupations; the Guide to Chemicals, which supplies information on over 2,000 chemicals; and the Guide to Units and Abbreviations, which summarizes the international system of units of measurement and lists the abbreviations and acronyms used throughout the *Encyclopaedia*. Volume IV also provides a subject index, an index by chemical substance name, and an index by author cited.

International Labour Organization (ILO) Web site, Geneva, Switzerland. <http://www.ilo.org/>

Summary: The International Labour Organization (ILO) is a specialized agency within the United Nations system that works to promote social justice and internationally recognized human and labor rights. It existed before the creation of the United Nations under the League of Nations, beginning in 1919. The *International Labour Organization* Web site provides statistics, databases, news, featured articles on topics, information from its yearly conferences, publications free online and for purchase, and much more on a variety of topics related to labor. Information is available on labor standards, such as treaties, labor rights, occupational safety, and workers' and employers' rights. The Web site includes a site map, thematic links, an ILO search engine, a photo library, and related links. The entire Web site is in English, French, and Spanish, and documents are provided in a number of other languages. Of special note are the categories Public Information and Resources which both lead to free online reports.

Detailed Description: The ILO's home page links to general information, publications, statistics, resources, meetings, and news. Links to local ILO Web sites are available for Arabic, German, Italian, Japanese, Portuguese, and Turkish languages from the home page. About the ILO links to online information and brochures about its history, constitution, and members. The ILO is a major and prolific publisher, and a great variety of information is available from the Publications link, including an online catalog of publications for ordering publications. The ILO publishes titles on employment, social protection, social dialogue, labor standards and the fundamental principles and rights at work, and child labor, some online and some for sale. One of its aims is to publish in the area of technical assistance it provides to its member governments, including vocational training and vocational rehabilitation, employment policy, labor administration, labor law and industrial relations, working conditions, management development, cooperatives, social security, labor statistics, and occupational safety and health. It publishes an index online to labor conferences. One reference title published regularly on labor conditions throughout the world is the ILO's *World Labour Report,* which is available in print only. The 2001 *World Labour Report,* entitled *Income Security and Social Protection in a Changing World,* covers social security expenditures, income protection, health care protection, the unemployment benefits systems, and conclusions about the social protection.

In addition to the information and publications accessible to users through the main ILO office, information is also available from the ILO regional offices, especially pertaining to specific geographic regions. What's New is a section from the home page that provides a list of hyperlinks to new documents and sites recently put on the Web site.

For more information about ILO publications, users can search the ILO Publications category alphabetically by title and by subject. Under Publications there is a link specifically for titles freely available online. Users may sign up for an e-mail newsletter on new titles. Information about library sales, *Ebrary* (a subscription online database of publications for libraries) and the International Labour Organization's depository library program is linked from this page. The *ILO Catalog* is available online in PDF format. Students and researchers should note that the home page category Public Information also provides access to online full-text publications, as well as to press releases and other media and news services.

For information about labor statistics, users may access the main page for the International Labour Organization's Bureau of Statistics. Users must first select between free on subscription, global or regional databases online, and external links. Major topics of information are listed which then link to more information on the ILO Bureau of Statistics programs, activities, databases, publications, free online publications, consumer price indices, conferences, meetings, and statistics. Under the databases link, users may find a major ILO statistical database called *LABORSTA (Labour Statistics Database)* <http://laborsta.ilo.org>, which is operated by the ILO Bureau of Statistics and contains statistics for over 200 countries and territories since 1945. It is a major labor research resource and is described separately in this chapter.

Information about ILO titles can be accessed through the home page category ILO Library. One primary catalog *LABORDOC* <http://labordoc.ilo.org/>, is the International Labour Office Central Library's main catalog of its books, reports, journals, and documents on the topic of labor, employment, and related economic and social activities. It covers these topics worldwide and provides detailed abstracts for titles. A CD-ROM version of *LABORDOC* is available for purchase at <http://ilis.ilo.org>, and it includes bibliographic information back to 1919. Under Library Services the ILO offers a literature search service for researchers. The ILO Library category also links to the ILO databases Workgate (a searchable database of best Internet labor resources), electronic resources, and research guides.

Researchers may note that in the past, the ILO published a series of print publications on labor issues called *World Employment Programme (WEP) Working Papers* that have also been published in microfiche format. Many research libraries in the United States own some or all of the titles in this important series of working papers.

Tracking labor legislation is one of the major activities of the ILO. Information is compiled by the ILO's International Observatory of Labour Law on the Web at <http://www.ilo.org/public/english/dialogue/ifp-dial/ll/ioll.htm>. This Web site is a gateway to labor law and legal information particularly interesting to labor law specialists. It exchanges information on trends and developments in labor law around the world with its *National Labor Law Profiles* database. A related database is *ATLAS,* which provides information on developments in labor administrations around the world and is searchable by country, field of activity, institution, and contacts <http://webfusion.ilo.org/public/db/dialogue/gllad/atlas/>. Related bibliographic databases are the International Labor Organization's *NATLEX,* <http://natlex.ilo.org/>, which features online full-text national laws on labor, social security, and related human rights and is searchable by country and law, and *ILOLEX,* a searchable database of international labor standards.

The home-page category Standards and Fundamental Principles and Rights at Work provides background information on global Labor Standards, including an online glossary. Much information is available on the 1998 ILO Declaration on Fundamental Principles and Rights at Work and on the ILO Convention No. 182 to ban the worst forms of child labor. This includes an explanation of the issues, information from meetings, and online documents and publications. The category Standards and Fundamental Principles and Rights at Work also links to the *NATLEX* and *ILOLEX* databases, as well linking to an online monthly bulletin *Legislative Information* <http://natlex.ilo.org/leginf/english/index.htm>, containing bibliographic records for the most recent and important legislation that has been added to the *NATLEX* database.

Under Resources on the home page, researchers may access ILO databases, which lists all of the ILO databases described here, including online databases of statistical information previously available in print form. Databases are also categorized by subject.

Labor conferences are an important part of the work of the ILO and are reported on its Web site under the section Meetings. Member states of the ILO meet yearly at an International Labour Conference held in

June in Geneva, Switzerland, the headquarters of the organization. Sometimes this conference is called an International Parliament of Labor. Each year, a report is issued on the central theme of the conference. The conference passes resolutions on policies and activities, budget, and work programs. More information about the conference, including reports and documents from the discussions at the conference, are available from 1987 to the current year on the *ILO* Web site.

The International Labour Organization (ILO) is the umbrella organization for the International Occupational Safety and Health Information Centre (CIS). CIS provides users with an updated, bilingual (English and French), bibliographic database entitled *CISILO*. This is a database that indexes titles on occupational safety and diseases and how to prevent them. Its emphasis is on training and policy documents from various countries. *CISILO* is available electronically through several subscription services.

New information added to this database is published in print in CIS's bimonthly bulletin, *Safety and Health at Work*. Each issue of *Safety and Health at Work* contains a News and Activities section, four bibliographic sections designed to highlight important aspects of safety and health, and an index section. Annual cumulative author and subject and chemical indexes are included in the sixth issue of the bulletin. A five-year cumulative index is published as a separate publication.

In recent years, International Occupational Safety and Health Information Centre (CIS) has also published free full-text information on its Web site providing practical information on occupational safety and health matters. CIS also offers personalized database searches for researchers.

The International Labour Organization is constantly addressing new challenges. In 2002 it established the World Commission on the Social Dimension of Globalization to respond to how globalization has affected people at work and in their families and societies. The Commission is charged to review the facts and identify policies that will improve negative affects of globalization. Its final report is due at the end of 2003, and it will include information gathered from national dialogues. The ILO also provides users with excellent links to external organizations concerning labor .

International Labour Review. Geneva: International Labour Organization (ILO), 1921– (ISSN 0020-7780) (print and online subscription title 1999–).

Summary: Published four times a year in English, French, and Spanish, this major scholarly journal pub-

lishes original research and analysis in short articles on labor and employment issues worldwide. Articles include bibliographical references, and the journal also includes reviews of recent publications on labor topics. Both a print and electronic edition of the journal are available. A major strength of the electronic version is that it is searchable online from the first electronic issue, volume 138, no. 1, 1999. All users may freely browse the table of contents online and buy individual articles from journal issues. The International Labour Organization reaches out to users such as economists, lawyers, sociologists, and policy makers in this publication on current labor issues of concern.

Detailed Description: Subjects covered in this multidisciplinary journal include a broad range of worldwide labor issues, including the nature and future of work, labor flexibility, globalization, sexual harassment, new technologies, social security reform, child labor, and much more. Emerging topics are covered in the Perspectives Section, which offers information on topics such as gender, innovations in labor statistics, parental leave, child labor, part-time work, women in management, and pension reform.

Key Indicators of the Labour Market (KILM).
Geneva: International Labour Organization (ILO), 1999–. <http://www.ilo.org/public/english/employment/strat/kilm/index.htm> (print, CD-ROM, and subscription online resource) or <http://www.ilo.org/> (select Resources, ILO Databases, KILM).

Summary: *Key Indicators of the Labour Market (KILM)* provides users with comparable data by countries, including 20 key crucial indicators in understanding and evaluating labor issues. The statistics are organized by country, and users can manipulate the output into comparative tables through the CD-ROM and Internet versions of *Key Indicators*. This resource is available in print version published every two years, on the Internet through a subscription version entitled *KILMnet,* or in a CD-ROM version. In 1999, ILO launched the Key Indicators program with the intention to provide researchers with a core set of labor market indicators and to improve the availability of data to monitor new employment trends.

Detailed Description: These are some of the key 20 indicators provided for each country covered: labor force participation rate, employment and unemployment statistics and status, hours of work, education attainment and illiteracy, manufacturing wage trends, hourly compensation costs, employment by sector and occupational wages, labor productivity, and labor market flows. The methodology behind the labor statistics is published, and the data is gathered from several reliable international intergovernmental agencies. Some estimates are included.

This title organizes information by the economic status of a country and its geographic status. An individual country's information will either be in one of two developmental groupings (developed or industrialized economies and transition economies) or under one of four geographic groupings (Asia and the Pacific, Latin America and the Caribbean, sub-Saharan Africa, and the Middle East and North Africa).

There are major differences between the versions available for this title. The biennial print version (the latest revised version is 2001–2002) offers users a comprehensive set of 20 "key" indicators of the labor market. It includes easy-to-understand explanations of what the indicators represent and how they can assist researchers in understanding labor market issues. The content is limited to the years 1980, 1990, and subsequent years. The content of both the Internet and CD-ROM versions contain all years from 1980 on. The Internet version, entitled *KILMNet,* allows individual users to definite their own queries and output. The greatest advantage is the frequent data updates online compared to data updated every two years with the print version. *KILMNet* promises to make the data available to users on the Internet as soon as latest year data or data to fill in current gaps become available to the ILO. The same data is available on the CD-ROM as well as including additional years.

LABORSTA Web site. <http://laborsta.ilo.org/>

Detailed Description: This title in print and database form is a major statistical reference for labor questions worldwide. It provides yearly statistics on employment, unemployment, hours of work, wages, labor cost, consumer price indices, occupational injuries, and strikes and lockouts from 1969 to current. In addition, the Internet database *LABORSTA* also provides monthly statistics from 1979 to current for unemployment, hours of work, wages, and consumer price indices. Users can extract data based on their choice of country, table, and year. Estimates and projects of working populations are also provided for 1950–2010 with access provided by regions of the world and countries. ILO plans to offer more information soon in this database: country population census data from 1945 and ILO's comparable annual estimates of labor and unemployment from 1981.

The print *Yearbook* appeared in a special retrospective edition still very useful for historical data on labor. Entitled *Yearbook of Labour Statistics, Retrospective Edition on Population Censuses 1945–1989,* the issue focused entirely on population censuses carried out through the world since 1945. It covers 184 countries, areas, and territories and 559 population censuses with data on the total and economically active population by sex and age group; the economically active population by industry, by status in employment and by sex; and the economically active population by industry, by occupation, and by sex.

World Employment Report. Geneva: International Labour Organization (ILO), 1998– (print biennial title, limited sections only are online). <http://www.ilo.org/public/english/employment/strat/stwer/>

Summary: A biennial title, published since 1995, the *World Employment Report* analyzes current employment issues and major global employment trends. These reports provide an introduction to a specific employment theme, up-to-date data, chapters on different aspects of the issues, and policy conclusions for the policy makers in nations. Only limited information is available online, not full text. The report consists of two main parts. Part I contains an up-to-date analysis of the global and regional employment and labor market and income trends and developments within and across countries. Part II provides a research analysis of a specific employment-related issue of major current interest.

A related biennial title *Global Employment Trends* (2002–) is published as a separate report in those years the *World Employment Report* is not issued. It is available online in PDF format at no charge from the *ILO* Web site.

World of Work: The Magazine of the ILO, by the International Labour Office, Geneva, Switzerland, 1992– (ISSN 1020-0010) (print and online title). <http://www.ilo.org/public/english/bureau/inf/magazine/index.htm>

Summary: This illustrated magazine provides general articles on current labor and worker information globally. Each issue focuses on a specific topic and provides several articles on the topic within an issue. Other articles and regular features and news are also included. Feature articles are often focused on a specific labor or worker concern in a country. *World of*

Work is available on the Internet in PDF format for current issues, with major articles also online in HTML back to no.17, September/October 1996. Frequency of publication varies from four to five times a year.

Regular features in the magazine include News, ILO: Then and Now, Planet Work, Around the Continents, ILO in the Press, and Media. ILO: Then and Now is a feature that compares an ILO issue in its history to current treatment. Planet Work is a regular feature on a review of trends and developments in labor issues globally, including such topics as workplace security. Around the Continents is another regular feature reporting on the International Labour Organization's activities and events taking place around the world. ILO in the Press, also a regular feature article, includes actual images of articles on the ILO in press around the world, in English and many other languages. Under the feature Media are annotated descriptions of recent publications of note from the International Labour Organization.

Users may reproduce texts and photographs freely, but must credit the source, except for photo agencies' photographs. Written notification is appreciated.

Copies of issues of *World of Work* are also available on request from an e-mail address at the ILO. This magazine is also published in Chinese, Czech, Danish, Finnish, French, German, Hindi, Hungarian, Japanese, Norwegian, Russian, Slovak, Spanish, and Swedish.

Yearbook of Labour Statistics. Geneva: International Labour Organization (ILO), 1936– (ISSN 0084-3857) (print and CD-ROM).

Summary: The International Labour Organization publishes labor data by country annually in the print *Yearbook of Labor Statistics* and updated regularly in the Internet database *LABORSTA*. Historical statistics are also available through the database. The CD version was made available in 2003 and includes over 40 years of data.

OECD Labor and Statistical Labor Resources

OECD Directorate for Employment, Labour, and Social Affairs Web site, Paris, France. <http:// www.oecd.org/> (search Browse: By Department).

Summary: The Web site of this Directorate of the OECD provides users with news, summaries of issues, and online publications concerning labor. It also provides an access point for the many labor-focused statistical databases and journals, although most of these are not freely available online, but through subscription or print only. Major titles are described separately in this chapter; however, this Web site is a rich resource for labor-related materials, especially for industrialized countries of the world.

Detailed Description: Under each listing of this OECD Directorate's subagencies, users will find documents, reports, and statistics covering a range of labor topics including employment, labor statistics in OECD countries, social expenditures, and social affairs. The OECD Statistical databases also include information related to labor. Some of the major labor publications from the OECD accessible through the Web site of this Directorate and described in this chapter are the online subscription and print annual title *OECD Employment Outlook,* the CD-ROM *OECD's Labor Market Statistics,* the print annual title *Labor Force Statistics,* the print title *Quarterly Labor Force Statistics,* and finally, the *Labor Force Statistics Online Databases.*

OECD Employment Outlook. Paris: Organisation for Economic Co-operation and Development (OECD), 1983– (print and online subscription title).

Summary: This annual publication, published in English and French, analyzes trends in employment statistics and labor supply for the industrialized OECD nation states and provides short-term prospects for short-term labor market developments. Areas of focus include women's employment, youth employment, temporary employment, the affect of long-term unemployment, and more. Users may also download some information free of charge from the 2002 report, including the editorial section, summaries of each chapter, the statistical annex, and the complete table of contents. The electronic version is accessible through the subscription online service entitled *SourceOECD,* available at many scholarly and research institutions, or through individual purchase. From this page, users are also linked to earlier reports from 1996–2001.

OECD's Labour Market Statistics (CD-ROM), by the Organisation for Economic Co-operation and Development.

Labour Force Statistics. Paris: Organisation for Economic Co-operation and Development, 1966– (ISSN 0474-5515) (print annual).

Labour Force Statistics Online Databases Web site. <http://www.oecd.org/> (search Find: Statistics).

Quarterly Labour Force Statistics. Paris: Organisation for Economic Co-operation and Development, 1983– (ISSN 0255-3627) (print).

Summary: The OECD publishes a related annual print title and quarterly print title and online databases with labor force statistics. The online database contains detailed statistics on working-age population (15–64), labor force, employment, and unemployment by age and sex, as well as employment/population ratios and participation rates. The CD-ROM title, *OECD's Labour Market Statistics* provides annual, quarterly, and monthly labor market statistics for OECD member countries. It contains some general data, data relating to policy decisions, and labor market outcome for the countries. Published in English and French, this subscription resource is a CD-ROM accessible through Windows software and can be networked.

Detailed Description: The statistical data series in the CD cover the following: annual hours of work data, gross earnings distributions for full-time workers by gender, minimum wage series compensation of employees and wage rates, taxation of wages, public expenditures on labor market programs, gross and net unemployment benefits replacement rates, newly developed indicators on the strictness of employment protection legislation, and finally, trade union density rates and collective bargaining coverage in member countries. Some macroeconomic indicators, such as GDP and Gross Domestic Product, are also included for countries.

The annual print title *Labour Force Statistics* provides historical labor statistics in each current issue from 1981 to the year of publication. It is published in English and French since 1956. It provides comparative detailed data between countries for major labor indicators, including statistics for OECD countries on population, labor force, employment and unemployment by gender, employment status and other characteristics, employment by sector, and part-time employment. The quarterly title provides recent labor data for 22 OECD countries on a monthly and quarterly basis, particularly for employment by sector and major indicators of labor force. Previously both single titles were available for purchase on CD-ROM and may be held by research libraries and institutions. Both titles are also available online through OECD's subscription resource, *SourceOECD.*

OECD's *Labor Force Statistics Databases* contain detailed statistics on working-age population (15–64); labor force; employment and unemployment broken down by age and sex; unemployment rates by age and sex; employment/population ratios; and labor participation rates. There are two databases: *Labour Force Statistic—Data* (Labor force characteristics from Labor Force Surveys) and *Labour Force Statistics—Indicators.* Comparing the CD-ROM product and the print product, users will find that the CD-ROM includes longer time series with more detail than the print. It has more comprehensive information on sources and definitions used by member countries and allows users to build customized tools for analysis (i.e., graphs and tables). The Windows TM-based software, Beyond 20/20TM, and its technical documentation is supplied with the CD-ROM. More information on purchasing the CD-ROM subscription product is available on the *OECD* Web site and in its catalog. The user may find more about how OECD handles labor statistics by searching the home page under Labour Statistics.

NONGOVERNMENTAL SOURCES

International Labor Rights Fund (ILRF) Web site, Washington, D.C. <http://www.laborrights.org/>

Summary: This advocacy organization dedicated to achieving just and humane treatment for workers worldwide posts information about human rights and workers' issues around the world in news and some reports. It tracks workers' organizations, human rights groups, and trade unions' complaints about current issues for six months under the category Urgent Actions.

Detailed Description: Free publications of the organization, news and press, current projects, information about the organization, related links, and jobs are available from this site. Recent newsworthy publications and news links are featured on the home page. The News and Press category is organized by theme, either by subject or area of the world, such as child labor or women in the workplace, and the news links are listed by date.

Current Projects feature the following projects: corporate labor rights abuses, child labor campaigns, labor rights in China, rights for working women, sweatshop monitoring, and workers and trade. Full text of the project's related complaints, publications, reports, and legislation are found here.

Although ILRF is a small publisher compared to the International Labour Organization, it offers reports and publications online, some for purchase and some free full text, under the ILRF Publications link located on the organization's home page. The current issue of its newsletter, *Workers' Rights News,* is available online in PDF format. Other publications are organized by theme under Papers and Speeches and by books available for purchase.

LabourNet: The International Labor Solidarity Web site, United Kingdom. <http://www.labournet. org/>

Summary: The *LabourNet* Web site, begun in November 1995, promotes electronic communications as a medium for building international labor solidarity—it is a portal for information on unions. Through its initial work to support Liverpool dock workers, the potential of the Internet for building labor solidarity, for communication, and for supporting activity was demonstrated. *LabourNet* has evolved into supporting solidarity globally and providing international cooperation through communication. Globalization of production and distribution by employers and transnational corporations has brought new issues and problems to labor throughout the world.

The *LabourNet* Web site organizes discussions on labor issues alphabetically by country and also on international labor events from the point of view of working toward international labor solidarity through unions, organization, and communication. It links to labor news, conferences, directory information, and union information and provides a Global Directory of Directories and also links to other labor solidarity sites for specific countries (e.g., LaborNet for the United States) and is available in German, Spanish, and Korean.

RESEARCH STRATEGIES

The ***International Labour Organization (ILO)*** Web site, with its extensive and comprehensive coverage on a variety of labor-related topics, is the best place to begin the research process. In the areas of occupational health and safety, the best source to consult is the International Labour Organization's *Encyclopaedia of Occupational Health and Safety.* Users should check the subscription title online for latest information. For other labor union and organized labor and worker information, researchers can also check a variety of research sites, especially the ILO, as well as the non-IGO Web site ***LabourNet,*** and for current information about the enforcement of labor rights for

the working poor, the ***International Labor Rights Fund (ILRF)*** Web site is a good resource to consult first.

For users interested in labor statistics, the three most important sources of international labor statistics, according to the U.S. Dept. of Labor Statistics, are the **International Labour Organization (ILO),** the **Organization for Economic Cooperation and Development (OECD),** and the **Statistical Office of the European Communities (EUROSTAT).** The ILO's print periodicals ***Yearbook of Labour Statistics*** and ***Key Indicators of the Labour Market (KILM)*** provide labor data by country for the largest number of countries. The ***Yearbook*** provides the most historical data and is now available in a CD-ROM. The OECD provides data primarily for the developed countries, whereas most EUROSTAT data are limited to the countries of the European Union. All of these organizations prepare special studies on a wide variety of labor-related topics. Users may search each organization's Web site to retrieve data of interest, but beginning researchers may find it easiest to consult the print periodical titles.[2]

Other international intergovernmental organizations that collect some labor statistics include the ***United Nations Statistics Division*** Web site <http:// unstats.un.org/unsd/>, the ***World Bank*** Web site <http://www.worldbank.org/>, and the ***United Nations Industrial Development Organization (UNIDO)*** Web site <http://www.unido.org>. ***The Foreign Labor Statistics Program (FSL)*** Web site, annotated following, is also a starting place for researchers interested in basic comparable employment and labor statistics by country.

For documents and titles published on labor topics globally, both ILO and the OECD publish prolifically in this area. Both provide some free titles on their Web sites, although OECD tends to provide the fewest free titles. For policy issues, researchers should check the OECD titles and Web site first or the online subscription resource ***SourceOECD.*** For labor law and standards, researchers should use the ILO documents first. Users may search the Web sites by following the publications links or the themes and subject links. Each organization provides a catalog of publications that can be searched.

Major periodicals on labor include the ***International Labour Review*** by the International Labour Organization, a scholarly journal, and also by the ILO, the magazine for workers issues, the ***World of Work.*** Both are available free online, are searchable, and cover global labor issues. Users should consult the *International Labour Review* for statistics and broad issues concerning labor and government policies about labor, whereas the *World of Work* is best for finding information on labor events and an analysis of those events in countries all over the world.

FOR FURTHER READING: COMPREHENSIVE WEB SITES AND OTHER REFERENCE SOURCES

Bureau of International Labor Affairs (ILAB) Web site, by the U.S. Department of Labor, Washington, D.C. <http://www.dol.gov/ilab/>

Of special note for this site is the Publications link on the home page, where users may link to specific subagencies and programs, for example, the International Child Labor Program. This subagency offers many of its reports and publications full text for free on the Internet, and many are free on request. The Bureau's Division of Foreign Economic Research also has comparative and country-level research reports. For listing of reports, users can consult <http://www.dol.gov/ILAB/media/reports/oiea/main.htm>.

Foreign Labor Statistics Program (FSL) Web site, by the U.S. Department of Labor, Washington, D.C. <http://www.bls.gov/fls/>.

This program provides comparative country statistics on hourly compensation costs, productivity and labor costs, labor force, employment and unemployment rates, and consumer prices. The comparisons relate primarily to the major industrial countries, but other countries are included in certain measures. Publications, including links to full-text articles on international labor issues in Department of Labor publications, and links to detailed statistics and statistical reports are available. Users can download tables, customize personal tables, or download flat files of statistical data. Links to other governmental sources for international labor statistics are provided.

Social Protection & Labor Web site, by the World Bank, Washington, D.C. <http://www1.world bank.org/sp/>

The World Bank is an international intergovernmental organization that publishes sector reports and issues briefs concerning labor-related topics. The World Bank also has a Web site devoted to the issue of Child Labor that includes the full text of a World Bank report on the issues of Child Labor and how the World Bank could take stronger action. A summary, appendices, and references are included. The report is also available free in PDF format from this Web site.

XPDNC Labour Directory Web site. <http://xpdnc.com/links/>

This Internet directory lists links to organizations and information under employment, rights at work, social protection (labor education, legal access, socioeconomic security), social dialogue (consumer goods, media outreach, corporate agenda, online labor), and other links.

NOTES

1. *European Foundation for the Improvement of Living and Working Conditions* Web site, Dublin, Ireland, <http://www.eurofound.eu.int/publications/publications.htm>.

2. *People Are Asking....What Are the Major Sources of International Labor Statistics?* by the U.S. Department of Labor Statistics, Bureau of Labor Statistics, Foreign Labor Statistics, <http://www.bls.gov/fls/peoplebox.htm#Q03>.

CHAPTER 15
Laws and Treaties

CHAPTER OVERVIEW

Sources described in this chapter focus on legal materials and treaties.[1] Because of the complexity of legal materials, this chapter is very dense. Included are the full text of legal opinions, judgments, and other related documents. Also included are publications of world sources such as the International Court of Justice, often referred to as the World Court, other United Nations bodies, and regional bodies such as the European Union and the Organization of American States. All of these sources are available via the Internet and, for the most part, at no charge.

The treaty sources are both index and full-text sources and include bilateral and multilateral international treaties from 1648 to the present. Much of these sources are in print format. Although the European Union provides full-text, free-of-charge access to its four founding treaties, access to others is only available via *CELEX,* an online subscription service. The Organization of American States provides full-text, electronic access to its treaties at no charge. The full text of United Nations treaties is available through the print version of *United Nations Treaty Series* and other United Nations' produced print publications. Full text of these treaties and other related publications are also available via the subscription *United Nations Treaty Collection.*

Because of the broad nature of legal materials, some resources that are more relevant to other subject areas have been described in other chapters, including Government and Politics, International Relations, and Trade.

Governmental Sources Discussed

CELEX database, by the European Communities. <http://europa.eu.int/celex/htm/celex_en.htm> (online subscription resource).

CURIA: Court of Justice of the European Communities Web site, by the Cour de justice des Communautés européennes, Luxembourg. <http://curia.eu.int/>

EUR-Lex: The Portal to European Union Law Web site, by the Office for Official Publications of the European Communities, Luxembourg. <http://europa.eu.int/eur-lex/en/>

Global Legal Information Network (GLIN) Web site, by the Law Library of Congress, Washington, D.C. <http://www.loc.gov/law/glin/>

Secretariat for Legal Affairs Web site, by the Organization of American States, Washington, D.C. <http://www.saj.oas.org>

United Nations Resources

International Court of Justice Web site, The Hague, Netherlands. <http://www.icj-cij.org/>

International Law Commission Web site, by the Office of Legal Affairs, United Nations, New York. <http://www.un.org/law/ilc/>

International Law Portal Web site, by the United Nations, New York. <http://www.un.org/law/>

Multilateral Treaties Deposited with the Secretary-General Status as at... New York: United Nations, 1981— (UN Document No.: ST/LEG./SER. E/ Document number) (ISSN 0082–8319) (print annual title).

Statement of Treaties and International Agreements Registered or Filed and Recorded with the Secretariat during the month of... New York: United Nations, 1946– (UN Document No.: ST/LEG/SER. A/United Nations document number) (print title).

United Nations Commission on International Trade Law (UNCITRAL) Web site, Vienna, Austria. <http://www.uncitral.org/>

United Nations Juridical Yearbook. New York: United Nations, 1962– (UN Document No.: ST/LEG/SER. C/document number) (ISSN 0082–8297) (print title).

United Nations Treaty Series: Treaties and International Agreements Registered or Filed and Recorded with the Secretariat of the United Nations (UNTS). New York: United Nations, 1946–(ISSN 0379–8267) (print and online subscription service).

Nongovernmental Sources Discussed

Consolidated Treaty Series, edited by Clive Parry. Dobbs Ferry, N.Y.: Oceana Publications, Inc., 1969–1981 (ISBN 0-37913-000-4).

Guide to International Legal Research, compiled by the editors and staff of George Washington University's *Journal of International Law and Economics.* 5th ed. Newark, N.J.: LexisNexis/Matthew Bender, 2003 (ISBN 0-32716-312-7).

Multilateral Treaties: Index and Current Status, edited by M. J. Bowman and D. J. Harris. London: Butterworths, 1984 (ISBN 0-40625-277-7).

World Legal Information Institute Web site, by the Australian Legal Information Institute, University of Technology Sydney (UTS) Faculty of Law, New South Wales, Australia. <http://www.worldlii.org>

World Treaty Index, edited by Peter H. Rohn, University of Washington. Santa Barbara, Calif.: ABC-Clio, 1974 (ISBN 0-87436-132-X).

GOVERNMENTAL SOURCES

CELEX database, by the European Communities. <http://europa.eu.int/celex/htm/celex_en.htm> (subscription online resource).

Summary: A subscription-based service, *CELEX* provides mainly full-text access, in HTML, PDF, and TIF formats, to European Union legislation, case law, preparatory documents, and parliamentary questions. Materials are available in all 11 official languages, and the database is updated weekly. Searching is available through cross-file, file category, document number, and publication reference. Results also link to earlier or subsequent acts.

CURIA: Court of Justice of the European Communities Web site, by the Cour de justice des Communautés européennes, Luxembourg. <http://curia.eu.int/>

Summary: The Court of Justice is the official judicial body of the European Communities. CURIA is its Web site and is divided into four main categories: The Institution, Proceedings, Judicial Cooperation, and News. In addition, there are icons on the bottom of the home page for Welcome, Press Releases, Research, Contacts, Links, Site Map, and Index. Welcome links back to the home page. Press Releases will be discussed in the News category. Research leads to searching and researching tools. A link to the four main categories as well as to the other icons is found on every page of this Web site. The site is available in all 11 of the official European Union languages: Danish, German, English, Spanish, Finnish, French, Greek, Dutch, Italian, Portuguese, and Swedish. Also found on the home page is a link to Practical Information, which provides contact information for the various departments along with information on visiting and accessing the building, a Frequently Asked Questions section, ordering information for multimedia products, and a photo gallery of buildings, official visits, and hearings.

Detailed Description: The Institution is the first main category, and here are found an Introduction, Departments, Texts, and Documents. The Introduction is especially useful in further understanding the Court, the Court of First Instance, and the European Community and in reading the full text, usually in PDF format, of the following documents: *Proceedings* (1998–), *Synopsis of Judgments Delivered* (1998–1999 in French, 2000 to current in English), *Synopsis of the Other Decisions of the Court of Justice* (2000–2001), *Statistics of Judicial Activity of the Court of Justice* (1999–), *Proceedings of the Court of First Instance* (1998–2001), *Synopsis of Judgments Delivered of the Court of First Instance* (1998–1999 in French, 2000–2001 in English), *Synopsis of the Other Decisions of the Court of First Instance* (2001), and *Statistics of Judicial Activity of the Court of First Instance* (1999–2001). Departments, another subcategory of Institution, is further subdivided into Registry of the Court of Justice, Registry of the Court of First Instance, Interpretation, Press and Information, Library, Research and Documentation, Translation, and Administration. Each of these subcategories includes a description of its activities, along with links embedded in the text to relevant documents and lists. Under the category Institution, Texts and Documents is a dense grouping and includes the following:

Provisions in force
   Extracts of Treaties
   Conventions on certain common institutions
   Statutes of the Court of Justice
   Special or additional jurisdiction
   Rules of Procedure of the Court of Justice,
      of the Court of First Instance
   Council Decision establishing a Court of
      First Instance
   Instructions to the registrar of the Court of First
      Instance of the European Communities

Court of First Instance Practice Directions
to parties
Sundry documents
Draft Council Decision Amending the Protocol
on the Statute of the Court of Justice
(Articles 51, 54, 62a, 62b, and 62c)
Intergovernmental Conference (IGC):
The future of the judicial system of the
European Union
Contribution by the Court of Justice and
the Court of First Instance to the inter-
governmental conference
The EC Court of Justice and the Institutional
reform of the European Union (April
2000)
Information note on references by national
courts for preliminary rulings
Notes for the guidance of Counsel before
the Court of Justice
Notes for the guidance of Counsel before the
Court of First Instance for the oral procedure
Documents
Publications
The Annual Report
FAQ: Your questions. <http://curia.eu.int/en/
instit/txtdocfr/index.htm>

Each of these entries provides specific documents in full text (PDF format). The FAQs are in French only.

Proceedings, the second category available from the *CURIA* home page, serves mainly an informational purpose in providing information that is not the "definitive version." Proceedings includes a Guide for Users, Case-Law, Research Tools, and Lodging of Procedural Documents. The Guide for Users explains the various parts of the Proceedings section, with embedded links in the text to various components. Case-law is subdivided into Search Forms (Case-law of the Court of Justice/Court of the First Instance and Case-law of the Court of First Instance in Staff Cases), Numerical Access to the Case-Law, Notices in the *Official Journal,* and Notice. The Search Forms provide access to the various search engines employed to locate these materials. The search forms for both Case-law of the Court of Justice/Court of the First Instance and Case-law of the Court of First Instance in Staff Cases is relatively the same. Both require that a choice of judgments, opinions, orders, or all documents be made in order to conduct the search. Both also allow searching by case number, date, and names of parties with an available list for each field. The search form for Case-law of the Court of Justice/Court of the First Instance is dated

from June 17, 1997, to the present and also provides searching by field (pull-down menu) and words in text. Searching in Case-law of the Court of First Instance in Staff Cases can also be done by words in text and words in abstract. This search form dates from July 9, 1997, to the present. Numerical Access to the Case-Law has cases lodged before the Court of Justice from 1953–1988 and since 1989 and cases lodged against the Court of First Instance since 1989. The title and page numbers from the *European Court Reports* is included, and many of the cases are in full-text format. Notices in the *Official Journal* contain new cases and cases removed from the register. However, at the time of this writing this was not hot-linked. Notices, the final subdivision of Case-law, documents changes in citations to the various legal instruments. Research Tools, another subsection of the Proceedings main category, is comprised of *Digest of Community Case-Law* (summaries of judgments and orders), alphabetical index of subject matter, annotations of judgments, and links to institutional and related Internet sites. Except for Links, all the sections are in French. Lodging of Procedures is the last subsection of Proceedings, and it contains contact information for both the Court of Justice and Court of First Instance, along with links to Rules of Procedure and Notes for the Guidance of Counsel.

Judicial Cooperation is the third main home page category, providing access to Case-law (national and international) and the Brussels and Lugano Conventions. Case-law has the full text, in PDF format, of the "Application of Community Law by National Courts: A Survey," a synopsis of excerpts from the relevant *Official Journal* (1997–2000) as well as the French version of the bulletin *Reflets,* a quick information source. The Brussels and Lugano Conventions subsections, in English and French, have the full text, in PDF format, of the conventions and protocols as well as the relevant cases.

The last main category, News, features Press Releases, Proceedings of the Institution, Diary, and News. Press Releases contains the full text, in all official languages, of releases related to cases, official visits, and information, dating from 1996 on. Proceedings of the Institution has the full text from 1997 to the present. The Diary is a quick reference to the events for the current month. News reports on events and site news.

EUR-Lex: The Portal to European Union Law Web
site, by the Office for Official Publications of the

European Communities, Luxembourg. <http://europa.eu.int/eur-lex/en/>

Summary: *EUR-Lex* is the Web portal for accessing European Union law and is arranged into eight major categories: *Official Journal,* Treaties, Legislation, Legislation in Preparation, Case-law, Parliamentary Questions, Documents of Public Interest, and Preparing Enlargement. Access is available in all the official languages: Danish, German, English, Spanish, Finnish, French, Greek, Dutch, Italian, Portuguese, and Swedish. The home page also has links to the major databases and portals, which are described in this chapter, as well as information about EU Law, a site map, glossary, and Frequently Asked Questions.

Detailed Description: *Official Journal (OJ),* the first major home page category discussed, links to this significant resource on European Union law and legislation that helps the organization conduct its business. The online version is searchable. Published daily in print format in all 11 official languages of the European Union, the *Official Journal (OJ)* consists of two main series, the L series (legislation) and the C series (information, preparatory acts, and notices). Some E series documents are available only electronically. The *OJ* is available in European Union depository libraries in the United States; researchers may consult the *European Union in the United States* Web site <http://www.erunion.org> for a list of depository libraries. The *TED* (Tenders Electronic Daily) database publishes the Supplement to the *OJ* (calls for tenders). There are links to the chronological list of available journals, list of available issues by language, and the link Supplement to the Official Journal-Public Procurement Notices is to the *TED* database. The rest of the *Official Journal* category contains a search engine that allows for searching by publication reference in the *Official Journal* with the required fields of publication year and *OJ* series and month or *OJ* number. Day and page are optional choices. Searching is also possible by word, with text being a required field and document date optional. An advanced search option is also included, however, it is through *CELEX,* the European Union's legal database, which is only available by subscription.

Treaties is the second major category from the *EUR-Lex* home page. Links from this category go to consolidated versions of the *Treaty Establishing the European Community* and *Treaty on European Union* (full text in HTML, PDF, or TIF formats), the *Treaty of Nice* (full-text in HTML, PDF, or TIF formats),

Other Treaties and Protocols (full text, TIF), Accession Treaties (full text, TIF), Founding Treaties (full text, TIF, some HTML), and Selected Instruments (full text, in PDF format, from the publication *European Union: Selected Instruments Taken from the Treaties*). A search engine is also included from this section, which allows searching by text (required) or advanced searching via *CELEX.*

The third major *EUR-Lex* home page category discussed is Legislation, which links to Directory of Community Legislation in Force, Consolidated Legislation, Application of Community Law in Member States, Euro Conversion Rates, and Searching. The Directory of Community Legislation in Force is arranged by topic (Analytical Structure), with links under each topic to the full text of the legislation. A how to use this directory is also included. Consolidated Legislation brings together, in one location, the basic legislation, amendments, and corrections. However, these are considered unofficial documents for legal citation purposes. Searching is available by publication reference from the *Official Journal* or by word. There is an About section along with a search engine. Application of Community Law details the progress in notification of national measures implementing directives, infringements, the annual report on monitoring the application of Community law, and State aids. Each section includes statistical information and an archive. The link Euro Conversion Rate provides the full text, PDF, of the legislation from 1998 and 2000 on this topic. The search engine that is included in this category is the same one found in the *Official Journal* category.

Legislation in Preparation is the fourth major category and is subdivided into: recent proposals not yet included in the Directory, Directory of Commission proposals, list of available Commission proposals, European Parliament activities, Council documents, European policies/summaries and legislative follow-up, and monitoring the decision-making progress between institutions. Recent proposals provides the full text, in PDF and WORD, for 2002 and only PDF for 1999–2001, along with more information, on Commission proposals. The Directory of Commission proposals links back to the topical arrangement found in the Legislation category. The list of available Commission proposals again provides the full text, in WORD and PDF, in all the official languages, of current proposals. European Parliament activities links to the *EUROPARL* home page, <http://www.europarl.eu.int/home/default_en.htm>, described in the Government and Politics chapter. Council documents links to the Council of the European Union section Access to Public Documents, also described in the Government and Politics chapter. European policies/summaries links to the Activities of the European Union page, where summary legislation can be accessed by clicking on the links of the main activities. Monitoring the decision-making progress links to *PreLex,* "the database on inter-institutional procedures" <http://europa.eu.int/prelex/apcnet.cfm? CL = en>. Found here are a description of the database, help guide, and the search forms. The search section of the Legislation in Preparation category is very complex. Searching is available by document number (required) with the options of selecting type of document. Searching by procedure (decision making or legislative observatory) is also available with the rest of the search function the same as that of the *Official Journal* category.

Case-Law, the fifth major category, is subdivided into Case-law since 1997, Competition Law, Court of the European Free Trade Association (EFTA), and European Court of Human Rights. Case-law since 1997 links to a search form, which allows searching by judgments, opinions, orders, or all documents for the Court of Justice and Court of First Instance, dating from June 1997 to the present. Competition Law (Commission-Competition Directorate-General) links to the *Citizen's Guide to Competition Policy* on the European Union Web site. This guide is divided into the topics of antitrust, mergers, liberalization, State aid, and international. At the time of this writing the EFTA link was not functioning. European Court of Human Rights links to the home page of this Court of the Council of Europe and includes pending cases, judgments and decisions, basic texts, and press releases. A search section is also part of the Case-Law category. This search form allows searching by case number with the year and number being required fields; searching by publication reference in the *European Court Reports* with searching by volume (Court of Justice, Court of First Instance, and Staff Cases) and year being required fields; searching by party, with the party a required field; and searching by word with text a required field. Advanced searching, via *CELEX,* is also included.

Parliamentary Questions is the sixth major category. This again links to the *EUROPARL* Web site with explanations and searching of various types of documents. The search section found on the Parliamentary Questions main page allows for text searching.

Documents of Public Interest, the seventh major category, has the full text, in PDF and WORD (current) formats, of documents subdivided into Communications from the Commission to the Council, Green Paper, Report, Commission Working Document, White Paper, and Other. These are arranged chronologically or numerically. The searching form allows searching by COM or SEC documents, with required fields of year and number or searching by word, with a required text field.

Also included on the *EUR-Lex* home page is Links, linking users to the sites of *CELEX, ŒIL, TED, CURIA,* and *PreLex.* Except for *ŒIL* and *CURIA,* the others have already been described in this resource. *CURIA* is described as a separate entry. *ŒIL* is the *Legislative Observatory* and is available from the *EUROPARL* site <http://wwwdb.europarl.eu.int/dors/oeil/en/default.htm>. Here are found news and general information, searching within legislative dossiers, subjects of current interest, and forecasts and results of institutional activities.

About EU Law is another section of the home page and is divided into Process and Players, *ABC of Community Law,* and a Glossary. Process and Players provides definitions and links to the major bodies, consultative bodies, and other EU institutions, along with an understanding of their roles. *ABC of Community Law* is the full text, PDF format, of a publication written by Dr. Klaus-Dieter Borchardt and published by the Directorate-General for Education and Culture. The Glossary is useful in defining the many terms associated with European Law and is arranged alphabetically by term.

Global Legal Information Network (GLIN) Web site, by the Law Library of Congress, Washington, D.C. <http://www.loc.gov/law/glin/>

Summary: Hosted by the Library of Congress, this database contains the official texts of laws, regulations, and other legal sources from international member governments. Only the members can access the full texts, but anyone can access the summaries (mainly in English) and citation information. The main menu from the *GLIN* home page is organized into Guest Search, Member Log On, *GLIN Thesaurus,* Membership Information, Jurisdictional Information, and Database Contents. A link to HELP is located at the bottom of the home page text. For the purpose of this discussion, the focus will be on Guest Search, *GLIN Thesaurus,* and Database Contents.

Detailed Description: Guest Search, a link from the home page, goes to a log-in screen, with guest or member being the log-in categories. Most researchers will be classified as guests. A search form for searching law summaries appears. Searching from this point can be done by country (pull-down menu), *GLIN Thesaurus,* subject terms from the *Thesaurus,* title of legal instrument, date of issuance, date of publication, instrument class, and instrument number. In addition, on the left-hand side of this page are links to Search Law Summaries, Search Legal Writing Summaries, and HELP sections for both of these as well as a contact link. The search form for searching legal writing summaries has the same country pull-down menu, the same link to the *Thesaurus* and subject terms from *Thesaurus* search box, and date of publication.

The *GLIN Thesaurus* also has a search form to find the terms and allows for keyword index searching and browsing. Database Contents, the other *GLIN* category to be discussed, is divided into Database Contents and Legislative Calendars. Databases Contents, the subsection, is arranged alphabetically by jurisdiction and has information on summary holdings, number of summaries, full-text holdings, number of full text, and notes. Legislative Calendars is arranged alphabetically by country name and provides an explanation for each country.

Secretariat for Legal Affairs Web site, by the Organization of American States, Washington, D.C.
<http://www.saj.oas.org/>

Summary: The Secretariat for Legal Affairs Web site, also available in Spanish, encompasses many of the legal resource and offices of the Organization of American States. Access to information is provided under the major headings of Inter-American Juridical Committee, Administrative Tribunal Office of the Assistant Secretary for Legal Affairs, Technical Secretariat for Legal Cooperation Mechanisms, Department of International Law, Inter-American Treaties Database, and Secretariat for Administrative Tribunal.

Detailed Description: The Inter-American Juridical Committee is the first main heading found on the home page of the Secretariat for Legal Affairs. With headquarters in Rio de Janeiro, this Committee is an international advisory body that advises the organization on juridical matters, promotes the progressive development and codification of international law, and studies juridical problems associated with the integration of the developing countries of the hemisphere. Included here are the sections Introduction, Members, Agenda, Reports, Recent News, and Department of International Law. Of special note is the Reports section, which provides the full text (PDF) of this Committee's *Annual Report* (2000–).

The second Secretariat main heading is Administrative Tribunal, a rich online resource of decisions, regulations, and documents. Established in 1971, "the principal purpose of the Tribunal is to settle—within the jurisdictional limits established in its Statute—disputes between staff members and the General Secretariat concerning the terms of their employment and other related questions, including the Retirement and Pension Plan. In 1976, provided a Special Agreement, the Tribunal's jurisdiction was extended to include the Inter-American Institute for Cooperation on Agriculture (IICA)."[2]

Included are Annual Reports, Decisions, Judges, Internal Regulations, Basic Documents, Tribunal Secretariat, IICA, Search, and E-mail. Annual Reports are in full text dating from 1999–2000 (English and Spanish only) through the present (in Spanish, English, Portuguese, and French). The Decisions section contains the full text of Judgments (1977-present) and Resolutions (1974-present). The earliest of each is in Spanish only. Internal Regulations provides the full text of the Statute and Rules of Procedure. Basic Documents is comprised of the full text of the *Charter; General Standards for the Operation of the General Secretariat,* Staff Rules, Executive Orders, Administrative Memorandums, Retirement and Pension Plan, Resolutions of the General Assembly, and Permanent Council. The IICA section pertains to the extension of jurisdiction of the Administrative Tribunal to the Inter-American Institute for Cooperation on Agriculture in the form of an "Informative Summary." The Search section contains a free-text search engine.

Office of the Assistant Secretary for Legal Affairs, another home page main heading, is subdivided into Mission Statement, Personnel, Reports and Documents, Legal Projects and Studies, Publications, Annual Report, Program Budget, and Internships. The Reports and Documents section provides the full text of speeches, remarks, and reports on a variety of topics. Legal Projects and Studies are the result of work by interns, staff, and/or the Assistant Secretary on topics pertaining to research and promotion related to international law and inter-American legal cooperation activities. The full text is included. Publications contains the reprints of full-text articles and book chapters written by the Assistant Secretary and published elsewhere. Annual Report contains the full text of the most recent annual report of this office. Program Budget is also the most recent and is presented in PDF full-text format.

The Department of International Law is the fourth main heading discussed and is subdivided into Private International Law, Public International Law, Treaties and Agreements, Courses and Seminars, Publications, Recent News, and the Inter-American Juridical Committee. The Private and Public International Law sections both contain a brief overview and links to relevant publications and other materials. Treaties and Agreements links to the *Inter-American Treaty Database,* which is also one of the main home page categories and described in that section. Publications features *Annual Reports,* workshop publications, the full text (PDF) of *Democracy in the Inter-American Juridical Committee* (February 1997), and also links to publications produced during the course on international law.

Technical Secretariat for Legal Cooperation Mechanisms is the fifth main heading, and for the purpose of this discussion the focus will be on the Menu and Projects sections of this heading. Menu, where much of the material is organized, is subdivided into *Charter of the OAS,* Inter-American Treaties, Resolutions and Declarations, and Publications. Resolutions and Declarations provides the full text of these documents for the OAS General Assembly, Permanent Council, Inter-American Juridical Committee, and Ministers of Justice. Publications for the Secretariat and the Inter-American Juridical Committee (IAJC) are found under the Publications subdivision. The IAJC publications have already been discussed. Those of the Secretariat are arranged by books, bulletins, and other, which consists of reports. Books features the various conventions, in full-text format, although a few other types of materials are also included. Each entry is annotated. The heading Bulletins provides the full text of *Legal Bulletin* (1997–).

Inter-American Treaties Database is the sixth main home page heading discussed. The text of treaties can be searched by year, by subject, and alphabetically. Signatories to treaties and ratifications can also be searched the same way. The full text of the treaties is available from 1948 on, although a few years are not hot linked. A search engine is also included to search for treaties dating before 1948. Also located here are links to full text of the *Inter-American Democratic Charter* and *The Inter-American Legal System: A Comparison of the Inter-American Treaties 1947–*

2001. In addition, there is a link to Other Databases of International Treaties, which includes the *United Nations Treaty Databases, Treaty Database of the Fletcher School of Law and Diplomacy* (Tufts University), *Political Database of the Americas* (Georgetown University), and *Global Legal Information Network.*

The last main heading is Secretariat for the Administrative Tribunal, which repeats Tribunal information already discussed.

United Nations Resources

United Nations Commission on International Trade Law (UNCITRAL) Web site, Vienna, Austria. <http://www.uncitral.org/>

Summary: Established in December 17, 1966, UNCITRAL serves as the legal body to curtail and end legal barriers to international trade. This Web site, available in all the official United Nations languages, is the primary source for global trade law information. The site is subdivided into 14 main categories: About UNCITRAL, News and Meetings, Adopted Texts, Status of Texts, Commission Sessions, Working Group, Technical Assistance, Frequent Questions, Case Law (CLOUT), *UNCITRAL Yearbook,* Bibliography, Research Guide, Search, and Online Resources. A pull-down menu to access related United Nations law resources is also included.

Detailed Description: The first main category discussed, About UNCITRAL, provides an introduction, quotes about the organization's work, the full text of the current and previous year's report on it's work, the working groups and commission meeting schedule for the coming year, and contact information. News and Meetings is the second main category and contains miscellaneous reports also linking to the work reports, along with some papers and program information from previous colloquia and symposia related to UNCITRAL (1994–).

The third main category discussed is Adopted Texts, which is subdivided into the topics of International Commercial Arbitration and Conciliation, International Sale of Goods and Related Transactions, Cross-Border Insolvency, International Payments, International Transport of Goods, Electronic Commerce, and Public Procurement and Infrastructure Development. Each of these topics has the full text of the related documents.

Status of Texts is the fourth main category. "As a service, UNCITRAL prepares a document containing the Status of Conventions and Enactments of UNCI-TRAL Model Laws. This document is updated when the Secretariat is informed of changes in status or new enactments. Readers are also advised to consult the *United Nations Treaty Collection* for authoritative status information."[3] The *Treaty Collection* or Series is described as a separate entry in this chapter.

Commission Sessions, the fifth main category, provides full-text coverage of the various documents produced from each session (1995–). Working Groups, the sixth main category, is divided into Groups I–VI and, when available, has the full text of the working documents (date coverage varies by Group).

Technical Assistance is the sixth main category discussed and includes various legal instruments that have been developed in compliance with the standards of other international legal systems. These instruments, in full text, are arranged into the subcategories of sales, dispute resolution, procurement and infrastructure development, banking and payments, transport, and electronic commerce. In addition, a pull-down menu provides choices for other technical assistance from the offices of Law of the Sea, Codification Division, Treaty Section, and Legal Affairs.

Case Law (CLOUT), another *UNCITRAL* home page main category, documents the Commission's work through the full text, PDF format, of court decisions and arbitral awards. Here are found a user's guide, thesauri, abstracts, and subscription information. Searching of CLOUT is also available and can be done by article, country, thesaurus issue, type of decision, and main view.

Of special note is the *UNCITRAL Yearbook*, the ninth major category. An annual publication available in English, French, Russian, and Spanish , it is comprised of documents produced by the Commission as well as the annual report (Supplement No. 17 of the *Official Records of the General Assembly*). Although all volumes are in print format, Volume I (1968)–Volume XXVI (1995) are also available electronically in full-text format.

Bibliography, the tenth main category, is divided into two sections: Consolidated, 1993–2002, and Newest Books and Articles, 2002–2003, and contains citations with some briefly annotated. Research Guide is the eleventh main category and should be consulted when conducting research within this organization. It discusses the types of materials included along with providing links to samples. The category Search UNCITRAL consists of a search engine for this site. Online Resources is the last main category and provides links to other intergovernmental and nongovernmental-related Web sites.

International Court of Justice Web site, The Hague, Netherlands. <http://www.icj-cij.org/>

Summary: As the United Nation's main judicial body, the International Court of Justice (ICJ) publishes a comprehensive Web site of the Court's information in both English and French. The page is divided into seven main headings: What's New, Docket, Decisions, General Information, Basic Documents, Publications, and Search. This site has mirror sites in Ithaca, New York; Paris, France; and Glasgow, Scotland.

Detailed Description: What's New, the first main home page heading discussed, provides the full text of press releases, categorized into latest, pending cases, and events and visits. An opportunity to subscribe to an e-mail service to receive notification of press releases is also available here. In addition, the full text of Statements of the President of the Court (1994–) is also included.

Docket is the second major heading and is categorized into Cases Currently Being Heard/Under Deliberation and List of Pending Cases Before the Court and Current Status. A listing of relevant cases is included for both categories. Each case description includes informational elements from the categories: Application, Request for Provisional Measures, Written Pleadings, Oral Pleadings, Orders, Judgment(s), Press Communiques, and Latest Developments. Not every case has text for each informational element.

Decisions, the third major heading, is subdivided into Contentious Cases and Advisory Cases and includes all cases that the Court has received since 1946. It links to an alphabetical listing, by country name, of these cases. Both types of cases are listed in chronological order with the newest cases first. The Contentious Cases group contains the same informational elements as the Docket heading. The Advisory Cases group provides the Advisory Opinion for each listed case.

General Information, the fourth main ICJ home page heading, provides a short history and overview of the Court under the subheading The Court at a Glance. A more in-depth description is found in *A Guide to the History, Composition, Jurisdiction, Procedure and Decisions of the Court,* which is based on a 50th anniversary booklet on the inaugural sitting of the Court (1946–1996). A list of the Court's members, with biographical information attached, and the full text to Annual Reports to the General Assembly (1998–) are also included.

The fifth main heading is Basic Documents, which are subdivided into two main categories: Constitutive

Instruments and Bases for Jurisdiction of the Court. Constitutive Instruments consist of the full text of the *United Nations Charter* (English and Spanish); *Statute of the Court* (English and Spanish); *Rules of the Court (1978)* as amended on December 5, 2000 (English and French), along with *Background Note by the Registry Indicating the Rules of Court,* also amended on the same day; *Practice Directions I–IX,* and other documents such as relevant resolutions; and an Index to Basic Documents, arranged alphabetically by topic. The Bases for Jurisdiction of the Court category contains the subcategories of Who Can Bring a Case Before the Court, Jurisdiction in Contentious Cases, and Advisory Jurisdiction. Here are found the full text of relevant statements from the official instruments pertaining to these issues.

Publications is the sixth main heading and is divided into Judgments, Orders, Advisory Opinions; Pleadings, Oral Arguments, Documents; Acts and Documents; Yearbook; and Bibliography. Each subcategory contains a listing of titles along with sales number and ISBN number, and in some cases, it notes if an item is out of print. Judgments, Orders, Advisory Opinions "contains the Reports of the decisions of the Court in both the English and the French texts. Each decision is published as soon as given, in an unbound fascicle which is sold separately. To allow for binding, a continuous system of pagination is adopted for all the fascicles of any one year. In January of each year, an analytical index is published of the previous year's decisions; this also may be purchased separately. The collected decisions, with index, for each year may also be obtained ready bound together in one volume with *I.C.J. Reports* [date] as the official title."[4] For Pleadings, Oral Arguments, Documents, "volumes in this series are published after the termination of each case and contain the documentation relating to the case in the original language, that is, in English or in French. This comprises the document instituting proceedings, the written pleadings, the verbatim record or the oral proceedings, any documents submitted to the Court after the closure of the written proceedings, and the correspondence. Official citation of the series: *I.C.J. Pleadings,* with the short title of the case."[5] *I. C. J. Acts and Documents* is the official title of publications under the Acts and Documents subcategory and includes titles such as *Rules of Court* and *Charter of the United Nations. I.C.J. Yearbook* [date], an annual publication, details the Court's work for the period August 1 to July 31. Lastly, the *I.C.J. Bibliography* includes a listing of Court-related documents and

works. This publication lags behind in currency and at this writing the most current volume was dated 1995.

Search is the last main home page heading discussed. Here is found a search box for free-text searching. Advanced Search is also an option and can be restricted to selected categories (Applications/Special Agreements, Written Pleadings, Oral Pleadings, Orders, Judgments, Summaries of Judgments and Orders, Press Communiques, and Basic Documents) or selected cases, with a listing of case names included. Help with searching is also available.

International Law Commission Web site, by the Office of Legal Affairs, United Nations, New York. <http://www.un.org/law/ilc/>

Summary: The Web site of the International Law Commission, which has as its mission the development and codification of international law, provides access to the full text of documents and reports of its work. In addition, information is given regarding its function, membership, and a guide to conducting research in this organization is available. The site itself is divided into eight main headings: Introduction, Activities, Conventions and Other Texts, Analytical Guide, Commission Reports and Other Documentation, Programme of Work, Sessions, and Membership.

Detailed Description: Introduction, the first main heading discussed from the *United Nations: International Law Commission* Web site, gives the history along with the text from relevant United Nations documents pertaining to the establishment of this Commission. Activities, the second main heading, is divided into four subdivisions: Cooperation with Other Bodies and Geneva International Law Seminar, both of which contain the full text of the reports, dating from 1996 on; 1998 Seminar to Celebrate the Fiftieth Anniversary of the Commission and Colloquium on the Progressive Development and Codification of International law (1997), both of which contain a brief overview only.

Conventions and Other Texts, the third main heading, contains full text of the Statute of the ILC, Completed Topics, and Topics Under Construction. Analytic Guide is the fourth main heading and contains the full text, as well as hard copy ordering information, of the *Analytical Guide to the Work of the International Law Commission.* The Web version is updated as needed. This publication is useful as a research tool to assess the Commission's work.

Commission Reports and Other Documentation, the fifth main heading discussed, has the full text of reports from the Commission, dating from 1998 to the present. Also provided is a listing of the reports, dating from 1949–1997, with the appropriate United Nations document symbol. The Commission also publishes an annual *Yearbook* and a list of the titles, again with the United Nations document number, is available here. Lastly, the full text of documents and reports for each session (1998–) is provided.

Programme of Work, the sixth main heading, describes what the Commission has done and is working on. Sessions, the seventh main heading, is comprised of the meeting records for each session, dating from 1996 to the present. Lastly, Membership, the final main heading, lists the current Commission make up by name and country.

International Law Portal Web site, by the United Nations, New York. <http://www.un.org/law/>

Summary: A comprehensive portal of relevant law-related Web sites of the United Nations, this site includes links to the Office of Legal Affairs, General Assembly's Sixth Committee, International Law Commission, UNCITRAL International Trade Law, Codification of International Law, Treaties, Laws of the Sea, Technical Assistance to State, International Court of Justice, Secretary-General's Trust Fund (ICJ), International Criminal Court, International Criminal Tribunal for Former Yugoslavia (ICTY), International Criminal Tribunal for Rwanda (ICTR), and Documents Research Guide. The site is available in all United Nations official languages: Arabic, Chinese, English, French, Russian, and Spanish. A text version is also available in all official languages except Arabic. **Detailed Description:** Office of Legal Affairs, the first major heading, is the Department that serves as the provider of legal advice to the Secretary-General, acting on his behalf in legal matters. There are six branches within this office: Office of Legal Counsel, General Legal Division, Codification Division, Division for Ocean Affairs and Law of the Sea, International Trade Law Branch, and Treaty Section. The Secretariat of the United Nations Administrative Tribunal is also under this Office administratively. On this section there is a link to each of these branches outlining their core functions, activities, and linking to related Internet sites, providing researchers with further documentation. The chief officer's name is also listed. The link for the United Nations Administrative

Tribunal goes to a page describing its organization and also includes the chief officer.

The second main United Nation: International Law Portal heading is the Sixth Committee of the General Assembly, which is devoted to legal issues before the United Nations. Contained here are links to the 52nd through current session (1997–), leading to the full text, usually in PDF format, of various documents and reports generated by this committee. In addition, there is a pull-down menu of links to related United Nation Web sites.

The International Law Commission is the third main heading and is also described separately in this chapter.

United Nations Commission on International Trade Law (UNCITRAL) is the fourth main heading and is described as a separate entry in this chapter. Codification of International Law, the fifth main heading, is a part of the Office of Legal Affairs. This site links to the Sixth Committee; International Law Commission; various relevant ad hoc committees; the International Criminal Court; the Programme of Assistance in the Teaching, Study; Dissemination and Wider Appreciation of International Law; the United Nations and the Development of International Law, 1990–1999 (a work in progress); and Recent Conventions Adopted by the Sixth Committee/General Assembly.

The Treaties section, the sixth main heading, will be described as a separate entry in this chapter. Oceans and Law of the Sea, is the seventh main heading. "The 1982 United Nations Convention on the Law of the Sea provides, for the first time, a universal legal framework for the rational management of marine resources and their conservation for future generations. Rarely has such radical change been achieved peacefully, by consensus of the world community. It has thus been hailed as the most important international achievement since the approval of the United Nations Charter in 1945."[6] Included here are links to the main convention, *United Nations Convention on the Law of the Sea of 10 December 1982,* further information about it as well as related conventions, agreements, reports, publications, listing of experts, and other United Nations agencies that pertain to this topic. A search engine is also available to search the Oceans and Law of the Sea site.

The eighth main heading is Technical Assistance and details the offerings of legal assistance for member states. Of particular interest in this section are the links to Web sites in the areas of Drug Control/Crime Prevention, Economic and Social Development, Environment, Governance, Human Rights, Legal Affairs, Outer Space, and Political Affairs. Many of these subject-based Web sites provide the full text of relevant reports and documents on a related subject.

Secretary General Trust Fund, the 10th main heading, provides assistance to countries in pursuit of International Court of Justice dispute settlement.

International Court of Justice is the ninth main heading and again is described separately in this chapter.

International Criminal Court, the 11th main heading, was established as a place to prosecute genocide and similar crimes. Found on this site are an overview and ratification status of the *Rome Statute* and *Agreement on Privileges and Immunities of the Court* (in English and French); information regarding the various bodies including Advance Team; Assembly of State Parties; Preparatory Commission for the International Criminal Court; and Documentation, mostly in full-text format.

The International Criminal Tribunal for Former Yugoslavia (ICTY), the 12th main United Nation: International Law Portal home page heading, provides an overview, latest developments, full text of indictments and proceedings (1994–), judgments (1994–), and basic legal documents of this Criminal Tribunal. Publications are also available, including the full text of judicial supplements and annual reports (1994–), along with citations to print publications and ordering information. Of special note is the video and audio of the trial of Slobodan Milosevic.

International Criminal Tribunal for Rwanda (ICTR) is the 13th main heading. This section is subdivided into About, Diary, Press Centre, Basic Legal Texts, Cases, Library, Links, and Public Judicial Records Database. About has a description of the Tribunal and its work along with the full text of annual reports to the General Assembly (1996–). Diary includes the full text of the *Daily Journal,* daily case minutes, and latest decisions. Press Centre contains the full texts of press releases (1995–), press briefings (2000–), *Handbook for Journalists,* speeches (2001–), and conference materials (2002–). Basic Legal Texts provides the full text of Security Council Resolutions, Statute of the Tribunal (in all six official UN languages), Rules of Procedure and Evidence, and Practice Directives. The subsection Cases is further subdivided into Completed and Cases in Progress. Each case file is comprised of relevant documentation. Library Resources under the International Criminal Tribunal for Rwanda (ICTR) is a particularly rich source of information. Although the data-

bases, CD-ROMs, and videos have total restricted access and the electronic references, news, and electronic journals have some restricted access, there are still enough useful resources that can be accessed by a nonaffiliated researcher. The library also publishes a full text, PDF format, of *Quarterly Bibliography,* which lists source titles and descriptors for each title. In addition, Library Resources provides annotated links to relevant Web sites subdivided into a variety of legal topics. Links to Other Sites has links to other relevant Web sites subdivided into ICTR Library, United Nations, International Criminal Court, Other International Organizations, Research Institutes and Libraries, Media Links, Non-Governmental Organizations, and Rwanda. The *Public Judicial Records Database* allows for searching by title word, record number, date created, and Thesaurus term. At the time of this writing, records were available up to September 30, 2001; however, the goal is to bring this current as soon as possible. The Tribunal site also contains a site map and is available in the native Rwanda language and French.

Documents Research Guide, the 14th main heading, was compiled by the United Nations' Dag Hammarskjöld Library and is divided into Courts and Tribunals, Principal Legal Bodies of the United Nations, Legal Documentation, Treaties, and International Law Pathfinder. Under the sections Courts and Tribunals and Principal Legal Bodies there is a link for each body to an explanation of that body, important documents, and its publications. Legal Documentation links to a description and to *UNBISnet,* the catalog of the library. Treaties links to an especially useful description of treaty research along with links to the *UN Treaty Database* and information about the annual print publication *Multilateral Treaties Deposited with the Secretary-General: Status as of 31 December*…Finally, the Pathfinder serves as a bibliography of relevant UN publications.

United Nations Juridical Yearbook. New York: United Nations, 1962– (UN Document No.: ST/LEG/SER.C/) (ISSN 0082–8297).

Summary: The annually published *Juridical Yearbook* provides the full text of legislative texts, treaty provisions, and legal activities pertaining to the United Nations and other intergovernmental organizations related to the United Nations. An index and a bibliography are also included. Except for the legislative texts and judicial decisions, which were distributed by the governments per the Secretary-General, all other texts were contributed by the organizations involved.

Detailed Description: The yearbook is divided into eight main chapters. Chapter I provides the legislative texts and is arranged by the relevant country names. Chapter II has the treaty provisions and is subdivided into those concerning United Nations and those of related intergovernmental organizations. Chapter III deals with legal activities, and Chapter IV pertains to "international law concluded under the auspices of the United Nations and related intergovernmental organizations." Decisions of the administrative tribunals are found in Chapter V. United Nations and other intergovernmental organization secretariats' legal opinions make up Chapter VI. Chapter VII contains international tribunals' advisory opinions and decisions, and in Chapter VIII are the Decisions of National Tribunals. Finally, there is a legal documents index and bibliography, published in the year of the yearbook, which is cumulative and also covers earlier years. In later years of the yearbook, this bibliography was prepared by the Dag Hammarskjöld Library.

Multilateral Treaties Deposited with the Secretary-General Status as at... New York: United Nations, 1981– (UN Document No.: ST/LEG./SER.E) (ISSN 0082–8319) (print annual title).

Summary: This annual publication, since 1981, includes the full text of multilateral United Nations and League of Nations treaties. Arranged in two parts with Part 1 containing United Nations treaties, it is organized, according to themes, and then chronologically by their conclusion dates. Part 2 has the League of Nations treaties, arranged by date "they first gave rise to formalities or decisions within the framework of the United Nations." [7] The predecessor publication was Multilateral Treaties in Respect of Which the Secretary-General Performs Depository Functions (1967–1979) and was available in loose-leaf format. This publication did not include the full text, but instead provided information about the treaty: name, entry into force, registration date and number, and reference to the Treaty Series volume number for the full text.

Statement of Treaties and International Agreements Registered or Filed and Recorded with the Secretariat during the month of... New York: United Nations, 1946– (UN Document No.: ST/LEG/SER.A) (print title).

Summary: Published monthly since December 1946/March 1947, by a succession of United Nations entities (Secretariat, March 1947–March 1949; Legal Department, June 1949–February 1955; and finally Office of Legal Affairs, March 1955–), this publication provides the full text of treaties for the particular month of a particular year. Treaties and international agreements are divided into two parts: those registered and those filed and recorded. Annexes are included for ratifications, accessions, prerogatives, and so on, along with corrigenda and addenda.

Each entry, in both English and French, is comprised of "registration or recording number, title, date of conclusion, date and method of entry into force, languages in which it was concluded, name of the authority which initiated the formality of registration of filing and recording and date of that formality." [8]

United Nations Treaty Series: Treaties and International Agreements Registered or Filed and Recorded with the Secretariat of the United Nations (UNTS). New York: United Nations, 1946– (ISSN 0379–8267) (print and online subscription database title).

Summary: Texts of treaties and international agreements are reproduced in this printed series, which dates from 1946 on. The treaties are in the original language, as well as translated into English and French. Access is provided via cumulative indexes.

The *Treaty Series* is divided into two parts: Part I, those treaties and international agreements registered with the Secretariat, and Part II, those filed and recorded. Each treaty contains a roman numeral to specify which part and an arabic numeral, which designates its individual *Treaty Series* number. League of Nations treaties are also included and have as their symbol, LoN. Volume numbers for UN treaties are in arabic numerals and those for the League of Nations in roman numerals.

The United Nations also offers the subscription-based electronic database *United Nations Treaty Collection. Databases* within this Collection include *Status of Multilateral Treaties Deposited with the Secretary-General, United Nations Treaty Series, Texts of Recently Deposited Multilateral Treaties, Summary of Practice of the Secretary-General as Depository of Multilateral Treaties, Treaty Handbook, Depository Notifications (CNs) by the Secretary-General, Notes Verbales from the Legal Counsel related to Article 102 of the Charter,*

Monthly Statement of Treaties, Cumulative Index, and Photographs-Treaty Action. The full text is provided.

The *Treaty Series* database allows for comprehensive searching by title/keyword or via a pull-down menu of International Agreements by Popular Name. Search results contain title, registration number, by, date, signed/adopted, entry into force, ICJ, participation, and the full text in English or French.

NONGOVERNMENTAL SOURCES

Consolidated Treaty Series, edited by Clive Parry. Dobbs Ferry, N.Y.: Oceana Publications, Inc., 1969–1981 (ISBN 0-37913-000-4).

Summary: The full texts of historical treaties dating from 1648 to 1918/1920 (establishment of the League of Nations) are contained in 226 volumes. These treaties were published "to reproduce such prints of treaties in their original languages as can be found in whatsoever collection along with such translations into English or French as again, which is very often the case, can be found."[9] When a translation is not available the text is summarized in the appropriate language. Some annotations are also included as well as the sources and information regarding its disposition.

Three types of indexes are also a part of this series: the five-volume chronology; the two-volume Special Chronology, which contains Colonial and Postal treaties; and the five-volume Party Index, which excludes Colonial and Postal treaties. Each entry in the General and Special Chronology Indexes contains the date of the treaty, title or descriptive headings, and reference to texts in the series. Entries in the Party Index refer the researcher by date to the volume in the main series containing the treaty text.

Guide to International Legal Research, compiled by the editors and staff of the George Washington University's *Journal of International Law and Economics.* 5th ed. Newark, N.J.: LexisNexis/Matthew Bender, 2003 (ISBN 0-32716-312-7).

Summary: Published originally in 1981 as an issue of the *Journal of International Law and Economics* (George Washington University, volume 15:1), it has been in book format since 1990, with other editions updating the original (1993, 1998, 2002, 2003). This publication serves as an excellent beginning point for international legal research.

The book content is divided into three parts: Introduction, Primary Sources/Secondary Sources, and Research by Geographic–Geopolitical regions. Each part is further subdivided and provides in-depth coverage of how to research as well as including an annotated listing of sources to consult.

Detailed Description: Part I, Introduction, discusses the basics of international legal research. Part II, Primary Sources/ Secondary Sources, is subdivided into Codified Law, Case Law, Serials/Analytical Tools, and Research Tools. Each subdivision is then further subdivided into related types of materials, with an explanation of how to use the sources and annotations for the sources themselves. Part III, Research by Geographic–Geopolitical Regions, is subdivided into Africa, Asia, Commonwealth of Independent States (former Soviet Union), European Union, International Organizations (especially the United Nations), and Latin America: Focusing on Mexico. Each heading includes constitutions, treaties, legislation, and case law.

Multilateral Treaties: Index and Current Status, edited by M. J. Bowman and D. J. Harris. London: Butterworths, 1984 (ISBN 0-40625-277-7).

Summary: Although the full texts of treaties are not included in this publication, it is an especially useful index to find citations for historical international treaties dating from 1856–1983. The entries are arranged chronologically and contain the title, concluded date, location (official and unofficial), entry into force date, duration, authentic texts, reservations, depository, open to, parties, territorial scope, and notes. Also found here is a table of multilateral treaties not included in the index as a main entry. These treaties are mentioned in the notes and amendments of the treaty entries found in the index. Subject and word indexes are also available.

World Legal Information Institute Web site, by the Australian Legal Information Institute, University of Technology-Sydney (UTS) Faculty of Law, New South Wales, Australia. <http://www.worldlii.org>

Summary: A source for no charge access to worldwide law, the World Legal Information Institute (WorldLII), officially launched in November 2002, is joint endeavor of the following institutes and universities:

• Australasian Legal Information Institute (AustLII) <http://www.austlii.org/> University of Technology, Sydney (UTS) & University of New South Wales (UNSW)

- British and Irish Legal Information Institute (BAILII) <http://www.bailii.org/> University of Cork, Institute of Advanced Legal Studies (IALS) & BAILII Trust
- Canadian Legal Information Institute (CanLII) <http://www.canlii.org/> University of Montreal & Federation of Law Societies of Canada
- Hong Kong Legal Information Institute (HKLII) <http://www.hklii.org/> University of Hong Kong (HKU)
- Legal Information Institute (Cornell) (LII (Cornell)) <http://www.law.cornell.edu/> Cornell Law School
- Pacific Islands Legal Information Institute (PacLII) <http://www.paclii.org/> University of the South Pacific (USP)
- WITS University School of Law <http://www.law.wits.ac.za/> University of the Witwatersrand (WITS) Law School
- Databases from East Timor, Cambodia, Viet Nam, the Philippines, and South Africa are hosted by the University of the Witwatersrand (WITS) <http://www.worldlii.org/worldlii/guides/brochure/html/>

The home page is divided into two main headings: Databases and Catalogs. News and Additions and Catalog Additions are also headings found on the home page. In addition, the entire site can be searched by keyword(s), phrase, document title, or Boolean query. The databases can also be searched from the home page. Help screens are available from the home page. A link to a translation program is also included. **Detailed Description:** Databases is one of the two main headings found on the home page. "WorldLII already has databases from 20 countries in six continents (at present mainly those with a common law tradition): from Australasia (120), Canada (61); Britain and Ireland (27), the Pacific Islands (25), Hong Kong (13) and other countries in Asia and Africa (6). All types of legal databases are included: case law (165), legislation (45), treaties (3), law reform (4), law journals (11), and specialist subject databases. In combination, the LII's accessible through WorldLII include 240 databases from 43 jurisdictions, with over 50 gigabytes of searchable text."[10] Databases is subdivided by region (Africa, Asia, Australasia, Europe, International, North American, Pacific Islands), as well as by Case Law, Law Reform, Law Journals, Legislation, Other Resources, Treaties, and those hosted on LII: International Deci-

sions and Countries. Under each region subdivision are links to resources for particular countries. However, each region does not include all the countries of that region. The topical subdivisions contain country-specific resources for that topic. Date spans vary according to the resource.

Catalogs, the second main home page heading, provides access to worldwide law-related Web sites linking users to as much full-text information as possible. Catalogs has been subdivided into: Categories, Countries, Other Indexes, Regions, Subjects, Courts and Case-Law, Education, International, Law Journals, Law Reform, Lawyers, Legislation, Parliaments, Research, and Treaties. Each subdivision allows searching by keyword(s), phrase, document title, or "Boolean query," and searching can be limited in three ways: to All WorldLII Catalog, All WorldLII Catalog-[topic], All WorldLII Databases. Links are also included to individual countries or material types, where relevant.

World Treaty Index, edited by Peter H. Rohn, University of Washington. Santa Barbara, Calif.: ABC-Clio, 1974 (ISBN 0-87436-132-X).

Summary: The *World Treaty Index* is a six-volume set that indexes historical League of Nations and United Nations treaties. Included for each entry is the type of instrument and number, signature and date, registered date and number, headnote, topic, concepts, and parties. If appropriate, some treaties also have a listing for treaty reference number, procedure, and international organization. Volume 1 includes a history of the project from which these volumes are produced, coverage, structure, search techniques, thesaurus, and League of Nations Treaty Series entries. Volume 2 contains entries for the *United Nations Treaty Series (UNTS).* Volume 3 continues the *UNTS* and also has the National Treaty Collection. Volume 4 contains chronological, party, intergovernmental organizations, and *UNTS* self-index sections. Volume 5 contains a topical section and each entry contains party one, party two, date, and citation number. Volume 6 is comprised of treaty profiles by country and intergovernmental organization.

RESEARCH STRATEGIES

For a beginning researcher, the best place to begin the research process is with the *Documents Research Guide* found online at the United Nation's **International Law Portal** and the print source ***Guide to International Legal Research,*** 5th edition. As the

United Nations provides comprehensive global legal coverage, the explanations found in its *Documents Research Guide* provides a clearer understanding of the processes for Courts and Tribunals, Principal UN legal bodies, legal documentation, treaties, and international law in general. The ***Guide to International Legal Research,*** 5th edition has comprehensive coverage of resources, arranged in a thematic approach, as well as an overview of international legal research, both generalized and subject-specific, which serves as a way to better understand the complexities of this type of research.

International Law Portal also serves as a launching pad for research with its extensive coverage of various types of international law, including trade, oceans and the environment, treaties, and genocide and similar crimes through the Web sites of the ***International Criminal Court, International Criminal Tribunal for Former Yugoslavia,*** and ***International Criminal Tribunal for Rwanda.*** Full texts of documents opinions, judgments, and reports, as well as some full text or at least bibliographic information for publications are included. The ***United Nations Juridical Yearbook*** recounts, in print format, some texts of legislation and judicial decisions. The ***International Court of Justice*** Web site provides comprehensive coverage of international justice with the full text of judgments and opinions available electronically and in print, although the print version lags behind in publication currency.

For more regional coverage both the European Communities and Organization of American States have comprehensive legal coverage. ***CELEX, CURIA,*** and ***EUR-Lex*** all have in-depth coverage. ***CELEX,*** a subscription service, has the most comprehensive full-text coverage of European Community legal materials. Although currently a fee-based subscription service, ***CELEX*** will soon provide free access to its holdings. ***CURIA*** covers the Court of Justice and has full-text access to proceedings and case law and provides a search engine. ***EUR-Lex*** is the European Union's law portal, and of particular importance is the full-text access it has to the *Official Journal (OJ)* from 1998 to the present. An advanced search engine is available in ***EUR-Lex*** to aid in identifying the relevant *OJ* entries. The *Organization of American States' Secretariat for Legal Affairs* Web site describes its various legal entities and provides the full text of judgments and resolutions, as well as reports, speeches, and publications. With its focus on Asia, Australia, Europe and the Pacific Islands the ***World Legal Information Institute*** Web site is another regional source to consult.

The online ***Global Legal Information Network*** from the Law Library on Congress is especially useful for its country-specific law summaries and citations. The *GLIN Thesaurus* can serve as a tool for developing a better search vocabulary in order to maximize efforts with both searching ***GLIN*** and the more comprehensive Web sites.

Treaty research can be especially complicated. The *Documents Research Guide* found under the ***United Nations: International Law Portal*** Web site is useful for researchers to consult first. The ***United Nations Treaty Series indexes, Multilateral Treaties Deposited with the Secretary-General Status as at....*** and ***Statement of Treaties and International Agreements Registered or Filed and Recorded with the Secretariat during the month of....,*** as well as the commercial ***Multilateral Treaties: Index and Current Status*** and ***World Treaty Index,*** provide citation information, including names, dates, and participants. The ***United Nations Treaty Collection*** subscription puts the citation as well as the full text at the researcher's fingertips. This service also brings many other relevant publications together for "one-stop" research. The print version of the ***Treaty Series*** and the predecessor ***League of Nations Treaty Series*** has the full text of treaties. For the full text of most international treaties that predate the ***League of Nations, the Consolidated Treaty Series*** and its indexes should be consulted.

The other Web resources listed under For Further Reading may also prove useful in the research process.

FOR FURTHER READING: COMPREHENSIVE WEB SITES AND OTHER REFERENCE SOURCES

FindLaw: International Resources: Countries Web site. <http://www.findlaw.com/12international/ countries/index.html>

Provides an alphabetical listing of countries of the world, with links for each country to relevant law-related Web sites.

International Commission of Jurists (ICJ) Web site, Geneva, Switzerland. <http://www.icj.org>

Founded in 1952, the International Commission of Jurists is dedicated to the primacy, coherence, and implementation of international law and principles that advance human rights. Of particular usefulness on this

Web site are the Publications and ICJ Legal Resource Center sections. Publications are arranged according to topic and county and include ordering information and titles, but no annotations. A search engine is available that searches by country, topic, or keyword. The ICJ Legal Resource Center is a searchable database of the ICJ's press releases, reports, legal documents, and key external legal materials with searching available by country, topic, section, or keyword. In addition, there is an Online Resources section, which links to relevant Web sites.

International Law Institute Web site, Washington, D.C. <http://www.ili.org>

Established in 1971 the Institute has trained more than 8,000 participants representing ca. 180 world countries. Of special note from this site is the link to its publications that includes the most recent catalog, complete with ordering information, titles, and annotations, and links, which links to relevant Web sites.

Law Association for Asia and the Pacific (LAWA-SIA) Web site, Darwin, Australia. <http://www.lawasia.asn.au/>

Established in 1966, LAWASIA is the Asia Pacific region's professional association for lawyers, firms, and corporations. Of particular importance on the Web site are the list of publications and links to member organizations' Web sites.

WashLaw Web: Foreign and International Law Web site. Topeka, Kans.: Washburn University School of Law Library. <http://www.washlaw.edu/forint/>

Links to primary international legal materials is available at this site, which is organized alphabetically by subject, author, country, and in some instances, title

Worldcourts Web site, by Anatoly Viasov. <http://www.worldcourts.com>

Created by an individual as a source for easy access to legal materials generated by international organizations, this site includes links to the Permanent Court of International Justice and International Court of Justice (both described under the ICJ entry), International Commissions of Inquiry, Central American Court of Justice, International Prize Court, European Court of

Human Rights, and European Court of Justice. The site is in English and Russian.

NOTES

1. "A treaty is a written international agreement concluded between states or other subjects of international law that is intended to create rights and obligations, or to establish relationships governed by international law. Treaties can be bilateral instruments, which are intended to promote or regulate matters of particular interest only to two states. Treaties may also be multilateral, having more than two parties, and often create new principles or rules of international law." Joel Krieger, *The Oxford Companion to Politics of the World,* 2nd ed. (New York: Oxford University Press, 2001), 841.

2. *Secretariat for Legal Affairs: Administrative Tribunal* Web site, Organization for American States, <http://www.oas.org/tribadm/default.htm>.

3. *United Nations Commission on International Trade Law (UNCITRAL)* Web site, Vienna, Austria, <http://www.uncitral.org/en-index.htm>.

4. *United Nations: International Court of Justice* Web site, The Hague, Netherlands, <http://www.icj-cij.org/icjwww/ipublications.htm>.

5. *United Nations: International Court of Justice* Web site, The Hague, Netherlands, <http://www.icj-cij.org/icjwww/ipublications.htm>.

6. Oceans and Law of the Sea Web site, Division for Ocean Affairs and the Law of the Sea, Office of Legal Affairs, United Nations, <http://www.un.org/Depts/los/index.htm>.

7. *Multilateral Treaties Deposited with the Secretary-General Status as at 31 December 1995* (New York: United Nations Secretary-General, 1996), p. iii.

8. *Statement of Treaties and International Agreements Registered or Filed and Recorded with the Secretariat during the Month of September 2002* (New York: United Nations Office of Legal Affairs, 2002), p. 5.

9. Clive Parry, *Consolidated Treaty Series,* Volume 1 (Dobbs Ferry, N.Y.: Oceana Publications, Inc., 1969), p. vi.

10. Brochure, *World Legal Information Institute* Web site, Australian Legal Information Institute, University of Technology–Sydney Faculty of Law, Australia, <http://www.worldlii.org/worldlii/guides/brochure/html/>.

CHAPTER 16
Science and Technology

CHAPTER OVERVIEW

International science organizations around the world can be categorized into national government ministries or agencies that set policy, agencies that fund science research and education, quasi-government organizations, nongovernmental organizations, science information organizations, and multilateral organizations or subunits of these, such as international governmental organizations that are concerned with science.[1] Due to the sheer magnitude of the information available, this chapter cannot be comprehensive, but will instead serve as an introduction to selected international intergovernmental organizations that focus in the areas of science and research. This chapter will review selected resources, major publications, scientific databases, journals, and Web sites of scientific governmental organizations from a variety of these international science organizations. Nongovernmental resources will be strictly limited as they are numerous. The resources included will lead users to national government sites in their particular area of focus in science. All of the Internet resources included have reliable links to related worldwide science organizations, for example, the United States' National Science Foundations' *Science Organizations Around the World* Web site is a very reliable electronic list of links to science organizations by country and region.

The type of scientific information described in this chapter includes astronautics, meteorology, nautical, nuclear, patents, science policy, space, statistics, sustainable development, and research. Although some the international intergovernmental agencies described here cover both science and technology, users seeking information on new technology should also consult the chapter on communication. Information on some core and natural sciences such as biology, physics, or chemistry are not included in this chapter, because international cooperation and research is more nongovernmental than governmental. However, in the fields of geology, meteorology, and astronautics (the study of space), there is high international inter-

government cooperation. Researchers should note that for all fields of science, in addition to using the following resources, they may search for individual nations' scientific agencies and their publications and information.

Governmental Sources Discussed

CERN (European Organization for Nuclear Research) Web site, Geneva, Switzerland. <http://public.web.cern.ch/>

CORDIS, Community Research & Development Information Service Web site, Luxembourg. <http://www.cordis.lu/en/home.html>

European Commission Research Web site, Brussels, Belgium. <http://europa.eu.int/comm/research/index_en.html>

European Patent Office (EPO) Web site, Munich, Germany. <http://www.european-patent-office.org/index.htm>

Organisation for Economic Co-operation and Development (OECD) Resources

Basic Science and Technology Statistics, by the Organisation for Economic Co-operation and Development (OECD). Paris: OECD, 1991– (ISSN 1024-7882) (print and online subscription).

OECD Science, Technology and Industry Outlook, by the Organisation for Economic Co-operation and Development (OECD). Paris: OECD, 1996– (paper biennial title and current edition online).

Science and Innovation Web site, by the Organisation for Economic Cooperation and Development, Paris. <http://www.oecd.org > (select by Topic: Science and Innovation).

Statistics on Science and Technology in Europe, by Eurostat. Luxembourg: Office for Official Publications of the European Communities, 1985/1999– (print, CD, and online subscription title and free online data). *Eurostat* Web site. <http://europa.eu.int/index_en.htm> (select Services: Statistics, Themes: Science and Technology).

United Nations Educational, Scientific, and Cultural Organization (UNESCO) Resources

UNESCO Natural Sciences Portal Web site, by the United Nations Educational, Scientific, and Cultural Organization (UNESCO), Paris. <http://www.unesco.org/science/>

World Science Report, by UNESCO, Paris, 1993–1998 (biennial print title subscription, with selections online). <http://www.unesco.org/science/publication/eng_pub/wsren.htm> (selections from the 3 editions).

United Nations Office for Outer Space Affairs (UNOOSA) Web site, Vienna, Austria. <http://www.oosa.unvienna.org/>

World Meteorological Organization (WMO) Web site, Geneva, Switzerland. <http://www.wmo.ch/>

Nongovernmental Sources Discussed

International Astronomical Federation (IAF) Web site, Paris. <http://www.iafastro.com/>

International Council for Science (ICSU) Web site, Paris. <http://www.icsu.org/>

Third World Academy of Sciences Web site, Trieste, Italy. <http://www.twas.org/>

GOVERNMENTAL SOURCES

CERN (European Organization for Nuclear Research) Web site, Geneva, Switzerland. <http://public.web.cern.ch/>

Summary: CERN is the European Organization for Nuclear Research, the world's largest particle physics center. Founded in 1954, the laboratory was one of Europe's first joint ventures and has become a shining example of international collaboration. CERN publishes information about its current research experiments on its Web site and is famous for its connection to the development of today's global information society. In 1990, Tim Berners-Lee, a scientist at CERN, invented the World Wide Web for automatic information sharing, which is at the basis of today's Internet. The *CERN* Web site, available in English and French, is searchable and provides a site map. An overview of CERN and its work is also included as well as an e-mail Ask-an-Expert service. The focus of this discussion will be on the Education and News home page categories.

Detailed Description: The Education home page category is an especially useful resource for teachers. The *CERN Education Portal,* published in English, French, and Spanish, provides a newsletter for teachers as well as a description of various programs. The CERN online resources section of the Education category leads to other educational resources, such as games on particle physics, an online tour of CERN, an interactive Web site on the Big Bang, live Web casts on the Internet viewable in QuickTime, and the Web Lecture Archive for students up through university level.

The News home page category has the latest headlines detailing CERN's work. The Press & Media link leads users to the full text of the monthly journal, *CERN Courier,* an international journal of high-energy physics. Online issues are available from October 1998 forward. Full-text press releases (1993–) are contained here and are searchable. There is also a searchable photograph database. In addition, links to other relevant research organizations are included.

CERN is one of the founders, along with the U.S. Department of Energy and other groups, of the Particle Data Group, <http://pdg.lbl.gov/>, which is an international collaboration that reviews particle physics and related areas of astrophysics and compiles and analyzes data on particle properties. The Particle Data Group publishes a major journal, *The Review of Particle Physics.* Particle physics information and databases are available from the Group's Web site.

CORDIS, Community Research & Development Information Service Web site, Luxembourg. <http://www.cordis.lu/en/home.html>

Summary: CORDIS is the European Commission's Research and Development Information Service, and this searchable Web site provides a gateway to the European Union (EU) information on research and development. Researchers can search across numerous databases, Web sites, and publications of the many EU science-based agencies. CORDIS also reports on current research, projects, and innovations in science on its Web site, which is available in English, German, French, Italian, and Spanish. The site is arranged into three major headings: Find, Explore, and Today, with each then containing numerous subheadings. A site map as well as links to news and press are also included. Some services are available at no charge, whereas others require registration.

Detailed Description: The Find home page heading contains the subheadings European Union-funded Research, Databases and Web Services, Interactive Services, and Guidance & Background Information. EU-funded Research provides access to the relevant materials pertaining to the various programs that have been conducted or are still in the process. Databases is subdivided into news, partners, projects, results, document library, programmes, Com documents, publications, acronyms, contacts, and *ERGO (European Research Gateways On-line)*. Each category is described and can be searched. Web Services is subdivided topically with access to relevant Web sites. Of special mention under the Interactive Services subheading is the e-mail notification system, online forums, and full-text access to the *CORDIS Express* weekly newsletter. The Guidance and Background Information subheading includes different searches on CORDIS databases and Web services: an A–Z index, a thematic index, separate keyword searching of Web pages and databases, and an acronyms and glossary dictionary. Also found here under Magazines is a link to the CORDIS Library, which helps users sign up free of charge for EU magazines on research and innovation, including: *CORDIS Focus* (latest information), *Research and Innovation* (projects and case studies), *RTD information* (industry information), and *EURO-Abstracts* (bibliographic information). All of these titles are archived online from 1997 on. The CORDIS Library also provides searching for publications and documents and provides a list of electronic full-text documents on research and technology. Researchers may sign up to receive key documents by e-mail.

The Explore home page heading has information regarding innovations under the subheading Innovation in Practice. The Research and Development Gateway is worth special mention as it links to relevant information pertaining to various initiatives. The Today home page heading provides access to current news and events.

European Commission Research Web site, Brussels, Belgium. <http://europa.eu.int/comm/research/index_en.html>

Summary: This is the European Union's research Web site, which serves as a gateway to news and information about Scientific Research and Technological Development in the European Union, with links by subject/theme and by type of publication. An A-Z index links users quickly to online documents. In contrast with *CORDIS*, the *European Commission Research* Web site is part of an international intergovernmental publishing agency, whereas *CORDIS* is a specific online gateway service, not an agency Web site or publisher. Thematic categories on this Web site include some specifically linking to more information on science: Pure Sciences, Science and Business, Science and Society, and Space. The home page links to the online editions (PDF) of the bi-monthly newsletter from the Innovation Directorate, *Innovation and Technology Transfer,* which reports up-to-date information on European Commission actions relevant to innovation and technology transfer and the bimonthly magazine on European Research, *RTD Info.*
Detailed Description: Categories of links to online publication information on the home page include: Articles, Briefings, Conferences, Consultations, Features, Leaflets (European Research in Action), Publications, and Working in Research. Publications links to sources of online documents and other Web sites and provides access to the annual report of the European Commission and periodicals, including the newsletter *Innovation and Technology Transfer,* the monthly newsletter of the Joint Research Center, and the magazine *RTD Info. Innovation and Technology Transfer* is archived online in PDF format back to 1998 and in HTML from 1996–July 1998, and is available in English, French, German, Italian, and Spanish. The newsletter's content *RTD Info* reports on current European research, is published every three months by the Directorate General for Research, and is archived online in PDF format back to October 1996. The paper edition may be ordered for free via an online subscription form. Also featured are links to data from the Commission's unit on European Commission's Science and Technology Research Indicators for the European Research Area (STI-ERA), found in full on the *CORDIS* Web site. The Joint Research Center, the European Union's scientific and technical research laboratory, reports on its activities in its monthly newsletter, archived online from 1998 on, in various languages.

European Patent Office (EPO) Web site, Munich, Germany. <http://www.european-patent-office.org/index.htm>

Summary: Established as a centralized patent grant system to create a uniform patent system in Europe, this international intergovernmental organization is based on a convention signed in 1973. The *European Patent Office (EPO)* Web site, available in English, French, and German, provides online searchable patent indexes; a searchable, alphabetical site map; a journal on patents; and reports, patent documents, and monographs online. Search tools and services for users needing patent information, including the text of patents, monographs on this topic, annual reports, and facts and figures are available here. News and official communications are also included as well as links to Patent Information Centers or libraries that assist users with European patent information.

Organisation for Economic Co-operation and Development (OECD) Resources

Basic Science and Technology Statistics, by the Organisation for Economic Co-operation and Development (OECD). Paris: OECD, 1991– (ISSN 1024-7882) (print and online subscription).

Summary: Statistical tables covering research and development are organized alphabetically by country in this title published biennially since 1991. Most of the tables provide information concerning research and development, including expenditures and personnel for businesses and for businesses by industry, for higher education, and for government. Also, it includes technology balance of payments for each country. The data is provided in both English and French in each edition. Where available, five years are provided for each statistical table. Detailed methodology for data by country is provided in an appendix. Abbreviations are included.

A related title, *Main Science and Technology Indicators,* published twice yearly, includes more statistical information about patents. Users who have access to *SourceOECD,* the organization's subscription service, may access the full publication electronically. Some data is available as free data downloads from the *OECD* Web site <http://www.oecd.org> under Statistics: Science, Technology and Patents. OECD may reissue the title *Basic Science and Technology Statistics* under a new title in 2003; however, researchers are encouraged to check online for many basic science indicators available for free. Also, publications such as the *Science and Technology Statistical Compendium 2004* (PDF format) are available online at no charge.

OECD Science, Technology and Industry Outlook, by the Organisation for Economic Co-operation and Development (OECD). Paris: OECD, 1996– (paper biennial title and current edition online). <http://www.oecd.org/EN/home/0,,EN-home-notheme-1-no-no-no,00.html>

Summary: This publication, also called the *OECD STI Outlook* and *Science, Technology and Industry Outlook,* reviews overall trends in science, technology, and industry and provides summaries and changes for national policies of the OECD member countries. The OECD Web site provides users with a free download of the latest edition of this title, along with the highlights, the table of contents, the national science and technology policies for countries, and sample statistics from chapters. Users who have access to *SourceOECD,* the organization's subscription service, may access the full publication electronically. Published biennially since 1996, it is also published with English and French text. A related title, *Industrial Structure Statistics,* provides industrial statistics for OECD member countries from 1982–1999.

Science and Innovation Web site, by the Organisation for Economic Co-operation and Development, Paris. <http://www.oecd.org/> (select By Topic: Science and Innovation).

Summary: This Web site reports on activities of the OECD Directorate for Science, Technology and Industry. Topics covered include industry issues, such as globalization; information and communications policy, especially those that arise from the digital economy and the global information society; science and technological policy and international cooperation; scientific, industrial, and health applications of biotechnology; transport issues; and statistical analysis of science, technology, and industry. The OECD is a major publisher in this area; some titles are available on their Web site at no charge, but the majority are subscription titles and are available electronically through the OECD's subscription service, *SourceOECD.* Major categories on this Web site are Statistics, Publication and Documents, Information by Country, and What's New.

Detailed Description: *STI Working Papers,* published by this Directorate, is a research series devoted to topics of science, technology, and industry. Indexes to the series are available from this Web site or through OECD catalogs and indexes. Users who prefer to access information through the thematic links will find links by the following topics: Innovation and Education, Measuring Science and Technology, S&T Policy, and Biotechnology.

Statistics on Science and Technology in Europe, by Eurostat. Luxembourg: Office for Official Publications of the European Communities,

1985/1999– (print, CD, and online subscription title and free online data). *Eurostat* Web site. <http://europa.eu.int/index_en.htm> (select Services: Statistics, Themes: Science and Technology).

Summary: Available in print and online via subscription, this publication contains interesting and easy-to-read analyses of science and technology in Europe in four parts accompanied by tables, diagrams, and maps. Although not described as a science resource, Eurostat, the publisher, is described in the chapter on Statistics and also provides some free data relating to science, technology, and research in Europe on its Themes: Science and Technology Web page.

Detailed Description: Part 1 of *Statistics on Science and Technology in Europe* summarizes the evolution of science and technology statistics and the methods that have been used in order to provide and improve the international comparability of science and technology data. Part 2 includes the statistics presented every year in Eurostat's R&D annual statistics (R&D expenditure, R&D personnel, government budget appropriations on R&D and patents) and also considers the role of Community RTD policy. In part 3, Eurostat presents, for the first time in such a format data on innovation, employments in high-technology sectors, human resources in science and technology, and external trade in high-technology products. Part 4 looks at the possible future directions for the development of a new generation of science and technology statistics. This title includes historical data and time-series data from 1985–1999.

Related information published by Eurostat on science includes online science databases and the title *Science and Technology in Europe: Statistical Pocketbook* 1991–2001 (print and online free PDF title), which presents key indicators describing science and technology in Europe and its main competitors. Data is available at the national and regional level and includes maps, figures, and statistical tables.

Users can also access free downloads of entire Eurostat publications through its Free Downloads page accessible through the Web site of Eurostat, under the category All Services, then Free Downloads. The free downloads (HTML or PDF format) are organized and searchable by types of publication such as data or publications.

United Nations Educational, Scientific, and Cultural Organization (UNESCO) Resources

UNESCO Natural Sciences Portal Web site, by the United Nations Educational, Scientific, and Cultural Organization (UNESCO), Paris. <http://www.unesco.org/science/>

Summary: The *Natural Sciences Portal* Web site of UNESCO organizes information under the broad categories Thematic Areas, Resources, News Events, Intergovernmental and International Programs, Main Events, and Regions/Countries. It is searchable with quick links to Web site archives. There also is a link to a new serial publication entitled *The World of Science,* a quarterly newsletter published in English and French by the Natural Sciences Sector of UNESCO (free subscription).

Detailed Description: Thematic Areas include Fresh Water, People & Nature, Oceans, Earth Sciences, Coastal Regions & Small Islands, Science Policy, and Basic and Engineering Sciences. The Intergovernmental and International Programs category links to programs such as:

- UN World Water Assessment Program (WWAP)
- International Hydrological Program (IHP)
- Man and the Biosphere (MAB)
- Intergovernmental Oceanographic Commission (IOC)
- International Geological Correlation Programme (IGCP)
- Management of Social Transformations (MOST) and topical subcategories such as:
- Gender, Science & Technology
- UNESCO Science Prizes
- Data Bases
- Field Offices
- Contacts

News Events provides general news articles that relate to UNESCO within the realm of science. Specific articles on scientific-related events, people, and current news releases are also included on the home page. The Archives category provides drop-down boxes by year and month of archival information from the Web site. Other special features on the Web site include Main Events section with links to current conferences and follow-up information on meetings such as the full report (PDF format) entitled *Harnessing Science to Society: An Analytic Report to Governments and International Partners on the Follow-up on the World Conference on Science* (1999).

World Science Report, by UNESCO, Paris, 1993–1998 (biennial subscription print title, with selections online). <http://www.unesco.org/science/publication/eng_pub/wsren.htm> (selections from 3 editions).

Summary: Published in English, French, and Spanish in a biennial series from 1993–1998, this title reports on the state of science around the globe, with issues, analysis, trends, and statistics in separate parts. The 4th edition was expected to have a 2002 publication date. Part I provides essays by individual experts on research and development trends, organization, and changes, as well as describing emerging trends in research, scientific investment, and science education, including region and country-specific issues. Statistics, tables, and graphs support the text. Part II examines contemporary global issues in science that affect society as a whole. Each issue is theme based, for example, the 1998 edition, Part II focuses on environmental stress on food and water and globalization, and the 1996 edition, Part II reported on the gender dimension of science and technology development, biodiversity, environmental degradation, and the ethics of science.

United Nations Office for Outer Space Affairs (UN-OOSA) Web site, Vienna, Austria.
    <http://www.oosa.unvienna.org/>

Summary: The objective of the Office is to promote international cooperation in the peaceful uses of outer space. It addition, it implements the United Nations Programme on Space Applications (PSA), an agency that works to improve the use of space science and technology for the economic and social development of all nations, especially developing countries. This resource highlights its major activities and resources within a textual introduction to the Office and then lists information on committee meetings, reports, and indexes; online documents; online presentations; and highlighted publications. Many documents, reports, and related conventions are in online full-text format. Other main categories found on the home page are the Office for Outer Space Affairs, Committee on the Peaceful Uses of Outer Space, Space Law, Register of Space Objects, Space Activities of Member States, Space Debris and Nuclear Power, Space Activities of the UN System, Reports and Publications, UN Space III, and World Space Week. Miscellaneous information also linked from the home page includes What's New, an online calendar, links, FAQ, and a search engine. This Web site has both a graphics and text versions for many pages.

Detailed Description: The home page category Office for Outer Space Affairs leads to many resources, including reports and studies prepared by the Office for the use of the United Nations' General Assembly Committee on the Peaceful Uses of Outer Space. These range from background information to substantive studies in various fields of space research, such as practical applications of space technology, space law, and organizational questions relating to international cooperation in those fields. Here are found comprehensive background papers for UNISPACE III on the current and future state of space science, technology and applications, and other information within the United Nations. An online searchable index to the Status of United Nations Treaties Governing Activities in Outer Space (international space law) is also available. The Committee on the Peaceful Uses of Outer Space section provides information on the UN sessions, including sessional documents. Reports of the Committee are available for downloading in HTML or PDF at no charge, such as *Status of International Agreements Relating to Activities in Outer Space* and *The Space Millennium: Vienna Declaration on Space and Human Development (Vienna Declaration),* also called the UNISPACE III report. The United Nations Programme on Space Applications category highlights this program's progress in furthering knowledge and experience of space applications around the world, particularly with developing countries. Remote sensing, communications, satellite meteorology, search and rescue, basic space science, and satellite navigation are examples of the work being done. A hot-linked index of online reports and documents is available.

Space Law, another home page category, provides many full-text online documents such as United Nations treaties and principles on space law, United Nations General Assembly resolutions relating to the peaceful uses of outer space, selected examples of national laws government space activities, selected treaties on governing space activities, legal studies and background documents on space law, and finally, a list of international agreements and other available legal documents relevant to space law (PDF format). The index to legal studies, a subcategory of Space Laws, contains a major online report entitled *Highlights in Space.* Published by UNOOSA and in print format since 1991 as *Highlights in Space: Progress in Science, Technology and Applications, International Cooperation and Space Law,* this yearly report covers space science, astronautics, and the international space year. The title continues a previous publication entitled: *Highlights in Space Technology and Applications...: Report Submitted by the International Astronautical Federation* (1982–1991). Users may also search only the Space Law Web pages. Another subsection of Space Law, the Register of Space Objects, contains the Online Index of Objects Launched into Outer Space, which includes data required under the United Nations' Register Convention from nations that launch satellites or other objects into space. The index is searchable by many fields, including name, state that launched the object, date of launch, status of object, and so on.

The category Space Activities of Member States includes online national reports on space activities submitted annually and voluntarily by nations. Likewise, the category on Space Debris features online national reports. Reports and Publications, another home page category, provides users with many indexes of online documents and reports on different space topics. These include indexes to the United Nations documents and resolutions of the General Assembly and a list of documents with UN document numbers, titles, and available languages, in PDF format. Also located here are the online reports from the Office's subcommittees.

Further investigation into outer space through the United Nations systems is provided in the online pathfinder of UN information, *Outer Space: United Nations System Pathfinder* Web site, available at <http://www.un.org/Depts/dhl/pathfind/frame/start.htm>.

World Meteorological Organization (WMO) Web site, Geneva, Switzerland.
   <http://www.wmo.ch/>

Summary: The World Meteorological Organization, a United Nations Specialized Agency, coordinates global scientific activity in the area of accurate weather information and prediction, air pollution research, climate change–related activities, ozone layer depletion studies, tropical storm forecasting, and other services concerning the climate for public, private, and commercial use. It is the authoritative scientific organization on the state and behavior of the Earth's atmosphere and climate. Official weather forecasts and warnings are available right from the home page. These Web pages also provide access to publications, public information, an online library, data, and information about the organization. Also featured are the categories of information under Hot Topics and Major Issues, summarizing topics for users and linking to further information. Available in English, French, and Spanish, the Web pages of this organization are searchable by WMO programs or by alphabetical topics, including a search engine for advanced searches.

Detailed Description: On the *World Meteorological Organization (WMO)* Web pages, users may link to information under public information, publications, links, meetings, members, hot topics, major issues, LTP (long-term plans), contacts, library, links, and organization information. Major WMO programs include World Weather Watch (WWW), the World Climate Programme, Atmospheric Research and Environment Programme (AREP), and other programs that assist in global water resources and atmosphere research and assessment, as well as the education and training needed for these areas. These programs support technical cooperation between developed and developing nations, including the WMO regional programs.

Under the drop-down box (Search by WMO Programs) on the home page, researchers may link to the AREP, which coordinates and stimulates research on the composition of the atmosphere, the physics and chemistry of clouds, weather modification techniques, tropical meteorology processes, and weather forecasting, particularly extreme weather events and socioeconomic impacts. It also coordinates the global monitoring of greenhouse gases, the ozone layer, major atmospheric pollutants, and urban environment and meteorological studies. Categories linking to AREP's responsibilities are: The Global Atmosphere Watch (GAW), World Weather Research Programme (links to research and development projects information), Tropical Meteorology Research Programme, Physics of Clouds and Weather Modification Research Programme, and Technical Library. The objectives of the Global Atmosphere Watch are to provide reliable long-term observations of the chemical composition of the atmosphere parameters in order to improve the understanding of atmospheric chemistry and to organize assessments in support of making environmental policy. Recent reports are available online in PDF format, such as the *Scientific Assessment of Ozone Depletion* (2002), as well as periodicals, such as the *WMO Antarctic Ozone Bulletin* (online in PDF format from 2000–). The Global Atmosphere Watch also provides background, history, and related acronyms information, as well as information on environmental conventions and international programs. Also from the Atmospheric Research and Environment Programme, the Technical Library section links to the reference services of the library, the library catalog, and a list of periodicals in their collection.

The WMO's World Weather Watch (WWW) is the backbone of WMO's activities, and it links from the drop-down box (Search by WMO Programs) on the home page. "WWW offers up-to-the-minute worldwide weather information through Member-operated observation systems and telecommunication links with four polar-orbiting and five geostationary satellites, about 10,000 land observation and 7,000 ship stations and 300 moored and drifting buoys carrying automatic weather stations."[2] WWW combines observing systems, telecommunication facilities, and data-processing centers, all operated by members, to make available the needed meteorological and geophysical information to provide efficient services concerning weather in all countries. It is a rich source of information—categorized by type of program in the WWW (Global Observing System, etc.), or type of information (online reports, databases, periodicals, technical reports, maps, and much more).

The World Climate Programme collects and preserves climate data in order to help governments prepare national development plans and determine their policies in response to the changing climate situation. Established in 1979, the World Climate Programme (WCP) includes separate programs on data, application, impact assessment, and research. It also supports the Global Climate Observing System (GCOS), which encompasses observation of all components of the climate system, atmosphere, biosphere, cryosphere, and oceans.

NONGOVERNMENTAL SOURCES

International Astronautical Federation (IAF) Web site, Paris. <http://www.iafastro.com/>

Summary: A nongovernmental organization that seeks to promote the understanding and development of space, this association provides information about its activities on the Internet, including the congress it sponsors, the International Astronautical Congress. IAF is active in the arena of space law, founding the International Institute of Space Law (IISL) in 1960. The IISL holds annual colloquia on space law, the proceedings of which are published by the American Institute of Aeronautics and Astronautics. The International Astronautical Federation, together with the Committee on Space Research and the International Institute for Space Law, conducts an annual survey of *Highlights in Space* for the United Nations. Highlights of this report are available online under the IAF/UN report link. Publications are not published online in full-text format, although some titles and abstracts are provided.

Detailed Description: The home page categories include Federation IAF with sections on Membership, Awards, Publications, and Newsletters; Congress, with a section on Archives; Academy IIA (International Academy of Astronautics); Space Law IISL (International Institute of Space Law): Other Space Links; and Other Colloquia. Also included are other highlighted features linking to the latest news of the organization and reports from the IAF Committees. The Publications link describes publications for sale only, and Newsletters section provides access only to the tables of contents of the *IAF Newsletters* from no. 1, 1997, on. From the home page, Congress links to the most recent annual Congress of the International Astronautical Federation, which lists titles and sometimes provides abstracts of the many papers held at the Congress. Archives link to past Congresses and lists of papers presented at them.

International Council for Science (ICSU) Web site, Paris. <http://www.icsu.org/>

Summary: A nongovernmental organization founded in 1931, the ICSU has as its purpose to bring together natural scientists in international scientific endeavor, focused on major international, interdisciplinary, and complex issues. On its searchable Web site, ICSU provides information, including reports, proceedings, reviews, press releases, regulations, and recent publications, some in full text (PDF format) online at no charge. One particular series of significant reports published online are the reports prepared for the World Summit on Sustainable Development.

Detailed Description: Sections on the home page are About ICSU, Membership, Partners Info Centre and Services. Info Centre leads to information under ICSU Central, Reviews, Proceedings, Reports, and Statements of ICSU bodies and WSSD reports. The ICSU central subsection provides online access to resolutions, statutes and statements of the organization, and meeting reports and publications online (PDF). The WSSD reports refer to the *Series on Science for Sustainable Development,* reports made to the World Summit on Sustainable Development (WSSD) and available online in PDF. The Services section on the home page leads to an online calendar and rates of exchange.

Third World Academy of Sciences Web site, Trieste, Italy. <http://www.twas.org/>

Summary: This nongovernmental organization's strength is in its activities in supporting scientific capacity in developing countries, by partnering with many international intergovernmental organizations and other organizations involved with science in developing countries. The World Academy of Sciences reports on many scientific conferences and provides many other links to information in the field of science. The home page features current news, publications, and activities of interest and organizes information under the categories: Background, Membership, Council, Activities, Relations, Contacts, Newsletters, and more.

Detailed Description: Under the home page category Newsletter is an online bimonthly *TWAS Newsletter* (PDF format) and an online News archive (1998–). The *Newsletter* reports on people, places, and events in science in the third world, with editorials and articles on specific issues and countries. Information about its programs and its research grants are available under the category Activities.

In 1988 TWAS facilitated the establishment of the *Third World Network of Scientific Organizations (TWNSO)* Web site, <http://www.twnso.org/> a nongovernmental alliance of some 150 scientific organizations in certain regions of the world whose aim is to help build political and scientific leadership for science-based economic development and promote sustainable development through partnerships in science and technology. TWAS provides the secretariat for TWNSO and cosponsors a number of its activities. The World Academy of Sciences also links to SciDevNet, a not-for-profit company, whose development of a permanent Web site since 2001 was discussed and endorsed at a meeting of the Academy. The *SciDevNet* Web site at <http://www.scidev.net/> seeks to provide information to individuals and organizations for developing countries on science and technology issues that impact them socially and economically. It provides authoritative news and subject guides and information by region of the world. In addition to these links, researchers will find other links to academies of science and nongovernmental organizations in the field of science.

RESEARCH STRATEGIES

This discussion of scientific international and foreign government information will first cover a few general resources and will then describe subject-based resources. The discussion will focus on the areas of science and technology that have resources described in this chapter: astronautics, law and government policy, meteorology, natural sciences, nautical science, nuclear, patents, physics, research, space, statistics, and sustainable development.

For general resources, an excellent overall science report is the title *World Science Report* by UNESCO. This annual report is well researched and covers scientific progress throughout the world with chapters on different global issues and trends and includes statistics. Another excellent title is the annual *Science, Technology and Industry Outlook* by the **Organisation for Economic Co-operation and Development (OECD)**, which provides an overall summary of scientific and technology trends worldwide for the year in review and specific statistics and policies for the OECD member countries. It provides more information on current technological trends and cutting-edge technology than the *World Science Report,* and OECD provides much of the latest edition available free on the Internet. Also, the OECD's *Science and Innovation* Web site is an excellent general resource for analysis of issues in the scientific, technological, and industrial environment. OECD, a major publisher, publishes most of its electronic publications online via its subscription service, *SourceOECD,* although some of this information is available online at no charge.

For the information on astronautics, researchers can consult the *International Astronautical Federation (IAF)* Web site, which publishes online information concerning its activities and is especially strong in the area of space law. Another useful publication is its annual survey for the United Nations, *Highlights in Space.*

For science and sustainable development, researchers should consult the nongovernmental *International Council for Science (ICSU)* Web site that provides PDF documents and reports online in this area, including its *Series on Science for Sustainable Development,* and reports made to the **World Summit on Sustainable Development (WSSD).** One nongovernmental resource particularly good in this area is the *Third World Academy of Sciences* Web site, which provides researchers with information specifically about developing countries and provides an online newsletter with articles on specific issues.

UNESCO Natural Sciences Portal Web site is an excellent beginning resource for information on natural sciences. Topics covered include: Fresh Water, People & Nature, Oceans, Earth Sciences, Coast & Small Islands, Basic Sciences, Engineering, and Science Policy. Its online periodical, *The World of Science,* is also good for use in general science research.

For meteorological information, such as information on weather forecasts and warnings and climate information, researchers may want to consult the ***World Meteorological Organization (WMO)*** Web site, the leader in world weather monitoring, international cooperation in meteorology, and world climate monitoring. Their Web site is an excellent online source of weather data and other facts.

In the area of nuclear science and physics, researchers can consult the ***CERN (European Organization for Nuclear Research)*** Web site for reports on projects and experiments. The CERN Education Portal is a useful learning resource for teachers and students, providing a newsletter, teaching tips, facts, games, and more.

To find patent information regarding copyright-protected scientific and technical developments, users can search online patent indexes at the ***European Patent Office (EPO)*** Web site and also find excellent links to national patent offices for further information.

International space coordination, and space law research should begin with the ***United Nations Office for Outer Space Affairs (UNOOSA)*** Web site, which contains many online free full-text reports and document. Its yearly report on ***Highlights of Space*** has been providing a review of progress since 1982.

For research and innovation in science and technology, the ***European Commission Research*** Web site and the ***CORDIS*** Web site provides access as portals and gateways to Europe's research information on science and technology. ***CORDIS*** provides an Internet information service with specialized searching capabilities, projects, and databases. CORDIS has excellent indexes and is an especially good source for reporting on new developments in Europe's science and technology. The ***European Commission Research*** Web site is a more general gateway to themes on research within the European Union.

Statistical publications included in this chapter feature titles with a general, broad focus, and those focused on Europe. For Europe, researchers should consult ***Statistics on Science and Technology in Europe*** by Eurostat, whose Web site also provides free downloads of limited data. To find research statistics for a broader area, including industrialized countries of the world, an excellent resource is the ***Basic Science and Technology Statistics*** by the Organisation for Economic Co-operation and Development. More in-depth data and research may be found in additional OECD publications online at no charge and through the subscription database *SourceOECD.*

Other additional specific scientific topics, which are the focus of international governmental organizations, are listed following in Further Reading and include scientific subjects such as geology, observatories, agricultural research, animal research, and hydrographics.

A good way for users to navigate in country-level governmental Web sites pertaining to the sciences is to consult a national Web site and check its links or to check some of the interdisciplinary Web sites suggested following. Also, for links to national government scientific offices and global scientific associations, researchers can consult the National Science Foundation directory online, ***Science Organizations Around the World,*** which is described in For Further Reading.

FOR FURTHER READING: COMPREHENSIVE WEB SITES AND OTHER REFERENCE SOURCES

Commission on Science and Technology for Sustainable Development in the South (COMSATS) Web site, Islamabad, Pakistan. <http://www.comsats.org.pk/>

The Commission on Science and Technology for Sustainable Development in the South (COMSATS) is an international intergovernmental organization, with the mission of improving social and economic development of the third world through useful applications of science and technology. Established in October 1994, COMSATS currently represents 21 developing countries. Its Web site provides information through categories under Introduction, Programmes of Excellence, Member States, Working Partners, Upcoming Events, Archives (online full-text documents), and Latest Developments. It is currently developing an online Biotechnology Web portal to provide quick access to individuals and institutions on research on biotechnology.

European Southern Observatory Web site, Chilton, United Kingdom. <http://www.eso.org/>

The European Southern Observatory is an intergovernmental, European organization for astronomical research, with 10 member countries. Its Web site includes publications, reports, and information on science activities, such as the ESO's imaging survey, Astronomical Photos, links, and much more.

International Geological Correlation Programme (IGCP) Web site, Paris. <http://www.unesco.org/science/earthsciences/igcp/>

The International Geological Correlation Programme (IGCP) is interdisciplinary, covering the different fields in earth sciences and maintaining cooperate activities among geoscientists across frontiers in disciplines such as water, ecological, marine, atmospheric, and biological sciences. It is a joint endeavor of UNESCO (United Nations Educational, Scientific and Cultural Organisation), and the IUGS (International Union of Geological Sciences) and is linked with the other UNESCO scientific programs. Beginning 1972, its activities focus on bringing scientists from all over the world together and enhancing interaction through joint research work, meetings, and workshops. The organization's main objectives are:

(1) To **increase** the understanding of the different factors influencing the environment in order to improve human living conditions and wise management of the Earth as a human habitat.

(2) To **develop** more effective ways to search and assess natural resources of energy and minerals.

(3) To **enhance** knowledge of the Earth's geological processes and concepts through correlative studies of sites and locations around the globe.

(4) To **improve** standards of research methods and techniques.[3]

The IGCP operates in about 150 countries, involving thousands of scientists. Project leaders submit annual reports to the IGCP Secretariat, which are then forwarded to the Scientific Board for appraisal. The achievements of the projects are included in the annual "Geological Correlation" published by the IGCP Secretariat. The 28th issue of the "Geological Correlation" is available online and on paper. The Web site links to the annual International Geological Congress, which provides documents and links to many major geologic organizations, such as the IUGS, the International Union of Geological Sciences, a major nongovernmental scientific organization.

International Hydrographic Organization (IHO)
Web site, Monaco. <http://www.iho.shom.fr/>

The International Hydrographic Organization is an intergovernmental consultative and technical organization that was established in 1921 to support safety in navigation and the protection of the marine environment. The organization's objectives include the coordination of the activities of national hydrographic offices; implementation of uniformity in nautical charts and documents; adoption of reliable and efficient methods of carrying out and exploiting hydrographic surveys; and development of the sciences in the field of hydrography and in descriptive oceanography techniques. Some publications are available online at no charge, such as a catalog of documents, annual report, reference texts, and journals for training in hydrography; however, most online publications are restricted to members. Publications may be ordered from the organization. One subscription publication of note is the IHO's scientific journal *International Hydrographic Bulletin.*

Science Organizations Around the World Web site,
by the National Science Foundation, Arlington, Virginia. <http://www.nsf.gov/sbe/int/map.htm>

An online list of links by region of the world to global and national scientific organizations, this Web site features alphabetical country lists. Under each country is information pertaining to the major academy of science and government science agency or ministry for that specific region.

NOTES

1. *Science Organizations Around the World* Web site, by the U.S. National Science Foundation, <http://www.nsf.gov/sbe/int/map.htm>.

2. *Basic Facts About WMO* Web site, by the World Meteorological Organization, <http://www.wmo.ch/web-en/wmofact.html>.

3. *International Geological Correlation Programme (IGCP)* Web site, <http://www.unesco.org/science/earthsciences/igcp/background.htm>.

CHAPTER 17
Security, Peace, and Disarmament

CHAPTER OVERVIEW

Since the beginning of time, there have been issues relating to peacekeeping, security, and disarmament. The two World Wars and ensuing Cold War kept these concerns alive in the twentieth century. With the ending of the Cold War and the subsequent attack on the United States, a new alignment of thought and alliances has come into being.

Since its inception, a major focus of the United Nations has been world peace, security, and disarmament. The Web sites of the relevant United Nations bodies, as well as the print source *The Blue Helmets: A Review of United Nations Peace-keeping*, 3rd ed., comprehensively describe both historic and current efforts in this area. The regional organizations, **North Atlantic Treaty Organisation** and the **Organization for Security and Co-operation in Europe,** were established to oversee the security of these areas, and their Web sites provide important information on their efforts. With terrorism being a worldwide epidemic, the U.S. Department of State *Patterns of Global Terrorism* Web site is a valuable source of information regarding what events have transpired in what area of the world.

Governmental Sources Discussed

The Blue Helmets: A Review of United Nations Peace-keeping. 3rd ed. New York: United Nations Dept. of Public Information, 1996 (ISBN 9-21100-611-2).

North Atlantic Treaty Organisation Web site, Brussels, Belgium. <http://www.nato.int>

Organization for Security and Co-operation in Europe Web site, Vienna, Austria. <http://www.osce.org>

Patterns of Global Terrorism Web site, by the U.S. Dept. of State, Washington, D.C. <http://www.state.gov/s/ct/rls/pgtrpt/>

Peace and Security through Disarmament Web site, by the United Nations, Department of Disarmament Affairs, New York. <http://disarmament2.un.org/index.html>

United Nations Documentation: Research Guide: Special Topics: Disarmament Web site. <http://www.un.org/Depts/dhl/resguide/specdis.htm>

United Nations Documentation: Research Guide: Special Topics: Peacekeeping Web site. <http://www.un.org/Depts/dhl/resguide/specpk.htm>

United Nations Institute for Disarmament Research (UNIDIR) Web site, Geneva, Switzerland. <http://www.unidir.org/html/en/home.html>

United Nations: Peacekeeping Web site, New York. <http://www.un.org/Depts/dpko/dpko/home.shtml>

Nongovernmental Sources Discussed

FIRST: Facts on International Relations and Security Trends Web site. <http://first.sipri.org/>

GOVERNMENTAL SOURCES

The Blue Helmets: A Review of United Nations Peace-keeping. 3rd ed. New York: United Nations Dept. of Public Information, 1996 (ISBN 9-21100-611-2).

Summary: *The Blue Helmets* provides a history of United Nations (UN) peacekeeping efforts from the UN's inception to 1996. This is the third edition of this publication, with the first published in 1985 and the second in 1990. The term itself refers to the blue helmets worn by military peacekeeping officials.

Detailed Description: Organizationally, the book is divided into 11 major parts: Introduction, Middle East, India and Pakistan, Cyprus, Africa, Central America, Cambodia, the Former Yugoslavia, Republics of the Former Soviet Union, Haiti, and Other Peacekeeping Missions. Each part is comprised of a narrative background and discussion of the various initiatives for that area, and some parts also have maps. An Appendix, Facts and Figures, is also included. Here is found a listing of each mission with such information as authorization, function, headquarters, duration, strength, fatalities, and financing.

Some of the missions contain additional information such as mediators, chiefs of staff, commanders, contributors, and members of the observation group.

The Blue Helmets serves to furnish in-depth coverage on global peacekeeping initiatives. As is the case with print material, the information supplied here is not up to date.

North Atlantic Treaty Organisation Web site, Brussels, Belgium. <http://www.nato.int>

Summary: The North Atlantic Treaty Organisation (NATO), a military alliance, was founded in April 1949 and has a membership of 19 countries. The *NATO* Web site includes documents, publications, links to other sources, photographs, conference information, and much more. Most information is in the two official NATO languages, English and French. Some materials are also available in other languages. A search engine is found on the home page that searches NATO-related Web resources, the NATO archives, other organizations related to NATO, NATO/OTAN headquarters, NATO Military Commands, and NATO Kosovo Force (KFOR). The home page is updated daily. Other sections of the Web site are updated at different times. This is an important site for comprehensive coverage. However, as it has more of a regional focus, fewer countries are included. The home page of the *NATO* Web site is divided into the main categories of Organisation, Publications, Issues, Multimedia, and Services. In addition, there are links to the latest NATO materials and an introduction to NATO.

Detailed Description: The Organisation home page section contains information regarding organization and structure of NATO, itself, as well as subdivisions of civilian, military, agencies, independent member countries, and national delegations, as well as partner countries. Web sites, transcripts, texts of speeches, biographies, and other documents are included for some of the subsections.

Publications, another main home page section, is chock-full of the full text of NATO documents and other information and is arranged according to the categories of Basic Texts, Fact Sheets, Press Archives, Ministerial Communiques, *NATO Review, NATO Handbook,* Seminars, Speeches, News Articles, Fellowship Reports, and Standardization Agreements. Basic Texts provides full text documents organized into three subcategories: Antecedents of the Alliance, Juridical Texts and Formal Agreements (1949–1997), and Key Policy Documents. Fact Sheets, also in full

text, contains embedded links to pertinent documents and Web sites. Press Archive, again in full-text format, contains NATO press releases (1996– in English and French; 1993–1995 in English only) and those from the International Military Staff (IMS) (1996–). Ministerial Communiques are in full-text format and date from 1949 to the present. Also included here are Ministerial Meetings, dating from 1996–, with links to the press releases, communiques, and speeches related to that particular meeting.

Issues of *NATO Review,* the official NATO journal, are also found in the Publications section. They are in full text format and date from 1997; the format varies. In addition, versions in 16 other languages are also included along with a chronological listing of articles by author. A major NATO publication is the *NATO Handbook.* The most current edition is available in full-text and PDF formats. Links to related documents are embedded in the text.

Although entitled Seminars, this subcategory actually includes conferences and symposia, both dating from 1997–. Each one contains a listing of events and participants. Speeches, dating from 1988–2001 with selected speeches from 1946 and 1947, provides the transcript of various speeches, delivered by NATO officials or at NATO functions. Some entries even include color photographs of the speaker. News Articles, 1997–2000, contains selected news articles about NATO affairs, sometimes from foreign publications. Fellowship Reports pertain to *NATO Research Fellowship Reports* (1994–2000, which have a two-year program cycle). These are arranged alphabetically by country, and some of the reports are available in full text via PDF format. Standardization Agreements include the actual agreements along with Allied Administrative Publications, Allied Ordnance Publications, Allied Quality Assurance Publications, and Allied Reliability and Maintainability Publications. Each group is arranged sequentially by group number and contains the full text in PDF format.

Issues, another of the home page main sections, is broken down into the subcategories Operations, Partnerships, and Topics. Operations provides in-depth coverage of the various global operations of NATO. Full-text documents, press releases, photographs, and maps are included for many of the sections under Operations. These sections include Bosnia, Kosovo, former Yogoslav republic of Macedonia, Turkey, and more. Partnerships include Euro-Atlantic Partnership, Mediterranean Dialogue, Russia–NATO, Ukraine–NATO, and South East Europe Initiative. Partnerships, another main section, is subdivided into Euro-Atlantic Partnership Council, Partnership for Peace, Mediterranean Dialogue, Russia–NATO, and Ukraine–NATO. Each of the subdivisions has the full text of fact sheets, press releases, statements, and some documents.

Multimedia, the final main section, includes the TV and Radio Unit and the Media Library, with the Media Library the primary focus. It is an "extensive collection of photo and video material taken by free-lance photographers and cameramen and for which NATO has sole copyright."[1] The main types of items included here are photographs, videos, and audio. The photographs, dated 1949–, are arranged chronologically and can be downloaded. They depict NATO events and visits by dignitaries. A search engine is available, which searches caption keywords in English, French, Russian, German, and Italian. Additional photographs are listed under Who's Who, photos of NATO officials. Short videos and clips are found under videos, dated 1997–. Audio for 2000– press conferences and selected ministerial meetings is also found here. A map of NATO member countries, partner countries, and Mediterranean Dialogue countries is also included.

Services, the last of the main categories, contains links to other related organizations and sites. The home page itself also provides information and links on a variety of short topics that relate to the work of NATO.

The *NATO* Web site serves as an important source of comprehensive coverage. However, it has a more regional focus, as fewer countries are represented. Having the full text of documents and publications along with photographs, video, and audio available via a few keystrokes, makes the *NATO* Web site a rich resource. Because these various formats are found in different categories, having a search engine, found on the home page, is a real necessity.

Organization for Security and Co-operation in Europe Web site, Vienna, Austria. <http://www.osce.org>

Summary: Originally established in 1973 and now comprised of 55 countries from the world regions of North America, Europe, and Central Asia, the Organization for Security and Co-operation in Europe (OSCE) is the largest regional security organization in the world. The Web site, updated daily, contains official records, other documents, reports, publications, news releases, fact sheets, and maps. Most of these are in full-text format, usually as PDF files. The official languages of the OSCE are English (EN), French (FR), German (DE), Italian (IT), Russian (RU), and Spanish (ES). Much of the materials found here are in more than one language. Extensive search engines are found throughout this site and described in depth in the appropriate section. There is also a search engine that searches the entire OSCE site. Because of its importance, this site is also very comprehensive. The *OSCE* Web site has several components. However, for this discussion the focus will be on the News, Events, Documents, Publications, Institutions, and Field Activities sections.

Detailed Description: The News home page section encompasses news, press releases, and statements. A search engine allows for searching by sources, date, region, category, and keyword. Current press releases are listed on this page.

The Events section lists the current calendar. A search engine is also available here. Searching is by sources (institutions/bodies or field activities), regions (all, South-Eastern Europe, Baltic & Eastern Europe, Caucasus, and Central Asia), categories, and date (current calendar, 2000–).

The Documents home page section is arranged according to the categories of Listings, Negotiating Bodies, and Services. The category Listings provides access to final documents, reports, journals, and decisions from 1993 on. Negotiating Bodies links to full-text, PDF format documents, divided into summits, ministerial meetings, Senior Council/Economic Forum, Permanent Council, and Forum for Security Co-operation. The Services category is more complex. Here are found the subcategories of List, OSCE Publications, ODIHR Election Reports, ODIHR Documents, HCNM (High Commissioner on National Minorities) Documents, Parliamentary Assembly Documents, and FoM (Freedom of Media). Lists contains publications available on request, including the *OSCE Handbook*, annual reports, and Official Verbatim Records. OSCE Publications contains links to the full text, sometimes in PDF format, of the OSCE Handbook, video documentary For Human Dignity, newsletter, fact sheets, mission survey, feature publications, and publications from related European organizations. Three search engines are also a part of the OSCE Publications subcategory. The news archive search engine has already been described in the News main section. The features archive search engine searches by source, region, category date, and keyword. The photo search engine searches by region, category, keyword, and events. The ODIHR (Office for Democratic Institutions and Human Rights) Election Reports subcategory of Services has information about this organization and its activities, publications, and election observations including reports. The election reports are arranged alphabetically by country and have the full text of statements and reports related to elections within that country. The ODIHR Library provides full text access, sometimes in PDF format, to fact sheets, newsletters, reports, background papers, handbooks, press releases, and periodicals related to this Office.

Also of interest in the Services subsection of the Documents home page section are the various publications of High Commissioner on National Minorities, Parliamentary Assembly, and the OSCE's Representative on Freedom of the Media. Many full-text yearbooks, reports, and fact sheets are included.

Institutions, another home page section, is organized into two subsections: Negotiating and Decision-making Bodies and Structures and Institutions. Under each subsection is a link to the particular body. Negotiating and Decision-making Bodies has links to the full text, in PDF format, of official publications such as journals and decisions. The groups listed under Structures and Institutions are varied in what they do and who they are, and therefore they have varied resources. Some have full-text descriptions. Others go a step further and include news releases, publications, and fact sheets.

The Field Activities section is divided into four subsections: South-Eastern Europe, Eastern Europe, Caucasus and Central Asia, and closed missions. Each subsection is further divided by individual country. Information for each individual country includes a description, statistics, maps, and news releases. Many of the country listings also contain publications and other news source information. Closed missions links to information for each specific mission.

Patterns of Global Terrorism Web site, by the U.S. Dept. of State, Washington, D.C. <http://www.state.gov/s/ct/rls/pgtrpt/>

Summary: Produced by the U.S. Department of State Publications and Office of the Secretary of State, released by the Office of the Coordinator for Counterterrorism, this site provides the full text of the publication *Patterns of Global Terrorism,* dating from 1995 on. Each publication is divided into Introduction, Year in Review, Africa Overview, Asia (this region may be further subdivided), Overview, Eurasia Overview, Europe Overview, Latin America Overview, Middle East Overview, and Overview of State-Sponsored Terrorism. Each region division is then subdivided by country and contains a brief description of the events for that year of coverage. Not every region may be covered for a particular year. Appendices may also be included, which focus on a particular aspect. With the tragic events of September 11, 2001, and the increased intensity of concern regarding terrorism in the world, these reports take on greater importance in keeping the world abreast of the events unfolding.

Peace and Security through Disarmament Web site, by the United Nations, Dept. of Disarmament Affairs, New York. <http:// disarmament2.un.org/ index.html>

Summary: International peace and security was one of the most important founding principles of the United Nations. The *Peace and Security through Disarmament* Web site describes the United Nations' work in this important, global area. The site itself provides a tremendous amount of useful online information, which is grouped into the main categories of Disarmament Issues, Disarmament Resources, Disarmament Machinery, UNIDIR (United Nations Institute for Disarmament Research), and Meetings/ Conferences/Events. Current highlights are included on the home page as well as news. A site index provides alphabetically arranged access to the topics covered by this comprehensive site.

Detailed Description: The home page category Disarmament Issues encompasses Weapons of Mass Destruction, Conventional Weapons, *Convention on Certain Conventional Weapons,* Land Mines, Regional Disarmament, Disarmament and Development, Terrorism, Gender and Disarmament, and Disarmament and Children. The Weapons of Mass Destruction, Conventional Weapons, and Regional Disarmament subcategories link to branches of the Department of Disarmament Affairs pertaining to these areas and provide descriptions and links to other sites. The *Convention on Certain Conventional Weapons* subcategory describes this document and provides the full text, in all official United Nations languages, of the *Convention.* The subcategories of Terrorism, Gender and Disarmament, and Disarmament and Children discuss work in these areas and have links to relevant information.

Disarmament Resources, another home page main category, provides access to relevant General Assembly resolutions and decisions (52nd session–). The UN Register of Conventional Arms, a subcategory of Disarmament Resource, contains the full text, in PDF, of *Annual Reports* (2000–), with most entries in all UN official languages. The Database (1992–2000) link provides information regarding weapon exports and imports, arranged alphabetically by country name. Other documents, publications, and press releases are also available under this subcategory. Another subcategory is Instrument for Reporting Military Expenditures, and this gives access to full-text, PDF, reports of the Secretary-General in all official languages (1998–) as well as resolutions, press releases, and the reporting form. *Article 7: Mine-Ban Convention,* another subcategory, contains the full text of the treaty, status, and individual country reports. The Status of Treaties subcategory provides the full text of these agreements as well as country, signature, and deposit date for each. The Education Resources subcategory has Microsoft PowerPoint presentations and the full-text, PDF, of the *Disarmament: A Basic Guide.* Statements and Press Releases, another subcategory, are the full text of statements by the Under-Secretary-General for Disarmament Affairs (1998–), the Secretary-General and Deputy-Secretary General on disarmament issues (1999–), and Press Releases (1999–). The DDA Publications subcategory features the table of contents for *United Nations Disarmament Yearbook* (1997–), full text of the *DDA Update* (1998–), some full text of Occasional Papers (1999–), and mainly full text, PDF, of Ad Hoc Publications (1999–), as well as ordering information and a link to UNIDIR publications. The last subcategory is Links, which provides access to other relevant sites.

The third major home page category discussed is Disarmament Machinery and includes the subcategories of General Assembly First Committee, Disarmament Commission, Conference on Disarmament, Department for Disarmament Affairs, SG's Advisory Board, and UNIDIR. Each of these subcategories provides access to information about its specific work as well as relevant documents and publications, many in full text.

UNIDIR (United Nations Institute for Disarmament Research) is included under the home page category of Disarmament Machinery as well as being its own home page category. However, it is discussed as a separate entry in this chapter.

United Nations Documentation: Research Guide: Special Topics: Disarmament Web site, by the United Nations Dag Hammarskjöld Library, New York. <http://www.un.org/Depts/dhl/resguide/specdis.htm>

Summary: This disarmament research guide is a product of the Dag Hammarskjöld Library and provides access to relevant materials published by the United Nations on the topic of disarmament. A short introduction of the history of peacekeeping is found here along with links to relevant General Assembly, Disarmament Commission, Conference on Disarmament, and United Nations Institute for Disarmament Research (UNIDIR) documentation complete with brief explanations of the various components. A discussion of research on disarmament and treaties is also provided, along with links to the full text, in PDF format, to major international instruments on disarmament and related issues. A pathfinder of UN reference sources is also included that gives a list of UN sources complete with bibliographic information and keywords.

United Nations Documentation: Research Guide: Special Topics: Peacekeeping Web site, by the United Nations Dag Hammarskjöld Library, New York. <http://www.un.org/Depts/dhl/resguide/specpk.htm>

Summary: Another product of the Dag Hammarskjöld Library, this research guide provides access to relevant materials published by the United Nations on the topic of peacekeeping. There is a short introduction of the history of peacekeeping, as well as links to pertinent Security Council and General Assembly documentation. A pathfinder of UN reference sources is also included, subdivided into the categories of general issues, specific conflicts and political issues, and decolonization. Each category contains a list of UN sources complete with bibliographic information and keywords.

United Nations Institute for Disarmament Research (UNIDIR) Web site, Geneva, Switzerland. <http://www.unidir.org/html/enhome.html>

Summary: Established in 1980 as a research center to study and assist United Nations member countries in the areas of security and disarmament, the *UNIDIR* Web site details this vital work through its three main focus areas: global security and disarmament, regional security and disarmament, and human security and disarmament. The Web site contains publications, links to other materials, and a unique feature, e-di@logue, which allows for online discussion. The UNIDIR home page, also available in French, contains the main categories About, Activities, Publications, Roundtable, Links, UNIDIR Highlights, Latest

Publications, and Databases. Searching for activities and publications is available from the home page, and a site map is also included. At the bottom of each major category are links to bibliographic information on books and reports classified into the subject areas of nuclear issues, biological issues, chemical issues, missiles, small arms, land mines, peacekeeping, and education. The same subjects are found on each page.

Detailed Description: The home page category About provides information on UNIDIR's background, mandate, stature, funding, and personnel. Activities, the next home page category, contains a detailed description as well as relevant materials relating to the three main focus areas outlined in the summary. Reports, some in full text, can be accessed here arranged by type: Research Projects, Conferences, Fellowships, and Geneva Forum. A search engine is available to search for specific titles or subject areas.

The Publications home page category contains a listing of books and reports as well as a search engine to look for specific titles or subject areas. Some publications are available online in full text. Ordering information is included. The quarterly journal *Disarmament Forum* (1999–) is available in PDF at no charge, and a researcher can subscribe to automatically receive notification when each issue is posted.

The Roundtable category allows for participation in an online discussion, e-di@logue. In addition, the full text of research papers are posted here and comments are invited. Links, another home page category, provides a listing of related international organizations and research institutes, with the name of each hot linked. The home page category UNIDIR Highlights has the latest news of UNIDIR activities and can be received via e-mail notification. The Latest Publications category has access to the most current issue of *Disarmament Forum* and a description of new books and reports. The last category, Databases, provides access to the *Database on Research Institutes (DATARIs)*, with searching available by the topics of institutes, research projects, publications, databases, or documentation centers. *UN Small Arms Conference Database* is also accessible here and reports on small arms status for member country. The database consists of three smaller databases: government documents and statements, voting records, and implementation of the UN Programme of Action. Publications and resources pertaining to small arms are also included.

United Nations: Peacekeeping Web site, New York.
    <http://www.un.org/Depts/dpko/dpko/home.shtml>

Summary: The *Peacekeeping* Web site, available in all six official UN languages, contains extensive information on the UN's 50 plus years of efforts. The site itself is subdivided into the categories of Current Operations, Past Operations, Overview, Facts and Figures, About, and Further Information.

Detailed Description: Current Operations, a home page category, is divided into Middle East, Europe, Asia, and Africa. Within each of these subdivisions are links to information pertaining to the specific operations for that region. This information usually includes background, mandate, facts and figures, United Nations documents, maps, and photographs, as well as access to the search engine for news and press releases. Some operations provide other documentation. The Past Operations home page category is also divided into the same regions and contains much of the same types of materials.

Overview, another home page category, provides much useful information for beginning research and background. There is the full text of *An Introduction to United Nations Peacekeeping,* which is followed by a topical Questions and Answers subsection. An interactive timeline dating from 1948 is arranged by decade, with a link to the operations during that period. Rapid Deployment discusses Standby Arrangements System, which pertains to commitment of forces and materials and Mission Planning, which is not yet available. The Facts and Figures category provides a PDF map of peacekeeping operations from 1948 on, as well as statistics on personnel and financial aspects. There are also full-text monthly summaries of contributor reports (2001–) and fatality statistical charts (1948–) by nationality and mission, mission and appointment type, mission and incident type, and year.

About the Department of Peacekeeping Operations category has links to the Best Practices Unit, Head of Department, Mine Action, Training and Evaluation services, Civilian Police Division, Military Division, Situation Center, and Medical Support. Each of these areas contains information about its work as well as relevant publications. An organizational chart and mission statement are also included.

The final home page category, Further Information, provides access to the subcategories of Special Committee, Special Representatives, Special Report, Deployment Maps, Medals, Publications/Archives, Glossary, and Photographs. Special Committee includes links to press releases, documents on peacekeeping, and selected General Assembly documents. Special Representatives lists the name, title, and appointment date of Special and Personal Representatives and Envoys of the Secretary-General according to area of the world. Special Reports has the full text, PDF, of relevant General Assembly and Security Council reports. Publications/Archives has the full text of important publications: *Year in Review United Nations Peace Operations 2002, Year in Review United Nations Peace Operations 2001, United Nations Peacekeeping 1991 to 2000, Background Note on Peacekeeping Operations,* and *Fifty Years of United Nations Peacekeeping.* Deployment Maps links to the UN Cartographic Section, which includes deployment maps in its holdings. These maps, in PDF format, are arranged according to mission. Medals features color images and a description of the various peacekeeping medals that are issued. Glossary is especially useful as it provides an alphabetically arranged listing of peacekeeping terms and definitions. A link to a UN peacekeeping monograph bibliography (1945–1996) is also available here. Photographs are selected photographs of UN peacekeeping missions. The UN gives permission for reproduction for editorial purposes from this page and includes inquiry information for prints.

NONGOVERNMENTAL SOURCES

FIRST: Facts on International Relations and Security Trends Web site. ISN: International Relations and Security Network, Center for Security Studies and Conflict Research and SIPRI: Stockholm International Peace Research Institute. <http://first.sipri.org/>

Summary: This integrated database system is a "free-of-charge service for politicians, journalists, researchers and the interested public. It covers areas in the field of international relations and security, such as hard facts on armed conflicts and peace keeping, arms production and trade, military expenditure, armed forces and conventional weapons holding, nuclear weapons, chronology, statistics and other reference data."[2]

Detailed Description: The database allows for searching three different ways: country profile (individual countries from an alphabetical listing of countries in a pull-down menu box), multiple country profile, and advanced searching (entire regions and free text). The date coverage is not specified. The main areas covered are Armed Forces, Conventional Weapon Holdings, and Military Activities; Arms Production, Trade, Embargoes, and Export Controls; Conflicts and Peace Keeping Activities; Country Indicators and Statistics; Government, Memberships, and

Agreements; Military Expenditure; Nuclear Weapons and Ballistic Missiles; and News, Events, and Reference Data. Each category has several subcategories to choose from. The user can select any number of subcategories from each main category. The results are posted first as a Table of Contents with individual results following. The results include relevant information along with the source.

RESEARCH STRATEGIES

Because of its more global focus, sources produced by the United Nations are probably the most useful for beginning research in the areas of security, peacekeeping, and disarmament. In particular, the Peacekeeping and Disarmament research guides produced by the Dag Hammarskjöld Library, may best serve as a starting point because they provide an introduction to the topic, links to documentation, and a pathfinder to additional sources.

For more in-depth research on a global basis, the *Peace and Security through Disarmament* Web site, and *United Nations Institute for Disarmament Research (UNIDIR)* Web site provide in-depth, comprehensive coverage on these topics. Many of the materials located on these sites are in full-text format with statistics and photographs also included. *The Blue Helmets: A Review of United Nations Peacekeeping,* is another useful tool on the subject of peacekeeping as it provides in-depth coverage on global peacekeeping initiatives. The downside of using a print resource is the issue of currency. Online resources are usually more up to date.

The *NATO* and *OSCE* Web sites also serve as important sources of comprehensive coverage; however, as they have more of a regional focus, fewer countries are represented. Both include search engines, which provide quicker access to finding relevant materials within the Web site. Like the UN sites, both have provided the full text to many of their documents and publications. In addition, NATO has included short video and audio clips to their holdings.

The *FIRST: Facts on International Relations and Security Trends* Web site provides a different perspective as it is produced by a nongovernmental source. It is of particular importance because it makes concise country-by-country information available.

All of the Web sites discussed in this chapter contain links to other resources and contain much information in full-text format. Having all this available at the user's fingertips makes the research process more efficient.

The additional sources included in this chapter serve as supplemental information with history, regional, and background information. The encyclopedias/dictionary are a quick source for looking up definitions of terms and names.

FOR FURTHER READING: COMPREHENSIVE WEB SITES AND OTHER REFERENCE SOURCES

Encyclopedia of Arms Control and Disarmament, by Richard Dean Burns. New York: Charles Scribner's Sons, 1993 (ISBN 0-68419-281-0).

Consisting of three volumes, this publication covers the topics of National and Regional Dimension and Themes and Institutions (volume 1), Historical Dimensions to 1945 and Arms Control Activities Since 1945 (volume 2), and Treaties (volume 3).

Encyclopedia of International Peacekeeping Operations, by Oliver Ramsbotham and Tom Woodhouse. Santa Barbara, Calif.: ABC-Clio, Inc., 1999.

An alphabetical list of individuals, events, concepts, countries, organizations, and missions comprise this volume. Appendices of Force Commanders, 1948–1998; Special Representatives to the Secretary-General, 1948–1998; and International Peacekeeping Acronyms are also included.

Historical Dictionary of Multinational Peacekeeping. No. 9: International Organizations Series, by Terry M. Mays. Lanham, Md.: The Scarecrow Press, 1996.

Included in this volume are a narrative introduction on peacekeeping, specifically centering on efforts by the League of Nations, United Nations, and United States, and an alphabetically arranged dictionary of individuals, events, organizations, topics, and documents, along with a bibliography.

North Atlantic Treaty Organization. No. 8: International Organizations Series, by Phil Williams. New Brunswick, N.J.: Transaction Publishers, 1994.

This publication is a selective annotated bibliography of English-language materials that have been written about NATO. The main focus is on books and journal articles. Listings of doctoral theses and U.S. Congressional documents are also included; however, these are not annotated.

Report of the Panel on United Nations Peace Operations Web site, by the United Nations. <http://www.un.org/peace/reports/peace_operations/>

Also known as the Brahimi Report, named for the Chair of the Panel, Lakhdar Brahimi (Algeria), this document was released in August 2000. It came about from a request of the Secretary-General to the Panel on United Nations Peace Operations "to assess the shortcomings of the existing system and to make frank, specific and realistic recommendations for change."[3] Contained on this site is the full text of the Executive Summary, Summary of Recommendations, and the Full Report itself, which is available in HTML or PDF formats. A listing, with brief biographical information, of the panel members and the full text of Press Releases and Fact Sheets (PDF format), is also included. In addition, follow-up reports of the Secretary-General are also included.

The UN Action Against Terrorism Web site, by the United Nations. <http://www.un.org/terrorism/>

Latest developments within the United Nations and its specialized agencies in the Global Coalition against Terrorism are located on this Web site. Web casts, radio/photos/videos, and reports from the General Assembly, the Security Council, the Economic and Social Council, and the Secretary General are included, along with links to resolutions and conventions.

United Nations Disarmament Yearbook. Geneva: United Nations Department for Disarmament Affairs.

An annual publication (1976–), the *Disarmament Yearbook* focuses on current disarmament and weapons issues. Each volume also includes the full text of relevant guidelines, resolutions, and statutes, along with a table of resolutions and decisions complete with sponsors and voting.

Western European Union (WEU) Web site. <http://www.weu.int/>

The *Western European Union (WEU)* was created by the *Treaty on Economic, Social and Cultural Collaboration and Collective Self-Defence* signed at Brussels on March 17, 1948 (the Brussels Treaty) and amended by the Protocol signed at Paris on October 23, 1954, which modified and completed it. The treaty provides for the mutual defense and military support of the members of the Union in a time of crisis. There are 10 member states, 6 associate members, 5 observers, and 7 associate member states, all European countries that have committed to different obligations. The 10 member states include Belgium, France, Germany, Greece (1995), Italy, Luxembourg, Netherlands, Portugal (1990), Spain (1990), and the United Kingdom, with associate members, observers, and partners. Although the security and crisis management part of the mission of the WEU was transferred to the European Union, there still remain some residual functions of the WEU, especially concerning the administration of the Brussels Treaty. Included here are background information (organization, structure, and history) as well as key online legal texts and documents and historical and multimedia archives.

NOTES

1. *North Atlantic Treaty Organisation* Web site, Brussels, Belgium, <http://www.nato.int/multi/multi.htm>.

2. *FIRST: Facts on International Relations and Security Trends* Web site, <http://first.sipri.org/>.

3. *Report of the Panel on United Nations Peace Operations* Web site, by the United Nations, <http://www.un.org/peace/reports/peace_operations/>.

CHAPTER 18
Social/Cultural Issues

CHAPTER OVERVIEW

The intent of this chapter is to describe basic, significant reference resources for research on worldwide social issues and cultural affairs, including social affairs, economics, and development; social statistics; general cultural information; cultural property and heritage; migration; humanitarian affairs; and refugees. This chapter does not intend to be comprehensive. For example, the United Nations' rich resources on social and cultural affairs are covered by the description of several selected resources that will, in turn, lead researchers to more resources. They provide researchers access to lists of social and cultural sources and Internet sites, significant reports, texts online, and periodicals within the United Nations family that are focused on social affairs, statistics, and development.

This chapter includes many of the general statistical sources that are excellent for studying social statistical indicators and the social issues reports published by international intergovernmental organizations. However, many excellent titles that have a more general focus and will also provide good information to researchers are described in other chapters, under General Sources, Statistics, Communications, Education, Development, Economics and Business, Women and Children, and Health. Resources that analyze and report on these subjects often include significant content on social affairs and some cultural information.

Governmental Sources Discussed

Cultural Profiles Project, by Citizenship and Immigration Canada. <http://cwr.utoronto.ca/cultural/english/index.html>

Division for Social Policy and Development Web site, by the United Nations, New York. <http://www.un.org/esa/socdev/index.html>

EU Culture Portal Web site, by the European Commission. <http://europa.eu.int/comm/culture/index_en.htm>

European Heritage Network Web site, by the European Heritage Network. <http://www.european-heritage.net/>

European Social Statistics: Demography, by the European Commission and EUROSTAT, Luxembourg, 2000– (print periodical with accompanying CD-ROM).

International Cultural Property Web site, by the U.S. Department of State, Washington, D.C. <http://exchanges.state.gov/culprop/>

International Organization for Migration (IOM) Web site, Geneva, Switzerland. <http://www.iom.int/>

Report on the World Social Situation, prepared by the Division for Social Policy and Development of the Department of Economic and Social Affairs, United Nations, New York, 1952– (ISSN 0082-8068). <http://www.un.org/esa/socdev/rwss/index.html> (print annual title with selected sections only online).

UNESCO, the United Nations Educational, Scientific, and Cultural Organization, Resources

Culture Web site, by UNESCO. <http://www.unesco.org/culture/development/>

UNESCO New Courier (previously *UNESCO Courier*) (print and online periodical). <http://www.unesco.org/courier/>

World Culture Report, by UNESCO, Paris, 1998– (print biennial title, with latest 2000 edition online). <http://www.unesco.org/culture/worldreport/>

World Heritage Center Web site, by UNESCO. <http://whc.unesco.org/nwhc/pages/home/pages/homepage.htm>

United Nations Resources

Humanitarian Affairs Web site, by the United Nations. <http://www.un.org/ha/>

United Nations High Commissioner for Refugees
Web site, Geneva, Switzerland.
<http://www.unhcr.ch/>

United Nations Social Development Pathfinder
Web site, by the United Nations Dag Hammaskjöld Library, New York. <http://www.un.org/Depts/dhl/pathfind/social/0901.htm>

World Economic and Social Survey: Trends and Policies in the World Economy, by the United Nations Department of Economic and Social Affairs, New York, 1994–. <http://www.un.org/esa/analysis/wess/> (selected sections online, including Chapter 1, "The State of the World Economy").

Nongovernmental Sources Discussed

Culturelink Network Web site, by Culturelink.
<http://www.culturelink.org/culpol/>

GOVERNMENTAL SOURCES

Cultural Profiles Project, by Citizenship and Immigration Canada.
<http://cwr.utoronto.ca/cultural/english/index.html> <http://cwr.utoronto.ca/cultural/>

Summary: This Internet site provides profiles of each country with overviews on life and customs in each country. Available in English and French, the profiles provide summaries of information on countries with the objective to assist new immigrants from other countries to adapt to life in Canada. The summaries are not intended to cover all facets of life or equally describe the customs of all peoples in these countries. Profiles of countries are available in hard copy through the AMNI Centre, Faculty of Social Work, University of Toronto.[1] The countries are listed both in text and via a navigational map. Some summaries are illustrated with photographs.

Detailed Description: Countries in the profile are listed alphabetically. Researchers will find a summary profile of facts concerning the specific country highlighted. In addition, information for each country is presented with these categories, which vary from a few paragraphs to a page in length: landscape and climate, a look at the past, family life, world of work, sports and recreation, health care, education, food, communication, spirituality, holidays, and arts and literature. A bibliography of books and Web sites useful for additional information is included.

Division for Social Policy and Development Web site, by the United Nations, New York.
<http://www.un.org/esa/socdev/index.html>

Summary: This gateway provides researchers access to the information under the Division for Social Policy and Development of the United Nations, including social affairs topics, conference information; information by the Commission for Social Development; reports on social affairs worldwide; official texts, agreements, and documents; and publications, including a major journal. It links to conference information, including statements archived from one significant conference for this area entitled the *World Summit for Social Development,* held in Copenhagen, 1995, and reviewed in Geneva in 2000.

The main objective of the Division for Social Policy and Development is to strengthen international cooperation for social development, with particular attention to the three core issues of poverty eradication, employment generation, and social integration, in order to provide opportunities and build higher standards of living for all.

Detailed Description: Topics on social affairs are available on the home page under sections on the issues, programs, conferences, services, bulletins, and *DESA News.* Issues covered include social integration, aging, families, youth, youth employment, persons with disabilities, poverty, advisory services, and nongovernmental organizations. For these issues, researchers will find a variety of comprehensive information, including reports, online periodicals, forums, international standards and conventions, the activities of the United Nations, definitions or briefings of priority issues, and global actions.

From the home page, information provided under the Commission for Social Development, which meets yearly, is very broad and includes documents from their annual meetings back to 1996 and also links to full-text reports related to their meetings, such as "National and International Cooperation for Social Development," available fully in PDF format.

Under Bulletins, access to the organization's new quarterly periodical, the *Bulletin on Social Integration Policies,* begun in 2002, is included. The aim of the *Bulletin* is to report on advances in social integration issues and trends as reflected in strategies, policies, and plans concerning persons with disabilities, older persons, youth, the family, and persons in situations of conflict. These were objectives that came from the World Summit on Social Development. Each issue of the *Bulletin* focuses on special social topics, for example aging, persons in situations of conflict, or disability. This *Bulletin* merged three earlier titles, *Disabled Persons Bulletin, Youth Information Bulletin,* and *Bulletin on Ageing.*

The World Summit on Social Development (WSSD) has its own Web site at <http://www.un.org/esa/socdev/wssd/>. It links under Issues on this page and includes online agreements, official texts and documents of the Summit, and an archive of statements made at the Summit. It is one of the most significant gatherings of world leaders on social development.

The parent agency of this Division, the *United Nations Department of Economic and Social Affairs* Web site at <http://www.un.org/esa/desa.htm> is a comprehensive Web site providing access to social and economic data, thematic issues (women, youth, globalization), and reports and periodicals online. It links to significant periodicals, among them the *World Economic and Social Survey,* described in this chapter, which is the United Nations' annual analysis of current developments in the world economy and in emerging social and development policy issues. The *United Nations Department of Economic and Social Affairs* Web site is also described in the Economics chapter of this book.

EU Culture Portal Web site, by the European Commission. <http://europa.eu.int/comm/culture/index_en.htm>

Summary: Available in English, Spanish, German, Italian, and French, this Web site focuses on gathering information sources and summarizing action of the European Union in the field of culture and related activities (i.e., music, dance, heritage, restoration) of the member states. Information is linked under the categories: Fields of Activity, National Web Sites, Events, Europe in Action, and Funding. It is not a publishing body, but does link to many sources of information within the EU and its member states.

The European Union's action in the field of culture is defined by its founding treaty, and not by the national cultural policies of its member states. "With its respect for cultural diversity, the EU aims to help open up European cultures whilst at the same time enhancing the common heritage which Europeans share. EU action looks to encourage cultural cooperation and exchange amongst Europeans and to support shared knowledge of cultural production right across the board."[2]

Detailed Description: The category Fields of Activity explains the direction of the EU in cultural support of activities such as theater, dance, books, and digital information. The National Web Site category links to a list of the online sites of ministries of culture within the European Union member states, candidate countries, and European economic area countries. The category Europe in Action is an overview of the activities related to cultural issues and their support within the European Union, including regulations. The Funding category summarizes the research programs, services, and cooperation within the context of the theme.

European Heritage Network Web site, by the European Heritage Network. <http://www.european-heritage.net/>

Summary: The *European Heritage Network* Web site provides access to European national cultural policies and an online cultural portal of selected links, which is an annotated, bibliographical online resource organizing and linking researchers to online information on European countries, culture, environment, urban planning, international cooperation, communication, research, and resources. The entire Web site is available in English, Spanish, and French, and there is a site map. An online, searchable multilingual thesaurus of cultural terms is under construction.

First established in 1999, the *European Heritage Network,* which grew out of the *HEREIN* project, is an intergovernmental initiative linking authorities responsible for the heritage Europe-wide and providing them with a common working tool for exploiting advanced information technology resources. The *HEREIN* Project has been through two phases, became the foundation of the cultural portal of the *European Heritage Network,* and is currently supported by the European Union.

Detailed Description: The national heritage policies are an online databank of the cultural heritage reports, which are required by Treaty. The information can be searched by country and theme, and nations may submit their reports online at this site. The cultural portal, under Selected Links, provides links to official texts, documents, databases, virtual visits, and directories of resources. It is a free, searchable online database of European countries heritage Web Sites, with searching available by country, themes, and keywords. Other information available through the *European Heritage Network* site includes news, an online forum, a thesaurus, FAQs, and information on the European Heritage Program, as well as on the European and International cooperation.

European Social Statistics: Demography, by the European Commission and *Eurostat,* Luxembourg, 2000– (print periodical with accompanying CD-ROM).

Summary: This annual publication reports on the social situation in Europe through detailed statistical data covering population, employment, the cost of labor, vocational training, education, health, work-related accidents, social exclusion, and social protection. It is published in several parts focused on separate themes, entitled *European Social Statistics: Demography; European Social Statistics: Labour Costs; European Social Statistics: Labour Market Policy, Expenditure and Participants;* and *European Social Statistics: Migration.* Each edition is published in English, French, and German text. The detailed data in these titles are drawn from numerous statistical sources, such as household surveys, enterprise surveys, household panels, and administrative business records. An accompanying CD-ROM includes tables and national country reports not available in printed version. Information in the CD-ROM is formatted in PDF, WORD, and Excel for the data tables.

A related series with individual titles is called *European Social Statistics.* Some data may be available online through Eurostat at <http://europa.eu.int.comm/eurostat/>

International Cultural Property Web site, by the U.S. Department of State, Washington, D.C. <http://exchanges.state.gov/culprop/>

Summary: This Web site defines the problems of pillage, looting, theft, prosecution, and recovery of cultural property worldwide, and it provides full-text documents and reports, as well as an image database of restricted objects online. The site is searchable and provides a site index.

The U.S. Department of State is responsible for implementing the Convention on Cultural Property Implementation Act (the Treaty), the enabling legislation for the 1970 UNESCO Convention on the Means of Prohibiting and Preventing the Illicit Import, Export and Transfer of Ownership of Cultural Property. In accordance with the Treaty, the U.S. Department of State accepts requests from countries for import restrictions on archaeological or ethnological artifacts, the pillage of which places their national cultural heritage in jeopardy. The Cultural Property Advisory Committee, appointed by the president of the United States, reviews these requests and makes recommendations to the U.S. Department of State. Under the president's authority, the State Department makes a decision with regard to the request and may enter into a cultural property agreement with the requesting country. The cultural property staff supports these functions and re-lated activities and serves as a center of expertise on global cultural heritage protection issues.

Detailed Description: This site includes online reports and articles on topics such as Protecting Cultural Property Worldwide; the U.S. response, which includes a glossary and definitions; and U.S. and International Laws. The topic on Laws contains full text of U.S. laws and international bilateral and multilateral treaties and conventions on cultural property. It also provides an online directory of contacts and hot links to U.S. and international law enforcement agencies.

The site index provides a clear overview of what is contained under each major topic and also lists agreements, emergency actions, and import restrictions alphabetically by country. Under each country is an information page, an image collection, and online agreements. Researchers can also easily link to the image database from the home page. Only selected countries are available, including Bolivia, Cyprus, El Salvador, Guatemala, Italy, Mali, Nicaragua, and Peru, with more planned. Each country image collection page provides a chronological table, sources for the images, an outline of categories subject to import restriction, and links to thumbnail images.

International Organization for Migration (IOM) Web site, Geneva, Switzerland. <http://www.iom.int/>

Summary: A rich source of information concerning migration issues through the world, the IOM Web site provides information and news about the IOM's projects and reports on its activities in the field of migration. Some publications, books and magazines, are available at no cost electronically, although most are sales publications. Two special features are drop-down boxes with quick links to selected pages and documents, project Web sites, and IOM country Web sites. Simple and advanced searching is available. An online portrait gallery links to online documents of the session of its governing body, and briefing notes for the press are also included.

IOM is also concerned with migration management activities worldwide; research, particularly on policy-related issues; news; and publications. It is committed to the principle that humane and orderly migration benefits migrants and society. As the leading international organization for migration, IOM acts with its partners in the international community to: assist in meeting the growing operational challenges of migration management, advance understanding of migration issues, encourage social and economic development through migration, and uphold the human dignity and well-being of migrants.

Detailed Description: In addition to its major publications, described under the category What We Know and most of which are not available online, the *IOM* Web site features an online portrait gallery, links to online documents of the session of its governing body, and briefing notes for the press. Major publications of the International Organization on Migration include two journals, *International Migration* (1963–) (ISSN 0020-7985) and *Trafficking in Migrants,* a Migration Research Series, books, and studies and reports. *International Migration* is a scholarly journal published quarterly by Blackwell Publishers Limited that analyzes both theoretical and applied aspects of issues of international migration. Reports on recent conferences, workshops, and publications are included. The Migration Research Series publishes policy-relevant current research on migration. The Publications section also links to more information under multilateral migration issues, references, related sites, a calendar of events, and an archive. *IOM News* is its online newsletter.

Most IOM books are published through the United Nations Sales Office; however, researchers will find some free book titles available online at no charge from the Publications section link to books. Some examples of significant titles include its *Compendium of Intergovernmental Organizations Active in the Field of Migration,* 2002 (PDF) and a new annual serial title, *International Migration Report* (New York: United Nations, 2002–), which provides world, regional, and individual country statistical profiles of immigration and emigration, including refugees and basic demographic indicators. Researchers will also find free online reports in PDF format under Publications and the link to Studies and Reports, which links to free concise analyses of emerging migration issues. Other significant titles, available for purchase only, are published in its series entitled *International Migration Policy Program.*

Report on the World Social Situation, prepared by the Division for Social Policy and Development of the Department of Economic and Social Affairs, United Nations, New York, 1952– (ISSN 0082-8068). <http://www.un.org/esa/socdev/rwss/> (print annual title with selected sections only online).

Summary: This series of reports are devoted to in-depth discussion of specific worldwide social problems. The 2001 report is the 15th in a series dating from 1952 whose purpose is to provide a single-volume summary of global developments seen from a social perspective.

Some of the content, structure, and shape of the report have changed over the years, but most of the reports focus discussion on a special theme. Introductions, summaries, and conclusions are drawn.

The mission of this UN Division is to monitor global social trends, identify emerging issues, and assess their implications for social policy at the national and international levels. More information available from the home page of this Division is described separately in this chapter under the resource entitled *Gateway to Social Policy and Development* Web site.

Description: In 2001, the introduction and overview were downloadable from the Web (WORD and PDF), and the entire issue was devoted to social and economic development in relationship to globalization, social change, and social equity. Among the topics are assessing trends, institutional framework, living conditions, quality of life, social disruptions, discrimination, privacy, social protection, and new challenges, equity, and ethical considerations. Statistical tables and figures support the text.

The *2001 Report on the World Social Situation* is the 15th in a series of reports on the subject dating from 1952. The content, structure, and shape of the reports have undergone change, but the main purpose of the series continues to be to provide both participants in intergovernmental debates in the United Nations and a wider audience with a handy, single-volume, succinct summary of global developments seen from a social perspective. The subject matter covered in the series has changed over the years, expanding with successive reports.

Nine of the previous fourteen editions included an in-depth discussion of a special theme: social problems of urbanization in economically underdeveloped regions (1957); the interrelationship of social and economic development and the problem of "balance" (1961); practical methods of promoting social change at the local level (1965); patterns of government expenditure on social services (1978, supplement); removing obstacles to social progress (1982); forces of social change (1985); critical social situation in Africa (1989, annex); major issues and dilemmas (1993); and poverty, unemployment, and discrimination (1997).

UNESCO, the United Nations Economic, Social, and Cultural Organization, Resources

Culture Web site, by *UNESCO.* <http://www.unesco.org/culture/>

Summary: This searchable and comprehensive Web site on culture, available in English, French, and Spanish, categorizes information into thematic sections: Cultural Policy Resources, Issues on Cultural Development, Copyright, Cultural Enterprises and Industries, Tangible and Intangible Culture Heritage, World Heritage Centre, Culture and Youth, Culture: Women and Gender Equality, and others. It also provides a glossary, links, site map, news and events, press information, and FAQs in a drop-down box. The Publications category is a separate section that highlights special forum and conference information. The founders of UNESCO wrote these words in their constitution, adopted in London in 1945, post–World War II:

> …since wars begin in the minds of men, it is in the minds of men that the defences of peace must be constructed;…the wide diffusion of culture, and the education of humanity for justice and liberty and peace and indispensable to the dignity of man and constitute a sacred duty which all the nations must fulfill in a spirit of mutual assistance and concern.…[3]

Detailed Description: UNESCO is a major publisher and vendor of its own titles and has an online bookshop. The Publications link from the home page contains links to online periodicals including *UNESCO Sources,* <http://www.unescosources.org/>, which is archived back to no. 80, 1996. A searchable archive is provided. An alphabetical and a thematic index to publications are provided, as well as online bibliographies and downloadable brochures and documents. The *New Courier,* a major monthly periodical on culture, also published by UNESCO is available online through this Web site and described separately in this chapter. Also described separately in this chapter is its *World Culture Report,* a significant report on culture throughout the world, with accompanying statistics <http://www.unesco.org/culture/worldreport/>.

The Statutory Texts section from the home page links to online full-text UNESCO official documents. It contains key texts on international cultural policy arranged by type, in reverse chronological order. It contains action plans, agreements, charters, conventions, declarations, protocols, and recommendations, either issued by UNESCO or under its auspices.

UNESCO New Courier (previously *UNESCO Courier*) (print and online periodical). <http://www.unesco.org/courier/>

Summary: The monthly periodical *UNESCO New Courier* continues the earlier title *UNESCO Courier,* having changed its title in 2002, but continuing publication since 1948. It contains feature articles on topics covering culture, development, and society and is richly illustrated. Each issue focuses on a theme. This periodical is published in over 30 language editions. The online version also offers a searchable archive of online issues and links to UNESCO's online photo bank.

The General Conference of UNESCO unanimously adopted a Universal Declaration on Cultural Diversity maintaining that cultural diversity is one of the roots of development as necessary for humankind as biodiversity is for nature and affirming the importance of respect for the diversity of cultures, tolerance, dialogue, and cooperation in a climate of mutual trust and understanding. As a result, the monthly periodical was affected by a title change and by a greater focus on cultural diversity.

Description: The periodical contains feature articles on people and places, human rights, education, ethics, planet, culture, and media, as well as interviews. UNESCO in action and UNESCO in brief sections report and summarize activities of UNESCO. There is also a photo gallery and a Zoom photo awards section. The online archive of electronic issues is searchable back to 1998.

World Culture Report, by UNESCO, Paris, 1998– (print biennial title, with latest 2000 edition available online). <http://www.unesco.org/culture/worldreport/>

Summary: The issues of this irregularly published report focus on specific concerns with culture and diversity, which is an important focus of UNESCO to seek ways of preserving culture, customs, and language. The first report in 1998 focused on the message that conflicts are not necessarily an obstacle to development. It was subtitled "Culture, Creativity and Markets." The second issue of 2000 focuses on "Cultural Diversity, Conflicts and Pluralism" and explores cultural challenges worldwide. UNESCO provides information, statistical analysis, and policy recommendations about cultural diversity in the era of information and communications.

Detailed Description: The 1998 report has seven parts and subsections, all written by individual authors and with their own introductions. These parts cover culture and economic development, global sociocultural processes, creativity, markets and cultural policies, public opinion and global ethics, methodology, building cultural indicators, implications for policy, and statistical tables and culture indicators. Some of the subtopics include cultural heritage, world music, heritage and cyberculture, culture and democracy, and recasting cultural policy. This first issue defines some of the parameters of discussing culture indicators and the cultural policy of countries. The statistical tables include information on newspaper, radio, recorded music, arts, archives, tourism, communication, cultural trends, cultural trade, and much more.

The 2000 report <http://www.unesco.org/culture/worldreport/> focuses on cultural diversity, conflict, and pluralism. In seven parts with articles all written by individual authors, this title summarizes the concept of cultural diversity, analyzes the issues and current debates, discusses cultural policies and cultural heritage, covers new media and cultural knowledge, international public opinion and national identity, and measures culture (practice) and statistical tables, and culture indicators. Each part has a separate introduction. Acronyms and a list of tables and graphs accompany the text. New tables are included in the 2000 version, dealing with multicultural areas not in the first report, including leading languages, leading religions, national festivals, folk and religious festivals, most visited cultural sites, and most visited natural sites. If ordered in print, attached to the book is the CD-ROM *Guide to Cultural Resources of the World.*

World Heritage Center Web site, by UNESCO.
   <http://whc.unesco.org/>

Summary: This Web site provides the latest World Heritage List by UNESCO and also access to the periodical *World Heritage Review,* a print and online resource. The *World Heritage List* is available in English and many other languages and lists properties, cultural sites, natural sites, and others in member states to the World Heritage Convention. The site also lists the newly inscribed sites on the *World Heritage List* and provides news, reports, and a kids' and an educational subsection online. It also links to other worldwide sites on culture. Researchers may access these sites by world/country/detail maps. Also available on this Web site are virtual tours and other detailed information about the specific heritage sites. It is available in English and French.

World Heritage is a UNESCO program established in 1972. A Committee established by the convention decides on the sites to be inscribed on the list.

According to the World Heritage Convention, "cultural heritage" is a monument, group of buildings or site of historical, aesthetic, archaeological, scientific, ethnological or anthropological value. "Natural heritage" designates outstanding physical, biological, and geological features; habitats of threatened plants or animal species and areas of value on scientific or aesthetic grounds or from the point of view of conservation. UNESCO's World Heritage mission is to: encourage countries to sign the Convention and ensure the protection of their own natural and cultural heritage; encourage States Parties to the Convention to nominate sites within their national territory for inclusion on the World Heritage List.[4]

Detailed Description: The record of Decisions of the World Heritage Committee is included under special events on the Web site. There are also links to a World Heritage Calendar, a special *World Heritage List* for cultural sites in danger, information on the UN International Year for Cultural Heritage, information on the Virtual Congress: World Heritage in the Digital Age <http://www.virtualworldheritage.org>, and finally, information on the international congresses on world heritage sponsored by UNESCO.

Under the Sites subsection on the main home page, researchers will find virtual tours, links to the world heritage sites, conservation methods, travel diaries, success stories, and information on sustainable tourism. Earlier print versions of the *World Heritage List* were published in English under the title *Properties Inscribed on the World Heritage List.*

The *World Heritage Review* is a richly illustrated bimonthly periodical highlighting culture and heritage sites worldwide. It is available in print and online back to June 1996 in English, French, and Spanish. Articles may focus on a type of site, such as sacred mountains or world heritage railways, or specific sites. Each issue covers a variety of regions and includes many beautiful photographs. New heritage sites named and the world heritage sites in danger are highlighted regularly.

United Nations Resources

Humanitarian Affairs Web site, by the United Nations (UN). <http://www.un.org/ha/>

Summary: A comprehensive Web site that organizes information on humanitarian assistance worldwide under the specific UN offices, the Humanitarian Affairs Web site is subdivided into these topics: Relief-Web, Landmines, Chernobyl disaster, Special Representative for Children and Armed Conflict, the Iraq Programme, and more. All of the links lead to useful research information online, such as publications, data, reports, and documents. Of special note, *ReliefWeb* <http://www.reliefweb.int/> organizes information online to serve the needs of the humanitarian relief community under the categories highlights, resources, and links. It also lists information and background on humanitarian assistance by country of the world.

Under ReliefWeb is the *Humanitarian Information Network (HIN)* searchable online resource. One of the still useful titles published under the reorganized United Nations Department of Humanitarian Affairs on the *ReliefWeb* page is the title *Humanitarian Report, 1997,* which covers in two parts the evolution of humanitarian coordination 1992–1997 and major developments in emergency relief coordination, complex emergencies, and natural disasters. The *HIN* online archive and online newsletters are also useful sources of information.

United Nations High Commissioner for Refugees (UNHCR) Web site, Geneva, Switzerland. <http://www.unhcr.ch/>

Summary: As the major UN agency dealing with refugee issue and problems, the materials found here provide comprehensive coverage in the form of online reports, magazines, documents, conventions, basic facts and other statistics, research, publications, and news. An online photo gallery and a pictorial history are also available on this searchable site. Search options include advanced searching, quick links to subjects through a drop-down box and a site map. It also offers a thematic Web site on the protection of refugees. Major publications include periodicals, including the online *Refugees Magazine* and annual reports, such as the online *State of the World's Refugees.*

The Office of the United Nations High Commissioner for Refugees was established on December 14, 1950, by the United Nations General Assembly. The agency is mandated to lead and coordinate international action to protect refugees and resolve refugee problems worldwide. Its primary purpose is to safeguard the rights and well-being of refugees. It strives to ensure that everyone can exercise the right to seek asylum and find safe refuge in another State, with the option to return home voluntarily, integrate locally, or to resettle in a third country.

Detailed Description: Three major categories from the home page, Statistics, Publications, and Research/Evaluation, link to documents and reports. From publications, researchers may access several of this organization's main reference publications, its

monthly *Refugees Magazine* and *The State of the World's Refugees. The State of the World's Refugees* is issued irregularly, and the latest edition (2000) is available online in PDF format in English, French, Italian, and Russian. It summarizes the state of displaced persons worldwide and the activities of the UNHCR and also provides an overview, the changing dynamics of the current situation, and a statistical annex.

Under Statistics, the *Statistical Yearbook* is available online in HTML or PDF format, with statistical tables and maps available for download. The series is online from the 2001 edition, the first of a series. A print copy may be requested free of charge. Its main purpose is to provide relevant, consistent data on refugees worldwide, as well as analysis of basic trends, patterns, issues of concern, and challenges to refugees and asylum seekers and provides a chapter with statistical indicators by country. Maps are provided in PDF format.

The quarterly *Refugees Magazine* is available linked from the Publications category, and most of the articles from it are provided free online back to March 1994 (HTML and PDF, format varies). Another periodical *Refugee Survey Quarterly* is a scholarly journal, only available in print. It includes statements, articles, conference reports, United Nations documents, bibliographies, reports on selected international and regional instruments, and selected United Nations resolutions and reports on refugees.

Many other documents are provided on the UNHCR Web site. Under the category Statistics, researchers will find the *UNHCR Statistical Reports* (online documents), *Asylum Trends, Global Refugee Trends* (annual statistics), special research reports, and a subsection entitled Statistics at a Glance. From the category Maps on the home page are online maps (PDF format) by region of the world, in a listing that is searchable by title, country, and full texts. Included are country maps, aerial maps, and satellite images. The category Protection Publications contains UNHCR legal handbooks and guidelines covering refugee protection issues.

From the home page, the Research/Evaluation category contains the Archives, Library, the Evaluation and Policy Analysis Unit, and Country of Origin and Legal Information. Archives leads to information concerning the archives services available at the UNHCR. The Library's holdings are searchable online. The Evaluation and Policy Analysis Unit provides electronic versions of all evaluation reports produced by UNHCR from 1994 on (full text). These are evaluations on UNHCR projects, programs, practices, and policies. Also available is reporting on issues, such as Afghan refugees and child refugees, and a series of online full-text research reports entitled *New Issues in Refugee Research.* Other miscellaneous categories from the home page include Special Events (linking to a kids' page), Teaching Tools, Partnership Guides, and Questions and Answers.

United Nations Social Development Pathfinder Web site, by the Dag Hammarskjöld Library, New York. <http://www.un.org/Depts/dhl/pathfind/social/0901.htm> (select Social Development).

Summary: Prepared by the Dag Hammarskjöld Library, this pathfinder, available in English and French, provides an online annotated bibliography for researchers interested in social development reference materials published by the organizations within the United Nations systems. Included are bibliographic information and brief annotations for the resources. Both current and historical titles are included, and if available on the *United Nations* Web site, a direct link is provided. This Pathfinder identifies major publications of the organizations comprising the United Nations system. Materials included were selected on the basis of currency, relevance, and usefulness, such as: global studies and reports, handbooks and guides, bibliographies and indices, international statistical publications, compilations of treaties, resolutions and documents, annual reports of UN bodies and specialized agencies, and some reference works.

Detailed Description: Researchers must first select Social Development from the list of the general United Nations Pathfinder site. Under the section Social Development, researchers will find information on the following categories: general issues, sustainable development, women, children, disabled persons, refugees, poverty, humanitarian assistance, crime prevention, narcotic drugs, education, health, and aging persons. Under the section Culture, researchers will find an online bibliography of titles on the topic of culture.

World Economic and Social Survey: Trends and Policies in the World Economy, by the United Nations Department of Economic and Social Affairs, New York, 1994–. <http://www.un.org/esa/analysis/wess/> (selected sections online, including Chapter 1, "The State of the World Economy").

Summary: A reference title published in two parts, this report is the United Nations' annual analysis of current developments in the world economy, emerging policy issues, review of major developments in international trade, and financial resources of developing countries. It contains a forecast of short-term global and regional economic trends. Statistical tables give standardized data on macroeconomic, international trade, and finance. This annual title has been published in print since 1949 under various titles, and under this title since 1994.

Detailed Description: Part I of this report is a textual overview of the world economy, the international economy, and the current situation in the world economies for the year. Part II analyzes economic, social, and development trends worldwide, including globalization, natural disasters, and other forces. It is a very rich source of statistical tables, which are provided in an annex and throughout the text in boxes, tables, and figures.

Chapter 1, "The State of the World Economy," is available online in PDF format, back to 1997, and Table of Contents of this title is available online back to 1993, with some press releases. The chapter is a textual summary of economic trends in the world (the executive summary). The entire report analyzes economic and social trends and effects and supports the analyses with data. Conclusions are drawn. Part II provides an overview of the worldwide forces to be discussed and especially discusses the question of vulnerability of countries and their economic and social fortunes. From 1949–1954 this title was published as *World Economic Report,* and from 1955–1993 it was published as *World Economic Survey.*

NONGOVERNMENTAL SOURCES

Culturelink Network Web site, by Culturelink. <http://www.culturelink.org/culpol/>

Summary: A searchable site that provides a database of cultural policies since 1997, *Culturelink* also features country profiles in HTML or PDF formats. *Culturelink* also publishes a CD-ROM version of its online network. Databases cover institutions, resources, and policies. *Culturelink* also provides news, research, publications, and conference reports online, as well as directories of cultural institutions worldwide. A member-supported organization, *Culturelink,* the Network of Networks for Research and Cooperation in Cultural Development, was established by UN-

ESCO and the Council of Europe in 1989 in Paris. Its mission is

to strengthen communication among its members, encouraging international and intercultural communication and collaboration, as well as joint research projects.

The long-term objective is the development of a world-wide information system for the study of cultural development and cooperation. To this end, Culturelink collects, processes and disseminates information on cultural development, cultural life and policies.[5]

Detailed Description: Under the subsection Publications, *Culturelink* describes its paper and electronic publishing and provides online publications regularly. The paper publications include the journal *Culturelink Review,* published quarterly in English, which researches and disseminates information on new concepts; research challenges; meetings and conferences; and reports on trends, experiences, and practice in the field of cultural development, cultural life, and policies. It also publishes the *Culturelink Joint Publications Series,* which are the published proceedings from conferences organized by the Network; the *Culturelink Directory Series,* which are directories of institutions and databases in the field of cultural development; and also the *Guide to the Culturelink Network,* which describes information on institutions and networks in the field of cultural development from around the world. Published regularly as a selection from the printed edition, the fully searchable online edition of the *Culturelink Review* is archived back to 1994. Also of interest to cultural researchers is the list published of e-resources for culture on the Internet, at <http://www.culturelink.org/dbase/links.html>, under the subsection Resources.

RESEARCH STRATEGIES

The reference resources described in this chapter will be approached separately in this section under social resources and cultural resources. General, research, regional, and specific resources are evaluated for both cultural and social resources. Under culture, one general resource is the periodical the ***UNESCO New Courier,*** by the United Nations, Educational, Scientific and Cultural Organization. As it provides articles and illustrations on specific cultural topics, places, policies, and events throughout the world, it is an excellent general resource for beginning research.

The ***Courier*** is online beginning in 1998, and there is a searchable archive.

Another excellent beginning resource is the ***Culture*** Web site by UNESCO. Researchers can use this resource either as a beginning resource or as a guide to research information. Consult this Web site specifically for a very comprehensive overview of culture in the world, also for a glossary, a guide to issues, and information on legal statutes relating to culture. UNESCO is a major publisher, and this Web site offers a mix of online titles and titles that can be ordered through its online bookshop or found in libraries.

Specific resources in the area of culture include UNESCO's ***The World Heritage Center*** Web site, which offers the ***World Heritage Review,*** an online journal, and a ***World Heritage List*** of cultural and natural significant heritage sites worldwide. Researchers will find links to specific sites and virtual tours. Another specific resource is the ***Cultural Profiles Project,*** by Citizenship and Immigration Canada, which assists citizens with understanding cultural backgrounds of new immigrants to Canada. Although this is specific to Canada, it may be useful to beginning research on world cultural backgrounds. In addition, it is an example of what researchers may find on a national level—national government offices dealing with cultural issues that may have information with a very broad scope. The ***International Cultural Property*** Web site, by the U.S. Department of State, publishes reports and other information on the theft and recovery of cultural property worldwide.

Regional resources in the area of culture include the ***EU Culture Portal*** Web site, by the European Commission, which gathers information on cultural activities in Europe and links to the ministries of culture in Europe, as well as the ***European Heritage Network*** Web site, by the European Heritage Network, which provides access to national heritage policies in a database ***(HEREIN),*** regulations, and online documents. Both of these Internet resources are gateways to information published by countries and agencies within the European Union.

A more advanced, research-oriented resource on culture is UNESCO's ***World Culture Report,*** an annual title providing an overview of cultural awareness, diversity, and protection worldwide since 1998. It is a scholarly reference title that also reports on government policies on culture in a constantly changing world and includes statistical tables. Another research resource is the nongovernmental ***Culturelink Network*** Web site, which provides databases, publications, and conference reports online, as well as directories through which researchers will find national offices responsible for cultural development and cooperation and cultural policy.

Under the topic of social affairs, one general research resource is the annual report *World Economic and Social Survey: Trends and Policies in the World Economy,* by the United Nations Department of Economic and Social Affairs. This reference report, published since 1949 under various titles, provides an excellent overview of social and economic trends and policies, major developments, and issues of concerns. Statistical tables support the text. Only selected information is available online, and although it has a global scope, it is not particularly easy to use. Even beginning researchers will find the overview in Part I understandable and a good way to put economic developments in relationship with social trends.

Another general resource is the *Report of the World Social Situation,* prepared by the Division for Social Policy and Development of the Department of Economic and Social Affairs, United Nations. It also is a scholarly resource and focuses even more on social trends than the *World Economic and Social Survey.* Published in a series since 1952, parts of the latest reports are online, specifically an overview that is appropriate for even the most beginning of researchers. Each title focuses on a theme in social trends worldwide of global concern.

Specific social resources include the United Nations Web site on *Humanitarian Affairs,* the *International Organization for Migration (IOM)* Web site, and the *United Nations High Commissioner for Refugees* Web site. Users may expect to find online titles and discussion and analysis of the issues.

In the area of regional social resources, the United Nations also publishes excellent statistical yearbooks and surveys covering specific regions of the world (i.e., the Arab world, Asia, Africa). Researchers may consult the *United Nations Social Development Pathfinder* Web site, where these resources are listed and annotated. Often social and economic data or social and development data are presented in one publication. For example, for social statistics in Europe, researchers should consult the annual *European Social Statistics: Demography;* however, this is just the beginning of research. The main publishing body of the *European Union* publishes many documents, books, and statistical data for social statistics. To search for titles related to European social statistics, researchers can refer to the publications portal of the

EU at <http://europa.eu.int/publications/index_en.htm> or they can consult EUROSTAT for statistics published by the European Union at <http://europa.eu.int/comm/eurostat/>

For a research Web portal on government social policy and development, researchers may consult the *Division for Social Policy and Development* Web site, by the Division for Social Policy and Development, Department of Economic and Social Affairs, United Nations, which leads to comprehensive information in the United Nations system published in this area. This same Division also publishes the *Report on the World Social Situation.*

FOR FURTHER READING: COMPREHENSIVE WEB SITES AND OTHER REFERENCE SOURCES

Cultural Co-operation Web site, by the Council of Europe, Strasbourg, France.
   <http://www.coe.int/t/e/Cultural_Co-operation/>

This Web site reports and links to cultural information and topics available through the Council of Europe, including culture, heritage, environment, education, sport, youth, cinema, modern languages, and photographic exhibitions. Full text of some reports is published on its Web site, such as *Forty Years of European Cultural Co-operation.* The Statute of the Council of Europe, signed in 1949, says that the organization's aims are to work toward greater unity between its members for protecting their joint heritage and for social and economics progress.

Interamerican Conference on Social Security (CISS) Web site, Mexico City.
   <http://www.ciss.org.mx/>

This agency is a specialized international and regional agency whose objective is to contribute to the development of social security in the countries of America, cooperating and coordinating with other international agencies. Of special interest is the Publications section, available from the home page, which links to the bimonthly *Social Security Journal,* available at no charge electronically since 1992, and its current featured report, *The Americas Social Security Report 2002.*

Social Indicators of Development. Baltimore: Published for the World Bank [by] the Johns Hopkins University Press, and Washington, D.C.: World Bank, 1987– (ISSN 1012-8026).

Published annually from 1987–1996, this is an excellent resource for statistical tables with social and development indicators within this time frame. Most of the information is organized under country name, with data given over five years for these categories: poverty, short-term income indicators, social indicators, human resources, natural resources, income, expenditure, and investment in human capital. Some charts accompany the statistical tables. It was also published on diskette. For a related current World Bank statistics, users may check the *World Bank* Web site <http://www.worldbank.org> or consult the Development chapter.

United Nations Economic and Social Development
Web site. <http://www.un.org/esa/>

This thematic Web site links to the organizations within the United Nations systems that deal with topics such as development and social development, crime, women, drugs, environment, human rights, statistics, environment, and more. Researchers may access information online concerning meetings, documents, research, and analysis on these issues. It includes an index, and its National Government Information link, <http://www.un.org/esa/national.htm>, links to national governments' information agencies Web sites.

UNRISD (United Nations Research Institute for Social Development)
Web site, Geneva, Switzerland. <http://www.unrisd.org/>

UNRISD is an autonomous United Nations agency that carries out research on the social dimensions of contemporary problems affecting development. Unpublished reports may be found online full text under the Publications category, which features for-sale publications. Reports on projects and case studies may be found online under the Research category. Quick Links is a category linking to about 20 topics on social development. This site is more fully described in the Development chapter of this book.

World Social Science Report,
edited by Ali Kazancigil and David Makinson. Paris: UNESCO/Elsevier, 1999 (UNESCO(058)/S678) (ISBN 9-23103-602-5).

This report provides an overview and global picture of the social science as practiced, including infrastructures and situations in the regions of the world, data and its utilization, and issues and applications. It covers social sciences applications in professional fields, technology, and natural sciences.

NOTES

1. For more information about the cultural profiles, contact the AMNI Centre, Faculty of Social Work, University of Toronto, 246 Bloor Street West, Room 100, Toronto, Ontario M5S 1A1, Tel: 416-978-3273.

2. *EU Culture Portal* Web site, by the European Union (EU), <http://europa.eu.int/comm/culture/about_en.htm, Dec. 2002>.

3. *Constitution of the United Nations Educational, Scientific, and Cultural Organization* (adopted 1945 and amended through the 31st session), UNESCO Web site, PDF, <http://www.unesco.org> (The Organization: Constitution: Official Text) p. 7.

4. *World Heritage Center* Web site, by UNESCO, <http://whc.unesco.org/nwhc/pages/doc/main.htm, Dec. 2002>.

5. *Culturelink Network* Web site, by Culturelink, <http://www.culturelink.org/network/index.html>.

CHAPTER 19
Statistics

CHAPTER OVERVIEW

Statistical sources can be found in every chapter of this book. The sources described in this chapter focus mainly on three broad subject areas of statistical indicators: social, demographic, and economic. These sources are included in this chapter because they:

- Are general statistical titles with broad data coverage of the world or a large region of the world
- Cover general subject areas, particularly in the three areas—demographic, social, and economic

Researchers interested in more statistical information in the economic and social subject areas should consult these two chapters in this book. Within the statistical resources of this chapter are many subdivisions with different sources focusing on different aspects. Researchers should pay close attention to the dates of the information within these resources, because date coverage varies widely among the sources and even within the same sources.

Representing the governmental point of view are the European Union, Organisation for Economic Co-operation and Development (OECD), and the United Nations, three of the largest suppliers of international statistical data. Unlike the United States, which spreads statistical reporting out among the various agencies, the European Union, the OECD, and the United Nations each have a centralized statistical body: Eurostat for the European Union; the Statistics Directorate of the OECD; and the Statistics Division for the United Nations. Each of these makes statistics available electronically, although some require a subscription or a fee, and through annual print publications. Statistics for regions of the world are detailed in the various regional statistical yearbooks published by the United Nations and publications of the European Union, and all are described in this chapter. Although many countries publish their own statistical yearbooks, there simply is not enough space in this chapter to mention them all. Under the For Further Reading: Web Sites section of this chapter is an online list of countries with links to each nation's national statistical office compiled by the U.S. Census Bureau. Another way to access this information is through *Current National Statistical Compendiums*, a nongovernmental source, which will be described in this chapter. Additionally, other international organizations also publish their own statistics. Although many of these sources have been described in other chapters, the print and online resource *Index to International Statistics,* which will also be described in this chapter, captures this information and provides an index/abstract as well as a subscription microfiche collection of the documents themselves.

Governmental Sources Discussed

European Union Resources

Basic Statistics of the European Union. Brussels: Statistical Office of the European Communities, 1995– (ISSN 0081-4873).

Eurostat Web site, by the Statistical Office of the European Communities, Luxembourg. <http://europa.eu.int/comm/eurostat/>

Eurostat Yearbook: A Statistical Guide to Europe. Luxembourg: Office for Official Publications of the European Communities, 1995–.

Regions Statistical Yearbook. Luxembourg: Office for Official Publications of the European Communities, 1995– (print, CD, and online subscription publication).

Organisation for Economic Co-operation and Development (OECD) Resources

OECD Statistics Portal Web site, by the OECD Statistics Directorate, Paris. <http://www.oecd.org/statsportal/>

United Nations Resources

African Statistical Yearbook. Addis Ababa, Ethiopia: Economic Commission for Africa, 1974– (ISSN 0252-5488).

Demographic Yearbook/Annuaire Déemographique. New York: Dept. of Economic and Social Affairs, Statistical Office, United Nations, 1948– (ISSN 0082-8041) (print and CD-ROM title).

Monthly Bulletin of Statistics. New York: Dept. of Economic and Social Affairs, Statistics Division, United Nations, 1947– (print and online resource).

Population Information Network (POPIN) Web site, by the United Nations, New York. <http://http://www.un.org/popin/>

Statistical Abstract of the ESCWA Region. New York: Economic and Social Commission for Western Asia, 1974– (ISSN 0252-4333).

Statistical Yearbook / Annuaire Statistique. New York: Dept. of Economic and Social Affairs, Statistics Division, 1948– (ISSN 0082-8459) (print and CD-ROM title).

Statistical Yearbook/Annuaire Statistique/UNESCO. Paris: UNESCO, 1963–1999 (ISSN 0082-7541).

Statistical Yearbook for Asia and the Pacific. Bangkok, Thailand: Economic and Social Commission for Asia and the Pacific, 1973– (ISSN 0252-3655).

Statistical Yearbook for Latin America, 1973–1984 (ISSN 0251-9445).

Statistical Yearbook for Latin America and the Caribbean, Santiago, Chile: Economic Commission for Latin America, 1985– (ISSN 1014-0697).

Statistics Division Web site, by the United Nations Dept. of Economic and Social Affairs, New York. <http://unstats.un.org>

UNESCO Institute for Statistics Web site, by the UNESCO Institute for Statistics, University of Montreal, Quebec, Canada. <http://www.uis.unesco.org>

World Statistics in Brief/World Statistics Pocketbook. New York: Dept. for Economic and Social Information and Policy Analysis, Statistical Division, United Nations, 1976–.

Nongovernmental Sources Discussed

Current National Statistical Compendiums. Bethesda, Md.: Congressional Information Service, 1974– (microfiche collection).

Index to International Statistics (IIS). Bethesda, Md.: LexisNexis (ISSN 0737-4461) (previously published by Congressional Information Service, now a part of LexisNexis) (print/online index to a microfiche set; subscription online service).

OFFSTATS: Official Statistics on the Web Web site, by the University of Auckland, New Zealand. <http://www.library.auckland.ac.nz/subjects/stats/offstats.OFFSTATSmain.htm>

GOVERNMENTAL SOURCES

European Union Resources

Basic Statistics of the European Union. Brussels: Statistical Office of the European Communities, 1995– (ISSN 0081-4873).

Summary: Originally entitled *Basic Statistics of the Community* (ca. 1959–1994), renamed *Basic Statistics of the European Union* (1995–), an annual statistical pocketbook publication available in eight languages, English, Danish, German, Greek, French, Italian, Dutch, and Portuguese, contains information on all 15 of the European Union countries (Austria, Belgium, Denmark, Finland, France, Germany, Greece, Ireland, Italy, Luxembourg, Netherlands, Portugal, Spain, Sweden, and the United Kingdom). General statistics are included as well as those on Economy and Finance, Population and Social Conditions, Energy and Industry, Agriculture/Forestry/Fisheries, Foreign Trade, Services and Transport, and Environment. No commentary on the data is available. Statistics are at the country level except for Population and Social Conditions, which goes down to the region within country level. There are also some graphs. Comparison data are available for Canada, United States, Japan, and USSR. Beginning in 1996 the member countries of CESTAT (Central European Cooperation in Statistics), consisting of Czech Republic, Slovakia, Poland, and Hungary, are also included for comparison purposes.

Eurostat Web site, by the Statistical Office of the European Communities, Luxembourg. <http://europa.eu.int/comm/eurostat/>

Summary: The premier online site for European Union statistics, Eurostat, is both a combination of pay-for service and no-charge site, depending on the types of statistics or online resource being accessed. The first-time user has to register by completing the in-depth registration form. An e-mail notification is sent out when the registration is received and access authorized. The site itself is divided into 10 main headings: Themes, Publications, Data, Metadata, Free and Online, Eurostat Activities, Data Shop Services, Help and FAQ, Contact, and All Services. In addition, current releases, news, and product information can be accessed from the home page.

Detailed Description: The best place to begin using Eurostat is to first visit the Help and FAQ home page heading, which provides a site map and frequently asked questions, but, most importantly, a first visit area. Questions such as content, fee and free services, accessibility, services offered, and how to begin are addressed in this section.

Themes is the first main home page heading discussed, and this is the way all of Eurostat's statistical information is arranged. The themes are General Statistics (by geographic area), Economy and Finances, Population and Social Conditions, Industry/Trade/ Services, Agriculture and Fisheries, External Trade, Transport, Environment and Energy, and Science and Technology. These themes are found on the pages of every heading along with a search engine, which allows for searching by browsing or keyword. Each theme includes relevant free data, news releases, Eurostat news, an alert service, database information, ask for statistics (a pay for service), essential products, and available products. Whether there is a fee attached or it is free depends on the type of product being accessed.

Publications, the second main home page heading, allows for online access to Eurostat print publications such as *Panorama of the European Union,* pocket books, detailed tables, methods and nomenclatures, research in official statistics, working papers and studies, *Statistics in Focus,* and catalogues. Access to these publications is via a fee structure, except for working papers and studies, *Statistics in Focus,* and catalogues. Free publications are usually in full-text, PDF format.

Data is the third main heading, and most of the statistical data is available for free. However, what is found is limited. Eurostat operates on a fee-for-service plan, so in order to obtain in-depth data, a fee must be paid. Information regarding the types of fee-based database information offered and how to request statistics for purchase is included here. Both long-term and short-term indicators are included. Short-term indicators are focused on economics in the form of euro information. Long-term indicators encompass the areas of economics, employment, social, and environment. Also found here are database information and ask-for statistics. Database information allows for mapping using various applications, with a fee attached. Ask-for statistics, a fee-based service, re-

quires the user to go through the registration process if this has not already been done.

Metadata is the fourth main heading. Contained here are classification and definitions, methods and explanatory texts, related publications and legal acts, and projects and links, all related to metadata.

Free and Online, another home page heading, provides an introduction, ordering information for the latest *Eurostat Yearbook,* euro-indicators, euro-yield curve (free), structural indicators (free), and create your own maps using relevant databases.

Eurostat Activities, the sixth main heading discussed, details the background work of Eurostat, including a description of some of the various components and initiatives. Data Shop Services, main heading number seven, has a listing of locations, along with information on how to purchase and license the various products. Help and FAQ, the eighth main heading, has already been described. Contact is the ninth main heading. All Services is the last main heading and provides an additional access point for much of the sources previously described.

Eurostat Yearbook: A Statistical Guide to Europe.
Luxembourg: Office for Official Publications of the European Communities, 1995– (print title).

Summary: A recent Eurostat publication, with the first issue published in 1995, the *Yearbook* covers 10 years of data in the categories of people, land and environment, national income and expenditure, enterprises and activities in Europe, and the European Union. Information about countries considered for membership is found in later editions. The data for each country is either compiled in the same statistical manner or harmonized by Eurostat.

Regions Statistical Yearbook. Luxembourg: Office for Official Publications of the European Communities, 1995– (print, CD, and online subscription publication).

Summary: Published since 1995 the annual *Regions Statistical Yearbook* contains statistics based on the Statistics in Nomenclature of Territorial Units (NUTS) classification. A table is included in the explanatory notes, found at the beginning of the book, explaining this system and detailing the three levels for the 12 EU countries included. Main statistical headings are demography, population activity and unemployment, economic aggregates, agriculture, industry, transport, and living standards. Each heading is then further subdivided. Countries are listed alphabetically with the regions next. Date coverage varies, but is usually only for a single year, although occasionally two years will be available. The explanatory notes are in Danish, Greek, English, French, and Dutch. The actual statistical information is in English and French. A glossary of terms is also included.

Beginning with the 2001 edition, a CD-ROM of the most recent data drawn from the REGIO Database is included with the print version. The data in the CD-ROM are more complete than those in the electronic publication, which is available for a fee in PDF format; however, the electronic publication is half the cost of the print/CD publication. A Table of Contents to the latest edition is available online.

Organisation for Economic Co-operation and Development (OECD) Resources

OECD Statistics Portal Web site, by the OECD Statistics Directorate, Paris. <http://www.oecd.org/statsported/>

Summary: With a membership of more than thirty countries and a working relationship with approximately another seventy, the OECD is a premier source of statistical data. The *OECD Statistics Portal* Web site, available in English and French, brings together various statistical resources together in one location. The home page is divided into the headings Browse, Find, Resources for, and Online Services. Each heading is then further subdivided. Searching and a site map are available.

Detailed Description: Browse is the first main heading discussed and allows browsing by topic, country, or OECD department. Relevant publications and documents are included for each. Find, another home page heading, with the subdivisions of statistics, publications and documents, and news releases is the major focus of this portal. The statistics section contains topics that are categorized as Agriculture/Fisheries, Demography/Population,Development,Education/Trainig Energy, Environment, Finance, Health, Industry/Services, Information and Communication Technology, International Trade, Labour, Leading Indicators and Tendency Surveys, National Accounts, Non-member Economies, Prices and Purchasing Power Parities, Public Management, Science/Technology/Patents, Short-term Economic Statistics, Social and Welfare Statistics, Statistical Methodology, Territorial Statis-

tics, and Transport. Each topic is then further divided into subcategories with links to relevant OECD sites and other web resources.

The Publications & Documents section of the Find home page heading provides links to various annual reports, newsletters, working papers, guidelines, best practices, and legal instruments, most of which are full-text (PDF) format, as well as publications available for sale. A search engine is also available.

The Online Services home page heading is also of importance. The Online Bookshop is located here, where books, periodicals, electronic publications, and electronic periodical titles can be browsed or searched. Online Library links to *SourceOECD,* a subscription service to the full text of OECD-produced books and periodicals. This service is described in the General Sources chapter. However, in regards to statistics, *SourceOECD* has the full-text, PDF, of annual publications, periodicals, *At a Glance* series, OECD databases, and IEA databases. An e-mail alert service and the customizable, MyOECD are also included under the Online Services home page heading.

Quick links are available from the home page under the heading Don't Miss listed as Key Upcoming Events and Frequently Requested Statistics, which features links to the most downloaded OECD statistics files for a current month. A researcher can quickly select and link to the full text of major statistical periodicals, reports, and data files.

United Nations Resources

African Statistical Yearbook. Addis Ababa, Ethiopia: Economic Commission for Africa, 1974– (ISSN 0252-5488) (print title).

Summary: Published annually since 1974, the data covers all 53 member countries of the United Nations Economic Commission for Africa. Country names are arranged alphabetically within each region: North Africa, West Africa, Central Africa, East Africa, and Southern Africa. Topics include population, national accounts, agriculture/forestry/fishing, industry, transport/communications/international tourism, foreign trade, price, finance, and social statistics. The text is in both English and French.

Demographic Yearbook /Annuaire Démographique. New York: Dept. of Economic and Social Affairs, Statistical Office, United Nations, 1948– (ISSN 0082-8041) (print and CD-ROM title).

Summary: An annual publication since 1948, the *Demographic Yearbook* provides statistical information, including a world summary of population and vital statistics, fertility, mortality, and marriage, termed nuptiality, and divorce data. Coverage is of 229 countries or areas and is in both English and French. Statistics are provided by national statistical offices and compiled by the Population Division, Department of Economic and Social Affairs, of the United Nations. Technical notes accompany each table for further explanations. Tables are arranged first by world, then by region, and then by individual country per region.

Special topics are also a focus of each annual addition. Topics include: Population Census (1949–1950, 1955, 1962–1964, 1971–1973, 1979, 1983–1984, 1993–1994); Mortality (1951, 1957, 1961, 1966, 1967, 1974, 1980, 1985, 1992, 1996); Natality (1954, 1959, 1965, 1969, 1975, 1981, 1986); Marriage and Divorce (1958, 1968, 1976, 1982, 1990); International Migration (1977, 1989); Population of Elderly (1991); General Demography (1948, 1953); Population Distribution (1952); General Tables (1978, 1991, 1997–1999); Historical (1978, 1997); Population Trends (1960, 1870); Ethic and Economic Characteristics (1956); and Household Composition (1987, 1995).

A CD-ROM version was issued in 2000 that contains 50 years' worth of statistics in time series. A print version, *Historical Supplement,* was published in 1979 covering a 30-year period. An update to the *Historical Supplement* came out in 1984 as a *Special Supplement.*

Monthly Bulletin of Statistics. New York: Dept. of Economic and Social Affairs, Statistics Division, United Nations, 1947– (print and online resource).

Summary: Published monthly since 1947 and also available online through a subscription, the *Monthly Bulletin of Statistics* provides current economic statistics on a monthly basis for the world's countries. The online version is updated on the first of every month. Statistics are compiled from official sources of individual countries as well as other specialized agencies of the United Nations. The countries are listed alphabetically. Special statistical tables are also included and then reprinted in the annual *Statistical Yearbook.* Topics covered include population, industrial production, price indices, manufacturing, food, external trade, transport, finance and in later years also employment and earnings/unemployment, energy commodities, production and fuel imports, iron ore production, and construction. Date coverage varies. Technical notes are included for each table, and data definitions and references are found at the end of the publication. The *Bulletin* is in English and French.

Population Information Network (POPIN) Web site, by the United Nations, New York. <http://http://www.un.org/popin/>

Summary: As the United Nations resource on population, this Web site is divided into four main headings: Data, Publications, Organizations, and Conferences. A link to the old version of the *POPIN* Web site is available under Archive, however, the external links are no longer being maintained. A Frequently Asked Questions, search engine, and site map are also found on the home page. In addition, there are links to relevant functional commissions, regional commissions, programmes-funds-other, specialized agencies, and regional POPINs: Economic Commission for Africa (Africa POPIN); Economic and Social Commission for Asia and the Pacific (Asia-Pacific POPIN); Economic Commission for Europe (Europe POPIN); Economic Commission for Latin America and the Caribbean (IPALCA POPIN); and Economic and Social Commission for Western Asia (Western Asia POPIN).

Detailed Description: Data is the first main heading discussed from the POPIN home page and is subdivided into Global and Regional Data. The online title *World Population Prospects: The 2000 Review* is one part of Global Data. Here are found population estimates (1950–2000) and projections (2000–2050) along with another 28 population and demographic indicators. The highlights and tables are available in full-text, PDF format, and there is also an online database with pull-down menus for variables and regions. Other topics included under Global Data are Other Population Data Sources (Statistics Division); Children (UNICEF); Cities and Urbanization (Population Division); Education and Literacy (UNESCO); Health (WHO, UNAIDS); Refugees (UNHCR); and Women (Statistics Division). Regional Data sources are from the UN regional agencies: ECA, ESCAP, ECE, ECLAC, and ESCWA. Included for each are an annotation and links to the agency's home page.

Publications, the second main home page heading is further subdivided into Major Recurring Population Publications and Major Recurring Population-Related

Publications. Each entry includes an annotation and link to the publishing organization. A few publications are available in full-text format.

Organizations is the third main heading. Here are found links to the Economic and Social Council and Secretariat, as well as functional and regional commissions, special program funds, and other specialized agencies.

The last main home page heading is Conferences. Included here are links to Intergovernmental Conferences on Population and other conferences, meetings, and workshops by name.

Statistical Abstract of the ESCWA Region. New York: Economic and Social Commission for Western Asia, 1974– (ISSN 0252-4333).

Summary: Published annually since 1974, but with an English title since 1983, this publication tracks statistics in the subject areas of population, education, national accounts, agriculture and fishery, industry, energy, transport, communication/tourism, foreign trade, and financial statistics/prices for the ESCWA countries. Data is derived from national statistical sources in the form of answers to a questionnaire or from other official publications. Countries are listed in alphabetical order, and the date coverage varies by subject area. Information is in both Arabic and English.

Statistical Yearbook / Annuaire Statistique. New York: Dept. of Economic and Social Affairs, Statistics Division, 1948– (ISSN 0082-8459) (print and CD-ROM title).

Summary: An annual comprehensive statistical source, in English and French, covering more than 200 countries and areas of the world, the *Statistical Yearbook* was first published in 1948 under the auspices of the United Nation's Department of Economic and Social Affair's Statistics Division. Beginning with the 2001 issue, the amount of statistical tables included was reduced from 140 tables to 80, covering 19 topics.

The *Yearbook* is arranged into four main parts: World and Region Summary, Population and Social Statistics, Economic Activity, and International Economic Relations. Each part is further subdivided into subtopics. For example, in the 2001 *Yearbook,* the most recent one at the time of this writing, the Population and Social Statistics part was comprised of population, education and literacy, health and nutrition, and culture and communication. The Economic Activ-

ity part encompassed national accounts and industrial production; financial statistics; labour [sic] force; wages and prices; agriculture, hunting, forestry, and fishing; manufacturing; transport; energy; environment; and intellectual property. The part on International Economic Relations contained international merchandise trade, international tourism, balance of payments, international finance, and development assistance. Data is grouped according to region and then individual countries within that region.

At the end of each chapter are technical notes pertaining to the various statistical sources and methodology. Annexes are also included containing such information as nomenclature, conversion information, statistical reference sources, and a listing of tables added or deleted from the previous *Yearbook* issue, as well as an index.

A CD-ROM version is also available for each year beginning with the 37th edition. It contains more than 400 statistical data that can be viewed, manipulated, and exported. In addition, a CD-ROM version of all the *Yearbooks* from 1946–1999 became available in 2003.

Statistical Yearbook / Annuaire Statistique/UNESCO. Paris: UNESCO, 1963–1999 (ISSN 0082-7541).

Summary: Published annually since 1963 and ceased in 1999 by UNESCO's Division of Statistics, *Statistical Yearbook* is an excellent statistical source in the areas of education, science and technology, and culture and communication. Statistics are based on answers to a UNESCO questionnaire, official publications and reports, and special surveys. Statistics are grouped by world region and then reported by the individual countries within that region: Africa, North America, South America, Asia, Europe, and Oceania. The historical time series varies according to statistical category. With the reorganization of the statistical division into the UNESCO Institute for Statistics, UNESCO is reevaluating their statistical products and made the decision to cease publishing the *Yearbook* in 1999.

Statistical Yearbook for Asia and the Pacific. Bangkok, Thailand: Economic and Social Commission for Asia and the Pacific, 1973– (ISSN 0252-3655).

Summary: Originally entitled *Statistical Yearbook for Asia and the Far East* (1968–1972) and renamed in

1973, this annual publication provides statistical information arranged alphabetically by country name. Topics covered include population, manpower, national accounts, agriculture/forestry/fishing, industry, energy, transport/communication, external trade, wages/price/consumption, finance, and social statistics. Data is published in the form available, with annexes listing the principle sources of information and conversion information.

Statistical Yearbook for Latin America, 1973–1984 (ISSN 0251-9445) (print title).

Statistical Yearbook for Latin America and the Caribbean, Santiago, Chile: Economic Commission for Latin America, 1985– (ISSN 1014-0697) (print title).

Summary: This publication, available in both Spanish and English, details the statistics of 25 of the 33 countries associated with the Economic Commission for Latin America. Covering only Latin America from 1973–1984, the Caribbean was added in 1985, although the data for this region is less complete.

The *Yearbook* is divided into two parts. Part 1 is comprised of Indicators of Economic and Social Development and includes social development and welfare, economic growth, domestic prices, capital formation and financing, and external trade. Part 2 is the Statistical Series, which includes statistical data on population, national accounts, domestic prices, balance of payments, external financing, external indebtedness, external trade, natural resources and production of goods, infrastructure services, employment, and social conditions.

The technical notes are found at the beginning of the volume. Date coverage varies according to subject. The countries are listed alphabetically for each subject area.

Statistics Division Web site, by the United Nations Dept. of Economic and Social Affairs, Statistics Division, New York. <http://unstats.un.org/>

Summary: The home page of this comprehensive Web site of statistical information is divided into 11 main topics: Statistical Databases, Publications, Methods and Classifications, Statistical Commission, Millennium Profiles, Demographic & Social, Energy, Environment, Industry, National Accounts, and Trade. In addition, there are links to Hot Topics, What's New, and Important Events. A search engine is available to search the entire site as well as a site map. Some of the data is available at no charge, whereas others can only be accessed through a subscription.

Detailed Description: Statistical Databases is the first main topic of the Statistical Division's home page. Both unrestricted and subscriber access databases are found here. The unrestricted access databases are Millennium Indicators, Social Indicators, Population of Capital Cities and Cities of 100,000 and More Inhabitants, and InfoNation. Millennium Indicators is the measurement tool to mark the progress of the Millennium Goals and consists of 8 goals, 18 targets and 48 indicators, with each goal and its targets linked to the accompanying indicators. Social Indicators contains country or area specific statistics, arranged alphabetically by country or area name for population, youth and elderly populations, human settlements, water supply and sanitation, housing, health, childbearing, education, illiteracy, income and economic activity, and unemployment. Most of the data can be found on the *Women's Statistical Indicators (WISTAT)* CD, described in the Women and Children chapter. The database entitled *Population of Capital Cities and Cities of 100,000 and More Inhabitants* is divided into regions: Africa, North America, South America, Asia, Europe, and Oceania and then alphabetically by countries within each region. The date of the data for each city varies. *InfoNation,* a statistical Web resource for school-age children, provides comparisons of up to five countries in the areas of population, economy, environment, health, and technology. Statistical Databases that required subscription access include *United Nations Common Database (UNCDB), Monthly Bulletin of Statistics Online (MBS Online), Population and Vital Statistics on Internet,* and *Commodity Trade Statistics Database (COMTRADE).*

Publication is the second main home page topic. Here is found a listing of the latest publications as well as annotations, pricing, and ordering information. Browsing of titles by topic is available. A search engine allows searching by title, series, methods, statistical data, and electronic format. A printable version of the results is also an option.

Methods and Classifications, the third main homepage topic discussed, provides links to the various types of classifications used by the Statistical Division. Statistical Commission is the fourth main topic and includes the full-text, PDF format, of meeting reports as well as presenting background information and membership.

Millennium Profiles, the fifth main topic, has already been discussed under Statistical Databases. Demographic and Social, main heading number six, contains links to sources already mentioned or methodology.

However, two sources are included here that have not been previously mentioned: *World's Women 2000: Trends and Statistics* and *Disability Database. World's Women 2000* is a print publication, but highlights are available online. The *Disability Database* contains a pull-down menu of countries and the date of their survey. The date coverage varies by country.

Energy, Environment, Industry, National Accounts, and Trade are the last main topics. Each contains an explanation of the type of coverage and work being done as well as providing lists of applicable print and online resources.

UNESCO Institute for Statistics Web site, by the UNESCO Institute for Statistics, University of Montreal, Quebec, Canada. <http://www.uis.unesco.org>

Summary: Established in 1999 to improve the collection, compilation, and maintenance of statistics related to UNESCO's mission, the UNESCO Institute for Statistics Web site is devoted to global statistics for the areas of education, literacy, culture and communication, science and technology, and facts and figures. The statistical tables are from the print publication *UNESCO Statistical Yearbook 1999* and are in Excel format. Graphs, technical guidelines, publications, projects, events, strategies, and links are also included for each area.

World Statistics in Brief/World Statistics Pocketbook. New York: Dept. for Economic and Social Information and Policy Analysis, Statistical Division, United Nations, 1976–.

Summary: *World Statistics in Brief* (1976–1992) and *World Statistics Pocketbook* (1995–) provide quick statistical data. *World Statistics in Brief* is divided into two parts, world and regional data and data on countries. Data on countries is arranged by region: world, Africa, America, North America, South Asia, Europe, Oceania, and USSR, and then by relevant country. Included are data on population, national accounts, agriculture/forestry/fishing, manufacturing, consumption, transport/communication, international tourist travel, external trade, education, and culture.

World Statistics Pocketbook is arranged alphabetically by country and has data subdivided into population, economic indicators, social indicators, and environment listed under each country. No data comparisons are available.

NONGOVERNMENTAL SOURCES

Current National Statistical Compendiums. Bethesda, Md.: Congressional Information Service, 1974– (microfiche collection).

Summary: First published in 1974, the bibliographic guides provide access to an accompanying microfiche set of the actual statistical titles. "A national statistical compendium is a serial publication of a national government that contains yearly summary data for the country as a whole. If a country does not issue a publication that fully corresponds to this description, coverage may be provided for one that has similar characteristics in most respects."[1]

Publications from more than 165 countries, including the publications of nonsovereign territories treated as separate entities, are contained in this collection, focusing on social, economic, and demographic data. However, the level of detail, types of specific information, as well as presentation, vary. Publications are dated from 1970 forward, but historical data coverage also varies. Information is either originally in English or translated English. Periodically, new subscription groups are released that contain varying country and compendium coverage.

Each new bibliographic guide supersedes the earlier edition. Entries are arranged according to an accession code stem, which is derived from the country's name or abbreviation, with the title following the accession number. The country's name is next, and then the authoring agency's name. Language, place of publication, accession code, date of publication, issue designation, subscription group, and bibliographic data are also elements of each entry. The accompanying microfiche are arranged by "continental subset."

Index to International Statistics (IIS). Bethesda, Md.: LexisNexis (ISSN 0737-4461) (previously published by Congressional Information Service, now a part of LexisNexis) (print/online index to a microfiche set; subscription online service).

Summary: Statistics from international intergovernmental organizations as well as social, demographic, economic, and industrial statistics are found in this index, which began publication in 1983. Indexed publications include official publications, both sales and nonsales, some working papers, those of limited distribution, and mimeographed documents in the form of books, journals, annuals, biennials, series, and special one-time studies. Statistical types are primary data, research data, secondary data, and bibliographic and methodological works. Indexing is by subject, names, geographical location, categories, issuing sources, titles, and publication numbers (as assigned by the European Union, Organization of American States, and the United Nations). Each entry is given a unique accession number that contains the publication name and type and issuing source. The issuing agencies have four-digit identifying codes. Publication types fall into four categories: document (D), monograph (M), periodical (P), other serials, such as annuals, (S). The index and accompanying abstracts are issues on a monthly basis, cumulated quarterly and then annually. The publications indexed can be purchased as a subscription microfiche set. *IIS* indexing can also be accessed via the subscription service LexisNexis™ Statistical.

OFFSTATS: Official Statistics on the Web Web site, by the University of Auckland, New Zealand. <http://www.library.auckland.ac.nz/subjects.stats/offstats/OFFSTATSmain.htm>

Summary: This Web site provides links to official online organizational sources for statistical information on a wide variety of topics. Information is accessible via pull-down menus to world countries, regions, and topic. An alphabetical list of information by country and region is also available. This resource is continually updated, with the aim of being a comprehensive directory.

RESEARCH STRATEGIES

In order to gain a worldwide perspective, the *United Nations Statistics Division* Web site provides the best place to begin the research process, using both the print resources and Web site. All of the UN titles included in this chapter are excellent general statistical references sources with global coverage. Both the *Statistical Yearbook* and *Demographic Yearbook* are published annually and date back to 1948. Both have each produced a CD-ROM product that contains at least 50 years of statistical data. Although the *Demographic Yearbook* focuses mainly on population, marriage, natality, and mortality, the *Statistical Yearbook* includes some of the same information as well as economic

statistics. The *Monthly Bulletin of Statistics,* both print and online versions, continually update some of the tables found in the *Statistical Yearbook,* with current information. Having more than 50 years of statistical data, both at the fingertips via the CD-ROM or through the annual printed volumes, allows for greater ease in studying historical statistical trends. The *World Statistics in Brief/World Statistics Pocketbook* provides quick access to some of this same information. The *Statistics Division* Web site by the United Nations Department of Economic and Social Affairs contains several databases, although some are subscription-based only, to current social, demographic, and economic data. This site is also an excellent source for locating other useful print and electronic sources through its Publications section.

For more specific population statistical information, the *Population Information Network (POPIN)* Web site, another product of the United Nations, is the place to go. Here is found both global and regional data as well as relevant publications, some available in full text.

The *African Statistical Yearbook, Statistical Abstract of the ESCWA Region, Statistical Yearbook for Asia and the Pacific, Statistical Yearbook for Latin America and the Caribbean,* and *UNESCO Statistical Yearbook,* also United Nations products, provide a more specialized focus. The first four titles contain much of the same type of data found in the *Statistical Yearbook,* but focus on specific regions only. The *UNESCO Statistical Yearbook* and the *UNESCO Institute for Statistics* Web site, which provides online access to some of the tables found in the *UNESCO Statistical Yearbook,* is more specialized in its focus, concentrating on education, science and technology, and culture and communication only.

Although the United Nations Statistics Division provides information for all regions and countries of the world, Eurostat, the official European Union statistical organization, is mainly concerned with the 15 European Union countries; however, some other major countries are included in some publications for comparison purposes. The *Eurostat* Web site contains both fee-based and free statistical resources centered around statistical themes. The print publications, such as *Basic Statistics of the European Union* and *Eurostat Yearbook,* provide a quick method of accessing statistical data on a variety of topics. The *Regions Statistical Yearbook* contains narrative essays and was written for schools and also is available in CD-ROM and in a sales electronic (PDF) version. The Organisation for Economic Co-operation and Development, with a membership of 30 countries, also has a narrower focus. Several countries are members of all three organizations. The ***OECD's Statistical Portal*** Web site is a valuable Web site with its theme-based approach to statistical coverage that includes links to relevant OECD resources.

Current National Statistical Compendiums, a subscription-based, nongovernmental resource, is an important source of country statistical sources. The print *Bibliographic Guide* provides the indexing necessary to locate the publications, which are then available through the accompanying microfiche collection. The ***Index to International Statistics (IIS),*** another subscription-based, nongovernmental source, indexes and abstracts international intergovernmental statistical publications such as books, journals, annuals, biennials, and special one-time studies. These publications can be accessed via the accompanying microfiche collection. However, for a higher subscription fee, the online IIS with live links and some data electronically can also be purchased. ***OFFSTATS: Official Statistics on the Web*** Web site is a useful, continually updated current directory of links to official organizational sources for statistical information on a wide variety of topics.

Historical statistics are available not only through the publications already mentioned but also in the print volumes of ***International Historical Statistics: Europe, 1750–1993,*** 4th ed., ***Africa, Asia, and Oceania, 1750–1993,*** 3rd ed., and ***The Americas, 1750–1993,*** 4th ed. described under For Further Reading in this chapter.

FOR FURTHER READING: COMPREHENSIVE WEB SITES AND OTHER REFERENCE SOURCES

Facts through Figures: Eurostat Yearbook at a Glance. Luxembourg: Office for Official Publications of the European Communities, 1996, 1998.

This report provides a quick look at statistics by country and overall European Union. The 1996 edition is divided into people, men and women, education and employment, economy, day-to-day life, and on the European Parliament. The 1998 edition is categorized into people, land and the environment, national income and expenditures, enterprises and activities in Europe,

European Union, and Central European Countries. Both are useful, especially in tracking time series.

International Historical Statistics

Europe, 1750–1993, 4th ed. New York: Grove's Dictionaries, 1998 (ISBN 1-56159-236-6).

Africa, Asia, and Oceania, 1750–1993. 3rd ed. London: Macmillan Reference, 1998 (ISBN 1-56159-234-X).

The Americas, 1750–1993, 4th ed. London: McMillan, 1998 (ISBN 1-56159-235-8).

Divided into 10 main headings: population and vital statistic, labour force, agriculture, industry, external trade, transport and communications, finance, prices, education, and national accounts. Each subject heading includes the relevant countries, listed alphabetically, with the time series for that heading.

Statistical Abstract of the World. 3rd ed. New York: Gale Research, 1997 (ISSN 1077-1360).

Also published in 1994 and 1996, this publication contains statistical data on all 185 United Nations member countries, as well as Hong Kong, Switzerland, and Taiwan. Countries are arranged alphabetically, and statistics are categorized by geography, demographics, health and human factors, education, science and technology, government and law, labor force, production sectors, manufacturing sector, and finance, economics, and trade. Date coverage varies.

Statistical Agencies (International) Web site, by the U.S. Census Bureau, Washington, D.C. <http://www.census.gov/main/www/stat_int.html>

This electronic directory is an alphabetical listing of nations of the world, with a link to the national statistical office of each country. Most statistical offices publish economic and demographic country statistics. Many have searchable online databases and online full-text statistical reference sources.

NOTE

1. *Current National Statistical Compendiums: Bibliographic Guide to the Microfiche Collection* (Bethesda, Md.: Congressional Information Service, 1998), iii.

CHAPTER 20
Trade

CHAPTER OVERVIEW

The subject of trade encompasses information on exporting, importing, marketing, investment, government policies, regulations, and trade agreements. "International trade is a catalyst in transforming countries, policies, and trends."[1] This chapter is intended to aid students, librarians, researchers, and businesspeople in identifying major sources of trade information broadly defined. Some resources include details about commodities traded, but they do not include individual company detail. Only some of the major statistical titles are covered. Some U.S. government resources are covered because they include trade information for individual countries.

For more information about statistics, and also on trade directories, and trade classification codes, users should check recommended sources For Further Reading later in the chapter. The reference materials recommended on the *World Trade Organization* Web site, the *United Nations Conference on Trade and Development* Web site, and the *U.S. International Trade Administration* Web site are also useful.

Governmental Sources Discussed

Country Commercial Guides, by the U.S. Embassy Staff and the U.S. Trade Administration, published online by Stat-USA and U.S. Trade Administration. <http://www.export.gov> (select Market Research: Country and Industry Market Reports; free subscription to researchers) and <http://www.stat-usa.gov/tradtest.nsf> (online subscription service; free to U.S. depository libraries).

The Development Economics Research Group of the World Bank on International Trade Web site, by the World Bank Research Group and the World Bank Institute. <http://www.worldbank.org/research/trade/index.htm>

Direction of Trade Statistics Quarterly and *Direction of Trade Statistics Yearbook,* by the International Monetary Fund, Statistics Department (print and CD-ROM) (quarterly, ISSN 1017-2734; yearly, ISSN 0252-3019).

External Trade Web site, by the European Commission Directorate-General for Trade. <http://europa.eu.int/comm/trade/index_en.htm>

International Trade by Commodities Statistics, by the Organisation for Economic Co-operation and Development (OECD), Paris. <http://www.oecd.org/> (select Browse: By Department, ECH: Trade Directorate) (annual print report, current edition only online at no charge or through an online subscription).

International Trade Centre (UNCTAD/WTO) Web site, by the International Trade Centre, Geneva, Switzerland. <http://www.intracen.org/index.htm>

International Trade Statistics, by the World Trade Organization, Statistics Division. 2000–. <http://www.wto.org/english/res_e/statis_e/statis_e.htm> (print annual report with online highlights) or <http://www.wto.org> (select Resources, Trade Statistics).

International Trade Statistics Yearbook, by the United Nations Department of Economic and Social Affairs, Statistical Division, New York, 1950– (print annual title).

Monthly Statistics of International Trade, by the Organisation for Economic Co-operation and Development (OECD) (print periodical and online subscription title).

OECD Trade Web site, by the Organisation for Economic Co-operation and Development (OECD), Washington, D.C. <http://www.oecd.org/> (select Browse: By Department, ECH: Trade Directorate).

Search Market Research (Market Research Reports) Web site, by the U.S. Department of Commerce and the U.S. & Foreign Commercial Service, and published by the U.S. Trade Administration. <http://www.export.gov> (select Country and Industry Market Reports) (free online subscription service) and also available on *Stat-USA/Internet,* <http://www.stat-usa.gov>

STAT-USA Internet, by the U.S. Dept. of Commerce (online subscription service, available free to U.S. depository libraries). <http://www.stat-usa.gov>

Trade & Development Centre Web site, joint venture of the World Bank Institute and the World Trade Organization. <http://www.itd.org/>

Trade Unit, Organization of American States Web site, by the Organization of American States, Washington, D.C. <http://www.oas.org/> (select OAS Issues: Trade and Integration) or <http://www.sice.oas.org/tunit/tunite.asp>

UNCTAD Handbook of Statistics, by the United Nations Conference on Trade and Development (UNCTAD), Geneva, Switzerland. <http://www.unctad.org/> (select Statistics, UNCTAD Handbook of Statistics) (print, CD, and online title).

United Nations Conference on Trade and Development Web site, by the United Nations Conference on Trade and Development, Geneva, Switzerland. <http://www.unctad.org>

World Trade Organization (WTO) Web site, Geneva, Switzerland. <http://www.wto.org>

Nongovernmental Sources Discussed

IATP Trade Observatory Web site, by the Institute for Agriculture and Trade Policy, Minneapolis, Minn. (previously ***WTOWatch.org*** Web site). <http://www.tradeobservatory.org/>

Lex Mercatoria: The International Trade/Commercial Law and E-Commerce Monitor Web site, hosted by the University of Oslo, Norway. <http://www.jus.uio.no/lm/>

GOVERNMENTAL SOURCES

Country Commercial Guides, by the U.S. Embassy Staff and the U.S. Trade Administration, published online by Stat-USA and U.S. Trade Administration. <http://www.export.gov> (select Market Research: Country and Industry Market Reports; free subscription to researchers) and <http://www.stat-usa.gov/tradtest.nsf> (online subscription service; free to U.S. depository libraries).

Summary: This up-to-date U.S. government guide to the trade environment and economic and business conditions of countries provides access to current and retrospective reports on individual countries. Each country report in this series includes an executive summary and chapters that provide a comprehensive look at the country's commercial environment. Because the reports are clearly organized, it is easy for users to go right to the section they are interested in from the table of contents, particularly the economic, commercial, trade statistics, or political analysis. These annual reports provide users with the information they need to understand a country's trade environment. This includes analysis of the market trends and strategies that would affect businesses engaged in trade and other political, economic, and legal factors affecting trade in a specific country.

Detailed Description: Users may link to the URL of each chapter or to the entire report for a country. Note that the left sidebar of the Market Research section allows the user to link back and forth from the *Country Commercial Guides* resource to the *Search Market Research,* a complementary database. Each chapter includes analysis and statistics of previous fiscal years in a dense form, but not too difficult to read and understand. Each report includes chapters on economic trends and outlook, political environment, marketing U.S. products and services, leading U.S. imports and exports, trade regulations, investment climate, financing, business travel, statistics, contacts (directory information), and even a trade events schedule.

The executive summary has an easy-to-understand explanation of the country's commercial environment, current markets, and issues of a political, trade, or business nature. Jump from the Table of Contents to the chapters for more specific information. The text of each country report is more difficult to understand than the executive summary because of the way the statistics and analysis are interwoven. In addition to the countries of the world, the *Guides* include: the Bahamas, EBRD (European Bank for Reconstruction and Development), European Union, and the West Bank.

Country Commercial Guides is also provided online through the *Stat-USA Internet* subscription service. *Stat-USA,* a private fee-based service, provides free access to databases including *Country Commercial Guides* to U.S. Depository Libraries. A list of the depository libraries may be found at the ***U.S. Government Printing Office*** Web site at <http://www.gpoaccess.gov/libraries.html>.

The Development Economics Research Group of the World Bank on International Trade Web site, by the World Bank Research Group and the World Bank Institute. <http://www.worldbank.org/research/trade/index.htm>

Summary: This Internet resource covers trade policy research and topics with many links to specific documents and resources on these issues. Information on the objectives and activities of the international trade work of the World Bank is the centerpiece of the page. The Web site was created as a research, training, and outreach tool for people interested in trade policy and developing countries, with particular emphasis placed on the new trade agenda of the World Trade Organization. Formed in 1944, the World Bank was developed to fight poverty, and it is the world's largest development assistance organization. Trade is one of the many issues the World Bank focuses on in its programs, and it works cooperatively with the World Trade Organization on research projects. This site features working papers, research activities, publications, *Trade Notes,* projects, and a glossary of terms.

Detailed Description: The Working Papers page documents research projects devoted to international trade and are available in full text (1996–) or can be ordered free of charge. These working papers are published under the *Policy Research Working Paper Series,* which focuses on trade, economic, and development issues.

The Research section links directly to information about various projects, but no documents, publications, or links are provided. *Trade Notes* are irregular full-text publications on various topics. Publications provides information on all World Bank Publications. Of special mention is the *Glossary of Trade-Related Terms* with definitions of relevant terms.

Direction of Trade Statistics Quarterly and ***Direction of Trade Statistics Yearbook,*** by the International Monetary Fund, Statistics Department (print and CD-ROM) (quarterly, ISSN 1017-2734; yearly, ISSN 0252-3019).

Summary: This quarterly periodical provides, for about 150 countries, tables with current data or estimates on the value of imports from and exports to their most important trading partners. Also included are similar summary tables for the world, industrialized countries, and developing countries. The yearbook provides seven recent years' worth of detailed trade data by country for about 182 countries, the world, and major areas.[2] These periodicals are available in English, French, and Spanish, and they are only available in a paper subscription and CD-ROM. The paper title has undergone several title changes since its first issue in 1964 and the first issues of the *Yearbook,* which covered 1958–1962.

The International Monetary Fund (IMF) is an international organization of member countries established in 1946 to promote monetary cooperation, economic growth, balanced trade growth, and to provide financial assistance to countries. The home page of the IMF is at <http://www.imf.org> and is available in English, Arab, French, German, and Spanish.

Detailed Description: The quarterly issues of this title are mainly organized into country tables, alphabetically by country. For about 150 countries, users can find figures on the value of merchandise exports and imports for seven years, with the latest year's figures also given quarterly. Estimates are used where necessary. The statistical tables provide the value of imports and exports by year, by major trading partner, thus providing a world trade figure for the country. Under each country, figures are detailed by the trading partners in the categories of industrialized countries and developing countries, by region. The term *country* is used in a broad sense, not just as a territory, as understood by international law, but also some that are not sovereign nations but for which statistical data are maintained. World and area tables precede the country tables and include about 37 small countries for which individual country tables are not made available.

Both the quarterly and especially the yearbook provide methodological information on the collection of the data, the origin of the data, and symbols and abbreviations in their introductions. Users should note that the data is expressed in terms of U.S. dollars, although most of the countries report in their national currency. The IMF provides the standards it follows to convert and aggregate the data. All years of these periodicals are included in the CD-ROM product *International Financial Statistics (IFS).*

External Trade Web site, by the European Commission Directorate-General for Trade. <http://europa.eu.int/comm/trade/index_en.htm>

Summary: Available in English and French, this Web site is the official site for Trade for the EU, one of the world's largest trading entities. It covers all aspects of the trade interests of the Union, including trade in goods and services, trade defense (issues such as dumping, subsidies, and export loans), intellectual property, investment, competition, upcoming World Trade Organization negotiations, trade relations of the member countries of the Union, trade policy, and more. It provides many documents full text on the Web and links to categories of documents, such as speeches, articles, and press releases.

The member states of the European Union share a common trade policy toward nonmember countries based on Article 133 of the Treaty of Amsterdam (1997). As the executive body of the European Union, one of the European Commission's main tasks is to secure the free movement of goods, services, capital, and persons throughout the Union to initiate new legislation and carry out Community policy. The Directorate-General for Trade conducts the Union's commercial policy throughout the Union. This site has three main headings: What We Do, Trade Issues, and I-Centre. Additional headings are listed for Statistics, Public Dialogue, Enlargement, and Latest News links to full-text press releases.

Detailed Description: The first home page heading discussed, What We Do, provides an online *Beginner's Guide to Trade* and information about the staff, organization, and mission of the Directorate. More information is included under the sections Frequently Asked Questions (FAQs), Glossary, Updates, Events Calendar, Image Library, Downloads, Links, and Work Programmes. The Image Library contains digital images and video. The Glossary provides definitions of trade terms, acronyms, and abbreviations. Downloads contains a few online documents and PowerPoints on trade issues, and finally, the Directorate's Work Programme discusses the Directorate's most recent agenda and focus for its activities.

The second major home page heading, Trade Issues, includes information by the following trade topics: EU and WTO, Harnessing Globalization, Sectoral Issues (agricultural, trade in services, intellectual property rights), Bilateral Trade Relations, and Respecting the Rules. Bilateral Trade Relations is an interactive online resource with a drop-down box by country and a clickable map. Researchers may select individual countries to see a summary of the trade relations of that country and the European Union. Respecting the Rules links to EU legislation and regulations concerning trade under the topics: Dispute Settlements, Trade Policy Instruments, and Monitoring of Third Country Commercial Defence [sic] Actions. The subsection Trade Policy Instruments explains Trade Defense Instruments and Trade Barriers Regulations used to regulate unfair trade practices within the European Union. Harnessing Globalization contains information on the social responsibilities of trade in the European Union, trade with developing countries, sustainability impact, and much more.

Another home page heading discussed, I-Centre, leads to an online searchable database of full-text documents. Searching is available by document type, year, key word, country, and sector. The database links to the full text of documents under the categories: Press Releases, Submissions to the WTO, Speeches & Articles, Policy & Issues Papers, and Legislation. Most documents are in HTML or PDF formats.

The Statistics heading on the home page provides researchers with the main economic and trade data for the European Union and its trading partners. PDF and XCEL formats are available for individual countries. Public Dialogue is an online forum with information about meetings. Full interaction requires a free login, but otherwise, the public has access to meeting information and documents reports generated from this forum. Finally, the heading on the Enlargement of the European Union contains background information on the impact of enlargement on trade defense by concern, whether a producer, importer, exporter, or user.

The *External Trade* Web site also links to an online database, the *Market Access Database.* This service informs about market conditions in non-EU countries and provides many other services that aim to reduce the obstacles faced by European exporters.

International Trade by Commodities Statistics, by the Organisation for Economic Co-operation and Development (OECD), Paris. <http://www.oecd.org/> (select Browse: By Department, ECH: Trade Directorate) (annual print report, current edition only online at no charge or through an online subscription).

Summary: *International Trade by Commodities Statistics* is an annual compilation of foreign trade statistics of OECD member countries with six years of detailed data on the value of trade in specific commodities by partner country. The Statistics Directorate maintains three main databases of statistics on international trade collected from its member countries. These are standardized in order to make them internationally comparable. They are: *International Trade by Commodities Statistics (1999–),* previously published as *Foreign Trade by Commodities; OECD Statistics on International Trade in Services,* previously published as *Services: Statistics on International Transactions;* and *Monthly Statistics of International Trade,* previously published as *Monthly Statistics of Foreign Trade.* Subsets of these databases are published in electronic form. The first two titles are covered in this description, but the *Monthly Statistics* is separately described.

The OECD Directorate usually publishes information in both printed and electronic subscription form, with only the current edition available in PDF at no charge from the OECD Web pages. OECD membership comprises industrialized countries worldwide.

Detailed Description: This is the main foreign trade statistical data source for the OECD, giving the imports and exports of its member countries in value (U.S. dollars) and in quantities, by type of commodity and by partner country. Users will find information organized by OECD member country with the categories of country origin or destination for the statistical tables of imports and exports under each country. Country notes are provided on the first page of every country. Additional data for totals is published for groupings of member countries, including OECD, North American Free Trade Agreement countries, OECD Asia and the Pacific, and OECD Europe. The SITC (Standard International Trade Classification) is used to classify data. Users should note that there have been three revisions of this classification. The introduction to the issue will provide information on the classification used. Historical data is available back to 1961, when this title was issued as *Statistical Bulletin Series C: Trade by Commodities,* but users will probably find the electronic versions provide easier access to the data.

This title is also available through OECD's subscription service to its databases and publications, *SourceOECD,* described in the Economics and Business chapter. Ingenta.com makes *International Trade by Commodities Statistics* available as an e-journal through subscription or provides access to articles through pay-per-view. This title is also available on a set of four CD-ROMs, *ITCS—International Trade by Commodities Statistics,* which is updated quarterly. They provide complete and detailed data on commodities and partner countries in value and quantity from 1961 to present. Several versions are available according to the Standard Industrial Trade Classification (SITC) used and the length of the time series. More information about the four industrial classifications used for international trade is available in either print or electronic formats of the *Industrial Trade by Commodity Statistics.*

International Trade Centre (UNCTAD/WTO) Web site, by the International Trade Centre, Geneva, Switzerland. <http://www.intracen.org/index.htm>

Summary: The ITC Web site includes much directory and bibliographic information, as well as information about the activities of the organization in many countries. ITC's main objective is assisting developing and transition economies to improve trade capacity and promote trading and the trade performance of businesses. ITC publishes trade promotion handbooks, directories, market surveys, international trade bulletins, and technical materials. The Web site is searchable, and it provides a few titles full text online. Its periodical *International Trade Forum: The Magazine of the International Trade Centre* provides trade development perspectives, often focusing an issue on a topic.

The ITC works with individual enterprises and is involved in technical support and research and development. ITC was created by the General Agreement on Tariffs and Trade (GATT) in 1964 and since 1968 has been operated jointly by GATT (now by the World Trade Organization, or WTO) and the UN, the latter acting through the United Nations Conference on Trade and Development (UNCTAD). The Web site is organized into the categories of Products & Services, Countries, Business Supports, Partners & Networks, Compendium of Tools & Services, E-shop, and About ITC. The Web design does not permit easy user access to ITC products as of 2001. For the purposes of this chapter, the discussion will focus on the information under Countries and the home page category of E-shop.

Products & Services provides general aggregated trade statistics and market product research. Not all the information is fully developed on the Web, but there are some full-text reports.

Detailed Description: The Countries section leads to directories on trade support institutions and trade information sources for individual countries. The link to References & Contacts Databases lets the user search the library holdings of the *ITC (International Trade Documentation Database)* with access to online bibliographic databases including publications, statistics, Web resources, and trade documents.

E-shop, another home page category, provides links to Publications and Products, including the online quarterly magazine *International Trade Forum: The Magazine of the International Trade Centre,* ITC List of Publications, Technical Papers, Trade Statistics, and Market Briefs. Users will find *Forum* has the most content in this section. Current and back issues are online and are searchable from 1999 on. The print periodical began in 1964 and is indexed in *Business Periodicals Index,* among others. Listings of books and CDs, technical materials, and trade bulletins (some available in full text) are also included.

International Trade Statistics, by the World Trade Organization, Statistics Division, 2000–. <http://www.wto.org/english/res_e/statis_e/statis_e.htm> (print annual report with online highlights) or <http://www.wto.org> (select Resources, Trade Statistics).

Summary: This detailed report contains up-to-date statistics on international trade for the current year together with an outlook for the upcoming year. The Web page provides a press release for highlights and explanations. It is also available in French and Spanish. The World Trade Organization has a specific role in collecting and disseminating data to fulfill its mission. Its Statistics Division compiles statistics required by the Secretariat for the regular analysis of world trade in merchandise and commercial services and for special studies on particular aspects of international trade.

Detailed Description: Prior to 2000, these statistics were published in a section of the WTO annual report entitled *World Trade Organization Annual Report: International Trade Statistics,* available both in print and CD-ROM (1998–). *International Trade Statistics* provides an overview, covers world trade in the previous year, long-term trends, trade by region, and trade by sector. Appendices and a table of acronyms are included. The appendices include world trade figures, product by region, and imports and exports by country, for a range of years. Online, a user may download the entire document in PDF, or selected sections either in Excel or PDF.

The main contents included are statistical highlights of international trade, detailed figures for world trade growth, world exports including world merchandise exports, and exports of commercial services. International capital flows and foreign direct investment are included.

The home page of the *World Trade Organization* Web site, under Resources, Trade Statistics, also links to *Historical Series* data from the Statistics Division, other links such as national statistical offices and other statistical information, and previous WTO *Annual Reports,* back to 1998. The Historical Series provides this historical information on international trade at the aggregate level, by country, region, and economic grouping from 1980 onward in Excel format, along with world trade and output indices available as of 1950; Merchandise trade by region and selected economies, 1980, 1985, 1990, and 1995–1999 (value and volume); Commercial services trade by region and selected economies, 1980, 1985, 1990, and 1995–1999; and Merchandise exports, production, and gross domestic product, 1950–1999.

Researchers should note that the *Annual Report* of the World Trade Organization extends back to 1995 when the WTO was established. Annual reports of an earlier trade organization General Agreement on Tariffs and Trade (GATT, 1948–1994) would also be an excellent source for historical policies and issues and statistical information.

The complete publication, *International Trade Statistics,* can be ordered from WTO publications in print, CD-ROM, or may be downloaded in PDF. Users should note that they can download individual chapters in PDF format or individual tables in Excel format from the tables. Copyright use information is available from this page; permission for personal or classroom use is granted.

International Trade Statistics Yearbook, by the United Nations Department of Economic and Social Affairs, Statistical Division, New York, 1950– (print annual title).

Summary: This publication of statistical tables provides trade information for 170 countries from around the world. It is issued in two volumes, with Volume I covering trade by country and Volume II trade by commodity. External trade performance, trading partners, and individual commodities imported and exported are included. From 1950–1983, this yearbook was issued under the title *Yearbook of International Trade Statistics.*

Detailed Description: Volume I of the *International Trade Statistics Yearbook* is trade by country. It is organized alphabetically by country with the same five statistical tables under each country. The first table provides historical imports and exports statistics yearly back to 1963. The second table is for imports by broad economic category and exports by industrial origin for seven years. The third table is trade by principal countries or origin and destination, with value in U.S. dollars. The fourth and fifth tables under each country cover imports and exports for four years broken down by general commodity category (Standard Industrial Trade Classification [STIC]).

Volume II covers trade by commodities. The statistical tables are organized by general commodity by STIC showing total world trade of those commodities for five years. It breaks down trade into exports and imports and provides world, region, and country figures. Volume II also includes special tables showing the contribution of the trade of each country to the trade of its region and the world and the flow of trade between countries and regions, as well as the fluctuations of the prices of goods.

The national statistical authorities compile the statistics, mostly consistent with U.N. recommendations, and submit them to the United Nations to compile. External trade data for the majority of the countries from 1962 are available on CD-ROM from the United Nations Statistics Division.

Monthly Statistics of International Trade, by the Organisation for Economic Co-operation and Development (OECD) (print periodical and online subscription title).

Summary: Previously published under the title *Monthly Statistics of Foreign Trade,* this periodical provides detailed data about trade for OECD member countries. There are four parts to the data: main indicators, indices, trade by SITC, and more detailed trade by partner countries. A CD-ROM version of this title gives all available details of the series and provides longer time series. The paper title has undergone several title changes since 1961, when it was originally issued as *Foreign Trade. Series A: Overall Trade by Origin and Destination.*

The OECD was established in 1961 to contribute to the development of the world economy; to improve employment, economic growth, and living standards for member countries; and to provide economic expansion for all world countries. In the area of trade, it was formed to contribute to the expansion of world trade, on a multilateral, nondiscriminatory basis.

Detailed Description: In each monthly issue, Part I includes aggregate trade indicators and the value of trade for each OECD member country. Part II includes value indices, which reflect the changes in the commodity composition of trade and prices. Part III, Trade by SITC section, provides data on each country's trade classified by five major commodity classifications: food, animals, and beverages; crude materials and inedible oils and fats; mineral fuels; chemicals and manufactured materials; and machinery and transport equipment. Part IV comprises foreign trade of OECD member countries by partner countries. An

annex contains OECD's geographic nomenclature, currency exchange rates, and country specific notes.

This title is available through OECD's subscription service to its databases and publication, *Source OECD,* described in the Economics and Business chapter. Other related major statistical periodical titles from the OECD are described in this chapter; see *International Trade by Commodities Statistics.*

OECD Trade Web site, by the Organisation for Economic Co-operation and Development (OECD), Washington, D.C. <http://www.oecd.org/> (select Browse: By Department, ECH: Trade Directorate).

Summary: In addition to providing detailed statistical information on trade, the OECD provides online publications and documents about trade on its Internet site. It provides documents concerning trade activities within the OECD as the promotion of trade liberalization, and understanding international trade issues is central to OECD's mission. The OECD Trade Committee and its Working Party were created to assist OECD's goal in contributing to the expansion of world trade on a multilateral basis in accordance with international obligations.

Detailed Description: The main body of the page links to the OECD Trade Committee meetings documents and summaries and information about other forums. The right and left sidebars lead to the following sections: Main Activities, About Us, Other Trade Links, On-line Documents, Trade Publications, and Feedback. Once the user enters a section, these links remain as choices on a sidebar. The Other Trade Links section provides information on National Trade Agencies, National Statistical Agencies, and International and Regional Organizations. Online full-text documents may be found in the On-Line Documents Section, whereas information and abstracts about subscription titles is available in the Publications Section.

Search Market Research (Market Research Reports) Web site, by the U.S. Department of Commerce and the U.S. & Foreign Commercial Service, and published by the U.S. Trade Administration. <http://www.export.gov> (select Country and Industry Market Reports) (free online subscription service) and also available on *STAT-USA/Internet,* <http://www.stat-usa.gov>

Summary: This online searchable database is an in-depth index of market research by country and by industry, made available by a U.S. agency. It is kept very up to date because this resource is geared toward business users who depend on current information. It is a partner resource to the *Country Commercial Guides,* a major resource also described in this chapter and available from the *USATrade.gov* Web site. The information is subject to international copyright laws and is the property of the U.S. Dept. of Commerce and the U.S. & Foreign Commercial Service.

Detailed Description: The *Market Research Reports* database provides a Search All Market Research feature. Researchers have the option to select either a specific country or an industry sector, such as apparel, iron and steel, computer services, and so on. Other search options include combining specific countries and specific industries and searching by Boolean operators, "AND," "OR," and "NOT."

It is made freely available on the U.S. Trade Administration Web pages, if a user registers for free use and meets certain requirements. *STAT-USA,* a privately run, fee-based service described in this chapter, also provides *Market Research Reports.*

STAT-USA Internet, by the U.S. Dept. of Commerce (online subscription service, available free to U.S. depository libraries). <http://www.stat-usa.gov>

Summary: This online resource of many databases provides authoritative trade information geared toward U.S. businesses. The focus for this chapter is on the trade resources, especially for international market research and country commercial analysis. *STAT-USA Internet* is a fee-based subscription service of the Economics and Statistics Administration, U.S. Department of Commerce, which is funded solely by its revenues. However, free access to the public is available through the U.S. Federal Depository Libraries.

Detailed Description: From the *STAT-USA Internet* home page, the user should link to *GLOBUS&NTDB* for trade information and databases. *GLOBUS* stands for Global Business Opportunities, and *NTDB* for *National Trade Data Bank. GLOBUS&NTDB* provides Trade News; a Trade News archive; current and historical trade leads in the areas of agriculture, defense, commerce, and program; and the United Nations trade leads. Also available is very detailed information, weekly, monthly, and annually, about current exchange rates. Researchers should note that the *National Trade Data Bank* is published in CD format and online.

The Market and Country Research section provides access to the databases Country Commercial Guides, Best Research Reports, Global Agriculture Information Network, and Industry Sector Analysis Reports.

Best Research Reports include information on markets by date and by country and analysis on industries by date and by country. Historical reports are available. The *Country Commercial Guides* and *Market Reports* are described as separate resources in this chapter because the current versions of the reports are available free online from the U.S. Trade Administration. Country Commercial Guides are available back to 1996 on the U.S. State Department's country information page. The International Trade Library is especially useful as it contains over 40,000 full-text titles related to trade.

EuroTrade Online is a new subscription database provided by *STAT-USA Internet* with the most current, official trade data of the European Union member countries, from Europe's authoritative statistical agency, *Eurostat. EuroTrade Online* also provides access to the European Union's ComExt (Commerce Exterieur) data series, which includes import and export data for each of the 15 major European countries with over 12,000 commodities up to the eight-digit European Harmonized System classification level.

Users can also find information on U.S. trade with other countries, including exports and imports through a current press release section and the major database *USA Trade Online.*

The United States Department of Commerce publishes a special Web site for trade with former Soviet countries called *BISNIS,* <http://www.bisnis.doc.gov>, and researchers will find reports, news stories, industry reports, trade leads, and much more information on this site, which is more fully described in the Economics and Business chapter.

Trade & Development Centre Web site, joint venture of the World Bank Institute and the World Trade Organization. <http://www.itd.org/>

Summary: This Internet resource was created to provide information on international trade, particularly as it relates to social and economic development. It offers information, analysis, comments, and an online exchange concerning international trade issues. Of specific note are Development Gateway resources and links. This Center is designed primarily for use by individuals from developing countries, but is open to all. It is run jointly by the World Trade Organization and the World Bank's Economic Development Institute under the program Information Technologies for Development (ITD). The Issues/Event, Guides, and Links home page categories will be the focus of this description.

Detailed Description: The Regions Overview section provides region-specific information on developing countries. The researcher can find regional information about tariffs, import and export flows, balance of payments, external debts, and other subjects. Guides is currently in beta version and contains guides about the WTO. Other regional organization pages can be accessed via the Links category.

Trade Unit, Organization of American States Web site, by the Organization of American States, Washington, D.C. <http://www.oas.org/> (select OAS Issues: Trade and Integration) or <http://www.sice.oas.org/tunit/tunite.asp>

Summary: To access this Web site, users need to go to the OAS home page and select Trade & Integration from the drop-down box or use the search engine to search your trade topic. This Web site is rich in analysis, news, publications, and data. Under Publications users may find many titles available free full text, downloadable in PDF or Word formats, especially the *Trade Unit Study Series,* which focuses on trade and integration in Latin America. Its SICE (Foreign Trade Information System, short for its Spanish acronym, Sistema de Información al Comercio Exterior) makes many documents available about the Free Trade Area of the Americas, trade agreements, articles, studies, and data about countries. The site is available in English, Spanish, French, and Portuguese, the four official languages of OAS. The Trade Unit of the Organization of American States (OAS) was created in 1995 to assist the member countries of this international intergovernmental agency in trade matters and particularly the Free Trade Area of the Americas (FTAA), in order to raise living standards for the people by strengthening free trade and to provide information about trade. Home page categories are OAS and the FTAA, Trade Capacity Building, Publications & Studies, and SICE (Foreign Trade Information System).

Detailed Description: The OAS and the FTAA home page category provides information about the role of the OAS in these issues, including Trade Unit mandates and reports and links to the FTAA official Web site and other information about it. The Trade Capacity Building category makes information about courses and seminars available and links to the *Trade Education Database (TED).*

Publications & Studies is a rich section for users, with abstracts of books privately published and full texts of OAS Trade Unit publications, especially in the *Trade Unit Study Series.* Some books no longer in print are available full text on the Web. It also contains the FTAA Official Publications Prepared by the Trade Unit, which are technical documents prepared on official request and approved for public release. These are listed by main topic and often contain very detailed information; for example, the title *Compendium of Antidumping and Countervailing Duty Laws in the Western Hemisphere* is available in online and Word format and provides information on legislation, regulations, and guides by country. Finally, the last section of Publications & Studies includes the articles by Trade Unit Staff Members from 1996 on.

SICE (Foreign Trade Information System) provides data, full texts of trade agreements, analysis, and links. It is searchable and has a Site Map, What's New, and a Calendar. The FTAA Process section gives full text of official documents from the beginning in 1994. The Trade Agreement section provides full text of trade agreements between nations of the Western hemisphere. Investment Treaties are also full text, and SICE provides summaries of many of the agreements. Trade Related Links provides links to current information needs for trade leads, directories, guides, private sources, and more. The Dispute Settlement section provides information on disputes concerning trade agreements and treaties.

UNCTAD Handbook of Statistics, by the United Nations Conference on Trade and Development (UNCTAD), Geneva, Switzerland. <http://www.unctad.org/> (select Statistics, UNCTAD Handbook of Statistics) (print, CD, and online title).

Summary: This annual title began in 2000 and continues the *Handbook of International Trade and Development Statistics,* 1967–1999. It provides a comprehensive source of data on world trade, investment, and development. The statistics cover the volume of trade by year and country, regional information, commodity prices, exports and imports, growth of world trade, trade balances, and some basic development and financial indicators. It is available in print (English and French), on CD-ROM, and online 2003– in PDF.

Detailed Description: This report of statistical tables has an introduction, appendices, and special tables and is organized into parts by topic covered. Many of the tables report data historically back to 1950. Also tables report trade statistics by year and by country.

Topics covered include value of exports and imports, trade indices, export by destination and major commodity group, and import by origin and by major commodity group. Also reported are tables on the export and import structure by commodity and by country. Commodities are reported using the Standard International Trade Classification (SITC). Basic indicators of development, population, and gross domestic product are reported by country. Special tables cover groupings of industrial or developing countries.

The online version allows downloads (PDF) in English and French. Highlights and tables of contents are also available to view separately for each edition. Some of the information included in this title is available on the main *UNCTAD* Web site, under Statistics, <http://www.unctad.org/>. For historical statistics and information, researchers should consult the paper or CD title, available in UN depository libraries and in some major university libraries and law libraries. The CD-ROM provides full time series of the data back to 1950.

United Nations Conference on Trade and Development Web site, by the United Nations Conference on Trade and Development, Geneva, Switzerland. <http://www.unctad.org>

Summary: This resource is an Internet site of an organization devoted to trade that provides many online titles of interest to everyone from beginning student to expert researcher. One of many major periodicals about trade that UNCTAD provides online is its annual *Trade and Development Report* (1981–). The Web site is available in English, French, and Spanish, and it links to information About the Organization, Events and Meetings, Technical Cooperation, Press, Statistics, Digital Library, and Programmes. It also provides a section on new offerings and links to the UNCTAD project sites.

UNCTAD assists countries by participating in worldwide policy discussions and promoting technical cooperation measures that assist countries in practical ways. Established in 1964 as a permanent intergovernmental body, UNCTAD is the principal organ of the United Nations General Assembly for trade, investment, and development issues.

Detailed Description: The focus of this discussion will be on the Digital Library home page category which provides online access to its major publications, including annual reports on the worldwide trade and investment situation. All of these annual report titles

are rich resources to beginning students and researchers alike, depending on subject, and are excellent resources for issue, country, and subject reference. Only the current issues are available free online, and sometimes only part of the text is available, otherwise these titles are available in print. Check the Web site for each title's availability in other major languages.

- *Trade and Development Report* (1961–) covers and analyzes current global economic performance, regional trends, interaction of trade, investment, and financial flows. Developing countries are covered particularly with development strategies and current policy issues.
- *World Investment Report* (1991–) analyzes trends in foreign direct investment and its relationship with transnational corporations and policies that impact development.
- *The Least Developed Countries Report* (1984–) identifies major challenges facing these countries and reports on international support. It provides comprehensive and authoritative analysis and data organized by country on the 49 least-developed countries related to quality of life.
- *E-Commerce and Development Report* identifies the prospects and challenges of e-commerce for developing countries.

Other resources on UNCTAD's Digital Library category include full-text access to basic documents, newsletters, and discussion papers. A search engine, which allows searching by document symbol or keyword, is also available. *Guides to the UNCTAD Publications* (1995–2002) provides a listing of publications and documents for each particular year. A link to statistical databases leads to the online version the *UNCTAD Handbook of Statistics,* also described in this chapter.

Statistical resources are available from UNCTAD's Statistics heading on the home page. It links to Statistics in Brief, Millennium Indicators, Statistical Databases, and Sources & Notes. Statistical Databases contains the *Commodity Price Bulletin* (1960–), *UNCTAD-TRAINS (Trade Analysis and Information System),* and the *Foreign Direct Investment* database.

The *UNCTAD* home page is a rich resource for information on trade meetings, worldwide trade events, and current publications. However, the researcher with historical needs will *not* find older titles, only the current years are free on the Internet and available to order in paper or on CD-ROM through the UN Sales

Publications Program. For older periodical titles and documents, researchers are advised to find UN depository libraries in the United States. Also some law libraries and academic libraries may have UN microfiche sets that provide this information.

World Trade Organization (WTO) Web site, Geneva, Switzerland. <http://www.wto.org>

Summary: WTO is the premier organization to search for trade information, as it conducts formal international negotiations on trade. Its Web site is intended for a wide range of users, from students, to general users, to researchers. Its home page features an A–Z list, a site map, a search engine, organizational news, and a community forum. It provides links to content including news, resources, documents, data, and trade topics. It is available in its official languages: English, Spanish, and French.

Previously called GATT (General Agreement on Tariffs and Trade) from 1948, the World Trade Organization was renamed in 1998. WTO is the only global international organization dealing with the rules on trade between nations, and its main function is to ensure that trade flows as smoothly, predictably, and freely as possible.

Detailed Description: The A–Z list on the home page is a quick way to get into a topic, because it lists publication titles, trade subjects, and general topics, such as publications, speeches, or FAQs. Researchers may link to a significant series of reports entitled *Trade Policy Reviews;* individual titles in this series are available full text online in Word format (1995–). The trade policy review process began in 1989, and print publications for specific countries began at this time. The *Trade Policy Reviews* series reports track and analyze individual countries' trade policies. For each year, by country, the WTO provides online access to the policy statement from the governments under WTO review, as well as to the separate detailed WTO report for the country, and press releases. Also of special note is a link to information about the WTO's major journal, *World Trade View.* Although not online in full text, abstracts and a sample issue are available.

The Documents section from the top of the home page links to legal texts (available full text in part), official documents, and dispute settlement reports, which are all downloadable. The official Documents Database contains official documentation in the three official languages, English, French, and Spanish, from

1995. Users can browse or search titles and search the full text of the documents. It does not contain WTO publications. The legal texts are only partly available from the Documents. Documents are in Word format, except for those before June 1998, which are in WordPerfect. Some selected material from 1986–1994 is included, mostly on the Uruguay Round and some GATT materials. Dispute settlement reports are downloadable in various and multiple formats, including Word, WordPerfect, and PDF.

Users should note that one of the major trade statistics resources has a link to a downloadable version from WTO's home page. This is the current issue of WTO's annual periodical *International Trade Statistics,* described separately in this chapter.

The Trade Topics section from the home page includes issues handled by the WTO Councils and Committees and its trade agreements, including those on goods, services, intellectual property, environment, investment, electronic commerce, development, regionalism, and dispute settlements. The Community Forum section is for the media, NGOs, and the general public, and it provides an opportunity for the public to comment on the WTO, its activities, and the trading system.

The World Trade Organization has depository libraries throughout the world at which WTO publications can be consulted by users. A list is available at <http://www.wto.org/english/res_e/booksp_e/db_e.htm>.

NONGOVERNMENTAL SOURCES

IATP Trade Observatory Web site, by the Institute for Agriculture and Trade Policy, Minneapolis, Minn. (previously ***WTOWatch.org***). <http://www.tradeobservatory.org/>

Summary: The *IATP Trade Observatory* serves as an observatory of global trade issues and the World Trade Organization (WTO), with comprehensive information and links on its Web pages. Most information is in online periodicals, but there are also some full-text reports online at no charge. The Institute monitors trade rules and WTO negotiations and encourages public participation in its activities.

In 2003, the *IATP Trade Observatory* absorbed *WTOWatch*, a private global information center earlier started by the same Institute to cover trade and sustainable development issues originally launched November 22, 1999, in conjunction with the third ministerial meeting of the World Trade Organization (WTO) in Seattle.

The home page is divided into the main categories of Headlines, Event Calendar, Fast Facts, Document Center, News Bulletins, What's News, and Related Sites. Also available from the home page are a search engine, a sign-up for e-mail subscriptions to electronic titles including *WTO Agriculture & Trade* and *WTO Activist,* and other trade updates. Check the Web site for more information about these titles. For the purposes of this chapter on trade, the discussion will focus on the Document Center, Multimedia Page, Fast Facts, and News Bulletins.

Detailed Description: The Document Center posts an online library of trade related titles listed by date posted, which includes title, author, brief title, and size. These are available in English, French, German, and Spanish. Documents are mainly in full text with varying formats, each with an abstract at the beginning of the document. This database of documents is searchable under the link Search Library. Users may also request a list of titles by broad subject category such as human rights, agriculture, trade, and the World Trade Organization among them.

The Multimedia page displays an annotated title list. Subject category lists are available from the left sidebar. The length of the document is given (i.e., running time in minutes), and date recorded. Searching Multimedia is available. Also, users have free access to the RealPlayer software that allows the user to run the individual recordings and media titles.

Fast Facts is an educational resource section that may be especially attractive to users who need definitions and explanations to understand the information on this Web site. It is listed under the tabs at the top of the page. Fast Facts lists frequently asked questions (FAQs) by general subject category, such as World Trade Organization, WTO and Trade, WTO and Labor, and WTO and Agriculture. Users may submit their own questions for response, and their submissions may be edited for use on the Fast Facts.

News Bulletins is a section under the tabs on the home page linking to *WTO News: The Road From Seattle* and *Bridges Weekly Trade News Digest.* Both of these are free electronic bulletins through e-mail. The bulletins link to the latest edition and to back issues. Each title has a searchable archive of issues. The *WTO News* reports analysis, follow-up, and future directions from the WTO Ministerial Meetings. *Bridges Weekly Trade News Digest,* published by the International Centre for Trade and Sustainable Development, pro-vides a weekly review of trade-related articles and information relevant to the sustainable development and trade communities. It is funded through foundations and various governments and organizations.

Lex Mercatoria: The International Trade/Commercial Law and E-Commerce Monitor Web site, hosted by the University of Oslo, Norway. <http://www.jus.uio.no/lm/>

Summary: This research- and professional-oriented Internet resource has provided extensive law links and materials free of charge since around 1993. It also links to journals that are free on trial, but are cost subscriptions, and gives abstracts of books to order. It includes country implementation details of important conventions and other important trade documents, including legal texts on trade. Its mission is to provide information on international commercial law, with related interests in commerce and information technologies. One of the first law sites on the Internet, *Lex Mercatoria,* is supported by the Law Faculty of the University of Tromsø, where it began, the Institute of International Commercial Law of Pace University School of Law, USA, and the Australasian Legal Information Institute, a.k.a. AustLII, and is hosted by the Law Faculty of the University of Oslo, Norway.

Detailed Description: Users can link to information by format: books, journals, or conferences, or by legal subject on the left sidebar. Some of the subject links that relate to trade are International Trade Law, Intellectual Property Law, "Treaties": International Trade Instruments, Electronic Commerce and Encryption Law, and other trade related topics. This site provides materials of a highly complex and legal nature. These links lead to lists of material that are often provided in full text, but are not explained or categorized. Users should have some background information in this area to fully utilize this site.

RESEARCH STRATEGIES

Country Commercial Guides is a recommended first source for all students and researchers who need general discussion on trade and an overview for a specific country. From the perspective of the U.S. Trade Administration, it provides clear summaries of a country's trade potential with partners and detailed chapters on the economic and commercial climate of that country. *Market Research Reports* is a recommended source for all users, including high school students who require country-specific and market-specific information, for example, on the beverage industry in Brazil. Although it is a more difficult source to access online than the *Country Commercial Guides,* for market research it is excellent, and it is available from U.S. federal depository libraries and other Web sites at no charge.

For trade statistics in a general world context, with discussion of world issues, users of all levels can first consult the periodical titles produced annually by the **United Nations Conference on Trade and Development.** These periodicals are also the place to start for comparative country trade statistics, and most of them can be easily found on the Internet on the UNCTAD Web pages. Users should take a look at the current edition online and if necessary consult the older editions in paper.

For detailed trade statistics, a very comprehensive source is OECD's *Internal Trade by Commodities statistics.* It may best meet the needs of users starting at an upper undergraduate level because of its detailed treatment by commodity and geography. Users will need to consult paper periodicals from the OECD for statistics covering older years. Also, for specific countries' trade statistics when the country is not an OECD member, researchers should try the more general sources listed earlier and then consult the country's agency or ministry responsible for trade. Most industrialized countries have statistical databases on the Internet with trade statistics. For example, for detailed trade statistics between the U.S. and a country, a user should consult the U.S. Trade Administration, <http://www.trade.gov>, under Trade Statistics. Its *Global Data Links,* <http://infoserv2.ita.doc.gov/otea/wdl.nsf?openDatabase>, links to specific countries or subject trade links compiled by the U.S. Trade Administration. Further information by national governments is available through the online list of U.S. Trade Offices by country. The subjects are economic indicators, finance, foreign trade payments, national accounts, and prices.

For the context of trade with finance, and for those interested in financial information and its relationship to trade, the *International Trade Centre* (UNCTAD/WTO) Web site by the International Trade Centre is the most in-depth, after trying the other resources for general information. The *Trade and Development Centre* by the World Bank institute and the World Trade Organization is best used as a second source, especially for trade issues and policies concerning developing countries as its mission focuses specially on these countries.

FOR FURTHER READING: COMPREHENSIVE WEB SITES AND OTHER REFERENCE SOURCES

Andean Community Web site, Lima, Peru. <http://www.comunidadandina.org/endex.htm> (English language).

This subregional organization has international legal status and is comprised of five countries of the region and the institutions and organizations of the Andean Integration System (AIS), including Bolivia, Colombia, Ecuador, Peru, and Venezuela. One of its goals is to create an internal common market of trade by 2005. The Documentation Center, a category on the home page, provides access to the full text of documents. A link to digital libraries is also included along with a video library. Statistics are also available and of special note is the full-text current issue of its *Monthly Indicators of the Andean Community* and other statistical indicators online. These are not necessarily kept up-to-date.

Business Guide to the World Trading System. 2nd ed. Geneva: International Trade Centre (UNCTAD/WTO), and London: Commonwealth Secretariat, 1999 (ISBN 0-85092-621-1).

This beginning guide to the world trading system published in English, French, and Spanish explains the legal framework for international trade resulting from trade agreements, treaties, and other international rules. It covers the World Trade Organization role and function, other international rules and agreements, rules on exports and imports, rules of origin, agreement on agriculture, and the general agreement on trade in services. It also analyzes world trade issues of concern such as trade and environment, investment, competition policy, government procurement, and much more and includes some statistics.

Dictionary of International Trade: Handbook of the Global Trade Community Including 12 Key Appendices, by Edward G. Hinkleman. 4th ed. Novato, Calif.: World Trade Press, 2000 (ISBN 1-88507-384-4).

This dictionary of trade terms includes appendices with acronyms; abbreviations; resources for international trade including books, periodicals, and directories; maps; and Web resources. Web resources lists general sites, international trade-related sites, and sites by country. A new edition is regularly published.

International Merchandise Trade Statistics: National Compilation and Reporting Practices Web site, by the United Nations Statistics Division. <http://unstats.un.org/unsd/tradereport/introduction.asp>

Resulting from an initial survey conducted between 1992 and 1995 by the International Trade Statistics Branch of the United Nations Statistics Division, this Web site is periodically updated to make available information on national compilation and reporting practices in international merchandise trade statistics. It includes an introduction with explanations and links to concepts and definitions and information about countries and their practices in collecting data, as well as the United Nations recommendations. Researchers should note that the Harmonized Commodities Description and Coding System, a six-digit code describing goods and used in data dissemination, was entered into force January 1, 1988 (the countries that entered into agreement to use this system account for nearly 100% of world trade).

International Trade Policies: Volume I, The Uruguay Round and Beyond: Principal Issues. Volume II, Background Papers (World Economic and Financial Surveys), by Naheed Kirmani. Washington, D.C.: International Monetary Fund, 1994 (ISBN 1-55775-469-1, vol.1) (ISBN 1-55775-457-8, vol.2).

This is an overview of the major issues and developments in world trade and the involvement of the International Monetary Fund. The first volume is the overview and the second the background staff papers on specific trade issues. Each volume contains statistics, appendices, and a bibliography. Vol. I contains a glossary, and Vol. II has bibliographies after each chapter on a trade subject.

International Trade Sources: A Research Guide, by Mae N. Schrieber. New York: Garland Publishing, Inc., 1997 (ISBN 0-81532-109-0).

This research handbook includes descriptions of about 800 sources in the field of International Trade in electronic and paper formats. It focuses on the American perspective and covers industry, markets, countries, products, and regulations for doing business internationally. It is intended to meet research needs of inter-national marketing students, librarians, researchers, and businesspeople.

Southern Cone Common Market (MERCOSUR) Web site (Spanish, Portuguese, and English). <http://www.merconet.org.uy/>

The MERCOSUR treaty signed in 1991 established a common market among four countries: the governments of the Argentine Republic, the Federative Republic of Brazil, the Paraguayan Republic, and the Republic of Uruguay. Joining later were Chile (1996) and Bolivia (1997). Their aim was to promote trade expansion, liberalization, and the free movement of goods. Although this is an important regional trade organization, with online publications and documents, particularly with statistics and information relating to trade, little information is available in English; this Web site is in Spanish and Portuguese. For easy-to-understand information in English on *MERCOSUR,* researchers may want to consult the *MERCOSUR-NETWORK Information* Web site at <http://www.idrc.ca/lacro/investigacion/mercosur.html>, which links to country Web pages, organization Web pages, the MERCOSUR Economic Research Network, and other MERCOSUR-related research, trade, and business information.

NAFTA Secretariat Web site. <http://www.nafta-sec-alena.org/DefaultSite/home/index_e.aspx>

This Organization administers the dispute processes and settlements under the North American Free Trade Agreement between the United States, Mexico, and Canada and links to the national secretariats in charge of NAFTA. The site provides rules, decisions, status reports of disputes, and the text of the agreement. It is available in English, French, and Spanish.

World Customs Organization Web site. <http://www.wcoomd.org/ie/En/en.html>

Available in English and French, this organization provides information about customs topics and links to customs Web sites, with press information. "Customs manages the physical movement of goods, people, and conveyances, across borders and frontiers."[3] This organization is an independent, intergovernmental body that promotes communication and cooperation and assists customs administrations with standardization and legislation. It provides an online magazine, *WCO News.*

World Trade Organization Archives. Geneva, Switzerland: WTO, 1995–.

This is a microfiche collection of documents issued by the World Trade Organization from 1995 on, when the organization changed its name from the General Agreement on Tariffs and Trade.

NOTES

1. Mae N. Schreiber, *International Trade Sources: A Research Guide* (New York: Garland, 1997), p. ix.

2. "International Trade by Commodities Statistics", by the Organisation for Economic Cooperation and Development (OECD), *Direction of Trade Statistics Quarterly* (International Monetary Fund, March 1999), p. iv. <http://www.oecd.org/document/18/0,2340,en_2649_34235_1906706_1_1_1_1,00.html>.

3. *World Customs Organization* brochure, <http://www.wcoomd.org/ie/En/AboutUs/OMD_GB.pdf>, p. 2.

CHAPTER 21
Transportation

CHAPTER OVERVIEW

Rapid technological innovation has changed the transport sector over the last century, often enabling it to grow faster than overall economic activity. The demand for mobility has greatly increased. Regulation, deregulation, standards, and statistics are of increasing importance in policy. "The sector is changing as a result of economic integration at regional and world levels but also because of stricter environmental regulations and the drive for sustainable, seamless transport systems."[1] Transportation information included in this chapter is both general and specific, covering the areas of aviation, rail, marine, public transportation, roads, transportation safety, and the transport of dangerous goods. The resources described range from transportation statistical resources, government periodicals that cover global transportation issues, and government and institutional Web sites. The Web sites included are produced by government agencies and organizations that either focus on transportation or provide transportation information for countries of the world. Web sites of sub-agencies of large international intergovernmental agencies that focus on transportation are also discussed in this chapter. Researchers should note that these Web sites are excellent sources for linking further to an area of transportation that may not be covered. A U.S. source the *Worldwide Transportation Directory* by the U.S. Bureau of Transportation Statistics, is included because it gives directory information for organizations whose responsibilities and transportation expertise cover two or more countries on a worldwide or regional scale. Also researchers should note that although many of the major governmental resources selected for this chapter are from organizations that focus on North America and Europe, the resources still have good information about other areas of the world.

Governmental Sources Discussed

***Annual Bulletin of Transport Statistics for Europe and North America**. New York: United Nations,* Economic Commission for Europe (print and online subscription title).

European Conference of Ministers of Transport (ECMT) Web site, hosted and administered by the Organization for Economic Cooperation and Development, Paris. <http://www1.oecd.org/cem/>

International Aviation Online Web site, by the Federal Aviation Administration (FAA), Washington, D.C. <http://www.intl.faa.gov/index.cfm>

International Civil Aviation Organization Resources

ICAO Journal, by the International Civil Aviation Organization, Montreal, Canada (ISSN 0018-8778) (print and online). <http://www.icao.int/> (select the link ICAO Journal) or <http://www.icao.int/cgi/goto.pl?icao/en/jr/jr.cfm>

International Civil Aviation Organization (ICAO) Web site Montreal, Canada. <http://www.icao.int/>

International Maritime Organization Web site, London. <http://www.imo.org/>

North American Transportation in Figures, by the Bureau of Transportation Statistics, 2000 (print and online title). <http://purl.access.gpo.gov/GPO/LPS7023>

OECD Transport Directorate Web site, by the Organisation for Economic Cooperation and Development, Paris. <http://www.oecd.org/transport/>

Panorama of Transport, by the European Commission and Eurostat (the Statistical Office of the European Communities) (print title, some summary sections online, some related data online). <http://www.eu-datashop.de/download/EN/inhaltsv/thema7/transp.pdf>

Transport Division Web site, by the United Nations Economic Commission for Europe. (UNELE), Geneva, Switzerland. <http://www.unece.org/trans/>

Worldwide Transportation Directory, by the Bureau of Transportation Statistics, U.S. Dept. of Transportation, 1997– (free online title). <http://www.bts.gov/programs/international/wtd/>

Nongovernmental Sources Discussed

International Association of Public Transport (UITP) Web site, Brussels, Belgium. <http://www.uitp.com/>

International Road Transport (IRU) Web site, Geneva, Switzerland (online subscription resource available from the Web site of IRU). <http://www.iru.org/>

World Road Statistics, by the International Road Federation (print title available online via membership in IRF).

GOVERNMENTAL SOURCES

Annual Bulletin of Transport Statistics for Europe and North America. New York: United Nations, Economic Commission for Europe (print and online subscription title).

Summary: The Transport Division of the United Nations Economic Commission for Europe publishes this annual *Bulletin,* available in English, French, and Russian, providing general and specific statistics for European and North American countries on roads, rails, inland waterways, maritime, oil pipeline transport, and intermodal transportation. Intermodal transportation is defined as transport involving more than one type of transportation, where the goods are not handled in the exchange from one type to another type.[2] Information on subscribing to the online version is available at <http://www.unece.org/trans/main/wp6/transstatpub.html>.

Among its other purposes, the UN's Economic Commission for Europe's Transport Division focuses on the collection of transport statistics and promotion of transport methodologies. Although most statistics are regional, some worldwide statistics are gathered.

Detailed Description: This *Bulletin* organizes statistics in the categories of general statistics; railway transport; road transport; inland waterways; oil pipeline transport; maritime transport; and intermodal transport. Most tables provide data by the last two years and the earlier 10th year for each country. An appendix provides selected definitions from the glossary for transport statistics, which is available on the Internet at <http://www1.oecd.org/cem>. In the introductory material, a country guide shows the table numbers for which each individual country is included.

European Conference of Ministers of Transport (ECMT) Web site, hosted and administered by the Organisation for Economic Cooperation and Development, Paris. <http://www1.oecd.org/cem/>

Summary: This international intergovernmental organization focuses on transportation in Europe. The Conference provides access to documents, statistics, bibliographies, and transportation topics from its home page. Also available are a site map, news and events, and links to related sites. The conference has many working groups focused on specific topics of transportation, including road transport, road safety, railroads, transport and environment, urban travel, combating crime in transport, and others, and it provides information in these areas from the annual reports of its working groups, which are linked from its home page. It publishes some major statistical reports on transportation.

The European Conference of Ministers of Transport (ECMT) is an intergovernmental organization established in 1953 with a mission to help create an integrated, economically and technically efficient transport system throughout the enlarged Europe that meets high safety and environmental standards and takes full account of the social dimension. The organization also provides a forum for analysis and discussion of innovative transportation policy issues.

Detailed Description: From the *ECMT* home page the researcher can link to information related to mainly road and railway transportation in the form of documents, statistics, full-text publications, and bibliographies. Proceedings of conferences, meetings, and seminars are published electronically on the *European Conference of Ministers of Transport (ECMT)* Web site. ECMT resolutions, arranged by topic, with date coverage varying, are included, as well as speeches, press releases, articles, and interviews. In addition, there are online versions of the newsletter *ECMT News* (1996–), and it is possible to sign up to receive these via e-mail. Some documents available from the ECMT's home page are only accessible to members and are therefore password protected. The Publications section includes new, annual, forthcoming, free, and full text (in PDF format). In addition, it provides a link to the Catalogue of Publications. Not all significant publications are online in full-text format.

The Documents section contains the full text, mainly PDF, of proceedings, resolutions, newsletters, press releases, articles and interviews, speeches, and a glossary. Bibliographic references, with citation and ordering information, are also included.

The Statistics section contains four headings: Trends; Passenger and Freight; Short-Term Trend Survey, which includes individual country statistics; and Road Accidents. The organization publishes several statistical reports, including *Statistical Trends in Transport, Trends in the Transport Sector,* and *Statistical Report on Road Accidents.* It also links to statistical databases on transportation and a directory list of transport ministers of its member countries.

International Aviation Online Web site, by the Federal Aviation Administration (FAA), Washington, D.C. <http://www.intl.faa.gov/index.cfm>

Summary: The Federal Aviation Administration (FAA), U.S. government agency, provides a wealth of online information about transportation in countries and regions of the world, because according to its purpose as an organization, it works closely with other aviation organizations on harmonizing global aviation standards. Current news, topics, links to international aviation organizations, and general information about international transportation are available on its searchable site. It also provides information on specific programs and projects in regions of the world and information by type of traveler, whether officials, operators, or personal travelers. Current international aviation news is highlighted, and news archives of the agencies announcements and regulations are provided back to September 2001. For additional news, researchers may sign up for e-mail announcements.

Detailed Description: The *International Aviation Online* Web site of FAA provides services such as information by type of traveler, including civil aviation officials, FAA officials, non-U.S. operators, travelers, and U.S. operators. The information for officials includes regulations, information on training, and foreign travel guidelines for officials (password protected). Operators' information includes manuals, regulations, and fees. Travelers' information includes links to the U.S. Department of State travel warnings and consular information. The travel warnings are issued when the State Department recommends Americans avoid travel to a certain country. The Consular information sheets are available for every country of the world and link to general information about the country and its conditions and to the U.S. embassy in the country. The subsection Travelers' information from the home page links to travelers' health information from the Centers for Disease Control and Prevention, which fully covers travelers' health concerns about specific diseases and geographic destinations.

Also linked from this home page is information about regional programs, plans, and projects listed by continent of the world. The link Frequent Questions answers questions on international aviation such as, "Are there ratings on the safety of foreign airlines?" and "What are the requirements for flying in a particular foreign country?"

Much detailed information is provided under the International Topics pull-down menu, located at the top of the home page. It provides links to such topics as civil aviation authorities of the world and other organizations; the Global Aviation Information Network; the Global Positioning System; the International Aviation Safety Assessment; International Flight Information Manual: a gateway to flight planning outside the U.S. a regulatory document to help countries develop or review laws and regulations to meet international standards; the Foreign Airport Security Assessment Program; research; aviation restrictions including trade sanctions, flight bans, and regulations affecting U.S. operators; Bilateral Aviation Safety Agreements and Bilateral Airworthiness Agreements; testing programs; and training activities.

The *Civil Aviation Authorities of the World* database at <http://www.intl.faa.gov/civilauths.cfm> is a comprehensive directory of links to the Web sites of civil aviation authorities across the globe. These authorities are the FAA-equivalent organizations in other countries responsible for civil aviation safety matters. The database is searchable by country. Finally, the database *Restrictions on International Aviation,* <http://www.intl.faa.gov/restricthome.cfm>, is searchable by country name, providing information about the regulations, restrictions, or sanctions imposed by U.S. agencies affecting air travel between the United States and foreign countries or between two foreign points.

International Civil Aviation Organization Resources

ICAO Journal, by the International Civil Aviation Organization (ISSN 0018-8778) (print and online title). <http://www.icao.int/> (select the link ICAO Journal) or <http://www.icao.int/cgi/goto.pl?icao/en/jr/jr.cfm>.

Summary: Published monthly, this journal provides articles on air safety worldwide and also on a broad variety of air management concerns. Articles are scholarly and contain bibliographic references. Statistics are also included, along with illustrations, graphs, and charts. Government agencies are frequent authors of individual articles. Issues are available online since volume 5, 1996. (DjVu format, a free plug-in is available). Researchers should check under the link "e-archives" for volumes older than the current volume. *ICAO Journal* began in 1946 under the title *ICAO Bulletin.* French, Spanish, and Russian versions are published, and some issues are also available electronically in these languages. The objective of the *Journal* is to report on the activities of the International Civil Aviation Organization and to feature additional information of interest to contracting states and the international aeronautical world.

Detailed Description: Each issue focuses on one specific theme, and the feature articles are related to it. For example, the June 2002 issue focused on global strategies to improve the aviation security net, including security developments and the public's confidence in aviation security. In addition to thematic feature articles, there is a monthly column entitled "ICAO Update," which makes varied reports on the organization, sometimes covering statistics, and sometimes reports or meetings.

ICAO Journal began in 1946 under the title *ICAO Bulletin.* French, Spanish, and Russian versions are published, and some issues are also available electronically in these languages.

International Civil Aviation Organization (ICAO)

Web site, Montreal, Canada. <http://www.icao.int/>

Summary: The Web site of this organization provides information about aviation worldwide and publishes its journal online, *ICAO Journal,* also described in this chapter. Online reports and working papers are available, but most of the information is the documents of the organization and its member bodies. The Web site is searchable and provides a site index, news, and information about the organization and its division under the category ICAO Secretariat. Publications are available through a subscription service *ICAO eCOMMERCE* and some are free online. Users can order publications online through an online sales catalog. From the home page users can access information by subject, by member body of the organization (including its regional offices), by service, and by type of publication.

ICAO is a specialized agency of the United Nations whose focus is on promoting safe and equitable international civil aviation. Its aims include standardization, regional planning, air navigation, facilitation, economics, technical cooperation for development, and law within worldwide and regional context.

Detailed Description: Under the ICAO Publications link from the home page, this organization offers *ICAO Journal* (2002–), *ICAO eCommerce,* online free publications, a subscription directory, *Directory of National Civil Aviation Administrations,* annual reports full text (1995–), a Training Directory, and meeting information. Free online publications are in PDF, DjVu, and HTML formats. *ICAO eCOMMERCE* is a service providing online access to publications for a subscription fee. These include International Conventions and Protocols, Annexes to the Convention on International Civil Aviation, Procedures for Air Navigation Services—Air Traffic Management, and Annual Reports of the Council. The online *Aviation Training Directory of ICAO* is available as a searchable database. Meetings contains information about the Worldwide Air Transportation Conference and the ICAO Global Safety Aviation Plan (GASP).

The category Regional Offices from the home pages links to regional offices in major cities on all continents of the world. As an example, Paris links to the ICAO Europe and North Atlantic Regional Office, whose Web site contains organization, history, objectives, activities, and publications under the category E-documents.

The category Focus On from the home page links to thematic information under the sections aviation security and alerts, environment, aviation medicine, and TRAINAIR. Although information is gathered in these pages and includes statements, summary of the issues, and links, many of the publications are not free available. The TRAINAIR program's objective is to improve safety and efficiency of air transportation through training and it does provide free online documents in PDF.

The ICAO Secretariat category from the home page links to information about the divisions of the organization. Of particular note is the Web, Library, and Archives section, located under the Administration subcategory, which provides much further access to information in this area, linking to an e-library, an *eARCHIVES,* its *ICAO Library Bulletin,* other online bibliographies, and its free online library catalog,

ATLAS. ICAO has implemented an *eARCHIVES* project to provide lasting preservation of its electronic documents.

International Maritime Organization Web site, London. <http://www.imo.org/>

Summary: This searchable Web site provides information on the legal and human side of shipping and maritime transportation, including publications, and information resources. A major publisher, it provides an online catalog of titles with a separate link to publications available online. A site index is available. This is a rich source of information for current and hot topics and news, but users should not expect many full-text publications online. This specialized agency of the United Nations is responsible for improving maritime safety and preventing pollution from ships. It promotes international technical cooperation and helps develop international regulations and recommendations in these areas.

From the home page, users may link to specific types of information, such as safety, legal, human element, technical cooperation, and marine environment. Other major headings include Publications, Information Resources, IMO documents (online full text), Circulars (online full text), Newsroom, Conventions, IMO FAQ (frequently asked questions), hot topics, meetings, and SeaLibrary Online. The search tool is a magnifying glass symbol on the upper right of the Web pages.

Detailed Description: The Publications heading links to an online bookshop with print, CD, and virtual sales publications from the IMO catalog. It also links to browsing online titles, which provides a search engine and an A–Z index of titles. The home page heading IMO Documents leads to full-text online documents such as the objectives of IMO, its history and structure, a kids' page, and documents in other languages. IMO Circulars are online full-text fact sheets on a variety of maritime topics.

Information Sources guides researchers to find IMO information and general maritime industry information. Also available are bibliographies, *Current Awareness* Bulletins (providing titles of articles and brief extracts back to 2000), Information Resources on Current Topics, IMO Resolutions, new resources, and Papers and Articles by IMO Staff. One major resource available here is the *IMO Directory of Maritime Links,* an up-to-date resource of links to Internet sites of interest to the maritime community, particularly in the field of maritime safety and prevention of pollution.

This directory is an online database searchable by subject, country, and specific links.

North American Transportation in Figures, by the Bureau of Transportation Statistics, 2000 (print and online). <http://purl.access.gpo.gov/GPO/LPS7023>

Summary: This title, available in English, French, and Spanish, provides key summary statistics on transportation in the United States, Canada, and Mexico. It contains mostly statistical tables supported by figures, maps, and technical documentation with data sources. A bibliography and country-specific technical references are provided in the appendices. Topics covered include the economies and demographics, trade and travel, safety, freight and passenger activity, infrastructure, and energy use of transportation. Notes describe definitions relating to each country. The report was developed under the framework of the North American Transportation Statistics Interchange representing the transportation and statistical agencies of Mexico, the United States, and Canada. Participating agencies include the Secretaría de Comunicaciones y Transportes, the Instituto Mexicano del Transporte, and the Instituto Nacional de Estadística Geografía e Informática from México; the Bureau of Transportation Statistics and the Census Bureau from the United States; and Statistics Canada and Transport Canada.

Detailed Description: A pull-down menu on the home page allows for the selection of a particular section of this title. Sections are divided into Introduction; A Country Overview, with basic economic and population statistics for the North American countries; Transportation and the Economy; Transportation Safety; Transportation, Energy, and the Environment; Domestic Freight Activity; North American Merchandise Trade, by mode of transportation, value, and top ports; International Merchandise Trade between North America and the Rest of the World by Value and Weight and Top International Commodities; Domestic Passenger Travel; North American Passenger Travel; International Passage Travel between North America and the Rest of the World; Transportation Infrastructure; Transportation Vehicles; and Appendices. A related statistical reference title is published by the United States Bureau of Transportation Statistics: *North American Transportation Highlights.*

OECD Transport Directorate Web site, by the Organisation for Economic Cooperation and

Development, Paris, <http://www.oecd.org/transport/>

Summary: This site provides information on these areas of transportation, particularly for OECD countries: aviation, environmentally sustainable transport, maritime transport, shipbuilding, road, and intermodal transport. OECD focuses particularly on the economics and policy of transportation, research, and statistics within its member countries. The agency is a rich resource for research materials on transportation, as it covers both current and emerging transportation issues for OECD countries and countries worldwide. Users need to be aware that some titles are provided full text and some are available only through sales or a subscription such as *SourceOECD*. Some key issues covered by OECD are regulatory reform, trade liberalization, competition policy, transport safety, and substandard transportation. OECD's aim is to provide input for policy debates on these issues, and it works closely with other international organizations, including the United Nations, World Bank, and the World Trade Organization.

Detailed Description: The *OECD Transport Directorate* Web site provides detailed news about current transportation trends and activities that the agency is working on. Recent publications from OECD on transportation issues are announced and described on this page with a link to OECD's online bookshop. Theme-related information is linked from the home page under the topics energy, environment, and sustainable development. These pages provide users links to OECD publications related to transportation under the specific topics, links to other international organizations on the topic, links to databases, and news within OECD. Many publications also are only available through subscription.

Panorama of Transport, by the European Commission and Eurostat (the Statistical Office of the European Communities) (print title, some summary sections online, some related data online). <http://www.eu_datashop.de/download/EN/inhaltsv/thema7/transp.pdf>

Summary: First published in 1999 in print, this title provides annual statistics of the most important features of transport in the European Union, including economic features of transportation, quantities of freight and passengers moved, and vehicles used. Available in English and French, it includes trends in energy consumption, pollutants, safety, and other statistics that can be used to measure the impact of transport. *Eurostat* compiles and publishes data from the member countries of the European Union and has much additional data collected on transportation.

Detailed Description: The information in this title is organized by transportation sector, with analysis and data under each sector. A separate statistical references list is provided. Each issue covers 30 years of historical data on transportation of the European Union member countries. After the 2001 issue, the intent is to cover all main modes of transportation.

The Publications Section of the *Eurostat* home page provides access to the Table of Contents for this title <http://europa.eu.int/comm/eurostat/>. It also links to a related electronic title *Highlights of Panorama of Transport 1970–1999* (PDF) which provides an executive summary and some data on transportation for these years.

Eurostat has also published a related significant title in transportation research, *Everything on Transports Statistics,* 2002, a DVD product, available in English, German, and French, that includes all public documents and statistics related to transportation issued by *Eurostat* since 1998. This first edition provides time-series data from 1970 to 2001, and it is intended for annual publication. In addition to detailed tables, it contains maps, graphs, and charts. More about this title and ordering information is available from *Eurostat* home page under the Publications section.

The European Commission also publishes other information about transportation. Researchers may consult its *Transport Research Program Knowledge Center* at <http://europa.eu.int/comm/transport/extra/>, which serves as a library for transport policy for decision makers. This Center provides online publications, project reviews, and thematic reports. Searching by theme or mode is available for final project results.

Transport Division Web site, by the United Nations Economic Commission for Europe (UNECE), Geneva, Switzerland. <http://www.unece.org/trans/>

Summary: This organization's online information is organized by transportation topics, including: road transport, road traffic safety, vehicle regulations, safety in tunnels, rail transport, inland water transport, combined transport, border crossing and customs, transport of dangerous goods, transport of perishable foodstuffs, transport trends and economics, transport statistics, monitoring scrap metal radiation, and the work of its Inland Transport Committee (ITC). Each topic provides online working documents, informal documents, reports, agendas, and meetings of that particular working group. The site also provides searching, news, a site map, links to transport Web sites of European and North American countries, and online legal instruments.

The work of the Transport Division of the Economic Commission for Europe is a priority activity for all UNECE governments because economic development and integration of UNECE countries require international transport and therefore intergovernmental cooperation. The overall objective of this cooperation is to facilitate and develop international transport while improving its safety and environmental performance. To fulfill this objective, the Transport Division supports the activities and work programs of the ITC (Inland Transportation Committee), the UNECE's guiding body for transport policy.

Detailed Description: Legal Instruments, a main heading of the *Transport Division* Web site, provides information pertaining to the conventions or treaties, under which the Commission works. The full text (PDF format) of the conventions is available in several languages, including English, French, and Russian. The conventions are organized under topic, along with a document entitled *Status of UNECE Transport Agreements and Conventions,* available in English and Russian, that provides more detail about convention signatures, ratifications, accessions, and acceptances by countries members of the United Nations.

The Transport Statistics section provides the online working documents of the Transport Division and also reports, agendas, and statistics (statistics are under construction). Most of the documents are available in English, French, and Russian. Online documents and reports are available for such current topics as road traffic accidents caused by cell phone use.

A significant title published under the auspices of the United Nations Economic Commission for Europe (UNECE) is the *Glossary for Transport Statistics* (2nd edition), by the Intersecretariat Working Group on Transport Statistics, Eurostat, ECMT, UNECE, 1998, available online in English and French (PDF) at <http://www.unece.org/trans/main/wp6/transstat-glossmain.html>. This title contains definitions of common standard terms used by these three organizations' statistical divisions to report transport statistics in these areas: railway, road, maritime, intermodal transport, inland waterways, and oil pipeline. These organizations jointly developed this glossary as well as a "Statistical Common Questionnaire" in order to improve internationally comparable data and to avoid duplication.

Worldwide Transportation Directory, by the Bureau of Transportation Statistics, U.S. Dept. of Transportation, 1997– (free online title). <http://www.bts.gov/programs/international/wtd/>

Summary: This title provides a transportation profile for every country of the world, along with contact points for general statistics, transportation statistics, highway statistics, air statistics, tourism statistics, and more specifically, for a U.S. audience. Searching by country is available for online users. Also included in a separate section are contact points for foreign embassies and transnational organizations. Not every country has a contact point for all the statistics. Originally published in 1997, it has been reissued online with updates.

Detailed Description: The directory is available from the home page under a list of continents that leads to a drop-down menu of country choices. A search box, also on the home page, allows for searching by individual country name. Each country transportation profile provides basic statistics and directory contact information for type of transportation information. Contacts include governments' transport statistics offices and tourism offices, hot linked to the offices' Web sites where available. Also, from the home page, the original transportation profile for countries in the 1997 edition can be downloaded in Microsoft Excel format.

NONGOVERNMENTAL SOURCES

International Association of Public Transport (UITP) Web site, Brussels, Belgium. <http://www.uitp.com/>

Summary: This worldwide network of public transport professionals provides a forum for transport policy, analysis, and research on transportation and is an advocate for public transport. This organization organizes congresses and conferences on the theme of transport and provides information, research, and analysis on all aspects of Public Transport including infrastructure, rolling stock, organization, and management. Major sections of information provided on its Web site include Events Publications; Media Room; Forum; Projects and Studies; its magazine, *PTI*

Magazine; and Mobi+ E-Library. The Web page is available in English, French, and German, and the association publishes its magazine, *PTI Magazine,* in these languages and also in Italian, Russian, Chinese, and Japanese.

Detailed Description: Under the Events section, the conference material is mostly published and available to members and nonmembers online, whereas the information from the congresses is available only to members. Also from the home page, UITP publishes the current issues of *PTI Magazine* full text online and selected articles from back issues (PDF) from 1999 on. The magazine covers human resources, urban transport, technology in public transport, and other issues relating to public transportation. UITP also makes other documents available online from the Publications section on its home page; however, most publications are not free.

The Mobi+ E-Library is an electronic library that contains full text of recent UITP conferences and congresses reports, organization reports and minutes, and some online documents. A pictures library and also a database with key figures about public transport operators are available on request.

The Media Room section provides press releases, articles, Frequently Asked Questions, and awards. The Projects and Studies section reports on ongoing and completed projects, which in general are not published online, but can be requested through e-mail. One significant project is a database the UITP compiled in collaboration with partners on 100 of the world's cities, entitled the "Millennium Cities Database for Sustainable Transport." Data includes population, the economy and urban structure, the number of road vehicles, taxis, the road network, parking, public transport networks (offer, usage, and cost), individual mobility and choice of transport mode, transport system efficiency and environmental impact (duration and cost of transport, energy consumption, accidents, pollution, and more from the year 1995 on).

International Road Transport (IRU) Web site, Geneva, Switzerland (online subscription resource available from the Web site of the IRU). <http://www.iru.org/>

Summary: The Web site of the International Road Transport Union is available in English and French, and it provides free downloadable publications from its Publications and Resources Section, under its Bookshop. Some titles are available in full text online and others only in summary. It also provides road transport news and bulletins. The International Road Transport Union represents the entire road transport industry worldwide and tries to maintain close working relationships with national, intergovernmental, and nongovernmental organizations to achieve its aim. IRU provides representation of the road transport industry at the Inland Transport Committee of the United Nations Economic Commission for Europe and consults with the UN Economic and Social Council and has consultative status with the Council of Europe. It takes an active role in the work of other international governmental organizations. including the Economic Commissions for Latin America, for Africa, and for Asia and the Pacific; the UN Conference for Trade and Development (UNCTAD); the European Economic Community; the International Labour Organisation (ILO) (with regard to social matters and professional training); the European Conference of Ministers of Transport (ECMT); the International Institute for the Unification of the Private Law (UNIDROIT); the Customs Cooperation Council (CCC); and the World Touring Organisation (WTO).

Detailed Description: The *IRU* Web site provides electronic access only through subscription to its *Handbook,* under the section IRU Information Resources. The IRU Information Centre provides constantly updated information to transport operators concerning national legislation relating to international road transport and includes customs road traffic regulations and fiscal charges. It also provides information on international transport agreements and conventions, road traffic regulations, fiscal charges, and the maximum permitted weights and dimensions of road vehicles in over 50 countries. This information was previously published in print in *IRU Handbook of International Road Transport.* The print title, which evolved into the online *Handbook,* the *World Transport Statistics,* is still a useful reference tool for researchers. The 6th edition of *World Transport Statistics,* 1996, covers 178 countries and includes official statistical data on road and railway networks; railway rolling stock and number of motor road vehicles; employment of road transport enterprises; and freight and passenger traffic by road, rail, inland waterway, sea, and air. It was published in both English and French.

World Road Statistics, by the International Road Federation (print title available online via membership in IRF).

Summary: This annual publication is a global compilation of road and vehicle statistics and is based on data compiled from official sources within national statistics offices and national road administrations in more than 185 countries and in cooperation with international institutions such as Eurostat and Afristat and the UN Economic Commissions for Europe. It is published in paper, electronic (e-mail PDF file), and CD, all for purchase.

The International Road Federation is a nongovernmental, not-for-profit organization with public and private-sector members in some 70 countries. Established in 1948, the organization's objective is to assist the international community to cooperate on the issue of developing safer and better road networks and to help rehabilitate Europe's damaged road systems.

Detailed Description: *World Road Statistics* is a collection of data tables that are a reliable source statistics on roads, particularly on a country level. The statistics are authoritative and are used by such agencies as the United Nations Development Programme, the World Bank, and the CIA for their own publications (i.e., the World Bank uses *World Road Statistics* to prepare a part of its own publication *World Development Indicators*). Chapters cover such topics as road networks (km); production and export of motor vehicle; first registration and import of motor vehicles; vehicles in use; road traffic; multimodal traffic comparisons; motor fuels; road accidents; rates and basis of assessment of road user taxes; examples of taxation for five common categories of motor vehicles; and annual receipts from road user taxation and road expenditure.

RESEARCH STRATEGIES

There are four ways of approaching the transportation information provided in this chapter: general or introduction resources; resources that provide access by transportation type; statistical resources; and resources that provide analysis of transportation issues. All researchers may want to start first by checking an overall general guide to give them background and statistics that they need. All the Web site resources can serve as general guides, for many have informational pages under transport topics. The *Panorama of Transport,* by the European Commission and *Eurostat* (print title, with some summary sections online and some related data online), is a general guide for transportation in the European Region. For researchers interested in a type of transportation, it is best to first consult the general reference materials before moving on to the specific resources. Also the free online directory *Worldwide Transportation Directory* by the Bureau of Transportation Statistics, U.S. Dept. of Transportation, <http://www.bts.gov/programs/international/wtd/>, can lead users to a national transportation office whose Web site or publications can be consulted for country-specific information. In many cases, it will be obvious to users that a specific resource covers the transportation topic contained in the title. Most of the following Web sites provide free full-text online documents in addition to other subscription material.

- Shipping/Marine Transport: *International Maritime Organization* Web site, <http://www.imo.org/>
- Civil Aviation (excluding military aviation): Both the *International Civil Aviation Organization (ICAO)* Web site, <http://www.icao.int/>, and the *International Aviation Online* Web site, by the Federal Aviation Administration (FAA). Washington, D.C. <http://www.intl.faa.gov/>
- Roads: Two nongovernmental sources, the *World Road Statistics,* by the International Road Federation, and the *International Road Transport (IRU)* Web site, by International Road Transport Union. (online subscription resource available from the Web site of the IRU), <http://www.iru.org/>
- Public Transportation: the nongovernmental *International Association of Public Transport (UITP)* Web site, <http://www.uitp.com/>. Although this resource is not strong in its online documents, it does have an online magazine on issues of public transportation and reports on projects online.

For statistical resources on transportation, a useful source to begin with is the International Road transport Union's *World Transport Statistics* because of its global approach. However, it is only available in print. A free online title with a regional focus is the *North American Transportation in Figures,* by the Bureau of Transportation Statistics, 2000. Even greater statistical depth is offered in the title *Annual Bulletin of Transport Statistics for Europe and North America,* by the United Nations, Economic Commission for Europe, which is excellent for historical data series. It is available in print title and electronic only by subscription.

Major government transportation periodicals and Web sites are a great source for analysis and reporting on global transportation issues. The *OECD Transport Directorate* Web site is an outstanding resource for transportation policy for industrialized countries of the world, not just including Europe. Although tending to focus on issues of concern to the member countries of its organization, it provides much analysis and reporting for free. The publications of the OECD are available through its online subscription, *SourceOECD,* and as print titles for purchase, therefore researchers may check library catalogs for titles that they find. The *Transport Division* Web site, the United Nations Economic Commission for Europe Web site, and the European Conference of Ministers of Transport (ECMT) Web site all provide online documents and statistics for transportation topics. The European Conference of Ministers of Transport has a more narrow, regional focus compared to the United Nations organization.

FOR FURTHER READING: COMPREHENSIVE WEB SITES AND OTHER REFERENCE SOURCES

EUROCONTROL: European Organization for the Safety of Aviation Navigation Web site. <http://www.eurocontrol.be/>

This intergovernmental European organization has a goal of improving coordination of air traffic control in Europe and of researching air traffic control capacity and safety in Europe in order to improve it. It provides flow management, air traffic services, safety management and regulation, training, and research and development. The Web site includes a site map and access to online publications, press releases, news, and reports on activities and projects. Online publications include its quarterly publication, *Skyway: The EURO-CONTROL Magazine,* which reports on European aviation issues, as well as statistics and project reports. *Skyway* is online from 1998 on and hard copies are available free on request. Other publications include informational brochures, its annual report (from 2000 in English and French), and ATM (Air Traffic Management) strategy reports for 2000 plus and the new millennium from the ECAC Transport Ministers.

International Labour Organization Transport Sector (ILO) Web site. <http://www.ilo.org/public/english/dialogue/sector/sectors/transp.htm>

The ILO provides research in the area of transport and its effect on employment and coordination among member states. Online reports linking transport and labor are available full text on its Web site. Selected ILO publications are highlighted. One feature of the Web site is Recent Developments, which reports on recent publications, conferences, meetings, reports, and other activities of the Transport Sector.

International Transportation Safety Council Web site. <http://www.itsasafety.org/>

This association of independent transportation accident safety boards focuses on independent investigation and reporting of transportation accidents and improving transport safety in member countries. Other objectives include improving transportation safety in each member country by sharing experiencing of the investigation boards; to promote independent investigations into transportation accidents; to exchange information on transportation safety and implementing transportation recommendations; and to identify common concerns, problems, and solutions and share this nationally and internationally.

International Transportation Web site, by the U.S. Bureau of Transportation Statistics. <http://www.bts.gov/itt/>

This U.S. agency's mission is to take a leadership role in developing international transportation data and information of high quality by conducting research and analysis on international transportation, trade, and travel. It also focuses on advancing the effective use of its data and information in transportation decision making either on a public or private level.

Journal of Transportation and Statistics, by the Bureau of Transportation Statistics, U.S. Dept. of Transportation, Washington, D.C. <http://purl.access.gpo.gov/GPO/LPS511> (online HTML journal with some sections only in PDF). <http://www.bts.gov/publications/journal_of_transportation_and_statictics/> (ISSN 1094-8848).

This journal provides articles on U.S. transportation, but also on worldwide transportation issues and trends. It provides an index, and users may find references to international information and statistics under the following headings: Europe, international perspectives, and specific country names.

Sources of Information in Transportation: General Information: Websites International, compiled by Ann R. Sweeney, European Commission Delegation. 5th edition. U.S. Department of Transportation, Bureau of Transportation Statistics, Transportation Library (online title). <http://www.ntl.bts.gov/ref/biblio/>

This electronic document provides an overall guide of individual bibliographies, arranged in subject sections, to the literature of transportation in North America and internationally. Prior were only published in print. Categories of transportation covered include: general transportation, hazardous materials, highways, inland water transportation, intelligent transportation systems, intercity bus, maritime transportation, nonmotorized transportation, pipelines, railroads, trucking, and urban transportation.

NOTES

1. *Transport Sector, International Labor Organization* Web site, <http://www.ilo.org/public/english/dialogue/sector/sectors/transp/background.htm>.

2. *Glossary for Transport Statistics,* by the Intersecretariat Working Group on Transport Statistics, Eurostat, ECMT, UN/ECE, 2nd ed., PDF document, p. 88, <http://www.unece.org/trans/main/wp6/pdfdocs/glossen2.pdf>.

CHAPTER 22
Women and Children

CHAPTER OVERVIEW

Throughout history the rights of women and children have been either nonexistent or of relative unimportance. Since its inception, the United Nations has lead the way in protecting and promoting the rights of women and children. However, it was not until the latter part of the twentieth century that this movement really gained international acceptance through the adoption of the United Nation's *Convention on the Elimination of All Forms of Discrimination against Women* (1979) and the *Convention on the Rights of the Child* (1989).

Because the United Nations has been so instrumental in the promotion of women's and children's rights, most of the sources described in this chapter, especially in regard to women, are affiliated agencies of the United Nations.

However, the United Nations has not been the only intergovernmental organization working to make a difference. The Inter-American Commission of Women of the Organization of American States is an invaluable resource for the Americas and a discussion of this organization is also included. Nongovernmental bodies also play a role for both women and children. Madre is one example of an organization focused on human rights for women, whereas Child Rights Information Network and Childwatch International are nongovernmental organizations working for children's rights. All three will be described in this chapter.

The chapter has been subdivided into two main categories: women and children. These resources detail the condition of women and children in the world, provide statistics, and report and analyze issues that concern them.

Women Governmental Sources Discussed

Inter-American Commission of Women Web site, by the Organization of American States, Washington, D.C. <http://www.oas.org/cim/default.htm>

United Nations Development Fund for Women (UNIFEM) Web site, New York. <http://www.unifem.org>

United Nations: Division for the Advancement of Women Web site, New York. <http://www.un.org/womenwatch/daw/>

United Nations International Research and Training Institute for the Advancement of Women (INSTRAW) Web site, Santa Domingo, Dominican Republic. <http://www.un-instraw.org/>

United Nations: WomenWatch Web site, New York. <http://www.un.org/womenwatch/>

WISTAT: Women's Indicators and Statistics Database. United Nations: New York. Version 3 CD-ROM (ISBN 9-21161-375-2) (UN Sales Publication No. E.95.XVII.6); (subscription) Version 4 CD-ROM (ISBN 9-21161-419-8) (UN Sales Publication No. E.00.XVII.4) (subscription).

Women Nongovernmental Source Discussed

MADRE: An International Women's Human Rights Organization Web site, New York. <http://www.madre.org/>

Children Governmental Sources Discussed

United Nations Children's Fund (UNICEF) Web site, New York. <http://www.unicef.org>

UNICEF: Innocenti Research Centre Web site, Florence, Italy. <http://www.unicef-icdc.org/>

The State of the World's Children. New York: Oxford University Press, 1980– (ISSN 0265-718X) (print and online). <http://www.unicef.org/infores/pubstitle.htm>

Children Nongovernmental Sources Discussed

Child Rights Information Network Web site, London, United Kingdom. <http://www.crin.org/>

Childwatch International Web site, by the University of Oslo, Norway. <http://www.childwatch.uio.no/>

WOMEN GOVERNMENTAL SOURCES

Inter-American Commission of Women Web site, by the Organization of American States, Washington, D.C. <http://www.oas.org/cim/default.htm>

Summary: The Web site of the Inter-American Commission of Women (CIM), "the first official intergovernmental agency in the world created expressly to ensure recognition of the civil and political rights of women,"[1] is a very comprehensive resource detailing the organization's work in protecting and promoting women's rights. The site, also available in Spanish, is divided into 12 main categories: About, History, Directory, Conventions, Documents, Assemblies, Seed Fund, What's New, Calendar, Priorities, Newsletter, and Publications. In addition, there are law updates, videos, media sources, and links to other related Web sites.

Detailed Description: The first two major categories discussed are About and History, and these are fairly self-explanatory. Directory, the third major category, provides a listing of participating countries, along with contact information.

Conventions is the fourth major category. Here are found the full text of the four major conventions of CIM. Documents, main category number five, is subdivided into reports, projects, programs/plans of action, and CIM's legal instruments with the full text of the relevant documents. Category six is Assemblies and found here are details of these meetings held in 1998, 2000, 2002, and 2004, including reports and resolutions. Seed Fund, the seventh main category, deals with the 1999 and 2001 projects supported by this special fund to improve access to needed resources to further the CIM's work.

What's New, the eighth major category discussed, provides information regarding ongoing projects by providing descriptions and the full text of relevant documents and reports. Calendars is the ninth major category, and here are found listings of events, including links to further information when available, to the activities of CIM, arranged sequentially by year (1999–). Priorities, category number ten, outlines the current work of the organization and includes the full text of reports. Newsletter is the eleventh main category and makes available the full text, PDF, of the newsletter *Mujer Interamericana,* in English, for 1999 and 2000. Publications is the last major category. Here are found citations and pricing information for various OAS publications related to women's issues.

Of special note is the Videos section. Here the researcher can view videos online of various roundtable discussions on the topics of violence against women and trafficking of women and children along with a discussion with women political leaders.

United Nations Development Fund for Women (UNIFEM) Web site, New York. <http://www.unifem.org>

Summary: The United Nations Development Fund for Women's (UNIFEM) was established as an outgrowth of the 1975 UN First World Conference on Women and has as its focus financial and technical assistance in the promotion of women's rights. The home page is subdivided into five major categories: About Us, Areas of Work, At Work Worldwide, Newsroom, and Resources. In addition, a section entitled Priorities discusses various initiatives of Economic Security and Rights; Women's Human Rights; and Government, Peace and Security. There are also links to online portals on Women, War, and Peace; Gender Equality and Millennium Development Goals; and Gender and HIV/AIDS. A drop-down menu at the top of the page links to UNIFEM information on regions of the world: Pacific, East/Southeast Asia, Andean Region, Arab States, South Asia, Central American, Commonwealth of Independent States, Southern Cone, and Eastern Africa. Each regional site contains information relevant to that area, but much of it is in the vernacular, not in English. The home page also features links to significant publications, such as the reference title the *Progress of the World's Women 2002* (full text, PDF).

Detailed Description: About Us, the first major category discussed, provides an overview of the organization as well as its mandate. In addition, there is a frequently asked questions section, key documents, and contact, vacancies, and internship information. Areas of Work, the second category, contains the same links as in the Priorities section from the UNIFEM home page, plus UNIFEM in the UN, Beijing Platform for action, and Emerging Areas of Work.

For another home page category, At Work Worldwide, "UNIFEM's thematic priorities, economic security and rights, women's human rights and governance and leadership are addressed in relation to regional realities in Africa, Asia and the Pacific, Latin America and the Caribbean, and Central and Eastern Europe and the Commonwealth of Independent States (CEE/CIS)."[2] This section is subdivided into the areas of Africa, Asia/Pacific, Latin America/Caribbean, and Central and Eastern Europe. Each of the regional subsections contains a description of the work of UNIFEM within the region, along with a list of the highlights.

Newsroom, the fourth category discussed, is comprised of the full text of press releases (1997–); speeches (1997–); *Currents,* UNIFEM's monthly electronic newsletter (2002–); Media Kits; Voices from the Field (articles by UNIFEM participants); events (current); and annual reports. Resources, the fifth category, is the location for UNIFEM publications, many of which are available in full-text format here. Women, Ink. is the exclusive distributor. The *Progress of the World's Women,* 2000, is a significant biennial reference report on tracking gender equality for the world, with statistics and analyses (print and online). The focus is on women in developing countries.

United Nations: Division for the Advancement of Women Web site, New York.

<http://www.un.org/womenwatch/daw/>

Summary: The United Nations Division for Women, the UN body most involved in women's issues and originally established in 1946, includes on its Web site much useful information in the form of reports, documents, and other publications for various United Nations bodies devoted to issues of women. This site is divided into nine major sections: About DAW, Beijing+5, News, CEDAW, CSW, Meetings and Documentation, Publications, Country Information, and Calendar.

Detailed Description: About DAW, the first major home page section discussed, comprises the mission statement, history, contact information, and organizational structure. Beijing+ 5, the second major section, provides in-depth coverage of the Women 2000 Gender Equality, Development and Peace for the 21st Century conference held on June 5–9, 2000 (23rd Special Session of the General Assembly) and is available in Arabic, Chinese, English, French, Russian, and Spanish. Included are documents, the Web cast of the conference, summaries of panel discussions, and daily press releases, along with the real-time online coverage, documents, and photographs from the Fourth World Conference on Women (Beijing, September 1995) under the link FWCW. The Beijing Declaration and Platform for Action from the Conference is available, along with other related information. News, the

third major section, contains the full text of news releases and speeches (1996–).

CEDAW, the fourth major section discussed, pertains to the *Convention on the Elimination of All Forms of Discrimination against Women,* adopted in 1979 by the UN General Assembly and "often described as an international bill of rights for women. Consisting of a preamble and 30 articles, it defines what constitutes discrimination against women and sets up an agenda for national action to end such discrimination."[3] The full text of the treaty, along with a listing of those countries who have ratified it, and the reservations are found here, as are the meeting records of the State Parties (11th and 12th). In addition, a listing of the committee membership from 1982 on is included. Also included are reporting guidelines, general recommendations, and a link to country reports (described in the Country Reports section); and the text, ratification, and signatures for the Optional Protocol. Lastly, the full text of official documents, press releases, statements, and concluding comments for Sessions 13– are also located at this site.

CSW, Commission on the Status of Women, is the fifth major section. "The Commission on the Status of Women (CSW) was established as a functional commission of the Economic and Social Council by Council resolution 11(II) of 21 June 1946 to prepare recommendations and reports to the Council on promoting women's rights in political, economic, civil, social and educational fields."[4] Its focus became the Fourth World Conference on Women in Beijing (1995) and the subsequent Platform for Action. This section contains an Overview with a description of its function and membership; information relating to the Follow Up to Beijing in critical areas, emerging issues, and gender mainstreaming; and the full text of official documents, statements, press releases, resolutions and decisions for Sessions 36–present (not all sessions have all types of materials).

Meetings and Documentation, the sixth major section, contains relevant documents from the Economic and Social Council (ECOSOC), General Assembly, CEDAW, CSW, Expert Group Meetings, Workshops, Consultations, Colloquiums, Forums, and Panel Discussions. Material types include reports, statements, background information, and sessional meeting documents.

Publications, the seventh major section, provides annotated descriptions and ordering information for various related publications such as commission reports, issues of *Women 2000,* and protocols. Some of these publications are available here in full text format.

Country Information, the eighth major section, includes National Action Plans and CEDAW country reports. These country reports are required reports of practice for all countries that have implemented the *Convention.* They are arranged in alphabetical order by country. Also included is At-a-Glance Table on Country Information, formally called *Implementation of the Beijing Platform for Action and Compliance with International Legal Instruments on Women,* again arranged alphabetically by country and kept current. Calendar, the last major section, provides a description of each event along with contact information and Web site URL.

Also available on the DAW home page is a link to the *WomenWatch* Web site, an information resource gateway. This resource is described separately in this chapter.

United Nations International Research and Training Institute for the Advancement of Women (IN-STRAW) Web site, Santa Domingo, Dominican Republic. <http://www.un-instraw.org/>

Summary: "INSTRAW works towards gender equality and the empowerment of women through its Gender Awareness Information and Networking System (GAINS), an internet-based research and training environment driven by a worldwide network. By facilitating collaborative work it seeks to create and share knowledge to improve development policy and practice."[5] Included on INSTRAW's home page are links to Research and Training, GAINS Network, Resources, and About INSTRAW. The home page itself includes an introduction, news, and contact information. This Web site is available in English, Spanish, and French.
Detailed Description: Research and Training, the first main section from the home page, discusses three main "strategic areas": Women and Men Building Partnerships for Gender Equality, Women and Men in the Information Society, and The Impact of Globalisation on Women. Included for each strategic area are relevant documents and publications. There are also links to Research and Training Strategy and Philosophy, and recent and current Projects.

GAINS, the second major section discussed, "consists of four networks of gender research, training and information organizations and individuals that form user-driven virtual communities for producing and sharing knowledge to improve development policy and practice for gender equality. Currently, there are over 250 members from 92 countries."[6] The Networks, including regional and national organizations; Research and Training Networks, already described; and Searchable Databases, described in the Resources section, are the main components of GAINS.

Resources, the third major section, features a Searchable Database, Special Collection of Resources, and INSTRAW Publications. The Searchable Database contains more than 2,000 international gender-related resources and includes citations to articles, papers, books, and reports; Web sites; newsletters; and discussion forums. Searching can be done by simple and advanced keyword searching and by searching UN critical areas and the INSTRAW Special Resources Collection via keyword or from the pull-down menu of subject choices. The Special Collections of Resources is subdivided into relevant subtopics and includes publications and Web sites. INSTRAW Publications provides an annotated listing of selected titles complete with ordering information and a link to contents titles. In addition, one can subscribe to the electronic newsletter. About INSTRAW, the last major section, provides information about the organization and its mission and networks.

United Nations: WomenWatch Web site, New York. <http://www.un.org/womenwatch/>

Summary: Founded by the United Nations Development Fund for Women (UNIFEM), United Nations International Research and Training Institute for the Advancement of Women (INSTRAW), and the United Nation's Division for Women (DAW), *WomenWatch* is a searchable gateway to information and resources on gender equality and the empowerment of women in the countries of the world. Included on the home page are the main categories About *WomenWatch,* News and Highlights, Latest Updates, Documents and Publications, International Instruments and more, Meetings and Events, New Web Sites, and New UN Publications. Also featured are quick links to related IGO sites and a Directory of UN Resources by theme and type. A site map aids in navigating the site.
Detailed Description: About *WomenWatch,* one of the home page categories, provides information regarding the formation of this site along with links to the home pages for founding partners UNIFEM, INSTRAW, DAW, and contributing partners United Nations Children's Fund (UNICEF), International Labour Organization (ILO), United Nations Educational, Scientific, and Cultural Organization (UN-

ESCO), World Bank, Sustainable Development Networking Programme, United Nations Development Programme-Gender in Development Programme, and Instituto de la Mujer-Ministerio de Trabajo y Asuntos Sociales de Espana, all of which contain a component related to women's issues.

The News and Highlights category highlights specific aspects. At the time of this writing these included United Nations documents on Palestinian Women, Situation of Afghan Women, and Gender Mainstreaming Information Kit, all of which have links to relevant materials.

Extensive links to information resources may be found under the home page category the Directory of UN Resources, which is organized into 10 subsections. Each links to comprehensive information and full-text United Nations resources concerning women. They include United Nations Entities; Gender Mainstreaming; UN Conferences, Meetings, and Special Days; International Instruments and Treaty Bodies; Thematic Issues and Critical Areas of Concern; Women of the World; Regions and Countries; UN Publications and other Media Resources; Statistics and Indicators; and Gender Training and Women in the UN System. The Statistics and Indicators subsection further links to online reports, databases, and archives on gender equality and women's human rights in an annotated list of resources. The *World's Women 2000: Trends and Statistics* is the first database under Statistics and Indicators and is actually not a database. It is a statistical reference book,[7] and the online version highlights important findings from each chapter of the print version, along with full text of the main findings and the statistical tables from the book. Also available is the *Good Practices Database,* which is a searchable and browsable database on gender mainstreaming and the United Nations system institutional processes such as training, policy commitments, and resource allocations, along with good practices worldwide in responding to the concerns about women and development defined as critical by the Beijing Platform for Action (Fourth World Conference on Women).

From one of the quick links on the home page, CEDAW, researchers may find information on *The Convention on the Elimination of All Forms of Discrimination against Women (CEDAW),* adopted in 1979 by the United Nations General assembly. Under the Publications heading is another significant database *Fact Sheet on Women in Government,* a "statistical database on women in the executive branch of governments,... extracted from the 1996 *Edition of the World-*

wide Government Directory,"[8] also not a searchable database but rather a listing of statistics (as of January 1996) and Explanatory Note, and a chart of Percentage of Women in Government (as of the same date). Women in Parliament: World and Regional Averages and Women in Parliament: Percentage of Women in Each National Parliament are two other topics, again not searchable databases but data "compiled by the Inter-Parliamentary Union on the basis of information provided by National Parliaments."[9] The data is current, and archived data, back to 2001, is also included along with a link to the PARLINE database, which allows searching by country, region, subregion, and free-text, produced by the Inter-Parliamentary Union. Lastly, a listing of female UN ambassadors in New York, Geneva, and Vienna is included, along with their contact information, in the Statistical Indicators section.

Gender Training information, under the Directory of UN Resources on Gender and Women's issues on the home page, provides enhanced access to gender mainstreaming capacity support materials from the United Nations and Commonwealth systems, including material, program information, and methodologies. Lastly, there is a link to selected United Nations publications, which includes selected titles and links to the publications listings/catalogs of DAW, UNIFEM, related women's studies and family issues publications, and Publicaciones de las Naciones Unidas: Ciencias Sociales—La Mujer.

The International Instruments and Treaty Bodies subsection of the Information Resources home page category features the full text of especially important conventions and declarations pertaining to women's rights, dating from 1942 to the present.

The News and Highlights home page category provides links to Web pages, reports, speech texts, and documents for conferences and meetings that have some relevance to women's issues. In addition included here are full-text news (press releases, statements, and other odds and ends, 1997–) and calendar of events (2002–), as well as links to the audio of women's issues on UN radio. These are also accessible from the quick links section on the home page.

WISTAT: Women's Indicators and Statistics Database. United Nations: New York. Version 3 CD-ROM (ISBN 9-21161-375-2) (UN Sales Publication No. E.95.XVII.6) (subscription); Version 4 CD-ROM (ISBN 9-21161-419-8) (UN Sales Publication No. E.00.XVII.4) (subscription).

Summary: Developed by the Statistical Division, Department for Economic and Social Information and Policy Analysis of the United Nations Secretariat, as a result of recommendations from the World Plan of Action for the Implementation of the Objectives of the International Women's Year, *WISTAT* provides statistical information on a variety of topics regarding the social and economic life of women and men.

Detailed Description: The first version of *WISTAT* was issued in 1988 as a diskette. Version 3, the first version to be found in CD-ROM format, provides data from 1970–1993 and has some population and demographic indicators projected to 2025.

Version 4 is the latest update of *WISTAT.* Main subjects covered include Population Composition and Distribution; Learning and Education; Economic Activity; Households, Marital Status and Fertility; Health and Health Services; Reproductive Health and Reproductive Rights; Public Affairs and Political Participation; Violence; and National Product and Expenditure. Each subject is then further subdivided. Most subject areas contain data on 1970, 1980, 1990, and the latest year available. Some contain data for only the latest year available, and some contain projections to 2010. Data can be browsed using Excel 97 or Beyond 20/20 and can be graphed.

WOMEN NONGOVERNMENTAL SOURCE

MADRE: An International Women's Human Rights Organization Web site, New York. <http://www.madre.org/>

Summary: As an organization focused on human rights for women, the *MADRE* Web site documents efforts of programs and projects through overviews and writings. The Web site itself is arranged into seven major headings: Mission and History, Programs by Country, International Advocacy, Articles & Factsheets, Travel with MADRE, Get Involved, and Links. Contact information is also included.

Detailed Description: Mission and History, the first major heading, provides background history and the work of the organization. Programs by Country, heading number two, lists the individual countries (Chiapas, Mexico, Colombia, Cuba, Guatemala, Kenya, Nicaragua, Palestine, and Rwanda) with a link from each country name to an overview and related material. The related material contains full text of articles written by *MADRE.*

International Advocacy, the third major heading, gives an overview of these efforts with links to more related materials of the same type previously discussed. There is also a menu to articles on training themes that are in both English and Spanish. The fourth major heading, Articles and Factsheets, contains titles in full-text format organized into Current Newsletter *(MADRE Speaks),* Latin America and Caribbean, Middle East, Africa, Balkans, U.S. Foreign Policy, Globalization & Economic Justice, International Advocacy, and Women's Health. Date coverage varies within each category, but is mainly from 1998 to the present. Some titles are also available in Spanish.

Travel with MADRE, the fifth major heading, details future trips to Peru, Guatemala, and Nicaragua under *Voyages with a Vision.* In addition, photographs from a previous visit to these areas are included. Get Involved is the sixth major heading and outlines how to join and become involved with its work. Links is the last major heading and provides access to other relevant Web sites, with brief annotations, arranged by Human Rights and Social Justice Organizations Links, Africa, Latin America and the Caribbean, Middle East, Selected UN Sites, and Research Sites.

CHILDREN GOVERNMENTAL SOURCES

United Nations Children's Fund (UNICEF) Web site, New York. <http://www.unicef.org>

Summary: Created in 1946, the United Nations Children's Emergency Fund (UNICEF) served to assist in alleviating sickness and hunger for European children caused by World War II. UNICEF became a permanent agency of the United Nations, with the mission of working with poverty-stricken children in developing nations. The *United Nations Children's Fund (UNICEF)* home page is composed of the major headings Information By Country; What We Do; Why We Do It; UNICEF People; Voices of Youth; Support UNICEF; and Press Centre. The home page also contains a pull-down menu of what's new topics and has links to current hot topics at the very top of the page. A search engine is also available here, as well as Spanish and French versions of the Web site.

Detailed Description: Information by Country, the first major heading discussed, is a list of links by country to UNICEF's goals, programs, and accomplishments in individual countries. Under each country is an explanation of the state of the child in the country, along with basic statistics, a detailed map, and further links to information. In effect, this is an online database version of UNICEF's significant report *State of the World's Children.*

What We Do, the second major heading, is subdivided into thematic priorities for UNICEF, including Girls Education, Child Protection, Immunization Plus, HIV/AIDS, and Early Childhood and also into sections under How We Work, including Adolescence, Communities and Families, Countries in Crisis, Evaluation and Good Practices, Gender Equality, Health, Life Skills, Monitoring and Statistics, Nutrition, Policy Analysis, Procuring Supplies for Children, Research, Rights and Results, and, finally, Water, Environment and Sanitation. These sections link further to online reports, full text of treaties, conventions and publications, and more under the subsection for each, including Introduction, the Big Picture, UNICEF in Action, Real lives, Resources, and Statistics.

Also on the home page under What We Do: Child Protection, researchers may find statistical information via the *Childinfo* database <http://www.child-info.org>. *Childinfo* is where "you will find UNICEF's key statistical databases with detailed country-specific information that was used for the end-decade assessment of progress and setbacks in implementing the 1990 World Summit for Children Declaration and Plan of Action."[10] This data is updated when possible. Topics include child survival and health, child nutrition, maternal health, water and sanitation, education, and additional child rights (birth registration and child labor). Each of these topics contains statistical indicators. A drop-down menu is available for quick access to a particular indicator or World Summit for Children goal. Another statistical instrument included here is the Multiple Cluster Indicator Survey. This instrument was created to collect data on the World Summary of Children goals, and topics covered include health and education, nutrition, family environment, child work, HIV/AIDS, and birth registration. Both mid-decade and end-decade assessment information is included here, along with the questionnaire. Additionally, information on monitory methods, evaluation methods and tools, *Education Technical Notes Series,* and links to other UNICEF evaluation bodies are found here. A link to the Innocenti Research Centre, the main research body of UNICEF, is also included, but this will be discussed as a separate entry. Lastly, the Evaluation Database, consisting of evaluation reports and studies, searchable by region, country, and date, are also a part of this subsection.

Another home page heading Voices of Youth is UNICEF's program of child rights for youth, and it provides for learning and the exchange of ideas for youth and teachers. Researchers may note that conferences and meetings are under topics; however, one conference of note is the *Special Session on Children* held May 8–10, 2002. Found here are an introduction, including links to relevant sites; an agenda and activities, again with links to relevant sites; preparatory information, including the full text of reports; listing of participating NGOs; the full text of press releases; child's rights, with an explanation and link to the full text, with supporting documentation, of the *Convention on the Rights of the Child;* How is Your Country Doing, which provides the full text (PDF and Word) of national reports; What Can you Do?, which provides information and links to two campaigns, *Global Movement for Children* and *Say Yes to Children;* press center, which contains the full text of press releases and a press kit; Under18-Zone, which includes the full text of the *Young Person's Guide to the Special Session,* child-friendly version of the draft outcomes, which includes the first-hand accounts of four children plus dictionary, and summary of *We the Children.* Of special note for the *Special Session on Children* section is the documents subsection. Here is found the full text, in PDF and Word formats, of the outcome document, *A World Fit for Children; We the Children: Meeting the Promise of the World Summit for Children,* issued by Secretary-General Kofi Annan; and *We the Children: Decade Review of the Follow-Up to the World Summit for Children* (May 2001, with some of the data updated). Web cast coverage is available under Official Coverage (United Nations).

The Highlights featured on the UNICEF home page contain links to various subjects addressed by UNICEF. The topics included here change over time. At the time of this writing topics included measles vaccination, HIV/AIDS, polio, football, *State of the World's Children* and other various campaigns, and information for broadcasters. Each topic has different material included such as publications, fact sheets, and statistics.

The Press Centre home page category is subdivided into Latest (Information, Hot Topics, Our Positions), Tools (Video and Media), Facts on Children, and an e-news alert. Video and audio clips and speeches are available online under Tools. Users may link further to a video catalog and archive. Searching can be done by subject, region, title, type of production, and also by *In-*

ternational Children's Day of Broadcasting, an annual event, as they have their own index, with a link provided. The previous catalogue is also available. Press Centre also includes the full text of current press releases, with an archive back to 1996, and the full text of executive speeches, dating back to 1999. Also found here are links to the full texts of the publications *State of the World's Children* (1997–) and *Progress of Nations* (1997–). Statistics link back to Childinfo, described earlier, and the statistical databases included at this site.

The Support UNICEF home page category provides an opportunity for online shopping for UNICEF products, along with information on donations to the organization. Press Centre, the fifth major section, contains the same elements as described under Information Resources. In addition, current headlines and highlights are supplied along with the annual report and tools for reporters, comprised of links to subject experts by topic, video b-rolls (Beta cam video tapes), and fast facts.

UNICEF: Innocenti Research Centre Web site, Florence, Italy. <http://www.unicef-icdc.org/>

Summary: The home page of the Innocenti Research Centre, established in 1988 as a research center for UNICEF, is comprised of five major sections: About the Centre, Publications, Research, Press Centre, and Resources. A site guide and search engine are also available on the home page.

Detailed Description: About the Centre, the first major section discussed, includes information on projects; staff, including contact information and biographies; a frequently asked questions section; overview; and information on the Innocenti Library, a collaborative project between the Innocenti Research Centre (IRC) and Instituto Degli Innocenti (IDI). The Library subsection links to the IRC and IDI catalogues. The IRC catalogue allows for browsing and simple and advanced searching. Searching can be done on title, title keyword, author, publisher, series title, subject word, subject, classification, and thesaurus term. Limits can be made on types (i.e., books, serials, and articles), languages (i.e., English, Italian, French, German, and Spanish), or formats. An online thesaurus does not seem to be available. The IDI catalogue is in Italian only, but information about the library and its resources are in English.

Publications, the second major home page section, provides a searchable catalogue of IRC publications. The full text of featured publications can be downloaded. Research, the third major section, focuses on the two areas of IRC research: economic and social policy analysis and application of human rights instruments. These two areas are hyperlinked from the Research page, linking to topical coverage. Press Centre, the fourth major section discussed, includes full-text press releases (2000–), press kits, a frequently asked questions section, and online news, including links to other news agencies covering IRC activities. The publication on specific issues, the *Innocenti Digest,* is publicly accessible through the Press Centre (2000–, PDF).

Resources, the last major section, includes satellite sites; the *TransMONEE Database*; the library, previously discussed; Virtual Library, and Links. Satellite sites provides links to Web sites of related research projects. The *TransMONEE Database* "is a public-use database of socio-economic indicators for Central and Eastern Europe and the Commonwealth of Independent States (CEE/CIS/Baltics). The database allows the rapid retrieval and manipulation of economic and social indicators for 27 transition countries in the region."[11] The database must be downloaded to the user's computer. Virtual Library is a hyperlinked list of subject-based Internet sites, including multidisciplinary databases, economics, human rights, international organizations, law, health, social policy, social science, and statistics. Links provide access to additional Web sites devoted to the topic of children's rights.

The State of the World's Children. New York: Oxford University Press, 1980– (ISSN 0265-718X) (print and online). <http://www.unicef.org/infores/pubstitle.htm>

Summary: Published annually since 1980, *The State of the World's Children* focuses each issue on a different topic. Each issue includes not only articles on that topic, but also panel information, maps, figures, and statistics. These reports are also available electronically from 1997 on in PDF and HTML formats. Sections of this reference report are available online in a database by country on the UNICEF Web site under the home page heading Information By Country.

CHILDREN NONGOVERNMENTAL SOURCES

Child Rights Information Network Web site, London, United Kingdom. <http://www.crin.org/>

Summary: The *Child Rights Information Network (CRIN)* Web site provides access to additional resources on child's rights through the filter of both

NGO and IGO participation. A description of its purpose and work is included on the home page. The *CRIN* home page is divided into five main categories: Child Rights, Resources, Organisations [sic], Regional Information, and Themes. A search engine is also available.

Detailed Description: Child Rights, the first category, is composed of information pertaining to the *Convention on the Rights of the Child,* NGO Alternative Reports, and International Treaties. The *Convention on the Rights of the Child* section includes links to the United Nations Office of the High Commissioner for Human Rights (OHCHR) and the Committee on the Rights of the Child, a description of the *Convention,* and additional links to the texts of the *Optional Protocols* and NGO Alternative Reports to the Committee on the Rights of the Child. NGO Alternative Reports, also the second subsection of Child Rights, are submitted to the Committee on the Rights of the Child detailing their efforts in implementing the *Convention.* The reports can be searched by country, session, or organization. However, a sequential sessional listing (1993–), with country name, document number, and when available, link to the report, comprises the bulk of this subsection. International Treaties, the third subsection of Child Rights, links to official instruments pertaining to rights of the child as well as to the Committee on Human Rights .

Resources, the second main home page category, is subdivided into Publications Catalogue, News, Events, and Email Lists. The first three subdivisions link to an individualized search engine; however, the same search elements are included as options for each one: information type, country, theme, language, or keywords. Each of the three subdivisions also has links to the latest of each type of source (publications, news, or events), selected readings, and view all. The latest of each type and selected readings contain listings of links to online resources. The Email Lists subdivision allows a researcher to subscribe to three list services: CRIN MAIL, CRIN Children and Armed Conflict, and CRIN Special Session. A description of each is included along with a link to the archives.

Organisations, the third main category discussed, provides links to the CRIN Members: Directory of Child Rights Organisations, CRIN, NGO Group for CRC *(Convention on the Rights of the Child),* Child Rights Caucus, and Children as Partners. The CRIN section is composed of the *CRIN Newsletter* (published three times a year and available here in full-text format from 2000 on), e-mail list services, coverage

of the *Special Session on Children,* and the full text of annual reports, research papers, and working papers. The other organizations listed on the home page include descriptions of various projects and materials that pertain to them. Each organization also has a link to online resources, available in English, French, and Spanish.

The fourth main category is Regional Information and it is divided into Africa, Americas, Asia, Europe, and Oceania. Each region has a search engine allowing for searching by resource, country, language, or keywords. In addition, there are links to other resources under latest, selected readings, and view all.

Themes, the last main category, is divided into the topics About Child Rights, Armed Conflict, Child Labour [sic], Disability, Discrimination, Education, Health, HIV/AIDS, Juvenile Justice, Macroeconomics, Media, Sexual Exploitation, UN Special Session on Children, and Violence Against Children. The Themes category has the same individualized search engine set up as the Resources category and also includes latest materials, selected readings, and view all.

Childwatch International Web site, by the University of Olso, Norway. <http://www.childwatch.uio. no/>

Summary: Childwatch International is a nongovernmental research network. The Web site provides research sources in the area of children's rights. It is a rich resource of information in the form of titles and additional Web sites. The home page is divided into five major categories: What is CWI, Key Institutions, Activities, News, and Resources. Current highlights of events and publications is included on the home page as well as a search engine.

Detailed Description: What is CWI, the first home page category discussed, provides detailed information on the organization along with its structure. In addition, the full text (PDF format) of annual reports (1993–) are found here.

Key Institutions, the constituency of Childwatch International, is the second major category and a rich source for information on institutions involved in research for children. Institutions can be located three ways: via a pull-down menu at the top, through a regional search (Africa, Asia, Europe, Latin America and the Caribbean, North Africa and the Middle East, North America, and the Pacific Region), or by clicking on the map of the world that is included. Each region includes those institutions involved in the organization. A detailed description is available for each institution that includes contact information, e-mail and Web addresses, main lines of research, staff profiles and disciplines, and affiliated networks.

Activities, the third major category discussed, describes the various research projects undertaken by the key institutions. Subjects covered at the time of this writing include children and media, monitoring children's rights, political and economic transformation, growing up in cities, and more. Each project has a description, but other materials included vary according to the subject. Reports, bibliographies, and conferences are some of the materials that may be found under the various topics.

News, the fourth major category, is comprised of listings for conferences, publications, and activities. A section at the beginning provides links to news and events outside the Childwatch International arena. The Conferences subcategory describes relevant conferences and, where applicable, has additional information links. Publications, another subcategory, is subdivided into journals and bulletins, research reports, books, and publications from specific key institutions. Annotations and ordering information are included, as well as links to full-text articles online. Activities, the last subcategory, is a miscellaneous collection of information on some of the activities undertaken by the key institutions.

Resources, the last major home page category, is subdivided into Child Research, Child-Related Matters, News and Events, and Electronic Newsletters. Child Research is further subdivided into institutions and organizations, online research reports and journals, and catalogs and data. Child-Related Matters is a listing of relevant Web sites organized by topic. News and Events covers the same conference coverage as found in the News category previously discussed. Electronic Newsletters provides an alphabetical listing of appropriate newsletters with brief annotations and Web and e-mail addresses.

RESEARCH STRATEGIES

For comprehensive research on the subject of women, the best place to begin is the *United Nations Division for the Advancement of Women* Web site. Not only does this site contain in-depth coverage of two of the most important women's rights conferences, *Fourth World Conference on Women* (1995) and *Women 2000: Gender Equality, Development and Peace for the 21st Century* (2000), but it also has in-depth coverage of the most important women's rights document, the *Convention on the Elimination of All Forms of Discrimination against Women* (1979). This site also provides a link to the Commission on the Status of Women (Economic and Social Council). In addition, the full text of relevant documents from the Economic and Social Council, General Assembly, and other meetings, colloquiums, and forums are available here along with an annotated listing of publications. Reports from various countries pertaining to the implementation of the *Convention* can also be found here.

Another source for in-depth research on women is the *United Nations WomenWatch* Web site, which is a gateway to information resources. Not only does this site contain useful statistical information on women in government and social and economic statistics, but it also has coverage of projects and programs on gender mainstreaming. Of special mention are the links from this page to many other UN specialized agencies that relate to women's issues.

The other resources highlighted in this chapter have a more specialized focus. The *UNIFEM* Web site provides information on United Nations financial and technical assistance for relevant regional programs. Also, the *United Nations International Research and Training Institute for the Advancement of Women (INSTRAW)* Web site deals with gender awareness and equality through strategic direction. The *WISTAT: Women's Indicators and Statistics Database* CD-ROM is a source for time-series statistical information on women's issues. Not all libraries may carry *WISTAT*. It will probably only be found in larger academic libraries. The *Inter-American Commission of Women* Web site concentrates on the specific work in the Americas region of the world. The *MADRE* Web site focuses on international human rights issues for women in Latin America, the Middle East, Africa, and the Balkans. Researchers should be alert to the bias of this nongovernmental organization.

The United Nations is also the major research organization in the area of children's rights. *UNICEF*'s Web site is the primary comprehensive source. It contains in-depth coverage on the United Nation's *Convention on the Rights of the Child* (1989) as well as on other campaigns and meetings. The UNICEF site also provides in-depth reporting of programs, humanitarian aid efforts, publications, and statistics.

The *UNICEF: Innocenti Research Centre* Web site links to an online catalog useful for searching publication titles related to research projects and children's rights issues. The full text of the *Social Monitor* is available here, which provides "socio-economic development" information. Of special mention is the **TransMONEE Database,** a source of socioeconomic statistics for Central and Eastern Europe and the Commonwealth of Independent States.

Two nongovernmental organization Web sites are also included, **Child Right Information Network** and **Childwatch International.** Both are sources of research project information and related publications. When using these resources, users should be especially alert about the objectives and bias of the nongovernmental organization.

NOTES

1. *Inter-American Commission of Women (CIM)* Web site, by the Organization of American States, Washington, D.C., <http://www.oas.org/cim/English/About.htm>.

2. *United Nations Development Fund for Women (UNIFEM)* Web site, New York, <http://www.unifem.org/index.php?f_page_pid=5/>.

3. *United Nations: Division for the Advancement of Women* Web site, New York, <http://www.un.org/womenwatch/daw/cedaw/index.html>.

4. *United Nations: Division for the Advancement of Women* Web site, New York, <http://www.un.org/womenwatch/daw/csw/index.html>.

5. *United Nations International Research and Training Institute for the Advancement of Women (IN-STRAW)* Web site, Santa Domingo, Dominican Republic, <http://www.un-instraw.org/en/index.html>.

6. *United Nations International Research and Training Institute for the Advancement of Women (IN-STRAW)* Web site, Santa Domingo, Dominican Republic, <http://www.un-instraw.org/en/gains/index.html>.

7. *World's Women 2000: Trends and Statistics,* UN Publications No. E.00.XVII.14 (ISBN 9-21161-428-7).

8. *United Nations: WomenWatch* Web site, New York, <http://www.un.org/womenwatch/daw/public/womeningov.htm>.

9. *United Nations: WomenWatch* Web site, New York, <http://www.un.org/womenwatch/resources/stats.htm>.

10. *Child Protection* Web site, by UNICEF, Geneva, Switzerland, <http://www.childinfo.org/index2.htm>.

11. *UNICEF: Innocenti Research Centre* Web site, Florence, Italy, <http://www.unicef-icdc.org/resources/>.

APPENDIX I
Selected Acronyms of International Organizations

ARRANGED BY ACRONYM

ADB	Asian Development Bank
APEC	Asian–Pacific Economic Cooperation
ASEAN	Association of South East Asian Nations
BIS	Bank for International Settlements
CEC	Commission for Environmental Cooperation
CEDAW	Convention on the Elimination of all Forms of Discrimination Against Women
CERN	European Organization for Nuclear Research
CGIAR	Consultative Group on Agriculture Research
CORDIS	Community Research & Development Information Service
CTBTO	Comprehensive Test Ban Treaty Organization
DDA	United Nations Department for Disarmament Affairs
EBRD	European Bank for Reconstruction and Development
ECB	European Central Bank
ECLA	United Nations Economic Commission for Latin America and the Caribbean
ECOSOC	United Nations Economic and Social Council
EEA	European Environment Agency
ESCAP	United Nations Social and Economic Commission for Asia and the Pacific
EU	European Union
EUROPOL	European Police Organization
FAO	Food and Agriculture Organization
GA	United Nations General Assembly
GEF	Global Environment Facility
HELCOM	Helsinki Commission
IACD	Inter-American Agency for Cooperation and Development
IACHR	Inter-American Commission on Human Rights
IADB	Inter-American Development Bank
IAEA	International Atomic Energy Agency
IBRD	International Bank for Reconstruction and Development (World Bank)
ICC	International Criminal Court
ICJ	International Court of Justice
ICSU	International Council for Science
ICTR	United Nations International Criminal Tribunal for Rwanda
ICTY	United Nations International Criminal Tribunal for the Former Yugoslavia
IDA	International Development Association (World Bank)
IFAD	International Fund for Agriculture Development
IFC	International Finance Corporation (World Bank)
ILO	International Labour Organization
IMF	International Monetary Fund
IMO	International Maritime Organization
INCB	International Narcotics Control Board
INTERPOL	International Criminal Police Organization
IOM	International Organization for Migration
IPU	Inter-Parliamentary Union
ISO	International Organization for Standardization
ITU	International Telecommunication Union
LN	League of Nations
MIGA	Multilateral Investment Guarantee Agency (World Bank)
NAFTA	North American Free Trade Agreement
NATO	North Atlantic Treaty Organization
OAPEC	Organization of Arab Petroleum Exporting Countries
OAS	Organization of American States
OAU	Organization of African Unity

OECD	Organisation for Economic Co-operation and Development	UNFCC	United Nations Framework Convention on Climate Change
OPEC	Organization of Petroleum Exporting Countries	UNFPA	United Nations Population Fund
OSCE	Organization for Security and Cooperation in Europe	UNHCHR	United Nations High Commissioner for Human Rights
PAHO	Pan American Health Organization	UNHCR	United Nations High Commissioner for Refugees
SAARC	South Asian Association for Regional Cooperation	UNICEF	United Nations Children's Fund
SC	United Nations Security Council	UNIDO	United Nations Industrial Development Organization
SEAMO	Southeast Asian Ministers of Education Organization	UNIFEM	United Nations Development Fund for Women
UNCHS	United Nations Centre for Human Settlements	UNODCCP	United Nations Office for Drug Control and Crime Prevention
UNCITRAL	United Nations Commission on International Trade Law	UNOPS	United Nations Office for Project Services
UNCTAD	United Nations Conference on Trade and Development	UNRISD	United Nations Research Institute for Social Development
UNDCP	United Nations International Drug Control Programme	UNRWA	United Nations Relief and Works Agency for Palestine Refugees in the Near East
UNDP	United Nations Development Programme	UNU	United Nations University
UNECA	United Nations Economic Commission for Africa	UNV	United Nations Volunteers
UNECE	United Nations Economic Commission for Europe	UPU	Universal Post Union
UNEP	United Nations Environment Programme	WFP	World Food Programme
		WHO	World Health Organization
UNESCO	United Nations Educational, Scientific and Cultural Organization	WIPO	World Intellectual Property Organization
		WMO	World Meteorological Organization
UNESCWA	United Nations Economic Commission for Western Asia	WTO	World Trade Organization

APPENDIX II
Selected International Organization Web Sites

Asian Development Bank   http://www.adb.org

Asian-Pacific Economic Cooperation
http://www.apec.org/

Association of Southeast Asian Nations
http://www.aseansec.org/home.htm/

Bank for International Settlements
http://www.bis.org/

CERN: European Organization for Nuclear Research   http://public.web.cern.ch/public/

Convention on the Elimination of all Forms of Discrimination Against Women
http://www.un.org/womenwatch/daw/cedaw/

CORDIS (Community Research & Development Information Service)
http://www.cordis.lu/en/home.html

CURIA: Court of Justice of the European Communities   http://curia.eu.int/

European Bank for Reconstruction and Development   http://www.ebrd.com/

European Central Bank   http://www.ecb.int/

European Environment Agency
http://www.eea.eu.int/

European Parliament   http://www.europarl.eu.int/

European Police Office   http://www.europol.eu.int/

European Union (Europa)   http://europa.eu.int/

Eurostat   http://europa.eu.int/comm/eurostat/

Food and Agriculture Organization of the United Nations   http://www.fao.org/

G8 Information Centre (University of Toronto)
http://www.g7.utoronto.ca/

Inter-American Agency for Cooperation and Development   http://www.iacd.oas.org/template-ingles/entrance-english.htm

Inter-American Commission on Human Rights
http://www.cidh.oas.org/

Inter-American Development Bank
http://www.iadb.org/

International Atomic Energy Agency
http://www.iaea.or.at/

International Bureau of Education
http://www.ibe.unesco.org/

International Court of Justice   http://www.icj-cij.org

International Criminal Police Organization (INTERPOL)   http://www.interpol.int/

International Finance Corporation
http://www.ifc.org/

International Labour Organization
http://www.ilo.org/

International Maritime Organisation
http://www.imo.org/index.htm

International Monetary Fund
http://www.imf.org/

International Narcotics Control Board
http://www.incb.org/

International Organization for Migration
http://www.iom.int/

International Organization for Standardization
http://www.iso.ch/iso/en/ISOOnline.openerpage

International Telecommunication Union
http://www.itu.int/home/

Inter-Parliamentary Union
http://www.ipu.org/english/home.htm

North Atlantic Treaty Organisation
http://www.nato.int/

Organisation for Economic Co-operation and Development   http://www.oecd.org

Organization of American States
http://www.oas.org/

Organization of Arab Petroleum Exporting Countries   http://www.oapecorg.org/

Organization of the Petroleum Exporting Countries   http://www.opec.org/

Organization for Security and Cooperation in Europe   http://www.osce.org/

Pan American Health Organization
http://www.paho.org/

South Asian Association for Regional Cooperation
http://www.saarc-sec.org/

United Nations   http://www.un.org

United Nations Children's Fund
http://www.unicef.org/

United Nations Commission on International
Trade Law   http://www.uncitral.org/

United Nations Conference on Trade and Development   http://www.unctad.org

United Nations Department for Disarmament Affairs   http://disarmament2.un.org/dda.htm

United Nations Development Fund for Women
http://www.unifem.org

United Nations Development Programme
http://www.undp.org/

United Nations Economic and Social Council
http://www.un.org/esa/coordination/ecosoc/

United Nations Economic Commission for Africa
http://www.uneca.org/

United Nations Economic Commission for Europe
http://www.unece.org/

United Nations Economic Commission for Latin
America and the Caribbean
http://www.eclac.cl/default.asp?idioma=IN

United Nations Economic Commission for Western Asia   http://www.escwa.org.lb/

United Nations Educational Scientific and Cultural Organization   http://www.unesco.org/

United Nations Environment Programme
http://www.unep.org/

United Nations General Assembly
http://www.un.org/ga/

United Nations High Commissioner for Refugees
http://www.unhcr.ch/

United Nations Human Settlements Programme
http://www.unhabitat.org/

United Nations Industrial Development Organization   http://www.unido.org/

United Nations International Criminal Tribunal
for the Former Yugoslavia
http://www.un.org/icty/

United Nations International Criminal Tribunal
for Rwanda   http://www.ictr.org/

United Nations: Office of the United Nations High
Commissioner for Human Rights
http://www.unhchr.ch/

United Nations Office on Drugs and Crime
http://www.unodc.org/unodc/index.html

United Nations Population Fund
http://www.unfpa.org/

United Nations Research Institute for Social Development   http://www.unrisd.org/

United Nations Relief and Works Agency for
Palestine Refugees in the Near East
http://www.un.org/unrwa/

United Nations Security Council
http://www.un.org/Docs/sc/

United Nations Social and Economic Commission
for Asia and the Pacific
http://www.unescap.org/

Universal Postal Union   http://www.upu.int/

The World Bank Group
http://www.worldbank.org

World Food Programme   http://www.wfp.org/

World Health Organization
http://www.who.int/en/

World Intellectual Property Organization
http://www.wipo.int/

World Meteorological Organization
http://www.wmo.ch/

World Trade Organization   http://www.wto.org

Index